FOURTH EDITION

Schools
and **Society**

To the next generation, our grandchildren,
Cosette, Chloe, Joseph, Daniel, and Corinne
Hannah, Caleb, Kai, and One-on-the-Way

FOURTH EDITION

Schools and Society

A Sociological Approach to Education

EDITORS

Jeanne H. Ballantine
Wright State University

Joan Z. Spade
The College at Brockport, State University of New York

Los Angeles | London | New Delhi
Singapore | Washington DC

Los Angeles | London | New Delhi
Singapore | Washington DC

FOR INFORMATION:

Pine Forge Press
An Imprint of SAGE Publications, Inc.
2455 Teller Road
Thousand Oaks, California 91320
E-mail: order@sagepub.com

SAGE Publications Ltd.
1 Oliver's Yard
55 City Road
London EC1Y 1SP
United Kingdom

SAGE Publications India Pvt. Ltd.
B 1/I 1 Mohan Cooperative Industrial Area
Mathura Road, New Delhi 110 044
India

SAGE Publications Asia-Pacific Pte. Ltd.
33 Pekin Street #02-01
Far East Square
Singapore 048763

Acquisitions Editor: David Repetto
Editorial Assistant: Maggie Stanley
Production Editor: Kelle Schillaci
Copy Editor: Trey Thoelcke
Typesetter: C&M Digitals (P) Ltd.
Proofreader: Andrea Martin
Cover Designer: Gail Buschman
Marketing Manager: Erica DeLuca
Permissions Editor: Karen Ehrmann

Printed in the United States of America

Library of Congress Cataloging-in-Publication Data

Schools and society : a sociological approach to education / editors, Jeanne H. Ballantine, Joan Z. Spade. — 4th ed.

p. cm.
Includes bibliographical references and index.

ISBN 978-1-4129-7924-5 (pbk.)

1. Educational sociology. 2. School management and organization—Social aspects. I. Ballantine, Jeanne H. II. Spade, Joan Z.

LC191.S268 2012 306.43′2—dc22 2010051007

This book is printed on acid-free paper.

11 12 13 14 15 10 9 8 7 6 5 4 3 2 1

CONTENTS

PREFACE

The challenge we struggled with as we selected material for this book was how to present sociology of education to students in a way that contains both a synopsis and a balanced picture of a complex field. As a result, we created this text to provide students with an overview of the scope, perspectives, and issues in the sociology of education. We drew on our many years of experience in researching, publishing, and teaching sociology of education. Our goal was to involve students by presenting well-rounded and provocative summaries of major areas in the field. Individual readings include a combination of classical foundations in the field, noted contemporary authors, and current issues most often discussed by instructors. The most frequently taught topics, according to recent survey data are stratification, the social context of education, schools as organizations, and diversity in education (American Sociological Association, 2004). Issues related to these topics are addressed throughout the book.

Schools and Society is designed to appeal to both graduate and upper-level undergraduate students. The text is divided into eleven chapters that begin with introductions outlining issues in the topic area and summarizing the readings that follow. The readings, written by leading scholars, are presented within a systematic framework that provides an overview of the field. These readings introduce major theoretical perspectives and include classic studies, current issues, and applications of knowledge to particular educational problems. Although this book is not about educational policy per se, many of the readings have practical and policy implications for education.

To accomplish the goal of presenting a comprehensive and theoretically balanced overview of the field, we selected readings that:

1. Illustrate major concepts, theoretical perspectives, and the complexity of education, including how to study it and how it has been studied;

2. Blend classic studies with newer, sometimes controversial topics;

3. Apply to students who are likely to take the course in various majors—sociology, education, and others;

4. Exhibit writing at a level of sophistication appropriate to students in advanced undergraduate or graduate courses;

5. Concentrate on materials drawn from a wide range of sources, including books, journals, scientific studies and reports, and commentaries; and

6. Use the open systems approach to provide a framework for an overview of the field and analysis of a disparate group of topics.

The readings selected were tested for readability and interest level with graduate and undergraduate students. Those readings included were seen as useful and important contributions to understanding the field. Changes were made in both selections and the introductions to the readings as a result of students' comments. Each chapter begins with an introduction to show the interrelationships between the various issues in education. Each reading is preceded by introductory remarks and questions to guide students to key aspects of the article and to tie it to other articles.

NEW TO THIS EDITION

The fourth edition of *Schools and Society* introduces 27 new readings, plus revisions of seven readings original to this book. In addition, we added a new chapter on the research methods used to study education. This new chapter on methods is structured to connect the methodological design to particular readings found in this book. Finally, chapters were renamed and reorganized to better portray the new materials in each section of the book and some readings from the previous edition were moved to new chapters to reflect the new organizational structure. This reader can be used alone, with a text, or with other readings or monographs. The readings included are appropriate for a variety of courses focusing on the study of education, such as sociology of education, social foundations of education, social contexts of education, and the like. This book may be used in departments of sociology, education, social sciences, or others as appropriate.

REFERENCE

American Sociological Association. (2004). *Teaching sociology of education.* Washington, DC: Teaching Resources Center.

ABOUT THE EDITORS

The editors, Jeanne Ballantine and Joan Spade, have known each other for many years through their involvement in the American Sociological Association (ASA) and Sociology of Education Section activities. This project started when Joan asked if Jeanne planned to update her reader. Thus, a collaboration began more than 10 years ago, with the two meeting in hotel rooms at conferences and visiting each other to develop and conceptualize this anthology. This collaboration continues with the publication of the fourth edition.

Jeanne H. Ballantine is professor of sociology at Wright State University in Dayton, Ohio. She received an MA from Columbia University and a PhD from Indiana University, with a specialty in sociology of education. She has been teaching and writing for more than 30 years and has written or coauthored several texts, including *Sociology of Education: A Systematic Analysis*, *Teaching Sociology of Education*, *Sociological Footprints*, and *Our Social World: Introduction to Sociology*. She has also published in other areas, including gender and teaching of sociology, and has been an active member of sociology of education organizations, including the ASA Section on Sociology of Education, the American Educational Research Association (AERA), and the International Sociological Association (ISA) Research Committee on Sociology of Education. She has won numerous awards, including the ASA Distinguished Contributions to Teaching Award.

Joan Z. Spade is professor of sociology at The College at Brockport, State University of New York, in Brockport, New York. She received her MA from the University of Rochester and her PhD from the University of Buffalo. She has been teaching and writing in the field for more than 30 years, including a semester teaching in Budapest, Hungary, as a Fulbright Scholar, and is coeditor of *Implementing Educational Reform: Sociological Perspectives on Educational Policy* and coauthor of articles in sociology of education on stratification and grouping practices in education. She also publishes in other areas, including gender and family, and is coeditor with Catherine G. Valentine of *The Kaleidoscope of Gender: Prisms, Patterns, and Possibilities*. Currently she is researching academic governance in higher education. She is a member of the ASA, including the ASA Section on Sociology of Education, the Eastern Sociological Society, and Sociologists for Women in Society.

INTRODUCTION

Schooling is ubiquitous in the world, making education a major institution in societies. Indeed, it is difficult to imagine any developed or developing society without a system of schools, from preschool to graduate level. Sociologists who study education examine schools from a variety of perspectives. The readings in this book introduce the primary sociological perspectives on educational systems and survey major issues in the field. The following illustrates some topics and questions addressed by sociologists of education:

In what ways do the informal relationships and expectations in schools affect student learning and experiences in school? (Chapter 4)

How is the knowledge that we teach our children constructed and selected for our schools? (Chapter 6)

What external ideas and organizations affect the way we teach our children? (Chapter 3)

How do students' race, social class, and gender affect their school experiences and reflect systems of inequality in society? (Chapters 7 and 8)

How is higher education organized, and how has that system evolved? (Chapter 9)

How do schools in the United States compare to those in other countries? (Chapter 10)

What factors bring about changes in societies' educational systems? (Chapter 11)

We address these and many other questions by providing an overview of major theoretical perspectives in Chapter 1 and end by considering change and reform of educational institutions in Chapter 11. Throughout this book, readings look at how schools work, how they affect students and society, and how they might work differently. We look at the current condition of education and consider educational change and policy issues, all of which help us to understand the complex matrix of relationships and activities within schools. We hope this knowledge about educational issues will help you make more effective decisions as students, parents, taxpayers, and perhaps educators. After reading this book, you should have gained some understanding of the fields of sociology and education, what both fields contribute to the study of educational systems, and some specific educational issues of concern to sociologists and education professionals.

What Can Sociologists Tell Us About Education?

Sociological analyses of education give us a deeper understanding of the form and purpose of education in a society and the interactions of people within educational organizations. Sociologists study structures and organizations of social systems, including education, family, religion, economics, politics, and health. Social institutions, such as education, constitute the major structural components of any society. Sociologists of education focus on the institution of education and the structure, processes, and interaction patterns within it. These aspects of education vary greatly across societies. In some societies, children learn their proper roles primarily by observing elders and imitating or modeling adult behavior. In other societies, children attend formal schools from a young age and learn the skills and knowledge needed for survival within the school and societal context.

Education and other institutions are interdependent in a society. Change in one brings change in others. For instance, a family's attitudes toward education will affect the child's school experience, as you will read in this book. Therefore, the sociological analysis of education is different from the approach taken by many people in society because sociologists begin by looking at the larger picture of society and the role that education plays in society rather than on individuals in that system. As a result, change in education is more likely to be based in structural rather than personal factors.

The Educational System

The analysis of educational systems falls into two main areas: process and structure. At whatever level of analysis we study the educational system of a society, processes are at work. These are the action parts of the system, bringing the structure alive. Examples of processes include teaching, learning, communication, and decision making, as well as those formal and informal activities that socialize students into their places in school and later life roles. These are the dynamic parts of the educational system.

However, we cannot ignore the structure of a system, including the hierarchy or roles people play—administrators, teachers, staff, parents, and, of course, students—as well as the organization of learning—classroom and school layout, types of schools, and structure of curriculum. Nor can we ignore the school's environment, which consists of groups, organizations, other institutions, and even the global society outside the school, all of which influence school functioning. For instance, parents may put pressure on schools to select particular books (Chapter 6), communities may provide unequal academic opportunities to different groups of students (Chapter 7), and the federal and state political and economic structures shape policies and resources available to schools (Chapters 3, 4, 8, 9, 10, and 11). In short, no school exists in a vacuum. This open systems perspective is the uniting theme in this book.

The Open Systems Perspective

The open systems perspective looks at the educational system as a whole, integrated, dynamic entity. Unfortunately, most research studies focus on only parts of the whole system, and most theoretical perspectives have biases or limitations by focusing on one part. An open systems perspective is not a panacea for all the problems we face when trying to get the total picture, but this perspective can help us conceptualize a whole system and understand how the small pieces fit together into a working unity. The open systems perspective provides a useful way of visualizing many elements in the system; it helps to order observations and data and represents a generalized picture of complex interacting elements and sets of relationships. The perspective modeled in Figure I.1 refers to no one particular organization or theoretical perspective, but rather to the common characteristics of many educational settings.

Figure I.1 Open Systems Approach to Education

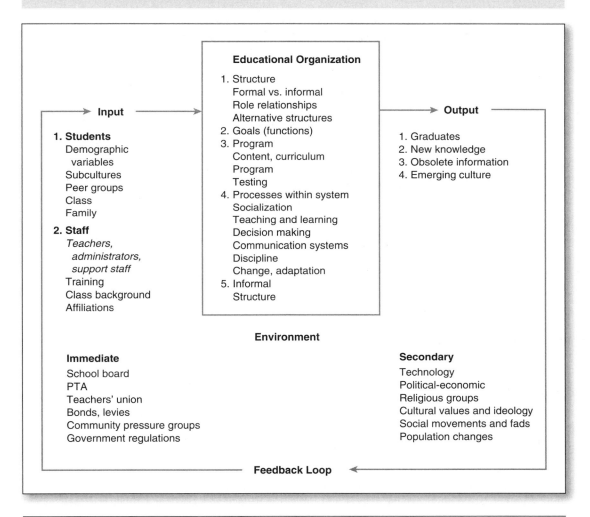

Note. From *The Sociology of Education: A Systematic Analysis* (6th ed., p. 27), by J. H. Ballantine and F. M. Hammack, 2009, Englewood Cliffs, NJ: Prentice Hall. Copyright 2009 by Pearson Education. Reprinted with permission.

Although this figure lists the component parts of a total system, it does not imply that one theory is better than another for explaining situations or events in the system. Neither does it suggest the best methodology to use in studying the system. The figure does allow you to visualize the parts you will read about in this book and help you to see where they fit and what relationship they bear to the system as a whole.

Figure I.1 shows the basic components or processes in any social system. These components are the organization, the environment, input, output, and feedback. In the following sections, we briefly discuss each of these parts as it relates to the educational system.

Step 1: Organization

Focus your attention on the center box, the organization. This refers to the center of activity and is generally the central concern for the researcher. This box can represent a society (such as the United States), an institution (such as the public education system), an organization (such as a particular school), a subsystem (such as a classroom), or an interaction (such as between teachers and students or between peers). For purposes of discussion, we shall refer to this as *the organization.* It is in the organization that many activities related to education take place, illustrating that the organization is more than structure, positions, roles, and functions. Within the organizational boundaries is a structure consisting of parts and subparts, positions and roles. Although we speak of the organization as though it were a living entity, we are really referring to the personnel who carry out the activities of the organization and make decisions about organizational action. The patterns of processes in the system bring the organization alive. Decision making and formulation of rules by key personnel, communication between members of the organization, socialization into positions in the organization, teaching in the classroom—these are among the many patterns of activities that are constantly taking place.

These patterns of processes do not take place in a vacuum. The decision makers holding positions and carrying out roles in the organization are constantly responding to demands from both inside and outside the organization. For example, the principal of a school must respond to many different constituencies, including federal, state, and local agencies; district personnel; parents; teachers; students; and even neighbors who live near the school. The boundaries of the organization are not solid but rather remain flexible and pliable in most systems to allow the system to respond to its environment. We call this *open boundaries*, or an open system.

Capturing the relationships in the school can tell us as much about its functioning as observing formal roles and structure. For example, students' experiences depend on their social class backgrounds, the responses of school staff to their behavior within schools, and the actions of students and staff that create school cultures.

Step 2: Environment

An open system implies that there is interaction between the patterns within the organizations and the environments outside the organizations. The environment refers to everything that surrounds the organization and influences it in some way. Typically the environment includes other surrounding systems. For schools, an important aspect of the environment is financial—where they get their money. What rules are imposed on schools is another critical factor, as schools exist within a maze of social, political, and legal expectations, such as the recent No Child Left Behind and Race to the Top legislation. Another is the employment market and job skills needed at a particular time. For each school organization, the crucial factors in its environment will differ and change over time.

Organizations depend on their environments to meet many of their resource requirements and to obtain information. Every school and school district faces a different set of challenges from its environment. There are many necessary and desired interactions with the environment, and some that are not so pleasant. The interaction of the school with the environment takes place in our systems model in the form of input and output.

Step 3: Input

The organization receives input from the environment in such forms as information (including textbooks and classroom materials), raw materials, personnel, finances, and new ideas. Furthermore, persons who are members of the organization are also part of surrounding communities and bring into the organization influences from the environment.

Some environmental inputs are mandatory for the organization's survival; others vary in degree of importance. For most organizations, some inputs are undesirable but unavoidable: new legal restrictions, competition, or financial pressures. The organization can exert some control over inputs. For instance, schools have selection processes for new teachers, textbooks, and other curricular materials. Schools have less control over other inputs, such as which students they serve. Certain positions in the organization are held by personnel who act as buffers between the organization and its environment. For example, the secretary who answers the phone has a major controlling function and so, too, in a very different manner, does the principal of a school.

Step 4: Output

Output refers to the material items and the nonmaterial ideas that leave the organization, such elements as completed products, wastes, information, evolving culture, and new technology. There may be personnel who bridge the gap between organizations and their environment. Personnel with responsibility for selling the organization's product serve this function, whether they work in a placement office for college graduates or in the central administrative offices of a school district creating newsletters and funding solicitations for local taxpayers and others.

The normal production of new knowledge in colleges and universities in the form of research papers and articles represents output from these educational institutions. As you will read in Chapter 9, the country saw a critical need for this production of scholarly knowledge when the former Soviet Union launched a space vehicle, Sputnik, well before the United States was prepared to do so, thus imposing new demands for the amount and types of knowledge generated by higher educational institutions in order to be competitive.

Step 5: Feedback

A key aspect of an open systems model is the process of feedback. This process implies that an organization's leaders are constantly learning about and adapting to changes and demands in the environment as a result of news they receive. For instance, the organizational personnel compare the current state of affairs with desired goals and environmental feedback to determine new courses of action. The feedback may be positive or negative, requiring differing responses. Top administrators of our educational institutions are, in many ways, managers of this system of feedback.

ORGANIZATION OF THE BOOK

The open systems perspective described above and in Figure I.1 can serve us in many ways. Not only does it provide an organizing framework for this book, but this perspective can also help to promote interdisciplinary study, as illustrated in many readings in this book. As Marvin Olsen (1978) has said:

> It is not a particular kind of social organization. It is an analytical model that can be applied to any instance of the process of social organization, from families to nation. . . . Nor is [it] a substantive theory—though it is sometimes spoken of as a theory in sociological literature. This model is a highly general, content-free conceptual framework within which any number of different substantive theories of social organization can be constructed. (p. 228)

A discussion of the fields of education and sociology must include numerous related fields: economics and school financing; political science, power, and policy issues; the family and child; church-state relationships; health and medical care for children; humanities and the arts; and the school's role in early childhood training, among others.

We structured this book to embrace the complexity of education, in terms of both what is studied and how it is studied, within the open systems perspective. Each chapter in the book focuses on an aspect of the open systems perspective and contributes to the overview of educational systems. In selecting readings for the book, we sought to blend theory and classical readings with recent studies and current issues to provide background for current arguments as well as an understanding of new directions in sociology of education. Though we focus primarily on research within sociology of education, we also include relevant readings from other areas. The readings herein represent a broad range of topics in the field; however, an attempt to cover all areas is not possible because the topic of education is multifaceted and very complex. When we leave out topics, we try to address them briefly in the chapter introductions.

For each chapter, we provide an introduction to both the area of education being covered and the research in that area. Each reading also includes an introduction and questions for you to consider as you read. We encourage you to read individual chapters within the whole as exemplified by the open systems perspective presented in this introduction.

Chapter 1 presents an overview of major classical and contemporary theoretical perspectives to understanding educational systems—from functionalism to branches of conflict and interaction theory. These theoretical perspectives provide different explanations for why schools operate the way they do. This chapter provides the frameworks that are used to understand how schools work and to explain why things are as they are in schools.

Chapter 2 illustrates the relationship between theory and methods in sociology of education and provides examples of different methodological approaches. These approaches cover issues from microlevel to macrolevel analyses, interaction between individuals to examinations of global systems. Readings discuss qualitative and quantitative approaches to understanding educational systems.

Chapter 3 moves to the environment, the larger context within which the educational system operates. The environment can influence the educational system through control of finances, law, public opinion, and attitudes toward schools.

Chapter 4 focuses on schools and educational systems as organizations including the formal and informal aspects of schools. This is Step 1 in the open systems model: what goes on within the educational organization. The readings provide a sample of the rich literature on formal and in-formal organizations and structures.

Chapter 5 also focuses inside the educational organization, but on the roles and responsibilities of administrators, teachers and students. The readings illustrate several methods of research, including survey research, use of large data sets, and ethnography.

Chapter 6 considers what knowledge is presented in schools and how that knowledge is selected. These readings illustrate how the processes of determining curricula are affected by the cultural and environmental factors external to schools.

Chapter 7 delves into a key process in schools and societies—stratification by race, class, and gender. Readings explore how the stratification process in the larger society shapes the inputs and outputs as well as educational organizations themselves. This chapter examines inequalities of social stratification in schools and school-related relationships.

Chapter 8 looks at programs and policies established to bring equality and equity into educational systems. The attempts at equality and equity include laws, changes in school structures, and attempts to override the dynamics of inequality in society. However, as you will read, these efforts toward equality are not always successful. This chapter explores both the development of the reform efforts and the consequences.

Chapter 9 considers the top tiers of the educational system—higher education. The readings illustrate how this part of the educational system also includes both formal and informal structures and is reflected in the larger environment. Again, issues of inequality are addressed, both historically and in current contexts, as we consider the role of higher education in the United States and globally.

Chapter 10 illustrates that educational systems around the world are interrelated through the needs of the global community. Aspects of educational systems around the world are becoming increasingly similar. However, features of local and national environments also influence curricula, testing, and preparation of young people for their roles in a complex world.

Chapter 11 considers how educational systems change and may change in the future. It is important to understand how educational systems work. It is also important to understand why alternatives to current educational systems are difficult to design and implement.

As you read about the different parts of educational systems in this book, we hope you develop a deeper understanding of the role of education both in your life and in the society as a whole.

REFERENCES

Ballantine, J. H., & Hammack, F. M. (2009). *The sociology of education: A systematic approach* (6th ed.). Englewood Cliffs, NJ: Prentice Hall.

Ballantine, J. H., & Hammack, F. M. (2012). *The sociology of education: A systematic approach* (7th ed.). Upper Saddle River, NJ: Prentice Hall.

Olsen, M. E. (1978). *The process of social organization: Power in social systems* (2nd ed.). New York: Holt, Rinehart and Winston.

1

WHAT IS SOCIOLOGY OF EDUCATION?

Theoretical Perspectives

A whole new perspective on schools and education lies in the study of sociology of education. How sociologists understand education can contribute to informed decision making and change in educational institutions. Sociologists of education focus on *interactions* between people and *structures* that provide recurring organizations, that bring the structures such as schools alive—teaching, learning, communicating. As one of the major structural parts, or *institutions*, of society, education is a topic of interest to many sociologists. Some work in university departments of sociology or education, others work in government agencies, and others advise school administrators. Whatever their role, sociologists of education provide valuable insights into the interactions, structures, and processes of educational systems.

Sociologists of education examine many parts of educational systems—interaction, classrooms and peer groups, school organizations, and national and international systems of education. Consider some of the following questions of interest to sociologists of education: What school settings are best for learning? How do peers affect children's achievement and ambitions? What classroom structures are most effective for children from different backgrounds? How do schools reflect the neighborhoods in which they are located? Does education "reproduce" the social class of students, and what effect does this have on children's futures? What is the relationship between education, religion, and political systems? How does access to technology affect students' learning and preparation for the future? How do nations compare on international educational tests? Is there a global curriculum? These are just a sampling of the many questions that make up the broad mandate for sociology of education, and it is a fascinating one. Sociologists place the study of education in a larger framework of interconnected institutions found in every society, including family, religion, politics, economics, and health, in addition to education. In this chapter we examine the basic building blocks for a sociological inquiry—the theories that are used to frame ways of thinking about education in society.

With this focus on people in group situations, studying educational systems means that sociologists study the organization of schools and education; the dynamics that take place within schools; the roles people hold in schools, such as teachers, students, and administrators; the processes that take place in schools, including those that result in unequal outcomes for students; how different racial/ethnic groups, genders, and social class backgrounds of students can affect educational outcomes; the influences from the environment surrounding schools (such as community pressures, financial status, and government regulations); and national and international comparisons of learning and achievement in different regions and countries. No other discipline has the broad approach and understanding provided by sociology of education.

THEORIES

Sociologists of education start with perspectives or *theories* that provide a framework to search for knowledge. Theories are attempts to explain and predict patterns and practices between individuals and in social systems, in this case educational systems. Theories are carefully structured explanations or arguments that are applied to real-life situations. Since theories are not descriptions of what is happening in schools but only carefully thought out explanations, we can apply more than one theory to explain educational phenomena. An understanding of several theoretical approaches gives us different ways of thinking about educational systems. Theories guide research and policy formation in the sociology of education and provide logical explanations for why things happen as they do, helping to explain, predict, and generalize about issues related to schools. It is from the theories and the resulting research that sociologists of education come to understand educational systems. This chapter provides an overview of sociological theories as they are related to sociology of education, followed by classical and contemporary readings on the major theories. These theories also appear in readings throughout the book. Following the open systems model discussed in the Introduction enables us to visualize the school system and its relationships with other organizations in its social context, or environment. By visualizing the dynamics inside a school, we can use theories to explain various situations within schools, such as the roles individuals play in schools and interactions between administrators, teachers, students, and other staff; equal opportunity within individual school organizations; social class dynamics as played out between peers in schools; formal and informal dynamics within schools; and the organization of school systems.

WHAT YOU WILL FIND IN CHAPTER 1

The purpose of the first chapter is to introduce you to the sociology of education through some key perspectives and theories in the field. The first reading is by the book's editors, Jeanne Ballantine and Joan Spade, and outlines early theories in sociology of education and how they have influenced contemporary theories and theorists. This provides an introduction to the remaining readings, which are original works in various theories of sociology of education. The second reading provides a classical excerpt from Emile Durkheim, generally considered to be the first sociologist to write about education. He was a French professor of pedagogy at the Sorbonne in Paris and used sociology to study education, a field in which he wrote and lectured for much of his career, until his death in 1917. Durkheim defined the field of sociology of education and contributed to its early content. He was particularly concerned with the functions or purposes of education for society, the relationship between education and social change, the role of education in preparing young people to adhere to societal norms, and the social system that develops in classrooms and schools. In the reading in this chapter,

Durkheim discusses the role that schools play in socializing the young. *Moral education,* the focus of Durkheim's excerpt, helps lay the foundation for more recent functional theorists.

Defining the main purposes or functions of educational systems, Durkheim provided the foundation for functional theory today and for much sociological work, both classical and modern. As laid out by Durkheim and others, these functions are the important purposes of education, especially in preparing the young to become members of society. These functions are at the root of functional discussions of education, and you will see them reflected in readings throughout the book. Sociologists using the functional perspective see the survival of society at stake—if a society fails to train its members in the skills and knowledge necessary for perpetuating that society, order and social control will be compromised. Durkheim and other functionalists were concerned with how educational systems work in conjunction with other parts of society to create a smooth-running social system.

An illustration of functional theory's application to education is found in the excerpt from a classical article by functionalist Talcott Parsons in the third reading in this chapter. This reading focuses on the workings of a school classroom and the roles performed by each position holder. In describing the functions of schools, Parsons focuses on the school class and its purposes in meeting the goals for schools. These activities contribute to socializing children into the expectations and knowledge needed for participation in society, preparing them for adult roles and contributing to a stable society.

Historically, the second major theoretical perspective to develop was conflict theory. It became a dominant theory in response to functional theory's focus on the need to preserve stability in society, sometimes at a cost to disadvantaged groups in society. Conflict theorists ask how schools contribute to unequal education and distribution of people in stratification systems (such as social classes). A major issue for sociologists of education in the conflict tradition is the role education plays in maintaining the prestige, power, and economic and social position of the dominant group in society. They contend that more powerful members of society maintain the most powerful positions in society and the less powerful groups (often women, disadvantaged racial and ethnic groups, and lower social classes) are "allocated" to lower ranks.

Karl Marx and Max Weber set the stage for contemporary conflict theories, and the reading in this chapter by Samuel Bowles and Herbert Gintis provides an example of this perspective applied to education. Classical conflict theorists argue that those who dominate capitalist economic systems also control other institutions in society, such as education. Capitalists use these institutions to maintain power and enhance their own profits, although not without resistance by some students and community groups.

In their reading, Bowles and Gintis present a classical Marxist conflict perspective as they argue that schools reproduce the economic class structure by providing more opportunities for students from privileged backgrounds. The few who dominate in schools and society repress the many who have primarily their wage labor to sell. For the few to maintain their positions, they reinforce distinctions of sex, ethnic origin, social class, and status; using the educational system is one means of dominating.

Contemporary sociologist Randall Collins (1971) also provides an overview of another approach to conflict theory, discussing the use of Weber's concept of "status groups" to point out the strong relationship between students' social class origins, their preparation in school, and the jobs they move into after school. Weber argued that schools teach and maintain particular "status cultures," that is, groups in society with similar interests and positions in the status hierarchy. Located in neighborhoods, schools are often rather homogeneous in their student bodies and teach to the local constituency, thus perpetuating status cultures.

Functional and conflict theorists have been debating how to explain what happens in schools since Marx, Weber, and Durkheim's times. Each function of education (discussed in the first reading) has generated controversy. For example, functionalists argue that schools prepare young members of society for their adult roles, thus allowing for the smooth functioning of society, whereas conflict theorists counter that the powerful members of society control access to the best educations, thus preparing only their children for the highest positions in society and retaining their positions of power.

The third major theoretical perspective in sociology of education is interaction theory, a microlevel theory that focuses on individual and small group experiences in the educational system: the symbols, processes, and interactions that take place in schools. In *interaction* or *interpretive theory*, individuals are active players in shaping their experiences and cultures, and not merely shaped by societal forces. By studying the way participants in the process of schooling construct their realities, researchers can better understand the meaning of education for participants. The final reading in the chapter, by Ray Rist, comes from the interaction theory tradition, and it focuses on *labeling theory*.

One important factor in the teaching and learning process is what teachers come to expect from their students. The concept of *self-fulfilling prophecy* applied to the classroom was made famous by Rosenthal and Jacobson's book *Pygmalion in the Classroom* (1968). They studied how teachers form judgments about their students and label them based on objective but also subjective factors, such as social class, appearance, and language patterns. The reading by Rist argues that utilizing labeling theory, and an outcome of labeling called the *self-fulfilling prophecy,* helps us to understand school processes from the standpoint of both teachers and students.

As you read about these theories in this chapter, try to picture the open systems perspective (discussed in the Introduction) with its many parts, activities, participants, structures, contexts or environments, and processes, such as conflict. These readings provide an overview and examples of theoretical perspectives that will help you to understand parts of the education system, interrelationships between parts, and many of the issues in the book that use these theories. In the following chapters, other parts of the open systems model are examined. Some readings take an institutional perspective, looking at how social structure affects the institution of education; others take a more microlevel focus on individuals, classrooms, and interactions in schools. All can be placed in the context of the open systems model, and all can be better understood with knowledge of the theories that are discussed in this chapter.

REFERENCES

Collins, R. (1971). Functional and conflict theories of educational stratification. *American Sociological Review, 36*(6), 1002–1019.

Rosenthal, R., & Jacobson, L. (1968). *Pygmalion in the classroom.* New York: Holt, Rinehart, and Winston.

GETTING STARTED

Understanding Education Through Sociological Theory

Jeanne H. Ballantine and Joan Z. Spade

Each of us has opinions about schools. These opinions, particularly if held by people in powerful positions in society, often translate into policy decisions related to schools and votes on tax levies. Theories provide sociologists and policy makers with a choice of frameworks to view educational systems in more depth than simple opinions and help us to understand the research that sheds light on what happens in schools, enabling informed decisions about school policies. In this reading, we outline key elements of several major theoretical approaches in sociology of education to provide multiple frames from which to view educational issues discussed in this book.

Questions to consider for this reading:

1. How can theories in the sociology of education help us understand educational systems?

2. What are some research questions that microlevel and macrolevel theorists might address? How do they differ?

3. Think of a current issue in education of interest to you and consider how each of the theories discussed in this reading would help to explain that issue.

To understand how education systems work—or don't work—social scientists develop theories providing logical, carefully structured arguments to explain schools and society. Theories inform research on education and provide valuable insights into all parts of education discussed and represented by the open systems model in the introduction to this book. Some theories have limited use, but others stand the test of time and have relevance beyond the immediate circumstances that generated them.

The purpose of this discussion is to review some of the leading theoretical approaches in the sociology of education used to understand how scholars develop questions about educational systems that organize their research. The discussion of theories in this reading is divided by levels of analysis. Microlevel explanations focus on the individual and interactions between individuals, such as how teachers, administrators, students, parents, or others perceive and respond to educational settings and how their responses

Revision of "Social Science Theories on Teachers, Teaching, and Educational Systems," in *The New International Handbook of Teachers and Teaching* (pp. 81–102), by A. G. Dworkin and L. J. Saha (Eds.), 2009, New York: Springer. Copyright 2009 by Springer. Adapted with permission.

shape interactions. For example, we can use microlevel theories to understand how teachers respond differently to some children based on their gender or social class of their families. Macrolevel explanations, on the other hand, focus on the institution of education and how schools fit into the larger social structure. As such, macrolevel theorists might study why different educational structures emerge in different societies, looking at the role of schools in society as a whole. Our discussion of these theories begins with microlevel explanations and moves to macrolevel theoretical perspectives.

For over a half century, *Why Johnny Can't Read* (Flesch, 1955) and numerous other books explored problems in school systems, from teachers' expectations of students to classroom dynamics and school policies such as tracking and testing. These issues continue to be debated today in both national and international contexts. We use the problem of "why Johnny can't read" to illustrate the theories we introduce in this article.

MICROLEVEL THEORIES OF EDUCATION

Efforts to understand why Johnny can't read are typically found at the microlevel of analysis. They focus on interactions and experiences in the classroom between the student and others, often attributing failure to the students themselves or to their teachers. *Interaction theorists* focus on the interpersonal dynamics of the situation and assume that individuals socially construct their lives based on the environments in which they find themselves. With origins in the field of social psychology, symbolic interaction theories link individuals with the symbols they use to understand the situations they are in. These symbols are developed and understood in their immediate social contexts, groups, and society. For example, the names students in each school or classroom call each other or the meanings they give to their school work vary both within and between schools and are often linked to the social class backgrounds of students and their peers.

Nothing is taken for granted in interaction theory; what most people accept as given is questioned and studied. Thus, the question of why Johnny can't read begins with Johnny's "social construction of reality," as well as the socially constructed realities of his teachers, school administrators, parents, and others in his social world and embedded in all interactions Johnny has (Berger & Luckmann, 1963). Add to the puzzle complications from the social construction of race, class, and gender, socially constructed categories themselves, and we have the context for symbolic interaction theory (as illustrated in the readings by Morris in Chapter 7). Interaction theories focus on what teachers and students *do* in school. These theories grew from reactions to the macrolevel structural-functional and conflict theories, which focus on society and how schools as institutions fit in the big picture. The criticism is that macrolevel approaches miss the dynamics of everyday school interactions and life in classrooms that shape children's futures. Interaction theorists question things most people don't question, such as how students get labeled and tracked in schools; they ask questions about the most common, ordinary interactions between school participants. Sociologists of education using this approach are likely to focus on students' attitudes, values, and achievements, such as their motivations to do well in school; students' self-concepts; and how interactions between peers, students, teachers, and principals are shaped by the social class backgrounds of all participants (see Lareau and Horvat in Chapter 2).

Among the several approaches taken by interaction theorists are symbolic interaction, role theory, and labeling theory; dramaturgy and ethnomethodology; and phenomenological sociology. The following discussion gives an overview of several of these approaches.

Symbolic Interaction Theory

Symbols are the concepts or ideas that we use to frame our interactions. These concepts can be expressed by words or gestures; they define reality and affect our sense of self and the social hierarchies which surround us. As such, children are viewed as active participants in making distinctions between one another and are therefore agents in creating the social reality in which they live. For example, popularity is a major issue for many children, especially in middle-school years. Popularity is mostly a function of being visible and having everyone know who you are, but it also specifies a symbolic hierarchy of social power. Sometimes popularity is gained by representing the school in an athletic contest, by being attractive, or by being in a leadership position. The difficulty is that positions of popularity are scarce. Thus, competition is created, and some individuals are going to be "losers," with negative social power, while a few others are "winners" in this socially defined popularity contest. Consider also the example of academic grouping. No matter what teachers or administrators call reading groups and different levels of English, mathematics, or science classes, children quickly learn whether they are "good" or "bad" students. Symbols define students' and teachers' interactions—specifying who is "bright," "cooperative," "trouble," and so forth. Symbols define what experiences are "good" or "bad," In other words, symbols create our social reality.

Considerable inequality occurs in the symbols students bring with them to school. Children from families who cannot afford to purchase desired clothing or other status symbols, or send their children to sports training or camp, are more likely to be the "losers." Those who "win" are more likely to have access to symbolic resources, including higher class-based language patterns and social experiences; they are valued, and given special privileges in the classroom or school. These students, who exude privilege in the symbols they bring with them, are more likely to develop leadership skills and generally feel good about themselves (Eder, Evans, & Parker, 1995).

Symbolic interaction theory has its roots in the works of G. H. Mead and C. H. Cooley on the development of the self through social interaction, whether in school or in other areas of life. People within a culture generally interpret and define social situations in similar ways because they share experiences and expectations (Ballantine & Roberts, 2011). Students look to others, particularly their teachers, to understand their place in this culture. Common norms evolve to guide behavior. Students learn through interaction how they are different from others based on individual experiences, social class, and status.

Labeling Theory

Labeling theory is closely related to the symbolic interactionist perspective (Goffman, 1967). If Johnny is told often enough that he is stupid and can't do the work, the label of "stupid" can become a self-fulfilling prophecy as he comes to incorporate that label into his sense of self. Then, teachers and others who create and reinforce the label continue to respond to Johnny as if that symbol is an accurate reflection of his abilities. Using labeling theory, we can better understand how teachers' expectations based on students' race, class, ethnic background, gender, religion, or other characteristics affect students' self-perceptions and achievement levels.

Labeling theory helps us to understand how microlevel interactions in the school contribute to individuals' formations of their sense of self. Young people from 6 to 18 years old spend much of their time in school or school-related activities; therefore, *student* is a status that has enormous impact on how one sees oneself. Interaction with others in school affects the student's sense of self. The image that is reflected back to someone—as student or as teacher, for example—can begin to mold one's sense of competence, intelligence, and likeability. The school creates a symbolic structure that influences how individuals make sense of their reality and interact with others. Official school positions such as president of the student council, lower-level reader, or athlete can become important elements of a student's self.

The powerful interactions between labelers and labeled have been studied in schools. A classic study found that students in classrooms where the teachers were told that students in their classes were "late bloomers" and would "blossom" that year achieved much more academically than students in classrooms where the teacher had no expectations for students, even though students in both classrooms were similar in ability (Rosenthal & Jacobson, 1968).

The processes of labeling by assigning students in academic and nonacademic tracks and ability groups serve to reproduce inequalities in society. Low-income students are often placed in low-ability groups, which can become a "life sentence" affecting achievement and future opportunities. Interactions between participants in the school and classroom give insight into the labeling process. For example, in another classic study, Rist found that teachers formed expectations for students based on their race, class, ethnicity, and gender and that these expectations had long-term effects on students' achievement and sense of themselves (Rist, 1970, 1977). The result is that low-income students are more likely to be placed in lower-ability groups that do not reflect their actual ability (Rist, 1970, 1977; Sadovnik, 2007).

Outside-of-school statuses can be an important basis for interactions in schools. In addition to social class, gender is reinforced in social interactions in the classroom, as shown in research findings indicating that girls struggle more with self-esteem, especially in middle school, than do boys (AAUW, 2001). Sadker and Sadker (1994) have found clear and distinct patterns in the way teachers interact with boys and girls in the classroom. Teachers tend to call on boys more, wait longer for boys' responses to questions, and expect boys to act out more in the classroom. Girls, on the other hand, are expected to be quiet and compliant, and teachers tend to do things for girls, rather than push them to succeed. Given how gendered expectations shape interactions in the classroom, it is not surprising that girls tend to struggle with self-esteem issues at adolescence. In Chapter 7, Roslyn Mickelson discusses gender differences in classrooms for boys and girls and how these differences are changing.

Furthermore, these patterns of gender and class differences vary by race and ethnicity (Carter, 2006; Grant, 2004). The point is that schools are powerful institutions, and the interactions within

them heavily influence how children think about themselves and their futures. Students from different social classes, races, genders, and sexual orientations bring different orientations, patterns, and behaviors into the schools, resulting in unique symbolic and interactional experiences.

Dramaturgy

Erving Goffman looked for connections between the microlevels and macrolevels of sociology. Stemming from Durkheim's ideas of the importance of rituals and symbols in everyday life, the messages they transfer, and the collective conscience that develops from them, Goffman wrote that everyday interactions are based on codes or systems that represent rules of the larger society (Antikainen et al., 2010). He compared social life for individuals to frontstage and backstage behavior on which people perform differently depending on the impressions they wish to project to the audience (Goffman, 1959). Goffman's influence is also seen in the study of school interactions with his concepts of "encounters"—conscious and planned interaction (Goffman, 1990). As Johnny comes to school, he goes "on stage" and presents himself through his clothing and other symbols that he adopts. He attempts to manage the impressions he gives to others, including teachers and peers, in order to manipulate how they define him as he struggles with learning to read.

Rational Choice Theory

While rational choice theory does not ignore symbols and interactions, this theory focuses primarily on the assumption that there are costs and rewards involved in our individual decisions within the classroom and school. According to rational choice theory, if benefits outweigh costs, the individual is likely to make the decision to act in order to continue receiving benefits. If costs outweigh benefits, the individual will seek other courses of action. In education, the question is how weighing of costs and benefits influences decisions about educational choices by students, teachers, and administrators in the conduct of school experiences.

For example, students who consider dropping out of school likely go through some analysis, comparing benefits of staying in school such as ability to get a better job, versus costs to themselves, for instance their battered self-esteem in schools. And, for Johnny, deciding whether to do what is necessary to learn to read or to focus on behaviors that gain him esteem in other areas may be part of his school day. Whether we would agree that individuals have assessed the costs and the benefits correctly is not the point; the issue is how individuals evaluate the benefits and costs at a given moment in making what theorists describe as a *rational choice.*

Rational choice theory can also be applied to the issue of teacher retention. Teachers have an extremely high dropout rate, with roughly half of all new teachers in the United States currently leaving the profession within 5 years (Lambert, 2006). Rational choice theorists would explain this in terms of the perceived costs—relatively low salary for a college graduate; minimal respect from parents, students, and administrators; long days for 9 months of the year; little opportunity to participate in teaching- and job-related decisions (Dworkin, Saha, & Hill, 2003). Teachers compare these costs to the benefits of teaching—the feeling of making a contribution to society and helping children; time off in the summer; and enjoying aspects of teaching, coaching, or directing. When costs are seen as higher than benefits, teachers leave the profession, resulting in high teacher burnout and dropout rates (Dworkin, 2007; also see the Dworkin and Tobe reading in Chapter 5). Rational choice theory extends interactionist theories and is useful as we try to understand decision making of individuals in schools.

MACROLEVEL THEORIES OF EDUCATION

Whereas microlevel theories focus on individual's construction of reality in educational settings and interpersonal interactions between individuals and in small groups within schools, macrolevel explanations focus on larger societal and cultural systems. As such, schools as organizations, the processes of teaching and learning, and the interactions within schools and classrooms are viewed as part of larger social contexts (Brookover, Erickson, & McEvoy, 1996).

Functional Theory

Functional theory helps us to understand how education systems work and what purpose education serves in societies. While this is not a leading theory in sociology of education today, we describe it here because of its historical importance and influence on the field today, and because other theories arose as reactions to or modifications of functional theory. Functional theory starts with the assumption that education, as an institution in society, operates, along with other institutions, to facilitate the stability of society. There is a relationship between schools and other institutions in society, as all institutions must fulfill necessary societal functions to maintain society. Each part of a society—education, family, political and economic systems, health, religion—works together to create a functioning social system. Each part contributes necessary elements to the functioning and survival of the whole society, just as multiple parts of the body work together to keep us healthy and active. As such, in functional theory, schools are analyzed in terms of their functions, or purposes, in the whole system (see the discussion of school functions below). The degree of interdependence among parts in the system relates to the degree of integration among these parts; all parts complement each other, and the assumption is that a smooth-running, stable system is well integrated. Shared values, or consensus, among members are important components of the system, as these help keep it in balance. In terms of why Johnny can't read, it may be that it is not important to society for Johnny to read, or it is simply not functional for all students to know how to read.

Functional theories of education originated in the work of Emile Durkheim (1858–1917), who contributed a method for viewing schools and an explanation of how schools help to maintain order in societies. According to Durkheim, a major role of education in society was to create unity by providing a common moral code necessary for social cohesion. Durkheim's major works in education were published in collections titled *Moral Education* (1925/1961), *The Evolution of Educational Thought* (1938/1977), and *Education and Society* (1903/1956), all written in the early 1900s. In these works, he set forth a definition of education that has guided the field.

In *Moral Education*, Durkheim outlined his beliefs about the function of schools and their relationship to society (see Reading 2 in this chapter). Moral values are, for Durkheim, the foundation of the social order, and society is perpetuated through its educational institutions, which help instill values and a sense of moral order in the youngest members of society. In this work, he analyzed classrooms as "small societies," or agents of socialization, reflecting the moral order of the social system at that time. The school serves as an intermediary between the *affective morality* (or a morality related to emotion or feeling) of the family and the rigorous morality of society. Discipline is the morality of the classroom, and without it the classroom can become like an undisciplined mob, according to Durkheim. Because children learn to be social beings and develop appropriate social values through contact with others, schools are an important training ground for learning social skills and the "rules" of the larger society, as opposed to the more emotional character of families. Functionalists also argue that the passing on of knowledge and behaviors is a primary function of schools, one necessary to maintain order and fill needed positions in society. Following Durkheim, sociologists see the transmission of moral and occupational education, discipline, and values as necessary for the survival of society. Thus, schools play a very important role in maintaining functioning of the larger society.

Durkheim was concerned primarily with value transmission for the stability of society. He did not consider the possible conflict between this stable view of the values and skills, and what is necessary for changing emerging industrial societies. He argued also that education should be under the control of the state, free from special interest groups; however, as we know, most governments are subject to influence from interest groups and changes in society, as you will read throughout this book.

Instrumental in the development of modern functional theory was the work of Talcott Parsons (1959). He saw education as performing certain important tasks or "functions" for society, such as preparing young people for roles in a democratic society. Parsons argued that female elementary school teachers (he assumed all elementary school teachers should be female) play a role in transitioning children from the home and protection of mother to schools where a more impersonal female role socializes children to meet the less personal and more universal demands of society (Parsons, 1959). This linking of teachers to their role in the larger society is only one example of how functionalists have viewed the role of teachers (see the reading by Ingersoll and Merrill in Chapter 5).

Other functionalists argued that some degree of inequality is inevitable in society because the most challenging positions required attracting the most talented individuals who must spend time and money educating themselves to fill these important roles. These theorists saw schools as part of a large system in which individuals who dedicate themselves to training for these higher-level occupations would receive greater rewards in terms of income and prestige (Davis & Moore, 1945). This functionalist view sees achievement in schools as based on merit, not one's status. Thus, the function of education is to support capitalism through the distribution of labor, allowing those with the most "merit" to achieve and fill higher-level positions in society.

Later functional theorists build on the base provided by Durkheim, Parsons, and others. For example, Dreeben (1968) considered the social organization of schools, while others examined the values taught in school and how these lead to greater societal consensus and preparation for one's role in society (Cookson & Sadovnik, 2002). To summarize, social scientists who research and interpret events from the functional perspective focus on the central functions of education for society as a whole (Ballantine & Hammack, 2012). We briefly summarize those functions as follows:

Socialization: Teaching Children to Be Members of Society

Most people remember their first day of elementary school, marking a transition between the warm, loving, accepting world of the family and a more impersonal school world that emphasizes discipline, knowledge, skills, responsibility, and obedience. In school, children learn that they must prove themselves; they are no longer accepted regardless of their behaviors as they were in their families. They must meet certain expectations and compete for attention and rewards. They also must prepare to participate in their society's political and economic systems, in which a literate populace is necessary to make informed decisions on issues. Citizens expect schools to respond to the constant changes in societies. In heterogeneous societies with diverse groups and cultures, school socialization helps to integrate immigrants by teaching them the language and customs of the larger society and by working to reduce intergroup tensions. This provides cohesion and order in society as a whole.

Teaching Children to Be Productive Members of Society

Societies use education to pass on values, skills, and knowledge necessary for survival. Sometimes this process occurs in formal classrooms, sometimes in informal places. For example, in West African villages children may have several years of formal education in a village school, but they learn future occupational roles informally by observing their elders in their families and by "playing" at the tasks they will soon undertake for survival. The girls help pound cassava root for the evening meal while boys build model boats and practice negotiating the waves. It is typically only the elite—sons and daughters of the rulers and the wealthy—who receive formal education beyond basic literacy in most developing countries (Ballantine & Roberts, 2011). However, elders and family members in developed societies cannot teach all the skills necessary for survival. Formal schooling emerged to meet the needs of industrial and postindustrial societies, furnishing the specialized training required by rapidly growing and changing technology. Schools in industrialized societies play a major part in placing students into later work roles.

Selection and Training of Individuals for Positions in Society

Most people have taken standardized tests, received grades at the end of a term or year, and asked teachers to write recommendation letters. Functionalists see these activities as part of the selection process prevalent in competitive societies with formal education systems. Schools distribute credentials—grades, test scores, and degrees—that determine the college or job opportunities available to individuals in society, the fields of study individuals pursue, and ultimately individual status in society. For example, selection criteria determine who gets into the "best" colleges or even into college at all, thereby sealing one's place in society. As you will read later in this book, countries today are competing against each other to provide the best education in our global society.

Promoting Change and Innovation

Institutions of higher education are expected to generate new knowledge, technology, and ideas, and to produce students with up-to-date skills and information required to lead industry and other key institutions in society. In a global age of computers and other electronic technology, critical thinking and analytical skills are essential as workers face issues that require problem solving rather than rote memorization. Thus, the curriculum must change to meet the needs of the social circumstances. Familiarity with technological equipment—computers,

Internet resources, electronic library searches, and so forth—becomes a critical survival skill for individuals and society. As Gamson describes in Chapter 9, colleges and universities are called on to provide ideas and innovation as well as skilled workers. Consider the example of India, which has top-ranked technical institutes training their graduates to meet changing world needs. The highly skilled graduates are employed by multinational companies around the world, and companies in Europe and the United States send information to India for processing and receive it back the next morning because of the time difference. Well-trained, efficient engineers and computer experts working in India for lower wages than in many developed countries have become an essential part of the global economy (Drori, 2006; Friedman, 2005).

Latent Functions of Education

In addition to these intended functions that are filled by schools, education also provides unseen latent functions. These are unintended consequences of the educational process. For example, schools keep children off the streets until they can be absorbed into productive roles in society, serving an informal "babysitting" function. In fact, in the United States, children now stay in school well into their 20s and the age at which they join the labor force or start families is much later than it was in previous generations. Schools also provide young people with a place to congregate, which in turn fosters a youth culture of music, fashion, slang, dances, dating, and sometimes gangs. At the ages when social relationships are being established, especially with the opposite sex, colleges serve as "mating" and "matching" places for young adults. Education also weakens parental control over youth, helps them begin the move toward independence, and provides experiences in large, impersonal secondary groups (Ballantine & Roberts, 2011).

Functional theorists believe that when the above social functions are not adequately addressed, the educational system is ripe for change. The structure and the processes within the educational institution remain stable only if the basic functions of society are being met.

Functionalists arguments, therefore, look to how the structure of schooling functions within the larger societal context. Understanding why Johnny can't read, thus, is not as important as understanding how Johnny's inability to read functions within the larger social order.

Conflict Theory

Conflict theorists challenge the functionalist assumptions that schools are ideologically and politically neutral and that schools operate based on meritocracy, with each child able to achieve to the highest level of his or her own ability so as to better meet the needs of society. Conflict theorists, instead, argue that inequality is based on one's position in the social system, not merit, and that schooling privileges some children and disadvantages others. There are several branches of conflict theory, which include different explanations of the role education systems play in maintaining inequality. Recent theories integrate ethnicity, race, and gender issues and add politics and culture to the traditional Marxist class and economic issues. In addition, issues of "reproduction and resistance" are recent additions to the conflict perspective. Origins of conflict theory are situated in the writings of Marx (1971) and later Max Weber (1958a, 1958b, 1961).

In contrast to functional theory, conflict theory assumes a tension in society created by the competing interests of groups in society. Conflicts occur even when teachers, students, parents, and administrators agree on the rules. Each group obeys the rules even though the rules are not in their best interests because they may not see alternatives or fear the consequences of not obeying. However, conflict theorists disagree on whether participants in the education system generally conform to the rules, rebel against them, or feel they have no choices. The roots of conflict thought are outlined below, and contemporary conflict theory, originating in the 1960s and 1970s, is discussed.

The foundation for conflict theory begins with the writings of Karl Marx (1818–1883). He was outraged over the social conditions of the exploited workers in the class system that resulted from the French Revolution and the growth of capitalism. He contended that the economic structure of capitalism created competing groups, the "haves" and the "have-nots," who lived in a constant state of tension (conflict) over resources that one had and the other wanted. The basis of this struggle is that the haves (or the owners of the means by which goods are produced in a society) control economic resources and thus have power, wealth, material goods, privilege (including access to the best schools and education), and influence. The have-nots (or the people who work for those who own the factories that produce goods in society) present a constant challenge as they seek a larger share of economic resources (wages) for their own survival. According to Marx, the haves often use coercive power and manipulation to hold society together. However, power can also be maintained by ideology—controlling ideas, or what people believe to be true. Conflict theorists view change as inevitable, as conflicts of interest should lead to the overthrow of existing power structures. Marx believed that class conflict would continue until the capitalist system of economic dominance was overthrown and replaced by a more equitable system. However, this revolution has yet to happen.

Marx argued that schools create and maintain inequality by teaching students an ideology that serves the interests of the rich and instills in students a sense of "false consciousness." That is, students in schools learn to accept the myth of meritocracy, that all have an equal chance of achieving. Those who buy into this ideology and fail often believe that their failure is due to their own shortcomings and lack of ability. Students learn to internalize their own lower position in society and their lowly fate, thus accepting a false consciousness and legitimizing the wealth and power of capitalists. Marx would also argue that the organization of schooling is set up in such a way that all students will not receive the same quality of education; thus, some students coming out of the educational system will work in factories for less pay.

Weber's Contributions to the Sociology of Education

Max Weber (1864–1920) was said to have argued with Marx's ghost because he believed that conflict in society was not based solely in economic relations as Marx had argued. Weber contended that inequalities and potential conflict were sustained in different distributions of status (prestige), power (ability to control others), as well as class (economic relations). While Weber also felt that conflict was a constant possibility, he focused more on power relationships between groups and differences in status that create a structure of inequality in societies.

Weber provided a less systematic treatment of education than Durkheim. His work in the field of sociology, however, has contributed to our understanding of many aspects of education. He is noted for his contributions to the understanding of bureaucracy and for the concept of *status groups*. In fact, he writes that the primary activity of schools is to teach particular "status cultures." Status cultures can be thought of as subcultures based on the social status of the group in society, such as working-class culture or upper-class culture. Each status group has its own set of symbols (e.g., sneakers that are "cool"), values (how important it is to go to college), and beliefs (whether or not studying is important) that are known to the individuals in the group, but not fully understood or available to those outside the group. Power relationships and the conflicting interests of individuals and groups in society influence educational systems, for it is the interests and purposes of the dominant groups in society that shape the schools.

Weber (1961) spoke of the "tyranny of educational credentials" as a prerequisite for high-status positions. This theme is discussed by Randall Collins (see his reading in this chapter), another conflict theorist following in Weber's tradition. Collins focuses on *credentialism,* or the increased requirements for higher-level positions used by more advantaged individuals to further their status (Collins, 1979). The rapid expansion of educational qualifications, faster than the number of jobs, has led to "credential inflation," yet what the school curriculum teaches is not necessary for most jobs. The result is that the credentials required for jobs keep increasing.

Within the school there are "insiders" whose status culture, Weber believes, is reinforced through the school experience, and "outsiders" who face barriers to success in school. As we apply these ideas to school systems today to explain the situation of poor and minority students, and why Johnny can't read, the relevance of Weber's brand of conflict theory becomes evident. His theory deals with conflict, domination, and status groups struggling for wealth, power, and status in society. Education is used by individuals and society as a means to attain desired ends. Relating this to Karl Marx's writings on conflict theory, education produces a disciplined labor force for military, political, or other areas of control and exploitation by the elite. Status groups differ in property ownership; cultural status, such as ethnic group membership; and power derived from positions in government or other organizations.

Weber, however, can also be considered a functionalist whose writings, using cross-cultural examples and exploring preindustrial and modern societies, shed light on the role of education in different societies at various time periods (Weber, 1958a). In preindustrial times, education served the primary purpose of a differentiating agency that trained people to fit into a way of life and a particular station in society. With industrialism, however, new pressures faced education from upwardly mobile members of society vying for higher positions in the economic system. Educational institutions became increasingly important in training people for new roles in society (Weber, 1958b).

Conflict Theory Today

Marx and Weber set the stage for the many branches of conflict theory advocated by theorists today. Research from the conflict theorists' perspective tends to focus on those tensions created by power and conflict that ultimately cause change. Some conflict theorists, following from Marx's emphasis on the economic structure of society, see mass public education as a tool of powerful capitalists to control the entrance into higher levels of education through the selection and allocation function. Marx argued that schools contributed to a "false consciousness," the equivalent of teaching students that the oppressive conditions that shape their lives cannot be changed. They must simply accept their situations, or even believe that they are not as worthy as others who are more powerful or have more advantages. Many conflict theorists believe that until society's economic and political systems are changed, school reform providing equal access to all children will be impossible (Bowles & Gintis, 1976; also see their reading in this chapter).

Conflict theorists studying education systems point out that differences in the achievement of students are not based on their ability or intelligence; rather, schools reflect the needs of the powerful, dominant groups in society and serve to perpetuate a capitalistic system that reproduces social classes. Teacher expectations based on characteristics of children, such as race and social class background, shape students' learning experiences and affect their achievement. For instance, teacher expectations may differ for poor students who have more limited language skills or speak with a dialect and lack middle-class dress, appearance, and manners. Some also argue that differential funding and resources for schools affect achievement of students. Poor and minority students are also more likely to be placed or tracked into lower reading and academic groups, placements which are hard to change. These groups are given different curricula. The higher class students receive more mentally challenging curricula that prepare them to think creatively and make decisions, and lower class students experience less challenging curricula that prepares them for manual labor. They are more likely to lead students to drop out of school. All of the above factors make it harder for Johnny to learn to read and serve to reproduce inequalities in society as a whole.

Other theorists apply early conflict theory arguments to the school and classroom level of analysis. For example, Willard Waller believes that schools are in a state of constant potential conflict and disequilibrium; teachers are threatened with the loss of their jobs because of lack of student discipline; academic authority is constantly threatened by students, parents, school boards, and alumni who represent other, often competing, interest groups in the system; and students are forced to go to schools, which they may consider oppressive and demeaning (Waller, 1932/1965). Although larger conflicts between groups in society may be the basis for these within-school patterns, the focus of some conflict theorists is not on these larger societal relationships. Many of these examples reinforce the concept of reproduction, discussed next.

Reproduction and Resistance Theories

In the second half of the 20th century, reproduction and resistance theories further expanded the ideas of conflict theories. The argument of cultural reproduction and resistance theories, very generally, is that those who dominate capitalistic systems mold individuals to suit their own purposes. These theorists considered how forms of culture are passed on by families and schools to shape individuals' views of their worlds (Bowles & Gintis, 1976).

The concept of *social reproduction* was developed in the late 1960s and early 1970s in Europe to explore the claim that schools actually *increase* inequality through the process of "teaching." At this time when equality was a central interest, the idea that schools might be contributing to societies' inequalities led to studies of the possibility that schools and families were actually perpetuating social class structures. Following from Marx, schools were viewed as part of a superstructure, along with family, politics, religion, culture, and economy, organized around the interests of the dominant capitalist group. The dominant group needs workers with good work habits, skills, and loyalty to produce products and services needed

by capitalists in exchange for wages for their labor. Schools served the needs of the dominant group by teaching students their roles in society and perpetuating the belief that the system was a fair and merit-based way to select workers.

An example is seen in Bowles and Gintis's (1976) "correspondence theory," which takes a macro view of schools, arguing that schools reproduce inequality and create class and power differences in societies. The reproduction process takes place through the student selection and allocation processes. These processes create hierarchies within schools and societies, socializing students into these hierarchies of power and domination, and legitimizing the hierarchies by claiming they are based on merit. Following the assumptions of Marx, Bowles and Gintis argue that school structure is based on the needs and standards of the dominant capitalist group in society and thus serves the purposes of that group. Students both bring into and take away different cultural competencies. The bottom line is that schools motivate higher class students to achieve and decrease ambitions of others, creating a false consciousness (Apple, 1993, 1996; also see the reading by Bowles and Gintis in this chapter).

Resistance theorists go beyond social reproduction theories by arguing that teachers and students are not passive participants in the school process and that they do not always follow the expectations that result in social reproduction. For example, students may resist their socialization into certain roles in society (Willis, 1979), just as teachers do not have to accept their role in facilitating reproduction. Teachers may work with all students to give them more equal chances in the system. Teachers can empower students with curricula that are participatory, affective, problem solving, multicultural, democratic, interdisciplinary, and activist (Shor, 1986).

CONTEMPORARY THEORIES IN SOCIOLOGY OF EDUCATION

Two concepts related to the development of reproduction and resistance theories are social capital and cultural capital. As you can see from the above, conflict theory started to move from strictly a macro/societal focus to more of a focus on interaction that maintains power and privilege. The concept of *cultural capital* was introduced in the 1970s, primarily by Pierre Bourdieu, and *social capital* was introduced by James S. Coleman (1988). These two concepts bridged macrolevel and microlevel explanations, attempting to understand how larger societal structures were maintained in day-to-day interactions.

Social capital refers to the social resources students bring to their education and future involvement in school or community, resulting in building of networks and relationships they can use as contacts for future opportunities. Ultimately, these networks are connections that make achievement possible and connect individuals to the larger group. Several researchers have applied this concept to the study of students, teachers, and teaching. For instance, connections students make in elite private schools and alumni connections through private schools and colleges enhance future economic status. Coleman's concept of social capital was used to explain the role of schools in reproducing social class.

Bourdieu's *cultural capital* is used in many research studies today. Trained as a sociologist, anthropologist, and philosopher, Pierre Bourdieu (1931–2002) delved into education's influences on stratification and social class, trying to reconcile the influences of social structures on the subjective experiences of individuals. Among the many concepts attributed to Bourdieu and in use today are *cultural and symbolic capital, symbolic violence*, and *habitus* (Bourdieu, 1973). He saw individuals as having different cultural capital based on their social settings. *Social capital* (referred to above) included the sum of resources held by individuals or groups because of their respective contacts or networks. *Symbolic capital* referred to the prestige, honor, or attention an individual held. These were each sources of individual power. *Cultural capital* refers to cultural practices, including dress and manners, language patterns and expressions, and knowledge of the world derived from life experiences such as visits to museums, all of which provide knowledge of middle-class and upper-class culture; that is, the culture of schools. Cultural capital does not refer to knowing about "culture," commonly thought of in terms of art, music and theater. Rather cultural capital allows students from middle and upper classes to use patterns of talking, common words, general knowledge, and values from their lives outside of school to fit into the patterns of interaction in school (Lareau, 1989). All individuals have cultural capital, and the form of cultural capital one has is generally related to one's social class background. A child who can speak the teacher's "language" is likely to fare better in school than one who has not been exposed to the cultural capital of the schools. Unfortunately, the cultural capital of children from working-class backgrounds is rarely valued in schools. Dominant groups pass on exposure to the dominant culture that their children take to school. Not only do their children know how schools work but they also come to school with the knowledge of what to do to be successful there. Working-class children generally do not go to school with this advantage (Bourdieu & Passeron, 1977).

The important point here is that higher social, cultural, and symbolic capital result in more power for the holder. Over time these power relationships come to be seen by individuals as legitimate. Consider how working-class children in schools might see the educational success of middle-class children as "legitimate" because they work hard or have more natural ability, whereas these advantages are bestowed on middle-class and upper-class children because of their advantaged position in the social structure (Bourdieu & Passeron, 1977).

Cultural capital inadvertently gets used by schools to reproduce inequality both in the interactions and the structure of education. For example, different curricula in different tracks create a system of educational inequality for students. While the assignment of students to learning groups is supposed to be based on explicit criteria (merit) such as test scores or completion of previous work, in actuality cultural capital plays a considerable role in who is assigned to groups. As early as pre-school, children experience different expectations from teachers (Lubeck, 1985). As noted earlier, Rist (1977) found that children were assigned to groups in kindergarten based on dress and speech patterns. Vanfossen, Jones, and Spade (1987) and Lucas (1999) found that family social class background was a strong predictor of the high school "track" in which students were placed. The end result is that students from working-class backgrounds end up learning more basic skills under stricter rules because they are expected to cause problems in the classroom. Those from upper classes learn how to make decisions, be creative and autonomous, and prepare for college (Anyon, 1980; Miller, Kohn, & Schooler, 1985). At the college level, students are again tracked into two-year or four-year educations with differences in the curriculum, goals for educational outcomes, and economic results for students (Pincus, 1980, 2002). Therefore, schools end up perpetuating differences in cultural capital by maintaining groups in school that are generally homogeneous in terms of social class backgrounds. And, you thought Johnny couldn't read because he lacked the ability needed to read well!

Teachers also bring varying degrees of cultural capital to schools and classrooms. Some teachers come from working-class and middle-class backgrounds and bring that cultural capital to the education system, both in their own training and in how they teach others. However, in some cases, the students they teach may bring a different cultural capital to the classroom, cultural capital that is either higher or lower in the hierarchy of power and wealth. Parents with higher cultural capital tend to be more involved in their children's schooling and more able to provide their children with stronger educational experiences and more at ease with the cultural capital of the school (Lareau, 1989; see also the Lareau and Horvat reading in Chapter 2).

The concept of cultural capital has been used in a number of studies of schools and classrooms. Consider McLaren's study (1989) of his experiences as a middle-class white teacher teaching in an inner-city school, facing violence and hostile parents. The cultural capital mismatch he faced was one in which his middle-class cultural capital was ineffective in working with the children he taught. This situation is repeated over and over again because teachers, by the very fact that they have the credentials to teach, have adopted a cultural capital that is not compatible with the children they teaching in economically disadvantaged neighborhoods.

Another study of social capital shows how resources in the family, community, and school serve as capital assets for improving student academic performance and psychological well-being (Schneider, 2002). This study points out that active involvement of parents at home with their children on homework and educational decisions can influence social capital and future opportunities. The reading in Chapter 9 by Portes and Fernández-Kelly further illustrates the value of cultural capital. They found that children of Mexican immigrants gained cultural capital in different ways so as to ensure that they went on to succeed in college. This study illustrates that the cultural capital children get from their social class backgrounds does not always have to hold them back. However, only a very few students in Portes and Fernández-Kelly's larger study actually made it to college and successful professional careers.

Code theory was developed around the same time as cultural capital. Code theory is presented in several volumes that lay out the sociolinguistic theory of language codes envisioned by Basil Bernstein (1924–2000). *Codes* refer to organizing principles used by members of a social group. The idea is that the language we use reflects and shapes the assumptions we hold about our relationship to a certain group. Our relationship with that group influences the way we use language.

Bernstein conceptualizes two types of codes—*restricted* and *elaborated*. Restricted codes are those we use with others that share the same knowledge base. It allows us to shortcut language because of assumptions and knowledge we share with those close to us. When we use restricted codes our language is brief and we expect the person or persons with whom we are speaking to fill in the rest of our meaning; for example, when we say "Get that." With elaborated codes, on the other hand, we do not take shortcuts. Everything is spelled out in more detail to be sure the others understand what we are communicating (Bernstein, 1971). This form is used with people we do not know well and in formal speech, such as, "Please pick up the hat on the table" (Littlejohn & Foss, 2007). People learn their place in the society by the language codes they use. The codes come to symbolize social identity.

As applied to schools, Bernstein was interested in the poor performance of working-class students, especially in language-based subjects. Though their scores in math-related classes were similar to middle-class students, lower performance in language signified to him a relation between social class and language. The result is that language codes aid in the social reproduction of class and differences in power, not only in school but in politics and the workplace. Working-class children are at a disadvantage in schools because they do not share the dominant code of the middle-class and upper-class students. Even the curriculum and transmission of knowledge in schools reflects the dominant code. In trying to understand why Johnny can't read, it may be the codes he brings with him to the classroom.

Although code theory is used less often than cultural capital in understanding processes within schools, it provides an important perspective for us to think about as we study and try to understand inequality in educational achievement.

The last theoretical framework we discuss here is *feminist perspectives on education*. Feminist theorists have echoed the need to "hear" other voices in the education system, in particular women's voices, and to pay more attention to the situation of women. Much of the history of ideas is a history interpreted by men, generally white men in the European tradition. Feminists see the world from a different perspective, one that represents a sometimes forgotten element in past theoretical interpretations of education systems, one in which women were essentially denied education for most of the history of the United States. They are still denied education in

some countries of the world (Lewis & Lockheed, 2006; Spender, 1987). While there are many branches of feminist theory, we mention several general feminist ideas that influence the understanding of schools. Early writings on gender and schooling expressed the concern that girl students and female teachers faced certain injustices. Different theorists related inequalities faced by women to differential access, different treatment and exploitation, patriarchy, and male dominance. This led to examination of educational policy and how it affected girls, women, and their future opportunities (Dillabough & Arnot, 2002). Although women have made many gains in educational attainment over the past century, many inequalities remain. As late as 1994, Sadker and Sadker found that girls were treated differently in the classroom—that girls were not called upon as often as boys and essentially not challenged as much as boys in the same classrooms. This discrepancy in classroom treatment likely contributes to lower self-esteem for girls, and it may also explain why men are more likely to enter higher paying, more prestigious careers because women are less likely to pursue mathematics and science degrees (see the reading by Roslyn Mickelson in Chapter 7).

Not all feminist scholarship on education focuses on describing gender inequalities. Feminist theory can be used to criticize school practices, such as the assumptions that schools use to connect parents, but actually meaning mothers, to engage in their children's educational experiences. For example, Stambach and David (2005) argue that school choice programs operate on the gendered assumption about family and employment, implying that mothers should be involved in their children's education and schools. Even today, schools in many European countries send children home for an extended lunch hour during the middle of the day, making it difficult for mothers to work full-time. Much of feminist scholarship focuses on the critical perspective at the macro level with concern about gender issues in educational environments and reproduction of gender inequality in schools. Radical feminists also link their theory to practice, as is the case with critical theorists, resulting in connections between policy and research. Thus, feminist theory and pedagogy relies on "lived experience" and concerted efforts to change the system as it exists to disadvantage women and girls.

Early feminist theories of education were criticized for having a middle-class bias and not adequately recognizing issues of concern for women of color, women from other cultures, nontraditional gender and sexual orientations, different ethnic or global identities, or political persuasions. As a result, various branches of feminist theory of education have arisen (Weiner, 1997) to address gender issues as they intersect with other categories of difference and inequality. It is expected that these multiple feminisms will result in a variety of challenges to educational practices and systems in addressing the teaching and learning experiences of all young women.

These concerns have resulted in feminist theorists struggling to understand the intersection of different categories of difference and inequality. Students are not treated solely based on gender, but also on race and ethnicity, social class background, and other categories of difference and inequality, such as sexual orientation. These categories intersect to create complex patterns of oppression and suppression not captured by either early feminist theories or other theories discussed in this reading. For example, research by Grant (2004) finds that teachers use Black girls to run errands in the classroom and, with findings similar to Ferguson (2000), that Black boys are viewed by teachers as "trouble" long before they do anything wrong. Gender alone does not explain fully the experiences of children across categories of difference and inequality. Therefore, when trying to understand why Johnny can't read, we may want to consider effects of his gender and race.

CONCLUSION

There is a long and broad tradition of social science and sociological theories, beginning with the coining of the word *sociology* by August Comte in 1838. These theories provide a range of explanations that can be used to examine issues and problems in educational systems in order to better understand the roles and activities in schools and society. All theories evolve. As described, interaction, functional, and conflict theories have gone through stages that attempted to explain the educational systems of the time and to react to previous theories that were inadequate to explain concerns of the education system. Recent trends see schools as "contested terrain" for determining curricula that meet diverse needs. Race, class, and gender issues have become dominant themes in this recent literature.

In short, different theorists help us to think differently as we attempt to explain why schools work as they do. This broad range of theories presents many alternative ways of thinking about schools and is valuable as policy makers and researchers try to find solutions to the multitude of problems plaguing education today, in both developed and developing countries.

REFERENCES

American Association of University Women (AAUW) Educational Foundation. (2001). *Hostile hallways: Bullying, teasing, and sexual harassment in school.* Retrieved from http://www.aauw.org

Antikainen, A., Dworkin, A. G., Saha, L., Ballantine, J., Essacks, S., Teodoro, A., & Konstantinovshy, D. (2010). *The sociology of education.* Retrieved from http://www.sociopedia.isa

Anyon, J. (1980). Social class and the hidden curriculum of work. *Journal of Education, 162*(1), 67–92.

Apple, M. W. (1993). *Official knowledge: Democratic education in a conservative age.* New York: Routledge.

Apple, M. (1996). Power, meaning, and identity: Critical sociology of education in the United States. *British Journal of Sociology of Education, 17*(2), 125–144.

Ballantine, J., & Hammack, F. (2012). *The sociology of education, A systematic approach* (7th ed.). Upper Saddle River, NJ: Prentice-Hall.

Ballantine, J., & Roberts, K. (2011). *Our social world* (3rd ed.). Thousand Oaks, CA: Sage.

Berger, P., & Luckmann, T. (1963). *The social construction of reality.* Garden City, NY: Doubleday.

Bernstein, B. (1971). *Class, codes, and control* (Vol. 1). London: Routledge & Kegan Paul.

Bourdieu, P. (1973). Cultural reproduction and social reproduction. In R. Brown (Ed.), *Knowledge, education, and cultural change* (pp. 71–112). London: Tavistock.

Bourdieu, P., & Passeron, J. C. (1977). *Reproduction in education, society and culture.* London: Sage.

Bowles, S., & Gintis, H. (1976). *Schooling in capitalist America.* New York: Basic Books.

Brookover, W. B., Erickson, E. L., & McEvoy, A. (1996). *Creating effective schools: An in-service program.* Holmes Beach, FL: Learning Publications.

Carter, P. L. (2006). Straddling boundaries: Identity, culture, and school. *Sociology of Education, 79*(4), 304–328.

Coleman, J. S. (1988). Social capital in the creation of human capital. *American Journal of Sociology, 94,* 95–120.

Collins, R. (1979). *The credential society.* New York: Academic Press.

Cookson, P. W., Jr., & Sadovnik, A. R. (2002). Functional theories of education. In D. L. Levinson, P. W. Cookson, Jr., & A. R. Sadovnik (Eds), *Education and society: An encyclopedia* (pp. 267–271). New York: Routledge/Falmer.

Davis, K., & Moore, W. (1945). Some principles of stratification. *American Sociological Review, 10*(2), 242–245.

Dillabough, J., & Arnot, M. (2002). Sociology of education—Feminist perspectives: Continuity and contestation in the field. In D. L. Levinson, P. W. Cookson, Jr., & A. R. Sadovnik (Eds.), *Education and sociology: An encyclopedia* (pp. 571–585). New York: Routledge/Falmer.

Dreeben, R. (1968). *On what is learned in school.* Reading, MA: Addison-Wesley.

Drori, G. S. (2006). *Global e-litism: Digital technology, social inequality, and transnationality.* New York: Worth.

Durkheim, E. (1956). *Education and society* (S. D. Fox, Trans.). Glencoe, IL: Free Press. (Original work published 1903)

Durkheim, E. (1961). *Moral education* (E. K. Wilson & H. Schnurer, Trans.). Glencoe, IL: Free Press. (Original work published 1925)

Durkheim, E. (1977). *The evolution of educational thought* (P. Collins, Trans.). London: Routledge. (Original work published 1938)

Dworkin, A. G. (2007). School reform and teacher burnout: Issues of gender and gender tokenism. In B. Bank, S. Delamont, & C. Marshall (Eds.), *Gender and education: An encyclopedia* (pp. 69–78). Westport, CT: Greenwood.

Dworkin, A. G., Saha, L. J., & Hill, A. N. (2003). Teacher burnout and perceptions of a democratic school environment. *International Education Journal, 4*(2), 108–120.

Eder, D., Evans, C. C., & Parker, S. (1995). *School talk: Gender and adolescent culture.* New Brunswick, NJ: Rutgers University Press.

Ferguson, A. A. (2000). *Bad boys: Public schools in the making of black masculinity.* Ann Arbor: University of Michigan Press.

Flesch, R. F. (1955). *Why Johnny can't read—and what you can do about it.* New York: Harper.

Friedman, T. L. (2005). *The world is flat: A brief history of the twenty-first century.* New York: Farrar, Straus, & Giroux.

Goffman, E. (1959). *The presentation of self in everyday life.* New York: Anchor Books.

Goffman, E. (1967). *Interaction ritual.* Garden City, NY: Doubleday.

Goffman, E. (1990). *Asylums.* New York: Anchor Books.

Grant, L. (2004). Everyday schooling and the elaboration of race-gender stratification. In J. H. Ballantine & J. Z. Spade (Eds.), *Schools and society* (2nd ed., pp. 296–307). Belmont, CA: Wadsworth.

Lambert, L. (2006, May 9). Half of teachers quit in five years: Working conditions, low salaries cited. *Washington Post*, p. A7.

Lareau, A. (1989). *Home advantage.* Philadelphia: Falmer Press.

Lewis, M. A., & Lockheed, M. E. (2006). *Inexcusable absence: Why 60 million girls still aren't in school and what to do about it.* Washington, DC: Center for Global Development.

Littlejohn, S. W., & Foss, K. A. (2007). *Theories of human communication* (9th ed.). Belmont, CA: Centage Learning.

Lubeck, S. (1985). *Sandbox society: Early education in black and white America.* London: Falmer Press.

Lucas, S. R. (1999). *Tracking inequality: Stratification and mobility in American high schools.* New York: Teachers College Press.

Marx, K. (1971). *The poverty of philosophy.* New York: International Publishers.

McLaren, P. (1989). *Life in schools.* New York: Longman.

Miller, K. A., Kohn, M. L., & Schooler, C. (1985). Education self-direction and the cognitive functioning of students. *Social Forces, 63*(4), 923–944.

Parsons, T. (1959). The school as a social system. *Harvard Education Review, 29*(4), 297–318.

Pincus, F. L. (1980). The false promises of community colleges: Class conflict and vocational education. *Harvard Education Review, 50*(3), 332–361.

Pincus, F. L. (2002). Sociology of education: Marxist theories. In D. L. Levinson, P. W. Cookson, Jr., & A. R. Sadovnik (Eds.), *Education and sociology: An encyclopedia* (pp. 587–592). New York: Routledge/Falmer.

Rist, R. (1970). Student social class and teacher expectations: The self-fulfilling prophecy in ghetto education. *Harvard Education Review, 40*(3), 411–451.

Rist, R. (1977). On understanding the processes of schooling: The contributions of labeling theory. In J. Karabel & A. H. Halsey, *Power and ideology in education* (pp. 292–305). New York: Oxford University Press.

Rosenthal, R., & Jacobson, L. (1968). *Pygmalion in the classroom.* New York: Holt, Rinehart and Winston.

Sadker, M., & Sadker, D. (1994). *Failing at fairness: How our schools cheat girls.* New York: Simon & Schuster.

Sadovnik, A. R. (2007). Theory and research in the sociology of education. In A. R. Sadovnik (Ed.), *Sociology of education: A critical reader* (pp. 3–22). New York: Routledge.

Schneider, B. (2002). Social capital: A ubiquitous emerging conception. In D. L. Levinson, P. W. Cookson, Jr., & A. R. Sadovnik (Eds.), *Education and sociology: An encyclopedia* (pp. 545–550). New York: Routledge/Falmer.

Shor, I. (1986). *Culture wars: School and society in the conservative restoration, 1969–1984.* Boston: Routledge & Kegan Paul.

Spender, D. (1987). Education: The patriarchal paradigm and the response to feminism. In M. Arnot & G. Weiner (Eds.), *Gender and the politics of schooling* (pp. 143–154). London: Hutchinson.

Stambach, A., & David, M. (2005). Feminist theory and educational policy: How gender has been "involved" in family school choice debates. *Signs: Journal of Women in Culture and Society, 30*, 1633–1658.

Vanfossen, B. E., Jones, J. D., & Spade, J. Z. (1987). Curriculum tracking and status maintenance. *Sociology of Education, 60*(2), 104–122.

Waller, W. (1965). *Sociology of teaching.* New York: Russell and Russell. (Original work published 1932)

Weber, M. (1958a). The Chinese literati. In H. H. Gerth & C. Wright Mills (Eds.), *From Max Weber: Essays in sociology* (pp. 422–433). New York: Oxford University Press.

Weber, M. (1958b). The rationalization of education and training. In H. H. Gerth & C. Wright Mills (Eds.), *From Max Weber: Essays in sociology* (pp. 240–244). New York: Oxford University Press.

Weber, M. (1961). The three types of legitimate rule. In A. Etzioni (Ed.), *Complex organizations: A sociological reader* (pp. 4–14). New York: Holt, Rinehart and Winston.

Weiner, G. (1997). Feminisms and education. In A. H. Halsey, H. Laudner, P. Brown, & A. S. Wells (Eds.), *Education: Culture, economy, and society* (pp. 144-153). Oxford, England: Oxford University Press.

Willis, P. (1979). *Learning to labor: How working class kids get working class jobs.* Adlershot, Hampshire, England: Saxon House.

Moral Education

Emile Durkheim

Emile Durkheim was an educator and sociologist. He wrote extensively on the functions of education in society, including the function of discipline for socializing the child to be a good citizen. In this reading, Durkheim provides insights into the education system, insights that guided later generations of theorists. First, he points to what he considers inevitable inequalities in educational outcomes as children come into the system from different backgrounds and exit with preparation for specialized positions in society. However, all children must learn a common base of knowledge to provide a common foundation that holds people together in society. Durkheim argues that leaders in each society have an idea of what skills and knowledge people need to develop, and education's responsibility is to help the child understand the importance of collective life. Durkheim also discusses the importance of rules, or discipline, in classrooms. If it is lacking, the class is like a "mob" of agitated students. Families are less disciplined by nature, but schools mirror adult society and prepare the young for their parts in society.

Questions to consider for this reading:

1. What is the role of discipline in schools, according to Durkheim? Does discipline serve the same function today? Explain.

2. How do schools instill discipline? Give an example.

3. What does Durkheim mean when he says we must develop the "habit" of self-control and constraint? Give an example.

There is a whole system of rules in the school that predetermine the child's conduct. He must come to class regularly, he must arrive at a specified time and with an appropriate bearing and attitude. He must not disrupt things in class. He must have learned his lessons, done his homework, and have done so reasonably well, etc. There are, therefore, a host of obligations that the child is required to shoulder. Together they constitute the discipline of the school. It is through the practice of school discipline that we can inculcate the spirit of discipline in the child.

Too often, it is true, people conceive of school discipline so as to preclude endowing it with such an important moral function. Some see in it a simple way of guaranteeing superficial peace and

From *Moral Education: A Study in the Theory and Application of the Sociology of Education* (pp. 148–151), by E. Durkheim, translated by E. K. Wilson and H. Schnurer, 1973, New York: Free Press. Copyright 1961, 1973 by The Free Press, a division of Simon & Schuster Adult Publishing Group. All rights reserved. Reprinted with permission.

order in the class. Under such conditions, one can quite reasonably come to view these imperative requirements as barbarous—as a tyranny of complicated rules. We protest against this kind of regulation, which is apparently imposed on the child for the sole purpose of easing the teacher's task in inducing uniformity. Does not such a system evoke feelings of hostility in the student toward the teacher, rather than the affectionate confidence that should characterize their relationship?

In reality, however, the nature and function of school discipline is something altogether different. It is not a simple device for securing superficial peace in the classroom—a device allowing the work to roll on tranquilly. It is the morality of the classroom, just as the discipline of the social body is morality properly speaking. Each social group, each type of society, has and could not fail to have its own morality, which expresses its own make-up.

Now, the class is a small society. It is therefore both natural and necessary that it have its own morality corresponding to its size, the character of its elements, and its function. Discipline is this morality. The obligations we shall presently enumerate are the student's duties, just as the civic or professional obligations imposed by state or corporation are the duties of the adult. On the other hand, the schoolroom society is much closer to the society of adults than it is to that of the family. For aside from the fact that it is larger, the individuals—teachers and students— who make it up are not brought together by personal feelings or preferences but for altogether general and abstract reasons, that is to say, because of the social function to be performed by the teacher, and the immature mental condition of the students. For all these reasons, the rule of the classroom cannot bend or give with the same flexibility as that of the family in all kinds and combinations of circumstances. It cannot accommodate itself to given temperaments. There is already something colder and more impersonal about the obligations imposed by the school: They are now concerned with reason and less with feelings; they require more effort and greater application. And although—as we have

previously said—we must guard against overdoing it, it is nevertheless indispensable in order that school discipline be everything that it should be and fulfill its function completely. For only on this condition will it be able to serve as intermediary between the affective morality of the family and the more rigorous morality of civil life. It is by respecting the school rules that the child learns to respect rules in general, that he develops the habit of self-control and restraint simply because he should control and restrain himself. It is a first initiation into the austerity of duty. Serious life has now begun.

This, then, is the true function of discipline. It is not a simple procedure aimed at making the child work, stimulating his desire for instruction, or husbanding the energies of the teacher. It is essentially an instrument—difficult to duplicate— of moral education. The teacher to whom it is entrusted cannot guard it too conscientiously. It is not only a matter of his own interest and peace of mind; one can say without exaggeration that the morality of the classroom rests upon his resolution. Indeed, it is certain that an undisciplined class lacks morality. When children no longer feel restrained, they are in a state of ferment that makes them impatient of all curbs, and their behavior shows it—even outside the classroom. One can see analogous situations in the family when domestic education is overly relaxed. In school, this unwholesome ferment of excitement, the result of a failure of discipline, constitutes a more serious moral danger because the agitation is collective. We must never lose sight of the fact that the class is a small society. Thus, no member of this small group acts as though he were alone; each is subject to the influence of the group, and this we must consider most carefully.

A class without discipline is like a mob. Because a given number of children are brought together in the same class, there is a kind of general stimulation deriving from the common life and imparted to all the individual activities—a stimulation that, when everything goes along normally and is well directed, emerges as more enthusiasm, more concern about doing things well than if each student were working individually. But if the teacher has not developed the necessary authority, then this hyperactivity degenerates into an unwholesome ferment, and a genuine demoralization sets in, the more serious as the class is larger. This demoralization becomes obvious in that those elements of least moral value in the class come to have a preponderant place in the common life; just as in political societies during periods of great flux, one sees hosts of harmful elements come to the surface of public life, while in normal times they would be hidden in the shadows.

It is important, therefore, to react against the discredit into which, for a number of years, discipline has tended to fall. Doubtless when one examines the rules of conduct that the teacher must enforce, in themselves and in detail, one is inclined to judge them as useless vexations; and the benevolent feelings, which childhood quite naturally inspires in us, prompt us to feel that they are excessively demanding. Is it not possible for a child to be good and yet fail to be punctual, to be unprepared at the specified time for his lesson or other responsibilities, etc.? If, however, instead of examining these school rules in detail, we consider them as a whole, as the student's code of duty, the matter takes on a different aspect. Then conscientiousness in fulfilling all these petty obligations appears as a virtue. It is the virtue of childhood, the only one in accord with the kind of life the child leads at that age, and consequently the only one that can be asked of him. This is why one cannot cultivate it too conscientiously.

General Influence of the School Environment

To understand clearly the important role that the school environment can and should play in moral education, we must first realize what the child faces when he comes to school. Up to that point he has only been acquainted with two kinds of groups. In the family the sentiment of solidarity is derived from blood relationships; and the moral bonds that result from such relationships are further re-enforced by intimate and constant contact of all the associated minds and by a mutual interpenetration of their lives. Then there are little groups of friends and companions—groups that have taken shape outside the family through free selection. Now, political society presents neither of these two characteristics. The bonds uniting the citizens of a given country have nothing to do with relationships or personal inclinations. There is therefore a great distance between the moral state in which the child finds himself as he leaves the family and the one towards which he must strive. This road cannot be travelled in a single stage. Intermediaries are necessary. The school environment is the most desirable. It is a more extensive association than the family or the little societies of friends. It results neither from blood relationships nor from free choice, but from a fortuitous and inevitable meeting among subjects brought together on the basis of similar age and social conditions. In that respect it resembles political society. On the other hand, it is limited enough so that personal relations can crystallize. The horizon is not too vast; the consciousness of the child can easily embrace it. The habit of common life in the class and attachment to the class and even to the school constitute an altogether natural preparation for the more elevated sentiments that we wish to develop in the child. We have here a precious instrument, which is used all too little and which can be of the greatest service.

It is the more natural to use the school to this end since it is precisely groups of young persons, more or less like those constituting the social system of the school, which have enabled the formation of societies larger than the family. With respect to animals, Espinas has already demonstrated that groupings of birds and mammals could not have taken shape if, at a certain moment in their lives, the young had not been induced to separate from their parents and formed societies of a new type, which no longer have domestic characteristics. Indeed, wherever the family keeps its members to itself it is easily self-sufficient; each particular family tends to live its own life, an autonomous life—tends to isolate itself from other families so as to provide more easily for itself; under these conditions, it is clearly impossible for another society to be formed. The small group appears only where the new generation, once it has been brought up, is induced to free itself from the family setting to lead a collective life of a new sort. Similarly, if, from the very beginning, inferior human societies are not limited to one household, if they comprise even in their humblest form a number of families, it is largely because the moral education of children is not undertaken by their parents, but by the elders of the clan. The elders would assemble the young, after they had reached a given age, to initiate them collectively into the religious beliefs, rites, traditions—in a word, to everything constituting the intellectual and moral patrimony of the group. Because of this gathering of the young into special groups, determined by age and not by blood, extrafamilial societies have been able to come into being and perpetuate themselves. The school is precisely a group of this kind; it is recruited according to the same principle. The gatherings of young neophytes, directed and taught by the elders, which we can observe in primitive societies, are already actual school societies and may be considered as the first form of the school. In asking the school to prepare children for a higher social life than that of the family, we are only asking something that is quite in accord with its character.

Furthermore, if there is a country in which the role of the school is particularly important and necessary, it is ours [France]. In this respect, we are living under quite special conditions. Indeed, with the exception of the school, there is no longer in this country any society intermediate between the family and the state—that is to say, a society that is not merely artificial or superficial. All the groups of this kind, which at one time ranged between domestic and political society—provinces, communes, guilds—have been totally abolished or at least survive only in very attenuated form. The province and the guild are only memories; communal life is very impoverished and now holds a very secondary place in our consciousness.

For morality to have a sound basis, the citizen must have an inclination toward collective life. It is only on this condition that he can become attached, as he should, to collective aims that are moral aims par excellence. This does not happen automatically; above all, this inclination toward collective life can only become strong enough to shape behavior by the most continuous practice. To appreciate social life to the point where one cannot do without it, one must have developed the habit of acting and thinking in common. We must learn to cherish these social bonds that for the unsocial being are heavy chains. We must learn through experience how cold and pale the pleasures of solitary life are in comparison. The development of such a temperament, such a mental outlook, can only be formed through repeated practice, through perpetual conditioning. If, on the contrary, we are invited only infrequently to act like social beings, it is impossible to be very interested in an existence to which we can only adapt ourselves imperfectly.

If, then, with the exception of the family, there is no collective life in which we participate, if in all the forms of human activity—scientific, artistic, professional, and so on—in other words, in all that constitutes the core of our existence, we are in the habit of acting like lone wolves, our social temperament has only rare opportunities to strengthen and develop itself. Consequently, we are inevitably inclined to a more or less suspicious isolation, at least in regard to everything concerning life outside the family. Indeed, the weakness of the spirit of association is one of the characteristics of our national temperament. We have a marked inclination toward a fierce individualism, which makes the obligations of social life appear intolerable to us and which prevents us from experiencing its joys.

The school is a real group, of which the child is naturally and necessarily a part. It is a group other than the family. Its principal function is not, as in the case of the family, that of emotional release and the sharing of affections. Every form of intellectual activity finds scope in it, in embryonic form. Consequently, we have through the school the means of training the child in a collective life different from home life. We can give him habits that, once developed, will survive beyond school years and demand the satisfaction that is their due. We have here a unique and irreplaceable opportunity to take hold of the child at a time when the gaps in our social organization have not yet been able to alter his nature profoundly, or to arouse in him feelings that make him partially rebellious to common life. This is virgin territory in which we can sow seeds that, once taken root, will grow by themselves. Of course, I do not mean that education alone can remedy the evil—that institutions are not necessary demanding legislative action. But that action can only be fruitful if it is rooted in a state of opinion, if it is an answer to needs that are really felt. Thus, although we could not at any time do without the school to instill in the child a social sense, although we have here a natural function from which the school should never withdraw, today, because of the critical situation in which we find ourselves, the services that the school can render are of incomparable importance. . . .

To bind the child to the social group of which he is a part, it is not enough to make him feel the reality of it. He must be attached to it with his whole being. There is only one effective way of doing this, and that is by making his society an integral part of him, so that he can no more separate himself from it than from himself. Society is not the work of the individuals that compose it at a given stage of history, nor is it a given place. It is a complex of ideas and sentiments, of ways of seeing and of feeling, a certain intellectual and moral framework distinctive of the entire group. Society is above all a consciousness of the whole. It is, therefore, this collective consciousness that we must instill in the child.

Of course, this penetration of the child's consciousness is effected in part by the mere fact of living, by the autonomous play of human relations. These ideas and sentiments are all around the child, and he is immersed in them by living. But there is another operation much too important to leave to chance. It is the business of the school to organize it methodically. An enlightened mind must select from among the welter of confused and often contradictory states of mind that constitute the social consciousness; it must set off what is essential and vital; and play down the trivial and the secondary. The teacher must bring this about and here again history will furnish him the means to this end.

The point is that to imbue children with the collective spirit it is useless to analyze it abstractly. On the contrary, they must be put in direct contact with this collective spirit. Now, what is the history of a people if not the genius of that people developing through time? By making the history of their country come alive for the children, we can at the same time make them live in close intimacy with the collective consciousness. Is it not through intimate and prolonged contact with a man that we finally get to know him? In this respect, a history lesson is the lesson of experience. But since our national character is immanent in historical events, the child would neither see nor feel them if the teacher did not try to set them off in bold relief, especially highlighting those events that merit it. Once again, the point is not to give a course on the French character. All that is needed is a knowledge of what it is and how to disentangle it from the welter of facts.

The School Class as a Social System

Talcott Parsons

Looking at the school classroom as a social system, Talcott Parsons provides an example of function-alist theory's approach to education. In these excerpts from a classic 1959 piece in the functionalist tradition, Parsons considers functions of schools that help hold society together, such as passing on knowledge and skills necessary for children to fit into society. In focusing on the school class, he looks at the function of school as an agency of socialization, preparing the young members of society for their adult roles. Schools sort students into college and noncollege groups early in the student's career. Parsons also points out the relationships between family, peer groups, and schools. As you read his description of the school class, keep in mind the functionalist perspective and how it is presented in his discussion.

Questions to consider for this reading:

1. What functions of school are carried out in the classroom? How are they carried out?

2. How do family and family background interact with a child's school experience?

3. What factors affect the elementary child's achievement in school? How does achievement relate to future chances?

4. How does the perspective presented in this reading compare to the discussion of functionalism as presented in the readings by Ballantine and Spade and by Durkheim?

This essay will attempt to outline, if only sketchily, an analysis of the elementary and secondary school class as a social system, and the relation of its structure to its primary functions in the society as an agency of socialization and allocation. While it is impor-tant that the school class is normally part of the larger organization of a school, the class rather than the whole school will be the unit of analysis here, for it is recognized both by the school system and by the individual pupil as the place where the "business" of formal education actu-ally takes place. In elementary schools, pupils of one grade are typically placed in a single "class" under one main teacher, but in the sec-ondary school, and sometimes in the upper ele-mentary grades, the pupil works on different subjects under different teachers; here the complex of classes participated in by the same pupil is the significant unit for our purposes.

THE PROBLEM: SOCIALIZATION AND SELECTION

Our main interest, then, is in a dual problem: first, of how the school class functions to internalize in its pupils both the commitments and capacities for successful performance of their future adult roles, and second, of how it functions to allocate these human resources within the role-structure of the adult society. The primary ways in which these two problems are interrelated will provide our main points of reference.

First, from the functional point of view the school class can be treated as an agency of socialization. That is to say, it is an agency through which individual personalities are trained to be motivationally and technically adequate to the performance of adult roles. It is not the sole such agency; the family, informal "peer groups," churches, and sundry voluntary organizations all play a part, as does actual on-the-job training. But, in the period extending from entry into first grade until entry into the labor force or marriage, the school class may be regarded as the focal socializing agency.

The socialization function may be summed up as the development in individuals of the commitments and capacities which are essential prerequisites of their future role-performance. Commitments may be broken down in turn into two components: commitment to the implementation of the broad values of society, and commitment to the performance of a specific type of role within the structure of society. Thus a person in a relatively humble occupation may be a "solid citizen" in the sense of commitment to honest work in that occupation, without an intensive and sophisticated concern with the implementation of society's higher-level values. Or conversely, someone else might object to the anchorage of the feminine role in marriage and the family on the grounds that such anchorage keeps society's total talent resources from being distributed equitably to business, government, and so on. Capacities can also be broken down into two components, the first being competence or the skill to perform the tasks involved in the individual's roles, and the second being "role-responsibility" or the capacity to live up to other people's expectations of the interpersonal behavior appropriate to these roles. Thus a mechanic as well as a doctor needs to have not only the basic "skills of his trade," but also the ability to behave responsibly toward those people with whom he is brought into contact in his work.

While on the one hand, the school class may be regarded as a primary agency by which these different components of commitments and capacities are generated, on the other hand, it is, from the point of view of the society, an agency of "manpower" allocation. It is well known that in American society there is a very high, and probably increasing, correlation between one's status level in the society and one's level of educational attainment. Both social status and educational level are obviously related to the occupational status which is attained. Now, as a result of the general process of both educational and occupational upgrading, completion of high school is increasingly coming to be the norm for minimum satisfactory educational attainment, and the most significant line for future occupational status has come to be drawn between members of an age-cohort who do and do not go to college.

We are interested, then, in what it is about the school class in our society that determines the distinction between the contingents of the age-cohort which do and do not go to college. Because of a tradition of localism and a rather pragmatic pluralism, there is apparently considerable variety among school systems of various cities and states. Although the situation in metropolitan Boston probably represents a more highly structured pattern than in many other parts of the country, it is probably not so extreme as to be misleading in its main features. There, though of course actual entry into college does not come until after graduation from high school, the main dividing line is between those who are and are not enrolled in the college preparatory course in high school; there is only a small amount of shifting either way after about the ninth grade when the decision is normally made. Furthermore, the evidence seems to be that by far the most important criterion of selection is the record of school performance in elementary school. These records are evaluated by teachers and principals, and there are few cases of entering the college preparatory course against their advice. It is therefore not stretching the evidence too far to say broadly that the primary selective process occurs through differential school performance in elementary school, and that the "seal" is put on it in junior high school.

The evidence also is that the selective process is genuinely assortative. As in virtually all comparable processes, ascriptive as well as achieved factors influence the outcome. In this case, the ascriptive factor is the socioeconomic status of the child's family, and the factor underlying his opportunity for achievement is his individual ability. In the study of 3,348 Boston high school boys on which these generalizations are based, each of these factors was quite highly correlated with planning college. For example, the percentages planning college, by father's occupation, were: 12 per cent for semi-skilled and unskilled, 19 per cent for skilled, 26 per cent for minor white collar, 52 per cent for middle white collar, and 80 per cent for major white collar. Likewise, intentions varied by ability (as measured by IQ), namely, 11 per cent for the lowest quintile, 17 per cent for the next, 24 per cent for the middle, 30 per cent for the next to the top, and 52 per cent for the highest. It should be noted also that within any ability quintile, the relationship of plans to father's occupation is seen. For example, within the very important top quintile in ability as measured, the range in college intentions was from 29 per cent for sons of laborers to 89 percent for sons of major white collar persons.[1]

The essential points here seem to be that there is a relatively uniform criterion of selection operating to differentiate between the college and the non-college contingents, and that for a very important part of the cohort the operation of this criterion is not a "put-up job"—it is not simply a way of affirming a previously determined ascriptive status.

To be sure, the high-status, high-ability boy is very likely indeed to go to college, and the low-status, low-ability boy is very unlikely to go. But the "cross-pressured" group for whom these two factors do not coincide[2] is of considerable importance.

Considerations like these lead me to conclude that the main process of differentiation (which from another point of view is selection) that occurs during elementary school takes place on a single main axis of achievement. Broadly, moreover, the differentiation leads up through high school to a bifurcation into college-goers and non-college-goers.

To assess the significance of this pattern, let us look at its place in the socialization of the individual. Entering the system of formal education is the child's first major step out of primary involvement in his family of orientation. Within the family certain foundations of his motivational system have been laid down. But the only characteristic fundamental to later roles which has clearly been "determined" and psychologically stamped in by that time is sex role. The postoedipal child enters the system of formal education clearly categorized as boy or girl, but beyond that his role is not yet differentiated. The process of selection, by which persons will select and be selected for categories of roles, is yet to take place.

On grounds which cannot be gone into here, it may be said that the most important single predispositional factor with which the child enters the school is his level of independence. By this is meant his level of self-sufficiency relative to guidance by adults, his capacity to take responsibility and to make his own decisions in coping with new and varying situations. This, like his sex role, he has as a function of his experience in the family.

The family is a collectivity within which the basic status-structure is ascribed in terms of biological position, that is, by generation, sex, and age. There are inevitably differences of performance relative to these, and they are rewarded and punished in ways that contribute to differential character formation. But these differences are not given the sanction of institutionalized social status. The school is the first socializing agency in the child's experience which institutionalizes a differentiation of status on nonbiological bases. Moreover, this is not an ascribed but an achieved status; it is the status "earned" by differential performance of the tasks set by the teacher, who is acting as an agent of the community's school system. Let us look at the structure of this situation.

THE STRUCTURE OF THE ELEMENTARY SCHOOL CLASS

In accord with the generally wide variability of American institutions, and of course the basically local control of school systems, there is considerable variability of school situations, but broadly they have a single relatively well-marked framework.[3] Particularly in the primary part of the elementary grades, i.e., the first three grades, the basic pattern includes one main teacher for the class, who teaches all subjects and who is in charge of the class generally. Sometimes this early, and frequently in later grades, other teachers are brought in for a few special subjects, particularly gym, music, and art, but this does not alter the central position of the main teacher. This teacher is usually a woman.[4] The class is with this one teacher for the school year, but usually no longer.

The class, then, is composed of about 25 age peers of both sexes drawn from a relatively small geographical area—the neighborhood. Except for sex in certain respects, there is initially no formal basis for differentiation of status within the school class. The main structural differentiation develops gradually, on the single main axis indicated above as achievement. That the differentiation should occur on a single main axis is insured by four primary features of the situation. The first is the initial equalization of the "contestants'" status by age and by "family background," the neighborhood being typically much more homogeneous than is the whole society. The second circumstance is the imposition of a common set of tasks which is, compared to most other task areas, strikingly undifferentiated. The school situation is far more like a race in this respect than most role-performance situations.

Third, there is the sharp polarization between the pupils in their initial equality and the single teacher who is an adult and "represents" the adult world. And fourth, there is a relatively systematic process of evaluation of the pupils' performances. From the point of view of a pupil, this evaluation, particularly (though not exclusively) in the form of report card marks, constitutes reward and/or punishment for past performance; from the viewpoint of the school system acting as an allocating agency, it is a basis of selection for future status in society.

Two important sets of qualifications need to be kept in mind in interpreting this structural pattern, but I think these do not destroy the significance of its main outline. The first qualification is for variations in the formal organization and procedures of the school class itself. Here the most important kind of variation is that between relatively "traditional" schools and relatively "progressive" schools. The more traditional schools put more emphasis on discrete units of subject-matter, whereas the progressive type allows more "indirect" teaching through "projects" and broader topical interests where more than one bird can be killed with a stone. In progressive schools there is more emphasis on groups of pupils working together, compared to the traditional direct relation of the individual pupil to the teacher. This is related to the progressive emphasis on co-operation among the pupils rather than direct competition, to greater permissiveness as opposed to strictness of discipline, and to a de-emphasis on formal marking. In some schools one of these components will be more prominent, and in others, another. That it is, however, an important range of variation is clear. It has to do, I think, very largely with the independence-dependence training which is so important to early socialization in the family. My broad interpretation is that those people who emphasize independence training will tend to be those who favor relatively progressive education. The relation of support for progressive education to relatively high socioeconomic status and to "intellectual" interests and the like is well known. There is no contradiction between these emphases both on independence and on co-operation and group solidarity among pupils. In the first instance this is because the main focus of the independence problem at these ages is vis-à-vis adults. However, it can also be said that the peer group, which here is built into the school class, is an indirect field of expression of dependency needs, displaced from adults.

The second set of qualifications concerns the "informal" aspects of the school class, which are always somewhat at variance with the formal expectations. For instance, the formal pattern of nondifferentiation between the sexes may be modified informally, for the very salience of the one-sex peer group at this age period means that there is bound to be considerable implicit recognition of it—for example, in the form of teachers' encouraging group competition between boys and girls. Still, the fact of coeducation and the attempt to treat both sexes alike in all the crucial formal respects remain the most important. Another problem raised by informal organization is the question of how far teachers can and do treat pupils particularistically in violation of the universalistic expectations of the school. When compared with other types of formal organizations, however, I think the extent of this discrepancy in elementary schools is seen to be not unusual. The school class is structured so that opportunity for particularistic treatment is severely limited. Because there are so many more children in a school class than in a family and [because] they are concentrated in a much narrower age range, the teacher has much less chance than does a parent to grant particularistic favors.

Bearing in mind these two sets of qualifications, it is still fair, I think, to conclude that the major characteristics of the elementary school class in this country are such as have been outlined. It should be especially emphasized that more or less progressive schools, even with their relative lack of emphasis on formal marking, do not constitute a separate pattern, but rather a variant tendency within the same pattern. A progressive teacher, like any other, will form opinions about the different merits of her pupils relative to the values and goals of the class and will communicate these valuations to them, informally if not formally. It is my impression that the extremer cases of playing down relative evaluation are confined to those upper-status schools where going to a "good" college is so fully taken for granted that for practical purposes it is an ascribed status. In other words, in interpreting these facts the selective function of the school class should be kept continually in the forefront of attention. Quite clearly its importance has not been decreasing; rather the contrary. . . .

NOTES

1. See table from this study in J. A. Kahl, *The American Class Structure* (New York: Rinehart & Co., 1953), p. 283. Data from a nationwide sample of high school students, published by the Educational Testing Service, show similar patterns of relationships. For example, the ETS study shows variation, by father's occupation, in proportion of high school seniors planning college, of from 35 per cent to 80 per cent for boys and 27 per cent to 79 per cent for girls (From *Background Factors Related to College Plans and College Enrollment Among High School Students* [Princeton, NJ: Educational Testing Service, 1957]).

2. There seem to be two main reasons why the high-status, low-ability group is not so important as its obverse. The first is that in a society of expanding educational and occupational opportunity the general trend is one of upgrading, and the social pressures to downward mobility are not as great as they would otherwise be. The second is that there are cushioning mechanisms which tend to protect the high-status boy who has difficulty "making the grade." He may be sent to a college with low academic standards, he may go to schools where the line between ability levels is not rigorously drawn, etc.

3. This discussion refers to public schools. Only about 13 per cent of all elementary and secondary school pupils attend non-public schools, with this proportion ranging from about 22 per cent in the Northeast to about 6 per cent in the South. U.S. Office of Education, Biennial Survey Education (*Biennial Survey of Education in the United States, 1954–56*, Washington: U.S. Government Printing Office, 1959, Chapter ii, "Statistics of State School Systems, 1955–56," Table 44, p. 114).

4. In 1955–56, 13 per cent of the public elementary school instructional staff in the United States were men (*Ibid*, p. 7).

SCHOOLING IN CAPITALIST SOCIETIES

Samuel Bowles and Herbert Gintis

Samuel Bowles and Herbert Gintis introduce us to conflict theory in this excerpt from their application of Marxist theory to the institution of education. Bowles and Gintis argue that schools reproduce the social class system by educating students to fit into their social class. This means that advantaged students are provided with the best educations money can buy, while poor, disadvantaged students often attend poor schools, thus locking in their social class status. This occurs because students from higher status families have more opportunities to attend expensive schools, visit cultural venues, and develop contacts and networks with those who can help them get ahead. Structuring school systems to mirror social status is but one means, but an important one, by which the privileged class maintains its status in society.

Questions to consider for this reading:

1. What is the basic Marxist argument described by Bowles and Gintis?

2. How does Marxism view the role of schools in society?

3. Why do some students get ahead and others stay locked in their social class status?

The most critical aspect of U.S. capitalism is that a few people own and control the bulk of productive resources, while most—aside from personal possessions—own only their labor power. The U.S. economy exhibits the most extensive and complete wage-labor system in the history of civilization. This system, which emerged historically as a progressive force in the service of economic productivity and the ethos of individuality and personal freedom, has long become repressive and anachronistic, an obstacle to further human progress. The many must daily acquiesce to domination by the few, giving rise to the systemic perpetuation of extensive inequalities—not only between capital and wage labor, but among working people as well. The stability and security of these economic power relationships require the creation and reinforcement of distinctions based on sex, race, ethnic origin, social class, and hierarchical status.

The educational system, basically, neither adds to nor subtracts from the degree of inequality and repression originating in the economic sphere. Rather, it reproduces and legitimates a preexisting pattern in the process of training and stratifying the work force. How does this occur?

The heart of the process is to be found not in the content of the educational encounter—or the process of information transfer—but in the form: the social relations of the educational encounter. These correspond closely to the social relations of dominance, subordination, and motivation in the economic sphere. Through the educational encounter, individuals are induced to accept the degree of powerlessness with which they will be faced as mature workers.

The central prerequisite for personal development—be it physical, emotional, aesthetic, cognitive, or spiritual—lies in the capacity to control the conditions of one's life. Thus a society can foster personal development roughly to the extent that it allows and requires personal interaction along the lines of equal, unified, participatory, and democratic cooperation and struggle. Needless to say, these very conditions are those most conducive to social and economic equality. The U.S. educational system, in the present nexus of economic power relationships, cannot foster such patterns of personal development and social equality. To reproduce the labor force, the schools are destined to legitimate inequality, limit personal development to forms compatible with submission to arbitrary authority, and aid in the process whereby youth are resigned to their fate.

Hence we believe—indeed, it follows logically from our analysis—that an equal and liberating educational system can only emerge from a broad-based movement dedicated to the transformation of economic life. Such a movement is socialist in the sense that private ownership of essential productive resources must be abolished, and control over the production process must be placed in the hands of working people.

The goals of such a revolutionary socialism go beyond the achievement of the Soviet Union and countries of Eastern Europe. These countries have abolished private ownership of the means of production, while replicating the relationships of economic control, dominance, and subordination characteristic of capitalism. While the abolition of private property in the means of production has been associated with a significant reduction in economic inequality, it has failed to address the other problems with which we have dealt. The socialism to which we aspire goes beyond the legal question of property to the concrete social question of economic democracy as a set of egalitarian and participatory power relationships. While we may learn much about the process of building a socialist society from the experiences of the Soviet, Cuban, Chinese, and other socialist peoples— and indeed, may find some aspects of their work downright inspiring—there is no foreign model for the economic transformation we seek. Socialism in the United States will be a distinctly American product growing out of our history, culture, and struggle for a better life. . . .

Just as the philosophers of ancient Greece could not conceive of society without master and slave and the Scholastics of medieval times without lord and serf, so, today, many cannot conceive of society without a controlling managerial hierarchy and a subservient working class. Yet neither technology nor human nature bar the way to democratic socialism as the next stage in the process of civilization. Unalienated work and an equal distribution of its products is neither romantic nostalgia nor postindustrial Luddism. The means of achieving social justice and of rendering work personally meaningful and compatible with healthy personal development are as American as apple pie: democracy and equality.

What is the role of education in this process? In the context of U.S. capitalism, a socialist education is a revolutionary education. Our objective for U.S. schools and colleges here and now is not that they should become the embryo of the good society but that struggles around these institutions, and the educational process itself, should contribute to the development of a revolutionary, democratic socialist movement. An ideal education for a socialist society may, in some respects, be irrelevant to the task of bringing that society into existence. This danger is not intrinsically great, however, for the struggle to liberate education and the struggle to democratize economic life are inextricably related. The social relations of education can be altered through genuine struggle for a democratic and participatory classroom, and for a reorganization of power in education. The process of creating a socialist educational system for the United States, if successful, renders the contradictions among administrators, teachers, and students nonantagonistic in the sense that the day-to-day outcomes of their struggles may be the positive, healthy development of both structures and individuals beneficial to all parties concerned. The experience of struggle and control promotes personal growth, forges solidarity, and prepares the student for a future of political activity in factory and office. The consciousness nurtured in such an integrated educational encounter is one of self-worth, cooperation, and an implacable hostility to arbitrary authority.

Even following a successful transformation of formal power relationships in the economic sphere, education will be part of the struggle for democratization of substantive social relationships. The educational system will be set the task of preparing youth for a society which, while geared toward the progressive realization of revolutionary goals, still bears the technological and cultural heritage of the present system. In this setting, the social relations of education will themselves be transitional in nature. For instance, the elimination of boring, unhealthy, fragmented, uncreative, constraining, and otherwise alienated but socially necessary labor requires an extended process of technological and organizational change in a transitional phase. The shift to automated, decentralized, and worker-controlled technologies requires the continuous supervision and cooperation of the workers themselves. Any form this takes in a transitional society will include a constant struggle among three groups whose ultimate interests may converge, but whose daily concerns remain distinct: managers concerned with the development of the enterprise, technicians concerned with the scientific rationality of production, and workers concerned with the impact of innovation

and management on job satisfaction and material welfare. The present educational system does not develop in an individual the capacities of cooperation, struggle, autonomy, and judgment appropriate to this task. The need for developing innovative educational forms is here paramount. . . .

The drive for an egalitarian and liberating educational system must be an essential element of a socialist movement. Indeed, the process-oriented nature of the educational encounter can render political activity in the school system exemplary for the rest of society. We offer five guidelines toward a socialist strategy for education. First, revolutionary educators—teachers, students, and others involved in education—should vigorously press for the democratization of schools and colleges by working toward a system of participatory power in which students, teachers, parents, and other members of the community can pursue their common interests and rationally resolve their conflicts. Second, the struggle for democratization should be viewed as part of an effort to undermine the correspondence between the social relations of education and the social relations of production in capitalist economic life. Socialist educational reform must consciously move toward equating liberated education with education for economic democracy. Third, a movement for socialist education must reject simple antiauthoritarianism and spontaneity as its guiding principles. We must develop and apply a dialectical educational philosophy of personal development, authority, and interpersonal relationships as sketched above. Fourth, revolutionary educators must be in the forefront of the movement to create a unified class consciousness. Socialist teachers must not only demand control over their activities; we must also extend this control to students and to the broader community. We must fight for curriculum which is personally liberating and politically enlightening; we must reject our pretentions as professionals—pretentions which lead only to a defeatist quietism and isolation—and ally with other members of the working class. We must expand their demands to include the use of educational resources by parents, workers, community groups, and the elderly; and finally, we must fight for egalitarian educational practices which reduce the power of the schools to fragment the labor force. Fifth, socialist educators should take seriously the need to combine a long-range vision with winning victories here and now. In the long march through the institutions, reforms must be sought which satisfy the immediate needs of students, teachers, and parents. Pie-in-the-sky politics must be rejected in favor of a program of revolutionary reforms built around such issues as democracy, free classrooms, open enrollment, adequate financial aid for needy students, and development of a critical anti-discriminatory and socialist content of education.

We cannot move forward through the Band-Aid remedies of liberal educational reform. The people of the United States do not need a doctor for the moribund capitalist order; we need an undertaker. Nor can the political challenge facing us be met through the spontaneous efforts of individuals or groups working in isolation. The development and articulation of the vision of a socialist alternative, as much as the ability to meet today's concrete human needs, requires a mass-based party able to aid in the daily struggles of working people throughout the United States and committed to a revolutionary transformation of the U.S. economy.

CONFLICT THEORY OF EDUCATIONAL STRATIFICATION

Randall Collins

Education prepares students for their position and roles in society. In the excerpt that follows, Randall Collins relates education to occupations by using conflict theory, showing how students receive educations common to their status group. Max Weber's concept of status groups corresponds to the idea that schools prepare the young to fit an occupational position commensurate with their status in society. The type of education students receive seals their future status because their education is viewed as appropriate preparation for future jobs.

Questions to consider for this reading:

1. What is the meaning of *status groups* and how are they related to the education of children?

2. What role does education play in preparation for membership in a status group?

3. According to Max Weber's conflict theory (see Ballantine and Spade's reading as well as this one), how are education and occupation related?

4. What is the role of conflict theory in Collins's discussion?

STATUS GROUPS

The basic units of society are associational groups sharing common cultures (or "subcultures"). The core of such groups is families and friends, but they may be extended to religious, educational, or ethnic communities. In general, they comprise all persons who share a sense of status equality based on participation in a common culture: styles of language, tastes in clothing and decor, manners and other ritual observances, conversational topics and styles, opinions and values, and preferences in sports, arts, and media. Participation in such cultural groups gives individuals their fundamental sense of identity, especially in contrast with members of other associational groups in whose everyday culture they cannot participate comfortably. Subjectively, status groups distinguish themselves from others in terms of categories of moral evaluation such as "honor," "taste," "breeding," "respectability," "propriety," "cultivation," "good fellows," "plain folks," etc. Thus the exclusion of persons who lack the ingroup culture is felt to be normatively legitimated.

There is no a priori determination of the number of status groups in a particular society, nor can the degree to which there is consensus on a rank order among them be stated in advance. These are not matters of definition, but empirical variations,

From "Conflict Theory of Educational Stratification," by R. Collins, 1961, *American Sociological Review, 36*(6), pp. 1002–1019. Copyright 1961 by the American Sociological Association. Reprinted with permission.

the causes of which are subjects of other developments of the conflict theory of stratification. Status groups should be regarded as ideal types, without implication of necessarily distinct boundaries; the concepts remain useful even in the case where associational groupings and their status cultures are fluid and overlapping, as hypotheses about the conflicts among status groups may remain fruitful even under these circumstances.

Status groups may be derived from a number of sources. Weber [1968] outlines three: (a) differences in life style based on economic situation (i.e., class); (b) differences in life situation based on power position; and (c) differences in life situation deriving directly from cultural conditions or institutions, such as geographical origin, ethnicity, religion, education, or intellectual or aesthetic cultures.

STRUGGLE FOR ADVANTAGE

There is a continual struggle in society for various "goods"—wealth, power, or prestige. We need make no assumption that every individual is motivated to maximize his rewards; however, since power and prestige are inherently scarce commodities, and wealth is often contingent upon them, the ambition of even a small proportion of persons for more than equal shares of these goods sets up an implicit counter-struggle on the part of others to avoid subjection and disesteem. Individuals may struggle with each other, but since individual identity is derived primarily from membership in a status group, and because the cohesion of status groups is a key resource in the struggle against others, the primary focus of struggle is between status groups rather than within them.

The struggle for wealth, power, and prestige is carried out primarily through organizations. There have been struggles throughout history among organizations controlled by different status groups, for military conquest, business advantage, or cultural (e.g., religious) hegemony, and intricate sorts of interorganizational alliances are possible. In the more complex societies, struggle between status groups is carried on in large part within organizations, as the status groups controlling an organization coerce, hire, or culturally manipulate others to carry out their wishes (as in, respectively, a conscript army, a business, or a church). Organizational research shows that the success of organizational elites in controlling their subordinates is quite variable. Under particular conditions, lower or middle members have considerable de facto power to avoid compliance, and even to change the course of the organizations (see Etzioni, 1961).

This opposing power from below is strengthened when subordinate members constitute a cohesive status group of their own; it is weakened when subordinates acquiesce in the values of the organization elite. Coincidence of ethnic and class boundaries produces the sharpest cultural distinctions. Thus, Catholics of immigrant origins have been the bulwarks of informal norms restricting work output in American firms run by WASPs, whereas Protestants of native rural backgrounds are the main "rate-busters" (Collins, Dalton, & Roy, 1946). Selection and manipulation of members in terms of status groups is thus a key weapon in intraorganizational struggles. In general, the organization elite selects its new members and key assistants from its own status group and makes an effort to secure lower-level employees who are at least indoctrinated to respect the cultural superiority of their status culture.

Once groups of employees of different status groups are formed at various positions (middle, lower, or laterally differentiated) in the organization, each of these groups may be expected to launch efforts to recruit more members of their own status group. This process is illustrated by conflicts among whites and blacks, Protestants and Catholics and Jews, Yankee, Irish and Italian, etc., found in American occupational life (Dalton, 1951; Hughes, 1949). These conflicts are based on ethnically or religiously founded status cultures; their intensity rises and falls with processes increasing or decreasing the cultural distinctiveness of these groups, and with the succession of advantages and disadvantages set by previous outcomes of these struggles which determine the organizational resources available for further struggle. Parallel processes of cultural conflict may be based on distinctive class as well as ethnic cultures.

EDUCATION AS STATUS CULTURE

The main activity of schools is to teach particular status cultures, both in and outside the classroom. In this light, any failure of schools to impart technical knowledge (although it may also be successful in this) is not important; schools primarily teach vocabulary and inflection, styles of dress, aesthetic tastes, values, and manners. The emphasis on sociability and athletics found in many schools is not extraneous but may be at the core of the status culture propagated by the schools. Where schools have a more academic or vocational emphasis, this emphasis may itself be the content of a particular status culture, providing sets of values, materials for conversation, and shared activities for an associational group making claims to a particular basis for status.

Insofar as a particular status group controls education, it may use it to foster control within work organizations. Educational requirements for employment can serve both to select new members for elite positions who share the elite culture and, at a lower level of education, to hire lower and middle employees who have acquired a general respect for these elite values and styles.

Tests of the Conflict Theory of Educational Stratification

The conflict theory in its general form is supported by evidence (1) that there are distinctions among status group cultures—based on both class and ethnicity—in modern societies (Kahl, 1957, pp. 127–156, 184–220); (2) that status groups tend to occupy different occupational positions within organizations (see data on ascription cited above); and (3) that occupants of different organizational positions struggle over power (Crozier, 1964; Dalton, 1959). The more specific tests called for here, however, are of the adequacy of conflict theory to explain the link between education and occupational stratification. Such tests may focus either on the proposed mechanism of occupational placement, or on the conditions for strong or weak links between education and occupation.

Education as a Mechanism of Occupational Placement

The mechanism proposed is that employers use education to select persons who have been socialized into the dominant status culture: for entrants to their own managerial ranks, into elite culture; for lower-level employees, into an attitude of respect for the dominant culture and the elite which carries it. This requires evidence that: (a) schools provide either training for the elite culture, or respect for it; and (b) employers use education as a means of selection for cultural attributes.

Historical and descriptive studies of schools support the generalization that they are places where particular status cultures are acquired, either from the teachers, from other students, or both. Schools are usually founded by powerful or autonomous status groups, either to provide an exclusive education for their own children, or to propagate respect for their cultural values. Until recently most schools were founded by religions, often in opposition to those founded by rival religions; throughout the 19th century, this rivalry was an important basis for the founding of large numbers of colleges in the U.S., and of the Catholic and Lutheran school systems. The public school system in the U.S. was founded mainly under the impetus of WASP elites with the purpose of teaching respect for Protestant and middle-class standards of cultural and religious propriety, especially in the face of Catholic, working-class immigration from Europe (Cremin, 1961; Curti, 1935). The content of public school education has consisted especially of middle-class, WASP culture ([Becker, 1961; Hess & Torney, 1967]; Waller, 1932, pp. 15–131).

At the elite level, private secondary schools for children of the WASP upper class were founded from the 1880s, when the mass indoctrination function of the growing public schools made them unsuitable as means of maintaining cohesion of the elite culture itself (Baltzell, 1958, pp. 327–372). These elite schools produce a distinctive personality type, characterized by adherence to a distinctive set of upper-class values and manners (McArthur, 1955). The cultural role of schools has been more closely studied in Britain (Bernstein, 1961; Weinberg, 1967) and in France (Bourdieu & Passeron, 1964), although Riesman and his colleagues (Jencks & Riesman, 1968; Riesman, 1958) have shown some of the cultural differences among prestige levels of colleges and universities in the United States.

Evidence that education has been used as a means of cultural selection may be found in several sources. Hollingshead's (1949, pp. 360–388) study of Elmtown school children, school dropouts, and community attitudes toward them suggests that employers use education as a means of selecting employees with middle-class attributes. A 1945–1946 survey of 240 employers in New Haven and Charlotte, N.C., indicated that they regarded education as a screening device for employees with desirable (middle-class) character and demeanor; white-collar positions particularly emphasized educational selection because these employees were considered most visible to outsiders (Noland & Bakke, 1949, pp. 20–63).

A survey of employers in nationally prominent corporations indicated that they regarded college degrees as important in hiring potential managers, not because they were thought to ensure technical skills, but rather to indicate "motivation" and "social experience" (Gordon & Howell, 1959, p. 121). Business school training is similarly regarded, less as evidence of necessary training (as employers have been widely skeptical of the utility of this curriculum for most positions) than as an indication that the college graduate is committed to business

attitudes. Thus, employers are more likely to refuse to hire liberal arts graduates if they come from a college which has a business school than if their college is without a business school (Gordon & Howell, 1959, pp. 84–87; see also Pierson, 1959, pp. 90–99). In the latter case, the students could be said not to have had a choice; but when both business and liberal arts courses are offered and the student chooses liberal arts, employers appear to take this as a rejection of business values.

Finally, a 1967 survey of 309 California organizations (Collins, 1971) found that educational requirements for white-collar workers were highest in organizations which placed the strongest emphasis on normative control over their employees. Normative control emphasis was indicated by (i) relative emphasis on the absence of police record for job applicants, (ii) relative emphasis on a record of job loyalty, and (iii) Etzioni's (1961) classification of organizations into those with high normative control emphasis (financial, professional services, government, and other public service organizations) and those with remunerative control emphasis (manufacturing, construction, and trade). These three indicators are highly interrelated, thus mutually validating their conceptualization as indicators of normative control emphasis. The relationship between normative control emphasis and educational requirements holds for managerial requirements and white-collar requirements generally, both including and excluding professional and technical positions. Normative control emphasis does not affect blue-collar education requirements. . . .

HISTORICAL CHANGE

The rise in educational requirements for employment throughout the last century may be explained using the conflict theory, and incorporating elements of the technical-functional theory into it at appropriate points. The principal dynamic has centered on changes in the supply of educated persons caused by the expansion of the school system, which was in turn shaped by three conditions:

Education has been associated with high economic and status position from the colonial period on through the twentieth century. The result was a popular demand for education as mobility opportunity. This demand has not been for vocational education at a terminal or commercial level, short of full university certification; the demand has rather focused on education giving entry into the elite status culture, and usually only those technically oriented schools have prospered which have most closely associated themselves with the sequence of education leading to (or from) the classical bachelor's degree (Collins, 1969, pp. 68–70, 86–87, 89, 96–101).

Political decentralization, separation of church and state, and competition among religious denominations have made founding schools and colleges in America relatively easy, and provided initial motivations of competition among communities and religious groups that moved them to do so. As a result, education at all levels expanded faster in America than anywhere else in the world. At the time of the Revolution, there were nine colleges in the colonies; in all of Europe, with a population forty times that of America, there were approximately sixty colleges. By 1880 there were 811 American colleges and universities; by 1966, there were 2,337. The United States not only began with the highest ratio of institutions of higher education to population in the world, but increased this lead steadily, for the number of European universities was not much greater by the twentieth century than in the eighteenth (Ben-David & Zloczower, 1962).

Technical changes also entered into the expansion of American education. As the evidence summarized above indicates: (a) Mass literacy is crucial for beginnings of full-scale industrialization, although demand for literacy could not have been important in the expansion of education beyond elementary levels. More importantly, (b) there is a mild trend toward the reduction in the proportion of unskilled jobs and an increase in the promotion of highly skilled (professional and technical) jobs as industrialism proceeds,

accounting for 15% of the shift in educational levels in the twentieth century (Folger & Nam, 1964). (c) Technological change also brings about some upgrading in skill requirements of some continuing job positions, although the available evidence (Berg, 1970, pp. 38–60) refers only to the decade 1950–1960. Nevertheless, as Wilensky (1964) points out, there is no "professionalization of everyone," as most jobs do not require considerable technical knowledge on the order of that required of the engineer or the research scientist.

The existence of a relatively small group of experts in high-status positions, however, can have important effects on the structure of competition for mobility chances. In the United States, where democratic decentralization favors the use of schools (as well as government employment) as a kind of patronage for voter interests, the existence of even a small number of elite jobs fosters a demand for large-scale opportunities to acquire these positions. We thus have a "contest mobility" school system (Turner, 1960); it produced a widely educated populace because of the many dropouts who never achieve the elite level of schooling at which expert skills and/or high cultural status is acquired. In the process, the status value of American education has become diluted. Standards of respectability are always relative to the existing range of cultural differences. Once higher levels of education become recognized as an objective mark of elite status, and a moderate level of education as a mark of respectable middle-level status, increases in the supply of educated persons at given levels result in yet higher levels becoming recognized as superior, and previously superior levels become only average.

Thus, before the end of the nineteenth century, an elementary school or home education was no longer satisfactory for a middle-class gentleman; by the 1930s, a college degree was displacing the high school degree as the minimal standard of respectability; in the late 1960s, graduate school or specialized professional degrees were becoming necessary for initial entry to many middle-class positions, and high school graduation was becoming a standard for entry to manual laboring positions. Education has thus gradually become part of the status culture of classes far below the level of the original business and professional elites.

The increasing supply of educated persons . . . has made education a rising requirement of jobs. . . . Led by the biggest and most prestigious organizations, employers have raised their educational requirements to maintain both the relative prestige of their own managerial ranks and the relative respectability of middle ranks. Education has become a legitimate standard in terms of which employers select employees, and employees compete with each other for promotion opportunities or for raised prestige in their continuing positions. With the attainment of a mass (now approaching universal) higher education system in modern America, the ideal or image of technical skill becomes the legitimating culture in terms of which the struggle for position goes on.

Higher educational requirements, and the higher level of educational credentials offered by individuals competing for positions in organizations, have in turn increased the demand for education by populace. The interaction between formal job requirements and informal status cultures has resulted in a spiral in which educational requirements and educational attainments become ever higher. As the struggle for mass educational opportunities enters new phases in the universities of today and perhaps in the graduate schools of the future, we may expect a further upgrading of educational requirements for employment. The mobilization of demands by minority groups for mobility opportunities through schooling can only contribute an extension of the prevailing pattern.

CONCLUSION

It has been argued that conflict theory provides an explanation of the principal dynamics of rising educational requirements for employment in America. Changes in the technical requirements of jobs have caused more limited changes

in particular jobs. The conditions of the interaction of these two determinants may be more closely studied.

Precise measures of changes in the actual technical skill requirements of jobs are as yet available only in rudimentary form. Few systematic studies show how much of particular job skills may be learned in practice, and how much must be acquired through school background. Close studies of what is actually learned in school, and how long it is retained, are rare. Organizational studies of how employers rate performance and decide upon promotions give a picture of relatively loose controls over the technical quality of employee performance, but this no doubt varies in particular types of jobs.

The most central lines of analysis for assessing the joint effects of status group conflict and technical requirements are those which compare the relative importance of education in different contexts. One such approach may take organization as the unit of analysis, comparing the educational requirements of organizations both to organizational technologies and to the status (including educational) background of organizational elites. Such analysis may also be applied to surveys of individual mobility, comparing the effects of education on mobility in different employment contexts, where the status group (and educational) background of employers varies in its fit with the educational culture of prospective employees. Such analysis of "old school tie" networks may also simultaneously test for the independent effect of the technical requirements of different sorts of jobs on the importance of education. International comparisons provide variations here in the fit between types of education and particular kinds of jobs which may not be available within any particular country.

The full elaboration of such analysis would give a more precise answer to the historical question of assigning weight to various factors in the changing place of education in the stratification of modern societies. At the same time, to state the conditions under which status groups vary in organizational power, including the power to emphasize or limit the importance of technical skills, would be to state the basic elements of a comprehensive explanatory theory of the forms of stratification.

REFERENCES

Baltzell, E. D. (1958). *An American business aristocracy.* New York: Macmillan.

Becker, H. S. (1961). Schools and systems of stratification. In A. H. Halsey, J. Floud, & C. A. Anderson (Eds.), *Education, economy, and society* (pp. 93–104). New York: Free Press.

Ben-David, J., & Zloczower, A. (1962). Universities and academic systems in modern societies. *European Journal of Sociology, 31,* 45–85.

Berg, I. (1970). *Education and jobs.* New York: Praeger.

Bernstein, B. (1961). Social class and linguistic development. In A. H. Halsey, J. Floud, & C. A. Anderson (Eds.), *Education, economy, and society* (pp. 288–314). New York: Free Press.

Bourdieu, P., & Passeron, J.-C. (1964). *Les heritiers: Les etudiants et la culture.* Paris: Les Editions de Minuit.

Collins, O., Dalton, M., & Roy, D. (1946). Restriction of output and social cleavage in industry. *Applied Anthropology, 5*(3), 1–14.

Collins, R. (1969). *Education and employment.* (Unpublished doctoral dissertation). University of California, Berkeley.

Collins, R. (1971). *Educational requirements for employment: A comparative organizational study.* Unpublished manuscript.

Cremin, L. A. (1961). *The transformation of the school.* New York: Knopf.

Crozier, M. (1964). *The bureaucratic phenomenon.* Chicago: University of Chicago Press.

Curti, M. (1935). *The social ideas of American educators.* New York: Scribner's.

Dalton, M. (1951). Informal factors in career achievement. *American Journal of Sociology, 56*(5), 407–415.

Dalton, M. (1959). *Men who manage.* New York: Wiley.

Etzioni, A. (1961). *A comparative analysis of complex organizations.* New York: Free Press.

Folger, J. K., & Nam, C. B. (1964). Trends in education in relation to the occupational structure. *Sociology of Education, 38,* 19–33.

Gordon, R. A., & Howell, J. E. (1959). *Higher education for business.* New York: Columbia University Press.

Hess, R. D., & Torney, J. V. (1967). *The development of political attitudes in children.* Chicago: Aldine.

Hollingshead, A. B. (1949). *Elmtown's youth.* New York: Wiley.

Hughes, E. C. (1949). Queries concerning industry and society growing out of the study of ethnic relations in industry. *American Sociological Review, 14*(April), 211–220.

Jencks, C., & Riesman, D. (1968). *The academic revolution.* New York: Doubleday.

Kahl, J. A. (1957). *The American class structure.* New York: Rinehart.

McArthur, C. (1955). Personality differences between middle and upper classes. *Journal of Abnormal and Social Psychology, 50*(2), 247–254.

Noland, E. W., & Bakke, E. W. (1949). *Workers wanted.* New York: Harper.

Pierson, F. C. (1959). *The education of American businessmen.* New York: McGraw-Hill.

Riesman, D. (1958). *Constraint and variety in American education.* New York: Doubleday.

Turner, R. H. (1960). Sponsored and contest mobility and the school system. *American Sociological Review, 25*(6), 855–867.

Waller, W. (1932). *The sociology of teaching.* New York: Russell and Russell.

Weber, M. (1968). *Economy and society.* New York: Bedminster Press.

Weinberg, I. (1967). *The English public schools: The sociology of elite education.* New York: Atherton Press.

Wilensky, H. L. (1964). The professionalization of everyone? *American Journal of Sociology, 70*(2), 137–158.

On Understanding the Process of Schooling

The Contributions of Labeling Theory

Ray C. Rist

The final reading in this chapter on sociology of education and theory moves to the microlevel, dealing with interactions between participants in schools. This is in contrast to the previous discussions of theories that more often deal with large groups, educational systems, or even societal systems of education. Recall the discussion of interaction theory in the first reading in this chapter by Ballantine and Spade. Ray C. Rist goes into detail to describe labeling theory, one type of interaction theory. He first points out the value of labeling theory for understanding what is happening in schools. In the first part of this reading, Rist explains how teachers label students as bright or slow, and the consequences of these labels for the students in school and in the future. He explains the importance of understanding how and why individuals are labeled—who applied the label to whom—and the results for the labeled person. In applying this to school settings, Rist focuses on teacher expectations of students that are based on the labels given to a student. He also points out the research on the relationship between class, race, and ethnicity and labels. Often teachers expect less of lower-class children than they do of middle-class children. Finally Rist explains the self-fulfilling prophecy as it applies to schools—the idea that teacher expectations held for students influence the actual behavior of the students. Labeling theory and the self-fulfilling prophecy are commonly used theories in sociology of education studies of school interactions.

Questions to consider for this reading:

1. What is the importance of labeling theory for understanding interaction dynamics in schools?

2. Explain the relationship between labeling theory and self-fulfilling prophecy as they relate to students and classrooms.

3. Of what use do you feel labeling theory might be for understanding the relationship between teachers and students?

4. How does labeling theory overlap with some of the arguments in conflict theories discussed in this reading?

I. Becoming Deviant: The Labeling Perspective

Those who have used labeling theory have been concerned with the study of *why* people are labeled, and *who* it is that labels them as someone who has committed one form or another of deviant behavior. In sharp contrast to the predominant approaches for the study of deviance, there is little concern in labeling theory with the motivational and characterological nature of the person who committed the act.

Deviance is understood, not as a quality of the person or as created by his actions, but instead as created by group definitions and reactions. It is a social judgment imposed by a social audience. As Becker (1963: 9) has argued:

> The central fact of deviance is that it is created by society. I do not mean this in the way it is ordinarily understood, in which the causes of deviance are located in the social situation of the deviant, or the social factors, which prompted his action. I mean, rather, that social groups create deviants by making the rules whose infraction constitute deviance, and by applying those rules to particular people and labeling them as outsiders. From this point of view, *deviance is not the quality of the act the person commits, but rather a consequence of the application by others of rules and sanctions to an "offender." The deviant is one to whom the label has been successfully applied. Deviant behavior is behavior that people so label* [emphasis added].

The labeling approach is insistent on the need for a shift in attention from an exclusive concern with the deviant individual to a major concern with the *process* by which the deviant label is applied. Again citing Becker (1964: 2):

> The labeling approach sees deviance always and everywhere as a process and interaction between at least two kinds of people: those who commit (or who are said to have committed) a deviant act, and the rest of the society, perhaps divided into several groups itself. . . . One consequence is that we become much more interested in the process by which deviants are defined by the rest of the society, than in the nature of the deviant act itself.

The important questions, then, for Becker and others, are not of the genre to include, for example: Why do some individuals come to act out norm-violating behavior? Rather, the questions are of the following sort: Who applied the deviant label to whom? Whose rules shall prevail and be enforced? Under what circumstances is the deviant label successfully and unsuccessfully applied? How does a community decide what forms of conduct should be singled out for this kind of attention? What forms of behavior do persons in the social system consider deviant; how do they interpret such behavior; and what are the consequences of these interpretations for their reactions to individuals who are seen as manifesting such behavior? (See Akers, 1973.)

The labeling perspective rejects any assumption that a clear consensus exists as to what constitutes a norm violation—or for that matter, what constitutes a norm—within a complex and highly heterogeneous society. What comes to be determined as deviance and who comes to be determined as a deviant is the result of a variety of social contingencies influenced by who has the power to enforce such determinations. Deviance is thus problematic and subjectively given. The case for making the societal reaction to rule-breaking a major independent variable in studies of deviant behavior has been succinctly stated by Kitsuse (1964: 101):

> A sociological theory of deviance must focus specifically upon the interactions which not only define behaviors as deviant, but also organize and activate the application of sanctions by individuals, groups, or agencies. For in modern society, the socially significant differentiation of deviants from the nondeviant population is increasingly contingent upon circumstances of situation, place, social and personal biography, and the bureaucratically organized activities of agencies of social control.

Traditional notions of who is a deviant and what are the causes for such deviance are necessarily reworked. By emphasizing the processual nature of deviance, any particular deviant is seen to be a product of being caught, defined, segregated, labeled, and stigmatized. *This is one*

*of the major thrusts of the labeling perspective—
that forces of social control often produce the
unintended consequence of making some persons defined as deviant even more confirmed as
deviant because of the stigmatization of labeling. Thus, social reactions to deviance further
deviant careers.* Erikson (1966) has even gone
so far as to argue that a society will strive to
maintain a certain level of deviance within itself
as deviance is functional to clarifying group
boundaries, providing scapegoats, clearing out-
groups who can be the source of furthering ingroup solidarity, and the like.

The idea that social control may have the paradoxical effect of generating more of the very
behavior it is designed to eradicate was first elaborated upon by Tannenbaum. He noted (1938: 21):

> The first dramatization of the "evil" which sepa-
> rates the child out of his group . . . plays a greater
> role in making the criminal than perhaps any other
> experience. . . . He now lives in a different world.
> He has been tagged. . . . The person becomes the
> thing he is described as being.

Likewise, Schur (1965: 4) writes:

> The societal reaction to the deviant then, is vital to an
> understanding of the deviance itself and a major ele-
> ment in—if not the cause of—the deviant behavior.

The focus on outcomes of social control mechanisms has led labeling theorists to devote considerable attention to the workings of organizations
and agencies which function ostensibly to reha-
bilitate the violator or in other ways draw him
back into conformity. Their critiques of prisons,
mental hospitals, training schools, and other people-changing institutions suggest that the results
of such institutions are frequently nearly the opposite of what they were theoretically designed to
produce. These institutions are seen as mechanisms by which opportunities to withdraw from
deviance are sealed off from the deviant, stigmatization occurs, and a new identity as a social "out-
sider" is generated. There thus emerges on the part
of the person so labeled a new view of himself
which is one of being irrevocably deviant.

This movement from one who has violated a
norm to one who sees himself as a habitual norm
violator is what Lemert (1972: 62) terms the
transition from a primary to a secondary deviant.
A primary deviant is one who holds to socially
accepted roles, views himself as a nondeviant,
and believes himself to be an insider. A primary
deviant does not deny that he has violated some
norm, and claims only that it is not characteristic
of him as a person. A secondary deviant, on the
other hand, is one who has reorganized his
social-psychological characteristics around the
deviant role. Lemert (1972: 62) writes:

> Secondary deviation refers to a special class of
> socially defined responses which people make to
> problems created by the societal reaction to their
> deviance. These problems . . . become central facts
> of existence for those experiencing them. . . . Actions,
> which have these roles and self-attitudes as their
> referents make up secondary deviance. The second-
> ary deviant . . . is a person whose life and identity
> are organized around the facts of deviance.

A person can commit repeated acts of primary
deviation and never come to view himself or
have others come to view him as a secondary
deviant. Secondary deviation arises from the
feedback whereby misconduct or deviation initiates social reaction to the behavior which then
triggers further misconduct. Lemert (1951: 77)
first described this process as follows:

> The sequence of interaction leading to secondary
> deviation is roughly as follows: (1) primary devia-
> tion; (2) societal penalties; (3) further primary
> deviation; (4) stronger penalties and rejections;
> (5) further deviations, perhaps with hostilities and
> resentments beginning to focus upon those doing
> the penalizing; (6) crisis reached in the tolerance
> quotient, expressed in formal action by the com-
> munity stigmatizing of the deviant; (7) strengthen-
> ing of the deviant conduct as a reaction to the
> stigmatizing and penalties; and (8) ultimate accep-
> tance of deviant social status and efforts at adjust-
> ment on the basis of the associated role.

Thus, when persons engage in deviant behavior
they would not otherwise participate in and when

they develop social roles they would not have developed save for the application of social control measures, the outcome is the emergence of secondary deviance. The fact of having been apprehended and labeled is the critical element in the subsequent construction of a deviant identity and pursuit of a deviant career.

II. The Origins of Labeling: Teacher Expectations

Labeling theory has significantly enhanced our understanding of the process of becoming deviant by shifting our attention from the deviant to the judges of deviance and the forces that affect their judgment. Such judgments are critical, for a recurrent decision made in all societies, and particularly frequent in advanced industrial societies, is that an individual has or has not mastered some body of information, or perhaps more basically, has or has not the capacity to master that information. These evaluations are made periodically as one moves through the institution of school and the consequences directly affect the opportunities to remain for an additional period. To be able to remain provides an option for mastering yet another body of information, and to be certified as having done so. As Ivan Illich (1971) has noted, it is in industrial societies that being perceived as a legitimate judge of such mastery has become restricted to those who carry the occupational role of "teacher." A major consequence of the professionalization of the role of teacher has been the ability to claim as a near exclusive decision whether mastery of material has occurred. Such exclusionary decision-making enhances those in the role of "teacher" as they alone come to possess the authority to provide certification for credentials (Edgar, 1974).

Labeling theorists report that in making judgments of deviance, persons may employ information drawn from a variety of sources. Further, even persons within the same profession (therapists, for example) may make divergent use of the same material in arriving at an evaluative decision on the behavior of an individual. Among the sources of information available to labelers, two

appear primary: first-hand information obtained from face-to-face interaction with the person they may ultimately label, and second-hand information obtained from other than direct interaction.

The corollary here to the activities of teachers should be apparent. Oftentimes, the evaluation by teachers (which may lead to the label of "bright," "slow," etc.) is based on first-hand information gained through face-to-face interaction during the course of the time the teacher and student spent together in the classroom. But a goodly amount of information about the student which informs the teacher's evaluation is second-hand information. For instance, comments from other teachers, test scores, prior report cards, permanent records, meetings with the parents, or evaluations from welfare agencies and psychological clinics are all potential informational sources. In a variation of the division between first-hand and second-hand sources of information, Johnson (1973) has suggested that there are three key determinants of teacher evaluations: student's prior performance, social status characteristics, and present performance. Prior performance would include information from cumulative records (grades, test scores, notes from past teachers or counselors, and outside evaluators) while social status and performance would be inferred and observed in the on-going context of the classroom.

What has been particularly captivating about the work of Rosenthal and Jacobson (1968) in this regard is their attempt to provide empirical justification for a truism considered self-evident by many in education: School achievement is not simply a matter of a child's native ability, but involves directly and inextricably the teacher as well. Described succinctly, their research involved a situation where, at the end of a school year, more than 500 students in a single elementary school were administered the "Harvard Test of Inflected Acquisition." In actuality this test was a standardized, relatively nonverbal test of intelligence, Flanagan's (1960) Test of General Ability (TOGA). The teachers were told that such a test would, with high predictive reliability, sort out those students who gave strong indication of being intellectual "spurters" or "bloomers" during the following academic year. Just before the beginning of school the following fall, the teachers were given lists with the names of between one and nine of their students. They were told that these students scored in the top twenty percent of the school on the test, though, of course, no factual basis for such determinations existed. A twenty percent subsample of the "special" students was selected for intensive analysis. Testing of the students at the end of the school year offered some evidence that these selected children did perform better than the nonselected.

The findings of Deutsch, Fishman, Kogan, North, and Whiteman (1964); Gibson (1965); Goslin and Glass (1967); McPherson (1966); and Pequignot (1966) all demonstrate the influence of standardized tests of intelligence and achievement on teachers' expectations. Goaldman (1971), in a review of the literature on the use of tests as a second-hand source of information for teachers, noted: "Although some of the research has been challenged, there is a basis for the belief that teachers at all levels are prejudiced by information they receive about a student's ability or character." Mehan (1971, 1974) has been concerned with the interaction between children who take tests and the teachers who administer them. He posits that testing is not the objective use of a measurement instrument, but the outcome of a set of interactional activities which are influenced by a variety of contingencies which ultimately manifest themselves in a reified "test score." Mehan suggests (1971):

> Standardized test performances are taken as an unquestioned, non-problematic reflection of the child's underlying ability. The authority of the test to measure the child's real ability is accepted by both teachers and other school officials. Test results are accepted without doubt as the correct and valid document of the child's ability.

Characteristics of children such as sex and race are immediately apparent to teachers. Likewise, indication of status can be quickly inferred from grooming, style of dress, need for free lunches, information on enrollment cards, discussion of family activities by children, and visits to the school by parents. One intriguing study recently reported in this area is that by two sociologists, Clifford and Walster (1973: 249). The substance of their study was described as follows:

> Our experiment was designed to determine what effect a student's physical attractiveness has on a teacher's expectations of the child's intellectual and social behavior. Our hypothesis was that a child's attractiveness strongly influences his teachers' judgments; the more attractive the child, the more biased in his favor we expect the teachers to be. The design required to test this hypothesis is a simple one: Teachers are given a standardized report card and an attached photograph. The report card includes an assessment of the child's academic performance as well as of his general social behavior. The attractiveness of the photos is experimentally varied. On the basis of this information, teachers are asked to state their expectations of the child's educational and social potential.

Based on the responses of 404 fifth grade teachers within the state of Missouri, Clifford and Walster concluded (1973: 255):

> There is little question but that the physical appearance of a student affected the expectations of the teachers we studied. Regardless of whether the pupil is a boy or girl, the child's physical attractiveness has an equally strong association with his teacher's reactions to him.

The variables of race and ethnicity have been documented, by Brown (1968), Davidson and Lang (1960), Jackson and Cosca (1974), and Rubovits and Maehr (1973), among others, as powerful factors in generating the expectations teachers hold of children. It has also been documented that teachers expect less of lower-class children than they do of middle-class children (cf. Becker, 1952; Deutsch, 1963; Leacock, 1969: Rist, 1970, 1973; Stein, 1971; Warner, Havighurst, & Loeb, 1944; Wilson, 1963). Douglas (1964), in a large-scale study of the tracking system used in British schools, found that children who were clean and neatly dressed in nice clothing and who came from what the teachers perceived as "better" homes, tended to be placed in higher tracks than their measured ability would predict. Further, when placed there they tended to stay and perform acceptably. Mackler (1969) studied schools in Harlem and found that children tended to stay in the tracks in which they were initially placed and that such placement was based on a variety of social considerations independent of measured ability. Doyle, Hancock, and Kifer (1971) and Palardy (1969) have shown teacher expectations for high performance in elementary grades to be stronger for girls than boys.

The on-going academic and interpersonal performance of the children may also serve as a potent source of expectations for teachers. Rowe (1969) found that teachers would wait longer for an answer from a student they believed to be a high achiever than for one from a student they believed to be a low achiever. Brophy and Good (1970) found that teachers were more likely to give perceived high achieving students a second chance to respond to an initial incorrect answer, and further, that high achievers were praised more frequently for success and criticized less for failure.

There is evidence that the expectations teachers hold for their students can be generated as early as the first few days of the school year and then remain stable over the months to follow (Rist, 1970, 1972, 1973; Willis, 1972). For example, I found during my three-year longitudinal and ethnographic study of a single, *de facto* segregated elementary school in the black community of St. Louis, that after only eight days of kindergarten, the teacher made permanent seating arrangements based on what she assumed were variations in academic capability. But no formal evaluation of the children had taken place. Instead, the assignments to the three tables were based on a number of socio-economic criteria as well as on early interaction patterns in the classroom. Thus, the placement of the children came to reflect the social class distinctions in the room—the poor children from public welfare families all sat at one table, the working-class children sat at another and the middle class at the third. I demonstrated how the teacher operationalized her expectations of these different groups of children in terms of her differentials of teaching time, her use of praise and control, and the extent of autonomy within the classroom. By following the same children through first and second grade as well, I was able to show that the initial patterns established by the kindergarten teacher came to be perpetuated year after year. By second grade, labels given by another teacher clearly reflected the reality each of the three groups experienced in the school. The top group was called the "Tigers," the middle group the "Cardinals," and the lowest group, the "Clowns." What had begun as a subjective evaluation and labeling by the teacher took on objective dimensions as the school proceeded to process the children on the basis of the distinctions made when they first began.

Taken together, these studies strongly imply that the notion of "teacher expectations" is multi-faceted and multi-dimensional. It appears that when teachers generate expectations about their students, they do so not only for reasons of academic or cognitive performance, but for their classroom interactional patterns as well. Furthermore, not only ascribed characteristics such as race, sex, class, or ethnicity are highly salient, interpersonal traits are also. Thus, the interrelatedness of the various attributes which ultimately blend together to generate the evaluation a teacher makes as to what can be expected from a particular student suggests the strength and tenacity of such subsequent labels as "bright" or "slow" or "trouble-maker" or "teacher's little helper." It is to the outcomes of the student's having one or another of these labels that we now turn.

III. An Outcome of Labeling: The Self-Fulfilling Prophecy

W. I. Thomas, many years ago, set forth what has become a basic dictum of the social sciences when he observed. "If men define situations as real, they are real in their consequences." This is at the core of the self-fulfilling prophecy. An expectation which defines a situation comes to influence the actual behavior within the situation so as to produce what was initially assumed to be there. Merton (1968: 477) has elaborated on this concept and noted: "The self-fulfilling prophecy is, in the beginning, a *false* definition of the situation evoking a new behavior which makes the originally false conception come true." [emphasis in the original]

Here it is important to recall a basic tenet of labeling theory—that an individual does not become deviant simply by the commission of some act. As Becker (1963) stressed, deviance is not inherent in behavior *per se,* but in the application by others of rules and sanctions against one perceived as being an "offender." Thus, the only time one can accurately be termed a "deviant" is after the successful application of a label by a social audience. Thus, though many persons may commit norm violations, only select ones are subsequently labeled. The contingencies of race, class, sex, visibility of behavior, age, occupation, and who one's friends are all influence the outcome as to whether one is or is not labeled. . . . Rosenthal and Jacobson's *Pygmalion in the Classroom* (1968) created wide interest in the notion of the self-fulfilling prophecy as a concept to explain differential performance by children in classrooms. Their findings suggested that the expectations teachers created about the children randomly selected as "intellectual bloomers" somehow caused the teachers to treat them differently, with the result that the children really did perform better by the end of the year. Though the critics of this particular research (Snow, 1969; Taylor, 1970; Thorndike, 1968, 1969) and those who have been unsuccessful in replicating the findings (Claiborn, 1969) have leveled strong challenges to Rosenthal and Jacobson, the disagreements are typically related to methodology, procedure, and analysis rather than to the proposition that relations exist between expectations and behavior. In the context of a single student facing the authority and vested interests of a school administration and staff, the most likely outcome is that over time, the student will increasingly move towards conformity with the label the institution seeks to establish. Good and Brophy (1973: 75) have elaborated upon this process within the classroom as follows:

1. The teacher expects specific behavior and achievement from particular students.

2. Because of these different expectations, the teacher behaves differently toward the different students.

3. This teacher treatment tells each student what behavior and achievement the teacher expects from him and affects his self-concept, achievement motivation, and level of aspiration.

4. If this teacher treatment is consistent over time, and if the student does not actively resist or change it in some way, it will tend to shape his achievement and behavior. High-expectation students will be led to achieve at high levels, while the achievement of low-expectation students will decline.

5. With time, the student's achievement and behavior will conform more and more closely to that originally expected of him.

The fourth point in this sequence makes the crucial observation that teacher expectations are not automatically self-fulfilling. For the expectations of the teacher to become realized, both the teacher and the student must move toward a pattern of interaction where expectations are clearly communicated and the behavioral response is consonant with the expected patterns. The vulnerability of children to the dictates of adults in positions of power over them leaves the negotiations as to what evaluative definition will be tagged on the children more often than not in the hands of the powerful. As Max Weber himself stated, to have power is to be able to achieve one's ends, even in the face of resistance from others. When that resistance is manifested in school by children and is defined by teachers and administrators as truancy, recalcitrance, unruliness, and hostility, or conversely denied as a lack of motivation, intellectual apathy, sullenness, passivity, or withdrawal, the process is ready to be repeated and the options to escape further teacher definitions are increasingly removed.

POSTSCRIPT: BEYOND THE LOGJAM

This paper has argued that a fruitful convergence can be effected between the research being conducted on the self-fulfilling prophecy as a consequence of teacher expectations and the conceptual framework of labeling theory. The analysis of the outcomes of teacher expectations produces results highly similar to those found in the study of social deviance. Labels are applied to individuals which fundamentally shift their definitions of self and which further reinforce the behavior which had initially prompted the social reaction. The impact of the self-fulfilling prophecy in educational research is comparable to that found in the analysis of mental health clinics, asylums, prisons, juvenile homes, and other people-changing organizations. What the labeling perspective can provide to the study of educational outcomes as a result of the operationalization of teacher expectations is a model for the study of the *processes* by which the outcomes are produced. The detailing over time of the interactional patterns which lead to changes in self-definition and behavior within classrooms is sadly lacking in almost all of the expectation research to date. . . .

To extend the research on the educational experiences of those students who are differentially labeled by teachers, what is needed is a theoretical framework which can clearly isolate the influences and effects of certain kinds of teacher reactions on certain types of students, producing certain typical outcomes. The labeling perspective appears particularly well-suited for this expansion of both research and theoretical development on teacher expectations by offering the basis for analysis at either a specific or a more general level. With the former, for example, there are areas of investigation related to (1) types of students perceived by teachers as prone to success or failure; (2) the kinds of reactions, based on their expectations, teachers have to different students; and (3) the effects of specific teacher reactions on specific student outcomes. At a more general level, fruitful lines of inquiry might include (1) the outcomes in the post-school world of having received a negative vs. a positive label within the school; (2) the influences of factors such as social class and race on the categories of expectations teachers hold; (3) how and why labels do emerge in schools as well as the phenomenological and structural meanings that are attached to them; and (4) whether there are means by which to modify or minimize the effects of school labeling processes on students.

Labeling theory provides a conceptual framework by which to understand the processes of transforming attitudes into behavior and the outcomes of having done so. To be able to detail the dynamics and influences within schools by which some children come to see themselves as successful and act as though they were, and to detail how others come to see themselves as failures and act accordingly, provides in the final analysis an opportunity to intervene so as to expand the numbers of winners and diminish the numbers of losers. For that reason above all others, labeling theory merits our attention.

References

Akers, R. L. (1973). *Deviant behavior: A social learning approach.* Belmont, CA: Wadsworth.

Becker, H. S. (1952). Social class variations in the teacher-pupil relationship. *Journal of Educational Sociology, 25*(8), 451–465.

Becker, H. S. (1963). *Outsiders.* New York: Free Press.

Becker, H. S. (1964). *The other side.* New York: Free Press.

Brophy, J., & Good, T. (1970). Teachers' communications of differential expectations for children's classroom performance: Some behavioral data. *Journal of Educational Psychology, 61,* 365–374.

Brown, B. (1968). *The assessment of self-concept among four year old Negro and white children: A comparative study using the Brown-IDS Self-Concept Referents Test.* New York: Institute for Developmental Studies.

Claiborn, W. L. (1969). Expectancy in the classroom: A failure to replicate. *Journal of Educational Psychology, 60*(5), 377–383.

Clifford, M. M., & Walster, E. (1973). The effect of physical attractiveness on teacher expectations. *Sociology of Education, 46*(2), 248–258.

Davidson, H. H., & Lang, G. (1960). Children's perceptions of teachers' feelings toward them. *Journal of Experimental Education, 29*(2), 107–118.

Deutsch, M. (1963). The disadvantaged child and the learning process. In H. Passow (Ed.), *Education in depressed areas* (pp. 147–162). New York: Teachers College Press.

Deutsch, M., Fishman, J. A., Kogan, L., North, R., & Whiteman, M. (1964). Guidelines for testing minority group children. *Journal of Social Issues 20*(2), 129–145.

Douglas, J. (1964). *The home and the school.* London: MacGibbon & Kee.

Doyle, W., Hancock, G., & Kifer, E. (1971). *Teachers' perceptions: Do they make a difference?* Paper presented at the meeting of the American Educational Research Association, New York, NY.

Edgar, D. E. (1974). *The competent teacher.* Sydney, Australia: Angus & Robertson.

Erikson, K. T. (1966). *Wayward Puritans.* New York: Wiley.

Flanagan, J. C. (1960). *Test of general ability: Technical report.* Chicago: Science Research Associates.

Gibson, G. (1965). Aptitude tests. *Science, 149*(3684), 583.

Goaldman, L. (1971). Counseling methods and techniques: The use of tests. In L. C. Deighton (Ed.), *The encyclopedia of education.* New York: Macmillan.

Good, T., & Brophy, J. (1973). *Looking in classrooms.* New York: Harper & Row.

Goslin, D. A., & Glass, D. C. (1967). The social effects of standardized testing on American elementary schools. *Sociology of Education, 40,* 115–131.

Illich, I. (1971). *Deschooling society.* New York: Harper & Row.

Jackson, G., & Cosca, C. (1974). The inequality of educational opportunity in the southwest: An observational study of ethnically mixed classrooms. *American Educational Research Journal, 11*(3), 219–229.

Johnson, J. (1973). *On the interface between low-income urban black children and their teachers during the early school years: A position paper.* San Francisco: Far West Laboratory for Educational Research and Development.

Kitsuse, J. (1964). Societal reaction to deviant behavior: Problems of theory and method. In H. S. Becker (Ed.), *The other side.* New York: Free Press.

Leacock, E. (1969). *Teaching and learning in city schools.* New York: Basic Books.

Lemert, E. (1951). *Social pathology.* New York: McGraw-Hill.

Lemert, E. (1972). *Human deviance, social problems and social control.* Englewood Cliffs, NJ: Prentice-Hall.

Mackler, B. (1969). Grouping in the ghetto. *Education and Urban Society, 2*(1), 80–95.

McPherson, G. H. (1966). *The role-set of the elementary school teacher: A case study.* (Unpublished doctoral dissertation). Columbia University, New York.

Mehan, H. B. (1971). *Accomplishing understanding in educational settings.* (Unpublished doctoral dissertation). University of California, Santa Barbara.

Mehan, H. B. (1974). *Ethnomethodology and education.* Paper presented to the Sociology of Education Association conference, Pacific Grove, California.

Merton, R. K. (1968). Social problems and social theory. In R. Merton & R. Nisbet (Eds.), *Contemporary social problems* (pp. 697–737). New York: Harcourt, Brace & World.

Palardy, J. M. (1969). What teachers believe—what children achieve. *Elementary School Journal, 69,* 370–374.

Pequignot, H. (1966). L'equation personnelle du juge. *Semaine des Hopitaux, 14*(20), 4–11.

Rist, R. C. (1970). Student social class and teachers' expectations: The self-fulfilling prophecy in ghetto education. *Harvard Educational Review, 40,* 411–450.

Rist, R. C. (1972). Social distance and social inequality in a kindergarten classroom: An examination of the "cultural gap" hypothesis. *Urban Education, 7,* 241–260.

Rist, R. C. (1973). *The urban school: A factory for failure.* Cambridge: MIT Press.

Rosenthal, R., & Jacobson, L. (1968). *Pygmalion in the classroom.* New York: Holt, Rinehart and Winston.

Rowe, M. (1969). Science, silence, and sanctions. *Science and Children, 6*(6), 11–13.

Rubovits, P., & Maehr, M. L. (1973). Pygmalion black and white. *Journal of Personality and Social Psychology, 25*(2), 210–218.

Schur, E. (1965). *Crimes without victims* Englewood Cliffs, NJ: Prentice Hall.

Snow, R. E. (1969). Unfinished Pygmalion. *Contemporary Psychology, 14*(4), 197–199.

Stein, A. (1971). Strategies for failure. *Harvard Educational Review, 41*(2), 158–204.

Tannenbaum, F. (1938). *Crime and the community.* New York: Columbia University Press.

Taylor, C. (1970). The expectations of Pygmalion's creators. *Educational Leadership, 28,* 161–164.

Thorndike, R. L. (1968). Review of *Pygmalion in the classroom. Educational Research Journal, 5*(4), 708–711.

Thorndike, R. L. (1969). But do you have to know how to tell time? *Educational Research Journal, 6,* 692.

Warner. W. L., Havighurst, R., & Loeb, M. B. (1944). *Who shall be educated?* New York: Harper & Row.

Willis, S. (1972). *Formation of teachers' expectations of student academic performance.* (Unpublished doctoral dissertation). University of Texas at Austin.

Wilson, A. B. (1963). Social stratification and academic achievement. In H. Passow (Ed.), *Education in depressed areas* (pp. 217–236). New York: Teachers College.

Projects for Further Exploration

1. Using the basic ideas of the theoretical perspectives discussed in this chapter, consider two theoretical perspectives that you could use to help understand a specific situation that influenced your schooling. What are the strengths and weaknesses of each approach in explaining this situation?

2. Go to your library (or library's databases for searching journals) and find the most recent issue of *Sociology of Education*. Look at one or two articles in this journal, glancing through the first part of each article, and see if you can figure out which theoretical approach the authors used in their research.

3. Look around your current classroom and see if you can see any outward evidence of the theoretical arguments presented in this chapter. For example, are students all from the same social class background? If so, why? Is the curriculum structured for particular purposes in terms of maintaining social stability or the power structure in society? Discuss this with others in your class to see if you came up with similar examples and explanations.

2

STUDYING SCHOOLS

Research Methods in Education

In Chapter 1, we introduced some of the theories that social scientists and educators use to explain how schools work. However, theories are not descriptions of what is happening in schools; they are explanations that can be applied to what is happening. Research is used to see if the theories are supported in real educational institutions. Researchers use the theoretical explanations to formulate questions that are the basis for systematic examinations of schools. There are a variety of different ways to study schools, all of which offer valuable insights into education today.

The articles on education that you will read in this book and elsewhere depend on these different methods of social science research, offering unique pictures of what is happening in schools. Understanding the research methods used in articles you read is important because the methods used to collect data can influence the descriptions of education. Furthermore, you may be in a position to work with research in education and this chapter provides information on some of the techniques used.

So, let's get down to work! Social science research methods are a very large area to study and we can only provide a brief overview here. These methods are often grouped into two large categories: quantitative and qualitative methods. We instinctively divide these two ways of collecting data based on the quantification of data using numbers. However, quantification of data can be used in qualitative as well as quantitative research. It is easier to distinguish between quantitative and qualitative methods if you focus on the way the data are collected, rather than the way the data are analyzed. For example, we can collect data on how students respond to new teaching techniques in a classroom by asking them to fill out a survey with questions. We might ask how much they have learned from using this new technique on a scale of 1 to 10 with 10 being "A great deal" and 1 being "Nothing." Or, we can go into the same classroom and observe the students in a lesson using this new technique. In the first instance, we are collecting data from the student that is already defined by using the numbers 1 to 10, which can be used later in a quantitative analysis. In the second instance, we are observing and must develop a way of analyzing what we see. For the most part, quantitative methods are coded ahead of time for later quantitative analysis, whereas qualitative methods may use some quantification, but the quantification emerges from the process of analyzing the data during or after it has been collected. Researchers who use quantitative data spend a great deal of time before collecting the data organizing the ways in which they will collect their data, whereas researchers using qualitative methods rely more on observation with emerging analysis.

Let's consider an example testing Bernstein's theory of *restricted and elaborated codes* (described in the last chapter) using quantitative and qualitative methods. Using a quantitative research design, we can develop a survey instrument with quantifiable measures of social class as well as measures of elaborated and restricted codes that Bernstein developed in his theory. Of course, we would spend a lot of time developing these measures, but if the measures are valid, we can easily give them to thousands of individuals, thus testing Bernstein's theory. On the other hand, we could also go into upper-class, middle-class, and working-class schools and observe classrooms to see how children respond to materials taught in schools. Although the classrooms cannot be identical—that would be impossible to find—we pick our classrooms carefully to study the same age and same subject matter and perhaps even the same area of the country. Then we may discover some interesting differences that may or may not support Bernstein's theory about the use of elaborated and restricted codes varying by the social class background of children in classrooms.

With this basic distinction between qualitative and quantitative research designs in mind, and an understanding that there are many variations that fall within these two categories, we move to describing in greater detail the nuances of these two approaches.

Issues in Quantitative Methods

Every research method has advantages and disadvantages, and quantitative methods are no exception. One major advantage of using quantitative methodology is that you can study a very large group of individuals or educational institutions. The coding of data before you begin, as represented by various forms of surveys (Internet, mail, or in-person), facilitates the use of larger numbers of individuals or groups in the research. Of course we cannot study everyone that we wish to study, so we select a sample from the larger population, ideally using random selection. Large random samples are likely to lead to more representative samples. Selecting a sample that is representative of the group you are studying is critical to being able to generalize your findings to a larger population. A large sample, however, does not always guarantee a representative sample. Therefore, as you read research studies, it is important that you understand how samples were selected. For instance, in our example above, would you have more confidence in a sample of 100,000 students whom teachers selected from schools in upper-class, middle-class, and working-class districts, or a sample selected randomly by the researchers in schools randomly selected in different social class neighborhoods? Sampling is an important step in quantitative research method design and it is important to understand how researchers obtain their samples.

In addition to sampling in research designs that use quantitative methods, researchers must pay special attention to how they ask questions about those things that they wish to measure. One issue is whether the questions are valid measures of that which is being studied. For example, does the measurement of school achievement reflect what the students in the study are actually achieving in school? Another question is whether the measure is reliable. That is, if you gave the same question to the same person at another time, would you get the same answer? Needless to say, invalid and unreliable measures do not help us to understand how schools work. Therefore, researchers work hard to develop accurate measures. As a result, you want to look carefully at the way concepts are measured in the studies you read.

Another issue that comes up in quantitative research is that of *causation*. In a cross-sectional survey of a group of students done at one point in time, it is difficult to say that one thing caused another. For example, in a survey of students looking at dropping out of school, does the correlation between dropping out and grades indicate that low grades *caused* the students in the study to drop out? Or could dropping out have resulted in low grades because the students left before the end of the year? Or could family issues such as illness or sudden homelessness interfere with some students' academic work and lead to both poor grades and the student dropping out? It is not always possible to figure out what happened unless you have data from more than one point in time.

Longitudinal studies are helpful in determining causation because data are collected over time. It is much better if data are collected from the same individuals over time. By collecting data this way, it is possible to follow patterns in the individuals' lives and identify things that may predict later outcomes. It would be easier to assess why students drop out in twelfth grade if you also had information from these students in earlier years.

Some quantitative data is collected by large research organizations and made available to researchers to analyze. Most of these large data sets are carefully designed longitudinal studies based on random samples of all students in the United States. Many of these data sets were collected by the National Center for Education Statistics (NCES), part of the U.S. Department of Education. Beginning in 1972, NCES began collecting longitudinal survey data starting with high school seniors (NLS-72). In 1980, NCES began collecting data from high school sophomores and seniors, a data set called High School and Beyond (HS&B). In 1988, another study was begun beginning with eighth graders (NELS-88). In 1990 and 1993, the Beginning Postsecondary Student Survey and the Baccalaureate and Beyond Survey began to follow postsecondary students (Schmidt, 2002). Individuals who completed the original survey are typically followed up every two years—not a small task as the samples are drawn to be representative of the entire United States and some of these data sets include data from more than 30,000 individuals at two or more points in time (Schmidt, 2002).

The most recent large data set collected by NCES (in collaboration with other federal agencies and organizations) is the Early Childhood Longitudinal Studies program. This includes three longitudinal studies. One is a representative sample of the kindergarten class of 1998–99 (ECLS-K) and the other of the birth cohort of 14,000 children born in the year 2001 (ECLS-B). NCES expects the two studies to "provide detailed information on children's health, early care and early school experiences" (NCES, 2010). The ECLS-K began in fall of 1998 with a nationally representative sample of approximately 21,000 kindergarteners. These children will be followed with testing in the fall and spring from kindergarten through fifth grade and then again in eighth grade. The birth cohort in ECLS-B will be followed yearly until the children are in kindergarten (NCES, 2010). NCES recently began a third study in 2010–2011 of the kindergarten cohort that year. Imagine the value of these large, longitudinal data sets for researchers. Therefore, don't be surprised if the methods sections of articles in this book list data collected by NCES or another agency.

The first reading in this chapter is by Bruce J. Biddle and David C. Berliner, who review mostly quantitative research on the effects of class size on students. While their findings are very important, pay special attention to their discussion of the various studies they reviewed and the detailed description of the longitudinal research on class size. This is a very interesting introduction to both the research on class size and the issues surrounding quantitative research.

The last reading, by Gerald W. Bracey, warns us to use caution when confronted with numbers. Although statistics are a normal part of analyzing quantitative data, Bracey provides excellent guidelines for reading those numbers so as not to be tricked by an argument that is "backed up by statistics."

ISSUES IN QUALITATIVE METHODS

As noted previously, qualitative methods, sometimes referred to as ethnographies, are also used to study education. And, as noted, qualitative methods rely primarily on observation or open interviews. Qualitative researchers typically do not spend a lot of time worrying about sampling methods, as virtually no qualitative studies use random samples. Nor do qualitative researchers have to worry about the accuracy or reliability of their measures, because they don't create measures ahead of time. Instead, most qualitative research begins with finding a site to observe or individuals to interview that fit the kinds of questions the researcher has in mind. For example, in the second reading in this chapter,

Annette Lareau and Erin McNamara Horvat observed in two classrooms in an elementary school in a small school district that was 52% white and 44% black. Collecting data in this case meant writing down observations of what they saw in the classrooms and in the school in general.

As you can see, their data analysis did not involve any statistics. Many researchers analyze their data as they begin their observations and continue to analyze the notes and materials for some time afterward. It is likely that data collected using qualitative data are more "valid" than quantitative data because researchers are reporting what they say from multiple observations and directly from the sources. However, it is not as easy to make a statement about what causes what when collecting qualitative data because a researcher cannot possibly observe as many people using this method and it is possible that the very question a researcher goes out to study may change in the course of the observations, as Edward Morris reports in Reading 35 in Chapter 7. In addition to this article by Morris, and the Lareau and Horvat reading in this chapter, there are many more examples of qualitative research in this book.

OTHER METHODS USED TO STUDY EDUCATION

Some researchers do a *meta-analysis* of a series of research studies on a particular topic. Meta-analysis takes quantitative findings from similar studies, and uses statistical analysis to get a statistic summarizing these previously published statistical findings. We do not include any research using this technique in our book because research using meta-analysis can be difficult to read and interpret, even though these studies can be quite powerful as well. Although Biddle and Berliner review multiple studies in their reading in this chapter, it is not a meta-analysis because they do not employ the statistical techniques of meta-analysis.

One other method that you will see in this book is *content analysis*. In Chapter 6, Stuart Foster and Jason Nicholls do a content analysis of history textbooks from England, Japan, Sweden, and the United States, focusing on the role of the United States in World War II. They selected books from all four countries and analyzed the text of each as related to U.S. involvement in World War II. We don't want to give away their findings just yet, but we promise you will find it very interesting.

At the close of this chapter, we hope you are better prepared to understand the basis for knowledge claims that you find in the readings in this book and in other research on education that you encounter. Understanding the types of methods researchers use to do their studies is important in being a good consumer of knowledge. For example, although you may get a deep understanding of a topic with an article that used qualitative techniques, it is not a good idea to generalize beyond the setting observed. However, ideas can be taken from that qualitative study and often are used to create a survey of a larger population and develop questions and causal statements (called *hypotheses*) that can be tested on a large number of individuals across settings. After reading this chapter, you have some basic information about the theories and methods that sociologists use to explore educational systems as portrayed by the open systems model discussed in the introduction.

REFERENCES

National Center for Education Statistics (NCES). (2010). *Surveys and programs.* Retrieved from http://nces.ed .gov/surveys/SurveyGroups.asp?Group=3

Schmidt, C. (2002). Longitudinal studies data collection program. In D. L. Levinson, P. W. Cookson, Jr., & A. R. Sadovnik (Eds.), *Education and sociology: An encyclopedia* (pp. 409–420). New York: Routledge Falmer.

SMALL CLASS SIZE AND ITS EFFECTS

Bruce J. Biddle and David C. Berliner

Debates over ideal class size have pitted policy makers and politicians against each other, and stimulated many researchers to study the issue. Politicians argue for larger versus smaller schools based on "the research," but the research presents a mixed picture. The question that is sometimes overlooked is the effect of large versus small classrooms on equality of educational opportunity, especially in overcrowded schools and classes. Biddle and Berliner present an overview of research and projects addressing size issues, especially the relationship of size to achievement of students. This study provides an overview of the advantages and disadvantages of using quantitative research to support policy issues on this important topic, the impact of class size on equal opportunity of academic achievement.

Questions to consider for this reading:

1. What does research show about class size and achievement?

2. What problems with quantitative research identified in the introduction to this chapter can you see in this description of the research on class size?

3. What features of quantitative research do the authors identify that lead to stronger studies on the effects of class size?

Studies of the impact of class size on student achievement may be more plentiful than for any other issue in education. Although one might expect this huge research effort to yield clear answers about the effects of class size, sharp disagreements about these studies' findings have persisted.

Advocacy groups take opposite stances. The American Federation of Teachers, for example, asserts that

> taken together, these studies provide compelling evidence that reducing class size, particularly for younger children, will have a positive effect on student achievement. (Murphy & Rosenberg, 1998, p. 3)

The Heritage Foundation, by contrast, claims that "there's no evidence that smaller class sizes alone lead to higher student achievement" (Rees & Johnson, 2000).

Reviewers of class size studies also disagree. One study contends that "large reductions in school class size promise learning benefits of a magnitude commonly believed not within the power of educators to achieve" (Glass, Cahen, Smith, & Filby, 1982, p. 50), whereas another claims that "the evidence does not offer much reason to expect a systematic effect from overall class size reduction policies" (Hanushek, 1999, p. 158).

That the American Federation of Teachers and the Heritage Foundation sponsor conflicting judgments is easy to understand. But why have reviewers come to such divergent views about the research on class size, and what does the evidence really say?

EARLY SMALL FIELD EXPERIMENTS

To answer these questions, we must look at several research traditions, beginning with early experiments on class size. Experiments have always been a popular research technique because investigators can assign their subjects randomly to different conditions and then compare the results of those conditions—and this human intervention can appear to provide information about causes and effects. Experiments on class size, however, are nearly always done in field settings—schools— where uncontrolled events can undermine the research and effect results.

Small experimental studies on the effects of class size began to appear in the 1920s, and scores of them emerged subsequently. In the 1960s, informal reviews of these efforts generally concluded that differences in class size generated little to no effect. By the late 1970s, however, a more sophisticated research method, meta-analysis, had been invented, which facilitated the statistical assembly of results from small-but-similar studies to estimate effects for the studies' populations. Reviewers quickly applied meta-analysis to results from early experiments in class size (Educational Research Service, 1980; Glass et al., 1982; Glass & Smith, 1979; Hedges & Stock, 1983) and eventually emerged with a consensus that short-term exposure to small classes generates—usually minor—gains in students' achievement and that those gains are greater in the early grades, in classrooms with fewer than 20 students, and for students from groups that are traditionally disadvantaged in education.

Most of these early class size experiments, however, had involved small samples, short-term exposures to small classes, only one measure of student success, and a single education context (such as one school or school district). Poor designs had also made results of some studies questionable. Researchers needed to use different strategies to ascertain the effects of long-term exposure to small classes and to assess whether the advantages of early exposure to small classes would generalize to other successes and be sustainable.

SURVEYS

Survey research has provided evidence on the effects of class size by analyzing naturally occurring differences in schools and classrooms and by asking whether these differences are associated with student outcomes.

Well-designed surveys can offer evidence about the impact of variables that experiments cannot manipulate—such as gender, minority status, and childhood poverty—but survey research cannot easily establish relationships between causes and effects. For example, if a survey examines a sample of schools where average class size varies and discovers that those schools with smaller classes also have higher levels of student achievement, has the survey ascertained that class size generated achievement? Hardly. Those schools with smaller classes might also have had more qualified teachers, better equipment, more up-to-date curriculums, newer school buildings, more students from affluent homes, or a more supportive community environment—factors that may also have helped generate higher levels of achievement. To use survey data to make the case for a causal relation between class size and student outcomes, then, researchers must use statistical processes that control for the competing effects of other variables.

Serious surveys of education achievement in the United States began in the 1960s with the famous Coleman report (Coleman et al., 1966). Written by authors with impressive reputations and released with great fanfare, this massive, federally funded study involved a national sample and took on many issues then facing education. Today, most people remember the report for its startling claim that student achievement is almost totally influenced by the students' families and peers and not by the characteristics of their schools. This claim was widely accepted—indeed, was greeted with dismay by educators and endorsed with enthusiasm by fiscal conservatives—despite flaws in the report's methods that were noted by thoughtful critics.

Since then, researchers have conducted surveys to establish whether differences in school funding or in the reforms that funds can buy—such as small class sizes—are associated with desired education outcomes. Most of these surveys, usually designed by economists, have involved questionable design features and small samples that did not represent the wide range of U.S. schools, classrooms, or students. . . .

Fortunately, a few well-designed, large-scale surveys have investigated class size directly (see, for example, Elliott, 1998; Ferguson, 1991; Ferguson & Ladd, 1996; Wenglinsky, 1997). These studies concluded that long-term exposure to small classes in the early grades can be associated with student achievement; that the extra gains that such exposure generates may be substantial; and that such gains may not appear with exposure to small classes in the upper grades or at the secondary school levels.

TRIAL PROGRAMS AND LARGE FIELD EXPERIMENTS

Other types of small class research have addressed some of the shortcomings of early experiments and surveys. In the 1980s, state legislatures in the United States began political debates about the effects of small class size, and some states began trial programs or large-scale field experiments. . . .

Tennessee's Project STAR

Such an experiment shortly appeared in Tennessee's Project STAR (Student/Teacher Achievement Ratio), arguably the largest and best-designed field experiment ever undertaken in education (Finn & Achilles, 1990; Finn, Gerber, Achilles, & Boyd-Zaharias, 2001; Folger, 1989; Grissmer, 1999; Krueger, 1999, 2000; Krueger & Whitmore, 2001; Mosteller, 1995; Nye, Hedges, & Konstantopoulos, 1999).

In the mid-1980s, the Tennessee legislature funded a four-year study to compare the achievement of early-grade students assigned randomly to one of three conditions: *standard classes* (with one certificated teacher and more than 20 students); *supplemented classes* (with one teacher and a full-time, noncertificated teacher's aide); and *small classes* (with one teacher and about 15 students). The study began with students entering kindergarten in 1985 and called for each student to attend the same type of class for four years. To control variables, the study asked each participating school to sponsor all three types of classes and to assign students and teachers randomly to each type. Participating teachers received no prior training for the type of class they were to teach.

The project invited all the state's primary schools to be in the study, but each participating school had to agree to remain in the program for four years; to have the class *rooms* needed for the project; and to have at least 57 kindergarten students so that all three types of classes could be set up. Participating schools received no additional support other than funds to hire additional teachers and aides. These constraints meant that troubled schools and those that disapproved of the study—and schools that were too small, crowded, or underfunded—would not participate in the STAR program, so the sample for the first year involved "only" 79 schools, 328 classrooms, and about 6,300 students. Those schools came from all corners of the state, however, and represented urban, inner-city, suburban, and rural school districts. The sample population included majority students, a sizable number of African American students, and students receiving free school lunches.

At the beginning of each year of the study, the sample population changed somewhat. Some participating students had moved away, been required to repeat kindergarten, or left the study because of poor health. Other families moved into the districts served by STAR schools, however, and their children filled the vacant seats. Also, because attending kindergarten was not then mandatory in Tennessee, some new students entered the STAR program in the 1st grade.

In addition, some parents tried to move their children from one type of STAR class to another, but administrators allowed only a few students to move from a standard class to a supplemented class or vice versa. By the end of the study, then, some students had been exposed to a STAR class for four years, but others had spent a shorter time in such classes. These shifts might have biased STAR results, but Alan Krueger's careful analysis (1999) concluded that such bias was minimal.

Near the end of each year, STAR students took the Stanford Achievement Test battery and received separate scores for reading, word-study skills, and mathematics. Results from these tests were similar for students who were in the standard and supplemented classes, indicating that the presence of untrained aides in supplemented classes did *not* contribute to improving student achievement. Results for small classes were sharply different, however, with long-term exposure to small classes generating substantially higher levels of achievement and with gains becoming greater the longer that students were in small classes.

. . . STAR investigators found that the students in small classes were 0.5 months ahead of the other students by the end of kindergarten, 1.9 months ahead at the end of 1st grade, 5.6 months ahead in 2nd grade, and 7.1 months ahead by the end of 3rd grade. The achievement advantages were smaller, although still impressive, for students who were only exposed to one, two, or three years of small classes. STAR investigators found similar (although not identical) results for word-study skills and mathematics.

Small-class advantages appeared for all types of students participating in the study. The gains were similar for boys and girls, but they were greater for impoverished students, African American students, and students from inner-city schools—groups that are traditionally disadvantaged in education.

These initial STAR findings were impressive, but would students who had been exposed to small classes in the early grades retain their extra gains when they entered standard size classes in 4th grade? To answer this question, the Tennessee legislature authorized a second study to examine STAR student outcomes during subsequent years of schooling.

At the end of each year, until they were in the 12th grade in 1997–1998, these students took the Comprehensive Tests of Basic Skills and received scores in reading, mathematics, science, and social science. The results showed that average students who had attended small classes were months ahead of those from standard classes for each topic assessed at each grade level. Figure 7.1 displays results from some of these tests, showing for example, that when typical students who had attended small classes in the early grades reached grade 8, they were 4.1 months ahead in reading, 3.4 months ahead in mathematics, 4.3 months ahead in science, and 4.8 months ahead in social science.

Students who had attended small classes also enjoyed other advantages in the upper grades. They earned better grades on average, and fewer dropped out or had to repeat a year. And when they reached high school, more small class students opted to learn foreign languages, study advanced-level courses, and take the ACT and SAT college entrance examinations. More graduated from high school and were in the top 25 percent of their classes. Moreover, initial published results suggest that these upper-grade effects were again larger for students who are traditionally disadvantaged in education.

. . . [O]f students who opted to take the ACT or SAT exams as high school seniors, roughly 44 percent of those from small classes took one or both of these tests, whereas only 40 percent of those from standard classes did so. The difference, however, was far greater for African American students. Instruction in small classes during the early grades had eliminated more than half of the traditional disadvantages that African American students have displayed in participation rates in the ACT and SAT testing programs.

Taken together, findings from the STAR project have been impressive, but they are not necessarily definitive. The STAR student sample did not quite match the U.S. population, for example, because very few Hispanic, Native American, and immigrant (non-English-speaking) families were living in Tennessee in the middle-1980s. Also, news about the greater achievement gains of small classes leaked out early during the STAR project, and one wonders how this may have

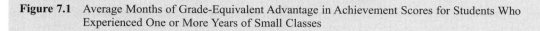

Figure 7.1 Average Months of Grade-Equivalent Advantage in Achievement Scores for Students Who Experienced One or More Years of Small Classes

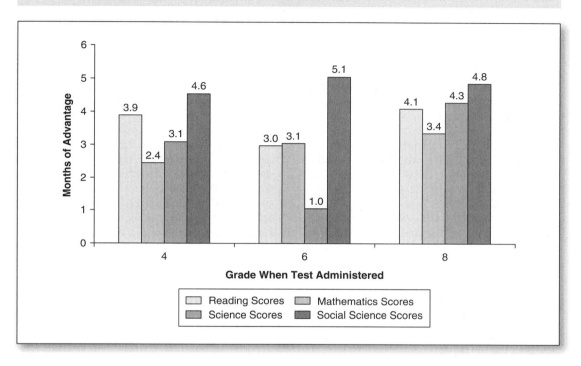

affected participating teachers and why parents whose children were in other types of classes did not then demand that their children be reassigned to small classes. Finally, the STAR schools had volunteered to participate, suggesting that the teachers and principals in those schools may have had strong interests in trying innovative ideas. Questions such as these should not cause us to reject the findings from the STAR project, but we should keep in mind that this was a single study and that, as always, other evidence is needed to increase certainty about class size effects. . . .

Like Project STAR, the SAGE program (Wisconsin's Student Achievement Guarantee in Education Program) studied schools that had volunteered for the program and provided them with sufficient funds to hire additional teachers. The SAGE program, however, involved more Hispanic, Asian, and Native American students than had the STAR project.

After the announcement of findings from the initial effort, the Wisconsin legislature extended the SAGE program to other primary schools in the state. Therefore, what began as a small trial project has now blossomed into a statewide program that makes small classes in the early grades available for schools serving needy students.

The California Class Size Reduction Program

In 1996, California began a class size reduction program that has been far more controversial than such programs elsewhere. In earlier years, California had experienced many social problems, and major measures of achievement ranked California schools last in the United States. That year, however, a fiscal windfall became available, and then-governor Pete Wilson announced that primary schools would receive $650 annually for each student (an amount later increased to $800) if they would agree to reduce class sizes in the early grades from the state-wide average of more than 28 students to not more than 20 students in each class (Hymon, 1997; Korostoff, 1998; Stecher, Bohrnstedt, Kirst, McRobbie, & Williams, 2001).

Several problems quickly surfaced. First, the California definition of a small class was larger than the size recommended in other studies. In fact, the size of small classes in California matched the size of standard classes in some other states. On the other hand, some California schools had been coping with 30–40 students in each classroom in the early grades, so a reduction to 20 students constituted an improvement.

The second problem was that the program's per-student funding was inadequate. Contrast the SAGE program's additional $2,000 for each student with the $650 or $800 offered by California. Nevertheless, the lure of additional funding proved seductive, and most California school districts applied to participate. This inadequate funding imposed serious consequences on poorer school districts, which had to abolish other needed activities to afford hiring teachers for smaller classes. In effect, then, the program created rather than solved problems for underfunded school districts.

In addition, when the California program began, many of its primary schools were overcrowded, and the state was suffering from a shortage of well-trained, certificated teachers. To cope with the lack of space, some schools created spaces for smaller classes by cannibalizing other needed facilities such as special education quarters, child care centers, music and art rooms, computer laboratories, libraries, gymnasiums, or teachers' lounges. Other schools had to tap into their operating budgets to buy portable classrooms, resulting in delays in paying for badly needed curricular materials or repairs for deteriorating school buildings. And to staff their smaller classes, many schools had to hire teachers without certification or prior training.

So far, results from the California program have been only modest. Informal evidence suggests that most students, parents, and teachers are pleased with their schools' smaller classes. And comparisons between the measured achievements of 3rd grade students from districts that did and did not participate in the early phases of the program have indicated minor advantages for California's smaller classes. These effects, however, have been smaller than those reported for the STAR and SAGE programs.

In many ways, the California initiative has provided a near-textbook case of how a state should *not* reduce class size. After failing to conduct a trial program, California adopted an inadequate definition of class size, committed insufficient funds to the initiative, and ignored serious problems of overcrowding and teacher shortages. This example should remind us that small classes are not a panacea for education. To be effective, programs for reducing class size need careful planning and consideration of the needs and strengths of existing school systems.

WHAT WE NOW KNOW ABOUT SMALL CLASSES

What should we conclude about the effects of small classes? Although the results of individual studies are always questionable, a host of different studies suggest several conclusions.

- When planned thoughtfully and funded adequately, small classes in the early grades generate substantial gains for students, and those extra gains are greater the longer students are exposed to those classes.
- Extra gains from small classes in the early grades are larger when the class has fewer than 20 students.
- Extra gains from small classes in the early grades occur in a variety of academic disciplines and for both traditional measures of student achievement and other indicators of student success.
- Students whose classes are small in the early grades retain their gains in standard size classrooms and in the upper grades, middle school, and high school.
- All types of students gain from small classes in the early grades, but gains are greater for

students who have traditionally been disadvantaged in education.

- Initial results indicate that students who have traditionally been disadvantaged in education carry greater small-class, early-grade gains forward into the upper grades and beyond.
- The extra gains associated with small classes in the early grades seem to apply equally to boys and girls.
- Evidence for the possible advantages of small classes in the upper grades and high school is inconclusive.

TENTATIVE THEORIES

Why should reducing class size have such impressive effects in the early grades? Theories about this phenomenon have fallen largely into two camps.

Most theorists focus on the teacher, reasoning that small classes work their magic because the small class context improves interactions between the teacher and individual students. In the early grades, students first learn the rules of standard classroom culture and form ideas about whether they can cope with education. Many students have difficulty with these tasks, and interactions with a teacher on a one-to-one basis—a process more likely to take place when the class is small—help the students cope. In addition, teachers in small classes have higher morale, which enables them to provide a more supportive environment for initial student learning. Learning how to cope well with school is crucial to success in education, and those students who solve this task when young will thereafter carry broad advantages—more effective habits and positive self-concepts—that serve them well in later years of education and work.

The need to master this task confronts all students, but doing so is often a more daunting challenge for students who come from impoverished homes, ethnic groups that have suffered from discrimination or are unfamiliar with U.S. classroom culture, or urban communities where home and community problems interfere with education. Thus, students from such backgrounds have traditionally had more difficulty coping with classroom education, and they are more likely to be helped by a reduction in class size.

This theory also helps explain why reductions in class size in the upper grades may not generate significant advantages. Older students normally have learned to cope with standard classrooms and have developed either effective or ineffective attitudes concerning academic subjects—and these attitudes are not likely to change just because of a reduction in class size.

The theory also suggests a caution. Students are likely to learn more and develop better attitudes toward education if they are exposed to well-trained and enthusiastic teachers, appropriate and challenging curriculums, and physical environments in their classrooms and schools that support learning. If conditions such as these are not also present, then reducing class size in the early grades will presumably have little impact. Thus, when planning programs for reducing class size, we should also think about the professional development of the teachers who will participate in them and the educational and physical contexts in which those programs will be placed.

A second group of theories designed to account for a class size effect focuses on the classroom environment and student conduct rather than on the teacher. We know that discipline and classroom management problems interfere with subject-matter instruction. Theories in this group argue that these problems are less evident in small classes and that students in small classes are more likely to be engaged in learning. Moreover, teacher stress is reduced in small classes, so teachers in the small class context can provide more support for student learning. Studies have also found that small instructional groups can provide an environment for learning that is quite different from that of the large classroom. Small instructional groups can create supportive contexts where learning is less competitive and students are encouraged to form supportive relationships with one another.

Theories such as these suggest that the small class environment is structurally different from that of the large class. Less time is spent on management and more time is spent on instruction, students participate at higher levels, teachers are able to provide more support for learning, and students have more positive relationships. Such processes should lead both to greater subject-matter learning and to more positive attitudes about education among students, with more substantial effects in the early grades and for those groups that are traditionally disadvantaged in education.

These two theories are not mutually exclusive. On the contrary, both may provide partial insights into what happens in small classes and why small class environments help so many students. Collecting other types of evidence to assess such theories directly would be useful, particularly observational studies that compare the details of interaction in early-grade classes of various sizes and surveys of the attitudes and self-concepts of students who have been exposed to classes of different sizes. Unfortunately, good studies of these effects have been hard to find.

POLICY IMPLICATIONS AND ACTIONS

Given the strength of findings from research on small classes, why haven't those findings provoked more reform efforts? Although many state legislatures have debated or begun reform initiatives related to class size, most primary schools in the United States today do not operate under policies that mandate small classes for early grades. Why not?

This lack of attention has several causes, among them ignorance about the issue, confusion about the results of class size research and ineffective dissemination of those results, prejudices against poor and minority students, the politicizing of debates about class size effects and their implications, and practical problems associated with adopting small classes.

Recent debates about class size have become quite partisan in the United States, with Democrats generally favoring class size reductions and Republicans remaining hostile to them. Responding to President Bill Clinton's 1998 State of the Union address, the U.S. Congress set up a modest program, aimed at urban school districts with high concentrations of poverty, which provided funds for hiring additional teachers during the 1999 and 2000 fiscal years. This program enabled some districts to reduce class sizes in the early grades, and informal results from those cities indicated gains in student achievement.

Republicans have been lukewarm about extending this program—some apparently believing that it is ineffective or is merely a scheme to enhance the coffers of teacher's unions—and have welcomed President George W. Bush's call for an alternative federal program focused on high-stakes achievement tests and using results from those tests to apply sanctions to schools if they do not perform adequately.

The major problems standing in the way of reducing class sizes, however, are often practical ones. In many cases, cutting class sizes means hiring more teachers. With the looming shortage of qualified teachers, recruiting more teachers may be even more difficult than finding the funds to pay their salaries. Further, many schools would have to find or create extra rooms to house the additional classes created by small class programs, which would require either modifying school buildings or acquiring temporary classroom structures.

In many cases, meeting such needs would mean increasing the size of public school budgets, a step abhorred by fiscal conservatives and those who are critical of public education. The latter have argued that other reforms would cost less and be more effective than reducing class sizes. In response to such claims, various studies have estimated the costs of class size reduction programs or compared their estimated costs with those of other proposed reforms. Unfortunately, studies of this type must make questionable assumptions, so the results of their efforts have not been persuasive.

Nevertheless, reducing the size of classes for students in the early grades often requires additional funds. All students would reap sizable education benefits and long-lasting advantages, however, and students from educationally disadvantaged groups would benefit even more. Indeed, if we are to judge by available evidence, no other education reform has yet been studied that would provide such striking benefits. Debates about reducing class sizes, then, are disputes about values. If citizens are truly committed to providing a quality public education and a level playing field for all students regardless of background, they will find the funds needed to reduce class size.

REFERENCES

Coleman, J. S., Campbell, E. Q., Hobson, C. J., McPartland, J., Mood, A. M., Weinfield, F. D., & York, R. L. (1966). *Equality of educational opportunity*. Washington, DC: U.S. Government Printing Office.

Educational Research Service. (1980). Class size research: A critique of recent meta-analyses. *Phi Delta Kappan, 70*(December), 239–241.

Elliott, M. (1998). School finance and opportunities to learn: Does money well spent enhance students' achievement? *Sociology of Education, 71*(3), 223–245.

Ferguson, R. F. (1991). Paying for public education: New evidence on how and why money matters. *Harvard Journal on Legislation, 28*(2), 465–498.

Ferguson, R. F., & Ladd, H. F. (1996). How and why money matters: An analysis of Alabama schools. In H. F. Ladd (Ed.), *Holding schools accountable: Performance-based reform in education* (pp. 256–298). Washington, DC: Brookings Institution.

Finn, J. D., & Achilles, C. M. (1990). Answers and questions about class size: A statewide experiment. *American Educational Research Journal, 27*(3), 557–577.

Finn, J. D., Gerber, B., Achilles, C. M., & Boyd-Zaharias, J. (2001). The enduring effects of small classes. *Teachers College Record, 103*(1), 145–183.

Folger, J. (Ed.). (1989). Project STAR and class size policy (Special issue). *Peabody Journal of Education, 67*(1).

Glass, G. V., Cahen, L. S., Smith, M. L., & Filby, N. N. (1982). *School class size: Research and policy*. Beverly Hills, CA: Sage.

Glass, G. V., & Smith, M. L. (1979). Meta-analysis of research on class size and achievement. *Educational Evaluation and Policy Analysis, 1*(1), 2–16.

Grissmer, D. (Ed.). (1999). Class size: Issues and new findings [Special issue]. *Educational Evaluation and Policy Analysis, 21*(2).

Hanushek, E. A. (1999). Some findings from an independent investigation of the Tennessee STAR experiment and from other investigations of class size effects. *Education Evaluation & Policy Analysis, 21*(2), 143–163.

Hedges, L. V., & Stock, W. (1983). The effects of class size: An examination of rival hypotheses. *American Educational Research Journal, 20*(1), 63–85.

Hymon, S. (1997). A lesson in classroom size reduction: Administrators nationwide can learn from California's classroom size reduction plan and how districts implemented it. *School Planning & Management, 36*(7), 18–23, 26.

Korostoff, M. (1998). Tackling California's class size reduction policy initiative: An up close and personal account of how teachers and learners responded. *International Journal of Educational Research, 29*(8), 797–807.

Krueger, A. B. (1999). Experimental estimates of education production functions. *The Quarterly Journal of Economics, 114*(2), 497–532.

Krueger, A. B. (2000). *Economic considerations and class size* (Working paper #447). Princeton, NJ: Princeton University, Industrial Relations Section.

Krueger, A. B., & Whitmore, D. M. (2001). The effect of attending a small class in the early grades on college-test taking and middle school test results: Evidence from Project STAR. *Economic Journal, 111*, 1–28.

Mosteller, F. (1995). The Tennessee study of class size in the early school grades. *The Future of Children, 5*(2), 113–127.

Murphy, D., & Rosenberg, B. (1998, June). *Recent research shows major benefits of small class size* (Educational Issues Policy Brief No. 3). Washington, DC: American Federation of Teachers.

Nye, B., Hedges, L. V., & Konstantopoulos, S. (1999). The long-term effects of small classes: A five-year follow-up of the Tennessee class size experiment. *Educational Evaluation and Policy Analysis, 21*, 127–42.

Rees, N. S., & Johnson, K. (2000, May 30). A lesson in smaller class sizes. *Heritage Views 2000*. Retrieved from http://www.heritage.org/views/2000/ed053000.html

Stecher, B., Bohrnstedt, G., Kirst, M., McRobbie, J., & Williams, T. (2001). Class-size reduction in California: A story of hope, promise, and unintended consequences. *Phi Delta Kappan, 82*(9), 670–674.

Wenglinsky, H. (1997). How money matters: The effect of school district spending on academic achievement. *Sociology of Education, 70*(3), 221–237.

MOMENTS OF SOCIAL INCLUSION AND EXCLUSION

Race, Class, and Cultural Capital in Family-School Relationships

Annette Lareau and Erin McNamara Horvat

In their qualitative study of parents' involvement in their children's educations, Annette Lareau and Erin Horvat found that race and social class come together to affect teachers' definitions of appropriate involvement for parents. They argue that those parents with more cultural capital (defined in Chapter 1) are in a better position to influence their children's educations. Because the cultural capital of school personnel is most likely to be of the middle or upper class, parents with similar social class backgrounds are likely to share that cultural capital and the expectations and meaning of education. This reading uses qualitative methods to examine how the concept of cultural capital influences the complex interactions of race and class in defining children's educational experiences.

Questions to consider for this reading:

1. How would this study be different if the researchers used quantitative methods to study cultural capital?

2. What are the strengths of using qualitative methods to explore how parental involvement is influenced by race and class?

3. What are the weaknesses of using qualitative methods to study this topic?

Scholars who are interested in how schools replicate existing social inequalities have found the concept of social reproduction to be useful, especially as articulated in the work of Bourdieu and his associates (Bourdieu, 1977a, 1977b, 1984, 1990; Wacquant, 1992, 1993). One of Bourdieu's major insights on educational inequality is that students with more valuable social and cultural capital fare better in school than do their otherwise-comparable peers with less valuable social and cultural capital. The social reproduction perspective has proved especially useful in attempts to gain a better understanding of how race and class influence the transmission of educational inequality.

However, a key dilemma that confronts those who seek to understand how the reproduction of inequality occurs in schools has been where to focus the debate. Exactly how is inequality perpetuated in school settings? Much of the literature has identified important class differences in parents' and students' attitudes or behaviors toward

From "Moments of Social Inclusion and Exclusion: Race, Class, and Cultural Capital in Family-School Relationships," by A. Lareau and E. M. Horvat, 1999, *Sociology of Education,* 72(1), pp. 37–53. Copyright 1999 by the American Sociological Association. Reprinted with permission.

schools and has shown that these class differences affect children's progress in school (Brantlinger, 1993; DiMaggio & Mohr, 1985; Lareau, 1989; McDonough, 1997; Useem, 1992). As valuable as this line of research has been, these theories do not always attend to individual interactions and interventions that more accurately characterize the students', teachers', and parents' interactions in schools. In other words, these studies have identified cultural and social factors that contribute to educational inequality but have not advanced knowledge of the process whereby social and cultural resources are converted into educational advantages. Thus, the picture that emerges from them is incomplete and overly simplistic.

Despite these difficulties, the overall perspective of social reproduction, with its focus on conflict, change, and systemic inequality, is still worthy of attention. Bourdieu's method allows for a more fluid interplay and better understanding of the relationship between structure and agency than do other theoretical perspectives. Although the theoretical potential of offering an intricate and dynamic model is embedded in Bourdieu's original conceptual work, the empirical research has often been disappointing. The translation of the theoretical model into "variables" has often decontextualized key concepts from the broader theoretical mission (see Wacquant, 1992, 1993, for a discussion of these issues).

Still, Bourdieu has always remained attuned to the strategies and actions that individuals follow in their daily lives. Nevertheless, he has not always been sufficiently aware of variations in the ways in which institutional actors legitimate or rebuff efforts by individuals to activate their resources. Nor has he given sufficient attention to the moments of reproduction and exclusion. Although both these points are clearly implied in Bourdieu's work, we see it as an important clarification.

In sum, the empirical work on social reproduction, despite the original theoretical richness of Bourdieu's writing, has not sufficiently recognized three important points. First, the value of capital depends heavily on the social setting (or field). Second, there is an important difference between the possession and activation of capital or resources. That is, people who have social and cultural capital may choose to activate capital or not, and they vary in the skill with which they activate it. Third, these two points come together to suggest that rather than being an overly deterministic continual process, reproduction is jagged and uneven and is continually negotiated by social actors.

We find it helpful to point to moments of "social inclusion" and "social exclusion" (Lamont & Lareau, 1988). To understand the character of these moments, one needs to look at the context in which the capital is situated, the efforts by individuals to activate their capital, the skill with which individuals activate their capital, and the institutional response to the activation. These factors, working together, can produce moments of reproduction or moments of contestation, challenge, and social change.

In this article, we highlight three aspects of the reproduction process: the value attached to capital in a particular social context, the process through which individuals activate their social capital, and the legitimacy the institutions accord these displays. In our analysis of these patterns, we explicate specific moments of inclusion and exclusion that have been muffled by the overly global approach to the process of social reproduction.

In exploring these theoretical issues, we investigate the complex topic of the relative influence of race and social class in aspects of children's school experiences. Although previous research (Lareau, 1989; Spade, Columba, & Vanfossen, 1997; Useem, 1992) stressed the importance of social class in shaping family-school relationships, in this article, we show how race acts to mediate the importance of class and has an independent theoretical significance in shaping family-school relationships. We suggest that it is more difficult for black parents than white parents to comply with the institutional standards of schools. In particular, educators are relentless in their demands that parents display positive, supportive approaches to education. The historical legacy of racial discrimination, however, makes it far more difficult for black parents than white parents to comply with such demands. Although social class seems to influence how black and white parents negotiate their relationships with schools, for blacks race plays an important role, independent of social class, in framing the terms of their relationship. . . .

METHOD

The study was conducted in Lawrence (a fictitious name, as are all the names used here), a small Midwestern town with a population of about 25,000. Located two hours from a metropolitan center, the town's commercial base is dominated by farming, coal mining, light manufacturing, retail stores, state government offices, and a university. At the time of the study, the public school system enrolled approximately 1,500 elementary and junior high school students in six schools. Of these students, 52 percent were white, 44 percent were black, 3 percent were Asian, and 1 percent were Hispanic. Forty percent of the children were classified as low income (eligible for the free-lunch program or receiving public assistance). . . .

Quigley Elementary School, with around 200 students in Grades 1–3, is located in an overwhelmingly white and affluent part of town. Most of the staff members—the superintendent, principal, teachers, and janitors—were white; only one first-grade teacher and the school secretary were black. The first author, a middle-aged white woman, conducted participant-observation in each of two third-grade classrooms twice a week from September to December 1989 and less frequently (for example, three times per month) from January to June 1990. Both teachers, Mrs. Erickson and Mrs. Nelson, were white middle-aged women, each with about 25 years of teaching experience. . . .

RESULTS

The educators thought that they enthusiastically welcomed parental involvement and believed that their requests for parental involvement were neutral, technically efficient, and designed to promote higher levels of achievement. In reality, from a range of potential socioemotional styles, they selected a narrow band of acceptable behaviors. They wanted parents not only to be positive and supportive but to trust their judgments and assessments—a pattern noted by other researchers (Epstein, 1986, 1987, 1991; Van Galen, 1987). One third-grade teacher stressed the importance of parents being "supportive" when asked about the qualities of an ideal parent. . . .

The teachers repeatedly praised parents who had praised them. They liked parents who were deferential, expressed empathy with the difficulty of teachers' work, and had detailed information about their children's school experiences. In addition, the teachers often stressed the importance of parents "understanding" their children's educational situations, by which they meant that the parents should accept the teacher's definitions of their children's educational and social performance.

Compliance With School Standards

The expected standard that parents should be positive and supportive was difficult for some black families to meet. One reason for the difficulty was the parents' understanding of the broader context of race relations and the ways in which it pervaded the school. In these cases, black parents' attempts to criticize educators directly were rebuffed. For example, the Mason family had a difficult and unhappy relationship with the school, partly because Mr. and Mrs. Mason criticized and expressed their anger directly to the educators. This display of parental concern and involvement through anger and criticism was deemed unacceptable and "destructive" by the educators.

Mr. Mason, a pastor of a small church, and his wife, a beautician and associate pastor, were troubled by patterns of racial injustice. Mrs. Mason thought that a "wave of prejudice" was sweeping the country and the community. . . .

Mrs. Mason complained that these broader patterns could be seen at Quigley, particularly in the ways the school lavished attention on some holidays and then systematically ignored the celebration of black heroes. . . .

The lavish attention to Halloween and little notice of Martin Luther King's birthday were noted in the field observations. Overall, however, the school officials were resistant to Mrs. Mason's arguments that there were patterns of racial injustice in the school. The principal rejected her claims of bias and found her accusations upsetting. . . .

The teachers also thought that the Masons' claims were undermining their authority by making it more difficult for them to educate their children. . . .

Mrs. Erickson found the Masons to be among the "most upsetting" parents in her teaching career. She was particularly disturbed by them raising their voices in conversation and "just out and out yelling." Because the Masons seemed always to be angry, Mrs. Erickson tried to avoid interacting with them. . . .

For the most part, the Masons' efforts resulted in moments of exclusion. Faith stayed in her reading group (below grade level), rather than being moved up, and hence was not exposed to the higher-level reading curriculum. Still, there were some changes. At the end of the year, Mrs. Erickson "boosted" Faith's English grade a few points because "I just didn't want to have a scene." Thus, rather than appreciate Mr. and Mrs. Mason's interest and concern for the school, the educators defined it as singularly unhelpful.[1] In this educational setting, open conflict and anger were not considered legitimate.

As we discuss shortly, there were variations in how the black parents activated their concern for race with the school. In addition, both the black and the white parents differed in their levels of concern. A few white parents presented a negative vision of racial interaction at the school; for example, one mother thought that the white children were being treated unfairly, and she "resented" it. Overall, however, the white parents' enthusiasm for busing for racial integration and levels of empathy and concern about the potential racial bias at school differed. But none of the white parents exhibited, in the interviews or observations, the wholesale suspicion, distrust, and hostility toward schools that we found among some of the black parents.

Thus, the white parents were privileged in the sense that they began to construct their relationships with the school with more comfort and trust than did the black parents. This lack of suspicion took on substantially more value (capital) in an institutional framework in which the educators stressed positive, affirmative, supportive family-school encounters. Had the school adopted the norms, for example, of a trial court or of a debating team, then the racial differences might not have been of value. In this setting, in which the educators were extremely hostile to expressions of criticism toward them, the membership of whites in a dominant race, without the risk of historical patterns of discrimination, was an advantage in complying with the school's standards.

Race Intertwining With Social Class

Other black parents also approached the school with a suspicion that the legacy of racial discrimination was continuing. There were, however, important social-class differences in how the black parents managed their concerns. The middle-class parents were much more likely than the poor parents to maneuver and "customize" (Lareau, 1989) their children's school experiences. At times, they diffused the risk of racial discrimination without the teachers ever knowing of their concern. These patterns point to the importance of differentiating between the possession and activation of capital. In addition, they point to variations (often by temperament) in the parents' skill and shrewdness in the activation process that have not always been noted in the empirical literature.

Some black parents were extremely skillful in fostering interactions with educators. For example, Mr. and Mrs. Irving, a middle-class couple, were apprehensive that black children were discriminated against in the school and actively monitored their daughter's schooling. But the teacher never knew the source of their concern because they shielded it from her.

Mr. and Mrs. Irving thought that some of the black children were being treated differently from the white children in the school. As members of a black middle-class church, they were friends with other middle-class blacks, including several teachers, who shared their criticisms with the Irvings of how some white teachers treated black students. . . .

When asked if he thought black children were being discriminated against, Mr. Irving said:

> It's probably happening. I'm just considering the ratio between black teachers and white teachers, I would say it's happening. I think as long as you have blacks and whites, there is going to be some kind of discrimination—some kind of problems; I don't think it's as bad as it used to be. You don't come out and see it now; it's more covert.

Indeed, his wife appeared to see her husband's bimonthly visits to the school as an activation of resources to prevent problems from developing. . . .

Mr. and Mrs. Irving kept a close eye on their daughter Neema's schooling. Mrs. Irving monitored Neema's homework closely and insisted that Neema read regularly. Mr. Irving would stop by to bring their daughter Neema her lunch, to volunteer, or just to check on how things were going. . . .

Not only did Mr. Irving supervise his daughter's progress, but he would occasionally make requests. When Neema was in the first grade, for example, he asked that she be tested for the academically talented program; Neema was tested and admitted to the program. In this case, Mr. Irving activated knowledge (from his days as a teacher) to improve his daughter's educational experience.

The teachers did not seem to know about the Irvings' apprehensions of racial discrimination. In both the interviews and the day-to-day chatter about parents after school, the teachers had only positive things to say about Mr. and Mrs. Irving and thought they were among the most supportive and helpful parents in the school. Thus, unlike the Masons, the Irvings were able to activate their cultural and social resources to intervene in their daughter's school career in a way the school defined as helpful and supportive. The Irvings' efforts to customize Neema's school career were partially motivated by their concern about the broader context of racial treatment in the schools. The Irvings were particularly masterful in gaining advantages for their daughter (for example, enrollment in the academically gifted program) and managing her schooling so they could be reassured that she was not subjected to unfair treatment without revealing their concern to the educators. The interventions provide a portrait of a series of moments of social inclusion in which parent-teacher contacts facilitated Neema's inclusion in high-status educational programs and her continuing success in school.

In contrast, some poor black parents who were concerned about racial discrimination handled the matter differently. Some saw a separation between home and school (Lareau, 1989) and did not seek to intervene in the school process. For example, Ms. Caldron had been an alcoholic and cocaine drug addict for most of her children's lives but had been sober for two months. She lived in a government-financed housing project with her children; on her welfare subsidy, she could not afford to have a telephone. Ms. Caldron was concerned that the school was treating the black children, especially those who lived in the housing project, unfairly. . . .

Ms. Caldron objected to children attending a school in the white part of town and thought it contributed to the racial discrimination at the school. When asked if she thought that the black children were being treated differently from the white children, she replied:

> I just feel that they do. They are being treated differently. For one thing they just got out there. They hadn't been there when the rest of that school was all white. So the kids that are still there get more seniority than these kids who are just coming in there. But it shouldn't be like that.

Ms. Caldron had little contact with the school during the academic year. Although Ms. Caldron requested spelling lists a few times, Mrs. Erickson complained that she did not return forms that required her signature or respond to notes that were sent home. Although Ms. Caldron had negative and hostile feelings toward the school, she did not discuss these concerns with other parents because she did not know any of the mothers of the other children in her children's classrooms. The only person she shared her concerns with was her friend Hope, whose child also attended the school. . . .

Unlike the Irvings, Ms. Caldron was not knowledgeable about her child's schooling (for instance, she did not know the name of his teacher or what reading group he was in), did not monitor and oversee the school experience through volunteer work, and did not attempt to intervene and change the character of the school experience.

In Bourdieu's terms, Ms. Caldron's habitus meant that she approached the educational field with fewer resources to influence her children's schooling successfully. It is also possible that because she was plagued with problems of substance abuse, she "played" her resources (Bourdieu, 1976) less successfully than did other parents with comparable resources. In any case, she felt (and appeared to be) excluded from the educational process. Her son, who had repeated a grade and was at the bottom of the class in educational performance, did not have promising educational prospects. The most important point, however, is that social class appears to mediate how parents with similar types of concern about racial discrimination seek to manage their children's school careers. The results point to the influence of social class on how families manage their concerns about racial injustice at school.

White working-class parents also experienced distance from or conflict with the school. However, they focused exclusively on their own children's experience independent of the political or racial climate at the school. These parents did not talk about "the school" having a particular attitude or stance; rather, they talked about teachers treating their children in a specific manner.

Chad Carson's parents are a case in point. His mother, a manager at a local motel, and his father, a car salesman, never married and do not live together. Ms. Carson had a number of conflicts with Chad's teacher, Mrs. Nelson, which centered on the communication between them. . . .

This pattern of difficult communication between the teacher and parent appeared in regard to other issues as well. Ms. Carson detailed the problems she had with the school in keeping Chad supplied with paper for school.

> Chad would call me here at work and say, "I ran out of paper." And I would say, "Chad, could you

borrow some from someone, and we'll be sure to get you some for tomorrow." [Chad replied]: "No, Mrs. Nelson won't let me do that. She made me call you." I said, "Chad, I can't leave work to bring you paper." The next day I sent four notebooks with Chad. Well, it happened again. So, the way I handled it the second time was I took two of those big 500-sheet things into the principal's office and said, "Here, if any child comes in here to call their parent for paper, please give them this." I said, "You know, I can't just leave work. If I don't know that Chad is out of paper, I can't do anything about it."

Even though the lack of communication between Mrs. Nelson and Ms. Carson involved a visit to the principal's office to drop off more paper, Ms. Carson remained focused on her and Chad's relationship with the teacher, not with the school in general.

Another white working-class couple, Mr. and Mrs. Jennings, attributed the problems that their daughter Lauren was having in third-grade mathematics to problems that began in the first grade. . . .

Despite her daughter's persistent problem in mathematics that was traceable to the first grade, Mrs. Jennings did not hold the school as a whole responsible.

These two families' experiences represent the most difficult conflicts that white working-class parents reported having with teachers or the schools. They clearly did not have the diffuse and pervasive race-based distrust of the school that some of the black parents identified. For them, conflict with the school was limited to and centered on their individual relationships with the teachers.

Variations in Parents' Perceptions

Black Parents

Not all the black parents and guardians had difficult and unhappy relationships with the educators at Quigley school. Some were very positive. One black grandmother, whose daughter died suddenly during the spring, was grateful to Mrs. Erickson. Saying she was "just super," the grandmother could not say enough good things about her. At the end of the year, she gave Mrs. Erickson a necklace as a thank-you gift.

Moreover, not all parents shared the view that black children at the school were subjected to unequal and less favorable treatment compared to the white children. A number of black parents stated that they did not know if there were problems at the school. For example, the grandmother of a child (the drug-addicted mother was unable to provide care) had not heard anything. . . .

Other black parents stated that children at Quigley school were not being treated unfairly on the basis of race. Some of these parents, from a range of social-class positions, were openly hostile to the black parents who complained about racial injustice. For example, one poor mother energetically defended the principal, Mrs. Hertman, from accusations of racism that she had heard in the public housing project in which she lived. . . .

A working-class father who worked as a laborer on the railroad was cautious as well:

> Tracking [of black students] is a problem, but I've got different feelings: A lot of parents don't take the time and make their kids do their part. If parents participated more, I don't think you [would] have a problem.

In a different vein, a middle-class father acknowledged that other parents were concerned that blacks were not sufficiently active in the schools but he, too, placed responsibility on the parents. He thought that the parents needed to take an active role in monitoring schooling: "My biggest thing is that a lot of black people just need to get more involved."

White Parents

The white parents' assessments of the existence of racial problems in the schools also varied. Some white parents agreed there were problems. As one white mother said:

> I think the teachers need to go, a lot of them, for a good semester, not a Friday workshop, and become sensitized to some of the problems these kids have.

This mother also noted that she would never discuss these issues with some parents because "I know that they are prejudiced."

Other white parents said that they did not know what to think about race relations in the schools. For example, one father had read of black parents' concerns in the newspaper, but he was not sure if they were happening in the school. . . .

Discussion

The conceptual model of social reproduction has been rightfully criticized for being overly deterministic. Although ethnographic research has stressed the meaning of daily life, the theoretical models have an "automatic pilot" quality to them. The skills that Bourdieu clearly pointed to in parents "playing their hands" are not brought to bear. The models also substantially underemphasize the crucial role of institutions in accepting or rebuffing the activation of capital by family members.

A more fruitful approach, we believe, is to adopt the conceptual framework of moments of inclusion and moments of exclusion. (One could also use the terms moments of reproduction and moments of contestation.) We define moments of inclusion as the coming together of various forces to provide an advantage to the child in his or her life trajectory. In the realm of school, these moments may include placement in an academically gifted program or the highest academic track (Oakes, 1985), enrollment in a suburban school (Wells & Crain, 1997), encouragement and preparation for applying to college (McDonough, 1997), attendance at an elite college, and use of networks for job placement. In contrast, moments of exclusion may include placement in a low reading group, retention, placement in remedial courses, and the failure to complete college-preparation requirements.

In this definition, we focus on the "objective" completion of or gaining access to a particular school task, not on the subjective experience attached to this task. Obviously, however, subjective experiences are integral to the entire process leading up to and through these critical moments in a life trajectory.

These moments are important. The social reproduction model has implied that the passing of privilege of family to child is relatively automatic. It is not. Although social class is heavily tied to educational outcomes, a student's performance is a core feature in determining educational access in the United States. Thus, even wealthy parents cannot guarantee admission to an elite university, such as Harvard, if their son or daughter has a combined SAT score of 780 and a grade point average of 2.2. By stressing the objective standards for entrance, this approach highlights more clearly the numerous strategies that parents, especially middle-class parents, take to gain advantages for their children in the educational system. For a strategy to be successful, however, it must be legitimated and accepted by the school officials. When it is, it can be termed a moment of inclusion.

To return to the parents, when Mr. and Mrs. Irving requested that their daughter Neema be tested for the academically gifted program, she was tested and admitted. This was a moment of inclusion, since the program was prestigious and exposed children to a higher level of academic work than in the regular classroom. Generally, teachers recommend that children be tested for the gifted program. In this instance, the Irvings were able to gain an advantage that, in all probability, would not have occurred otherwise.

In contrast, Mr. and Mrs. Mason's involvement was, for the most part, less successful. Mrs. Mason repeatedly asked her daughter Faith's third-grade teacher, Mrs. Erickson, to move Faith up to a reading group at grade level, but Mrs. Erickson, who thought that Faith's vocabulary was inadequate for a higher group, refused. Mrs. Mason also complained that Faith wasn't being called on enough during class. In addition, she was unhappy that the school library did not have enough books that celebrated black heroes and expressed concern about the uneven distribution of detentions by race.

The situation of these girls, is, of course, not strictly comparable, since there were important differences between the girls, especially in reading level. Our point, however, is not the girls' absolute level of performance in the class, but the ability of their parents to intervene in a fashion that the educators defined as appropriate and legitimate.

One can argue that, in Bourdieu's terms, Mr. and Mrs. Mason were drawing on their habitus and seeking to activate cultural capital for their daughter within the educational field. Most of their efforts were rebuffed. For example, the school (with elaborate special decorations, a special program, and a special school assembly) devoted far more time and energy to the celebration of Halloween than to Martin Luther King's birthday, and their daughter's reading group was not changed. These interactions, which further compounded the Masons' feelings of alienation and anger, should be characterized as moments of social exclusion. Although Mrs. Erickson "boosted" Faith's grade on her report card, an action that could theoretically be considered a moment of social inclusion, this action was the exception, and the Masons did not know about it.

Moreover, these moments of social exclusion were heavily (but not entirely) connected to Mr. and Mrs. Mason's membership in a minority group with a history of legal discrimination. The Masons framed the issues with contestation and anger, but the school had a standard that emphasized positive, polite interactions. (The standard was not formally stated or made explicit.) In a setting (field of interaction) in which the educators defined a particular socioemotional style (calm voices, positive affirmations, and few criticisms) as legitimate, the anger and hostility that these black parents brought to bear were not recognized as legitimate.

Thus, we stress the value of particular cultural displays should not be presumed to be general, but should be linked to legitimated standards in specific social settings (fields). In the case of parental involvement in white-dominant schooling, being white is an advantage. Whiteness represents a largely hidden cultural resource that facilitates white parents' compliance with the standard of deferential and positive parental involvement in school. Even when white parents approach the school with suspicion and hostility, they are spared the concern over historically recognized patterns of racial discrimination of black children in schools.

CONCLUSION

What are the implications of this study for research in sociology of education? On a substantive level, the work points to the independent power of race in shaping key interactions in school settings. Although middle-class black families still benefit from their class position (and interact with schools in different ways than their less-privileged counterparts), they still face an institutional setting that implicitly (and invisibly) privileges white families. We assert that in this instance, the role of race is independent of the power of class. This study echoes, in some respects, other research that has suggested the primacy of race in shaping school experiences (Fordham & Ogbu, 1986; Ogbu, 1974, 1988). Similar to O'Connor's (1997) and Fordham's (1996) findings, we point to the interplay of the individual and the institution in mediating the complex ways that race shapes school experiences.

At the theoretical level, we suggest the value of using Bourdieu's theory to explore social reproduction. Our study sought to highlight the fluid nature of social interaction and the reproduction of inequality in society in a way hinted at, but often underdeveloped, in the literature on social reproduction. Relying on the theoretical purchase offered by Bourdieu's method, our results suggest three modifications to notions of social reproduction. First, researchers should pay more attention to the field of interaction and the explicit and implicit rules for interaction embodied in a given field. Any form or type of capital derives value only in relation to the specific field of interaction. Particular types of social capital do not have inherent value exclusive of what is accorded in a specific field. Second, individuals must activate capital in social environments, and they vary in the level of skills they have to do so.

Accepting these two points leads to our third and concluding point. The process of social reproduction is not a smooth trajectory based on individual characteristics that are seamlessly transmitted across generations. An individual's class and racial position affect social reproduction, but they do not determine it. Each person (in this instance, a parent), through the skill with which he or she activates capital or plays his or her hand, influences how individual characteristics, such as race and class, will matter in interactions with social institutions and other persons in those institutions. Thus, a closer focus on moments of the activation of capital situated in a field analysis that emphasizes how individual behaviors are recognized and legitimated or marginalized and rebuffed provides a more conceptually accurate picture of how social reproduction occurs.

The process of social reproduction is not a continual, deterministic one. Rather, it is shaped moment by moment in particular social fields. By not abandoning the concept of capital, but showing more forcefully the individual's use of strategies in their displays, as well as the nature of the field, researchers stand to develop more nuanced and accurate models of the continuing nature of social inequality.

NOTE

1. We do not want to paint an overly deterministic picture of the relationship between the Masons and Mrs. Erickson. Although they had clear periods of conflict, they also had times when relations were more cordial.

REFERENCES

Bourdieu, P. (1976). Marriage strategies as strategies of social reproduction. In R. Forster & O. Ranum (Eds.), *Family and society* (pp. 117–144). Baltimore: John Hopkins University Press.

Bourdieu, P. (1977a). Cultural reproduction and social reproduction. In J. Karabel & A. H. Halsey (Eds.), *Power and ideology in education* (pp. 487–511). New York: Oxford University Press.

Bourdieu, P. (1977b). *Outline of a theory of practice* (R. Nice, Trans.). Cambridge, England: Cambridge University Press.

Bourdieu, P. (1984). *Distinction: A social critique of the judgment of taste* (R. Nice, Trans.). Cambridge, MA: Harvard University Press.

Bourdieu, P. (1990). *In other words: Essays towards a reflexive sociology.* Stanford, CA: Stanford University Press.

Brantlinger, E. A. (1993). *The politics of social class in secondary school.* New York: Teachers College Press.

DiMaggio, P., & Mohr, J. (1985). Cultural capital, educational attainment, and marital selection. *American Journal of Sociology, 90*(6), 1231–1261.

Epstein, J. L. (1986). Parents' reactions to teacher practices of parent involvement. *Elementary School Journal, 86*(3), 277–294.

Epstein, J. L. (1987). Toward a theory of family-school connections: Teacher practices and parent involvement. In K. Hurrelmann, F.-X. Kaufmann, & F. Losel (Eds.), *Social interventions: Potential and constraints* (pp. 121–136). New York: Walter de Gruyter.

Epstein, J. L. (1991). Effects on student achievement of teachers' practices of parent involvement. In S. Silvern (Ed.), *Literacy through family, community, and school interaction* (pp. 261–276). Greenwich, CT: JAI Press.

Fordham, S. (1996). *Blacked out: Dilemmas of race, identity, and success at Capital High.* Chicago: University of Chicago Press.

Fordham, S., & Ogbu, J. U. (1986). Black students' school success: Coping with the burden of "acting white." *Urban Review, 18*(3), 176–206.

Lamont, M., & Lareau, A. (1988). Cultural capital: Allusions, gaps, and glissandos. *Sociological Theory, 6*(2), 153–168.

Lareau, A. (1989). *Home advantage: Social class and parental intervention in elementary education.* Philadelphia: Falmer Press.

McDonough, P. M. (1997). *Choosing colleges: How social class and schools structure opportunity.* Albany: State University of New York Press.

Oakes, J. (1985). *Keeping track: How schools structure inequality.* New Haven, CT: Yale University Press.

O'Connor, C. (1997). Dispositions toward (collective) struggle and educational resilience in the inner city: A case analysis of six African American high school students. *American Educational Research Journal, 34*(4), 593–629.

Ogbu, J. U. (1974). *The next generation: An ethnography of education in an urban neighborhood.* New York: Academic Press.

Ogbu, J. U. (1988). Class stratification, race stratification, and schooling. In L. Weis (Ed.), *Class, race, and gender in American education* (pp. 163–189). Albany: State University of New York Press.

Spade, J. Z., Columba, L., & Vanfossen, B. (1997). Tracking in mathematics and science: Courses and course-selection procedures. *Sociology of Education, 70*(2), 108–127.

Useem, E. (1992). Middle school and math groups: Parents' involvement in children's placement. *Sociology of Education, 65*(4), 263–279.

Van Galen, J. (1987). Maintaining control: The structure of parent involvement. In G. Noblit & W. T. Pink (Eds.), *Schooling in social context* (pp. 78–90). Norwood, NJ: Ablex.

Wacquant, L. J. D. (1992). Toward a social paxeology: The structure and logic of Bourdieu's sociology. In P. Bourdieu & L. J. D. Wacquant (Eds.), *An invitation to reflexive sociology* (pp. 1–59). Chicago: University of Chicago Press.

Wacquant, L. J. D. (1993). Bourdieu in America: Notes on the transatlantic importation of social theory. In C. C. Calhoun, E. LiPuma, & M. Postone (Eds.), *Bourdieu: Critical perspectives* (pp. 235–263). Chicago: University of Chicago Press.

Wells, A. S., & Crain, R. L. (1997). *Stepping over the color line: African American students in white suburban schools.* New Haven, CT: Yale University Press.

HOW TO AVOID STATISTICAL TRAPS

Gerald W. Bracey

How to Lie With Statistics and *Damned Lies and Statistics* are two books that point out the complications in interpreting the meaning of statistics. Data do not always support the conclusions drawn in research and reports, yet parents, educators, and policy makers rely on statistics to make sense of the educational scene and trends. Statistics are an essential part of quantitative methods because they are used to summarize data collected to test theories and to determine if the data collected from a sample are representative of the larger population that one would like to generalize to. Thus, as Bracey illustrates, knowing how to interpret statistics is crucial for understanding research on schools.

Questions to consider for this reading:

1. What role do statistics play in helping researchers understand educational systems?

2. Why is it important to have more than one statistical result?

3. What does Bracey recommend we do to ensure more accuracy in research results?

There are three kinds of lies: lies, damned lies, and statistics. This quote from Benjamin Disraeli, Prime Minister of England under Queen Victoria, demonstrates that the field of statistics has needed to defend its honor since its inception in Europe centuries ago.

The original term for statistics, *political arithmetic* (Best, 2001), might be more accurate. Statistics are rarely neutral. Those who collect them have a purpose—sometimes benign, sometimes not—and translate the information to serve that purpose. For example, some people, including representatives of the pharmaceutical industry, say that statistics reveal an "obesity crisis" in the United States. Other people, including some

financed by the food industry, allege that the "obesity crisis" is a false alarm spread by drug companies that want the standards for diseases constantly made stricter so that they can define more people as patients and sell them expensive drugs. It's true that the numbers accepted as indications of high cholesterol, high blood pressure, and high blood sugar have all become much lower in the last decade.

Contradictory claims like these may be one reason why people say that you can prove anything with statistics. You can't, but people will certainly try to prove their particular viewpoints by using only those numbers that serve their purposes.

From "How to Avoid Statistical Traps," by G. W. Bracey, 2006, *Educational Leadership, 63*(8), pp. 78–82. Copyright by the Association for Supervision and Curriculum Development (ASCD), a worldwide community of educators advocating sound policies and sharing best practices to achieve the success of each learner. To learn more visit http://www.ascd.org. Reprinted with permission.

MORE THAN ONE NUMBER

You need more than one statistic to get a full picture of just about anything. Educators whose performance is being judged solely by annual standardized test scores will appreciate this point.

As I was writing this, an article in *The New York Times* gave three statistics for various nations' greenhouse gas emissions: total emissions, per capita emissions, and emissions per industrial output (Barringer, 2006). Using total emissions, the United States is number one by far, with China second and Russia third. Using per capita emissions, the United States is still number one and Russia is still third, but Canada is second. (China has lots of people and is still largely a rural nation despite its rapid urbanization.) Using industrial output, Russia is first, China second, and the United States fifth. (Russian and Chinese industries are not as clean as U.S. industries.)

Which statistic is best? All of them together. Using only one would be like evaluating a center fielder only on his batting average or a quarterback only on yards gained per pass. You need more than one statistic to paint a complete picture.

Similarly, a recent e-mailer asked me whether a preschool program, which produced a four-month gain in vocabulary and math and cost $6,000 per kid per year, was worth it. I said that I couldn't tell. For one thing, the program likely produced health, socialization, and other outcomes besides the two mentioned. In addition, the real value of the program might not be clear for years: It took long-term evaluations of the outcomes of the Perry Preschool Project and the Chicago Family Centers project to establish that society gained about $7 for every dollar invested in these programs (Berrueta-Clement, Schweinhart, Barnett, Epstein, & Weikart, 1984; Reynolds, 2001).

PRINCIPLES OF DATA INTERPRETATION

Despite the limitations of individual statistics and public cynicism about being able to prove anything, people remain remarkably trusting when it comes to statistics. Best (2001) observes that "Most of the time, most people simply accept statistics without question" (p. 4). This acceptance would be dangerous at any time, but given today's polarized politicization of education (and virtually everything else), it is particularly hazardous now. Educators can avoid this danger by following some basic principles of data interpretation.

Go Back to the Data

Many people call the National Commission on Excellence in Education's 1983 report *A Nation at Risk* "the paper *Sputnik*" because it focused attention on education in the same way *Sputnik* did in 1954. Some still refer to it today as a "landmark" study. It's a landmark, all right: a golden treasury of selected, spun, distorted, and even manufactured statistics.

After opening with a blast of Cold-Warrior rhetoric, the good commissioners listed 13 indicators of the "risk," all referring to test scores. For example, "Over half the population of gifted students do not match their tested ability with comparable achievement in school." Given that achievement tests at the time were the principal means of selecting kids for gifted and talented programs, how could this possibly be true? When I sought an answer from some commissioners and their staff members, no one could remember where this statistic came from. How convenient.

Another statistic was, "Average tested achievement of students graduating from college is also lower." The United States has no program to test students graduating from college that would yield a statistic showing their "average tested achievement." What on earth could this mean? These examples illustrate a vital principle of data interpretation: If you find a statement the least bit suspect, ask to see the raw data.

Beware of Selectivity

Some of the other indicators in *A Nation at Risk* illustrate perhaps the most common misuse of statistics: selecting a statistic that, although accurate in itself, paints an incomplete and misleading picture. For instance, the report claimed that "there was a steady decline in science achievement scores of U.S. 17-year-olds as measured by national assessments in 1969, 1973, and 1977." This was true.

But the statement refers only to science, and only to 17-year-olds. What about the 9- and 13-year-olds also tested in national assessments? No "steady decline" in science for them. What about math? What about reading? No hint of any decline in either subject for any of the three age groups (National Center for Education Statistics [NCES], 2000).

The commissioners had nine trend lines available from NCES data (three ages times three subjects). Only one could be used to support crisis rhetoric, and that was the only one the commissioners mentioned.

Compare Rhetoric
With the Numbers

Perhaps the most dangerous statistic is the one that Joel Best calls the *mutant* statistic. This statistic begins life as a legitimate datum, but mutates into something new and wrong. Best (2001) gives the example of the claim, widely circulated, that 150,000 women die in the United States each year from anorexia. The U.S. Census Bureau's *Statistical Abstract of the United States* shows that 55,000 women ages 15–44 die each year of all causes. Even if anorexia had killed all 55,000, given that anorexia mostly affects young women, it is unlikely that we can find another 95,000 anorexia victims younger than 15 and older than 44. In fact, the proper statistic is that 150,000 women *suffer* from anorexia—and even this number is probably a bit inflated because it was produced by an activist group attempting to call attention to the problem.

Mutant statistics afflict education data as well. *Washington Post* pundit George Will wrote in one column that almost half of Chicago's public school teachers sent their own children to private schools (Will, 1993a). This was true. The figure was 43 percent at the time, and that was the highest

proportion in the United States. (Religion figured strongly in the Chicago teachers' decisions.) But over a period of six months, Will's neurons replaced "Chicago" with "the nation"; in another column, he wrote, "Nationally about half of urban public school teachers with school-age children send their children to private schools" (Will, 1993b). This was not true. According to data from the 2000 census, 17.5 percent of all urban families and 21.5 percent of urban public school teachers send their children to private schools. The rate ranges from 43.8 percent of teachers in the Philadelphia/Camden metro area down to 1.7 percent in Oklahoma City. In 21 of these top 50 cities, teachers use private schools less than urban families do (Doyle, DeSchryver, & Diepold, 2004).

Will's brain might have been addled by the work of Denis Doyle, whose reports using data from the 1980, 1990, and 2000 censuses have promoted the idea that public school teachers do send their kids to private schools in larger numbers than the general public does (Doyle, 1995; Doyle, DeSchryver, & Diepold, 2004; Doyle & Hartle, 1986). Doyle refers to teachers as "connoisseurs" of education, implying that if they send their kids to private schools, they must know something that the rest of us don't. He writes,

> With teachers choosing private schools, the truth is self-evident: While they work in public schools, they choose private schools for their own children because they believe they are better. (Doyle, 1995)

This statement creates the impression that all public school teachers in all types of communities use private schools. But if we look beyond the rhetoric to the actual statistics, we find these figures for the United States as a whole (Doyle, 1995; Doyle, DeSchryver, & Diepold, 2004):

	Teachers	General public
1990	12.1%	13.1%
2000	10.6%	12.1%

The numbers show that teachers made less use of private schools than the general public did. What's more, despite all the lionization of private schools and the demonization of public schools during the 1990s, a smaller proportion of both teachers and the general public had children in private schools in 2000 than in 1990.

Make Sure That Groups Are Comparable

The statistics on the percentages of children sent to private schools point to another principle of data interpretation: When comparing groups, make sure the groups are comparable. Teachers and the general public are not comparable. Teachers are more likely to have at least a bachelor's degree and less likely to live below the poverty line. We need to consider the implications of these and similar factors before we draw conclusions about the two groups' public school–private school choices.

This principle often comes into play in figuring out the impact of high-stakes graduation tests. In 2004, Massachusetts announced that 96 percent of its seniors had passed the state test and would graduate. This was true, but it was true only for people who had begun the 2003–2004 school year as seniors and who were still in school. Many in the class of 2004 were no longer present and accounted for. When that cohort of students started 9th grade, it contained 78,000 students; by the time it reached 12th grade, there were only 60,000. Eighteen thousand students had decamped (Wheelock, 2004).

We don't know what happened to these students. Some, of course, left the state and might well have passed the test and graduated if they had remained. But others were retained in grade and were no longer in the class of 2004. Some failed and dropped out or sought a General Equivalency Diploma. If we look at how many who started as 9th graders in the class of 2004 eventually graduated, we find rates ranging from

54 percent for Latino students to 80 percent for white students (Wheelock, 2004). We can't draw an accurate conclusion about the effects of high school graduation exams unless we consider all the groups, including those that did not graduate on time.

Know the Difference Between Rates and Scores

The Massachusetts example also illustrates another principle of data interpretation: Be aware of whether you are dealing with rates or scores. The two metrics can paint very different pictures of a situation. These days, most states are reporting some kind of rate: percent passing, percent proficient, or percent meeting state standards. But if we focus only on the proficiency cutoff, it doesn't matter whether the student exceeds it by one question or 40. We're looking at how many kids can jump over the barrier, not at how high they jump.

Moreover, using passing rates instead of scores can obscure the fact that the white-minority achievement gap may be increasing. Consider the theoretical data in Figure 9.1. If we look only at passing rates, black students have reduced the gap from 40 percent to 30 percent. But if we look at scores, the gap has actually increased from 16 points to 24 points.

This discrepancy might not be so important if the passing score actually meant something in terms of performance in the real world. But it doesn't. These passing scores are totally arbitrary. Some readers might recall that in my recent report on the condition of public education (Bracey, 2005), I awarded a Golden Apple to a student in Ohio because he refused to take the Ohio Proficiency Tests. It was not his act of defiance that garnered him a prize; it was the reasons he gave:

> In 13 years of testing, Ohio has failed to conduct any studies linking scores on the proficiency test to college acceptance rates, dropout rates, college

Figure 9.1 Pass Rates and Average Scores Tell a Different Story

Pass rate—Gap closed by 10 points

	2004	2005
Black students	60%	70%
White students	100%	100%
Gap	40	30

Average scores—Gap increased by 8 points

	2004	2005
Black students	62	68
White students	78	92
Gap	16	24

These are hypothetical data. Score needed to pass = 60.

grades, income levels, incarceration rates, scores on military recruiting tests, or any other similar statistic. [The student was admitted to several colleges.] (p. 140)

Do the Arithmetic

Here's a final principle of data interpretation to examine on your own: Do the arithmetic. In 1995, an article in an education periodical (not *Educational Leadership*) stated that "Every year since 1950, the number of American children gunned down has doubled." Sit down with a calculator and a sheet of paper on which you write in one column the years from 1950 to 1994. Then assume that one child was "gunned down" in 1950 and let the figure double for each successive year. Have fun.

REFERENCES

Barringer, F. (2006, January 26). United States ranks 28th on environment, a new study says. *The New York Times*, p. A3.

Berrueta-Clement, J. R., Schweinhart, L. J., Barnett, W. S., Epstein., A. S., & Weikart, D. P. (1984). *Changed lives: The effects of the Perry preschool program on youths through age 19*. Ypsilanti, MI: High/Scope Press.

Best, J. (2001). *Damned lies and statistics: Untangling numbers from the media, politicians, and activists*. Berkeley: University of California Press.

Bracey, G. W. (2005). The fifteenth Bracey report on the condition of public education. *Phi Delta Kappan, 87*(2), 138–153.

Doyle, D. P. (1995). *Where connoisseurs send their children to school*. Washington, DC: Center for Education Reform.

Doyle, D. P., DeSchryver, D. A., & Diepold, B. (2004, September 7). *Where do public school teachers send their kids to school?* Washington, DC: Thomas B. Fordham Institute. Retrieved from http://www.edexcellence.net/foundation/publication/publication.cfm?id=333

Doyle, D. P., & Hartle, T. W. (1986). *Where public school teachers send their children to school: A preliminary analysis.* Washington, DC: American Enterprise Institute.

National Center for Education Statistics (NCES). (2000). *NAEP 1999 trends in academic progress* (Report No. NCES-2000–469). Washington, DC: Author.

National Commission on Excellence in Education. (1983). *A nation at risk.* Washington, DC: Author. Retrieved from http://www.ed.gov/pubs/NatAtRisk

Reynolds, A. J. (2001, May/June). *Age 21 benefit cost analysis of the Chicago child-parent center program.* Paper presented to the Society for Prevention Research, Madison, Wisconsin.

Wheelock, A. (2004, June 8). *Massachusetts department of education "progress report" inflates "pass rates" for the class of 2004.* Retrieved from http://www.massparents.org/news/2004/passrate_2004.htm

Will, G. F. (1993a, March 7). When the state fails its citizens. *The Washington Post,* p. C7.

Will, G. F. (1993b, Aug. 26). Taking back education. *The Washington Post,* p. A27.

Projects for Further Exploration

1. As you read the articles in this book, keep a list of which methodology is used in each, even if a full discussion of the methods is not included in each one. This should sharpen your ability to evaluate information.

2. Pick a reading from this book that you find particularly interesting and do a library search for another article on the same topic. If possible, compare different methodologies to see if they come up with similar findings.

3. Do a library search for *"class size"* (use quotation marks around it) and *achievement* to see if the articles you find correspond to the arguments made in the article by Biddle and Berliner in this chapter.

3

SCHOOLING IN A
SOCIAL CONTEXT

Educational Environments

With the background on some theories and methods (Chapters 1 and 2) used to study educational systems, we can now begin our study of schools. We begin with examining the contexts that affect how schools work. No education system exists in a vacuum. In this chapter we consider the *environment* part of the open systems model (discussed in the Introduction) that influences schools from outside school walls. If schools ignore the contexts in which they are located, they do so at their own peril. Results could be loss of financing, accreditation, and community support. To focus only on what happens behind the closed doors of the school or classroom misses the total picture of the educational environment. Changing values in society and the community, political and economic constraints, home environments of students and school personnel, business and technology, special-interest groups, and other external influences affect what happens within school walls. In addition, the social context or environment helps to define the purpose, meaning, functions, and limitations of education.

Schools cannot ignore important aspects of their environments, especially those that are necessary for support of the school or those that conflict with the schools' goals. We will look at several of these environmental factors and how they can influence educational settings. Several environments, noted in italics, are discussed in this introduction. The readings in this chapter add to this discussion. For example, each of *the participants* in the school brings values, beliefs, attitudes, abilities, and behaviors into schools. Add home dynamics (including what each participant had for breakfast!), and we have a picture of some of the environmental complexities that affect schools. Students are processed in the school system. They are required to attend school to learn skills and knowledge that are necessary for success in the world outside school. Teachers and administrative staff members are also participants. They differ in age and educational background from the students, and they can differ in social class background from parents and their students, a factor that can add complexity to school interactions.

In addition, *the public* holds attitudes on school policies, curriculum, and funding. Attitudes reflect opinions of the parents who send their children to school, of community members who pay taxes to support schools, and of many political and religious interest groups that express their feelings about school policies. The significance of public opinion is that school policies and support for schools often reflect attitudes of the community. Each year the Phi Delta Kappa/Gallup Poll on "The Public's Attitudes Toward the Public Schools" surveys a sample of more than 1,000 U.S. adults on questions related to school issues. Responses to the survey indicate areas of most concern to the public. In 2009, key issues and attitudes included the following:

No Child Left Behind—public support is declining;

Charter Schools—strong support;

Teacher Pay—public supports merit pay;

Tenure—split support, but no support for lifetime contracts;

Dropouts—remains the top or almost top issue of concern;

Early Childhood Education—support for making kindergarten compulsory;

Innovation—public more open to innovations;

Economic Stimulus Money—support for use of these funds to retain teachers.

These public attitudes influence passage of levies and are the focus of other demands on schools (Highlights of the 2009 Phi Delta Kappa/Gallup poll, 2009).

Technological changes also affect what students and teachers bring into the school setting as well as what the schools teach students. Most studies of computer access and school achievement confirm that technology improves student achievement (North Central Regional Educational Laboratory, 2010). Yet keeping up to date with technology is a challenge for budget-strapped schools and busy teachers. Almost all schools with computers have Internet access, but often those schools are in more affluent areas. Even with computers, most schools use predominantly written texts, which some critics argue is not the best medium for passing on knowledge to tech students (Farris-Berg, 2005). The reading by Attewell discusses the problems created by the "digital divide"—differences between socioeconomic groups in access to and use of computers.

Federal, state, and local governments play a major role in the educational environment and policy, in part because the money they provide to schools is essential to operations. In the No Child Left Behind and Race to the Top policies, expectations are laid out for schools and districts, such as the requirement that schoolchildren pass proficiency tests; failure to do so places a red mark on the school district, as Kathryn Borman and Bridget Cotner describe in this chapter. These practices can disadvantage schools with high numbers of children living in poverty, especially immigrants and refugees (Winerip, 2010). The funding for schools is based on federal and state mandates, discussed in Reyes and Rodriguez's reading on patterns of school funding. Furthermore, over half of the states require high school exit exams, although their effect on curriculum and student achievement is mixed, as discussed in the reading by Warren and Grodsky.

Because all institutions in society are interrelated, influence and pressure on schools often come from other institutions, such as family. Children bring their home environments to school with them; if there are problems in the home, they affect the children's achievement. If parents are involved in their children's education by volunteering in school, attending parent-teacher conferences, or helping children with their homework, the children are likely to have higher achievement in school (Epstein, 1987, 1988). However, the amount and type of involvement of parents differs by social class.

Parents have direct interest in what their children are learning, and parents can be quite vocal about agendas for their children's schooling. Some schools require parental participation for students to attend, and many educational policy makers point out the value of parental involvement in and outside of school. However, how, when, and why parents are involved is important in determining the impact involvement will have on individual children's achievement (Pomerantz, Moorman, & Litwack, 2007).

One area of research for sociologists of education has been the effects of parental involvement in children's homework. Especially in elementary and high school, positive involvement can be effective in raising achievement; the effectiveness even varies by subject matter (Patall, Cooper, & Robinson, 2008). Summer experiences of children, those months when school is not in session, are also directly related to student achievement. Students from higher socioeconomic status tend to have experiences that enhance their academic performance. Music, sports lessons, camps, or visits to museums influence their achievement, as shown in the reading by Alexander, Entwisle, and Olson.

An example of environmental factors that cause conflict for schools is *religion*. Separation of church and state has been a guiding principle supporting freedom of religious practice since the founding of the United States. Yet where to draw the line has been a bone of contention in many communities. The line is challenged in discussions of what constitutes school prayer; whether to allow released-time for religious classes in public schools; what support from taxpayer monies can legally be spent on parochial school students for transportation, free meals, counseling, and other services; what standards private parochial schools should meet; and what curriculum and textbooks to use, especially when the topics are related to religious beliefs such as creationism.

Another example of the influence from school environments is the relationship between *business enterprises* and schools. To what extent should schools be influenced by pressures from the business community? Should businesses have a say in what schools teach? After all, they are the main source of jobs for students on completion of schooling. Many argue no, that education should remain independent of external influences, especially those with profit motives. One concern related to business interests and schools has been the advertising that crept into the hallways and classrooms. From soft drink companies providing incentives to schools to have their products be the only choice on school campuses to labels of popular consumer items found in textbooks, on book covers, and on clothing worn to school, business ventures have subtly inserted themselves into our schools. Many schools are now eliminating soda and candy machines due to concerns from parents and governmental agencies about the health and obesity of children.

The importance of any particular part of the environment changes over time. For example, when the school needs to pass a levy to obtain operating funds, the voters become a highly salient community. When school administrators face pressure from teachers' unions at contract time, their negotiations take on high salience. At other times, voters or unions take a secondary position in importance compared to other pressing issues in the environment at the time.

Each of the readings in this section focuses on an aspect of the educational system's environment. The first reading considers political involvement in educational systems. John Meyer and Brian Rowan discuss the institution of education as it operates in the larger political context. In most countries, control of schools is in the hands of the national political system. The dominant goal of governments is to incorporate students into society by meeting the educational and skill needs of the society. To find schools that are entities independent of or separate from the state is rare. In their book from which the reading in this chapter comes, Meyer and Rowan discuss the United States, a country that allows a degree of local control, "decoupling" schools from some external federal political and environmental pressures. The authors use the term *decoupling* to describe the discrepancy between what schools do and how schools and their environments evaluate the outcomes. In practice, U.S. schools are organized to meet different internal and external pressures. Decoupling also serves the purpose of protecting local schools from too much external scrutiny, resulting in more autonomy at the local level and little evidence of ineffectiveness, conflict, or inconsistency. Furthermore, decoupling occurs with the tacit agreement of all players, from the community to school personnel.

The readings in this chapter present examples of environmental influences and constraints on what happens in schools and classrooms and how the environment affects educational achievement. The bottom line is whether schools are preparing children to be productive members of society, a question that we discuss throughout this book and that is of much debate among experts, researchers, and the various public constituencies of schools.

References

Epstein, J. (1987). *Target: An examination of parallel school and family structures that promote student motivation and achievement* (Report 6). Baltimore: Johns Hopkins University, Center for Research on Elementary and Middle Schools.

Epstein, J. (1988). Effects on student achievement of teachers' practices of parent involvement. In S. B. Silvem (Ed.), *Literacy through family, community, and school interaction* (pp. 261–276). Greenwich, CT: JAI Press.

Farris-Berg, K. (2005). *Listening to student voices on technology: Today's tech-savvy students are stuck in text-dominated schools.* St. Paul, MN: Education/Evolving. Retrieved from http://www.educationevolving.org/pdf/Tech-Savvy-Students.pdf

Highlights of the 2009 Phi Delta Kappa/Gallup poll. (2009). Retrieved from http://www.docstoc.com/docs/52573873/Phi-DeltaKappaGallup-Poll

Natriello, G. (2006). *Bridging the second digital divide: What can sociologists of education contribute?* New York: EdLab, Teachers College, Columbia University.

North Central Regional Educational Laboratory (2010). *Critical issue: Technology: A catalyst for teaching and learning in the classroom.* Retrieved from http://www.ncrel.org/sdrs/areas/issues/methods/technlgy/te600.htm

Patall, E. A., Cooper, H., & Robinson, J. C. (2008). Parent involvement in homework: A research synthesis. *Review of Educational Research, 78*(4), 1039–1101.

Pomerantz, E. M., Moorman, E. A., & Litwack, S. D. (2007). The how, whom, and why of parents' involvement in children's academic lives: More is not always better. *Review of Educational Research, 77*(3), 373–410.

Winerip, M. (2010, July 18). A popular principal, wounded by government's good intentions. *The New York Times.* Retrieved from http://www.nytimes.com/2010/07/19/education/19winerip.html

THE STRUCTURE OF EDUCATIONAL ORGANIZATIONS

John W. Meyer and Brian Rowan

To begin our exploration of the social context of educational systems, John W. Meyer and Brian Rowan present a macrolevel interpretation of the school in modern society. Schools serve societal needs more than individual or family needs, and in many societies they are controlled by centralized political authorities. By preparing youth for positions in the economic and stratification system, educational bureaucracies serve the societies in which they are located. Educational systems prepare and credential individuals for participation in society, especially corporate society. By meeting the expectations of external political and corporate organizations, schools gain legitimacy and resources to carry out their missions and to be innovative. Whereas educational systems and authority in most societies are centralized, the U.S. system is decentralized, with controls at the local and state levels. This means that educators are less secure in their positions because they are beholden to sometimes-conflicting local interests.

Questions to consider for this reading:

1. How do schools serve the needs of the political and corporate sectors of society?

2. What theoretical approach or approaches relate most closely to the ideas in this reading?

3. How does credentialing link schools to other institutions in society, such as family and the economy?

THE ORGANIZATION OF SCHOOLING: ANOTHER INTERPRETATION

The explanation developed here begins with the context in which educational organizations are presently found. Modern education today takes place in large-scale, public bureaucracies. The rise of this kind of educational system is closely related to the worldwide trend of national development. The first step in our argument, therefore, is to relate national development to the organization of education.

The Growth of Corporate Schooling

[W]e know that bureaucratic schooling has not arisen from a need to coordinate and standardize instruction, for this is precisely what modern American educational organizations do not do. Nor do these bureaucratic organizations merely fund and administer an exchange between educational professionals and families needing educational services. Educational bureaucracies present themselves not as units servicing education but as organizations that embody educational purposes in their collective structure. A theory of their

---

emergence and dominance should explain why these bureaucracies assume jurisdiction over educational instruction.

The most plausible explanation is that modern schools produce education for society, not for individuals or families. In the nineteenth and twentieth centuries, national societies everywhere took over the function of defining and managing the socialization of their citizen personnel (Coombs, 1968; Meyer & Rubinson, 1975; Ramirez, 1974). In national societies, education is both a right and duty of citizenship (Bendix, 1964). It also becomes an important way of gaining status and respect (for example, see Blau & Duncan, 1967). For reasons that do not require elaborate discussion here, education becomes the central agency defining personnel—both citizen and elite—for the modern state and economy.

Since World War II, the trend toward corporate control of education has intensified. As nation-states have consolidated their control over a growing number of elements of social life, they have established educational systems to incorporate citizens into the political, economic, and status order of society. This incorporation is managed by a large public bureaucracy that uniformly extends its standardization and authority through all localities. Thus, educational organizations have come to be increasingly structured by centers of political authority (Meyer & Rubinson, 1975). Bailyn (1960), Field (1972), Katz (1968), and Tyack (1974) describe the steps of this process in pre-twentieth-century American history. First local, and later national, elites became concerned with the social control of peripheral citizen groups—who need control precisely because they are citizens. At first, the rural New Englanders who escaped from the control of clergy and town community (Bailyn, 1960), then the Irish immigrants (Field, 1972; Katz, 1968), and finally the great waves of nineteenth century immigration (Tyack, 1974) created the pressures to control, standardize, and coordinate the educational system. As these steps progressed, the impetus to organize schooling on a large scale—to certify and classify pupils, to certify teachers, to accredit schools, and to control formal curriculum—gained force.

The growth of corporate control of education has major implications for educational organizations. As citizen personnel are increasingly sorted and allocated to positions in the social structure on the basis of classified or certified educational properties, the ritual classifications of education—type of student, topic, teacher, or school—come to have substantial value in what might be called the societal identity "market." A workable identity market presupposes a standardized, trustworthy currency of social typifications that is free from local anomalies. Uniform categories of instruction are therefore developed, and there is a detailed elaboration of the standardized and certified properties comprising an educational identity.

The result of this social expansion of education is a basic change in social structure. Education comes to consist, not of a series of private arrangements between teachers and students, but rather of a set of standardized public credentials used to incorporate citizen personnel into society. Society and its stratification system come to be composed of a series of typifications having educational meaning—ordinary citizens are presumed to have basic literacy. Strata above ordinary citizens are composed of high school and college graduates. The upper levels contain credentialed professionals, such as doctors and lawyers.

Thus, as societies and nation-states use education to define their basic categories of personnel, a large-scale educational bureaucracy emerges to standardize and manage the production of these categories. The credentials that give individuals status and membership in the wider collectivity must come under collective control. Such collective control would not be necessary if instruction were conceived of as a merely private matter between individuals and teachers. But, as educational organizations emerge as the credentialing agency of modern society and as modern citizens see their educational and corporate identities linked—that is, as education becomes the theory of personnel in modern society—it is consequently standardized and controlled.

Society thus becomes "schooled" (Illich, 1971). Education comes to be understood by corporate actors according to the schooling rule: Education is a certified teacher teaching a standardized curricular topic to a registered student in an accredited school. The nature of schooling is thus socially defined by reference to a set of standardized categories the legitimacy of which is publicly shared. As the categories and credentials of schooling gain importance in allocation and membership processes, the public comes to expect that they will be controlled and standardized. The large-scale public bureaucracy created to achieve this standardization is now normatively constrained by the expectations of the schooling rule. To a large degree, then, education is coordinated by shared social understandings that define the roles, topics, and contents of educational organizations.

The Organizational Management of Standardized Classifications

The political consolidation of society and the importance of education for the allocation of people to positions in the economic and stratification system explain the rise of large-scale educational bureaucracies. These processes also explain why educational organizations focus so tightly on the ritual classifications of education. Educational organizations are created to produce schooling for corporate society. They create standard types of graduates from standard categories of pupils using standard types of teachers and topics. As their purposes and structures are defined and institutionalized in the rules, norms, and ideologies of the wider society, the legitimacy of schools and their ability to mobilize resources depend on maintaining congruence between their structure and these socially shared categorical understandings of education (Dowling & Pfeffer, 1975; Meyer & Rowan, 1977; Parsons, 1956).

Consider this matter from the viewpoint of any rational college president or school superintendent. The whole school will dissolve in conflict and illegitimacy if the internal and external understanding of its accredited status is in doubt: If it has too few Ph.D.'s or properly credentialed teachers on its faculty, it may face reputational, accreditational, or even legal problems. If it has one too many "economics" courses and one too few "history" courses (leave aside their actual content), similar disasters may occur as the school falls short of externally imposed accrediting standards. No matter what they have learned, graduates may have difficulty finding jobs. No matter what the school teaches, it may not be capable of recruiting funds or teachers. Thus, the creation of institutionalized rules defining and standardizing education creates a system in which schools come to be somewhat at the mercy of the ritual classifications. Failure to incorporate certified personnel or to organize instruction around the topics outlined in accreditation rules can bring conflict and illegitimacy.

At the same time, the creation of institutionalized rules provides educational organizations with enormous resources. First, the credentials, classifications, and categories of schooling constitute a language that facilitates exchange between school and society. Social agencies often provide local schools with "categorical funding" to support the instruction of culturally disadvantaged or educationally handicapped students or to support programs in bilingual or vocational education. Second, schools can exploit the system of credentials and classifications in order to gain prestige. They can carefully attend to the social evaluations of worth given to particular ritual classifications and can maximize their honorific worth by hiring prestigious faculty, by incorporating programs that are publicly defined as "innovative," or by upgrading their status from junior college to four-year college. Finally, the school relies on the ritual classifications to provide order. Social actors derive their identities from the socially defined categories of education and become committed to upholding these identities within the context of their school activities. To the degree that actors take on the obligation to be [a part of the system] (Goffman, 1967), the whole educational system retains its plausibility.

In modern society, then, educational organizations have good reason to tightly control properties defined by the wider social order. By incorporating externally defined types of instruction, teachers, and students into their formal structure, schools avoid illegitimacy and discreditation. At the same time, they gain important benefits. In schools using socially agreed-on classifications, participants become committed to the organization. This is especially true when these classifications have high prestige (McCall & Simmons, 1966). And, by labeling students or instructional programs so that they conform to institutionally supported programs, schools obtain financial resources. In short, the rewards for attending to external understandings are an increased ability to mobilize societal resources for organizational purposes.

The Avoidance of
Evaluation and Inspection

We have explained why schools attend to ritual classifications, but we have not explained why they do not attend (as organizations) to instruction. There are two [primary] ways that instructional activities can be controlled in modern education bureaucracies. First, many of the properties of educational identities may be certified in terms of examinations. Second, many of the ritual classifications involve a reorganization of educational activity, and some school systems organize an inspection system to make sure these implications are carried through. Thus, two basic kinds of instructional controls are available to educational organizations—the certification of status by testing, and/or the inspection of instructional activity to ensure conformity to rules.

Our explanation of the loose control of instruction in U.S. school systems must in part focus on specific features of U.S. society, since most other societies have educational bureaucracies that assignment to a classification such as student, graduate, or teacher is determined by various tests, most often controlled by national ministries of education. Also, national inspectors are often employed to attempt to make sure that teachers and schools conform to national standards of practice, regardless of the educational outcome. Thus, in most societies the state, through a ministry of education, controls systems of inspection or examination that manage the ritual categories of education by controlling either output or instructional procedure (Ramirez, 1974; Rubinson, 1974).

In American society, tests are used in profusion. However, most of these tests are neither national nor organizational but, rather, are devices of the individual teacher. The results seldom leave the classroom and are rarely used to measure instructional output. In the United States, the most common national tests that attempt to standardize local output differences—the Scholastic Aptitude Test (SAT) and the Graduate Record Examination (GRE)—are creatures of private organization. Further, only the New York State Board of Regents examination approximates (and at that in a pale way) an attempt to standardize curriculum throughout a political unit by using an examination system.

The apparent explanation for this lack of central control of instruction in American education is the decentralization of the system. Schools are in large part locally controlled and locally funded. While higher levels of authority in state and federal bureaucracies have made many attempts to impose evaluative standards on the educational system, the pressures of continued localism defeat them; category systems that delegate certification or evaluation rights to the schools themselves are retained. The reason for this is clear. A national evaluation system would define almost all the children in some communities as successes and almost all those in others as failures. This could work in a nationally controlled system, but it is much too dangerous in a system that depends on legitimating itself in and obtaining resources from local populations. Why, for instance, should the state of Mississippi join in a national credentialing system that might define a great proportion of its schools and graduates as failures? It is safer to adapt the substantive standards of what constitutes, say, a high school graduate to local circumstances and to specify in state laws only categories at some remove from substantive competence.

There is yet another way in which the institutional pattern of localism reduces organizational controls over instruction. In the United States, the legitimacy of local control in some measure deprofessionalizes school administrators at all levels (in contrast to European models). They do not carry with them the authority of the central, national, professional, and bureaucratic structures and the elaborate ideological backing such authority brings with it. American administrators must compromise and must further lose purely professional authority by acknowledging their compromised role. They do not have tenure, and their survival is dependent on laypersons in the community, not professionals. Their educational authority of office is, therefore, lower than that of their European counterparts, especially in areas dealing with central educational matters such as instruction and curriculum. This situation is precisely analogous to the "red" versus "expert" conflict found in many organizations in communist societies, where organizational managers must often act contrary to their expert opinion in order to follow the party line. The profusion of local pressures in American society turns school administrators into "reds" as it were. . . .

OVERVIEW OF THE ARGUMENT

With the growth of corporate society, especially the growth of nation-states, education comes into exchange with society. Schooling—the bureaucratic standardization of ritual classifications—emerges and becomes the dominant form of educational organization. Schools become organized in relation to these ritual categories in order to gain support and legitimacy. In America, the local and pluralistic control of schools causes these classifications to have little impact on the actual instructional activities of local schools. Thus the official classifications of education, although enforced in public respects, are decoupled from actual activity and can contain a good deal of internal inconsistency without harm. As a result, American schools in practice contain multiple realities, each organized with respect to different internal or exogenous pressures. These multiple realities conflict so little because they are buffered from each other by the logic of confidence that runs through the system.

In this fashion, educational organizations have enjoyed enormous success and have managed to satisfy an extraordinary range of external and internal constituents. The standardized categories of American society and its stratification system are maintained, while the practical desires of local community constituents and the wishes of teachers, who are highly satisfied with their jobs, are also catered to. As new constituents rise up and make new demands, these pressures can be accommodated within certain parts of the system

with minimal impact on other parts. A great deal of adaptation and change can occur without disrupting actual activity. And, conversely, the activities of teachers and pupils can change a good deal, even though the abstract categories have remained constant.

REFERENCES

Bailyn, B. (1960). *Education in the forming of American society*. Chapel Hill: University of North Carolina Press.

Bendix, R. (1964). *Nation building and citizenship*. New York: Wiley.

Blau, P. M., & Duncan, O. D. (1967). *The American occupational structure*. New York: Wiley.

Coombs, P. H. (1968). *The world educational crisis*. New York: Oxford University Press.

Dowling, J., & Pfeffer, J. (1975). Organizational legitimacy: Social values and organizational behavior. *Pacific Sociological Review, 18*(1), 122–136.

Field, A. (1972). *Educational reform and manufacturing development, Massachusetts 1837–1865* (Unpublished doctoral dissertation). University of California, Berkeley.

Goffman, E. (1967). *Interaction ritual*. Garden City, NY: Doubleday.

Illich, I. (1971). *Deschooling society*. New York: Harper & Row.

Katz, M. (1968). *The irony of early school reform*. Boston: Beacon.

McCall, G. J., & Simmons, J. L. (1966). *Identities and interactions*. New York: Free Press.

Meyer, J. W., & Rowan, B. (1977). Institutionalized organizations: Formal structure as myth and ceremony. *American Journal of Sociology, 83*(2), 340–363.

Meyer, J. W., & Rubinson, R. (1975). Education and political development. *Review of Research in Education, 3,* 134–162.

Parsons, T. (1956). Suggestions for a sociological approach to the theory of organizations. *Administrative Science Quarterly, 1*(1), 63–85.

Ramirez, F. O. (1974). *Societal corporateness and status conferral* (Unpublished doctoral dissertation). Stanford University: Palo Alto, California.

Rubinson, R. (1974). *The political construction of education* (Unpublished doctoral dissertation). Stanford University: Palo Alto, California.

Tyack, D. B. (1974). *The one best system*. Cambridge, MA: Harvard University Press.

NO CHILD LEFT BEHIND—AND BEYOND

The Federal Government Gets Serious About Accountability

Kathryn M. Borman and Bridget A. Cotner

Kathryn Borman and Bridget Cotner present an overview of the No Child Left Behind (NCLB) Act of 2001 and the Obama administration's policy, "Blueprint for Reform" for education. They also provide a brief historical overview of educational reforms that preceded the current policies. Since states are critical components for implementing federal policies, the authors examine what states are doing in response to the legislation and problems that schools and states are experiencing as a result. They also present criticisms of the policies and what sociologists are proposing as revisions to this legislation.

Questions to consider for this reading:

1. In what ways do NCLB and Obama administration plans for education build on prior educational reforms and legislation?

2. What are some of the main concerns states and schools have regarding federal policies?

3. How do federal policies such as the "Blueprint for Reform" change school practices?

On December 13, 2001, the No Child Left Behind Act of 2001 (NCLB) was proposed before the first session of the 107th Congress. This act was signed into law by President George W. Bush on January 8, 2002. As an amendment to the Elementary and Secondary Education Act (ESEA) of 1965, three principal areas were affected by NCLB: (1) changing the federal focus to all schools and students, not just disadvantaged students; (2) measuring academic performance versus providing additional resources to schools; and (3) enhancing the role of the federal government through federal spending and mandates at the state level (McGuinn, 2006). The changing focus and level of involvement of the federal government in education affected the national educational system in profound ways. In the next sections, we present an overview of NCLB

implementation from its inception in 2002 until today. We begin with a brief history of policies and critiques of educational reform policies and consider the recent policies now in place under the rubric of NCLB and the "Blueprint for Reform."

BRIEF HISTORY LEADING UP TO PRESENT POLICIES

The federal government in the United States has been deeply interested in influencing local policy at the school and school district level for some time. However, the extent to which the No Child Left Behind Act of 2001 reaches into the schoolhouse and classrooms is remarkable in many respects. Before our discussion of the extent of the NCLB legislation and its consequences, it is important to consider the path education policy has taken in recent years as the federal government dramatically ratcheted up its involvement in accountability systems at state and local levels. Some sociologists argue that as a nation we are headed toward a national system of education with a subsequent loss of local control over curriculum, teacher certification, and other critical policy dimensions. Others believe that increased federal control will lead to more equal outcomes for all students.

In considering the history of federal policy, most sociologists, especially those interested in educational policy, identify the publication of the federal mandate *A Nation at Risk* (National Commission on Excellence in Education, 1983) as the first intrusion by the federal government into what was until that time jealously guarded local control of both schools and the schooling process. Prior to the publication of *A Nation at Risk,* academics such as Harvard University Professor of Chemistry (and later Harvard president from 1933 to 1953) James Conant and others attempted to rally school leaders and universities to take up the charge of reforming the national educational system. Conant, for example, was appalled by what he saw as deplorable conditions in teacher education. He saw teacher preparation programs as devoid of intellectual content and in need of radical change. Conant launched a debate on teacher preparation programs that has still not been resolved, with colleges of education still arguing with critics over whether teacher education should include strong training in the disciplines teachers are preparing to teach.

Although the critiques of academicians such as Conant had limited impact on the educational system, the federal government through legislation is able to regulate and modify state and local educational policy in dramatic ways. A brief history of the Elementary and Secondary Education Act (ESEA, 1965) demonstrates the power of congressional authority and also tells the story of legislation that served as a precursor to NCLB and was drafted to amend the ESEA.

The 1954 *Brown v. Board of Education* decision declaring separate educational facilities for children of different racial/ethnic backgrounds illegal had not accomplished the desegregation of educational facilities the Supreme Court intended. Schools and school districts had been advised to proceed with "all deliberate speed" to desegregate the schools, but little desegregation occurred and poor and minority students were falling further behind in schools. President Johnson, himself a former teacher, was concerned about the role of education in preparing all children for successful careers and for citizenship roles. ESEA was drafted by the president and Congress in 1965 to perform a "redistributive" function and put in place a "floor under spending in the nation's poorest communities" as well as to lend federal clout to the improvement of educational delivery systems and services (McGuinn, 2006, p. 31).

The centerpiece of ESEA was Title I, designed to assist those communities, schools, and children most "educationally deprived." These were likely to be communities located in rapidly deteriorating central cities across the country, although rural schools and communities were also likely to be similarly resource-poor. Title I of ESEA provided large sums of money for the purpose of improving and expanding educational programs—more than $1.06 billion, an extraordinarily large sum at that time. Nonetheless, ultimately because of congressional members' interest in providing resources to their home constituents, a redistribution of funds resulted in the dilution of support overall to the neediest districts. The debates during this time involved sociologists and policy makers alike. Chief among these was New York State Senator Daniel Patrick Moynihan, a sociologist and an advocate for policies that shored up what he saw as weak and poorly equipped African American families. Thus began a debate that still continues on the origins and causes of inequalities in financial and social capital among the most distressed urban and rural poor.

As noted earlier, the release of *A Nation at Risk* during the presidency of Ronald Reagan, by Secretary of Education Terrell Bell, dramatically changed the federal government's role in educational policy, rather ironic since Reagan had toyed with the idea of eliminating the Department of Education altogether. The report caused a major sensation because of its eloquent appeal to business interests concerned with losing the trade wars to rising giants including Japan and Germany whose governments were far more invested in education than was the case in the U.S.

During the administration of George H. W. Bush in the early 1990s, federal policy emphasized the relationship between the local business community and local public schools. With leadership from the White House, Congress enacted the New American Schools reforms. In the 1990s additional federal versions of the standards-based movement emerged that influenced education policy. *America 2000* was issued in 1990 calling for "world class" education and "break the mold" schools ultimately under the control of the New American School Corporation. This reform movement was unique in several respects. First, the mandate called for a competition during which local businesses partnered with schools of education and a variety of groups including think tanks such as the Hudson Institute which spawned the Modern Red SchoolHouse design. In the end, a number of Comprehensive School Reform Models were funded and flourished for a number of years, but financial support for such programs virtually ended with the passage of the No Child Left Behind legislation. Then-governor Clinton of Arkansas was a strong supporter of these reforms. As president, Clinton continued to support standards-based reforms under the rubric of *Goals 2000,* in a reauthorization of ESEA.

Following on the heels of the Goals 2000 Act, which provided funds for the voluntary creation of state content and performance standards, Improving America's Schools Act (IASA), passed in 1994, *required* such standards and aligned assessments for students served by the act. Thus for the first time, accountability in the form of measurable student achievement in core subjects was mandated. There is little question that under this reauthorization of ESEA the federal government sought to encourage standards-based reform, an approach that was largely successful.

ESEA has been reauthorized by Congress six times since 1965. Under the first four reauthorizations, ESEA primarily provided supplementary services to poor and low achieving children using funding under Title I/Chapter 1 of the law. Standards-based reforms through curricular change and teacher certification requirements were thus in place before the arrival of NCLB and had become an acceptable aspect of state education policy. NCLB incorporated many of the standards-based principles in the 1994 reauthorization, but propelled the law's reach further into the classroom by instituting a specified timeline for improvement and by ratcheting up accountability criteria and consequences. Under NCLB, not only do schools need to demonstrate progress in student achievement, but states, districts, and schools are required to ensure that *all* students in their charge are proficient in reading and mathematics by the end of the 2013–14 school year.

According to sociologist of education Gary Dworkin (2007), the standards-based school reform movement rests on an array of assumptions about public schools and human motivation:

> The core premises of the movement have been that the public schools are broken and that only through *external* intervention can they be fixed. Further, the imposition of free market forces and competition, which advocates of the reforms suggest have worked well for American industry, will turn the schools into more efficient and effective systems for the delivery of educational services.

It is not surprising that No Child Left Behind was ushered onto the scene by the administration of George W. Bush in 2001, who was intent upon re-establishing the power of the executive branch in all areas of policy.

WHAT NCLB CALLS FOR

The NCLB Act continues the policies of the ESEA in Title I through Title X. The purpose of the act is "to close the achievement gap with accountability, flexibility, and choice, so that no child is left behind" (2002). Each title of the act focuses on a different educational aspect, such as accountability, teacher preparation, and limited English proficient students.

- **Title I** continues the emphasis on improving the academic achievement of disadvantaged students. To fulfill its purpose, Title I emphasizes accountability systems and high-quality assessments. States must define Adequate Yearly Progress and a timeline for change.
- **Title II** provides grants to State educational agencies, local educational agencies, State agencies for higher education, and eligible partnerships in order to:
  - ○ (1) increase student academic achievement through strategies such as improving teacher and principal quality and increasing the number of highly qualified teachers in the classroom and highly qualified principals and assistant principals in schools; and
  - ○ (2) hold local educational agencies and schools accountable for improvements in student academic achievement.
- **Title III** focuses on students who are limited English proficient, including immigrant children and youth. The Title supports attainment of English proficiency and of high levels of academic achievement.
- **Title IV** supports programs at the State, local educational agency and school levels that prevent violence in and around schools and prevent the illegal use of alcohol, tobacco, and drugs through the involvement of parents and communities.
- **Title V** provides funding for local educational agencies and State education agencies to implement and/or support reform programs in order to meet the educational needs of all students.
- **Title VI** provides funds to the states to pay the costs of developing State accountability assessments and standards and to administer those assessments.
- **Title VII** supports local educational agencies, Indian tribes and organizations, postsecondary institutions and other entities to meet the unique educational and culturally related academic needs of American Indian and Alaskan and Hawaiian Native students.
- **Title VIII** provides funds to local educational agencies in times of emergency and when modernization of a facility is needed due to overcrowding or other factors.
- **Title IX** provides guidelines on how states and local educational agencies may receive NCLB funds. Other provisions are described for school prayer, equal access to public school facilities (also known as the Boy Scouts of America Act, where as a patriotic society, they and other groups of that kind are allowed to use public schools as a venue), etc.
- **Title X** repeals or amends laws that have been affected by NCLB.

Together, these ten titles of NCLB create a new direction in education where states and local educational agencies are held accountable for the education of America's students, for high quality teachers and instructional practices, and producing high levels of achievement for all students. For those that succeed in meeting the requirements in the time frame outlined in these titles, incentives are issued; however, for those who do not meet the requirements, sanctions are also issued. Indeed, NCLB places greater control with the federal government as the "watch dog" of reform.

How States Have Coped

Despite the severity of federal Adequate Yearly Progress (AYP) requirements, states have taken it upon themselves to cope with AYP by "modifying" and developing their own approaches to AYP accountability, teacher certification and qualification requirements, as well as a host of other dimensions of NCLB reforms. In fact, many states have become quite innovative. As an example, Indiana public schools in 2006 implemented full day kindergarten to assure that all students received a boost early on in their student careers. Indiana serves as a useful case to consider as schools in that state have gradually improved since the enactment of NCLB. From 2006 to 2007, 60 percent of the state's Title I supported schools met AYP requirements compared to 55 percent the previous year.

A contrasting example for resisting this federal mandate is demonstrated by the tactic referred to as the "minimum n," the number of students tested under the accountability program in each state. According to LeFloch (2007), "The range of subgroup sizes among states varies from 5 students in Maryland, to 50 students in Virginia and West Virginia." States create plans aggregating data across subjects or years to achieve the "minimum n," and thus avoid too close scrutiny.

Accountability at the state level extends to the manner in which states set their measurable objectives on a yearly basis. This requirement has resulted in the establishment of annual measurable objectives (AMOs) that according to LeFloch (2007) "chart progress from the 'starting point' in 2001–02 to the NCLB target of 100% proficiency by 2013–14." States have varied in their responses with one group of 12 states following a linear path from a starting point to 100% proficiency. Another group of 13 states has organized their trajectory into a configuration more like a set of plateaus to be attained after a period of two or three years after which a leap in proficiency is projected. Again, according to LeFloch:

> It is not surprising that states and local school districts are finding ways to circumvent the punishing and frequently contradictory policies of the NCLB legislation. However, no state or locale is likely to stretch requirements for compliance too far since they are highly dependent on federal dollars. These dollars have become an increasingly large portion of state and local district budgets over the years, although by comparison with other revenue sources, these dollars still remain the smallest percentage (approximately 6% of expenditures) of these jurisdictions' revenue stream.

Whether states adopt a policy of resisting or embracing NCLB reforms, all are bound by requirements of the law to ensure that schools improve their progress from year to year. While there is little question that states have increased their burden in meeting the requirements of the legislation, it is also clear that to meet 100% proficiency by the year 2014 will be a stretch for most states, particularly states with high percentages of impoverished students and high numbers of English language learners.

WHAT SOCIOLOGISTS ARE PROPOSING FOR REVISIONS

Reauthorization of NCLB legislation was due in 2007, five years after its inception. While former U.S. Secretary of Education, Margaret Spellings, rallied for support for the reauthorization of NCLB by citing the impact it has had on education, there has been a rather muted response on the part of the current administration's Secretary of Education Arne Duncan. Then Secretary Spellings (U.S. Department of Education, 2007, p. 1) remarked, "No Child Left Behind helps kids by measuring their progress and holding schools accountable for results. It helps teachers by providing them with information and resources to better help their students. And it helps parents by giving them a more direct say in children's education."

However, NCLB would not be reauthorized until 2010, under President Barack Obama's administration with U.S. Secretary of Education Arne Duncan. In March 2010, the Obama administration released *A Blueprint for Reform: Reauthorization of the Elementary and Secondary Education Act* (U.S. Department of Education, 2010). According to the reauthorization (U.S. Department of Education, 2010, p. 3), the blueprint builds on reforms already made in response to the American Recovery and Reinvestment Act of 2009. The American Recovery and Reinvestment Act of 2009 was passed to address the economic crisis by encouraging economic growth, providing tax cuts and benefits to working families and businesses, increasing federal funds for education and health care, and making funds available for contracts, grants, and loans while encouraging transparency and accountability in federal spending. Authorized under the American Recovery and Reinvestment Act of 2009, the Race to the Top Assessment Program provides funding to consortia of states to develop assessments that are valid, support and inform instruction, provide accurate information about what students know and can do, and measure student achievement against standards designed to ensure all students gain the knowledge and skills needed to succeed in college and the workplace. A recent *New York Times* article (Lewin, 2010) argues that in the states that meet and exceed the national standards (including Massachusetts notably), the key to assuming successful adoption of more rigorous standards rested at least in part on having the states participate in their development. While Alaska and Texas did not participate in developing more rigorous standards, states motivated by the opportunity to compete for Race to the Top funds or for more altruistic reasons sought to stay in the game by developing rigorous standards.

The reauthorization of NCLB builds on the Race to the Top Assessment Program's efforts by focusing on four main areas:

1. Improving teacher and principal effectiveness to ensure that every classroom has a great teacher and every school has a great leader;

2. Providing information to families helping them evaluate and improve their children's schools, and to educators assisting them in improving their students' learning;

3. Implementing college- and career-ready standards and developing improved assessments aligned with those standards; and

4. Improving student learning and achievement in America's lowest-performing schools by providing intensive support and effective interventions.

These changes to NCLB strive to target funds more readily to the neediest schools and students. Nonetheless, sociologists remain skeptical about how far reaching this legislation will be in addressing the very lowest achieving students and schools. Schools, after all, are embedded in communities and in the larger society. Sociologists argue that an important corrective to current policy discussions must be interjected by the insistence that school level policies and reforms required by NCLB are only understood in their larger societal context and in relation to external social, economic, and political factors. Forty years of sociological research on the causes of the achievement gap demonstrate that educational inequalities are a result of both school-based and non-school factors. To ignore societal factors in policies aimed at reducing the achievement gap will inevitably limit the effectiveness of educational policies aimed primarily at the school level, as NCLB is, to adequately reduce the achievement gap.

Having said this, sociological research provides important evidence that school-based policies can improve schools and help reduce the achievement gap in the areas covered by the law under which NCLB operates. In addition, the sociological discipline provides research-based evidence for improving the implementation of NCLB and correcting unintended consequences of the law. Sociologists of education must continue to engage in research aimed at analyzing the various components of NCLB and this research should inform the larger policy debates about NCLB, especially with respect to its reauthorization (Sadovnik, Dworkin, Gamoran, Hallinan, & Scott, 2007).

While sociologists continue to critique the policies that make up the NCLB Act, Congress has passed the act's reauthorization. As long as the achievement gap between poor and rich, as well as the gap between different racial and ethnic groups, persists, there will continue to be a focus both among sociologists and among policy makers and the public on reducing these disparities. What may continue to be debated are the assumptions for why gaps persist and the strategies for reducing them.

REFERENCES

Dworkin, G. (2007). Accountability and assessment issues. In A. Sadovnik, J. O'Day, K. Borman, & G. Bohrenstedt (Eds.), *No Child Left Behind and the reduction of the achievement gap: Sociological perspectives on federal educational policy.* New York: Routledge.

LeFloch, K. C. (2007). State policy activity under NCLB: Adequate yearly progress and highly qualified teachers. In A. Sadovnik, J. O'Day, K. Borman, & G. Bohrenstedt (Eds.), *No Child Left Behind and the reduction of the achievement* gap: Sociological perspectives on federal educational policy. New York: Routledge.

Lewin, T. (July 21, 2010). States embrace core standards for the schools. *New York Times*, p. A1.

McGuinn, P. J. (2006). *No Child Left Behind and the transformation of federal education policy, 1965–2005*. Lawrence: University Press of Kansas.

National Commission on Excellence in Education. (1983). *A nation at risk: The imperative for educational reform* (Stock No. 065-000-00177-2). Washington, DC: U.S. Government Printing Office.

No Child Left Behind Act of 2001, Pub. L. No. 107-110, 115 Stat. 1425 (2002).

Sadovnik, A., Dworkin, A. G., Gamoran, A., Hallinan, M., & Scott, J. (2007). Conclusion: Sociological perspectives on NCLB and federal involvement. In A. Sadovnik, J. O'Day, K. Borman, & G. Bohrenstedt (Eds.), *No Child Left Behind and the reduction of the achievement gap: Sociological perspectives on federal educational policy* (pp. 359–373). New York: Routledge.

U.S. Department of Education. (2007, January 30). *Secretary Spellings highlights the importance of closing the achievement gap and preparing Georgia's students for the 21st century workforce. Meets with business leaders, students, and teachers to promote reauthorization of No Child Left Behind*. Retrieved from http://www.ed.gov/news/pressreleases/2007/01/01302007.htm

U.S. Department of Education. (2010). *A blueprint for reform: Reauthorization of the Elementary and Secondary Education Act*. Washington, DC: Author.

EXIT EXAMS HARM STUDENTS WHO FAIL THEM—AND DON'T BENEFIT STUDENTS WHO PASS THEM

John Robert Warren and Eric Grodsky

A major part of No Child Left Behind and Blueprint for Reform is examinations, usually mandated by state or federal agencies with a price tag attached for noncompliance. At various points in students' careers, they are given achievement exams to see if they are on grade level. Many states are also requiring expensive exit exams for students to graduate with a high school degree; currently approximately two in three U.S. students will have to pass an exit exam to graduate. In most cases the goal is to be sure students have mastered the knowledge expected by the time they graduate from high school, and that they have not just slid through high school without mastering basic skills. Among the problems pointed out by critics of exit exams are that these exams result in some students dropping out of school and others not being able to graduate. However, few alternatives to failure are offered for these students who slip through the net. Also, the curriculum in states with tests often changes to accommodate the material being tested, thus cutting time spent on other valuable subjects such as physical education, art, and music. The authors studied the effects of exit exams on students and report some surprising findings, as outlined in the following reading.

Questions to consider for this reading:

1. Why do the authors indicate that exit exams help no one?

2. Do exit exams really lower graduation rates? Why or why not?

3. Do exit exams improve learning or preparation for work?

4. How does the previous discussion by Borman and Cotner on federal mandates relate to the findings of Warren and Grodsky in this article?

A generation ago, high school students earned their diplomas by showing up for classes, keeping up their grades, and staying out of trouble. Since the late 1970s, a growing number of states have also required aspiring graduates to pass "exit exams"—standardized tests that assess mastery of basic skills—in order to graduate. This spring, about two in three American high school students will have to pass an exit exam on their way to earning their diplomas.

After evaluating the effects of high school exit exams on a variety of student outcomes using nationally representative data spanning nearly 30 years, we conclude that exit exams hurt students who fail them without benefiting students who pass them—or the taxpayers who pay for developing, implementing, and scoring them. Exit exams are just challenging enough to reduce the graduation rate but not challenging enough to have measurable consequences for how much students learn or for how prepared they are for life after high school. Political pragmatism rather than academic benchmarks have led states to implement fundamentally flawed exit exam policies. Policy makers should either revamp exit exams to be sufficiently challenging to make a real difference for how much students learn or abandon them altogether.

ARGUING ABOUT EXIT EXAMS

Proponents of exit exam policies say too many students simply get credit for "seat time," graduating without basic literacy and numeracy skills. With the decline in manufacturing and growth of the information economy, architects of exit exam policies have sought to bolster the value of the diploma. Supporters say these policies have increased pressure on students, parents, teachers, and school systems to boost academic achievement and to better prepare young people for college and the global economy.

Critics contend that such policies are fundamentally counterproductive and unfair. First, they assert, exit exams deny diplomas to some students and lead others to drop out of high school without offering much in the way of improved academic outcomes. Second, exit exams force educators to narrow the curriculum by "teaching to the test," neglecting to devote adequate time to subjects not covered on the exit exam. Third, these policies are expensive to develop, implement, and score, diverting resources from instruction. Finally, critics argue that these policies are unfair to students who haven't had sufficient opportunity to master the tested material, either because of disabilities or limited English proficiency or because of inequities in educational resources.

Besides the similarity of the rhetoric and claims for and against exit exam policies over time and across states, these debates have also

typically proceeded in the absence of sound empirical evidence on either side.

DO EXIT EXAMS LOWER GRADUATION RATES?

At first glance, it seems obvious that exit exam policies should reduce high school graduation rates, at least during the initial years of their implementation. By design, these policies deny diplomas to students who don't meet basic proficiency standards in core curricular areas and who, presumably, would have earned diplomas before the exit exam requirement.

On the other hand, there are reasons to suppose that exit exams may have very minimal consequences for graduation rates. First, it may be that the only students who can't exceed the low bar imposed by exit exam policies would have dropped out anyway. Second, it may be that the basic proficiency standards set by most states are so low that nearly all students who continue in high school through their senior year would eventually be able to meet those standards. Third, schools and districts may "game the system" to artificially increase test scores and graduation rates by selectively exempting students for whom exit exams would present a serious barrier to graduation.

Our analyses indicate that state exit exams reduce high school graduation rates (Warren, Jenkins, & Kulick, 2006). In states with "minimum competency" exit exams (assessing mastery of material that students should learn before 9th grade), graduation rates decline by about one percentage point. In states with "higher competency" exit exams, graduation rates decline by about two percentage points. Nationally, each percentage point reduction in the graduation rate means about 35,000 fewer young people leave high school with a diploma each year.

Exit exams have a greater impact on graduation rates in states that are more racially/ethnically diverse and have higher rates of poverty. This doesn't necessarily mean exit exams increase dropout rates of disadvantaged students more than advantaged students, but it is consistent with that claim.

Do Exit Exams Improve How Much Students Learn?

Exit exams deny diplomas to some students, but they may also increase the academic achievement of others by raising the bar. If diploma recipients learn more than they would have in the absence of exit exams, exit exams are redistributive rather than capricious. They may increase the rewards to those who succeed as well as the costs to those who fail. However, surprisingly little empirical research has investigated the impact of state exit exams on students' proficiency in core academic subjects.

Data from the long-term trend component of the National Assessment of Educational Progress (or LTT NAEP) help answer this question (Grodsky, Warren, & Kalogrides, [2009]). LTT NAEP includes a set of achievement test items that are the same from year to year in order to allow for methodologically sound assessments of trends over time in reading, mathematics, and science achievement. In combination with the detailed information that we collected about exit exam policies in each state, we asked whether exit exams increased the reading and math achievement of students between 1971 and 2004. Beyond asking whether exit exams improved *average* levels of achievement in reading and math, we also asked whether exit exams improved the achievement of students closer to the top and the bottom of the achievement distribution. Exit exams might do the most to improve the achievement of marginal students and the least to improve the reading or math test scores of already high-achieving students. We also asked whether exit exams matter more or less for racial/ethnic minority students and for students from different social class backgrounds.

We found no evidence for any effect of exit exams (minimum competency *or* higher competency) on reading or math achievement at the mean or at any of several cut-points of the

achievement distribution. These results hold for 13-year-olds and for 17-year-olds and don't vary across racial/ethnic or social class backgrounds, undermining claims of disparate impact.

Do Exit Exams Prepare Students for Work?

Although exit exams have no discernable effects for reading or math achievement, could exit exams still affect graduates' employment prospects and wages? Employers, like many other members of the public, may *believe* exit exams have increased the academic achievement of high school graduates. Employers of relatively less skilled workers—that is, those without a college education—generally value such traits as trustworthiness, reliability, and sound work ethics at least as much as they value academic skills in reading and math. Exit exams may signal to employers that diploma holders are able to follow through on a more rigorous set of high school graduation requirements and thus certify that graduates possess the noncognitive skills that employers value.

If exit exams produce graduates who are better prepared for work, then we should expect lower unemployment rates and higher wages among young people who passed exit exams to obtain their diplomas. These effects should be most pronounced among young people who don't go on to college; the effects of postsecondary training and credentials are probably much larger than any effect of exit exams.

We use data from the 1980 through 2000 U.S. Censuses and from the 1984 through 2002 Current Population Surveys to evaluate the labor market returns to exit exams (Warren, Grodsky, & Lee, 2008). Both data sources include large, nationally representative samples of American young people. We limited our focus to 20- to 23-year-olds with no college education (and along the way we found that exit exams have no bearing on 20- to 23-year-olds' chances of having attended college). Young high school graduates who obtained their diplomas in exit exam states fared no better in the labor market than their peers who obtained their diplomas in other states. These findings held in states with minimum competency exit exams and in states with higher competency exit exams. They also held for students from different racial/ethnic backgrounds.

HOW DID WE GET HERE? LESSONS FROM FLORIDA AND CALIFORNIA

Our research suggests that exit exams fail to improve either academic achievement or early labor market outcomes. At the same time, the direct costs of developing, implementing, and scoring exams, as well as the indirect costs of denying diplomas to thousands of otherwise eligible students each year, are substantial. How is it that 23 states (and counting) have implemented policies that appear to do such harm without doing any good?

The answer has more to do with political pragmatism than sound policy. Consider the history of exit exam policies in Florida and California. There, as in other states, exit exam policies were shaped by fears of unacceptably high exam failure rates, resulting in concerns about lowered graduation rates and legal challenges on behalf of various classes of students. These factors may very well minimize the potential benefits and costs of exit exams.

Florida tried to adopt an exit exam beginning with the graduating classes of 1979, but the exam was quickly challenged in court. In *Debra P. v. Turlington,* attorneys representing 10 African-American students argued that the test was racially biased and imposed without adequate notice. The U.S. District Court sided with the plaintiffs, delaying implementation of the exit exam requirement until the 1982–83 school year and compelling the state to demonstrate the instructional validity of the test, which it did. The class of 1983 was the first cohort of Florida students required to pass a high school exit exam. Florida revised and first administered a more difficult version of its exit exam in October 1994, first affecting students in the class of 1996.

Not surprisingly, far fewer students did well on the more difficult Florida exit exam. Two months after first administering and scoring the revised exit exam in fall 1994, the Florida Department of Education opted to set the passing threshold at the point on the test score distribution that would guarantee that the same percentage of students failed the revised (more difficult) exam as failed the previous year's (less difficult) exam. In the end, the state based decisions about which students had "mastered" key curricular materials on fear of politically unacceptable failure rates.

The California High School Exit Exam (CAHSEE) was originally scheduled to go into effect for the class of 2004. In the face of very high failure rates—just under half of the class of 2004 had passed both components of the exam by summer 2003—the state Board of Education voted unanimously to postpone the exit exam as a graduation requirement until the class of 2006. At that time, the board also opted to revise the CAHSEE, making the mathematics portion of the exam easier in order to ensure that the failure rate was lower.

As in Florida and other states, plaintiffs challenged California's exit exam in the courts based on claims that the state had inadequately prepared racial/ethnic minority and economically disadvantaged students for the exit exam. Weeks before the class of 2006 was to graduate, a superior court judge struck down the CAHSEE on these grounds. The CAHSEE was eventually upheld after a series of appeals.

This same basic pattern of exit exam policy evolution has played out in a number of states. States begin by setting moderate to high standards and then spend hundreds of thousands of dollars designing exit exams that purport to hold students to these standards. In short order, however, high failure rates and much-publicized legal challenges test the political will of policy makers to hold students to these standards. In the end, politics wins over principle and the exit exam, the passing threshold, or both are altered to increase the share of students who pass the exam. In the end, most states set the bar for passing exit exams at a point too low to make a real difference for academic achievement or workplace preparedness but just high enough to prevent a modest number of would-be graduates from obtaining diplomas.

Where Do We Go From Here?

State exit exams harm students who fail them and provide no discernable benefits to students who pass them. Obviously, states didn't intend to implement ineffective and punitive education policies. Exit exam policies are broken, and states should either fix them or get rid of them, but either option requires a political will that is in scarce supply among policy makers and politicians.

To fix exit exams, states would need to set substantially higher standards for passage—requiring mastery of more challenging and advanced curricular materials—and actually hold students to those standards. While educationally sound, the cost of raising standards would be daunting, especially in the current fiscal climate. More students will be initially unprepared to meet these higher standards, which means states will need to devote more time, money, and other resources to preparation and remediation. Such policies will reduce high school graduation rates, at least in the short term. The social costs of denying greater numbers of would-be graduates their high school diplomas should not be born lightly. The high school diploma is now a prerequisite for social and economic success in American society.

If states abandon exit exams, they would be on sound scientific ground. Many researchers question the wisdom of basing something as important as the decision about which students deserve diplomas on the score from a single standardized test. The ethics of high school exit exams are questionable at best. According to the American Educational Research Association (2000, p. 378), "Decisions that affect individual students' life chances or educational opportunities should not be made on the basis of test scores alone." As noted above, there are also persistent concerns about the disparate impact of such policies. However, public opinion determines the outcomes of elections, not science. Anyone with the courage to advocate for abolishing high school exit exams would likely be portrayed as "soft on education."

Conclusion

We came to our work on exit exams not as policy advocates but as researchers. We believed that the claims proponents made about the benefits of high school exit exams were just as plausible as those made by opponents of those policies. We still believe that arguments in favor of exit exams as policy levers may have merit. However, arguments in favor of the exit exam polices in place today do not. Exit exams, as currently implemented, appear to have real downsides and none of their purported upsides. After a quarter of a century of experience with exit exams, states have reached a crossroads. The policies that we have now aren't working. It's time to try something else.

References

American Educational Research Association (AERA). (2000). *Position statement on high-stakes testing in pre-K–12 education.* Retrieved from http://www.aera.net/?id=378

Grodsky, E., Warren, J. R., & Kalogrides, D. (2009). State high school exit examinations and NAEP long-term trends in reading and mathematics, 1971–2004. *Educational Policy, 24,* 589–614.

Warren, J. R., Grodsky, E., & Lee, J. C. (2008). State high school exit examinations and post-secondary labor market outcomes. *Sociology of Education, 81*(1), 77–107.

Warren, J. R., Jenkins, K. N., & Kulick, R. (2006). High school exit examinations and state-level completion and GED rates, 1973–2000. *Educational Evaluation and Policy Analysis, 28*(2), 131–152.

SCHOOL FINANCE

Raising Questions for Urban Schools

Augustina H. Reyes and Gloria M. Rodriguez

The economic environment of schools is as important as the political environment discussed in the articles above on federal policies such as No Child Left Behind and the Blueprint for Reform, as well as exit exams. Educational systems would not exist were there not funding from local and state taxes and federal allocations for special initiatives and programs, plus parent tuition for private schools and funding for special school events. Even bake sales and chili cook-offs help raise funds for school activities. Augustina Reyes and Gloria Rodriguez discuss funding options, structures, and systems used in school districts. The purpose of this reading is to provide insight into another crucial aspect of the education system's environment. Although funding formulas are established to cover needs of schools and school districts, equalization so that basic levels of funding are available for different school districts has been an ongoing concern and cause for judicial actions.

Questions to consider for this reading:

1. Explain the basic school funding structures discussed in the reading.
2. Why can funding structures result in inequality of educational opportunity?
3. If you were to design a funding structure for schools, what would be the components?

School finance drives policy and practice in public education, yet most citizens and some practitioners know very little about how their schools are funded. The purpose of this article is to address the financial issues related to urban schools and the challenge of balancing expectations of higher levels of education with the values of equity, efficiency, and economic growth.

In school finance theory and policy, there are a number of terms and concepts that are commonly used to discuss the mechanisms for directing funds to public schools. This section provides a brief definition of each term or concept and discussion of how it is used in policy and theoretical treatments of school finance issues.

One key component of any state or local system of school finance is *revenues*. Revenues are the dollars that are generated by either fees for various services or taxes on certain goods and services. At the state level, revenues are largely produced from a variety of taxes that are levied on things such as income, the sale of merchandise, and capital gains. To a lesser degree, states also collect fees for licensing, professional certificates, and so forth. Revenues are distributed to local governments and school districts and referred to according to the level of government from which they originated. For example, all school districts will generally have some combination of revenues from local, state, and federal sources, and they can either be referred to by source or by program (e.g., State Compensatory Education or Federal Title I).

Over the past 30 years, there has been considerable legal, legislative, and grassroots activity to address the disparities that exist among districts in terms of the revenues they are able to generate from property taxes. Indeed, the interdistrict variations in property wealth disparities have been at the crux of most school finance equity cases as discussed in the first section of this article. State policies designed to ameliorate the disparities among school districts in terms of property tax revenues generated are referred to as *equalization policies.*

Equalization policies include state methods for ensuring that there is provision for a basic level of educational funding supported by a combination of local and state revenues. In cases where large disparities exist relative to the local property tax revenue-raising capacity among districts, the state provides funding for school districts in an inverse relationship to their capacity to raise revenues. By doing so, states are able to ensure that low-property-wealth districts have access to at least a basic minimum level of funding for their schools, while high-property-wealth districts are able to maintain their basic funding from primarily locally raised revenues.

Very often, the starting point for figuring the available funding for schools is the foundation program or base amount that is allotted at a minimum basic level of funding for schools. In some cases, states may include a variety of adjustments to the funding distributed to districts based on factors that relate to either higher costs of education or variations in student needs among districts. States may use average daily attendance (ADA) or average daily membership (ADM) to distribute foundation funds. ADA systems tend to favor stable

suburban school districts with students who attend school regularly, have access to health care (which promotes healthy children), and role models that instill the economic importance of an education. ADA penalizes urban schools with large numbers of low-income students who have less access to health care; consequently, they experience lower attendance. For example, a state constitution may provide originating language guiding the state legislature or other agency to ensure that each district receive a flat grant or equal dollar figure in total or per pupil. The flat grant usually reflects the starting point of the funding available for all districts within a given state.

Additionally, the state may add funding to support the additional costs associated with transportation, special educational services, and so forth. Such adjustments may be made using an index or using weighted pupils, the latter of which is a method for counting students eligible for special services in a way that reflects the additional costs associated with providing them with a basic education. Although a state or district may determine the amount that reflects a minimum basic education, the student with special educational needs is typically assigned a weight that indicates the extra costs associated with his or her education. For example, it may be determined that a student who is eligible for certain extraeducational services costs twice as much to educate as a student who is not eligible. Such a student would count as two students in a weighted pupil system.

The funding most states distribute to local school districts is typically some balance of local, state, and federal support, with the latter often filtering through state-level structures. In cases where the local share is nearly or completely nonexistent, it is referred to as *full-state funding.* This means that the revenues that schools use to support their operations are composed virtually or entirely from state-collected taxes, fees, and other sources. The concept of full-state funding is also used to describe situations where, because of equalization efforts at the state level, local districts are no longer able to exert the same control over the generation, distribution, or expenditure of such funds.

The intricate mechanisms that determine the level of funding that public schools receive are referred to as *funding formulas.* Indeed, the structures used to systematically determine how much and what sources of funding districts and schools receive are generally very complex sets of mathematical operations grouped together and applied as a formula. The mathematical operations involve each of the different types of adjustments, upward and downward, that reflect the various factors that are acknowledged as necessary in appropriately distributing available funding to local school districts that exhibit wide variation in characteristics and challenges.

As mentioned above, revenues that states receive are, in turn, distributed to school districts for support of local educational services. When the revenues are distributed to districts, they are referred to as *district revenues.* Several factors can affect the level and variation of available district revenues. For example, in most states, revenues are distributed to districts based on some measure of students in attendance the previous year, including actual attendance or ADA (the methods used to determine how many students a district can count for funding purposes can likewise vary significantly). This is why, for many educators, attendance in school is such a huge concern—indeed, it drives district revenues to a great degree in many finance systems.

Within state school finance systems, considerable attention is paid to the tax policies that help to support reforms to ensure increased equity in the distribution of funding to school districts. In particular, one concept that has been useful to policy makers is the notion *of district power equalization.* District power equalization refers to state policies or structures that intervene in situations where large disparities exist in the property tax revenue-raising capacity among school districts. The idea is to enable districts with lower capacity to raise property tax revenues, especially in cases where the average property values are significantly lower than in other districts, and to benefit from policies that enable

them to more easily generate property tax revenues. Another term that is often used to refer to district power equalization is *guaranteed tax base,* where states ensure that districts can generate property tax revenues as though they had access to higher average property values.

One key component associated with a policy of district power equalization or guaranteed tax base is *guaranteed tax yield.* The guaranteed tax yield feature is tied to a district's taxpayers' willingness to tax themselves at higher levels to generate sufficient support for local schools. Under some state finance schemes, when a district's taxpayers approve a certain tax rate, this enacts a policy that guarantees a certain yield (level of revenues), given a certain tax rate, regardless of the average property wealth in the district. Typically, such features are applied only to lower property wealth districts using a very specific property value threshold to qualify for participation. In addition, the guaranteed yield is usually stated in dollar terms tied to specific tax rates. For example, in a given state system, low-property-wealth districts may have the option of taxing themselves at a slightly higher rate per $1,000 of property wealth, which, in turn, generates a set dollar amount in yield for every extra percentage of tax rate levied. That is, if a district taxes itself at $1.55 per $1,000 of property value and the guaranteed tax yield is enacted above a rate of $1.50 per $1,000, the district would enjoy the enhanced yield guaranteed for the additional .05¢ levied. In this way, districts are able to generate extra revenues at the margin that would reflect higher average property values in the absence of the guaranteed tax yield.

Finally, another concept that is often used in the distribution of funding to schools is the *categorical program.* Categorical programs, also referred to as targeted programs, are designed to address either a particular or targeted educational policy goal or the special needs of a category of eligible student populations. Very often, the existence of categorical programs within a school finance formula reflects an acknowledgement by policy makers that additional resources are needed in districts with several schools exhibiting certain characteristics or serving students with certain special needs. In other instances, the categorical programs through which resources are distributed to districts fall outside of the regular state school finance formula and are therefore under the scrutiny of other parties, such as the federal U.S. Department of Education. Some categorical programs operate as entitlements, meaning that the dollars follow the students who qualify under the programs' guidelines. In other cases, categorical programs are doled out to schools on a competitive basis, requiring a carefully presented school district (or state) proposal for the use of funds to advance the particular purposes of the program.

LASTING CONSEQUENCES OF THE SUMMER LEARNING GAP

Karl L. Alexander, Doris R. Entwisle, and Linda Steffel Olson

Karl Alexander, Doris Entwisle, and Linda Steffel Olson discuss what happens in the summer months between school years, a time in which the family and community context influences students far more than the school itself. They find that summer learning from family and community activities differ by families' socioeconomic status. Those students from more affluent families have advantages of camps, lessons, vacation trips, and museum visits. These differences that students bring from summer learning affect high school track placement, school completion rates, and school attendance. Thus, family and community play a key role in student achievement, including those nonschool months of summer.

Questions to consider for this reading:

1. Which children benefit from summer experiences and how do they affect their later school achievement?

2. What could be done to level the uneven playing field created by summer experiences?

3. What other types of experiences might children have that affect their school achievement?

Comparisons of school-year and summer learning inform fundamental questions of educational stratification and help parse school, family, and community influences on children's academic development. With children "in" their homes, schools, and communities during the school year, but just "in" their homes and communities over the summer months, the academic calendar approximates a natural experiment that affords leverage for isolating the distinctive role of schooling in children's cognitive development. This was the great insight exploited by Barbara Heyns in her 1978 book *Summer Learning,* which established that achievement gaps by family SES (socioeconomic status) and race/ethnicity widen more during the summer months than during the school year.

Although the detailed results of subsequent research on the seasonality of learning do not line up perfectly (see Cooper and colleagues' [1996] meta-analysis for an overview), the patterns documented by Heyns in the 1970s for middle school children in public schools in Atlanta, Georgia, appear to have considerable generality. This is especially the case for her conclusions regarding family socioeconomic background, which have been replicated in our Baltimore research on the early elementary years with data from the 1980s (e.g., Entwisle, Alexander, & Olson, 1997), in studies conducted in other localities (Murnane, 1975; O'Brien, 1998), and in national data from earlier ([Chin & Phillips, 2004]; Heyns, 1987; Karweit, Ricciuti, & Thompson, 1994) and more recent periods (Burkam,

[Ready, Lee, & LoGerfo], 2004; Downey, von Hippel, & Broh, 2004; Reardon, 2003).

Findings from this literature support two conclusions: (1) prior to high school, the achievement gap by family SES traces substantially to unequal learning opportunities in children's home and community environments; and (2) with learning gains across social lines more nearly equal during the school year, the experience of schooling tends to offset the unequalizing press of children's out-of-school learning environments. Schooling thus appears to play a compensatory role, although we caution that this conclusion holds only for the experience of schooling writ large. It does not imply parity, or even near equivalence, in access to particular school resources or opportunities to learn, which often are quite unequally distributed (e.g., Dougherty, 1996).

Two bodies of evidence suggest there *ought* to be lasting consequences of summer learning differences over the elementary grades—consequences that are likely substantial.

First, achievement scores at any level of schooling predict success at the next level. This holds for high school completion, college attendance, college completion (see Entwisle et al., 1997, table 7.2), and later successes in the labor market (e.g., Kerckhoff, Raudenbush, & Glennie, 2001). Second, cognitive achievement scores at the individual level are moderately to highly correlated across time. Most immediately relevant is the patterning of scores from the early elementary grades into middle school and high school.

Here, then, is the argument: (1) if the achievement gap by family SES during the elementary school years traces substantially to summer learning differences, and (2) if achievement scores are highly correlated across stages of young people's schooling, and (3) if academic placements and attainments at the upper grades are selected on the basis of achievement scores, then (4) summer learning differences during the foundational early grades help explain achievement-dependent outcome differences across social lines in the upper grades, including the transition out of high school and, for some, into college.

Using data from the Baltimore-based Beginning School Study (BSS) youth panel, our analysis examines consequences of seasonal learning differences during the elementary school years for children's later schooling. . . .

DISCUSSION

Our analysis adds an important practical dimension to research on the seasonality of learning, with implications for how the out-of-school institutional contexts of family and community that frame young children's academic development contribute to patterns of educational stratification. Stability in cognitive achievement over the course of young people's schooling is the bridge between summer learning shortfall over the elementary school years and later schooling outcomes. *Since it is low SES youth specifically whose out-of-school learning lags behind, this summer shortfall relative to better-off children contributes to the perpetuation of family advantage and disadvantage across generations.*

Low SES youth, we find, are less likely to find their way to a college-preparatory high school program, partly because their test scores are low at the very time these placements are made. And because their scores are low, they also are more prone to leave school without degrees and less likely to attend a four-year college. In light of these, and no doubt other, serious consequences, the question of why achievement levels at the start of high school are so disparate takes on great importance.

It is well established that there are vast differences across social lines in preschool children's out-of-school learning environments (e.g., Hart & Risley, 1995). This helps explain not just why disadvantaged youth start school already far behind in kindergarten or 1st grade (Lee & Burkam, 2002), but also why they continue to lag behind later (Farkas & Beron, 2004; Phillips, Crouse, & Ralph, 1998). Now we see that summer learning differences after children start school follow a like pattern, but what might not have been expected is the extent to which the *continuing press* of school-age children's family and neighborhood environments contributes to the year 9 achievement differential between high and low SES youth: summer shortfall over the five years of elementary school accounts for more than half the difference, a larger component than that built up over the preschool years. And too, these learning differences from the early years that present themselves in 9th grade reverberate to constrain later high school curriculum placements, high school dropout, and college attendance. This lasting legacy of early experience typically is hidden from view.

The BSS is a local study and the analytic sample before imputation is small, just over 300. This is obviously limiting. Yet, the local context is urban and high poverty and thus policy relevant. Though the analytic sample may not be, strictly speaking, representative, these nevertheless are typical urban youth. But more to the point, to our knowledge there is no better data source, *anywhere,* for informing the issues addressed in this article. The national ECLS data, for example, include fall tests in kindergarten and 1st grade only, and so cover just the summer between kindergarten and 1st grade. Other samples used to study learning patterns by season also typically include data for just one summer, and none offer the long-term perspective of the BSS. Our results are best considered suggestive, and certainly the detailed percentages and probabilities reported should not be generalized. That said, BSS findings align well with a now sizeable literature on summer learning differentials, and the links seen in this analysis to later outcomes certainly have surface plausibility. With these caveats understood, we now discuss several implications of the findings presented here.

Surely the point made by David Berliner (2006) in his Invited Presidential Speech at the 2005 American Educational Research Association (AERA) annual meeting is correct: to moderate the achievement gap, the most compelling need is to reduce family and youth poverty. However, there also is a critical role for school reform. Achievement differentials by race/ethnicity and along lines of family advantage/disadvantage over the last 50 years have exhibited more volatility than many seem to realize (e.g., Krueger, 1998; Lee, 2002). Using National Assessment of Educational Progress (NAEP) testing data, for example, Hauser (1995) estimates that the I.Q. gap separating white and black youths declined by almost a third between 1970 and 1990, while Grissmer and colleagues (1994) conclude that progress during this period was too great to be accounted for by improvements in family life alone. They, and the others mentioned, direct attention to the likely role played by school improvements, including increased funding and class size reduction.

It is unlikely school resources can compensate *wholly* for the limited learning opportunities outside school that hold back many minority and low SES youth. Nevertheless, seasonal comparisons of learning make a compelling case that schooling indeed "makes a difference" in these children's lives, echoing the "differential sensitivity" hypothesis originally advanced in the Equality of Educational Opportunity report (Coleman et al., 1966). But how and when can interventions be most effectively targeted? What is the role of schools in educational stratification? And how should schools be held accountable when achievement scores persist in falling short of expectations? These are large issues, and the realization that much of the problem traces to out-of-school time during the early-elementary years has implications for them all.

First, attempting to close the gap after it has opened wide is a rearguard action. Most of the gap increase happens early in elementary school, which is where corrective interventions would be most effective—or even before. To catch up, youth who have fallen behind academically need to make larger than average gains. That is expecting a great deal, perhaps too much, of struggling students. Early interventions to keep the achievement gap from opening wide in the first place should be a high priority, and the earlier the better, with the kinds of preschool compensatory education initiatives that have proven effective (e.g., Ramey, Campbell, & Blair, 1998; Reynolds & Temple, 1998; [Schweinhart & Weikart, 1998]).

Second, once in school, disadvantaged children need year-round, supplemental programming to counter the continuing press of family and community conditions that hold them back. The school curriculum in the elementary years often is self-consciously pursued at home, as when, for example, parents work with their children on letter and number skills or reading. Parents of means generally did well in school themselves. They understand the skills and behaviors valued there and exemplify them in family life. For their part, poor parents often themselves struggled at school and have low literacy levels, and thus they undoubtedly have difficulties cultivating valued educational skills in their children. While low income, low SES parents generally want the same kinds of enriching experiences for their children as do well-off parents, they often lack the means to provide them (e.g., Chin & Phillips, 2004).

Seasonal studies of learning suggest that schooling compensates, to some degree, for a lack of educationally enriching experiences in disadvantaged children's family life—these youth come closer to keeping up with better-off students during the school year than they do during the summer months. But if some school helps, does that mean more school is necessarily better? Summer and after-school programs are the most obvious approaches, but what counts is how that extra learning time is used. Summer schools that incorporate so-called best practice principles have proven effective (Borman & Dowling, 2006; Cooper, [Charlton, Valentine, & Muhlenbruck], 2000), but to address the achievement gap specifically, programs will need to target disadvantaged students specifically. All children can benefit from high quality "universal" programs—preschools for all; summer schools for all—but they will not benefit in equal measure. Families of privilege will tend to find their way to higher quality programs, and their children will be positioned to profit more from programs of like quality (e.g., Cooper et al., 2000). As a result, rather than moderate the achievement

gap, across-the-board programming for academic remediation and/or enrichment would likely exacerbate it, making the problem worse rather than better (Ceci & Papierno, 2005). This poses a challenge to policy: what to do when two educational goals, each commendable, are in conflict?

Third, the school-year pattern of achievement gain parity (or near parity) across social lines flies in the face of widely held (if often only whispered) assumptions about the learning abilities of poor and minority youth, It also flies in the face of widely held assumptions about the failures of the public schools and school systems burdened by high poverty enrollments. Perhaps these schools and school systems are doing a better job than is generally recognized (e.g., Alexander, 1997; Berliner & Biddle, 1995; Krueger, 1998), with family disadvantages mistaken for school failings (e.g., Rothstein, 2002) and the occasional but very real horror story (e.g., Kozol, 1991) overgeneralized.

Finally, a seasonal perspective on learning also has implications for school accountability. The No Child Left Behind (NCLB) standard of "adequate yearly progress" is intended to monitor school effectiveness based on annual achievement testing in grades 3 through 8. Schools that fail to meet local NCLB standards in math and reading for two consecutive years are designated "in need of improvement," with increasingly severe correctives required the longer they remain so designated. Certainly schools that chronically fall short need help; however, the punitive cast of NCLB may be misplaced. Indeed, annual assessments confound school-year and summer learning in unknown proportions, and schools that enroll mainly disadvantaged students will be held accountable not just for what happens to their pupils during the school year, but also for their students' summer learning, over which they have no control. If the BSS pattern is at all typical, this will show many schools in a poor light even when their students move ahead during the school year at a rate comparable to that of students in schools deemed to be performing adequately. An accountability system that monitors progress fall to spring, perhaps relative to an expected summer gain baseline (Downey, von Hippel, & Hughes, 2005), would be more appropriate for gauging a school's effectiveness. The current arrangement is useful for identifying need, but little more, and certainly not for apportioning blame.

REFERENCES

Alexander, K. L. (1997). Public schools and the public good. *Social Forces, 76*(1), 1–30.

Berliner, D. (2006). Our impoverished view of educational reform. *Teachers College Record, 108*(6), 949–995.

Berliner, D. C., & Biddle, B. J. (1995). *The manufactured crisis: Myths, fraud and the attack on America's public schools.* Reading, MA: Addison-Wesley.

Borman, G. D., & Dowling, N. M. (2006). The longitudinal achievement effects of multi-year summer school: Evidence from the Teach Baltimore randomized field trial. *Educational Evaluation and Policy Analysis, 28*(1), 25–48.

Burkam, D. T., Ready, D. D., Lee, V. E., & LoGerfo, L. F. (2004). Social-class differences in summer learning between kindergarten and first grade: Model specification and estimation. *Sociology of Education, 77*(1), 1–31.

Ceci, S. J., & Papierno, P. B. (2005). The rhetoric and reality of gap closing: When the "have-nots" gain but the "haves" gain even more. *American Psychologist, 60,* 149–160.

Chin, T., & Phillips, M. (2004). Social reproduction and child-rearing practices: Social class, children's agency, and the summer activity gap. *Sociology of Education, 77*(3), 185–210.

Coleman, J. S., Campbell, E. Q., Hobson, C. J., McPartland, J., Mood, A., Weinfeld, F. D., & York, R. L. (1966). *Equality of educational opportunity.* Washington, DC: U.S. Government Printing Office.

Cooper, H., Charlton, K., Valentine, J. C., & Muhlenbruck, L. (2000). Making the most of summer school: A meta-analytic and narrative review [Monograph]. *Society for Research in Child Development, 65*(1, No. 260). Ann Arbor, MI: Society for Research in Child Development.

Cooper, H., Nye, B., Charlton, K., Lindsay, J., & Greathouse, S. (1996). The effects of summer vacation on achievement test scores: A narrative and meta-analytic review. *Review of Educational Research, 66*(3), 227–268.

Dougherty, K. J. (1996). Opportunity-to-learn standards: A sociological critique. *Sociology of Education,* (extra issue), 40–66.

Downey, D. B., von Hippel, P. T., & Broh, B. (2004). Are schools the great equalizer? Cognitive inequality during the summer months and the school year. *American Sociological Review, 69*(5), 613–635.

Downey, D. B., von Hippel, P. T., & Hughes, M. (2005, August). *Are "failing" schools really failing? Using seasonal comparisons to evaluate school effectiveness.* Presentation at the American Sociological Association, Education Section, Montreal.

Entwisle, D. R., Alexander, K. L., & Olson, L. S. (1997). *Children, schools and inequality.* Boulder, CO: Westview Press.

Farkas, G., & Beron, K. (2004). The detailed age trajectory of oral vocabulary knowledge: Differences by class and race. *Social Science Research, 33*(3), 464–497.

Grissmer, D. W., Kirby, S. N., Berends, M., & Williamson, S. (1994). *Student achievement and the changing American family.* Santa Monica, CA: RAND.

Hart, B., & Risley, R. (1995). *Meaningful differences in the everyday experience of young American children.* Baltimore: Paul H. Brookes.

Hauser, R. M. (1995). The bell curve. *Contemporary Sociology, 24*(2), 149–153.

Heyns, B. (1978). *Summer learning and the effects of schooling.* New York: Academic.

Heyns, B. (1987). Schooling and cognitive development: Is there a season for learning? *Child Development, 58*(5), 1151–1160.

Karweit, N., Ricciuti, A., & Thompson, B. (1994). *Summer learning revisited: Achievement profiles of prospects' first grade cohort* (Unpublished manuscript). Washington, DC: Abt Associates.

Kerckhoff, A. C., Raudenbush, S. W., & Glennie, E. (2001). Education, cognitive skill, and labor force outcomes. *Sociology of Education, 74*(1), 1–24.

Kozol, J. (1991). *Savage inequalities: Children in America's schools.* New York: Crown.

Krueger, A. B. (1998). Reassessing the view that American schools are broken. *FRBNY Economic Policy Review, 4*(1), 29–43.

Lee, J. (2002). Racial and ethnic achievement gap trends: Revising the progress toward equity. *Educational Researcher, 31*(1), 3–12.

Lee, V. E., & Burkam, D. T. (2002). *Inequality at the starting gate.* Washington, DC: Economic Policy Institute.

Murnane, R. J. (1975). *The impact of school resources on the learning of inner city children.* Cambridge, MA: Ballinger.

O'Brien, D. M. (1998, October). *Family and school effects on the cognitive growth of minority and disadvantaged elementary students.* Presentation at the Association for Public Policy Analysis and Management, New York.

Phillips, M., Crouse, J., & Ralph, J. (1998). Does the black-white test score gap widen after children enter school? In C. Jencks & M. Phillips (Eds.), *The black-white test score gap* (pp. 229–272). Washington, DC: Brookings.

Ramey, C. T., Campbell, F. A., & Blair, C. (1998). Enhancing the life course for high-risk children: Results from the Abecedarian project. In J. Crane (Ed.), *Social programs that work* (pp. 163–183). New York: Russell Sage Foundation.

Reardon, S. F. (2003). *Sources of inequality: The growth of racial/ethnic and socioeconomic test score gaps in kindergarten and first grade* (Working Paper No. 03005). University Park, PA: Population Research Institute, Pennsylvania State University.

Reynolds. A. J., & Temple, J. A. (1998). Extended early childhood intervention and school achievement: Age thirteen findings from the Chicago longitudinal study. *Child Development, 69*(1), 231–246.

Rothstein, R. (2002). *Classes and schools: Using social, economic, and educational reform to close the black-white achievement gap.* Washington, DC: Economic Policy Institute.

Schweinhart, L. J., & Weikart, D. P. (1998). High/scope Perry preschool program effects at age twenty-seven. In J. Crane (Ed.), *Social programs that work* (pp. 148–162). New York: Russell Sage Foundation.

THE FIRST AND SECOND DIGITAL DIVIDES

Paul Attewell

The rate of advances in technology is mindboggling! Students entering our highly technological world without skills to keep abreast of new technology cannot be competitive in the global market-place. Thus, schools must not only keep on top of new technologies but prepare students for this ever-changing technological world. Paul Attewell discusses the effects of the digital divide that finds poor and minority families and students on "the other side" of the divide. Schools can play a signifi-cant role in preparing students for 21st-century jobs. Realizing the impact a digital divide could have on the United States, governments and businesses have donated computers and Internet connections to schools in low-income communities. However, access to computers is only half of the concern. Actual usage is also critical, and usage differs by socioeconomic status. As Attewell describes, working-class students use computers for different reasons than students of higher socioeconomic status, and that leaves these students at a disadvantage in the long run.

Questions to consider for this reading:

1. What does Attewell mean by the first and second digital divides?
2. What happens to those who are left behind in the digital world?
3. Why is the digital divide the biggest civil rights issue of our times?
4. How would conflict theorists interpret the digital divide?

A new social problem—the digital divide—has captured the attention of politicians and philanthropists in Amer-ica. Poor and minority families are less likely than other families to have access to computers or the Internet, creating a technology gap between "information haves" and "information have-nots."

Policy makers have responded to this threat in an unusually proactive way, trying to head off a new social problem before it has fully emerged. Former president Bill Clinton pro-posed a $2.1 billion tax incentive for busi-nesses to donate computers and related services to poor schools and communities (Lacey, 2000). The U.S. Senate considered a National Digital Empowerment Act that would double funding for school technology ([Digital Empow-erment Act of 2000]), and the governor of Maine announced a plan to provide every seventh-grade student in his state with a laptop computer (["A Governor Would Give,"] 2000).

Meanwhile, several corporations have initi-ated a home-computer benefit for employees who do not already own computers, and other high-tech firms and their philanthropies are financing the creation of computer clubhouses in minority communities and providing technology training for public school teachers. Trade unions are also becoming involved; two have already obtained home computers for their members during collective bargaining. Clearly, the challenge of bridging the digital divide appeals to political, business, and labor leaders alike.

The idea that many African Americans and other minorities are falling further behind in their ability to participate in a modern economy has seized the popular imagination on both sides of the color line. Unequal access to computing at home and in school provides fuel for this nightmare. It conjures up images of poor minority youths receiving an inadequate education because their schools lack computers and Internet access, later to be refused employment because they are unfamiliar with core technologies and skills required for manipulating information. Recent remarks by Henry Louis Gates, Jr., show the depth of African Americans' concern. Recalling historical repression that denied African Americans communicative freedom via the "mastery of letters and mastery of drums," Gates (2000, 72) argued: "Today, however, blacks are facing a new form of denial to the tools of literacy, this time in the guise of access to the digital-knowledge economy."

In a similar vein, the head of the Federal Communications Commission in the Clinton administration (who is an African American) contended that the digital divide constitutes "the main civil rights challenge of this new millennium" (Labaton, 2000, A12). However, this contention was derided by his successor in the Bush administration, who said that he thought that the *digital divide* is a dangerous term and joked: "I think there is a Mercedes Divide. I'd like to have one; I can't afford one" (Labaton, 2001, C1).

The effort to avoid what Gates (2000) termed "cyber-segregation" has energized wealthy individuals, corporations, philanthropies, and many in government. Schools in poor neighborhoods are being wired for the Internet. Companies are donating used computers, and libraries are providing technological outreach to those who cannot afford to own computers. As demonstrations of concern and social inclusion, these are honorable; as symbolic politics, they have captured the public's attention. But is providing access to computer technology an effective policy instrument for reducing social inequality?

THE FIRST DIGITAL DIVIDE: ACCESS

Recent evidence indicates that minorities and the poor are less likely to own computers and have Internet access at home than are whites and more affluent households. Equally disturbing, from 1994 to 2000, the technology gap between blacks and whites widened, giving the impression that the problem is not correcting itself over time (U.S. Department of Commerce, 2000). As computer prices have fallen substantially, however, Americans of all races are buying home personal computers (PCs) at a fast rate, suggesting that the racial gap in computer ownership and Internet access will close.

These disparities in access are driven, in large part, by income inequality and/or educational differences, rather than by race. At higher levels of income and education, there are minimal ethnic or racial differences in Internet access or computer ownership. If computer ownership continues its rapid spread among middle-income families, as seems likely, the digital divide will shift to the bottom fifth of the income distribution, demarcating families with incomes below $15,000 from the rest of our society. This is a racially heterogeneous stratum already facing severe educational and economic disadvantages. Nevertheless, roughly 19 percent of this poor group already have computers, and falling prices may bring this technology to more of them.

The availability of computers and Internet access in schools (grades K–12) provides another arena for disadvantage. At first glance, school technology fits a digital divide scenario quite well. The percentage of public schools with access to the Internet jumped from 35 percent in 1994 to 95 percent in 1999, but schools that serve the poor still have less computing equipment and slower web connections. Public schools that serve the poorest populations average 16 children per computer, while more affluent schools average 7 students per computer (Williams, 2000).

THE SECOND DIGITAL DIVIDE: COMPUTER USE

Studies of computer *use* in schools present a contrasting picture to the number of computers per student. Studies of the National Assessment of Educational Progress (NAEP) in the mid- to late 1990s found that African American and Hispanic fourth graders were *more likely* than white fourth graders to report almost daily use of computers in their school-work (Coley, Cradler, & Engle, 1997; Wenglinsky, 1998). Poor and urban students also reported more frequent computer use at school than did more affluent and suburban students. But not all uses of computers have equivalent educational benefits. These figures obscure the second digital divide: social differences in the ways computers are used at school and at home.

Computers at School

Whether the digital divide constitutes a caste-like division in society or is only a temporary feature of the rapid diffusion of computers, the question remains, Does the lack of access to computing seriously affect children's life chances? Here, the best guide is the research literature on the impact of computing on academic and work skills.

Unfortunately, what the public usually reads are the most extreme or striking statements. Publishers prefer prophetic statements that information technology will utterly restructure education and turn every child into an intellectual dynamo or the opposite, dystopian warnings that computers are warping children's minds. Despite their opposite prognoses, these extreme scenarios share certain characteristics. Both grossly underestimate the moderating influence of social institutions, which constrain new technologies and limit the amount of time that school-children spend with them.

Schools do not easily abandon their traditions and curricula or rebuild around new technologies even when they want to. They face competing demands from parents, teachers, children, and state testing agencies and suffer severe limitations on spending and staff time. Schools find it difficult to fulfill their current educational and social mandates, let alone embrace a visionary new one. The result is often a compromise: Educational computing adapts to schools at least as much as it "transforms" them (Cuban, 1986, 1999). Classroom teachers take from computing what they find immediately useful and practical and eschew the rest. Children do likewise.

Schools tend to build computer labs because they lack the funds to put a computer on every child's desk and because of a tradition of sending students to separate classes for subjects that require instruction by specialists. Nevertheless, thousands of "ordinary" teachers have been using computers in their nonlab classrooms for a decade or more. Children are obviously enriched by those experiences, and some exhibit positive but not startling advances in measurable skills. It is possible, then, that teachers have adopted computer technology in modest doses because they perceive it to be of modest utility. Unfortunately, that is not acceptable to visionaries. Self-seeking schools are sabotaging their vision. When there is one computer per child in regular classrooms and many teachers are computer savvy, the radically subversive educational potential of technology will be unleashed (Papert, 1993).

Technological dystopians are no less convinced of the powerful negative effects of technology on children. The most measured critique is the book *Failure to Connect* (Healy, 1998). Once the principal of an elementary school and a self-styled LOGO enthusiast, Healy has become a technological Cassandra. Although she discusses many potential dangers of children's computer use, from vision problems to bad posture, Healy's greatest concern is that computers will displace authentic childhood learning experiences. She asked: "Will our children ever be alone with their thoughts or emotions in an age when we perpetually clog their brains with artificial stimulation?" (p. 309). For young children, Healy worries that computer use will cut into the playtime and physical activities that are important for cognitive and emotional development. . . .

Although there is solid evidence of academic payoffs from school computing, success is by no means assured. Some well-financed interventions have yielded disappointment. The best known among them is Apple Computer's Classroom of Tomorrow project that initially created computing-intensive environments in five schools. Although students' attitudes toward learning improved over a five-year period, students' skills in tests of mathematics, reading, and vocabulary did not (Baker, Gearhart, & Herman, 1994).

Even the successful outcomes documented by researchers in demonstration projects are a poor guide to the effects of educational computing in ordinary classrooms and homes.

Demonstration experiments typically use highly motivated teachers, who have been properly trained in the use of the particular software being studied and who draw upon extensive technical support provided by the researchers. The children receive a lot of enthusiasm and attention, beyond just the computing. Consequently, these studies represent a best-case scenario, the upper bound to what one may reasonably expect of educational technology in a resource-rich school environment with well-trained teachers.

Most schools do not have plenty of powerful networked computers, however. Many make do with old software and hardware because their technology budgets are modest. Most teachers have limited time for training themselves on technology or for developing a curriculum tailored to computers. Finally, few schools can afford technicians to support educational computing. The real environment of computing in American public schools is therefore quite different from that provided in demonstration projects and experiments.

One large-scale study that provides insights into computing in "ordinary" schools analyzed data from the NAEP, which tests schoolchildren across the nation in subjects such as math, reading, and writing. Wenglinsky (1998) examined whether students' frequency of using computers at school was associated with higher scores on math tests. To assess the influence of computing per se, he first removed the confounding effects of parental education, race, and family income. The subsequent results were startling. For fourth graders, both home and school computing were associated with *lower* math scores. The more time a student spent with computers, the lower his or her scores. For eighth graders, the frequency of using school computers was also associated with lower math scores, while home computer use had a positive relationship.

There are two plausible interpretations for these surprising findings. Either current computing efforts are so educationally maladroit that they impair learning, or causation runs in the opposite direction, such that students with weaker skills are being given more time on school computers. I suspect the latter is true, that computer labs are being used to occupy the time of academically less-skilled children. Survey evidence also indicates that economically disadvantaged and minority students are more likely to use computers daily, use drill-and-practice more, and have teachers with less computer training (Coley et al., 1997; National Center for Education Statistics, 1999; Wenglinsky, 1998). Taken together such findings point to a second digital divide: unequal outcomes may stem from differences between affluent and disadvantaged students in what they do with the technology, once they have access.

Computers at Home

Studies of home computing further illustrate the danger of a second digital divide. In the mid-1980s, Giacquinta, Bauer, and Levin (1993) undertook a detailed observational study of children from affluent families using computers in their homes. Even among these privileged children, little educational computing was going on. About half these families had purchased computers with their children's education in mind. Nevertheless, most children avoided educational products and preferred playing noneducational games instead. About half the children were using word processing for homework assignments. At most, one in five children was using the technology to develop skills in math, reading, science, or critical thinking, and most of this use was sporadic and of short duration.

Those children who came the closest to involvement with academic computing had received substantial encouragement and involvement from their parents and older siblings. Most parents seemed content to allow their children to choose what to do with computers, and most children worked alone at the machines. The authors concluded, first, that almost all children turn home computers into game machines and word processors, rather than into learning resources, and second, that the "social envelope" around computing—the attitudes, competencies, and involvement of parents and siblings—is crucial to any kind of educational outcome. As one may imagine, this social envelope had a lot to do with parents' educational background and occupational standing. By implication, children in poor families would be disadvantaged when using home computers for education.

To test this idea, a colleague and I examined the consequences of having a computer at home for eighth graders' academic skills, as measured by reading and math scores (Attewell & Battle, 1999). Even among children whose families *did* own computers, the benefits of having a home computer were substantially greater for children from more affluent and educated families than from poorer and less educated ones. Boys benefited more than did girls and whites more than minorities. These disparities remained apparent even after parental involvement in a child's education, trips to museums, and several other forms of social and cultural capital were controlled.

It is therefore naive to expect the provision of computers to reduce educational differences among children in any simple or automatic way.

On the contrary, computers may, at least initially, exacerbate existing educational differences between social classes. Compounding this problem is a disheartening but real possibility that computing for already-disadvantaged children may be dominated by games at home and unsupervised drill-and-practice or games at school, while affluent children enjoy educationally richer fare with more adult involvement. If this is the case, all the resources, idealism, and goodwill that are being expended to make sure that our children have access to the technology will have been wasted.

The new policies on the digital divide grapple with the technological dimension of social exclusion and inequality, addressing this one strand of disadvantage separately from the larger complex of educational and economic woes that afflict the poor. Most current policy proposals provide the technology, assuming that access is the critical barrier. In the short run, that emphasis may make sense, but social inequalities will make themselves felt, even if we are able to provide a computer on every desk. Affluent children will leverage their ample resources of social and cultural capital to excel in this new arena of skill.

Computer literacy may prove a boon to some disadvantaged children, but computer skills are more mixed with conceptual and language abilities than the current idea of computer literacy envisions. It would be helpful to have a richer picture of the skills that separate computer virtuosi from ordinary computer users in the workplace, as a guide to training youths (and adults) in ways that will make them most employable. Lacking this understanding, current technology literacy courses are helpful but hardly powerful interventions that address only the basics.

In some respects, computer technology is serving as a Trojan horse. Politicians who are loathe to increase expenditures aimed at disadvantaged youths make an exception when interventions are draped in the mystique of new technology. The digital divide is the latest effort to encourage our reluctant social and political leaders to ameliorate inequality and social exclusion. We must wait to see whether "Let them have Pentiums" proves more practical than "Let them eat cake."

REFERENCES

Attewell, P., & Battle, J. (1999). Home computers and school performance. *The Information Society, 15*(1), 1–10.

Baker, E. L., Gearhart, M., & Herman, J. (1994). Evaluating the Apple classrooms of tomorrow. In E. L. Baker & H. F. O'Neil (Eds.), *Technology assessment in education and training* (pp. 173–198). Hillsdale, NJ: Lawrence Erlbaum.

Coley, R., Cradler, J., & Engle, P. (1997). *Computers and classrooms: The status of technology in U.S. schools.* Princeton, NJ: Educational Testing Service.

Cuban, L. (1986). *Teachers and machines.* New York: Teachers College Press.

Cuban, L. (1999, August 22). Don't blame teachers for low computer use in classrooms. *Los Angeles Times Education.* Retrieved from http://articles .latimes.com/1999/aug/22/opinion/op-2609

Digital Empowerment Act of 2000, S. 2229, 106th Cong. (2000). Retrieved from http://www.govtrack .us/congress/bill.xpd?bill=h106-3897&tab

Gates, H. L. (2000, January 12). Black to the future. *Education Week,* p. 72.

Giacquinta, J., Bauer, J., & Levin, J. (1993). *Beyond technology's promise: An examination of children's educational computing at home.* New York: Cambridge University Press.

A governor would give every student a laptop. (2000, March 3). *New York Times,* p. A12.

Healy, J. M. (1998). *Failure to connect: How computers affect our children's minds—for better and worse.* New York: Simon & Schuster.

Labaton, S. (2000, May 15). His civil rights challenge: Equal access in technology. *New York Times,* p. A12.

Labaton, S. (2001, February 7). New FCC chief would curb agency reach. *New York Times,* p. C1.

Lacey, M. (2000, February 3). Clinton enlists top-grade help for plan to increase computer use. *New York Times,* p. A25.

National Center for Education Statistics. (1999). *The condition of education 1999.* Washington, DC: U.S. Government Printing Office.

Papert, S. (1993). *The children's machine: Rethinking school in the age of the computer.* New York: Basic Books.

U.S. Department of Commerce. (2000). *Falling through the net: Toward digital inclusion.* Washington, DC: Author.

Wenglinsky, H. (1998). *Does it compute? The relationship between educational technology and student achievement in mathematics.* Princeton, NJ: Policy Information Center of the Educational Testing Service.

Williams, C. (2000). *Internet access in U.S. public schools and classrooms 1994–99.* Washington, DC: National Center for Education Statistics.

Projects for Further Exploration

1. Using an academic database, look up *"student"* and *"summer learning."* Relate this to family and community influences.

2. After reading the selections in this chapter, construct an interview form that includes various environmental influences on schools. Now interview a superintendent, principal, or several teachers in a school district in your area to learn how environmental (social context) factors influence them and the decision-making processes in the district. If you interviewed individuals in different school roles, how did their answers differ? Projects in later chapters will ask you to collect additional data on this school district.

3. After reading the Attewell article, discuss how technology affects different students. Now select a new type of technology, such as iPods, iPads, or iPhones, and write about how this is likely to have different impacts on different groups.

4

Schools as Organizations

Formal and Informal Education

The bell rings, lockers slam, conversations end, and classroom doors shut as the school day begins. We are all familiar with these signs that the formal school day is about to start. Schools provide the framework for meeting certain goals of societies and preparing young people for future statuses and roles. School organizations, just as other organizations, have formally stated goals, criteria for membership, a hierarchy of offices, and a number of informal goals, such as friendship and sharing of interests. Although individual schools around the world share a number of similarities in their structures and roles, they also have their own distinct personalities.

This chapter begins our analysis of the formal and informal parts of educational organizations: the structure, stated goals, and what "really" happens in schools. Organizationally, schools are divided into classrooms, the day into periods, teachers into subject areas and rank, and students into groups by grades or performance results on examinations (Hurn, 1993; Parsons, 1959). Like other formal organizations, schools have memberships composed of individuals holding different status positions necessary to carry out the functions and goals of the school. Each position holder has certain roles to perform—administrating, teaching, learning, and providing support functions such as driving the bus and preparing the meals. These activities are the processes of schools, the means to meet goals.

The broad functions and goals of schools are common knowledge and shared by many people as pointed out in the reading in this chapter by Mary Haywood Metz. However, there is conflict over how to carry out those functions and goals—what curriculum to teach, what courses to offer, and how to best prepare all students for society. As discussed in the previous chapter, conflicts can occur between the school and its environment, between the school and school board, with different groups in communities, and between schools and the government. Even religious and political interest groups want a say in what schools teach and how they teach it. These conflicting goals can be seen in readings throughout the text.

Although the organizational goals of schools call for educating all students, not all students meet the requirements for passing to the next grade level or for graduating, especially when exams are administered to promote and graduate students. However, to give up on the students—that is, to "fire" them—would be to lose societal resources. Therefore, schools cannot be run by the same rules and under the same efficiency model as business organizations. Schools are expected, according to their goals, to prepare students for the next generation by transmitting shared knowledge, societal values, and ideals;

foster cognitive and emotional growth; and sort and select students into different categories—college material, gifted, talented, slow, rebellious, and so forth—with consequences for future adult status.

The readings in this chapter discuss educational organizations from large systems to individual classrooms. Overseeing the schools are state and federal organizations that make decisions about laws governing schools and money spent in schools, as described in Chapter 3. Local school boards translate these broad mandates into policies to meet the goals of the local district. To begin our exploration of schools as organizations, Rebecca Barr and Robert Dreeben focus on schools and classrooms. Their reading covers events that take place in schools, the division of labor in schools, the roles of participants, the organization of classrooms, and how time structures the day in schools and classrooms.

Anthony S. Bryk continues the discussion in organizing schools for improvement, comparing school organizations that work with those that don't work. Based on a large study of Chicago schools, he points out the essential elements for school improvement and how these can lead to better student achievement. Debates continue over the role of school boards in determining the organization of schools and whether states or local governments should take control of schools. Gene I. Maeroff discusses the roles school boards can and should play in strong educational systems.

Discussion about how to make schools more effective for student achievement stimulate social science research. A key research question has focused on a defining dimension—the most effective size of schools and classrooms; policies and funding reflect this interest, if not always the research findings (Honig, 2009). The reading by Bruce Biddle and David Berliner in Chapter 2 reviewed studies of class size and the impact of class size on student learning, considering the effect of size on school organizations and processes of teaching and learning. Linda Darling-Hammond's reading in Chapter 8 also touches on class size, as well as a number of other school practices that can result in improving school quality.

Behind the formal rules, classroom and school size and structure, and goal statements is another layer to explore—the informal system, or what really happens in schools. Whenever you enter a classroom, especially for the first time, interact with peers or teachers, or determine what you really need to do for a class, you are dealing with the informal system. In the second part of this chapter we look at this aspect of what goes on in school organizations and its importance for the overall understanding of educational systems.

Students learn both the formal and informal systems, each quite important to understanding how schools work. In fact, Philip Jackson (1968) argues that success in school requires mastery of both systems, even though there are contradictions between them. Students who have problems in school are often the ones who have not learned to balance the two systems or to negotiate the contradictions. The "hidden curriculum," as labeled by Snyder (1971) in his book by the same name, defines this system as "implicit demands (as opposed to the explicit obligations of the visible curriculum) that are found in every learning institution and which students have to find out and respond to in order to survive within it" (p. 6). These unwritten regulations and unintended consequences are an education in themselves and determine how we learn to cope with the unspoken expectations in life.

Sociologists who study education ask numerous questions about the role of the informal system in selection and allocation of students: how students and teachers learn to cope with the expectations of school; feelings about themselves and others that students bring to school and develop in school; the classroom and school climate, or culture; and power relationships in schools between teachers, students, and peers.

The not-so-obvious aspects of the informal system of schooling include the subtle messages and power relationships inherent in any system. These aspects of schooling cannot be studied by looking at lists of goals, school documents, descriptions of role responsibilities, or recorded test scores. In fact, most studies of the informal system are ethnographies (as described in Chapter 2), or carefully documented observations of interactions, behaviors, and the atmosphere in schools that record the "school climate." Two examples are included in this chapter, one by Harry Gracey and another by Mary Haywood Metz.

School climate, or culture, which makes up one aspect of the informal system, refers to several parts of the school experience: the interactions that result from grouping students, the resistance of some students to schooling, and teachers' expectations of students that affect their achievement levels. Factors inside and outside the school influence school climate (Ballantine & Hammack, 2012). Sociologists refer to the school value climate, learning climate, and power dynamics, among other types of climate. For instance, "effective schools" studies consider both the formal and informal systems in school, making recommendations on how to change school climate to make schools more conducive to learning for all children (Brookover, Erickson, & McEvoy, 1996). These studies measure school climate by considering teacher expectations, academic norms, students' sense of futility (giving up on school), role definitions, grouping patterns, and instructional practices.

Several of the best-known studies of the informal system use ethnographic methods in which the researchers immerse themselves in the school settings to observe the more subtle workings of schools and messages students receive from schools. These studies have generally fallen into the categories of conflict theory or interaction or interpretive theory. Conflict theorists, as described in Chapter 1, see in the hidden curriculum a social control and power element that reproduces the social class of students. Working-class students find that they are not fully integrated into the educational system; they learn to cope with boredom in school, which prepares them for the boredom of future jobs. Consider the following examples.

In a now classic ethnography, Paul Willis (1979) describes the activities of two groups of English students, the "lads" and the "ear'oles." The lads experience an informal hidden curriculum that reinforces their working-class status and prepares them for factory work. The ear'oles suck up the knowledge from teachers in preparation for further education and success in higher level professional jobs in the work world. The lads show resistance to school in their "counterschool culture" and create a "shopfloor culture" of chauvinism, toughness, and machismo to cope with the unpleasant situations they face in the middle-class school culture and hidden curriculum. In another ethnography, Jay MacLeod (2009) provides a vivid description of two groups of kids from a poor Chicago housing project and their experiences negotiating the educational system. He talks about the differences in the groups, one group of boys with high aspirations and the other whose members have given up on the system, and how those differences are influenced by the messages and experiences they receive in the informal system of the school. Unfortunately, in both the Willis and MacLeod studies, whether they give up or have high aspirations, all students tend to have trouble succeeding in life in general.

The readings in this chapter continue the ethnographic tradition by taking us through the lives of children experiencing the informal system of education, starting with kindergarten. Students learn both the formal and informal rules of the classroom from their earliest experiences in schools. Harry Gracey describes a day in the life of a kindergarten class for the teacher and the students. He points out both the formal lesson plans and time schedule and the informal learning that takes place in lessons about punctuality, obedience, respect, and other rules that govern the informal aspects of the classroom. This illustrates the interaction between formal goals of schools and informal lessons learned by children from teachers and peers to prepare them to move to the next levels of schooling.

Mary Haywood Metz's ethnographic study of classrooms included interviews with teachers in eight diverse settings. In studying aspects of the informal system, Metz found a "common script" in schools. All the schools were recognizably similar in many respects, but she found clear differences in the way the script was carried out based on the dominant social-class background of the students and the informal system this created in the schools.

We end this chapter with a provocative view of school organizational decision making by Diane Ravitch, a former Assistant Secretary of Education under President Clinton. She examines the current organizational structure of schools, arguing that recent movement by districts toward using a business model that includes charter schools is depriving communities of their role in school policy decision making. After studying these readings, you should have a clearer idea of what the formal organization of schools means, what sociologists of education look for in the formal organization of schools, and an exploration of informal systems in schools.

REFERENCES

Ballantine, J., & Hammack, F. (2012). *The sociology of education, A systematic approach* (7th ed.). Upper Saddle River, NJ: Prentice Hall.

Brookover, W., Erickson, F. J., & McEvoy, A. W. (1996). *Creating effective schools: An in-service program.* Holmes Beach, FL: Learning Publications.

Honig, M. I. (2009). No small thing: School district central office bureaucracies and the implementation of new small autonomous schools initiatives. *American Educational Research Journal, 46*(2), 387–422. Retrieved from http://aerj.aera.net

Hurn, C. J. (1993). *The limits and possibilities of schooling: An introduction to sociology of education* (3rd ed.). Boston: Allyn & Bacon.

Jackson, P. E. (1968). *Life in classrooms.* New York: Holt, Rinehart and Winston.

MacLeod, J. (2009). *Ain't no makin' it: Leveled aspirations in a low-income neighborhood* (2nd ed.). Boulder, CO: Westview Press.

Parsons, T. (1959). The school class as a social system: Some of its functions in American society. *Harvard Educational Review, 29*(4), 297–318.

Snyder, B. R. (1971). *The hidden curriculum.* New York: Alfred A. Knopf.

Willis, P. (1979). *Learning to labor: How working class kids get working class jobs.* Aldershot, Hampshire, England: Saxon House.

How Schools Work

Rebecca Barr and Robert Dreeben

In this excerpt from Rebecca Barr and Robert Dreeben's book, *How Schools Work*, the authors discuss the functioning of schools and classrooms. They examine different levels of organization in school districts from district offices to instructional groups in classrooms; they identify distinct events that take place in each unit, and how what happens in one unit affects others. They also discuss the roles and division of labor among some participants. Within classrooms there are instructional groups, often by ability level of students. Organization of time is another determinant of how schools work. From the length of the class period and day to the number of days in a year, the way time is structured affects opportunities to learn. The importance of this excerpt is in providing the methods and framework needed to understand the organization of educational systems and how schools work. The reading provides an example of the levels of analysis in the open systems model.

Questions to consider for this reading:

1. What are topics to consider and methods that can be used to study how schools work?

2. How do these articles relate to the open systems model and levels of organization?

3. What is the division of labor that influences classroom activities, directly and indirectly?

4. Relate what you read here to a school system with which you are familiar.

Our formulation begins with the idea that school systems are organizations that like others can be readily subject to sociological analysis. In all organizations labor is divided, which means that different activities are carried out in the different parts and that the parts are connected to each other in a coherent way. The parts of school systems are very familiar. They consist of a central administration with jurisdiction over a school district as well as local administrations situated in each school with responsibility for what happens therein. The business of schooling, mainly instruction, takes place in classrooms run by teachers; and teachers preside not only over classes but over parts of them as well when they rely upon grouped forms of instruction. We will show how the work that gets done in district offices, schools, classes, and instructional groups is different in character, that these separate jurisdictions are locations for carrying on different sorts of activities. Indeed, this proposition is true for teachers as classroom instructors and as group instructors in that teachers do different things in organizing a class from what they do while instructing subgroups within it. Part of the answer to our question of how schools work, then, is to be found by identifying the distinct events happening at each level of school system organization.

A second part of the answer can be found by discovering how the events characteristic of one level influence those taking place at another. It would be a strange organization indeed if the parts were hermetically sealed off from each other; if, for example, what the principal did had no bearing on what teachers did and if what teachers did made no difference for what students did and learned. Yet it is precisely the failure to come up with satisfactory answers to these questions that has caused so much grief in our understanding of educational effects. The answer must come from identifying correctly what the activities are and from being able to trace their antecedents and effects across pathways that connect one level to another.

The third part of the answer pertains not so much to what to look for as it does to how to look for it. School systems, like other forms of social existence, are characterized by variability. We can learn about their workings by attending to the different ways that comparable parts act: different schools in the same system, different classes in the same school, different groups in the same class. What can vary in these levels of school organization is the way in which resources are allocated, transformed, and used. A particular resource, like books, may be purchased by the district office. All fourth grade mathematics texts, for example, can then be distributed to each elementary school, thence to be stocked in each fourth grade class. Thus, a simple process of resource transmission takes place. From there, teachers in the same school may use the text in almost identical ways or in vastly different ways depending on how they organize their instructional programs. The program itself determines the instructional use, and hence the meaning, of the resource. Accordingly, insofar as the school is no more than a transmission belt for transporting books from the district

office to the classroom, school-by-school comparisons will show similar activities. Class-by-class comparisons in textbook use, however, might show sharp contrasts. Depending upon the nature of those class contrasts, they may average out to show no school differences or bunch up to show marked school differences. In either case, it is the comparison of events at the same level—school and class in these examples—that tells us what is going on.

THE FORMULATION

Levels of Organization

Labor in school systems is divided; it is differentiated by task into different organizational levels in a hierarchical arrangement. While we customarily think about hierarchies as pertaining to relations of authority, rank, and power, they not only are manifestations of stratification and status distinction, but also represent organizational differentiation, a manifestation of labor being specialized and other resources distributed to different locations, of the elements of production having been both separated and tied together in some workable arrangement. We are concerned here with hierarchy in this latter sense.

In an educational division of labor, school systems comprise several levels of administrative and staff officers as well as "production" workers occupying positions with district, school, and classroom jurisdictions. In addition, school systems are differentiated according to the resources they use, such as time and physical objects—like books—that constitute instructional materials. As we shall indicate shortly, time is a resource that has meaning at all levels of the hierarchy, but its meaning has different manifestations at each level. Textbooks, by contrast, are productive resources only inside classrooms. School systems also contain one additional element: students who are both the clients of the organization, the intended beneficiaries of its services, and, because schools are engaged in effecting change in children, productive resources in their own right because they participate directly and actively in their own learning.

When organizations are differentiated, it is because their parts make distinct contributions to the overall productive enterprise. This means that people located hierarchically at different places perform different kinds of activities; it also means that resources come into play in different ways depending upon where they are utilized in the productive process. A complete formulation of school production, therefore, should identify all relevant combinations of people, time, and material resources at each hierarchical level.

More specifically, school systems characteristically contain a managerial component responsible for centralized financial, personnel, procurement, plant maintenance, and supervisory functions applicable to all their constituent elements. This component is also engaged in direct dealings with agencies of the federal and state governments as well as with locally based interest groups and units of municipal government. Activities occurring at this managerial level have nothing directly to do with running schools or teaching students but rather are concerned with the acquisition of resources, with general supervision, and with the maintenance of relations with the surrounding community including suppliers of labor. We refer to this as the district level of organization; its jurisdiction includes all schools in the district.

Even though districts are divided into levels (elementary and secondary) related to the ages of students, and some are also divided into geographical areas as well as functional units, we are primarily concerned—at the next lower hierarchical level—with schools. Contrary to conventional belief, schools are not organizational units of instruction. They are structures akin to switching yards where children within a given age range and from a designated geographical area are assigned to teachers who bring them into contact with approved learning materials, specified as being appropriate to age or ability, during certain allotted periods of time. Schools deal in potentialities; they assemble a supply of teachers, of students, and of resources over a given period of

time. Their central activities are the assignment of children to specific teachers, the allocation of learning materials to classrooms, the arrangement of a schedule so that all children in the school can be allotted an appropriate amount of time to spend on subjects in the curriculum, and the integration of grades so that work completed in one represents adequate preparation for the next.

These activities are the primary responsibility of school principals; they are core functions peculiar to the school level of organization. This is so because decisions affecting the fate of all classrooms in a school are not likely to be left to individuals (teachers) who have in mind primarily classroom interests rather than whole school interests and whose self-interest puts them in a poor position to settle disputes among equals. Nor are they likely to be left to district-wide administrators, whose locations can be too remote and jurisdictions too widespread to allow them to make informed decisions about local school events.

While these decisions constitute the peculiar core activities of school level administration, they by no means exhaust the responsibilities of school administrators, which frequently include such matters as planning curriculum; establishing disciplinary standards; and making school policies for homework, decorum in public places, and the like. But while such concerns are frequently characteristic of school administration, they are not peculiar to it because district-wide administrators and teachers also participate in them at the school level in fulfilling responsibilities within their own respective jurisdictions.

While instruction is not the business of the school, it is the business of classrooms and of teachers responsible for the direct engagement of students in learning activities. Aggregations of children are assigned to specific teachers who direct their activities and bring them into immediate contact with various sorts of learning materials. These activities are more than potentialities because children's active engagement working with teachers and materials is what enables them to learn.

Because classes contain diverse aggregations of children, it is not automatic that the instruction appropriate for one member of the aggregation will be appropriate for another. Hence, teachers in the lower grades characteristically create an additional level of suborganization to manage activities not easily handled in a grouping as large as the class. For example, in primary grade reading, there are suborganizations called instructional groups that represent still another level of organizational differentiation.

Finally, there are individual students. It is only individuals who work on tasks, and it is only they who learn; so that while work tasks might be set for all students in the class or in a group, the individual members vary in how much work they do and in how much they learn.

We argue here not only that school systems can be described by their constituent organizational levels, but that the events, activities, and organizational forms found at each level should be seen as addressing distinct as well as partially overlapping agendas. Districts, schools, classes, and instructional groups are structurally differentiated from each other; and what is more they make different contributions to the overall operation of the school system. We recognize that not all schools have precisely the same organizational pattern. In the upper elementary grades, for example, formalized instructional groups characteristically used for primary level reading might or might not be employed; and in secondary schools, which lack self-contained classrooms, a departmental level of organization usually appears as does formal tracking that distinguishes students largely on the basis of ability within schools but not within classes. Despite these variations, the general principle of differentiated structures and agendas holds.

Linkages Between Levels

If organizational levels are as distinct as this analysis suggests, how is it possible to think about a coherent production process for the whole school district organization? How should the connections between levels be formulated? We contend that each level of a school system has its own core productive agenda even though certain activities are performed at more than one level. That is, productive events of differing character occur at each level to effect outcomes that are themselves characteristic of each level. For example, a school outcome becomes a productive condition in classes yielding in turn a class outcome; the class outcome in turn becomes a productive element for instructional groups yielding a group outcome; and so on. We see, then, a set of nested hierarchical layers, each having a conditional and contributory relation to events and outcomes occurring at adjacent ones.

Consider an example of how levels of organization are connected to each other to constitute school production. As we observed earlier, classroom characteristics do not directly affect individual learning; they influence the formation of instructional groups. This might seem to be a strange statement since everyone knows that classroom teachers are responsible for instructing all children in a class. However, the teacher's job, we maintain, is first to transform an aggregation of children into an arrangement suitable for establishing an instructional program. In first grade reading, this usually means creating instructional reading groups. Hence, before any instruction takes place, decisions are made about how to arrange the class; whether to teach everyone together in one group, as in recitation; whether to establish subgroups in which only some children work intensively with the teacher while the others proceed by themselves with little supervision; whether to set everyone to work independently at their desks to perform at their own rate such more or less individualized tasks as are contained in workbooks.

The results of these classroom decisions are not instructional, nor do they appear as individual learning. They are alternative grouping arrangements which should be thought of as class outcomes, or values. We must draw a distinction between what teachers do in organizing classes for instruction and the instruction they actually provide for the groupings of children that make up classroom organization. Down the road, those grouping arrangements influence individual learning through a chain of connections consisting of instructional activities. Individual learning, however, is not itself a class outcome. As our story unfolds, we will show how class grouping arrangements determine certain characteristics of the groups composing them, in particular the level of children's ability characteristic of each classroom group. As it turns out, this level of ability is a direct determinant of certain instructional activities undertaken by teachers, who treat differently composed groups in different ways.

One form this treatment takes is the amount of material covered, which we construe as an outcome, or value, created by instructional groups. (Note again: individual learning is not a group outcome any more than it is a class outcome.) Then, depending on how much material children cover over a given span of time, in combination with their own characteristics, they learn proportionally more or less. In sum, group arrangements are the value created at the class level, coverage the value at the group level, and learning the value at the individual level. Note particularly that the activities and outcomes characteristic of each level are qualitatively distinct—grouping, coverage, learning—and that they are linked together in a coherent manner.

Most readers will have recognized that we have been describing aspects of the familiar phenomenon of ability grouping, but not in a familiar way. Instead of simply distinguishing students according to whether they belong to homogeneous or heterogeneous groups, which is the usual (and not very illuminating) way of studying grouping, we have tried to identify distinct though related activities that refer to sets of decisions that constitute class organization, grouped instruction, and individual learning.

This brief analysis shows the concatenation of distinct activities that constitute and surround classroom instruction. An implication of this analysis is that we can take any single educationally relevant resource and trace its manifestations across several hierarchical levels of school system organization. To illustrate the logic of the formulation, we will consider here the resource of time.

A school district administration makes three kinds of decisions about time. The first reveals its responsibilities of law enforcement to the state: the schools must remain open for a stipulated number of days to qualify for state aid. While this enforcement of state law places an outside limit on time available for teaching, it does not bear directly on teaching, instruction, or learning. Furthermore, when the length of the academic year is combined with a determination about the length of the school day, the second type of district decision is made: how much time teachers (and other employees) will work as part of a contractual agreement with suppliers of labor. The third type of decision pertains to when the schools will start and finish each academic year, open and close each day, and recess for vacations, decisions that determine when and whether parents can leave the household for work and arrange for the care of very young children. Basic time considerations, then, at the district level of organization are tied up with law enforcement, labor contracts, and the integration of the school system with households in the community; and district outcomes can be defined in these terms.

School systems, of course, do not hire teachers in general, but teachers who instruct in particular subjects in secondary schools and in a variety of basic skills in elementary schools. Hiring teachers by subject and skill presumes that curricular priorities have been established, which means that decisions have been made about how much time will be devoted to each segment of the curriculum: to English, mathematics, science, foreign languages, and so on, in secondary schools; to reading, arithmetic, science, social studies, and so on, in elementary schools. At the level of schools, these decisions become manifest in the time schedule, a formal statement written in fine-grained time units of how much time will be devoted to each subject matter and to extracurricular pursuits.

The school schedule is really a political document that acknowledges the influences of administrative directives and the preferences of teachers and parents expressing varying views about the welfare of the student body, of individual students, and of different types of students. It embodies past decisions about how much ordinary instruction there will be, in which subjects, at which more or less desirable times, and in which more or less desirable places. It expresses how segregated or desegregated classes will be in response to higher level administrative directives as well as the integration of the handicapped in regular and special classes. These resultant priorities conventionally expressed in the time schedule are an outcome of school level organization.

The curricular priorities expressed in the school time schedule represent temporal constraints upon the work of teachers in classrooms. While in secondary schools the order of classes throughout the day is established by the schedule itself, in elementary schools the teachers themselves arrange activities within the confines of daily time allotments, deciding which activities come earliest in the day, which next, and which last, with some flexibility about how long each successive activity will last. In addition to determining which activities take place during the "better" and "worse" times of the day, teachers also establish, within school guidelines and across parts of the curriculum (reading, arithmetic, science), how long instruction will last in each of a variety of classroom formats (whole class, grouped, individual instruction) and how much time gets wasted through interruptions, poor planning, and transitions between activities. At the classroom level, then, teachers allocate time in ways that bear directly upon instruction by determining the amount of time that students will have available for productive work in various subject areas.

Finally, given the time that teachers make available for productive work, students then decide how much of that time to use and to waste, and in so doing influence the amount they will learn.

What we have done here is to trace the allocation of time through the layers of school system organization to show how it takes on different manifestations as district, school, class, and individual phenomena. We have also shown how the nature of time at one level becomes a time condition for events occurring at the next lower level.

What our formulation does is very simple. It locates productive activities at all levels of the school system that in more common but less precise parlance are known as administration and teaching. It also states that productive activities specific to levels produce outcomes specific to levels. Accordingly, we distinguish carefully between the productive processes that constitute the working of school organization from the outcomes, or values, produced by those processes. They are not the same thing, although they have commonly been confused in discussions about educational effects. The distinction between production and value not only is important conceptually, but provides a principle that ties the parts of the levels of school organization into a coherent pattern.

The formulation also carries us some distance in thinking about how the effectiveness of schools should be viewed. The common practice of using individual achievement (or aggregations of individual achievement) as a primary index to gauge whether schools are productive is of limited value because there are other outcomes that are the direct result of productive processes occurring at higher levels of school system organization. There is no question that achievement is an important outcome at the individual level; it may or may not be an important outcome at other levels, as our previous analyses of time and grouping indicate. Perhaps, for example, the properly understood outcome of instructional groups is a group-specific rate of covering learning materials or the amount of time a teacher makes available for instruction, outcomes that when considered at the individual level are properly construed as conditions of learning. An important class level outcome may be the creation of an appropriate grouping arrangement or the establishment of a productive time schedule, both of which are conditions bearing on the nature of group instruction.

Similarly, at the school level, the important outcomes may be the allocation of time to curricular areas that makes enough time available for basic skill subjects, an assignment of teachers to classes that makes the most appropriate use of their talents or that provides equitable work loads, or the appropriate coordination of skill subjects from year to year so that children are prepared for the work of the succeeding grade. At the district level, perhaps negotiating labor contracts that satisfy employees, administrators, and the taxpayers, or having a satisfactory book and materials procurement policy represent significant outcomes.

ORGANIZING SCHOOLS FOR IMPROVEMENT

Anthony S. Bryk

Two of the worst schools in Chicago make efforts to raise student achievement. One is impressively successful, but one fails. What is the difference? Anthony Bryk addresses the differences between schools that succeed and those that fail, using findings from their major study results of hundreds of elementary schools. The researchers identify five essential supports for school improvement. These five essential supports touch on many aspects of school organization and relations to parents and community, the environment surrounding schools. The author reminds us that schools are complex organizations with many subsystems that must be considered in efforts to improve teaching and learning for students.

Questions to consider for this reading:

1. How do the five essential supports for school improvement work to help schools?

2. How do these five essential supports relate to levels of organizations described by Barr and Dreeban in the previous reading?

3. What are some challenges that we might encounter when applying these five essential supports to effect school reform?

Alexander Elementary School and Hancock Elementary School began the 1990s as two of the worst schools in Chicago in terms of math and reading achievement. Only two miles apart, the schools are in bordering neighborhoods and appear similar in many ways. Both enrolled nearly 100% minority students from families considered low income.

During the 1990s, both launched an array of initiatives aimed at boosting student achievement. Hancock moved impressively forward, while Alexander barely moved the needle on improvement. How did Hancock "beat the odds" while Alexander failed to do so?

This puzzle led us to undertake a systematic longitudinal investigation of *hundreds* of elementary schools in Chicago, just like Alexander and Hancock. Beginning in 1990, the Consortium on Chicago School Research initiated an intensive longitudinal study of the internal workings and external community conditions that distinguished improving elementary schools from those that failed to improve. That unique 15-year database allowed us to develop, test, and validate a framework of essential supports for school improvement. These data provided an extraordinary window to examine the complex interplay of how schools are organized and interact with the local

From "Organizing Schools for Improvement," by A. S. Bryk, 2010, *Phi Delta Kappan, 91*(7), pp. 23–30. Copyright 2010 by Phi Delta Kappa International. All rights reserved. Reprinted with permission.

community to alter dramatically the odds for improving student achievement. The lessons learned offer guidance for teachers, parents, principals, superintendents, and civic leaders in their efforts to improve schools across the country.

Five Essential Supports for School Improvement

Students' academic learning occurs principally in classrooms as students interact with teachers around subject matter. How we organize and operate a school has a major effect on the instructional exchanges in its classrooms. Put simply, whether classroom learning proceeds depends in large measure on how the school as a social context supports teaching and sustains student engagement. Through our research, we identified five organizational features of schools that interact with life inside classrooms and are essential to advancing student achievement.

1. **Coherent instructional guidance system.** Schools in which student learning improves have coherent instructional guidance systems that articulate the what and how of instruction. The learning tasks posed for students are key here, as are the assessments that make manifest what students actually need to know and provide feedback to inform subsequent instruction. Coordinated with this are the materials, tools, and instructional routines shared across a faculty that scaffold instruction. Although individual teachers may have substantial discretion in how they use these resources, the efficacy of individual teacher efforts depends on the quality of the supports and the local community of practice that forms around their use and refinement.

2. **Professional capacity.** Schooling is a human-resource-intensive enterprise. Schools are only as good as the quality of faculty, the professional development that supports their learning, and the faculty's capacity to work together to improve instruction. This support directs our attention to a school's ability to

recruit and retain capable staff, the efficacy of performance feedback and professional development, and the social resources within a staff to work together to solve local problems.

3. **Strong parent-community-school ties.** The disconnect between local school professionals and the parents and community that a school is intended to serve is a persistent concern in many urban contexts. The absence of vital ties is a problem; their presence is a multifaceted resource for improvement. The quality of these ties links directly to students' motivation and school participation and can provide a critical resource for classrooms.

4. **Student-centered learning climate.** All adults in a school community forge a climate that enables students to think of themselves as learners. At a minimum, improving schools establish a safe and orderly environment—the most basic prerequisite for learning. They endorse ambitious academic work coupled with support for each student. The combination allows students to believe in themselves, to persist, and ultimately to achieve.

5. **Leadership drives change.** Principals in improving schools engage in a dynamic interplay of instructional and inclusive-facilitative leadership. On the instructional side, school leaders influence local activity around core instructional programs, supplemental academic and social supports, and the hiring and development of staff. They establish strategic priorities for using resources and buffer externalities that might distract from coherent reform. Working in tandem with this, principals build relationships across the school community. Improving teaching and learning places demands on these relationships. In carrying out their daily activities, school leaders advance instrumental objectives while also trying to enlist teachers in the change effort. In the process, principals cultivate a growing cadre of leaders (teachers, parents, and community members) who can help expand the reach of this work and share overall responsibility for improvement.

Using extensive survey data collected by the consortium from teachers, principals, and students, we were able to develop school indicators for each of the five essential supports, chart changes in these indicators over time, and then relate these organizational conditions to subsequent changes in student attendance and learning gains in reading and mathematics. Among our findings:

- Schools with strong indicators on most supports were 10 times more likely to improve than schools with weak supports.
- Half of the schools strong on most supports improved substantially in reading.
- Not a single school weak on most supports improved in mathematics.
- A material weakness in any one support, sustained over several years, undermined other change efforts, and improvement rarely resulted.

This statistical evidence affords a strong warrant that how we organize schools is critical for student achievement. Improving schools entails coherent, orchestrated action across all five essential supports. Put simply, there is no one silver bullet.

Dynamics of Improvement

Schools are complex organizations consisting of multiple interacting subsystems (that is, the five essential organizational supports). Personal and social considerations mix deeply in the day-to-day workings of a school. These interactions are bound by various rules, roles, and prevailing practices that, in combination with technical resources, constitute schools as formal organizations. In a sense, almost everything interacts with everything else. That means that a true picture of what enables some schools to improve and others to stagnate requires identifying the critical interconnections among the five essential supports: *How do these five essential supports function together to substantially change the odds for enhancing student engagement and academic learning?*

Schools that improved student attendance over time strengthened their ties to parents and community and used these ties as a core resource for enhancing safety and order across the school. This growing sense of routine and security further combined with a better-aligned curriculum that continually exposed students to new tasks and ideas. Engaging pedagogy afforded students active learning roles in the classroom. High-quality professional development aimed to enhance teachers' capacity to orchestrate such activity under the trying circumstances that most confront daily. When this combination of conditions existed, the basic recipe for improving student attendance was activated.

In terms of the organizational mechanisms influencing academic achievement, this can be told in two contrasting stories. Schools that stagnated—no learning improvement over several years—were characterized by clear weaknesses in their instructional guidance system. They had poor curriculum alignment coupled with relatively little emphasis on active student engagement in learning. These instructional weaknesses combined with weak faculty commitments to the school, to innovation, and to working together as a professional community. Undergirding all of this were anemic school-parent-community ties.

In contrast, schools in which student learning improved used high-quality professional development as a key instrument for change. They had maximum leverage when these opportunities for teachers occurred in a supportive environment (that is, a school-based professional community) and when teaching was guided by a common, coherent, and aligned instructional system. Undergirding all of this, in turn, was a solid base of parent-community-school ties.

Leadership drives change in the four other organizational supports—but the actual execution of improvement is more organic and dynamic. Good teachers advance high-quality instruction, but developing good teachers and retaining them in a particular school depends on supportive school leadership and positive work relations with colleagues. Meaningful parent and community involvement can be a resource for solving problems of safety and order; but, in a reciprocal fashion, these ties are likely to be stronger in safe and orderly schools. This reciprocity carries over to leadership as the driver for change. While a principal commands formal authority to effect changes in the four other organizational supports, a school with some strengths in these four supports is also easier to lead.

Arguing for the significance of one individual support over another is tempting, but we ultimately came to view the five supports as an organized system of elements in dynamic interaction with one another. As such, primary value lies in their integration and mutual reinforcement. In this sense, school development is much like baking a cake. By analogy, you need an appropriate mix of flour, sugar, eggs, oil, baking powder, and flavoring to produce a light, delicious cake. Without sugar, it will be tasteless. Without eggs or baking powder, the cake will be flat and chewy. Marginal changes in a single ingredient—for example, a bit more flour, large versus extra-large eggs—may not have noticeable effects. But, if one ingredient is absent, it is just not a cake.

Similarly, strong local leadership acting on the four other organizational elements constitutes the essential ingredients for spurring school development. Broad-based instructional change and improved student learning entail coordinated action across these various domains. Correspondingly, student outcomes are likely to stagnate if a material weakness persists in any of the supports. The ensemble of supports is what's essential for improvement. Taken together, they constitute the core organizational ingredients for advancing student engagement and achievement. . . .

UNRECOGNIZED CHALLENGES

In many recent discussions about school reform, ideas about parent involvement and school community contexts fade into the background. Some school reform advocates believe only instruction and instructional leadership matter. This perspective assumes that a school's social and personal connections with local families and communities play a small role in reform. Our evidence, however, offers a strong challenge. To be sure, instruction matters—a lot. But social context matters too.

We have documented that strength across all five essential supports, including parent-school-community ties, is critical for improvement to occur in all kinds of urban schools. Unfortunately, we have also learned that this organizational development is much harder to initiate and sustain in some community contexts than others.

As data accumulated in Chicago and school-by-school trends in attendance and student learning gains became clear, a complex pattern of results emerged. Improving schools could be found in all kinds of neighborhoods varying by socioeconomic and racial/ethnic composition. Stagnating schools, in contrast, piled up in very poor, racially isolated African-American neighborhoods. We became haunted by the question, "Why? What made reform so much more difficult to advance in some school communities?"

Our analyses led us to two different answers. First, the social capital of a neighborhood is a significant resource for improving its local school. We found that the latter was much more likely in neighborhoods where residents had a history of working together. In contrast, the absence of such collective efficacy in the surrounding community increased the likelihood that a troubled school would continue to stagnate. Correspondingly, communities with strong institutions, especially religious institutions, were more supportive contexts for school improvement. These institutions afford a network of social ties that can be appropriated for other purposes, such as improving schools. They also create connections that can bring new outside resources into isolated neighborhoods.

So, differences among neighborhoods in their bonding and bridging social capital help explain why the essential supports were more likely to develop in some neighborhoods than others. But this was only a partial answer for a subset of the school communities.

A second mechanism was also at work. We found that the proportion of children who were living under extraordinary circumstances—neglect and abuse, homeless, foster care, domestic violence—also created a significant barrier to improvement in some schools. To be clear, these students were learning at about the same rates as their classmates in whatever school they were enrolled. So, the learning gains for these particular students were not depressing the overall results for their schools. But the odds of school stagnation soared when a concentration of these students appeared in the same place. On balance, schools are principally about teaching and learning, not solving all of the social problems of a community. However, when palpable personal and social needs walk through doors every day, school staff can't be expected to ignore those needs. Our evidence suggests that when the proportion of these needs remains high and pressing, the capacity of a school staff to sustain attention to developing the five essential supports falls by the wayside. A few schools managed to succeed under these circumstances, but most did not.

In sum, a nettlesome problem came into focus on improving student learning to truly disadvantaged communities where social capital is scarce and human need sometimes overwhelming. These schools face a "three-strike" problem. Not only are the schools highly stressed organizations, but they exist in challenged communities and confront an extraordinary density of human needs every day.

Our findings about schooling in truly disadvantaged communities offer a sobering antidote to a heady political rhetoric of "beating the odds" and "no excuses." To be sure, we believe that all schools can and must improve. Such claims represent our highest, most noble aspirations for our children, our schools, and systems of schools. They are ideas worthy of our beliefs and action. But there are also facts, sometimes brutal facts. Not all school communities start out in the same place and confront the same problems. Unless we recognize this, unless we understand more deeply the dynamics of school stagnation, especially in our most neglected communities, we seem bound to repeat the failures of the past.

Our concluding point is straightforward—it is hard to improve what we do not understand.

We need more attention on how to improve schools in these specific contexts. All plausible ideas for educational improvement deserve serious consideration. Absent systematic analysis of not only where we succeed but also where and why we fail, we will continue to relegate many of our students and their teachers to a similar fate.

SCHOOL BOARDS IN AMERICA

Flawed, but Still Significant

Gene I. Maeroff

Who should make decisions about school policies and operations? Traditionally, local governments in the form of school boards are elected to represent the views of community citizens. However, these boards have come under fire as governments and citizens look for explanations to why schools fail children. Some large school districts have shifted to mayoral control—with mixed results. Gene Maeroff discusses some concerns with this level of the school organization. He recommends careful consideration of the school board and its roles before dismissing its usefulness.

Questions to consider for this reading:

1. Who should make decisions for schools? Locally elected school boards? Mayors of cities? Other decision makers?

2. What impact do state and federal governments have on local board decision makers?

3. In what ways does the nation expect too much of school boards?

If the problems of school district governance lent themselves to quick repair, they would be fixed by now. But very little is easy when it comes to school boards and what ails them. . . . Some solutions require new commitments and radical changes. Even then, there are no guarantees that the future of school governance will be better than the past.

What reverberates strongest is the notion that school boards, like an old car past its prime, need attention and that the status quo won't suffice for those who want improved student outcomes. However, in some ways, school boards suffer a bum rap. They may be somewhat inconsequential, but sometimes circumstances leave school boards with few choices and limited autonomy. They've been stripped of some of their authority, they face competition in a world in which they were accustomed to enjoying a monopoly, and they simply lack the fiscal wiggle room to attempt some of the initiatives they might like to promote.

It wasn't supposed to turn out this way when towns in New England formed the first school committees of citizen volunteers not only to govern their local schools, but also to run them. Eventually, superintendents took over the operations, and the huge school boards of the 19th century—which needed many members so as to perform tasks ranging from stoking the wood stoves to interviewing teacher candidates—shrank in size. But the school board was still seen, literally, as the personification of democracy.

Now, the world of public education has been turned upside down and inside out. States and, increasingly, the federal government influence what occurs in classrooms. Teachers, especially in connection with collective bargaining, have assumed many of the prerogatives that school boards once reserved for themselves. New governance models threaten to make school boards in some locales as obsolete as yesterday's Pontiac. And financial pressures leave school boards less and less leeway in their spending decisions.

Think about the particulars. Fed up with low and uneven student performance, most of the states are collaboratively moving toward the creation of national standards. Organized teachers, not satisfied simply with bargaining for salaries and benefits, have greater input on working conditions. The largest school system in the country (New York City) has been operating without a school board for almost a decade, and the second-largest (Los Angeles) decided in August to explore how it might turn over 250 of its schools to private operators, which already happens in Philadelphia. With many school boards spending $4 of every $5 in their budgets on salaries and benefits for employees, the pot is shrinking for everything else, and board members have no idea where to turn for relief.

Such critics as Marc Tucker and Frederick M. Hess recommend radical surgery. Tucker would have the state, not the local district, hire teachers and would turn over the operation of schools to partnerships of teachers, organized as companies. Such changes, he maintains, would lift the caliber of school board members and shift their responsibility to improving or preserving the quality of education in their communities. Hess' way of putting the patient on the table reconsiders whether it makes sense for each of the more than 14,000 school districts to take responsibility for so many different tasks. He raises the possibility of individual school districts gaining expertise in a few specific areas and then making that expertise available to other districts so that those districts could focus on other specializations.

High Expectations

Ideas of this sort point to a major shortcoming of school boards. Society may expect too much of each of these small panels of citizen-volunteers. School boards oversee too many complex activities. Their governance extends to personnel, curriculum, and instruction—not to mention transportation, food services, and facilities. Every school board—whether it governs a district of 1,500, 15,000, or 150,000 students—is supposed to oversee the same conglomeration of duties. Furthermore, a great deal of the work of school boards is little more than window dressing, taking votes on matters on which the school board has no genuine authority.

Diane Ravitch cautions that we should be skeptical of critics of school boards who want to use the latest crisis to dilute or altogether eliminate the power of boards. Like snake oil salesmen, according to Ravitch, they have something to sell. She saves her sharpest criticism for Michael R. Bloomberg, who used the alleged failings of New York City's public schools as an excuse to shove the school board aside and take control of the system. In my opinion, the main questions to ask about any sort of change in school governance, such as mayoral control, is whether it's better than what it replaced, whether it improves student outcomes. Ravitch tells us that the result of no longer having a real school board in New York City is less accountability, a loss of a forum for parents, fewer checks and balances, and the end of budget transparency.

Whatever one feels about Mayor Bloomberg and the manner in which Schools Chancellor Joel I. Klein has operated the public school system in his behalf, it's doubtful that mayoral control will become widespread among the nation's thousands of school systems. Those searching for better forms of governance would do well to examine other possibilities.

A few school boards like New York City's may pass into irrelevance, but most are apt to remain on the scene for a long time, however hobbled they may be. I have found in my almost two years on a school board, reinforced by several decades of experience as a professional observer of education, that change comes slowly to the governance of public education and that some board members don't even know to be dissatisfied when they should be dissatisfied.

Yet, school boards have their supporters. While these supporters grant that there is room for improvement, they maintain that wholesale upheaval is neither necessary nor practical. Anne L. Bryant and Michael A. Resnick make the case for school boards, which they call "cornerstones of democracy." They maintain that no other arrangement for governing elementary and secondary education is likely to produce people with the knowledge, focus, and commitment possessed by members of local school boards. Members of boards as they are now constituted have an edge in engaging their friends and neighbors on behalf of the public schools simply because they are part of the local community, [with] communication and transparency as the results.

Hayes Mizell acknowledges that school boards have lost some of their former authority, but insists nevertheless that they retain the flexibility to do a lot more than they currently do to improve the skills, knowledge, and practice of the educators on their payrolls. This approach would presumably translate into higher student achievement. Mizell wants school boards to think more about human resources and how they can be strengthened. Probably, few school boards in the country have given the kind of thought to the professional education of educators that Mizell would like to see.

Professional development is but one area in which school boards, if they have not bargained away their ability, can set policies that make a difference. They may determine class sizes, as well as the length of the school day and the school year. They may have their districts offer prekindergarten, and they may call for literacy specialists in the early grades. They may mandate enrichment for the gifted, call for Advanced Placement courses, and set in motion various initiatives to close achievement gaps. School boards, in collaboration with superintendents, may determine the number of central administrators and whether there should be assistant principals in elementary schools. They may put capital

referendums on the ballot and approve or disapprove of almost every dollar spent by the system.

Given this latitude for action, Michael D. Usdan holds out the hope that school boards can still be instrumental in school reform. He says that business, political, and education leaders pushing for improvement have not paid enough attention to the potential of local school boards in these efforts. He urges advocates and practitioners of school reform not to write off school boards, but to reach out and engage them.

A multitude of forces, though, have limited school boards' options and lurk just outside the schoolhouse door to narrow their jurisdiction. Today, school boards must respond with increasing alacrity to the whims and orders of an array of officials seeking to influence the public schools—the U.S. Secretary of Education, state education departments, state boards of education, chief state school officers, members of the legislature, and even governors' education advisers in some states. Laws, regulations, and rules pour out like water from a broken main. State lawmakers and state officials who are hardly accountable to anyone are demanding that school boards be more accountable to them. Meanwhile, the federal government, wielding stimulus money like a cudgel, plays an ever more prominent role in local school board matters.

All in all, boards have less room to determine what to teach and how to teach it, though they remain responsible for making sure that broken furniture in the schools gets repaired and that copying machines have enough paper.

MANAGING THE MONEY

Money is the lifeblood of education, and school boards, like landlords handcuffed by rent control, have few options as costs mount. Public education is on an unsustainable financial course, especially when it comes to benefits for employees and retirees. School boards find little relief from fiscal pressures when they face the demands of teachers, who have bargaining rights in 75% of the states. Organized teachers and other public employee unions exert such control in these places that legislators surrender all pretense of independence. School boards are mere pawns on this financial chess board.

Special education is the 800-pound fiscal gorilla about which school board members and administrators moan in private but say little in public, not wanting to be politically incorrect. Congress didn't recognize it at the time, but passage in 1975 of the Education for All Handicapped Children Act, now known as IDEA (Individuals with Disabilities Education Act), set loose forces that have altered public education. Special education is an entitlement that can force school boards to find the money to send kids with the most severe disabilities to residential schools that can cost the taxpayers $100,000 per child annually.

Meanwhile, many school boards must authorize out-of-district daily placements for many more disabled children at an annual cost of anywhere from $30,000 to $80,000 per tuition. And this doesn't include the several hundred dollars that boards spend weekly on each child for transportation and the aide who must be on the bus, which sometimes is a van carrying a single student to a far-off location. It's all done in the name of a federally mandated "free and appropriate public education" for every disabled child, no matter the cost. Nonspecial education students, in effect, subsidize those classified for special education. School boards are confounded and stymied by these requirements.

In America of the 21st century, many school boards struggle to attract top-flight members who are willing to put up with the grief that comes with the job. Interest in and support for the public schools have ebbed as the percentage of households using the public schools has declined and the portion of public school students who look different from the people who pay most of the taxes has increased. The neighborhood school is no longer the focal point of the local community as people are less attracted to what it offers. School boards continue to consume the largest share of local taxes, but they find less support from taxpayers for what they try to do.

The nation's school boards are not at their zenith. But neither are they at their nadir. The coming decade, filled with challenge, may well determine if school boards regain their vitality or simply slip further into irrelevance, reduced to discharging hollow legal responsibilities.

LEARNING THE STUDENT ROLE

Kindergarten as Academic Boot Camp

Harry L. Gracey

The organizational structure of schools cannot be studied in isolation from the roles of individuals holding positions within the system. Part of the informal organization includes messages students learn about their expected roles. Bridging Chapter 4 on organizations and Chapter 5 on roles is Harry L. Gracey's classic discussion of young students learning their roles within the organizational structure. In his complete article, Gracey describes the socialization process into the role of "student" by documenting the organizational structure of the classroom and a day in the life of a kindergarten teacher and class. New initiates to formal schooling learn the expectations of school so that they will fit into the educational system and later into the world of work. In these excerpts from this classic article, some of the references may seem a bit old-fashioned; however, the article conveys a powerful message about the way students are socialized in school and for what purposes.

Questions to consider for this reading:

1. What are the formal and informal organizational structures of kindergarten classrooms and what role do they play in preparing kindergarten students for the next stages of school life?

2. Taking the message about learning the student role, how is this role perpetuated and expanded through other levels of schooling?

3. How might functional and conflict theorists described in Chapter 1 interpret the processes taking place in kindergarten?

Education must be considered one of the major institutions of social life today. Along with the family and organized religion, however, it is a "secondary institution," one in which people are prepared for life in society as it is presently organized. The main dimensions of modern life, that is, the nature of society as a whole, are determined principally by the "Primary institutions," which today are the economy, the political system, and the military establishment. Education has been defined by sociologists, classical and contemporary, as an institution which serves society by socializing people into it through a formalized, standardized procedure. At the beginning of this century, Emile Durkheim told student teachers at the University of Paris that education "consists of a methodical socialization of the younger generation." He went on to add:

> It is the influence exercised by adult generations on those that are not ready for social life. Its object is to

arouse and to develop in the child a certain number of physical, intellectual, and moral states that are demanded of him by the political society as a whole and by the special milieu for which he is specifically destined. To the egotistic and asocial being that has just been born, [society] must as rapidly as possible add another capable of leading a moral and social life. Such is the work of education.[1]

"The education process," Durkheim said, "is above all the means by which society perpetually recreates the conditions of its very existence."[2] The contemporary educational sociologist, Wilbur Brookover, offers a similar formulation in his recent textbook definition of education.

Actually, therefore, in the broadest sense education is synonymous with socialization. It includes any social behavior that assists in the induction of the child into membership in the society or any behavior by which the society perpetuates itself through the next generation.[3]

The educational institution is, then, one of the ways in which society is perpetuated through the systematic socialization of the young, while the nature of the society which is being perpetuated— its organization and operation, its values, beliefs, and ways of living—is determined by the primary institutions. The educational system, like other secondary institutions, serves the society which is created by the operation of the economy, the political system, and the military establishment.

Schools, the social organizations of the educational institution, are today for the most part large bureaucracies run by specially trained and certified people. There are few places left in modern societies where formal teaching and learning is carried on in small, isolated groups, like the rural, one-room schoolhouses of the last century. Schools are large, formal organizations which tend to be parts of larger organizations, local community school districts. These school districts are bureaucratically organized and their operations are supervised by state and local governments. In this context, as Brookover says:

The term education is used to refer to a system of schools, in which specifically designated persons are expected to teach children and youth certain types of acceptable behavior. The school system becomes a unit in the total social structure and is recognized by the members of the society as a separate social institution. Within this structure a portion of the total socialization process occurs.[4]

Education is the part of the socialization process which takes place in the schools; and these are, more and more today, bureaucracies within bureaucracies.

Kindergarten is generally conceived by educators as a year of preparation for school. It is thought of as a year in which small children, five or six years old, are prepared socially and emotionally for the academic learning which will take place over the next twelve years. It is expected that a foundation of behavior and attitudes will be laid in kindergarten on which the children can acquire the skills and knowledge they will be taught in the grades. A booklet prepared for parents by the staff of a suburban New York school system says that the kindergarten experience will stimulate the child's desire to learn and cultivate the skills he will need for learning in the rest of his school career. It claims that the child will find opportunities for physical growth, for satisfying his "need for self-expression," acquire some knowledge, and provide opportunities for creative activity. It concludes, "The most important benefit that your five-year-old will receive from kindergarten is the opportunity to live and grow happily and purposefully with others in a small society." The kindergarten teachers in one of the elementary schools in this community, one we shall call the Wilbur Wright School, said their goals were to see that the children "grew" in all ways: physically, of course, emotionally, socially, and academically. They said they wanted children to like school as a result of their kindergarten experiences and that they wanted them to learn to get along with others.

None of these goals, however, is unique to kindergarten; each of them is held to some extent by teachers in the other six grades at Wright School. And growth would occur, but differently, even if the child did not attend school. The children already know how to get along with others, in their families and their play groups. The unique job of the kindergarten in the educational division of labor seems rather to be teaching children the student role. The student role is the repertoire of behavior and attitudes regarded by educators as appropriate to children in school. Observation in the kindergartens of the Wilbur Wright School revealed a great variety of activities through which children are shown and then drilled in the behavior and attitudes defined as appropriate for school and thereby induced to learn the role of student. Observations of the kindergartens and interviews with the teachers both pointed to the teaching and learning of classroom routines as the main element of the student role. The teachers expended most of their efforts, for the first half of the year at least, in training the children to follow the routines which teachers created. The children were, in a very real sense, drilled in tasks and activities created by the teachers for their own purposes and beginning and ending quite arbitrarily (from the child's point of view) at the command of the teacher. One teacher remarked that she hated September, because during the first month "everything has to be done rigidly, and repeatedly, until they know exactly what they're supposed to do." However, "by January," she said, "they know exactly what to do [during the day] and I don't have to be after them all the time." Classroom routines were introduced gradually from the beginning of the year in all the kindergartens, and the children were drilled in them as long as was necessary to achieve regular compliance. By the end of the school year, the successful kindergarten teacher has a well-organized group of children. They follow classroom routines automatically, having learned all the command signals and the expected responses to them. They have, in our terms, learned the student role.

TRAINING FOR LEARNING AND FOR LIFE

The children [at the Wright School] learned to go through routines and to follow orders with unquestioning obedience, even when these make no sense to them. They have been disciplined to do as they are told by an authoritative person without significant protest. Edith Kerr, [the teacher] has developed this discipline in the children by creating and enforcing a rigid social structure in the classroom through which she effectively controls the behavior of most of the children for most of the school day. The "living with others in a small society" which the school pamphlet tells parents is the most important thing the children will learn in kindergarten can be seen now in its operational meaning, which is learning to live by the routines imposed by the school. This learning appears to be the principal content of the student role.

Children who submit to school-imposed discipline and come to identify with it, so that being a "good student" comes to be an important part of their developing identities, become the good students by the school's definitions. Those who submit to the routines of the school but do not come to identify with them will be adequate students who find the more important part of their identities elsewhere, such as in the play group outside school. Children who refuse to submit to the school routines are rebels, who become known as "bad students" and often "problem children" in the school, for they do not learn the academic curriculum, and their behavior is often disruptive in the classroom. Today schools engage clinical psychologists in part to help teachers deal with such children.

[It is interesting to look at Edith Kerr's] kindergarten at Wright School [and] to ask how the children learn this role of student—come to accept school-imposed routines—and what, exactly, it involves in terms of behavior and attitudes. The most prominent features of the classroom are its physical and social structures. The room is carefully furnished and arranged in ways adults feel will interest children. The play store and play kitchen in the back of the room, for example, imply that children are interested in mimicking these activities of the adult world. The only space left for the children to create something of their own is the empty center of the room, and the materials at their disposal are the blocks, whose use causes anxiety on the part of the teacher.

The room, being carefully organized physically by the adults, leaves little room for the creation of physical organization on the part of the children.

The social structure created by Edith is a far more powerful and subtle force for fitting the children to the student role. This structure is established by the very rigid and tightly controlled set of rituals and routines through which the children are put during the day. There is first the rigid "locating procedure" in which the children are asked to find themselves in terms of the month, date, day of the week, and the number of the class who are present and absent. This puts them solidly in the real world as defined by adults. The day is then divided into six periods whose activities are for the most part determined by the teacher. In Edith's kindergarten the children went through Serious Time, which opens the school day, Sharing Time, Play Time (which in clear weather would be spent outside), Work Time, Clean-up Time, after which they have their milk, and Rest Time after which they go home. The teacher has programmed activities for each of these times.

Occasionally the class is allowed limited discretion to choose between proffered activities, such as stories or records, but original ideas for activities are never solicited from them. Opportunity for free individual action is open only once in the day, during the part of Work Time left after the general class assignment has been completed (on the day reported, the class assignment was drawing animal pictures for the absent Mark). Spontaneous interests or observations from the children are never developed by the teacher. It seems that her schedule just does not allow room for developing such unplanned events. During Sharing Time, for example, the child who brought a bird's nest told Edith, in reply to her question of what kind of bird made it, "My friend says it's a rain bird." Edith does not think to ask about this bird, probably because the answer is "childish," that is, not given in accepted adult categories of birds. The children then express great interest in an object in the nest, but the teacher ignores this interest, probably because the object is uninteresting to her. The soldiers from "Babes in Toyland"

strike a responsive note in the children, but this is not used for a discussion of any kind. The soldiers are treated in the same way as objects which bring little interest from the children. Finally, at the end of Sharing Time the child-world of perception literally erupts in the class with the recollection of "the spooky house" at the zoo. Apparently this made more of an impression on the children than did any of the animals, but Edith is unable to make any sense of it for herself. The tightly imposed order of the class begins to break down as the children discover a universe of discourse of their own and begin talking excitedly with one another. The teacher is effectively excluded from this child's world of perception and for a moment she fails to dominate the classroom situation. She reasserts control, however, by taking the children to the next activity she has planned for the day. It seems never to have occurred to Edith that there might be a meaningful learning experience for the children in re-creating the "spooky house" in the classroom. It seems fair to say that this would have offered an exercise in spontaneous self-expression and an opportunity for real creativity on the part of the children. Instead, they are taken through a canned animal imitation procedure, an activity which they apparently enjoy, but which is also imposed upon them rather than created by them.

While children's perceptions of the world and opportunities for genuine spontaneity and creativity are being systematically eliminated from the kindergarten, unquestioned obedience to authority and role learning of meaningless material are being encouraged. When the children are called to line up in the center of the room they ask "Why?" and "What for?" as they are in the very process of complying. They have learned to go smoothly through a programmed day, regardless of whether parts of the program make any sense to them or not. Here the student role involves what might be called "doing what you're told and never mind why." Activities which might "make sense" to the children are effectively ruled out, and they are forced or induced to participate in activities which may be "senseless," such as calisthenics.

At the same time the children are being taught by rote meaningless sounds in the ritual oaths and songs, such as the Lord's Prayer, the Pledge to the Flag, and "America." As they go through the grades children learn more and more of the sounds of these ritual oaths, but the fact that they have often learned meaningless sounds rather than meaningful statements is shown when they are asked to write these out in the sixth grade; they write them as groups of sounds rather than as a series of words, according to the sixth grade teachers at Wright School. Probably much learning in the elementary grades is of this character, that is, having no intrinsic meaning to the children, but rather being tasks inexplicably required of them by authoritative adults. Listening to sixth grade children read social studies reports, for example, in which they have copied material from encyclopedias about a particular country, an observer often gets the feeling that he is watching an activity which has no intrinsic meaning for the child. The child who reads, "Switzerland grows wheat and cows and grass and makes a lot of cheese" knows the dictionary meaning of each of these words but may very well have no conception at all of this "thing" called Switzerland. He is simply carrying out a task assigned by the teacher because it is assigned, and this may be its only "meaning" for him.

Another type of learning which takes place in kindergarten is seen in children who take advantage of the "holes" in the adult social structure to create activities of their own, during Work Time or out-of-doors during Play Time. Here the children are learning to carve out a small world of their own within the world created by adults. They very quickly learn that if they keep within permissible limits of noise and action they can play much as they please. Small groups of children formed during the year in Edith's kindergarten who played together at these times, developing semi-independent little groups in which they created their own worlds in the interstices of the adult-imposed physical and social world. These groups remind the sociological observer very much of the so-called "informal groups" which adults develop in factories and offices of large bureaucracies.[5] Here, too, within authoritatively imposed social organizations people find "holes" to create little subworlds which support informal, friendly, unofficial behavior. Forming and participating in such groups seems to be as much part of the student role as it is of the role of bureaucrat.

The kindergarten has been conceived of here as the year in which children are prepared for their schooling by learning the role of student. In the classrooms of the rest of the school grades, the children will be asked to submit to systems and routines imposed by the teachers and the curriculum. The days will be much like those of kindergarten, except that academic subjects will be substituted for the activities of the kindergarten. Once out of the school system, young adults will more than likely find themselves working in large-scale bureaucratic organizations, perhaps on the assembly line in the factory, perhaps in the paper routines of the white collar occupations, where they will be required to submit to rigid routines imposed by "the company" which may make little sense to them. Those who can operate well in this situation will be successful bureaucratic functionaries. Kindergarten, therefore, can be seen as preparing children not only for participation in the bureaucratic organization of large modern school systems, but also for the large-scale occupational bureaucracies of modern society.

NOTES

1. Durkheim, E. (1956). *Sociology and education* (pp. 71–72). New York: Free Press.

2. Ibid., p. 123.

3. Brookover, W. (1957). *The sociology of education* (p. 4). New York: American Book.

4. Ibid., p. 6.

5. See, for example, Blau, P. M. (1956). *Bureaucracy in modern society* (Chapter 3). New York: Random House.

REAL SCHOOL

The Universal Drama Amid Disparate Experience

Mary Haywood Metz

In this reading, Mary Haywood Metz discusses the similarities and differences in American high schools and contrasts them based on the social-class differences of the students they serve. Looking at a range of public and Catholic high schools, Metz studied teachers' work by observing their classrooms, interviewing them, and reviewing documents about each school. What Metz found was a "common script." The roles and plots within the school organization were similar, and the settings and actor lines were recognizable but different. The importance of this reading for the discussion of schools as organizations lies in the way the common script is carried out across educational institutions. Although the setting and goals and even some of the rituals may be similar across schools, each school differs in the way the common script is actualized, based on social-class differences of students and expectations for their futures.

Questions to consider for this reading:

1. What were some differences in the common script found by Metz in the eight schools she studied?

2. How would you explain the process by which school organizations with common scripts can be so different?

3. How does this reading illustrate that schools play a role in reproducing social class?

4. Why is there a need for us to have a common script of "real schools"?

Variations on the phrase "The American High School" adorn the titles of popular recent reports on reform (Boyer, 1983; Cusick, 1983; Powell, Farrar, & Cohen, 1985; Sedlak, Wheeler, Pullin, & Cusick, 1986; Sizer, 1984), expressing a common belief that they address a single institution.

American high schools are indeed alike, strikingly so in many important respects. But they are also very different in other important respects.

Reformers have paid little attention to their differences; some ignore them, while others mention them almost reluctantly, hurrying on to describe what is common among schools. Still, the differences among schools are crucial to their daily practice and to their effects upon students, and so to reform. This article addresses the interplay of similarity and difference in American high schools, regarding their similarity, rather than their difference, as problematic and in need of explanation.

THE DATA

The chapter arises out of a study of teachers' working lives undertaken at the National Center of Effective Secondary Schools. In that study we took a close look at a set of teachers in "ordinary" or typical high schools spread across the social class spectrum. We chose eight schools in midwestern metropolitan areas. Six were public schools and two were Catholic. Of the six public schools, two were in high, two in middle, and two in low SES areas. One of the Catholic schools served a predominantly middle class clientele and the other a predominantly working class one. We chose schools varying in social class as sites to study teachers' work because previous research in sociology and anthropology suggests that differences in the social class of communities and student bodies have serious implications for the life of schools (e.g., Anyon, 1981; Bowles & Gintis, 1976; Connell, [Ashendon, Kessler, & Dowsett], 1982; Heath, 1983; Lubeck, 1985; Weis, 1985; Willis, 1977).

We visited each school in teams, spending more than two weeks, and a total of twenty or more person days in each school. At each school, we followed diverse students through a school day, spent a whole school day with each of eight teachers, and interviewed those eight teachers in depth, as well as ten others more briefly. We also perused and collected a number of documents and statistics about each school. While our fieldwork in each school was too brief to be genuinely ethnographic, the strength of the design lay in its comparative potential. We attended classes and interviewed teachers in situations that were formally parallel across the eight diverse schools. We could see their differences in clear relief.

THE COMMON SCRIPT

We chose the sample of schools we did because we expected to find some important differences among them. Our visits to the first schools quickly gave us dramatic evidence that our expectations were correct; participation in the varied schools provided us radically different experiences. The buildings varied from resembling a college campus, at suburban Maple Heights, to resembling a fortress, at low income, urban Charles Drew. The use of time varied from intent and taut to relatively relaxed. Maple Heights allowed students to go home for lunch or to roam its spacious lawns in small groups after eating, while the two low income urban schools, Grant and Drew, kept all but the main door locked and security guards at Drew checked students' picture identifications both at the door to the school and at the entrance to the lunch room. More important, the content and tone of classroom discourse varied widely, as did the style of interactions between students and teachers.

While this variation riveted our attention as we moved from school to school, the discourse of the reform movement—which the Center hoped to address—assumes commonality, even sameness, among schools. As we puzzled over the discrepancy between our diverse experiences and the reformers' assumption that schools are standard, we came to see that we were looking at different aspects of schools' lives. The reform movement emphasizes formal structure and technical procedures in schools. In these respects, the schools we saw were indeed very alike. The meaning of that structure and technology, the cultural assumptions of participants about their activities, and the place of the school in relation to the society and to children's life trajectories differed significantly among the schools we saw.

As we watched the schools in daily action, and talked with the actors who gave them life, it seemed that the schools were following a common script. The stages were roughly similar, though the scenery varied significantly. The roles were similarly defined and the outline of the plot was supposed to be the same. But the actors took great liberties with the play. They interpreted the motivations and purposes of the characters whose roles they took with striking variation. They changed their entrances and exits. Sometimes, they left before the last act. The outlines of the plot took on changing significance with the actors' varied interpretation of their roles. Directors had limited control over their actors; only a few were able to get the actors to perform as an ensemble that would enact the director's conception of the play. Directors often had to make the best of the qualities the actors brought to their roles and to interpret the play consistently with the players' abilities and intentions.

Just the same, the script was there, and the play was in some sense recognizable as the same play in all the schools. More important, the script was extremely important to some of the actors and some of the audiences. In fact, it was where the production was hardest to coordinate and perhaps least easily recognizable as the same play that was being produced at schools where action meshed more smoothly, that the school staffs were the most insistent that their production followed the script for "The American High School," varying from others only in details.

We found similarities in our schools that paralleled those recently noted by several writers (e.g., Goodlad, 1984; Sizer, 1984). There was little variation in school schedule and all schools had long hallways with nearly identical classrooms lined up along them. Class size and teachers' normal assignment to meet five groups of students for instruction five times a week varied little. The scope and sequence of the curriculum differed only in detail from school to school, though the number of sections available in subjects like advanced foreign language or vocational education varied significantly. Students were expected to attend all their classes promptly every day. There were extracurricular activities after school, or occasionally during the last hour of the day.

Textbooks were ubiquitous. We saw the same textbooks in use where students' scores on standardized tests were far below average and where they were concentrated well above the median. Instruction was conducted primarily through lecture, recitation, discussion, and seatwork, with occasional use of student reports, filmstrips, movies, and videotapes.

Teachers had undifferentiated roles. Department chairs held a slight measure of authority and engaged in some co-ordinating activities. A few teachers were temporarily released from some portion of their teaching for a variety of special responsibilities, but these variations in routine were not permanent and conferred no formal special status, though they often brought informal prestige.

Despite these very strong similarities among the schools, there was variation in the appearance and style of the buildings, the strictness of enforcement of routines, and the relationships built among flesh and blood individuals on the staff and in the student body. The curriculum actually in use varied also. The content of classroom interactions, the questions asked on tests, students' written work, and the deportment of students in class varied widely from school to school even when classes used the same books.

COMMUNITY AND STUDENT PRESSURES FOR DIFFERENCES

Among Schools

Differences among the schools arose in large part from differences in the communities surrounding them. The communities we studied varied markedly in the financial resources they gave schools and in the relationship between school and community. They also varied in the resources parents brought both to their relations with the school and to the task of assisting their children with education. These communities had developed differing visions of how the high schools should be run—within the parameters set by the common script—and of the place of a high school education in their children's life trajectories. The communities affected the schools most intimately as they shaped the students who entered their doors. Students' skills, their understanding of a high school education, and their vision of its place in their overall lives differed markedly between communities. The effects of the ties between the communities and schools in our project are discussed in detail in other papers (Hemmings & Metz, 1990; Metz, 1990).

Despite different resources and quite different ideas about the nature and uses of high school education, there was no evidence that any of the communities wanted or expected schools to depart from the basic common script for "The American High School." This support for the common script may seem "natural," but in fact it requires explanation. Why should people with such different backgrounds and experiences and such different ambitions for their children all expect and demand "the same" high school education for them? Why do they do so even as they also exert pressures for interpretations of that "standard" education that produce important differences in students' actual educational experiences?

The persistence of the common script seems most problematic when one looks inside the school at teachers and students engaged in the common work demanded by the script. Except at the three schools with the most skilled, best prepared students, large proportions of the students did poorly academically, including failing courses. At Drew, the school in the poorest neighborhood, the dropout rate was apparently over 50%; it approached 50% at Grant, the other school in a poor setting. Even at the two schools that had students from steadily employed blue collar and lower white collar families, the dropout rate was a worry to school officials and the failure rate substantial, though both were much lower than at the schools with students in poverty.

Furthermore, at all the schools where no more than half of the students were headed for college, students expressed alienation from the curriculum and from class and school procedures in various subtle or blatant ways. The favored forms for expressing alienation from the schools' academic endeavors, and their severity and frequency, varied from school to school. Especially at the schools in the poor neighborhoods, students cut classes or cut school; at these schools there were chronic problems with severe tardiness. Once in class at these schools, students often carried on social conversations or read or wrote on unrelated projects, or sat limply staring, or put their heads down and slept. At the predominantly working class schools, where most students wanted to graduate but did not expect to go to college, some objected to assignments or quibbled with teachers over small issues; a few engaged in expressive interactions with peers designed for maximum disruption. In a few classes some students carried on a running guerrilla warfare, teasing and badgering teachers in various ways. Especially at one of these schools, students in the majority of classes had successfully negotiated with teachers for time in class to do "homework" that became an open social hour. Students in tracked classes whose achievement was much higher or lower than average for their school tended to differ from their school in the direction of students in schools where their level of achievement was average.

TEACHERS' RESPONSES TO DIFFICULTIES WITH THE COMMON SCRIPT

Teachers' work consists of transforming the minds and perhaps the characters of their students. To succeed in their work they must, at a bare minimum, win the passive acquiescence of their students. Students' active co-operation will make the task far easier and the teachers' work more effective.

Consequently, students' expressions of distance and distaste for the academic undertaking created serious distress and frustration for their teachers. A few determined and skilled individuals were able to reduce or mitigate these patterns through imagination and force of character within the parameters of the common script. Some, equally dedicated, tried hard but were unable to do so. Some teachers simply blamed the difficulty of teaching on students; they considered those they worked with intellectually or morally deficient. They wished they had students "like the old days" or they wished they taught in their idealized conception of a "better" school: a magnet school, a suburban school, or a school in a different kind of suburb where families cared more about education. Many teachers seemed to use such blame to protect their own imperiled sense of craft. Even among teachers who did not reject students as unworthy, the overwhelming majority did not expect to tailor the institution or the learning to the students, but assumed that they must tailor the students to the institution.

Even where there was incontrovertible evidence that students were not learning well, both students and teachers were frustrated or alienated, and there was an evident lack of connection between students and standard structures and curricula, teachers did not respond by suggesting alternative strategies that would significantly change the common script. A few teachers did speculate about one or another possible change, but they did not seem fully to appreciate the systemic alterations their suggestions might imply.

Teachers did make informal, de facto adjustments in the script, however. Much of the difference between the schools in daily curriculum-in-use, in the sense of time, and in relationships resulted from adjustments in the common script that students and teachers created together through informal processes. Sometimes these were conscious adjustments on teachers' part. For example, teachers at one predominantly blue collar school said repeatedly that they had "to be realistic." They made the subject matter simpler and more practical, without departing altogether from the formal curriculum embodied in the common script.

Sometimes adjustments were gradual and formally unrecognized. For example, at some schools, teachers (and administrators) felt forced to put up with tardiness and truancy, as long as these stayed within reasonable limits, because they were too rampant to control. Some teachers simply sought strategies that would win students' attention to the lesson for at least part of the class hour.

In short, teachers were forced to adjust to their students, to change school practices to accommodate students' unwillingness to meet certain demands (e.g., for significant homework) or abide by certain procedures (e.g., consistent prompt appearance in class). They did in fact change the system to meet the students. But they did not, for the most part, do it in formal ways and they did not attempt to challenge the common script. For example, they did not argue for alternative pedagogical approaches, but simply "watered down"

the common curriculum or made it "more practical" or just "did the best I can to cover the material." They did not alter expectations for prompt class attendance; they just started getting the major business of the class going more and more slowly.

If one looks at students' learning simply as a technical problem, it is quite remarkable to see situations where a technical process (or the social structure which frames it) is clearly not effective on a massive scale, but no one in the organization calls for developing alternative technical or structural approaches. Should a company that produced inanimate objects have such difficulties in accomplishing its desired results—if, for example, bicycle wheels produced in a factory were not straight and strong—the company would soon be out of business unless it changed its procedures.

THE PERSISTENCE OF THE COMMON SCRIPT AS A REFLECTION OF SOCIETAL THOUGHT AND VALUES

While it is easy to blame teachers and administrators for being myopic in the production of this state of affairs, it is a grave mistake to do so. On the contrary, school staffs stand squarely in the mainstream of American educational thought in their reluctance to consider alternatives to the common script.

The schools we saw were typical of schools described throughout the literature, in their adherence to the common script, in students' alienation and distance from it in all but schools for the able and ambitious, and in teachers' informal adjustments that accommodated students without altering the script or supporting learning (Boyer, 1983; Cusick, 1983; McNeil, 1986; Powell et al., 1985; Sedlak et al., 1986; Sizer, 1984).

There are reasons for students' resistance to school that, in part, lie beyond the schools' control. There is by now a large literature on the ways that mainstream schools require minority children to learn through cultural patterns that are initially unfamiliar and often distasteful. Insistence on these patterns not only creates cognitive problems—that many can and do overcome—but problems of identity, of choice between home and school worlds. This choice leads many minority students intentionally to distance themselves from the school (Erickson, 1987; Fordham, 1988).

At the high school level minorities experience a second set of problems. John Ogbu (1978, 1987) has argued that minorities do not learn well because the economic experience of the adults they see around them has taught them that credentials do not yield the rewards for minorities that they do for majority students. They perceive a "job ceiling" that limits the rewards that can be gained from cooperation with the schools. Recently, he has noted that minority students who have just immigrated to this country often do not perceive these limitations, while for others even low end American jobs constitute improvements over their experience in their home countries. These immigrant students (Ogbu, 1987) do better in school than do native minority students.

Native minority students may often resist the common script of high school because embracing it signifies betrayal of the peer group (Fordham & Ogbu, 1986) and of ethnic identity, on the one hand, and promises little tangible reward, on the other. It is difficult for teachers, especially individual teachers, to break through such patterns of resistance.

Similar problems exist in the apparently increasing resistance of blue collar white students to the schools and the common script. A number of external social processes have undercut the claims to authority of the schools and their individual staff members over the last twenty years (Hurn, 1985). Probably more important, as Sedlak and his colleagues (1986) argue, a high school diploma has decreasing value for young people hoping to use it as their major ticket to a place in the labor market. Children of blue collar and even lower white collar families have been watching the economic prospects of adults and older siblings in their communities contract during the last ten years. For these students, the most minimal cooperation with the school needed to obtain a diploma often seems a fair bargain for the minimal benefits bestowed by its receipt.

In short, students' alienation from schooling has significant roots outside the schools that teachers and administrators can do little about. Nonetheless, in all of our schools there were some students making a visible effort to co-operate and do well. In all there were some teachers who were quite successful in drawing large parts of their classes into the academic enterprise, at least during class time. And some schools succeeded better than others at this task, despite roughly equivalent student bodies.

Students' resistance to school, then, must be understood as the result of a mixture of influences. A very important part of that mixture lies in economic and social processes beyond the schools' control—though not beyond the reach of intentional social change. Still, school practice and the practice of individual teachers, as well as the perspectives of individual students, also have important effects.

Given the erosion of extrinsic rewards for schooling that increasing numbers of blue collar white students, as well as minority students, are experiencing, it would seem logical to try to increase the intrinsic rewards of schooling. Since teachers are most aware of the students' resistance to the common script, why are teachers not pushing for education that will use their students' interests, experiences, and intellectual strengths to draw them into the enterprise? Why do they not press for a more flexible, adaptable, and less monotonous rhythm of activity?

One important reason is that teachers work within larger organizations that mandate much of the common script in non-negotiable terms. In most of our schools teachers had curriculum guides that outlined their formal curriculum, though they might be able to make a fairly broad range of choices within a given framework. The schedule of the school day was decided by the central district administration. State laws and Carnegie units for college admissions froze the larger outlines of the formal curriculum even beyond the district level. Architecture and union contracts shaped class size. In most cases district policy determined homogeneous or heterogeneous ability grouping. In other words, teachers were hemmed in by state laws, district directives, union contracts, and college admissions pressures—as well as societal expectations—all of which presumed or required that they follow the common script.

We have, then, to look beyond individual schools or the occupations of teaching and school administration to find the most important sources for the common script. It has deep historical roots. Several historical works (e.g., Callahan, 1962; Katz, 1971; Tyack, 1974) have traced the development of the forms we take as "natural" today. They stress the dominance of the factory model of organization at the time that compulsory schooling was being taken seriously, so that schools were increasing in number and public saliency, and being given what was to become their common form. Managers and bosses expected to have almost total control over subordinates. Schools were a mechanism for quick Americanization of diverse immigrants and efficient training of a labor force, most of whom were headed for menial jobs where bosses and managers intended to be the brains while they were simply hands. Such a system was not designed to be responsive to individual or cultural diversity. If it failed to develop sophisticated literacy and numeracy in poorer children or those who were culturally different, then they simply would be channeled into work where sophisticated skills were not required or even desired. The common script is, in some ways, a historical residue.

David Cohen (1987) has recently argued that the roots of the common script are historically deeper yet; they go far into European history. He focuses on schools' attachment to teaching through a corpus of revered written works and through telling. Western society learned to revere the few surviving written works of earlier great civilizations through the years of the middle ages when a few precious copies of these works were carefully preserved and laboriously copied. Protestant attachment to the Bible furthered this attitude. At the same time, he says, folk patterns of informal teaching in everyday life consist in telling, in instruction through didactic means. When the schools resist innovations that would make children more active learners or adjust the curriculum to the child, they are only following

deeply engrained cultural patterns of revering great books and of instruction by lecture.

While history may have shaped the form of the common script, it is important to seek the reasons that it is so widely embraced by contemporary actors. If the common script has not been able to produce good results with large proportions of students in recent years, it would seem reasonable to try altering the script. It requires explanation that neither teachers, nor other education professionals, nor policymakers, nor parent groups often consider such a possibility. Why, then, is the common script so persistent?

REAL SCHOOL AS A SYMBOL OF EQUITY

The symbols and rituals of Real School are important not only for the immediate school communities, but also for a regional, state, and national audience. These audiences want to be able to assume that all schools follow a common template and can be said to be offering the same, commonly understood and commonly valued, high school education. In the current rhetoric of the national reform movement and in the rhetoric of many local and regional commissions, it is axiomatic that high schools should be the same across communities. The reasons for this are so much taken for granted as to be little discussed, but preparation of a capable labor force and equity are the main reasons given where any become explicit.

In the United States we say we do not believe in passing privilege from parent to child; rather we [claim that we] expect individuals to earn favoured slots in society through talent and hard work. Equality of opportunity, mostly through education, is a central tenet of our social and economic system. The schools have been given the task of judging new citizens' talent and diligence. Consequently, it is important to our national sense of a social system that is fairly ordered that all children have an equal opportunity through education. If we are to say that success in education is a fair and just criterion by which to award each child a slot in an adult occupational hierarchy based upon individual merit, then the poorest child must have access to as good an education as the richest.

How, then, to guarantee an equal education? By guaranteeing the same education. State legislatures and large school districts standardize in the name of equity. The reform reports, with their bland references to "The American High School," reflect a strong public consensus on the importance of offering a standard high school experience to all American children. The common script and its enactment with symbols and rituals of Real School in all high schools gives a skeletal reality to the claim of equity through sameness.

But societal perceptions here bear some scrutiny. Just as the rituals of Real School create more social reassurance than technical substance in the daily life of some schools, so do they in the regional and national life of the society. Although the schools we studied served communities that differed widely in privilege and power, since all followed the common script they were similar in most formal respects: in social structure, in the use of time and space, in grouping of students and even in the formal curriculum. But they were very different in one formal respect. They had very different distributions of measures of student achievement. Grades, nationally standardized test scores, dropout rates, and rates of college attendance all varied significantly between schools and all were correlated with the socioeconomic status of the community.

Schools not only teach the young the content of the curriculum and some of the social graces required to be a member in good standing of a school community, they also sort young people into groups labeled as barely employable, possessing moderate skill, capable of much further development, or showing extreme promise. The public schools rank the students who emerge from their doors after thirteen years in ways which are fateful for those young people's work, their economic fortunes, and their status among other members of society.

Imagine what would happen if the goals that educators and reformers officially seek were actually accomplished. All students would become top performers. All of them would make perfect scores on the Scholastic Aptitude Test, not to mention having perfect A records throughout their schooling. Chaos would ensue. Colleges would not have room for all, but would have little ground on which to accept some and reject others. Employers looking for secretaries, retail salespersons, waiters, bus drivers, and factory workers would have jobs unfilled as every student considered such work beneath his or her accomplishments.

As long as education is used to rank young people and sort them into occupational futures that differ substantially in the money, status, power, and intrinsic rewards they can yield, good education, or students' success at education, must remain a scarce commodity. Those who do succeed have less competition for access to attractive occupations, if large numbers of others do not.

Families with the resources to affect the quality of their children's education have strong motivation both to provide a superior education to their children and to keep access to such a superior education limited, so that their children will face less challenge from others.

Consequently, an unspoken principle that opposes equality of opportunity through standardization of education is also at work. The public perceives schools to be in practice very unequal. Middle class parents will make considerable sacrifices to locate their children in schools they perceive to be better than others. Communities of parents with the economic and political means to do so will construct schools with special resources for their own children and will keep access to them exclusive. The social class and race of peers is often used by parents as a rough indicator of school quality.

Separate suburban school districts facilitate residents' ability to create superior schools based on selected peers, generous material resources, and teaching positions that attract many applicants from which to choose. Ordinances requiring certain sizes for lots, or only single occupancy housing, can keep out lower income families. Fair Housing groups across the country document the continued practice of racial steering by real estate agents; it can be used to keep many suburban communities all or mostly white. These districts can take advantage of their higher tax base to add the amenities of higher salaries for teachers, smaller class sizes, and richer stores of materials to their "standard" schools.

The six public schools we studied, although chosen to be ordinary and not including any really elite schools, provide eloquent testimony to the differences in public education that economic and racial housing segregation create in this country. In the communities they served, students received very different amounts of economic and educational resources from their parents and enjoyed very different levels of community safety and support. Students from different communities arrived at high school with visibly different skills, attitudes, and future plans. Different levels of funding available from local tax bases were visible in the schools' architecture, the nonteaching duties expected of their faculties, their extracurricular activities, and their supplies. Not only parents and students but school staff entertained very different visions of students' futures; these visions shaped the relationships of staff and students and the curricula-in-use (Hemmings & Metz, 1990; Metz, 1990). The differences among these schools remind us that more is hidden than revealed when one speaks in a single phrase of "The American High School."

Political scientist Murray Edelman (1977) argued that our political life is shot through with contradictory ideas that the public entertains simultaneously, but in alternation, so that no sense of inconsistency troubles our individual or collective consciousness. We perceive each side of the contradiction as it suits the context, or our social purposes and self-interests. In this way, Americans seem to live with a contradiction between officially equal education based on the common script for the drama of Real School, on the one hand, and tremendous variety in the quality and content of education resulting from schools' ties to socially and racially segregated communities, on the other. Middle class parents make sacrifices to buy houses where schools are supposed to be "better" and communities strongly resist moves for school consolidation

with neighboring communities, let alone proposals to desegregate schools or to introduce low income housing into suburbs. Despite continuous strenuous efforts to place children in superior schools and to preserve their exclusiveness, we rarely see, let alone openly acknowledge, the contradiction between these practices and equality of opportunity through the standardization of educational patterns.

Society's blindness to this contradiction serves the interests of the well-educated middle class. Children in schools with better prepared peers, which are attractive to better prepared teachers, have a considerable advantage in competition with the other products of America's supposedly standard and equal public schools. But middle class leaders feel no inconsistency in claiming that the young of the society are rewarded according to merit, even while they take care to place their own individual children in contexts that foster merit much more actively than those to which other children find themselves consigned.

The formal regulations and informal expectations that create the common script for high schools, and that lead school staffs to use that script to create some form of a Real School, reinforce the apparent equity of American education. The common script for a Real School thus becomes a guarantor of equity across schools. It has important symbolic value in this way to an outside audience of citizens and educational policymakers, as well as to participants. Thus not only do the staffs and parents of Drew and of Grant want to be reassured that these are Real Schools; so also do district administrators, state legislators, and leading citizens with an interest in educational equity—apparent or real.

CONCLUSION

The common script for high school practice with its standard social structure, technical routines, and curricular scope and sequence has taken on a deep cultural value in this country. Its enactment assures both participants and outsiders of the equity of public schooling in the nation as a whole, while it certifies teachers and students who follow it as legitimate and worthy participants in the academic and social life of the broader society. To follow the script is to accomplish these ends more clearly and surely than it is to effect students' mastery of geometry, chemistry, grammar, and clear written expression. The script serves as a symbol of unity and equity in American education. Participation in the drama it sketches out is participation in a ritual that affirms membership in mainstream American life.

The symbolic and ritual aspects of the play called "The American High School" are most visible where its routines are least technically effective in teaching geometry, chemistry, and English. We reached our insights into the symbolic and ritual aspects of the common script as we puzzled over its persistence in schools where it was manifestly not technically effective. Our conviction of the importance of symbol and ritual in maintaining Real School grew as we considered the outpouring of writing already cited which indicates that in recent years, not only in our schools for the poor and the working class, but in most American public high schools for students not headed for selective colleges, the script is no more than minimally effective while student alienation and even student failure are endemic.

This is not to say that the common script that we have developed for high school structure and instruction is irrelevant to its technical ends. It works with reasonable technical effectiveness in schools where certain unstated preconditions are met. In our study, it worked where students came to high school with strong literacy, numeracy, and writing skills and a rudimentary knowledge of history and science. Its effective operation also seemed to depend on students' having realistic hopes of at least modestly successful economic futures to give them extrinsic motivation to compete with each other and to accept the staff's agenda as worthwhile. These conditions apply to the majority of students in a decreasing number of schools, in only two of the six public schools we visited, and only three of the total eight. In our study, they applied where the majority of students expected to attend colleges with admissions standards that would eliminate some high school graduates.

Persons who are in a position to influence district, state, and national agendas for education are usually persons who were reasonably successful in learning through the patterns of Real School themselves. Most will expect it to work well for their own children, and for most it will indeed do so. These children will come to school from home prepared with relevant skills and a cultural style matched to school discourse. They will be able to expect later rewards for effort and good performance. They will be in schools with peers with similar advantages who will allow teachers to proceed with planned agendas and will stimulate one another to competition.

Many persons in policy-making positions have little direct experience from which to reflect on schooling processes and student reactions other than their own schooling and that of their children. Many have had little or no firsthand experience with schools for blue collar, let alone really poor or minority children, and little or no firsthand experience with the families or the life experience of students in such schools. If their images of what happens inside these schools are not clear and their diagnosis for the students and the schools not well-suited to the realities of their lives, no one should be surprised. Lacking this knowledge, they can easily believe that poor and minority and even blue collar children do not learn well in school because of defects in their characters that can be remedied with stronger demands and coercive pressures, with a sterner imposition of Real School. They can see differences between schools for poor children and the schools their own children attend in terms of talent and its lack, or effort and sloth, not in terms of advantages in their children's school experience. The system seems to them to offer equality of opportunity through the common script, while dramatic differences in patterns of student accomplishment between schools can be attributed to merit and fault in the individuals who attend them.

The lack of search for alternatives to the common script is a striking feature of current high school life—though some individual teachers do have successful alternative practices in place. But the many experiments that were tried in the 1960s and '70s, producing at least some anecdotal evidence of success, were rarely visible in the schools we studied. Some were still remembered. For example ethnic studies classes, like Afro-American history at Drew, had been discontinued within recent memory at some schools. This lack of alternatives feeds on itself, as schools that offer unconventional courses or teachers who follow unconventional practices become increasingly exceptional.

The pressures of the reform movement on the schools we studied strengthened the grip of Real School. Rising graduation requirements, increased standardized testing, and increased monitoring of drop-out rates and grading practices pushed teachers not only to use the script, but to follow it more slavishly and improvise less than they otherwise might have.

Once in place, the common script and the practice of Real School are reinforced by an interacting set of influences that overdetermine a conformist outcome. Broad societal support for these standardized patterns is frozen into bricks and mortar and into legal language. Thus school buildings, union contracts, and curriculum guides at the district level all support its patterns and are difficult to alter. Nationally distributed textbooks, college entrance requirements, state policies and laws, and nationally visible tests such as the ACT and college board achievement tests also play their parts.

These structural conditions and the less explicit expectations for curriculum and pedagogy that accompany them constrain teachers' practice directly but also set invisible boundaries around the content and style that teachers can easily claim to be legitimate. They significantly limit the range of teachers' ways of working. By legitimating, even certifying as required, a particular, apparently effective technical approach, they make teachers responsible both to use this approach and to make it successful. If teachers' practice is not then effective, the explanation seems evidently to lie in the actors within the school, in defects either in teachers' own performance of the script or in students' application of themselves to their parts. Teachers must blame themselves or blame the students—as will outsiders.

The institutionalization of Real School is embraced not only by powerful, well educated families for whom it usually works well, but by powerless and minimally educated families and their children as well. Even where students are not learning well, parents can be very insistent on the importance of traditional, Real, patterns of schooling (Joffe, 1977; Lubeck, 1985; Ogbu, 1974). Even the students who skip classes or refuse to do the written work when they come, may accept only the most traditional activities of Real School as authentic. James Herndon's (1969) description of his experience of teaching poor black children in junior high school in the late 1950s gives vivid evidence of this attitude. He describes how the children celebrated when a substitute teacher gave them grade level books, which they embraced, but never worked in. They wanted the books; so they could "not-do" them, as Herndon says. In our terms, the books gave them symbolic status as Real Students, but were not something they wanted to involve themselves in learning.

Nonetheless, there is some technical wisdom in the reluctance of school administrators and parents alike to open the flood gates of experimentation in poor areas. Standard curricular materials cut down the amount of work that teachers must do to present students a lesson that has at least minimal substance. Experimentation with genuinely alternative educational processes in an attempt to elicit students' intrinsic interest requires much more work from teachers. Many, perhaps most teachers, are likely to find the rewards unequal to the efforts such teaching requires. A good deal of skill and imagination is probably also required to succeed in such efforts, and not all teachers possess these requisites. Curriculum guides and texts support the efforts of the less than gifted. Poor and minority parents, who have been exposed to the low end of American schooling, are well aware of the effects of despair or malfeasance among teachers; they have experienced some of them in action despite the protections of the common script. They are probably not wrong in seeing some guarantee and insurance of education for their children in the patterns and rituals of Real School.

Alternatives to Real School exist; they have a history that extends well back into the nineteenth century (Cremin, 1964). Many have met with great success in particular situations. A few, like the Montessori method for young children, have become well-codified and have gained considerable social recognition. Especially at the elementary level, but also at the high school level, similar ideas keep being reinvented by teachers or founders of schools. They fade away, only to reappear again in a new guise a few years later in another place. But few have become fully institutionalized and widely recognized. Hence, when the obvious policy question "What method is better than Real School?" is raised, there is no systematic loyal opposition waiting to take over control, no alternative "one best system" (Tyack, 1974) standing in the wings.

A reason for the lack of [a] codified substitute plan for schooling system[s] lies in the emphasis of many alternative patterns upon responsiveness to students' prior experience and current interests. Such educational approaches must be relatively unstructured; they will take variable forms in varied settings. They also do not lend themselves to mass production with textbooks, standardized tests, and comparable credentials—all features that mass schooling and mass credentialing of students demand.

A concatenation of influences thus support the dominance of Real School and make its patterns extremely difficult to dislodge, even when their technical effectiveness falters and is clearly vulnerable to criticism. However ironic it may be, many dispossessed parents and students, together with their teachers, see in Real School a chance to maintain their pride and their sense of membership in the mainstream of American education, and so in American society. At the same time, precisely because Real School is not very effective in improving learning for more than small numbers of children from poor, minority, or even established blue collar families, the

relatively privileged educational decision makers who determine its content can support offering it to all students, and even intensifying its requirements for all, without fear that they will increase competition for the children of more educationally privileged parents like themselves. Offering the same education to all appears to be the essence of fairness—unless one has a sense of the interactive processes that transform the same structures and formal procedures into the diverse daily lives of schools in differing communities.

REFERENCES

Anyon, J. (1981). Social class and school knowledge. *Curriculum Inquiry, 11*(1), 3–42.

Bowles, S., & Gintis, H. (1976). *Schooling in capitalist America: Educational reform and the contradictions of economic life.* New York: Basic Books.

Boyer, E. L. (1983). *High school: A report on secondary education in America.* New York: Harper & Row.

Callahan, R. E. (1962). *Education and the cult of efficiency.* Chicago: University of Chicago Press.

Cohen, D. (1987). Educational technology, policy, and practice. *Educational Evaluation and Policy Analysis, 9*(2), 153–170.

Connell, R. W., Ashendon, D. J., Kessler, S., & Dowsett, G. W. (1982). *Making the difference.* Sydney: George Allen & Unwin.

Cremin, L. (1964). *The transformation of the school.* New York: Vintage Books.

Cusick, P. A. (1983). *The egalitarian ideal and the American high school.* New York: Longman.

Edelman, M. (1977). *Words that succeed and policies that fail.* New York: Academic Press.

Erickson, F. (1987). Transformation and school success: The politics and culture of educational achievement. *Anthropology and Education Quarterly, 18*(4), 335–356.

Fordham, S. (1988). Racelessness as a factor in black students' school success: Pragmatic strategy or Pyrrhic victory? *Harvard Educational Review, 58*(1), 54–84.

Fordham, S., & Ogbu, J. U. (1986). Black students' school success: Coping with the burden of acting white. *Urban Review, 18*(3), 176–206.

Goodlad, J. I. (1984). *A place called school: Prospects for the future.* New York: McGraw-Hill.

Heath, S. B. (1983). *Ways with words: Language, life and work in communities and classrooms.* Cambridge, England: Cambridge University Press.

Hemmings, A., & Metz, M. H. (1990). Real teaching: How high school teachers negotiate societal, local community, and student pressures when they define their work. In L. Valli & R. Page (Eds.), *Curriculum differentiation in U.S. secondary schools: Interpretive studies* (pp. 9–11). Buffalo: State University of New York Press.

Herndon, J. (1969). *The way it spozed to be.* New York: Bantam Books.

Hurn, C. (1985). Changes in authority relationships in schools: 1960–1980. In A. Kerckhoff (Ed.), *Research in sociology of education and socialization* (Vol. 5, pp. 31–57). Greenwich, CT: JAI Press.

Joffe, C. (1977). *Friendly intruders: Child care professionals and family life.* Berkeley: University of California Press.

Katz, M. B. (1971). *Class, bureaucracy, and schools: The illusion of education change in America.* New York: Praeger.

Lubeck, S. (1985). *Sandbox society: Early education in black and white America—A comparative ethnography.* Philadelphia: Falmer Press.

McNeil, L. (1986). *Contradictions of control.* New York: Routledge & Kegan Paul.

Metz, M. H. (1990). How social class differences shape the context of teachers' work. In M. McLaughlin & J. Talbert (Eds.), *The secondary school workplace* (pp. 40–107). New York: Teachers College Press.

Meyer, J., & Rowan, B. (1978). The structure of educational organizations. In M. W. Meyer & Associates, Environments and organizatons (pp. 78–109). San Fran: Jossey-Bass.

Ogbu, J. U. (1974). *The next generation: An ethnography of education in an urban neighborhood.* New York: Academic Press.

Ogbu, J. U. (1978). *Minority education and caste: The American system in cross-cultural perspective.* New York: Academic Press.

Ogbu, J. U. (1987). Variability in minority school performance: A problem in search of an explanation. *Anthropology and Education Quarterly, 18*(4), 312–334.

Powell, A., Farrar, E., & Cohen, D. (1985). *The shopping mall high school: Winners and losers in the educational marketplace.* Boston: Houghton Mifflin.

Sedlak, M., Wheeler, C. H., Pullin, D. C., & Cusick, P. A. (1986). *Selling students short: Classroom bargains and academic reform in the American high school.* New York: Teachers College Press.

Sizer, T. R. (1984). *Horace's compromise: The dilemma of the American high school.* Boston: Houghton Mifflin.

Tyack, D. B. (1974). *The one best system: A history of American education.* Cambridge, MA: Harvard University Press.

Weis, L. (1985). *Between two worlds: Black students in an urban community college.* New York: Routledge & Kegan Paul.

Willis, P. (1977). *Learning to labor: How working class kids get working class jobs.* New York: Columbia University Press.

WHY PUBLIC SCHOOLS NEED DEMOCRATIC GOVERNANCE

Diane Ravitch

As noted in the reading by Maeroff in this chapter, local public schools are most often governed by local school boards representing their communities, resulting in locally controlled schools. However, especially in some larger cities, the business model operates—city schools run by a business model with mayoral control and some degree of privatization, such as charter schools. Diane Ravitch considers the issues surrounding these two approaches and takes a strong stand in support of locally controlled schools. In her argument she points out that schools should be local institutions with local control. By removing control from local school boards, we take away that democratic institution—but for what? She argues that we do not know if privately run schools or "open market forces" will lead to better education. However, she argues that in the process of changing the authority structure of schools we are taking risks with children's lives. Ravitch points to the case of New York City, which is controlled by the mayor and is adding many new private charter schools, just as Cleveland and Chicago have done. Yet according to test scores, some of the higher performing school districts, such as Charlotte and Austin, are run by school boards. Thus, her argument is that we should not jump to new forms of school governance when the problems of schools are economic and demographic. No Child Left Behind and Race to the Top, federal government educational initiatives, advocate for more federal control in setting standards, teacher pay for performance, teacher tenure guidelines, and some privatization of schools through charters and choice. Beware the "crisis talkers" and the "latest fads" is Ravitch's advice.

Questions to consider for this reading:

1. What concerns does Ravitch have about the federal mandates discussed in the Borman and Cotner reading in Chapter 3?

2. Why does Ravitch argue that local control is necessary for democracy as opposed to mayoral or federal control of schools?

3. How does the business model affect democratic governance?

4. Based on articles by Maeroff and Ravitch, should school board structures be changed? If so, how?

E very time some expert, public official, or advocate declares that our public schools are in crisis, stop, listen, and see what he or she is selling. In the history of American education, crisis talk is cheap. Those who talk crisis usually have a cure that they want to promote, and they prefer to keep us focused on the dimensions of the "crisis" without looking too closely at their proposed cure.

The crisis talkers today want to diminish the role of local school boards and increase the privatization of public education. They recite the familiar statistics about mediocre student performance on international tests, and they conclude that bold action is needed and there is no time to delay or ponder. Local school boards insist on deliberation; they give parents and teachers a place to speak out and perhaps oppose whatever bold actions are on the table. So, in the eyes of some of our current crop of school reformers, local school boards are the problem that is blocking the reforms we need. The "reformers" want action, not deliberation.

Local school boards have not been enthusiastic, for example, about privatization of public schools. More often than not, they're skeptical that private entrepreneurs will be more successful running schools than experienced educators. Nor are they eager to open charter schools, which drain away resources and students from the regular schools and have the freedom to remove the students who are most difficult to educate. Local school boards have also been an obstacle to those who want to replace experienced principals and teachers with enthusiastic neophytes.

Local school boards are right to be wary of the latest fad. Our education system tends to embrace "reforms" too quickly, without adequate evidence of their value. Here's just one example from the many I could cite. In 1959, James Conant, the president of Harvard University, led a campaign against small high schools. He said they were inefficient and unable to supply a full curriculum. He called for consolidation of small districts and small high schools, so we could have the advantages of scale. Conant was featured on the cover of *Time,* and suddenly large high schools were the leading edge of reform. In our own time, the Bill & Melinda Gates Foundation poured $2 billion into breaking up large high schools and turning them into small high schools. Now, the Gates Foundation has decided that wasn't such a good idea, and it's off on another tangent, offering rewards to districts that evaluate teachers by their students' test scores.

Today, the public schools once again have a plethora of critics. Some say that public education itself is obsolete. There is a large and growing movement to dismantle public education. Some critics want to get rid of public education and replace it with a completely choice-based system of vouchers and charter schools. Proponents of this view say the market and choice are the only mechanisms that will produce high achievement. Government, they say, has failed. They believe—naively, I think—that in an open market, good schools would thrive and bad ones would die. Personally, I think this is a ludicrous analysis to apply to public education, which is a public good, not a private good or a commodity. As a society, we have a legal, moral, and social responsibility to provide a good public school in every neighborhood and not to leave this vital task to the free market and not to take unconscionable risks with the lives of vulnerable children.

First Line of Defense

The local school boards are the first line of defense for public education. Critics know this. In 2008, an article in *The Atlantic* was titled "First, Kill All the School Boards." It was written not by a right-wing extremist or a libertarian, but by Matt Miller of the Center for American Progress, whose president, John Podesta, led the Obama transition team. Miller argued that local control and local school boards are the basic cause of poor student performance. He said the federal government should take control of the nation's schools, set national standards, eliminate teacher tenure, and tie teacher pay to student performance. In an ideal world, he wrote, we would scrap local boards and replace them with mayoral control, especially in urban districts. This one act of removing all democratic governance, he claimed, would lead to better education.

This argument lacks logic and evidence. Some localities have high achievement, some have low, and the difference is economics and demography, not democracy. There is not a shred of evidence in Miller's article or in the research literature that schools improve when democratic governance ends.

In a similar vein, *Tough Choices or Tough Times,* a report prepared by the New Commission on the Skills of the American Workforce, proposed turning over all public schools to private managers. The role of school boards would be limited to approving performance contracts with these independent managers, monitoring their performance, and closing schools that didn't meet their goals. Under this proposal, signed by many of our most eminent leaders, local government would get out of the business of running public schools. In effect, every school would be a privately managed school.

Why would schools get better if they're managed by private companies? What secret do private sector organizations have that hasn't been shared with state and local education leaders? What's the logical connection between privatization and quality education? Why are they so certain that any privately managed school will be better than any regular public school?

The recommendation for universal privatization is irresponsible. You don't rip apart a vital part of the nation's social fabric—its public schools— because it sounds like a good idea. You don't destroy democratic governance of public education because of a hunch.

NEW YORK EXPERIENCE

As it happens, New York City has already created a test case of what happens when the local school board is rendered toothless. In 2002, the state legislature turned over control of the school system to the city's newly elected mayor, Michael Bloomberg. The legislation continued a central board, but abolished the city's 32 local school boards. The central board, however, consisted only of appointees who serve at the pleasure of the person who appointed them. Of its 13 members, eight serve at the pleasure of the mayor, and the remaining five serve at the pleasure of the borough presidents who appointed them.

The mayor immediately demonstrated that the new central board was of no importance. He renamed it the Panel for Educational Policy. When he introduced its members at a press conference, he made clear that they would not be speaking out on anything. He said, "They don't have to speak, and they don't have to serve. That's what 'serving at the pleasure' means" (Hernandez, 2009, [p. A1]). On a rare occasion, when two of his appointees planned to vote against his plan to end social promotion for 3rd graders, he fired them and replaced them on the same day. This central board, which was supposed to provide oversight and a check on the mayor's extraordinary power over the schools, was reduced to a rubber stamp.

Only one borough president appointed a representative who dared to ask questions. Patrick J. Sullivan, a business executive, was appointed to the central board in 2007 as a parent member. Before his term began, he sat in on a meeting and watched the board approve a $17 billion budget, a major labor contract, and a new database costing $80 million, all in less than an hour. He observed that, "The Panel for Educational Policy seemed more a misplaced relic of the Brezhnev-era Soviet Union than a functioning board of directors overseeing the education of 1.1 million children" ([Sullivan,] 2009).

The board exists to do whatever the mayor and chancellor want, not to exercise independent judgment. Sullivan reported that board members seldom had presentation materials in advance. Votes are cast before hearing public comments, not after, as is typical of other public boards. Although the law specified that the board would meet at least once a year in executive session, no such meeting was held in Sullivan's first two years on the board. Time and again, when controversial issues came up, Sullivan was the only dissenting voice on the panel.

When mayoral control of the schools came up for reauthorization before the New York state legislature in 2009, the mayor waged a heavily financed campaign to maintain his complete control of the school system. His advocacy group received millions of dollars from the Bill & Melinda Gates Foundation, the Broad Foundation, and other foundations. On one point, the mayor drew a line: He did not want any board members to serve for a fixed term, even if he appointed them. They must continue to serve at his pleasure. When Citizens Union, a respected civic organization, was considering the possibility of issuing a statement on behalf of fixed terms, it received a personal letter from U.S. Secretary of Education Arne Duncan, opposing fixed terms for any appointees and insisting that the mayor could be effective only if he had complete control.

Because New York City no longer has an independent board of education, it no longer has democratic control of its public education system. There is no forum in which parents and other members of the public can ask questions and get timely answers. Major decisions about the school system are made in private, behind closed doors, with no public review and no public discussion.

Because New York City no longer has an independent board of education, there are no checks or balances, no questioning of executive authority. A contract was awarded for nearly $16 million to the business consulting firm of Alvarez & Marsal to review operations and cut spending. This firm rearranged the city's complex school bus routes and stranded thousands of young children on one of the coldest days of the year without any means of getting to school. Some of the chaos they created might have been averted had there been public review and discussion of their plans. No one was held accountable for their mistakes; they were not chastised, and their contract was not terminated.

Similarly, the Department of Education imposed a grading system on every school in the city. In the name of accountability, each school is given a single letter grade from A to F, not a report card. The grade depends mainly on improvement, not on performance. Some outstanding schools, where more than 90% of the students meet state standards, got an F because they didn't make progress, while some really low-performing schools, even persistently dangerous ones, got an A because they saw a one-year gain in their scores. This approach was imposed without public discussion or review. The result was a very bad policy that stigmatizes some very good schools and helps none. The lesson is, or should be, that public discussion can prevent or mitigate policy errors.

In the absence of an independent board, there is no transparency of budget. There is no public forum in which questions are asked and answered about how the public's money is spent. Consequently, the number and size of no-bid contracts for consultants and vendors have soared into the hundreds of millions of dollars, with no public review or oversight. The education budget has grown from $12 billion annually to nearly $22 billion.

In the absence of a school board to oversee the actions of the executive, there is no accountability. The mayor can do as he wishes in the schools. The chancellor can adopt any policies he wishes; he serves at the pleasure of the mayor and answers to no one else. When a school fails or many schools fail, only the principal is held accountable. Those at headquarters who impose policies and programs are never held accountable.

All this unchecked authority has been used to turn New York City's public schools into a demonstration of choice and free markets in education. Children may choose among 400 or so high schools. They may choose from among 100 charter schools. If the school is successful or popular, students must enter a lottery or go onto a waiting list. In many of the poorest neighborhoods, the number of charter schools has increased, and many have been given space in neighborhood public schools. New York City might be the only district in the nation that places charter schools in public school buildings, taking away space previously allocated to art rooms, music rooms, computer rooms, and other activities. Parents and teachers have protested, but the mayor continues to place charters in public school buildings. By the end of the mayor's third term, there may be neighborhoods that have no public schools, just charters to which students seek entry.

The mayor has promised to open yet another 100 charter schools because he believes that schools should function like a marketplace, with choice and competition. Parents must struggle to get their child into the right high school, the right middle school, or the right charter school. Sustaining and improving regular public schools, neighborhood public schools, has low priority in the new world of the business model in education.

This business model has impressed the Obama Administration. Secretary Duncan has strongly endorsed mayoral control as a means to improve achievement, even though the results of the National Assessment of Educational Progress suggest caution: Two of the three lowest-performing districts in the nation (Cleveland and Chicago) are controlled by their mayors, while the highest performing districts (Charlotte and Austin) are managed by school boards. The Obama Administration has also required states to remove their caps on charter schools to be eligible for its $4.3 billion "Race to the Top" fund. In this time of budget cutting, every district wants new funding. But the price may be too high if public education is placed in jeopardy.

The business model assumes that democratic governance is a hindrance to effective education. It assumes that competition among schools and teachers produces better results than collaboration.

It treats local school boards as a nuisance and an obstacle rather than as the public's representatives in shaping education policy. It assumes that schools can be closed and opened as if they were chain stores rather than vital community institutions.

By endorsing mayoral control and privatization, the Obama Administration is making a risky bet.

REFERENCES

Hernandez, J. C. (2009, April 23). Schools panel is no threat to the mayor's grip. *The New York Times*, p. A1.

Miller, M. (2008). First, kill all the school boards. *The Atlantic* (January/February). Retrieved from http://www.theatlantic.com/magazine/archive/2008/01/first-kill-all-the-school-boards/6579/

Sullivan, P. J. (2009). Inside the panel for educational policy. In D. Ravitch (Ed.), *NYC schools under Bloomberg and Klein*. New York: Lulu.com.

Projects for Further Exploration

1. To gain a better understanding of schools as organizations in the United States, select indicators from the reading by Barr and Dreeben, or from others in this chapter. Using the Web pages in the Appendix, go to your state website and find school report card data. Locate a data set that allows you to compare schools in your areas using at least two of these indicators. There may also be information about schools on your state Web page.

2. The reading by Bryk in this chapter discusses ways to improve schools. Find a case study of a school that has improved its achievement levels on tests and graduation rates and describe what factors have made the difference. Compare this with the information provided by Bryk. Case examples can be found in Chicago, Anapolis, and other cities.

3. Replicate the study by Harry Gracey on the organization of the kindergarten classroom. Observe a nursery school or kindergarten class and keep notes on your observations. Write a summary that describes the lessons taught by the organization and the teacher, plus activities and interactions in the classroom.

4. Look for information on the number of charter schools in your state and in major cities. What can you learn about the structure and organization of these schools?

5

ROLES AND RESPONSIBILITIES

Administrators, Teachers, and Students

O rganizations provide the structure and goals, but people run organizations. For educational
systems, that involves people both inside and outside the organization. Outside influences on
schools were discussed in Chapters 3 and 4 where we explored some of the external organizations that influence schools, such as parents and local businesses. In this chapter we focus on positions
individuals hold in schools themselves and the responsibilities, or roles, that go with those positions.
For example, principals are responsible for the management of the local school building; their roles
put them in the middle between superintendents, school boards, and community members on the one
hand and teachers, staff, and students on the other. Principals must negotiate solutions to differences
between these other participants. Who has influence over what happens in schools is based in part on
the social, cultural, and economic capital held by school leaders (Spillane, Hallett, & Diamond, 2003).
Decisions on policies, practices, and reforms in schools come from leaders, often the principals. The
roles and responsibilities of principals are discussed in the first reading, which includes excerpts from
Dan Lortie's book, *School Principal* (2009).

About 3.2 million persons in the United States are employed as elementary and secondary school
teachers (National Center for Education Statistics [NCES], 2009). The number of public school
teachers has risen at a greater rate than that of students in the past 10 years, resulting in a decline in
student/teacher ratios from 17 to 15.7 students per teacher (NCES, 2009). In addition, 5 million
people served as professional, administrative, and support staff in schools and colleges.

Many sociologists of education have focused on the roles of teachers in educational organizations.
Two readings in this chapter review who teachers are, what conditions they face, how much control
they have in their jobs, and dissatisfaction and burnout resulting from, among other things, lack of
control. Richard Ingersoll and Elizabeth Merrill discuss the criteria for professional status, when
teachers meet these criteria, and where they fall short. Anthony Gary Dworkin and Pamela Tobe examine the effects of changing school accountability standards, federal and state mandates, school safety, and
student misbehavior on teachers' jobs and teacher burnout. Teachers have direct contact with the children
they are educating. Although they are responsible for their students, teachers are not completely autonomous. This presents a dilemma for many teachers, who feel they should have power to make decisions
for the children they teach (Dworkin, 2007; Dworkin & Townsend, 1994). Lack of control is one factor

leading to teacher burnout (Dworkin, Saha, & Hill, 2002). In addition, average teachers' salaries have held steady at around $50,000 for the past few years (NCES, 2009), not rising with inflation.

Because teachers are the front line in the classroom and are the main adults interacting with students, their influence has a major impact on the way students feel about their school experiences. If students like school, they have fewer disciplinary problems and higher achievement, plus they are less likely to drop out of school. The reading by Maureen Hallinan addresses the interaction between the roles of teachers and students and the influence of teachers on students' attitudes toward school.

Another important aspect of many students' school experiences and attachment to school is extracurricular activities. Just as teacher interactions with students can affect student attitudes toward school, extracurricular activities create a bond between the students and their schools. However, those who participate most in extracurricular activities are the higher socioeconomic status students who already bought into the achievement goals of schools, as discussed by Elizabeth Covay and William Carbonaro in their reading in this chapter.

Schools provide a gathering place for young people of similar ages. They facilitate the formation of peer groups that influence how the formal goals of schools are carried out. Students' experiences in schools vary greatly depending on their backgrounds, the school climate, and their roles in the school system. Some are leaders, some followers. Some are jocks, some brains. Some succeed, some fail. The informal aspects of schools discussed in Chapter 4 have great influence on students' experiences in school.

Probably the most difficult problem in schools, and one about which the public is most concerned, is violence, even though schools are one of the safest places for students to be (Addington, Ruddy, Miller, DeVoe, & Chandler, 2002). Some of this violence is brought into schools from the external environment by gang members. Some violence comes from isolated or alienated students, a cause made apparent by recent school shootings. Whatever the source, violence is perceived by the public and school personnel alike as a severe problem for schools, and debates about how to deal with school violence are the subject matter of many conferences. Violence finds its roots in the climate of schools. In their reading, David Dupper and Nancy Meyer-Adams illustrate the importance of school climate, in particular environments of intimidation and fear, in which some students have intolerable experiences. They suggest possible ways to change these toxic school climates.

When the education system fails students or students fail in the education system, policy analysts ask why and what can be done to correct the problem. Research tells us many of the problems that result in dropouts—high turnover in schools, problems with school resources, structure (including student-teacher ratios, quality of teachers, and school size), and student characteristics and composition (Rumberger & Thomas, 2000). In the last reading, Paul Barton discusses the situation of students for whom the educational system does not work. These "at risk" students and dropouts face reduced opportunities in life and are a considerable cost to society.

All of the readings in this section touch on aspects of roles held by participants in school systems. They also relate to both the formal and the informal school systems. Keep both the formal and informal organizations, plus the roles of participants in these organizations, in mind as you read other parts of this book and in your contacts with educational institutions.

REFERENCES

Addington, L. A., Ruddy, S. A., Miller, A. K., DeVoe, J. F., & Chandler, K. A. (2002, November). *Are America's schools safe? Students speak out* (U.S. Department of Commerce, National Technical Information Service, Technical Report, NTIS PB2003-101473, pp. 79–81). Washington, DC: U.S. Department of Education, National Center for Education Statistics.

Dworkin, A. G. (2007). School reform and teacher burnout: Issues of gender and gender tokenism. In B. Banks, S. Delamont, & C. Marshall (Eds.), *Gender and education: An encyclopedia* (pp. 69–78). New York: Greenwood Press.

Dworkin, A. G., Saha, L. J., & Hill, A. N. (2002). *Teacher burnout and perceptions of a democratic school environment.* Unpublished manuscript.

Dworkin, A. G., & Townsend, M. (1994). Teacher burnout in the face of reform: Some caveats in breaking the mold. In B. A. Jones & K. M. Borman (Eds.), *Investing in schools: Directions for educational policy* (pp. 68–86). Norwood, NJ: Ablex.

Lortie, D. C. (2009). *School principal: Managing in public.* Chicago: University of Chicago Press.

National Center for Education Statistics (NCES). (2009). Public elementary and secondary teachers, by level and state or jurisdiction (tables 63 and 65). *Digest of Education Statistics.* Washington, DC: U.S. Department of Education, National Center for Education Statistics. Retrieved from http://nces.ed.gov/programs/digest/d09/tables/dt09_065.asp

Rumberger, R. W., & Thomas, S. L. (2000). The distribution of dropout and turnover rates among urban and suburban high schools. *Sociology of Education, 73*(1), 39–67.

Spillane, J. P., Hallett, T., & Diamond, J. B. (2003). Forms of capital and the construction of leadership: Instructional leadership in urban elementary schools. *Sociology of Education, 76*(1), 1–17.

School Principal

Complications and Complexities

Dan C. Lortie

The school principal holds the role in the middle between government, superintendents and school boards, and teachers, staff, and students. Principals are the leaders of schools, and their roles involve balancing demands of multiple internal and external constituencies. The constraints and pressures on schools often fall to the principal to negotiate. In this excerpt from the newest edition of an old classic on school principals, Dan Lortie reviews the challenges elementary school principals face. Among the daily ongoing challenges are scarcity of time, interruptions to work, maintaining safety, and paperwork. More complex tasks include teacher evaluations and supervision, and problems or mistakes that need to be rectified. In their leadership positions, principals need to set the tone for the school. This excerpt provides an overview of the complex role of principals in schools.

Questions to consider for this reading:

1. Why is the role of principal a balancing act?

2. What are some ongoing challenges faced by principals in their day-to-day work?

3. With whom must principals interact in their roles as middle managers?

COMPLICATIONS AND COMPLEXITIES

What is hard about being an elementary principal? What is the downside? We will look at conditions that complicate the day, tasks that principals find difficult and/or dislike, and, finally, trouble that can strike as they go about doing their work. The progression in the discussion is from the least to the most serious challenges elementary principals face.

COMPLICATING CONDITIONS

Certain of the conditions under which principals work make that work more challenging than it

might otherwise be. Although no single problem is limited to the principalship, the combination of challenges may well be unique.

The Scarcity of Time

"What do you do all day long?" people ask my friend the Chicago principal. The questioners point out that since the children are dispersed among classrooms and supervised by teachers, she must surely have a lot of time on her hands. Perhaps memory plays a part in their raising the question; my informal inquiries, including discussion with persons who work in schools, suggest that many have little idea of how their elementary principals spent their time.

There is irony, therefore, in the fact that principals express a lot of anxiety about not having enough time, of feeling constant pressure as they try to complete their work. We mentioned earlier that classroom teachers have designated responsibilities that prevent them from being free to assist the principal in doing organizational jobs. That low "assignability" of staff members contributes to the long list of duties principals have to handle (McPherson, Salley, & Baehr, 1975). Empirical studies have pointed out that the principal's day tends to be fractured into numerous activities, which, on average, last only a few minutes (Peterson, 1977). This fragmentation of time, although not unique to school managers, is probably exacerbated by the nature of managerial work in schools (Mintzberg, 1973). Part of the difficulty lies in the fact that school officials find it difficult to persuade board members and the public at large to spend money on administrative assistance for principals.

What other aspects of the job produce principals' sense of time deprivation? There seem to be several. One is the rigidity of school schedules—the length of the day and number of weeks and the total time schools may operate—are all specified in advance and are extremely resistant to change. Whatever is going to be accomplished has to be done within the rigid parameters of overall schedules set by state authorities and specified by school district authorities. Collective bargaining has added to that rigidity by placing distinct limits on the amount of time that principals can ask teachers to meet outside regular school hours. Other causes grow out of the nature of principal tasks and their definition as public service, both of which limit the amount of time principals can use as they see fit. All compress the working day.

A lack of time flexibility is built into some of the major sets of tasks faced by principals, particularly, for example, in the responsibility to evaluate staff members. This area is highly formalized, an approach that is reinforced by the anxiety of officials to avoid legal action and the need to respect specifics worked out in collective bargaining contracts.

The steps in teacher evaluation illustrate how formalization reduces the control principals have over their time. Although districts differ in their specific requirements (e.g., how many members of the faculty to evaluate each year), the process normally demands many hours. The prescribed steps must be taken in a set order and, once initiated, must proceed at an appropriate pace: delays complicate communication and add anxiety for those being evaluated. Each step takes time—a preparatory conference between the principal and the teacher, observation in the classroom, writing up observations, and a conference to share the evaluation with the teacher. Tension can run high, for the results are entered in the teacher's permanent file. Principals quickly discover how prickly the process can be, leading them to adhere closely to district rules in case teachers who are dissatisfied with their evaluations fault them on procedural grounds (perhaps through the union) or central officials reprimand them for flouting district policies and practices. These rigidly prescribed sequences can stretch over many days during the academic year, particularly in schools with large faculties and/or in districts with particularly stringent procedures. Principals, as we shall see, express numerous doubts about evaluation; some of their dissatisfaction lies in the bureaucratic rigidities involved and the time spent at the expense of activities they consider more important.

On Interruption

Although research on managerial time indicates that interactions tend to come fast and often, there are respects in which principals are probably more vulnerable to interruption than is the case in many other organizational settings. Like middle managers in general, it is difficult for principals to resist demands from higher ranked officials; school heads complain that they are sidetracked by sudden deadlines for information and/or requests to attend meetings on matters in which they have little interest. In addition, the norms of public service deny them the right to privacy so prevalent in corporate affairs. Unlike the situation in private sector, it is difficult to erect barriers to limit access from their customers. Not for them, for example, are the elaborate, recorded responses to telephone calls found in businesses, which constrain access to officers by steering callers to "customer service representatives." In schools, however, to be seen as unresponsive to parents is a serious matter. In addition, many principals maintain an "open door" to teachers, a practice that is consistent with the emphasis we have seen on sustaining the approval and support of faculty members.

One way to underscore the weakness of barriers between principals and the public at large is to consider the scope of potential intervention by "customers" up to and including intervention in the processes of production. There are retail chains (e.g., Sears Roebuck) that control the manufacturing processes of some of the products they sell either through factory ownership or specifications in contracts with suppliers. Such retail firms deal with complaints in a routine fashion, usually by replacing products or refunding the dissatisfied customer's money. They would hardly agree, however, to a retail customer visiting and suggesting changes in the manufacture of, let's say, a washing machine—incredulity would greet any such request. Compare that, however, to the situation of a principal where parents insist that their child be transferred to another class, a demand that penetrates to the core of instructional practice. Granting the request may alienate not only one faculty member but, depending on the circumstances, other teachers as well. Simple rejection of parental requests ("That is none of your business") is not among the responses available to the principal. In fact, a parent who continues to be dissatisfied can appeal to officials in central office. Similar contrasts can be made, of course, to the ability of surgeons and other high-status professionals to restrict client influence on how they do their work.

The Maintenance of Order and Safety

The principal is a front-line supervisor with custodial responsibility (in loco parentis) for hundreds of young children. President Harry Truman's placard saying "the buck stops here" would be appropriate on the principal's desk, particularly in regard to maintaining good order and student safety. The principal serves as backup for teachers who need assistance in maintaining control and who refer individual students for final decisions. There are also occasions when the principal acts as the immediate supervisor of students, such as in the lunchroom or halls and play areas, which may not be supervised by teachers.

Outbursts of student misbehavior can be sudden and unpredictable—effective responses may demand immediate attention and allow little time for deliberation. The same applies, of course, to dealing with accidents in which a student is hurt. The risk of legal liability intensifies official concern, particularly if parents become alarmed and are ready to blame the school for injuries sustained by the children. Other tasks, even when interrupting them is costly, must be put aside. Principal work is marked by such unpredictable urgencies.

It is important to bear in mind the behavioral volatility of children, to recall that they are only gradually socialized into complying with the norms of orderly behavior which can usually be taken for granted among adults. Those charged with supervising children learn that lapses in adult control can produce disorder and that keeping order requires the physical presence of adults. That need results in "pinning down" many staff members and by reducing their mobility, also limiting the range of tasks they might otherwise undertake and preventing the formation of a more refined division of labor. It is another factor that affects the "assignability" of those who report to the principal.

Paperwork

The interviews make it clear that principals see various types of desk work as a constant, unremitting pressure on their time, a pressure many detest. If done at the office, it cuts off contact with teachers and students, but if taken home, affects relationships within the family. Some of the tasks result from the principal being the only (official) manager in the school who consequently has responsibility for overseeing the ordering and distribution of supplies, monitoring cash revenues, etc. Superintendents and boards also expect the principal to report on whatever information they consider relevant and urgent at a particular time—in addition, of course, to maintaining regular records such as attendance figures, which affect state revenues to the district. State and federal surveys are routinely shunted to principals who see such duties as contributing nothing to the instruction of their students. A small number of suburban principals mentioned that they had secretaries or assistants they could entrust with much of the paperwork; nationwide, there was a similar lack of help.

There are subjective costs in having to spend considerable amounts of time doing paperwork—tasks that are not only disliked but that block action on other tasks that are felt to be more urgent, important, or interesting. The load of paperwork also intensifies the principals' sense of too little time.

COMPLEX TASKS

One is hard put to think of any occupation that has no difficult or even distasteful tasks that have to be done. They may be difficult to do well or intrinsically complex. When we bear in mind that school management is fundamentally interactive in nature, it is not surprising that the major complexities that emerge focus on relationships with other people. Two questions that provoked talk about such difficulties will be discussed here; the first asked what aspect of the work is most difficult to do well and the second inquired into any mistakes the principal had made during the previous year. We will also explore responses to the question "Which of the tasks you do are least enjoyable?". Unrewarding tasks are difficult in a particular way; dealing with them requires mobilizing energy without the hope of pleasure and at the expense of tasks that are rewarding.

Challenges at the Core

The most frequent responses dealing with difficult tasks focus on the core of the principal's instructional responsibilities—that is, the formal evaluation and supervision of faculty members (Table 22.1). Within that large category, we find two central sources of difficulty: the lack of confidence principals have in the evaluative procedures they are required to use and the resistance teachers show to evaluation and to making whatever changes are proposed by the principal. (Less frequent but closely related responses include dismissing teachers, principal dislike of the evaluative process, and sustaining teacher morale.)

Principals mention several problems in evaluating teachers and using the assessments they make to supervise their work. The process, they say, is "too subjective." The appropriate criteria are not clear, and/or there is not enough time to visit classrooms and make solid judgments. ("It's hard to define what you are looking for and to get it across" [Male, 52].) Two kinds of uncertainty are evident—"How do I know what is best?" and "Do I have enough information to make a good judgment?" There are issues, then, in regard to the appropriateness of available standards and doubts about the empirical basis for their judgments.

Some principals felt caught between boards and superintendents who wanted corroboration for possible dismissal and teachers who wanted supportive evaluations; the first called for cool and detailed critiques, the second for more generous appraisals. Other principals saw a contradiction between representing evaluation as pedagogical assistance while, in fact, using it as the basis for retention or dismissal. Some principals rejected the assumption they perceived in evaluative procedures, namely, that there is only one right way to teach. Others reported that central office required them to use forms with specific and limited choices that constrained the quality of their judgments. Principals may, moreover, be required to state conclusions when unsure of their diagnoses; for example, they may not understand why a teacher is having particular problems and what steps might correct them.

Table 22.1 Most Difficult Task (Q. 20A)

	M	% Total M
A. Evaluation and supervision of teachers		
Weaknesses of evaluation process	31	27%
Dealing with teacher resistance	22	19%
Principal dislikes process	5	4%
Dismissing teachers disturbing	4	4%
Sustaining teacher morale	2	2%
Subtotal	64	56%
B. Other tasks		
Paperwork and "administrivia"	12	11%
Deciding without adequate knowledge	7	6%
Dealing with parents (resistant, angry)	6	5%
Resolving conflicts	5	4%
Living with time constraints	4	4%
Student discipline	3	3%
Miscellaneous (1 mention each)	12	11%
Subtotal	49	44%
Total mentions (N = 107)	113	100%

Recall, however, that principals, whatever their misgivings, have no choice in this matter—they must complete and submit formal evaluations; private reservations must be set aside and formal procedures carried out.

Given the variety of bases for discomfort mentioned by principals, it appears that being required to do formal evaluations imposes interpersonal and emotional "costs" on a substantial number of principals. Yet no respondent called for serious revision of the process or its elimination; it may be that despite those costs, principals see their evaluative responsibilities as supporting their authority in technical and professional realms. It concretizes the right of the principal to evaluate teacher behavior and to propose changes in their classroom activity; it underlines the important part played by principals in the district "chain of command." In a context of many limits on their authority, it remains valued by principals despite the problems it creates; the responses, taken together, point to considerable ambivalence toward the responsibility to evaluate teachers.

A substantial proportion of the principals' responses (19%) referred to the lack of cooperation shown by teachers when told to make changes in their behavior. The word "threatened" appears often in such responses, with principals varying in how broadly they apply the term to teachers—some generalize broadly while others restrict such references to a few. There are times when teacher resistance is portrayed sympathetically and times when it is not. Assisting teachers with some problems may face built-in difficulties, such as helping teachers to develop more control in the classroom.

I was against ranking teachers when I was a teacher and I still am.

The teacher union protects mediocrity. (Male, 61)

The more you intercede the more the children disrespect the teacher. (Female, 50)

Some principals mention the need for tact, the importance of taking teacher sensitivities into account. Whatever the specifics, teachers are not portrayed as welcoming evaluation and the supervision growing out of it. One of the challenges facing principals, therefore, is to exercise their instructional authority in ways that do not alienate the members of their faculties.

You have to keep a positive rapport with the person you are evaluating. Trying to get adults to change is a hell of a lot harder than getting children to change. (Male, 49)

The other responses to this question point to the variety of difficulties principals associate with their work. They may disdain the seemingly endless paperwork and administrative duties they define as trivial, and they are hard-pressed to maintain the energy to perform tasks that bore them or that seem unimportant. Some regretted their lack of knowledge: ignorance of cleaning techniques hampered one principal in supervising custodians, a former physical education teacher found it hard to cope with the academic curriculum, and another principal who knew little about budget matters had trouble dealing with the central office business manager. It can be taxing to interact with angry parents or those, at another extreme, who show little interest in what is happening to their children. Conflict, time constraints, and discipline problems round out the list of difficult tasks and situations.

What general observations can we derive from these responses? Two appear to be clear. Principals face considerable uncertainty in the course of their daily activities, uncertainty that makes their work harder; they are often unsure about the standards they should use and the reliability or validity of their judgments. The second overall theme is relational complexity. Teachers can and do fail to respond to the professional judgments of the principal. Parents produce unpredicted outbursts while students may exhibit puzzling and/or defiant behavior. Complexities around interaction account for a large proportion of the difficulties they mention. If their efforts to resolve problems with parents and subordinates fail, principals may be left with chronically dissatisfied parents and/or embittered faculty members, an unhappy and career-threatening state of affairs. Time and again we see principals emphasize the importance of good working relationships; at the same time, it is also evident that they cannot count on them to prevail.

Mistakes

Mistakes are, of course, considerably more likely to occur in difficult rather than easy situations; for that reason, they are cited here as another indicator of the particular tasks that principals find difficult to perform. Respondents were asked to talk about any mistakes they had made in the recent past. Seventy-one percent were ready to respond with actions they regretted or actions they wished they had taken and did not (Table 22.2).

The responses to this question are, in interesting ways, similar to those we just examined. Respondents ready to concede mistakes link most of them to day-in, day-out relationships; they connected 68% of the mistakes to interactions with others. Of those 63 relational errors, teachers stand out as the major source (32/61 of $N = 52\%$). The latter divide almost equally between employment issues of hiring and firing ($M = 14$) and problems that arise in the day-to-day management of faculty members ($M = 18$). The following quotation is a strong instance.

I have one teacher I think is crappy. I say some things, and weigh it. I wish she would take early retirement. I wish it, but I don't say it. I put kids in her classroom every year. Would I put my own kid in her classroom? No. I've been guilty for 22 years of not being able to get rid of bad teachers. (Male, 47)

This respondent is not alone in citing reluctance to let teachers go as a mistake. In nine of fourteen references to teachers, the principals regretted not having arranged their dismissal; the

Table 22.2 Types of Mistakes (Q. 55B)

	M	%Total M
1. Relational errors		
Teachers		
Managing faculty	18	20
Hiring and firing	14	16
Subtotal	32	36
Noncertified staff		
Hiring and firing	3	3
Parents		
Public relations	8	9
Allocation time and energy	2	2
Subtotal	10	11
Students		
Helped more	7	8
Disciplinary action	2	2
Subtotal	9	10
Central office		
Pushed harder	4	5
Avoided anger	2	2
Informed better	1	1
Subtotal	7	8
Subtotal of relational errors	61	68 (r.e.)
2. Other allocations of time and energy		
Instructional program	10	11
Other	3	3
Subtotal	13	14
3. Career-related regrets	3	3
4. Miscellaneous (1 mention each)	11	13
Grand Total mentions	88	98 (r.e.)
(N = 80/112: 71%)		

remaining five principals mentioned hiring teachers who did not work out. (The three mistakes with noncertified employees were also regrets about waiting too long to dismiss them.) Decisions about employment, and particularly the reluctance to dismiss staff members, can produce remorse. The most frequent regrets arise from omissions, from not acting rather than from acting too boldly; the others were based on poor predictions about how teachers would perform.

The responses classified under "managing faculty" include a variety of mistakes that can be made in supervising teachers. They must be assigned to particular classes, a process that can and does go wrong. There are issues with no clear answers. How should one use one's scarce resources of time and attention? Should one emphasize better performance from teachers, including more training opportunities, or devote more time and effort to increasing rapport with them? One principal may regret not going along with teacher preferences and another regret not having resisted them more strongly. Some principals may rue expressing anger at an uncooperative teacher where others wished they had not ignored the feelings of, and not helping, a new group of teachers displaced from a school that was closed. The perplexing choices involved in exercising authority in achieving an effective balance between "consideration" and "thrust," to quote terms used by Andrew Halpin (Halpin & Croft, 1963), are potential sources of remorse.

The mistakes made with parents consist almost entirely of not according them enough attention or not doing well in relating to them. You can be "too confrontational" said one, a sentiment voiced by two others as well who criticized themselves for being too "testy" and "authoritarian" with parents. Others regret mistakes such as being late in providing information about school changes and being slow to defuse the concerns of some parents. One idea summarizes these responses: the wise principal pays close attention to the parents of students and works hard to keep them well-informed and satisfied. Failure to do so can be costly.

Professional consciences are voiced when principals talk about mistakes with students; while two wish they had been somewhat sterner in disciplinary matters, others regretted occasions when they might have done more to help. Examples include the failure to seek outside expertise in a particular case, not fighting to prevent students from having to compete in an unfair (as she saw it) district competition and, in one tragic case, not trying harder to prevent a student from committing suicide. These mistakes exemplify what can be an important aspect of the principal's moral concerns—the obligation to

serve as the defender of, and advocate for, the students in his or her charge.

Mistakes vis-a-vis central office differ. Some say they should have pushed harder against central office decisions; a few regret occasions when they displayed negative feelings toward superordinates and their decisions.

Finally 14% of those mentions derive from what principals later see as poor judgments in allocating their own time and energy—mostly, insufficient attention devoted to instructional matters. Principals are exposed continuously to the idea that they should exercise "educational leadership," an injunction from authorities who do not necessarily accompany it with permission to slight competing obligations. Some look back, it seems, and blame themselves when they have not met whatever time and energy standards they associate with instructional leadership. One principal's regrets were echoed by others as well:

> Strengths for me are conferences, public relations, communications. Up to this year I have not concentrated on curriculum as much as I should have, perhaps. I want to mesh the two better. I'm not sure if it can be done, but I would like to. (Female, 40)

To summarize, the responses to our two questions on task difficulties undermine any view of the work of elementary principals as straightforward and uncomplicated. The difficulties they described arose in the central responsibilities laid on them, responsibilities, as we have seen, that included aims and relationships they considered important, for example, the oversight and improvement of instruction provided by faculty members. Substantial numbers doubted their own ability to make solid judgments on the quality of teacher performance; similar numbers found teachers did not respond affirmatively to their direction on how to improve their work.

Asked about mistakes they had made, these principals faulted themselves primarily in their managerial decisions in employment matters and where they chose to focus their attention and energy. They were too slow to dismiss ineffective teachers; they made mistakes in how they organized the work of their subordinates. Some did not, as they see it, do a good job in relating to parents and handling their relationship with central office. While none said they put too much emphasis on instructional matters, over a tenth wished they had concentrated more on teaching and learning. Some felt, after the fact, that they had not honored their obligation to take proper care of their students. It seems that recriminations come readily for these men and women—recriminations that grow out of the uncertainties and relational complexities that inhere in their work.

REFERENCES

Halpin, A. W., & Croft, D. B. (1963). *The organizational climate of schools.* Chicago: Midwest Administration Center, University of Chicago.

McPherson, R. B., Salley, C., & Baehr, M. F. (1975). *A national occupational analysis of the school principalship.* Chicago: Industrial Relations Center, University of Chicago.

Mintzberg, H. (1973). *The nature of managerial work* New York: Harper & Row.

Peterson, K. D. (1977). The principal's task. *Administrator's Notebook, 26*(8), 1–4.

THE STATUS OF TEACHING AS A PROFESSION

Richard M. Ingersoll and Elizabeth Merrill

Teachers are often considered the backbone of schools; without them there would be no school. Thus, understanding teachers' roles is key to understanding the educational system. Discussions of organizations often include information about the roles people occupy within them. One aspect of roles that distinguishes organizations is the type of workers they employ. Professionals have a high degree of control over their work environments, high prestige, and relatively high compensation compared to nonprofessionals. This designation is not without controversy, and it is often at the foundation of many labor disputes. Whether teachers qualify as professionals is one of these debates. Richard Ingersoll and Elizabeth Merrill evaluate the criteria of professionalization as they apply to teachers and conclude that teachers generally fall into a category called "semi-professionals."

Questions to consider for this reading:

1. What criteria differentiate professionals from other types of workers?
2. Where do teachers meet or fall short of these criteria?
3. Will teachers ever gain professional status?

Professionalization has long been a source of both hope and frustration for teachers. Since early in the 20th century, educators have repeatedly sought to promote the view that elementary and secondary teaching is a highly complex kind of work, requiring specialized knowledge and skill and deserving of the same status and standing as traditional professions, like law and medicine. This movement to professionalize teaching has, however, been marked by both confusion and contention, much of which centers around what it means to be a profession and to professionalize a particular kind of work. To some, the essence of a profession is advanced training and, hence, the way to best professionalize teaching is to upgrade teachers' knowledge and skills through professional development. For others, the essence of a profession lies in the attitudes individual practitioners hold toward their work. In this view the best

way to professionalize teaching is to instill an ethos of public service and high standards—a sense of professionalism—among teachers. For even others, the focus is on the organizational conditions under which teachers work; in this view, the best way to professionalize teaching is to improve teachers' working conditions. As a result of this wide range of emphases, it is often unclear whether education critics and reformers are referring to the same things when they discuss professionalization in teaching.[1]

Although education reformers often disagree over what is meant by profession, professionalism, and professionalization, students of occupations, notably sociologists, do not. The study of work, occupations, and professions has been an important topic in sociology for decades, and researchers in this subfield have developed what is known as the professional model—a series of organizational and occupational characteristics associated with professions and professionals and, hence, useful to distinguish professions and professionals from other kinds of work and workers.[2] These include rigorous training and licensing requirements, positive working conditions, an active professional organization or association, substantial workplace authority, relatively high compensation, and high prestige. From this viewpoint, occupations can be assessed according to the degree to which they do or do not exhibit the characteristics of the professional model. The established or "traditional" professions—law, medicine, university teaching, architecture, science, engineering, in particular—are usually regarded as the strongest examples of the professional model. There are, of course, large variations both between and within these professions in the degree to which they exhibit the professional model. Moreover, most professions have been and are currently undergoing change in the degree to which they exhibit the attributes of the professional model, that is, in their degree of professionalization or deprofessionalization.[3]

Sociologists have also been careful to distinguish professionalization from professionalism. The former refers to the degree to which occupations exhibit the structural or sociological attributes, characteristics, and criteria identified with the professional model. The latter refers to the attitudinal or psychological attributes of those who are considered to be, or aspire to be considered as, professionals. From the latter perspective, a professional is someone who is not an amateur, but is committed to a career and to public service. Although professionalism is often considered part of the professionalization process, sociologists do not consider it a reliable indicator of the professional model. Members of established professions do not necessarily exhibit a higher degree of the attitudes associated with professionalism than do those in less professionalized occupations. For instance, those with a strong service orientation—who place more importance on helping others and contributing to society and less importance on material rewards such as income and status—are less likely to be found in some of the traditional professions,

such as law, and more likely to be found in occupations such as nursing and teaching that traditionally have not been categorized as full professions (Ingersoll, 2003b; Kohn & Schooler, 1983; Rosenberg, 1981).

This chapter attempts to theoretically and empirically ground the debate over the status of teaching as a profession. Our purpose is neither explanatory nor evaluative. We do not seek to provide an historical account of the sources behind teachers' status, nor assess the benefits and costs, advantages, and disadvantages of professionalization. Moreover, our purpose is not normative; while we personally feel teaching should be treated as a profession, our purpose here is analytic and descriptive. That is our objective—to define and describe teaching's occupational status. The focus of this analysis is on professionalization or the characteristics of school workplaces and teaching staffs, and not on professionalism or the attitudes of individual teachers. Our primary point is that much of the educational discussion and literature on teaching as a profession has overlooked some of the most basic characteristics that sociologists have used to distinguish professions from other kinds of occupations. We empirically ground the subject by presenting a range of representative data from the best sources available. From these data we developed a series of indicators of the traditional characteristics of the professional model and used them to assess the professionalization of teaching. These include:[4]

1. Credential and licensing levels

2. Induction and mentoring programs for entrants

3. Professional development support, opportunities, and participation

4. Specialization

5. Authority over decision making

6. Compensation levels

7. Prestige and occupational social standing

These, of course, are not the only characteristics used to define professions, nor are they the only kinds of criteria used to distinguish or to classify work and occupations in general. But they are among the most widely used indicators of professions and professionals and are the subject of much discussion in reference to teachers and schools.

In a series of background analyses of these empirical indicators, we found large differences in professionalization among different kinds of schools. Consistent with other research on school organization, we found school sector (public/ private) and poverty level, in particular, to be the most significant factors related to professionalization (Ingersoll, 1997, 2003b).

Below, we will briefly describe each of the classic indicators of professionalization we examined, and then we will summarize what the data tell us about levels of professionalization in teaching and the extent to which it varies across these above different types of schools.

How Professionalized Is Teaching?

Credentials

To sociologists, the underlying and most important quality distinguishing professions from other kinds of occupations is the degree of expertise and complexity involved in the work itself. In this view, professional work involves highly complex sets of skills, intellectual functioning and knowledge that are not easily acquired and not widely held. For this reason, professions are often referred to as the "knowledge-based" occupations. But even if laypeople were to acquire these complex sets of skills and knowledge, rarely would they be able to practice as professionals. Entry into professions requires credentials. That is, entry into professions typically requires a license, which is obtained only after completion of an officially sanctioned training program and passage of examinations. Indeed, it is illegal to do many kinds of work, professional and not, from plumbing and hairstyling to law and medicine, without a license.

These credentials serve as screening or "gatekeeping" devices. Their rationale is protection of the interests of the public by assuring that practitioners hold an agreed-upon level of knowledge and skill, and by filtering out those with substandard levels of knowledge and skill. The importance of such credentials is evidenced by the practice, commonly used by professionals, such as physicians, dentists, architects, and attorneys, of prominently displaying official documentation of their credentials in their offices.

Given the importance of credentials to professions, not surprisingly, upgrading the licensing requirements for new teachers has been an important issue in school reform. (Licenses for teachers are known as teaching certificates and are issued by states.) But it has also been a source of contention. On one side are those who argue that entry into teaching should be more highly restricted, as in traditional professions. From this viewpoint, efforts to upgrade certification requirements for new teachers will help upgrade the quality and qualifications of teachers and teaching.

On the other side are those who argue that entry into teaching should be eased. Proponents of this view have pushed a range of initiatives, all of which involve a loosening of the entry gates: programs designed to entice professionals into mid-career changes to teaching; alternative certification programs, whereby college graduates can postpone formal education training, obtain an emergency teaching certificate, and begin teaching immediately; and Peace Corps–like programs, such as Teach for America, which seek to lure the "best and brightest" into understaffed schools. These alternative routes into the occupation claim the same rationale as the more restrictive traditional credential routes— enhanced recruitment of talented candidates into teaching—but the ultimate consequence of such initiatives, intended or not, can be deprofessionalization. That is, traditional professions rarely resort to lowering standards to recruit and retain quality practitioners.

Conflict over the ease of entry into teaching is reflected in the degree to which employed teachers actually hold a full state-approved certificate.[5] The data (the first row in Table 23.1) show that

Table 23.1   Level of Teacher Professionalization in Schools, by Type of District or School

	Public	Public Low Poverty	Public High Poverty	Private
Credentials				
% teachers with full certification	93	93	91	49
Induction				
% beginning teachers participating in induction program	78	79	78	32
Professional development				
% schools providing teachers with time for professional development activities	98	98	97	85
% teachers participating in professional organization activities	94	93	96	83
% teachers receiving funding for professional development activities	66	69	64	64
Specialization				
Mean % in-field teaching	77	81	71	58
Authority				
Over teacher hiring				
% with influential board	23	18	25	28
% with influential district staff	32	29	33	–
% with influential principal	91	92	88	94
% with influential faculty	27	27	27	33
Over teacher evaluation				
% with influential board	13	11	15	16
% with influential district staff	26	27	28	–
% with influential principal	94	93	94	95
% with influential faculty	19	22	20	18
Compensation				
% with retirement plan	88	87	90	57
Mean starting salary ($)	33,567	37,116	32,616	26,920
Mean maximum salary ($)	62,231	73,695	57,610	47,108

Source: From original analysis by the authors of the *Schools and Staffing Survey 1987–2007*. Washington, D.C.: Department of Education.

Note. Data for the first 6 indicators in the study are displayed in Table 23.1.

most, but not all, teachers in public districts do, indeed, hold full teaching certificates. In contrast, teachers in private schools are far less inclined to hold a full license to teach; just under half of private school teachers do so. This reflects different standards in public-private state regulations; many states do not require private school teachers to hold state certification (Tryneski, 2007). It also contrasts sharply with traditional professions. Hospitals, whether they are public or for-profit, for instance, would rarely hire unlicensed doctors and nurses to fill regular staff positions.[6]

This does not mean, of course, that private schools are not selective in who they hire as teachers. Private schools are, indeed, often very selective in their choice of teaching candidates, but they far less frequently use hiring criteria associated with professions. They are, however, not uniform in this deprofessionalization. There are distinct differences in the use of these hiring criteria among private schools, depending upon their orientation. Catholic schools, in particular, are far more likely than other private schools to require certificates and tests of their new hires.

Induction

In addition to initial formal training and preparation, professional work typically requires extensive training for new practitioners upon entry. Such training is designed to pick up where preservice training has left off. That is, while credentials and examinations in many professions are usually designed to assure that new entrants have a minimum or basic level of knowledge and skill, induction programs for practitioners are designed to augment this basic level of knowledge and skill. As a result, entry to professions typically involves both formal and informal mechanisms of induction—internships, apprenticeships, or mentoring programs. Sometimes these periods of induction can be prolonged and intensive, as in the case of physicians' internships. The objective of such programs and practices is to aid new practitioners in adjusting to the environment, to familiarize them with the concrete realities of their jobs and also to provide a

second opportunity to filter out those with substandard levels of skill and knowledge.

In teaching, mentoring, apprenticeship, and induction programs have been the subject of much discussion among reformers. The teaching occupation has long been plagued by high attrition rates among new staff (Ingersoll, 2003a) and, reformers argue, one of the best ways to increase the efficacy and retention of new teachers is to better assist them in coping with the practicalities of teaching, of managing groups of students and of adjusting to the school environment.

The data suggest these attempts at professionalization have had some success: over the past decade the numbers of schools with assistance programs has increased. Our background analysis of the data shows that in 1990 and 1991 in the public sector about one half of first-year teachers participated in formal induction programs of one sort or another. By 2007 and 2008 this had increased to almost 80% (see Table 23.1). The proportion of beginning teachers in private schools who participated in formal induction programs has been lower than public school teachers, but this percentage has also increased over the past decade. However, the data also show that induction programs vary widely in the number and kinds of activities and supports they include. The most comprehensive include a wide range of components, such as mentoring by veterans, structured planning time with teachers in one's field, orientation seminars, regular communication with an administrator, a reduced course load, and a classroom assistant. Moreover, in an advanced statistics analysis of these data, we have found that while induction makes a difference for teacher retention, it depends on how much one receives. Beginning teachers who receive comprehensive induction packages have far higher retention than those who receive fewer supports (see Smith & Ingersoll, 2004).

Professional Development

Beyond both preservice basic training and mentoring for beginners, professions typically require ongoing in-service technical development and growth on the part of practitioners throughout their careers. The assumption is that achieving a professional-level mastery of complex skills and knowledge is a prolonged and continuous process and, moreover, that professionals must continually update their skills, as the body of technology, skill, and knowledge advances. As a result, professionals typically belong to associations and organizations that, among other things, provide mechanisms, such as periodic conferences, publications, and workshops, for the dissemination of knowledge and skill to members. Moreover, professionalized workplaces typically both require and provide support for employee development. These include on-site workshops, financial support for conferences, coursework, skill development, and sabbaticals.

Professional development has been one of the most frequently discussed and advocated teacher reforms in recent years. In the 1990s improvement in the professional development of teachers was made one of eight major national education goals, introduced by a commission of governors and the president (National Education Goals Panel, 1997). Again, the data present a picture of success in the provision of support for, and teacher use of, professional development.

Data on three indicators of teacher professional development are displayed in Table 23.1: the percentage of schools that provided professional development programs for the teaching staff during regular school hours; the percentage of teachers who participated in workshops, seminars, or conferences provided by their school or by external professional associations or organizations; and the percentage of teachers who received financial support for college tuition, fees, or travel expenses for participation in external conferences or workshops during that school year.[7]

What is striking about the data on professional development is the consistency across schools. Most schools, both public and private, provide professional development, most teachers participate in workshops or activities either sponsored by their schools, or sponsored by external professional organizations, and most teachers also receive financial support of some sort for external professional development activities.

These data are an impressive set of indicators of this aspect of professionalization. However, they, of course, do not tell us about the quality or length of these professional development programs and activities.

Specialization

Given the importance of expertise to professions, it naturally follows that one of the most fundamental attributes of professions is specialization—professionals are not generalists, amateurs, or dilettantes, but possess expertise over a specific body of knowledge and skill. Few employers or organizations would require heart doctors to deliver babies, real estate lawyers to defend criminal cases, chemical engineers to design bridges, or sociology professors to teach English. The assumption behind this is that because such traditional professions require a great deal of skill, training, and expertise, specialization is considered necessary and good. In contrast, the other part of the assumption is that nonprofessions and semiskilled or low-skill occupations require far less skill, training, and expertise than traditional professions and, hence, specialization is assumed less necessary.

Despite the centrality of specialization to professionalization, there has been little recognition of its importance among education reformers, even among proponents of teacher professionalization. Indeed, some school reformers have argued that teacher specialization, especially at the elementary school level, is a step backward for education because it does not address the needs of the "whole child," unduly fragments the educational process and, hence, contributes to the alienation of students (e.g., Sizer, 1992).

To assess the degree of specialization in teaching and the degree to which teachers are treated as professionals with expertise in a specialty, we examine the phenomenon known as out-of-field teaching—the extent to which teachers are assigned to teach subjects which do not match their fields of specialty and training. Out-of-field teaching is an important but little understood problem. It is misunderstood because it is usually confused with teacher training. Most researchers and reformers assume, wrongly, that out-of-field teaching is due to a lack of training or preparation on the part of teachers. The source of out-of-field teaching lies not in a lack of education or training on the part of teachers, but in a lack of fit between teachers' fields of preparation and their teaching assignments. Out-of-field teaching is a result of misassignment—when school principals assign teachers to teach subjects for which they have little background. It is important because otherwise qualified teachers may become highly unqualified when assigned out of their fields of specialty.

Assessing the extent of in-field or out-of-field teaching is one way of assessing the importance of professional specialization in the occupation of teaching—it provides a measure of the extent to which teachers are treated as if they are semiskilled or low-skill workers whose work does not require much expertise or, alternatively, as if professionals whose work requires expertise in a specialty. Table 23.1 presents a measure of in-field/out-of-field teaching—the average percentage of secondary-level classes in which teachers do have at least a college minor in the fields taught.[8]

The data show that an emphasis on specialization in one's area of expertise often does not hold in secondary level teaching. Teachers at the secondary school level are assigned to teach a substantial portion of their weekly class schedules out of their fields of specialty. For example, in public schools, teachers, on average, spend only about three quarters of their time teaching in fields in which they have a college major or even a minor. This lack of specialization is more widespread in high-poverty schools. But, again, these comparisons are overshadowed by public/private differences.

Private school teachers are far more often assigned to teach subjects out of their fields of training than are public school teachers—just over half of a private school teacher's schedule is in fields for which they have basic training. However, there are differences among private schools (not shown here). Teachers in nonsectarian private schools have higher levels of in-field teaching than do teachers in other private schools. On average, teachers in nonsectarian schools spend about two thirds of their schedules teaching in field; in contrast, in-field levels in religious private schools are lower—about half their class loads.

Authority

Professionals are considered experts in whom substantial authority is vested and professions are marked by a large degree of self-governance. The rationale behind professional authority is to place substantial levels of control into the hands of the experts—those who are closest to and most knowledgeable of the work. Professions, for example, exert substantial control over the curriculum, admissions, and accreditation of professional training schools; set and enforce behavioral and ethical standards for practitioners; and exert substantial control over who their future colleagues are to be. Sometimes this control is exerted through professional organizations. For instance, gaining control over (and sharply limiting) medical school admissions by the American Medical Association was a crucial factor in the rise of medicine from a lower status occupation to one of the pinnacle professions (Starr, 1982). Other times control is exerted directly in workplaces and, as a result, professionalized employees often have authority approaching that of senior management when it comes to organizational decisions surrounding their work. In the case of hospitals, physicians traditionally were the senior management. Academics, for another example, often have substantially more control than university administrators over the hiring of new colleagues and, through the institution of peer review, over the evaluation and promotion of members and, hence, over the ongoing content and character of the work of the profession.

The distribution of power, authority, and control in schools is one of the most important issues in contemporary education research and policy. Indeed, this issue lies at the crux of many current reforms, such as teacher empowerment, site-based management, charter schools, and school restructuring. But it is also a source of contention. Some hold that schools are overly decentralized organizations in which teachers have too much workplace autonomy and discretion. Others hold the opposite—that schools are overly centralized in which teachers have too little influence over school operations. Part of this confusion arises because of differences in the domain analyzed; most focus on how much autonomy teachers have in their classrooms over the choice of their texts or teaching techniques. Others focus on how much power faculties collectively wield over schoolwide decision making, such as budgets.[9] Here we focus on faculty influence over two issues traditionally controlled by professionals—peer hiring and peer evaluation.

Table 23.1 displays the frequency of schools in which principals report the school board, the district staff if in the public sector, the faculty, and principals themselves, to have substantial decision making influence over two activities—staff evaluation and hiring.[10] The data paint a picture of a steep organizational-level hierarchy, with principals at the top.

Overall, principals clearly view themselves as powerful actors in reference to decisions concerning teacher evaluation and hiring and teachers as among the least powerful actors. In comparison to principals, boards, and district staff have far less authority over these school decisions, at least from the viewpoint of principals. In every kind of school, principals report faculty to be influential far less often than they are themselves. Teachers are also less often influential than district staff over these issues. However, in comparison to school boards, teachers' professional authority is equal or higher in both public and private schools.

Consistent with conventional wisdom, the hierarchy in some ways is less steep in affluent than in poor public schools; faculty in poor schools are less often reported to be influential, especially over hiring, and boards are more often influential. But, especially over hiring, private school teachers are less often empowered than those in public schools, counter to conventional wisdom that private school teachers are delegated more workplace influence

than public school teachers (e.g., Chubb & Moe, 1989).

Compensation

Professionals typically are well compensated and are provided with relatively high salary and benefit levels throughout their career span. The assumption is that, given the lengthy training and the complexity of the knowledge and skills required, relatively high levels of compensation are necessary to recruit and retain capable and motivated individuals.

Teacher salaries have been a much discussed topic amongst teacher reformers. But, unfortunately, data on teacher salaries have often been misleading. Teacher salary analyses typically focus on the average salary levels of teachers of particular types or in particular jurisdictions. Comparing average teacher salaries for different kinds of teachers or schools can be misleading because teacher salary levels are often standardized according to a uniform salary schedule, based on the education levels and years of experience of the teachers. Especially with an aging teaching workforce, it is unclear if differences in average salary levels are due to real differences in the compensation offered to comparable teachers by different schools, or are due to differences in the experience and education levels of the teachers employed. That is, schools with older teachers may appear to offer better salaries, when in fact they do not.

A more effective method of comparison across schools is to compare the normal salaries paid by schools to teachers at common points in their careers. Start-of-career salary levels provide some indication of how well particular kinds of workplaces are able to compete for the pool of capable individuals. End-of-career salary levels provide some indication of the ability of particular kinds of workplaces to retain and motivate capable individuals. The ratio between starting salaries and end-of-career salaries provides some indication of the extent of opportunity for promotion, and the range of monetary rewards available to employees as they advance through their careers.

Table 23.1 shows data on the normal starting and maximum teacher salaries offered in different kinds of districts or schools in the 2007–2008 school year. Of course, salary data such as these quickly get "old" due to inflation. However, our analysis is not concerned with absolute salary values, but with comparisons—which have shown little change over time. We make four comparisons: how salaries vary across different types of schools; the ratio between teachers' start-of-career and end-of-career salaries; how beginning teachers' salaries compare with those of other recent college graduates; and, finally, how teachers' annual salaries compare to those in other occupations. These are revealing comparisons to make and get at the status of teaching as a profession. Data on the provision of retirement benefits are also displayed.[11]

Consistent with conventional wisdom (Kozol, 1991), there are differences in the compensation afforded to teachers in public schools and public schools serving high-poverty communities pay less than schools in more affluent communities. But the differences between public and private schools are even greater. Teachers in private schools are paid far less than in public schools, and also are less likely to be provided with a retirement plan by their school. The average starting salary for an individual with a bachelor's degree and no teaching experience was about 25% more in public schools than in private schools. Moreover, the public-private salary gap widens as teachers progress through their careers. The average maximum salary (the highest possible salary offered) for public school teachers was more than 30% more than for private school teachers. We also found that among private schools, there are also large differences in compensation. Non-Catholic religious private schools pay their starting teachers a salary that is just above the official federal poverty line. Teachers' salaries, in both public and private schools, are also "front loaded." The ratio of teachers' end-of-career to start-of-career salaries in Table 23.1 is less than 2 to 1. This is far less than many other occupations and traditional professions. Front loading suggests limited opportunity for financial gains, can undermine long-term commitment to an occupation, and can make teaching less attractive as a career (Lortie, 1975).

In order to place teachers' salaries in perspective, it is useful to compare them to the salaries earned in other lines of work. Traditionally teachers have long been called the "economic proletarians of the professions" (Mills, 1951), and the data bear this out. Table 23.2 shows that the salaries of new college graduates who have become teachers are considerably below those of new college graduates who chose a number of other occupations. For instance, the average salary (one year after graduation) for 2000 college graduates who became teachers was almost 50% less than the average starting salary of their classmates who took computer programming jobs.

Table 23.2 Mean Annual Salaries of New Bachelor Degree Recipients in Selected Occupations (2000–2001)

Occupation	Salary
Managers/executives	$75,470
Computer programmers	$50,158
Engineers/architects	$47,205
Sales	$36,521
Military	$35,917
Mechanics	$35,818
Editors/writers/reporters	$29,506
Teachers (K–12)	$26,609
Laborers	$24,387
All occupations	$28,478

Note. From original analysis by the authors of the *Baccalaureate and Beyond Survey: 2000–2001*. Washington, DC: U.S. Department of Education.

These differences remain throughout the career span. For instance, data collected in 2008 by the Bureau of Labor Statistics show that the average annual salaries of teachers were far below those of traditional professionals, such as college professors, scientists, pilots, and lawyers (see Table 23.3).

Table 23.3 Mean Annual Salaries for Selected Occupations (2008)

Occupation	Salary
Surgeons	$206,770
Dentists	142,070
Lawyers	124,750
Pilots	119,750
Law professors	101,070
Physicists	106,440
Pharmacists	104,260
Veterinarians	89,450
Education administrators (K–12)	86,060
Architects	76,750
Chemists	71,070
Psychology professors	69,560
Sociology professors	68,900
Accountants	65,840
Secondary school teachers	54,390
Middle school teachers	52,570
Elementary school teachers	52,240
Kindergarten teachers	49,770
Preschool teachers	26,610

Note. From *National Occupational Employment and Wage Estimates*, 2009, Washington, DC: Bureau of Labor Statistics.

Prestige

Professions are high status, high prestige occupations. In other words, they are respected and envied. Prestige and status, unlike salary, power or professional development, at first glance, might seem very difficult to empirically assess because they are highly subjective. But, like other attitudes, public perceptions of which kinds of occupations are more or less prestigious can be assessed and, indeed, for more than 50 years sociologists have studied how the public evaluates the relative prestige of occupations. Table 23.4 presents some of the results from the best known studies of occupational prestige.[12] These data are useful to illustrate how the status of teaching compares to other occupations and also to compare the relative status of different levels of teaching. The

data clearly show that, as expected, the traditional professions are very prestigious. Teaching, like many of the other female dominated occupations, is rated in the middle. Teaching is less prestigious than law, medicine, and engineering, but it is more prestigious than most blue collar work, such as truck driving, and pink collar work, such as secretaries. The status of teaching also changed slightly from the early 1970s to the late 1980s. Both elementary and secondary teaching went up in prestige, but kindergarten and preschool teaching went down. The result is a distinct status hierarchy within the teaching occupation; secondary teachers are slightly higher status than elementary teachers. Both are substantially higher status than kindergarten and preschool teachers.

IMPLICATIONS

This article attempts to ground the ongoing debate over teacher professionalization by evaluating teaching according to a series of classic criteria used to distinguish professions from other kinds of work. The data show that, on the one hand, almost all elementary and secondary schools do exhibit some of the important characteristics of professionalized workplaces. On the other hand, and despite numerous reform initiatives, almost all schools lack or fall short on many of the key characteristics associated with professionalization. Clearly, teaching continues to be treated as, at best, a "semi-profession" (Lortie, 1969, 1975).

But there are also large variations in the degree of professionalization, depending on the type of school. Consistent with conventional wisdom, low-income schools are, in a number of ways, less professionalized than are the more affluent public schools. The most striking differences are those between public and private schools. The teaching job in private schools is in some important ways less professionalized than in public schools. Moreover, there are distinct differences within the private sector, often overlooked in public/private comparisons. Our background analyses show that in most ways, the least

Table 23.4 Relative Prestige of Selected Occupations (ranked by 1972 scores)

Occupation	Score 1972	Score 1989	Occupation	Score 1972	Score 1989
Physicians	82	86	Funeral directors	52	49
Professors	78	74	Athletes	51	65
Lawyers	76	75	Bank tellers	50	43
Judges	76	71	Police	48	60
Physicists and astronomers	74	73	Secretaries	46	46
Dentists	74	72	Mail carriers/postal service	42	47
Architects	71	73	Plumbers	41	45
Aerospace Engineers	71	72	Tailors	41	42
Psychologists	71	69	Carpenters	40	39
Chemists	69	73	Barbers	38	36
Clergy	69	69	Bakers	34	35
Chemical engineers	67	73	Truck drivers	32	30
Secondary school teachers	63	66	Cashier	31	29
Registered nurses	62	66	Painters/construction/maintenance	30	34
Elementary school teachers	60	64	Cooks	26	31
Authors	60	63	Waiters and waitresses	20	28
Pre-K/kindergarten teachers	60	55	Maids	18	20
Actors and directors	55	58	Garbage collectors	17	28
Librarians	55	54	Janitors/cleaners	16	22
Social workers	52	52			

Note. From *General Social Survey*, 1972 and 1989, Washington, DC: U.S. Census Bureau. Reprinted with permission.

professionalized of schools are non-Catholic religious private schools. This has important implications for current school reform and policy. It suggests there may be an overlooked but fundamental clash between teacher professionalization and school privatization reforms, such as some school choice initiatives. It also suggests that privatization may lead to an unintended consequence—the further deprofessionalization of teaching.

These data raise some obvious questions. What difference does professionalization make for those in schools? What are the implications of variations among schools in professionalization? To be sure, research and reform concerned with teacher professionalization typically assume that professionalization is highly beneficial to teachers,

schools, and students. The rationale underlying this view is that upgrading the teaching occupation will lead to improvements in the motivation, job satisfaction, and efficacy of teachers, which, in turn, will lead to improvements in teachers' performance, which will ultimately lead to improvements in student learning (e.g., Carnegie Forum on Education and the Economy, 1986; Holmes Group, 1986). If we accept this assumption, in other words if we assume that professionalization attracts capable recruits to an occupation, fosters their expertise and commitment, and, ultimately, provides assurance to the public of quality service to the public, then these data do not yield a reassuring portrait of the teaching occupation.

This logic and these assumptions seem reasonable enough. Indeed, equivalent arguments are regularly used by proponents of professionalization in any number of other occupations and also by defenders of the status quo in the traditional professions. However, just as in other occupations and professions, very little empirical research has ever been done to test such claims. It is difficult to find, for instance, empirical research examining the direct effects of the relatively high levels of training, power, compensation, and prestige accorded to physicians and professors.

It is important, however, to ask these kinds of questions because proponents of professionalization, in teaching and elsewhere, ignore an important stream of literature in the sociology of work, occupations and professions that illuminates the downside to professionalization. For instance, medicine, long considered among the pinnacle professions and the clearest example of work that has successfully become professionalized over the past century, has been the subject of a great deal of criticism. The focus of this criticism is the negative consequences of the power and privilege of professionalization—monopolistic control over medical knowledge and the supply of practitioners, antagonism toward alternative medical approaches, a power imbalance in the physician/client relationship (e.g., Abbott, 1988; Freidson, 1986; Starr, 1982). From this viewpoint, professionalization in medicine has brought many benefits, but it also incurs costs. The implication of this line of thought is that it is important to distinguish both the benefits and costs of professionalization and also to specify for whom both of these apply.

In other follow-up research projects, we and colleagues have analyzed the effects of various indicators of professionalization on teachers themselves—specifically their engagement or commitment to teaching; on conflict in schools and on teachers' actual rates of retention and turnover (see, e.g., Ingersoll, 1997, 2003b; Smith & Ingersoll, 2004). We found that most of the above indicators of professionalization do, indeed, positively affect teacher commitment, school climate, and teacher retention. Several, however, particularly stood out for their strong effects: faculty autonomy and decision-making influence; the effectiveness of assistance for new teachers; and teachers' salaries and benefits.

NOTES

1. For examples of the literature on teacher professionalism and professionalization, see Labaree (1992, 2004); Little (1990); Lortie (1969, 1975); Malen and Ogawa (1988); Rosenholtz (1989); Rowan (1994); Talbert and McLaughlin (1993).

2. For examples of the sociological literature on professions, see, e.g., Abbott (1988); Collins (1979); Etzioni (1969); Freidson (1984, 1986, 2001); Hall (1968); Hodson and Sullivan (1995); Hughes (1965); Larson (1977); Mills (1951); Starr (1982); Vollmer and Mills (1966).

3. There is an important stream of sociological research on the proletarianization, bureaucratization, and deprofessionalization of some traditional professions. See, for example, Freidson (1984, 1986, 2001).

4. Unless noted, the data for these indicators are from the U.S. Department of Education's Schools and Staffing Survey (SASS). This is the largest and most comprehensive data source available on elementary and secondary teachers. SASS was conceived to fill a long-noted void of nationally representative data on the staffing, occupational, and organizational aspects of elementary and secondary schools. To date, six independent cycles of SASS have been completed: 1987–1988, 1990–1991, 1993–1994, 1999–2000, 2003–2004, 2007–2008. Each cycle includes several sets of linked questionnaires: for each school sampled, for the principal or headmaster of each school, for the central district administration for each public school, and for a sample of teachers within each school. In each cycle, the effective sample sizes are about: 5,000 school districts, 11,000 schools, and 55,000 teachers. The SASS data presented in this analysis are primarily from the 2007–2008 cycle.

5. In Table 23.1, low poverty refers to schools where 10% or less of the students receive publicly funded free or reduced price lunches. High poverty refers to schools where more than 50% do so. In Table 23.1, "full" certification refers to all those with regular, standard, advanced, or probationary certification. It does not include temporary, emergency, or provisional certificates. Probationary refers to those having completed all of the requirements for a full certificate, except for a required probationary period.

6. Of course, many organizations, such as hospitals and universities, are characterized by a growing secondary labor market of "adjunct" jobs and positions. These are often very similar in work content to regular positions, but are otherwise highly deprofessionalized; i.e., with lower levels of compensation, authority, specialization, prestige, etc. For examples of the literature on primary and secondary labor markets, see Simpson and Simpson (1983).

7. Of the three indicators of teacher professional development displayed in Table 23.1, the first is from data collected in 2007–2008, the second and third are from 2003–2004 data.

8. The data on percentage in-field teaching are from the 1993–1994 SASS. For a detailed report of our research on out-of-field teaching, see "The Problem of Underqualified Teachers in American Secondary Schools" (Ingersoll, 1999).

9. For a more detailed discussion of the debate over school control and centralization/decentralization and a more detailed analysis of the data on decision-making influence, see Ingersoll (2003b).

10. The measures of decision-making influence are drawn from principals' answers to the question: "How much actual influence do you think each group or person has on decisions concerning the following activities: hiring new full-time teachers and evaluating teachers?" For four groups: school boards, district if public sector, principals themselves and faculty. Each group or person is defined as being "influential" if the mean score for the activity was equal to 4, on a scale of 1 = no influence to 4 = major influence.

11. The retirement plan measure indicates whether a school or district offers either a defined-benefit or a defined-contribution (with employer contribution) retirement plan. It does not account for differences in the worth or coverage of plans.

12. In the early 1960s, sociologists, working with the General Social Surveys (GSS) and Census data, developed an occupational prestige scale based on rankings of the social standing of occupations by a nationally representative sample of respondents. These scales were replicated and refined over subsequent years. For information on the GSS and the occupational prestige scales and data, see Davis and Smith (1996).

REFERENCES

Abbott, A. (1988). *The system of professions: An essay on the division of expert labor*. Chicago: University of Chicago Press.

Carnegie Forum on Education and the Economy. (1986). *A nation prepared: Teachers for the 21st century*. New York: Carnegie Forum.

Chubb, J. E., & Moe, T. M. (1989). *Politics, markets, and America's schools*. Washington, DC: Brookings Institution.

Collins, R. (1979). *The credential society*. New York: Academic Press.

Davis, J., & Smith, T. (1996). *General social surveys, 1972–1996: Cumulative codebook*. Chicago: National Opinion Research Center.

Etzioni, A. (Ed.). (1969). *The semi-professions and their organizations: Teachers, nurses, and social workers*. New York: Free Press.

Freidson, E. (1984). The changing nature of professional control. *Annual Review of Sociology, 10*(1), 1–20.

Freidson, E. (1986). *Professional powers: A study in the institutionalization of formal knowledge*. Chicago: University of Chicago Press.

Freidson, E. (2001). *Professionalism: The third logic*. Chicago: University of Chicago Press.

Hall, R. (1968). Professionalization and bureaucratization. *American Sociological Review, 33*(1), 92–104.

Hodson, R., & Sullivan, T. (1995). Professions and professionals. In *The social organization of work* (pp. 287–314). Belmont, CA: Wadsworth.

Holmes Group. (1986). *Tomorrow's teachers*. East Lansing, MI: Author.

Hughes, E. (1965). Professions. In K. Lynn & the editors of Daedalus (Eds.), *The professions in America* (pp. 1–14). Boston: Houghton Mifflin.

Ingersoll, R. (1997). *Teacher professionalization and teacher commitment: A multilevel analysis*. Washington, DC: National Center for Education Statistics.

Ingersoll, R. (1999). The problem of underqualified teachers in American secondary schools. *Educational Researcher, 28*(2), 26–37.

Ingersoll, R. (2003a). *Is there really a teacher shortage?* Philadelphia: Consortium for Policy Research in Education, University of Pennsylvania. Retrieved from http://www.gse.upenn.edu/pdf/rmi/Shortage-RMI-09-2003.pdf

Ingersoll, R. (2003b). *Who controls teachers' work? Power and accountability in America's schools*. Cambridge, MA: Harvard University Press.

Kohn, M., & Schooler, C. (1983). *Work and personality*. Norwood, NJ: Ablex.

Kozol, J. (1991). *Savage inequalities*. New York: HarperCollins.

Labaree, D. (1992). Power, knowledge, and the rationalization of teaching: A genealogy of the movement to professionalize teaching. *Harvard Educational Review, 62,* 123–154.

Labaree, D. (2004). *The trouble with ed schools.* New Haven, CT: Yale University Press.

Larson, M. (1977). *The rise of professionalism: A sociological analysis.* Berkeley: University of California Press.

Little, J. (1990). Conditions of professional development in secondary schools. In M. McLaughlin, J. Talbert, & N. Bascia (Eds.), *The contexts of teaching in secondary schools: Teachers' realities* (pp. 187–218). New York: Teachers College Press.

Lortie, D. (1969). The balance of control and autonomy in elementary school teaching. In A. Etzioni (Ed.), *The semi-professions and their organizations: Teachers, nurses and social workers* (pp. 1–53). New York: Free Press.

Lortie, D. (1975). *School teacher.* Chicago: University of Chicago Press.

Malen, B., & Ogawa, R. (1988). Professional-patron influence on site-based governance council: A confounding case study. *Educational Evaluation and Policy Analysis, 10,* 251–270.

Mills, C. W. (1951). *White collar.* New York: Oxford University Press.

National Education Goals Panel. (1997). *National education goals report.* Washington, DC: Government Printing Office.

Rosenberg, M. (1981). *Occupations and values.* New York: Arno Press.

Rosenholtz, S. (1989). *Teacher's workplace: The social organization of schools.* New York: Longman.

Rowan, B. (1994). Comparing teachers' work with work in other occupations: Notes on the professional status of teaching. *Educational Researcher, 23*(6), 4–17.

Simpson, I., & Simpson, R. (1983). *Research in the sociology of work.* Greenwich, CT: JAI Press.

Sizer, T. (1992). *Horace's compromise: The dilemma of the American high school.* Boston: Houghton Mifflin.

Smith, T. M., & Ingersoll, R. (2004). What are the effects of induction and mentoring on beginning teacher turnover? *American Educational Research Journal, 41*(3), 681–714.

Starr, P. (1982). *The social transformation of American medicine.* New York: Basic Books.

Talbert, J., & McLaughlin, M. (1993). Teacher professionalism in local school contexts. *American Journal of Education, 102*(2), 123–153.

Tryneski, J. (2007). *Requirements for certification of teachers, counselors, librarians, administrators for elementary and secondary schools* (71st ed.). Chicago: University of Chicago Press.

Vollmer, H., & Mills, D. (1966). *Professionalization.* Englewood Cliffs, NJ: Prentice Hall.

TEACHER BURNOUT IN LIGHT OF SCHOOL SAFETY, STUDENT MISBEHAVIOR, AND CHANGING ACCOUNTABILITY STANDARDS

Anthony Gary Dworkin and Pamela F. Tobe

Each U.S. presidential administration puts forth a plan to reform schools. Each proposed reform impacts the structures and roles in schools. Where the impact is most noticeable is in classrooms as reforms affect teachers—their lesson plans, curricula, classroom structure, discipline procedures, use of time, focus of lessons, and goals for students. Add to the teacher's role the responsibilities of dealing with student misbehavior and sometimes their own safety in schools, and individuals become disenchanted with what brought them into the field of teaching in the beginning of their careers. Because of the frequent policy changes, sometimes implying teachers are at fault for problems with our schools, and problems with some students, many teachers experience burnout resulting from alienation. Thus, the teaching profession loses its most experienced personnel. Anthony Gary Dworkin and Pamela Tobe discuss these conditions that result in burnout.

Questions to consider for this reading:

1. What school reforms initiated by politicians have taken place and are taking place in school classrooms across the United States?

2. What are the causes of teacher burnout?

3. What is the relationship of changes brought about by proposed school reforms and teachers' problems?

4. Compare the status of teaching as a profession in the previous reading with the description of teacher burnout in this article. Does this comparison support Ingersoll and Merrill's suggestion that teachers are semiprofessionals?

Job burnout has been symptomatic of many new employees in human service professions, including school teaching. Previous research has linked school reforms spawned by the Standards-Based School Accountability Movement with the expansion of feelings of burnout to more experienced teachers. Recent research has also tied the lack of school safety, including student bullying behaviors, and poor student discipline to increased teacher burnout. This reading links student misbehavior and school safety concerns to changes in teacher burnout over three waves of school reform.

Burnout, as a concept, was coined by the psychologist Freudenberger (1974) to describe a malaise or "wearing out" frequently experienced by human service professionals such as teachers, nurses and social workers. Soon after Freudenberger's initial publication other psychologists attempted to operationalize and measure the concept. The most often cited of the investigators, Christine Maslach, identified three central themes in burnout: emotional exhaustion, a sense of loss of personal accomplishment, and depersonalization where the student, patient or client was at fault (Maslach, 1978a, 1978b, 1993; Maslach & Jackson, 1981; and Cherniss, 1980, 1992). The malady leads workers to cease to perform their roles effectively, and sometimes become hostile or uncaring about those they are charged to assist. Most psychological models of burnout "blame the victim" or attribute to the victims an unwillingness to cope with multiple life stressors. Burnout, from a psychological perspective, is seen as a personal weakness rather than an institutional weakness; the solutions are therefore therapeutic or palliative. There are panoply of strategies to enhance individual coping skills (Abel & Sewell, 1999; Cedoline, 1982; Farber, 1991; Gold & Roth, 1993; Pines, 1993; Swick & Hanley, 1983) such as being taught stress and time management skills, holistic health care, and yoga.

Alaya Pines (1993), in another psychological approach, characterized burnout as an existential crisis, where the value of the individual's work and sense of self-worth are questioned. In this conception of burnout teachers come to question why they are doing this unappreciated and underpaid job and question what difference their efforts make. These questions reflect self-doubt, a diminished sense of self-worth, and similarly a diminished value of their work. Workers in developed nations often define themselves in terms of their work roles; diminished satisfaction with work represents diminished appraisal of their own worth.

As a sociological concept, burnout is explained in terms of the organizational and social causes of stress, and not the individual's ability to cope with stress. The initial sociological view arose from five dimensions of alienation (Seeman, 1959, 1975): powerlessness, normlessness, meaninglessness, isolation, and estrangement. In this conceptualization of burnout, teachers may feel powerless in the educational system or in their school; normless in that school rules may be perceived as dysfunctional, unenforceable or nonexistent; meaningless because they are unable to achieve their personal goals or incapable of making a difference in their

students' lives; and feel isolated or estranged from their colleagues and principal. Stress can still be a precipitating factor in teacher burnout but the causal elements are seen within the structure of the school or the structure of the educational system (Dworkin, 1987, 1997, 2001).

There is no universally accepted cause of "burnout." The different theories put forth for the causes of burnout range from psychological (identifying personal factors to blame) to sociological (organizational/work environment). Additionally, increased federal and state accountability demands have made teaching more stressful. The impact on teacher burnout of increased accountability demands and changing school reform efforts has been analyzed by Dworkin and colleagues (LeCompte & Dworkin, 1991; Dworkin, 2001, 2007; Dworkin, Saha, & Hill, 2003).

ACCOUNTABILITY AND SCHOOL REFORM EFFORTS

Teacher burnout, as a function of school reform legislation and the changing demands and roles required of teachers, was analyzed by Dworkin (1997) and Dworkin, Saha, and Hill (2003). Three major school reform movements were identified as evolving from the publication of *A Nation at Risk* (1983) by the National Commission on Excellence in Education. The report condemned the public educational system for producing low academic achievement in American students and declared that, unless student achievement improved and massive educational reforms were implemented, America's competitive edge in the global marketplace would be lost. These school reform efforts are based on the assumption that the public schools are failing to educate the nation's future labor force, thus endangering the economic future of the country. Reform efforts blame poor student achievement on poor teaching, and on incompetent and/or unmotivated school district personnel (teachers, administrators).

The first reform efforts sought "to introduce uniformity and conformity through standardized curricula, rigorous requirements for student performance, promotion, graduation, and teacher evaluation" (Smylie & Denny, 1990, p. 235). These reform efforts, referred to as the Standards Movement, sought to guarantee only competent teachers were in the classroom and that the students who graduated from high school were proficient at the skills that would make them competent employees in American industry. The first wave of reform also included establishing statewide uniform academic standards for students.

In response to *A Nation at Risk,* competency based testing of teachers began. Burnout had previously been a malady of novice teachers; the highest burnout rates occurred among teachers with less than 5 years experience. However, with the introduction of teacher competency testing, more experienced teachers (10 to 15 years) were challenged regarding their expertise. Additionally, uniform academic standards defied their autonomy by specifying the curriculum to be taught and narrowing its content to what was being assessed by standardized tests. During the Standards Movement, experienced teachers became more stressed than novices.

When teacher testing did not produce the desired increases in student test scores, a second stage of reforms were implemented. These reforms were often referred to as high-stakes testing. Schools were held accountable for the test scores of their students and repeated low achievement could result in the termination of teaching contracts and the closing of schools. The first Bush administration established America 2000 (1991) to establish "world-class standards" for education. Decentralization and site-based decision making (decision making made at the community and district level) was the proposed solution. The results engendered local conflicts and turf wars among teachers, administrators and communities, which further heightened teacher stress and burnout.

The Clinton administration in the Goals 2000 (1994) advocated high-stakes testing. Initially, high-stakes testing was aimed at teachers and schools where test passage rates would become public information. Making school academic achievement information public, affected housing

values and community attractiveness; neighborhoods whose schools produced high-test scores had increased property values while low test scores saw declines. Community pressure to maintain high property values provided support for employing severe measures to correct low student and school performance.

The third stage of reform efforts expanded the consequences of high-stakes testing to include the students. In this stage, not only could schools be closed and teachers fired, but a student's low standardized test performance could lead to being retained in grade. Many states passed laws eliminating social promotion thereby making test failure high stakes for both students and school personnel. The No Child Left Behind Act of 2001 (NCLB) represents a national implementation of the high-stakes testing movement begun under Goals 2000. NCLB specified a timetable and sequence under which schools could be deemed *In Need Of Improvement* (INOI) and ultimately subject to closing (faculty and staff terminated). The law included a public school choice option whereby parents could move their children out of low performing schools (INOI) to better performing schools. Schools and districts are measured by improvements in annual test score results. Statewide passage standards for all students and subgroups of students (minorities, limited English proficient, special education, and low-income) are used to determine whether a school or district is performing adequately. The passage rates for groups of students are to be raised each year until 2013–2014 when all students tested are expected to pass (with 95% of students being tested). The passage rates are expected to increase by state-specified increments, defined as adequate yearly progress (AYP). High-stakes testing and its attendant impact on school accountability, exacerbated teacher burnout (Dworkin, 2009; Sunderman, Tracey, Kim, & Orfield, 2004).

Prior to the reform waves, teacher burnout tended to be the malady of new teachers who often were unable to cope with the multiple demands placed upon them in the teaching role, especially in urban schools. Additionally, novice teachers were more likely to be assigned to the most troubled urban schools where administrators were unsupportive and considered them to be expendable employees (Dworkin, 1987). The pattern of burnout across cohorts in the pre-reform era was such that burnout was highest among the new teachers and progressively diminished with increased teaching experience. Following the imposition of school reforms, burnout became more widespread among the teaching population, with more experienced teachers also reporting attitudes indicative of burnout. However, it was not necessarily the case that the magnitude of burnout escalated, especially as reforms were replaced by more reforms. Teachers came to expect some form of accountability system and therefore learned to adapt to them (Dworkin, 2009).

Unsafe Schools

In the early 1990s, an assessment by the Education Economic Policy Center of the State of Texas reported that student test scores were highest in safe and secure schools, even controlling for other covariates such as student body composition, size, teacher characteristics, and socioeconomic status (Heller & Toenjes, 1993). Schools that are fraught with drug and gang problems, disruptive students, and bullying students create two categories of stressors that adversely affect teacher morale. The presence of danger heightens teacher job stress, a significant causal factor in burnout. In this current era of school accountability, teachers are assessed on the extent to which they raise student standardized test scores; campus insecurity and danger affect student achievement of the victims of school violence and bullying, and also the performance of the whole class, including the bullies (Bru, 2009). Thus, a school that is not safe and secure is likely to have depressed test scores amongst all students, resulting in elevated teacher stress due to fear of negative job appraisals.

A broad array of activities can make a school unsafe and insecure, some of which constitute illegal acts and others that diminish the effectiveness of teaching and learning. For the present analysis our focus will be on three elements of unsafe and insecure schools: the presence of legally defined crimes against the person or property, student bullying behaviors, and markedly disruptive student behaviors in class. Bullying behaviors may include acts that are categorized as crimes against the person, but also include more psychological attacks, including taunting and teasing.

The National Center for Education Statistics has issued a report on school crime and safety since 1992. From 1993 to 2008, the percentage of teachers nationally who have been victims of nonfatal crimes had been progressively diminishing from 12.8% in 1993–4 to 8.1% in 2007–8 (Bauer, Guerino, Nolle, & Tang, 2008; Dinkes, Kemp, & Baum, 2009). Student victimization statistics from the *School Crime and Safety Report: 2009* indicate an estimated 11% of urban high school students and 9% of elementary school students reported being victims of violent crimes during the 2007–8 academic year. High school students are more likely to report violent crimes off-campus, while younger students report more incidents occurring on campus. Schools that are persistently dangerous under NCLB can be deemed INOI. Dangerous schools impact teachers and exacerbate burnout in two distinct ways. The threat of teacher and student victimization is itself a stressor that can affect teacher morale and burnout. Additionally, dangerous schools tend to be low-performing schools, with teaching and learning disruptions depressing student performance.

In schools where gang violence and criminal activities spill over from dysfunctional neighborhoods, the level of job stress experienced by teachers and administrators significantly increases their burnout and diminishes their work commitment. Vettenburg (2002) noted how teachers who feel unsafe in their workplace have difficulty focusing their attention on teaching and the stress associated with the perception of physical danger diminishes their commitment to their students and their work. The investigator further noted that mitigating student aggressive behavior alone was less significant than changing the organizational climate. Likewise, Orpinas et al. (2000)

noted that both students and teachers who feel unsafe are more likely to miss class.

Cassidy (2009) reported that student victims of bullying displayed more stress reactions and had diminished problem solving abilities. Gavish and Friedman (2010) reported that disruptive students adversely affected the morale of novice teachers. Novice teachers usually have fewer classroom management and organizational skills to draw upon. However, Bru (2009) indicated that with the exception of the disruptive student, the rest of the class tends not to suffer academically from marked disruptions. The Bru study was conducted in Norway where student bodies are less likely to differ from their teachers in social class and ethnicity. Dworkin (1987) found that significant differences between students and teacher ethnicity and social class were associated with higher levels of stress and burnout.

There is considerable evidence that supportive principals can break the functional connection between job stress and teacher burnout (Blasé, 2009; Dworkin, 1987, 2009; Sarros & Sarros, 1992). Supportive principals can provide trust, respect, feedback, advice and information (Sarros & Sarros, 1992) to their teachers reducing stress and facilitating coping. However, in schools where the principal or other supervisors are abusive and create a toxic work environment, teacher morale is significantly diminished. Thus, the principal can play a substantial role in making even a stressful work situation less stressful and less likely to lead to burnout, or the principal can compound stress and burnout.

DISRUPTIVE STUDENTS

Some research on teacher morale has focused on the extent to which disruptive students increase job stress among teachers and, in turn, their level of burnout. Friedman (1991, 1995) reported that typical student behavior patterns (disrespect, inattentiveness and sociability) contributed to predicting teacher burnout. Studies by Brouwers and Tomic (2000) and Burke, Greenglass, and Schwarzer (1996) reveal that student disruptions divert teacher

attention away from instruction and thereby diminish the teachers' sense of accomplishment (a component of burnout). Further, disruptions can lead to confrontations that are stressful. Student disruptions tend to more adversely affect novice and/or poorly trained teachers (Friedman, 1995), whose own hold on classroom management and professional self-confidence may be weak.

Earlier work by Dworkin and his colleagues (Dworkin, 1997, 2001, 2009; Dworkin & Townsend, 1994) has shown that while school accountability systems became more punitive, teacher burnout patterns changed from a malady that affected novice teachers to one that affects teachers at all levels of experience. Career risk for teachers has increased from an accountability system that assesses teacher competency without a verifiable risk that teachers will lose their jobs, as in reforms associated with *A Nation at Risk* (1983) and site-based decision making reforms (early 1990s), to ones in which high-stakes testing can result in school closures and termination of staff (as in the Texas Accountability System of the late 1990s and the No Child Left Behind Act of 2001). In one sense, reforms that tested the competency of teachers did not actually detract from teachers' control over their fate. Their own performances were used to assess their abilities. By contrast, high-stakes testing places the fate of schools and teachers in the hands of their students. Thus, more consequential accountability is expected to heighten burnout levels for all teachers.

Prior work has also linked the lack of school safety and teacher burnout for two reasons. Increased risk of crime and victimization of teachers is in itself a job stressor, which can heighten burnout. However, victimization of students is associated with diminished academic performance of those victimized and those who are victimizers. Even if the safety issues are limited to psychological bullying behavior (as opposed to violent crime) or to disruptive student behaviors, the results are that students will learn less, perform less well on tests, including state-mandated standardized tests, and thereby increase the accountability risk to schools and teachers. Further, diminished student achievement adversely affects the teachers' sense of accomplishment, as the teacher has less evidence that her/his teacher practices have been effective in promoting learning. It is therefore expected, that in relatively unsafe schools, teacher burnout will be higher and that as the accountability system changes from minimally threatening to draconian (e.g., school closings and staff terminations), burnout levels among the teaching staff will increase.

There are two countervailing tendencies that may nuance the burnout levels. The occurrence of violent school behavior has been decreasing since 1992 (Dinkes, Kemp, & Baum, 2009), at least in part due to "zero tolerance" policies and the opening of alternative schools for students who do not comply with the rules enforced in conventional schools. This should result in decreased burnout associated with victimization, including problems of discipline and decreased safety. Nevertheless, it is expected that burnout will be higher in schools where gang activity, bullying, and neighborhood violence are prevalent. The second tendency is associated with accountability systems based on school reform efforts and the Standards-Based School Reform Movement (which began in 1983). While earlier work showed that when accountability systems were first put into place they heightened teacher stress and burnout. However, for most teachers the accountability systems have been a way of life throughout their careers. Only the most senior teachers in the post-NCLB cohorts would have ever taught in an era in which schools were not assessed using some accountability system. On balance we would expect that:

H_1: Teachers assigned to schools with higher levels of crime and safety risks and more discipline problems will display greater levels of burnout than teachers not assigned to such schools.

Rival Hypothesis H_{1a}: Since the creation of alternative schools and "zero tolerance" programs teacher burnout associated with disciplinary problems and school safety have diminished such that these stressors will have a lower effect size on burnout than before the development of these schools and programs.

H_2: Accountability systems that place teachers' careers and the continued operation of their schools at risk will be associated with higher levels of teacher burnout than those systems that do not create risks for schools and teachers.

Rival Hypothesis H_{2a}: The more years that teachers have functioned in schools affected by accountability systems the lower will be the effect of such systems on their level of burnout.

MEASURING TEACHER BURNOUT

The present study relies on a burnout scale developed by Dworkin (1987) and discussed in Lester and Bishop (2000). The burnout scale is made up of ten items that assess the concepts of alienation, including meaninglessness, powerlessness, normlessness, isolation, and estrangement. They represent components of burnout that Dworkin (1987, p. 28) had developed and reflect his definition of the construct:

> Burnout is an extreme form of role-specific alienation characterized by a sense that one's work is meaningless and that one is powerless to effect changes that would make the work more meaningful. This sense of meaninglessness and powerlessness is heightened by a belief that the norms associated with the role and the setting are absent, conflicting, or inoperative, and that one is alone and isolated among one's colleagues and clients.

The items were combined statistically through principal components analysis and yielded a unidimensional scale or single factor. Because the measure is expressed in z-score form, negative values represent lower levels of burnout and positive values represent high levels of burnout.

THE DATA SETS

The present analysis relies on three data sets collected in the Houston metropolitan area between 1986 and 2009. The initial data set consists of surveys administered to 1,060 urban public school teachers assigned to several large school districts. No subgroup of teachers was significantly under-represented in the obtained sample (as determined by the Bridge, 1974, sampling bias technique). The enumeration occurred soon after Texas had implemented an accountability system that required teachers to pass a competency test. These data supply information on burnout prior to the implementation of more severe accountability systems and the use of alternative schools and "zero tolerance" policies.

The second sample consists of 2,961 public school teachers drawn in 2002 from a large school district in the Houston area. Although the teachers were not from the same school district as in the first sample, the teacher characteristics and student demography (high poverty and predominantly minority) did not differ from those of the first sample. Additionally, the same colleges of education throughout the region and state supplied teachers to both of the school districts in the samples. The 2002 sample was collected immediately after the passage of The No Child Left Behind Act of 2001 and after Texas had imposed high-stakes testing with the potential of teacher terminations and school closures.

The third and final 2009 sample consists of 2,148 teachers from the same urban district enumerated in 2002. Again, the teachers did not differ significantly from the teaching population of 1986 or 2002. The 2009 data represent attitudes of teachers enumerated after the full implementation of The No Child Left Behind Act of 2001 and after Texas had eliminated social promotion by requiring students to pass the state-mandated TAKS (Texas Assessment of Knowledge and Skills) tests in specified subjects and grades. Test failure requires students to attend summer school and possibly repeat grades 3, 5, and 8. The test had become high-stakes for schools, teachers, and students, and in fact, there have been school closings and public school choice option afforded to students in low-performing schools. The second and third data sets (2002 and 2009) measure the effects of increasingly more severe accountability systems

on teacher burnout, as well as the implementation of systems designed to remove seriously misbehaving students from schools.

RESULTS

Table 24.1 presents the predictors of teacher burnout in each of the three sample years separately to clarify the relative effects of student discipline and school safety, as well as the consequences of subsequent accountability systems, pressuring teachers to improve student achievement, on teacher burnout. The table presents the results of an OLS (ordinary least squares) regression analysis of the various predictors of teacher burnout for the three sample years in which different accountability systems were operative, and then the results of the pooled data including all three years. The pooled data in *All Time Periods* provide a test of whether the type of accountability system made a difference in the level of teacher burnout. That is, examining the results for the pooled data tells us whether the reforms operative in 1986 promoted higher or lower levels of burnout than those in 2002 or 2009.

Each predictor variable listed in Table 24.1 was part of the regression model to help explain the level of teacher burnout observed. Using OLS regression permits the assessment of how each predictor (independent) variable affects burnout (dependent variable), while controlling for the effects of all other predictors. The table numbers in bold indicate that the predictor was statistically significant in the model. The larger the beta (a standardized coefficient using the same denominator) the more the predictor explains teacher burnout. Some variables are statistically significant even though their relative contributions (beta) in the model are small.

The results of the analysis are quite revealing. First, the model explained between 34 and 61 percent of the variance in teacher burnout depending on the time period. In 1986, good *Student Discipline* reduced burnout, but *Safe Schools* did not, while *Teacher Stress* and *Role Conflict/Role Ambiguity* increased burnout. *Principal Support*

Table 24.1 Predictors of Teacher Burnout Across the Three Time Periods

Predictors	Beta 1986	Beta 2002	Beta 2009	Beta All Time Periods
Student Discipline	−.073	−.239	−.086	−.137
Safe School	−.052	−.119	−.088	−.053
Teacher Stress	.103	.080	.342	.229
Role Conf./Ambig.*	.277	.046	.232	.287
Black Teacher	.115	−.019	.041	.054
Latino Teacher	.000	−.003	.066	.053
Other Teacher	.026	−.008	.066	.042
Female Teacher	.011	−.023	−.089	.050
Education	.040	−.006	−.009	−.007
Grade Level	.016	−.057	.000	.000
Principal Support	−.263	−.239	−.171	−.017
Peer Support	.055	−.108	−.068	−.008
Years Teaching	−.073	−.036	.000	−015
Accountability Year	N/A	N/A	N/A	−.559
Adjusted R^2 =	.405	.337	.552	.614

Source: "Survey of Houston Area Teachers: 1986, 2002, 2009," by A. G. Dworkin, Unpublished reports to Houston school districts.

Note. Statistically significant predictors ($p<.05$) are in **bold.**

*Role Conflict/Role Ambiguity

lowered burnout, but *Peer Support* had no significant effect on burnout. *African American Teachers* were more subject to burnout than were other teachers, and teachers with more years of experience were less likely to experience burnout.

In 2002, good *Student Discipline* and being in a *Safe School* reduced burnout, while *Teacher Stress* raised burnout. However, *Role Conflict/ Role Ambiguity* had no significant effect on burnout. *Principal* and *Peer Support* lowered burnout.

By 2009, good *Student Discipline* and *Safe School* lowered teacher burnout, while *Teacher Stress* and *Role Conflict/Role Ambiguity* elevated burnout. *African American, Latino,* and *Other teachers* were more likely to burn out than were *White Teachers*, but *Female Teachers* were less likely to burn out than male teachers. *Principal Support* and *Peer Support* were associated with lower burnout.

If the data across the three time periods are pooled, it is possible to make an assessment of the effects of the different waves of school accountability, from the implementation of competency testing of teachers (1986) through standardized testing which was high stakes for teachers (2002) and then high stakes for both teachers and students (2009). An independent variable identified as "Accountability Year" assessed the effect of the changing accountability systems on teacher burnout. While good *Student Discipline* and *Safe School* continued to be associated with lower burnout, the variable measuring changing accountability systems exerts the greatest impact on burnout. Over time, burnout has declined and the effect of *Accountability Year* on burnout is a beta of −.559. This large negative beta indicates that teacher burnout has substantially decreased over time. That is, accountability has had a significantly diminished effect on teacher morale as teachers have become accustomed to accountability and have adapted so that it is rare for the systems to actually jeopardize most teachers' career.

To summarize the regression analyses, *Student Discipline* and *Safe School* are generally both associated with diminished teacher burnout, as had been hypothesized in this study. However, the strongest predictor of teacher burnout is the year of the respective data sets. The negative regression coefficient describing *Accountability Year* indicates that the earlier the wave of reform the greater the amount of teacher burnout. Thus, even though later reforms since NCLB have called for more severe consequences for teachers and schools, it was the initial reform following *A Nation at Risk* (1983) that is associated with the most burnout. Quite simply, teachers have learned to cope with school reform and it less often provokes burnout than earlier. However, unsafe schools and schools in which there are disciplinary problems remain significant sources of teacher burnout.

Another way to display the effects of the different accountability systems on teacher burnout and to assess the relative roles of accountability systems and school safety and student discipline is to present the relationships with bar charts. These charts show how burnout levels among the samples of teachers have changed over the periods of school reform and also present the effects on burnout of school discipline and safety at each time period. While Table 24.1 provides an assessment of the effect of school safety and student discipline on burnout across the three periods of school accountability, Figures 24.1 and 24.2 provide information on how the mean burnout scores appear under different school conditions and over time.

Figure 24.1 displays the relationships between teachers' perceptions of student discipline (poor, moderate, and good) at their schools and their level of burnout, while Figure 24.2 presents the relationship between teachers' perceptions of the degree to which their schools are safe (unsafe, moderate, and safe) and their level of burnout. In both instances the figures present results over three periods of school reform. The first period, in 1986, was soon after states had implemented teacher competency testing in response to the release of *A Nation at Risk* in 1983. The second period was in 2002, soon after the passage of the reauthorization of the Elementary and Secondary Education Act known as No Child Left Behind.

High-stakes testing had been in place in Texas schools for several years and a new test and accountability system, with the prospect of school closures, was on the horizon. The third period was in 2009, when the accountability system had been in full operation and testing had been high-stakes for schools, teachers, and students, especially as the state had eliminated social promotion of students who failed the state-mandated standardized test, the Texas Assessment of Knowledge and Skills (TAKS).

It should be immediately apparent that burnout levels have been decreasing across the periods of reform. Regardless of how poor the student discipline or the extent to which a school is seen as unsafe, burnout scores are lower, more into the negative, in 2002 compared with 1986, and lower in 2009 compared with 2002. In each of the time periods, schools with *Poor Student Discipline* are associated with higher (more positive) teacher burnout scores than are those with *Moderate Student Discipline*. Schools with *Good Student Discipline* are associated with the least teacher burnout. The same is true for *School Safety*. *Unsafe Schools* are associated with higher amounts of teacher burnout than are *Moderately Safe Schools* and *Safe Schools* are associated with the lowest level of teacher burnout.

School safety and student discipline remain predictors of teacher burnout during the three time periods even when additional variables are considered. A set of OLS regression equations were calculated in which the dependent variable was teacher burnout and the independent (predictor) variables included teachers' gender, ethnicity, level of own education, number of years teaching, grade level taught, and such social psychological factors as principal and colleague support, job stress, the perception of role conflict and role ambiguity (being pulled in different directions by expectations of others and lacking clarity in one's job specification). In such analyses, school safety and student discipline remained statistically significant predictors of burnout. The more unsafe the school and the poorer the student discipline the greater the amount of teacher burnout. The effect sizes were relatively small, but statistically significant even with the inclusion of the other independent variables.

Figure 24.1 Student Discipline and Teacher Burnout Over Three Reform Periods

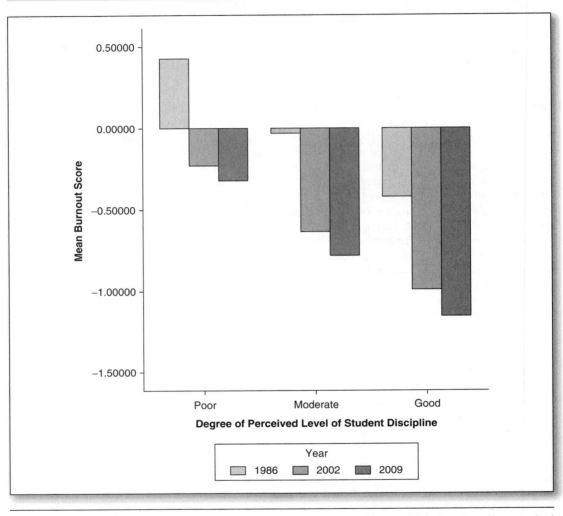

Note. From "Survey of Houston Area Teachers: 1986, 2002, 2009," by A. G. Dworkin, Unpublished reports to Houston school districts.

DISCUSSION AND CONCLUSION

It is apparent that the contention that increasing accountability has elevated teacher burnout may be overstated. Burnout levels have been dropping since they peaked during the initial implementation of school reform during the 1980s. Why might that be the case? Although accountability systems have been intended to improve teaching and learning and to reduce the number of low-performing teachers, it has become commonly known among school faculty that teacher shortages and increases in student populations, especially in the Sunbelt, have made it impractical to remove many teachers. Rather, school districts have opted to spend significant funds on teacher professional development to improve the quality of teaching. Furthermore, as reform upon reform

Figure 24.2 School Safety and Teacher Burnout Over Three Reform Periods

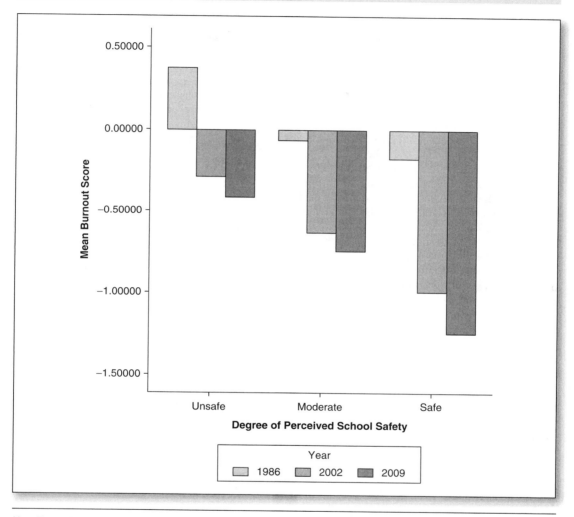

Note. From "Survey of Houston Area Teachers: 1986, 2002, 2009," by A. G. Dworkin, Unpublished reports to Houston school districts.

has been implemented, teachers have adapted to the changing demands. To secure the supply of needed teachers and to reduce the likelihood that many schools will be subjected to closing, much legislation has been weakened and state education agencies have "gamed" various reforms, including No Child Left Behind. A recent book on No Child Left Behind was produced by members of the Sociology of Education section of the American Sociological Association (Sadovnik, Dworkin, Gamoran, Hallinan, & Scott, 2007). Dworkin (2008) also explored the reasons why states have "gamed the NCLB system."

Faculty in schools that are seen as safe and in schools where students are not overly disruptive are less likely to experience burnout than those in schools that are less safe and where students are disruptive. Threats to safety and discipline diminish the capacity of teachers to accomplish their goals of improving student learning. In turn, reduced student learning both increases threats to schools and teachers under the three states of the school accountability systems and deprives teachers of a sense of accomplishment and job meaningfulness— an essential aspect of burnout. Nevertheless, it appears that over the three waves of school reform assessed in this chapter, teacher burnout is diminishing, even if the effect of school safety and student discipline has not substantially changed over the three reform periods. That is, while the level of burnout has diminished over the years 1986, 2002, and 2009, the extent to which school safety and student discipline impacts burnout has generally not declined. Safe schools and disciplined students continue to lead teachers not to burn out. That teachers' burnout scores in even unsafe schools and in schools with low levels of student discipline reflect lower levels of burnout may be the result of policies intended to make schools more effective in promoting student learning within the context of the accountability system. Policies that promote "zero tolerance" of student deviance and lead to the transfer of poorly disciplined students to alternative schools may heighten the sense of accomplishment of teachers and reduce overall burnout rates. It should not be assumed, however, that these newer policies are without problems. There are an abundance of reports of excessive use of zero-tolerance policies in schools and their application should be administered with substantial forethought.

REFERENCES

Abel, M., & Sewell, J. (1999). Stress and burnout in rural and urban secondary school teachers. *Journal of Educational Research, 92*(5), 287–293.

America 2000: An education strategy. (1991). Washington, DC: U.S. Department of Education.

Bauer, L., Guerino, P., Nolle, K. L., & Tang, S. (2008). *Student victimization in U.S. schools: Results from the 2005 school crime supplement to the national crime victimization survey* (NCES 2009-306). Washington, DC: National Center for Education Statistics, Institute of Education Sciences, U.S. Department of Education.

Blasé, J. (2009). School administrator mistreatment of teachers. In L. J. Saha & A. G. Dworkin (Eds.), *International handbook of research on teaching and teachers* (pp. 433–448). New York: Springer Science.

Brouwers, A., & Tomic, W. (2000). A longitudinal study of teacher burnout and perceived self-efficacy in classroom management. *Teaching and Teacher Education, 16*(2), 239–253.

Bru, E. (2009). Academic outcomes in school classes with markedly disruptive pupils [Electronic version]. *JSTOR: Social Psychology of Education, 12*(4), 461–479.

Burke, R. J., Greenglass, E. R., & Schwarzer, R. (1996). Predicting teacher burnout over time: Effects of work stress, social support, and self-doubts on burnout and its consequences. *Anxiety, Stress and Coping: An International Journal, 9*(3), 1–15.

Cassidy, T. (2009). Bullying and victimization in school children: The role of social identity, problem-solving style, and family and school context. *Social Psychology Education, 12*, 63–76.

Cedoline, A. J. (1982). *Job burnout in public education: Symptoms, causes, and survival skills.* New York: Teachers College Press.

Cherniss, C. (1980). *Professional burnout in human service organizations.* New York: Praeger.

Cherniss, C. (1992). Long-term consequences of burnout: An exploratory study. *Journal of Organizational Behavior, 13*(1), 1–11.

Dinkes, R., Kemp, J., & Baum, K. (2009). *Indicators of school crime and safety: 2009* (NCES 2010–012/NCJ 228478). Washington, DC: National Center for Education Statistics, Institute of Education Sciences, U.S. Department of Education, and Bureau of Justice Statistics, Office of Justice Programs, U.S. Department of Justice.

Dworkin, A. G. (1987). *Teacher burnout in the public schools: Structural causes and consequences for children.* Albany: State University of New York Press.

Dworkin, A. G. (1997). Coping with reform: The intermix of teacher morale, teacher burnout, and teacher accountability. In B. J. Biddle, T. L. Good, & I. F. Goodson (Eds.), *International handbook of teachers and teaching* (pp. 459–498). London: Kluwer Academic.

Dworkin, A. G. (2001). Perspectives on teacher burnout and school reform. *International Education Journal, 24*(2), 69–78.

Dworkin, A. G. (2007). School reform and teacher burnout: Issues of gender and gender tokenism. In B. J. Banks, S. Delamonte, & C. Marshall

(Eds.), *Gender and education: An encyclopedia* (pp. 69–78). New York: Greenwood Press.

Dworkin, A. G. (2008). School accountability and the standards-based reform movement: Some unintended consequences of education policies. *International Journal of Contemporary Sociology, 45*(2), 11–31.

Dworkin, A. G. (2009). Teacher burnout and teacher resilience: Assessing the impacts of the school accountability movement. In L. J. Saha & A. G. Dworkin (Eds.), *New international handbook of teachers and teaching* (pp. 491–509). New York: Springer Science.

Dworkin, A. G., Saha, L. J., & Hill, A. N. (2003). Teacher burnout and perceptions of a democratic school environment. *International Education Journal, 4*(2), 108–120.

Dworkin, A. G., & Townsend, M. (1994). Teacher burnout in the face of reform: Some caveats in breaking the mold. In B. A. Jones & K. M. Borman (Eds.), *Investing in United States schools: Directions for educational policy* (pp. 68–86). Norwood, NJ: Ablex.

Farber, B. A. (1991). *Crisis in education: Stress and burnout in the American teacher.* San Francisco: Jossey-Bass.

Freudenberger, H. J. (1974). Staff burn-out. *Journal of Social Issues, 30*(1), 159–165.

Friedman, I. A. (1991). High- and low-burnout schools: School culture aspects of teacher burnout. *Journal of Educational Research, 84*(6), 325–333.

Friedman, I. A. (1995). Student behavior patterns contributing to teacher burnout. *The Journal of Educational Research, 88*(5), 281–289.

Gavish, B., & Friedman, I. A. (2010). Novice teachers' experience of teaching: A dynamic aspect of burnout [Electronic version]. *JSTOR: Social Psychology of Education, 13*(2), 141–167.

Goals 2000: Educate America Act, Pub. L. 103-227. (1994).

Gold, Y., & Roth, R. A. (1993). *Teachers managing stress and professional burnout: The professional health solution.* London: Falmer Press.

Heller, T., & Toenjes, L. (1993). Analysis of Texas school effectiveness: EEPC school site survey interview and instrument results. In *A new accountability system for Texas public schools, vol. II.* Austin, TX: Educational Economic Policy Center.

LeCompte, M. D., & Dworkin, A. G. (1991). *Giving up on school: Student dropouts and teacher burnouts.* Newbury Park, CA: Corwin Press.

Lester, P. K., & Bishop, L. K. (2000). *Handbook of tests and measurement in education and the social sciences* (2nd ed.). Lanham, MD: Scarecrow Press.

Maslach, C. (1978a). The client role in staff burnout. *Journal of Social Issues, 34*(4), 111–124.

Maslach, C. (1978b). Job burnout: How people cope. *Public Welfare, 36*(2), 56–58.

Maslach, C. (1993). Burnout: A multidimensional perspective. In W. B. Schaufeli, C. Maslach, & T. Marek (Eds.), *Professional burnout: Recent developments in theory and research* (pp. 19–32). Washington, DC: Taylor and Francis.

Maslach, C., & Jackson. S. E. (1981). The measurement of experienced burnout. *The Journal of Occupational Behaviour, 2*(1), 99–113.

National Commission on Excellence in Education. (1983). *A nation at risk: The imperative for educational reform.* Washington, DC: U.S. Government Printing Office.

Orpinas, P., Kelder, S., Frankowski, R., Murray, N., Zhang, Q., & McAlister, A. (2000). Outcome evaluation of a multi-component violence-prevention program for middle schools: The students for peace project. *Health Education Research, 15*(1), 45–58.

Pines, A. (1993). Burnout: Existential perspectives. In W. B. Schaufeli, C. Maslach, & T. Marek (Eds.), *Professional burnout: Recent developments in theory and research* (pp. 33–52). Washington, DC: Taylor & Francis.

Sadovnik, A. R., Dworkin, A. G., Gamoran, A., Hallinan, M., & Scott, J. (2007). Sociological perspectives on NCLB and federal involvement in education. In A. R. Sadovnik, J. A. O'Day, G. W. Bohrnstedt, & K. M. Borman (Eds.), *No Child Left Behind and the reduction of the achievement gap* (pp. 359–373). New York: Routledge.

Sarros, J. C., & Sarros, A. M. (1992). Social support and teacher burnout. *Journal of Educational Administration, 30*(1), 55–69.

Seeman, M. (1959). On the meaning of alienation. *American Sociological Review, 24*(7), 83–91.

Seeman, M. (1975). Alienation studies. *Annual Review of Sociology, 1,* 91–123.

Smylie, M. A., & Denny, J. W. (1990). Teacher leadership: Tensions and ambiguities in organizational practice. *Educational Administration Quarterly, 26*(3), 235–259.

Sunderman, G. L., Tracey, C. A., Kim, J., & Orfield, G. (2004). *Listening to teachers: Classroom realities and No Child Left Behind.* Cambridge, MA: The Civil Rights Project at Harvard University.

Swick, K. J., & Hanley, P. E. (1983). *Teacher renewal: Revitalization of classroom teachers.* Washington, DC: National Education Association.

Vettenburg, N. (2002). Unsafe feelings among teachers. *Journal of School Violence, 1*(4), 33–49.

TEACHER INFLUENCES ON STUDENTS' ATTACHMENT TO SCHOOL

Maureen T. Hallinan

Teachers play a major role in determining how students feel about school. We can recall how some teachers inspired us to work hard and take school seriously, others were mean authoritarians, and others really didn't seem to care much about their students. Maureen Hallinan looks at the unique role teachers play in students' school experiences. The bottom line is that students who feel their teachers respect them, care about how they are doing, and praise them when they succeed like school more than students who receive little encouragement or support. Liking school correlates positively with staying in school and succeeding academically.

Questions to consider for this reading:

1. What is the relationship between teachers' behaviors and students' attachment to school?

2. What is the process of students developing an attachment to school, and what difference does this attachment make for students?

3. According to Hallinan, how can schools reduce truancy, absenteeism, discipline problems, and dropping out of school?

4. If you were a principal of a school trying to decrease the dropout rate, what message would you take from Hallinan?

Research has shown that students who like school have higher academic achievement and a lower incidence of disciplinary problems, absenteeism, truancy, and dropping out of school than do those who dislike school. Thus, one way to improve academic outcomes is to increase students' attraction to school. This study focused on the role of teachers in shaping students' feelings about school. The unique role that teachers play relative to students and the kinds of experiences that teachers create for students suggest that teachers may exert a powerful influence on whether students like school. Since attachment to school has been shown to affect students' academic performance, identifying the characteristics of teachers that have a positive effect on students' feelings about school is one way to increase students' academic achievement. The study estimated cross-sectional and longitudinal models of teachers' influences on students' feelings about school on data from 6th-, 8th- and 10th-grade students in public and Catholic schools in Chicago. It found that students who perceive that their teachers care about them, respect them, and praise them are more apt to like school than are those who do not, but that teachers' expectations for students' achievement have a negligible effect on whether students like school.

Most students spend 40 or more hours a week in school. This considerable time suggests that

From "Teacher Influences on Students' Attachment to School," by M. T. Hallinan, 2008, *Sociology of Education, 81*(3), pp. 271–283. Copyright 2008 by American Sociological Association. Reprinted with permission.

students' feelings about school likely influence how much they learn. While some studies have examined the consequences of students' feelings about school for academic and behavioral outcomes, little is known about the determinants of attachment to school. . . . In this article, the terms *liking school* and *attachment to school* are used most frequently because they seem closest to the way students discuss their feelings about school. . . .

DETERMINANTS OF LIKING SCHOOL

Teachers play a major role in shaping students' experiences in school. A large part of a student's school day is spent in verbal and nonverbal interactions with teachers. Two components of these interactions are expected to affect students' feelings about school: the extent to which teachers provide social and emotional support for students and the nature of teachers' expectations for students' academic performance.

Teachers' Support

Social psychological theory suggests that stable, positive interactions with one or more persons are essential for healthy socioemotional development. Noddings (1992, 2003) assigned the responsibility of engaging in positive interactions with students primarily to the teacher. She claimed that a teacher should first be one who cares about students and second, be one who instructs them.

The way that teachers interact with students is of considerable importance in shaping how students feel about themselves and their surroundings. If students feel ignored, misunderstood, devalued, or disrespected by their teachers, they are likely to react negatively. If they feel that their teachers have regard for them, approve of their behavior, and are interested in their welfare, they will react positively. For positive or negative teacher-student interactions to generalize to feelings about school, they need to occur consistently in a stable, enduring environment. Furthermore,

teachers' consistent positive or negative interactions with students need to occur both during formal instruction and, perhaps more important, on an informal basis to extend to feelings about school. For example, research on effective teaching has shown that teachers are more successful in motivating students to study when they demonstrate their concern about their students, both during and outside formal instruction (for a review, see Stronge, 2002).

Teachers demonstrate that they care about their students when they listen to the students, encourage their efforts, and provide a warm atmosphere that enables them to feel safe and secure. Teachers also show interest in students by respecting them and their familial and peer cultures and giving them a sense of inclusion in the school community.

Another way that teachers support students is by being fair in their dealings with them. Students, especially adolescents, have a keen sense of fairness. They judge their teachers by the way the teachers implement school rules and policies. When teachers follow norms of equity and treat everyone fairly and compassionately, students feel respected. If students perceive that their teachers are being unfair to them or their peers and are violating norms of equity, they feel that their teachers have low regard for them.

In addition to showing caring and respect and treating students fairly, supportive teachers praise students for their effort to learn, as well as for their academic and social accomplishments. Praise is important for all students but especially for those who find schoolwork difficult. Yet, Brophy (1981) cautioned teachers to praise students effectively. Ineffective praise is given after a task has been completed and focuses on the task itself. It represents an extrinsic reward, rather than the intrinsic gratification that is associated with the performance. Ineffective praise reduces a student's motivation and can create negative feelings about school. Appropriate praise is a teacher's response to a student's efforts without judging the student's work or suggesting that it has implications for the student's value as a person or status in the school or classroom. A teacher's recognition of a student's efforts sustains the student's motivation and reduces the likelihood of discouragement. Teacher's praise increases a student's effort, builds self-confidence, and contributes to a student's positive attitude toward school.

Teachers' Expectations

While teachers' support is expected to have a fairly straightforward relationship with students' attachment to school, the association between teachers' expectations and whether students like school is more complex. During childhood and adolescence, children are particularly sensitive to the evaluation of adults (Goffman, 1959). Students' reactions to meeting or failing to meet teachers' expectations are likely to have a significant effect on their attitudes toward learning and their feelings about school.

A teacher can have high or low expectations for a student, and a student may or may not be able to meet these expectations. When students live up to teachers' standards, they earn the teachers' approval (Kloosterman & Cougan, 1994). Teachers' approval builds students' self-confidence and motivates students to persist in their efforts to achieve. As a result, students experience greater academic success and become more attached to their school. If students fail to meet teachers' expectations, teachers usually convey disapproval, verbally or otherwise. In response, students lose self-confidence, their motivation declines, and the quality of their academic work suffers (Mulford & Silins, 2003; Pugh, 1976). Students are expected to like school less when they are aware that their teachers are dissatisfied with their schoolwork.

This argument suggests that students' attachment to school is positively associated with teachers' expectations. When students fail to meet teachers' high expectations, they become discouraged, lose confidence, and become disengaged from school. However, the argument fails to take into account students who react to their failure to meet teachers' expectations by working harder to improve their schoolwork. Other students may work harder to prove their teachers wrong. Either

reaction would break the negative cycle of students' failure, teachers' disapproval, and students' detachment from school.

Furthermore, if teachers set low expectations for students' academic performance, some students will feel that their teachers are underestimating their abilities. These students may try harder to show that they can do more challenging work and in an effort to win greater esteem from the teachers. On the other hand, they may react by putting less effort into their work because they believe that even a minimal effort will produce teachers' approval. In either case, students' reactions to teachers' expectations will affect their effort and achievement and, in turn, their feelings about their teacher and school.

Variability in teachers' expectations and students' reactions to these expectations makes it difficult to predict the impact of a teacher's expectations on a student's achievement and feelings about school. Unless contingency factors, such as students' reactions to teachers' approval or disapproval and the goodness of fit between teachers' expectations and students' ability, are taken into account, it is difficult to predict the effect of teachers' expectations on students' attachment to school. . . .

Discussion

Proponents of the NCLB (No Child Left Behind federal plan) claim that focusing on students' test scores is an effective way to improve students' achievement. However, learning is a cognitive and a social psychological process, and both these dimensions must be taken into account to maximize academic achievement. A broad conception of learning is necessary to inform the current debate among academics, educators, and policy makers concerning the reauthorization of the NCLB.

A comprehensive view of the learning process includes an understanding of what leads students to like school. Identifying factors that affect students' feelings about school is important for two reasons. First, students who like school gain significant social benefits. They become engaged in school activities that provide opportunities to develop social skills, establish friendships, learn respect for adults and peers, and engage in cooperative behaviors. These social skills foster students' social development. Second, liking school is important because it affects academic achievement. Students who like school perform better academically. Recognition of the social and cognitive effects of liking school motivates this effort to identify influences on students' feelings about school.

Many adults assume that students like school primarily because they enjoy learning or because they interact with their friends in school. Previous research has supported these beliefs. However, the study reported here identified another, often ignored, influence on students' feelings about school, namely, teachers. Even when students' school friendships and other personal and school-related factors, including school sector, are taken into account, the analyses reveal that certain characteristics of teachers have a significant influence on whether students like school.

This research examined two ways that teachers affect students' feelings about school, namely, the extent to which teachers support students socially and emotionally and the expectations that teachers hold for students' achievement. The results show that teachers who support their students by caring about them and by respecting and praising them satisfy students' needs and, in so doing, increase students' attachment to school.

The effect of teachers' expectations on whether students like school is less clear. This study found only a negligible effect of teachers' expectations on liking for school. This finding does not mean that teachers' expectations are unimportant or unrelated to students' feelings about school. Rather, it supports the argument that the magnitude and direction of the effect cannot be determined without taking into account a number of contingency factors, including students' ability. Given the complexity of students' responses to teachers' expectations, the relationship between teachers' expectations and students' feelings about school should be studied in greater depth in future research.

The most striking finding of this study is that even when other factors are taken into account, the extent to which teachers support students has a strong influence on their attachment to school. This result underscores an important dimension of the role that teachers play in the daily lives of students. By providing social and emotional support, teachers increase students' liking for school, which, in turn, improves students' academic and social outcomes.

References

Brophy, J. (1981). Teacher praise: A functional analysis. *Review of Educational Research, 51*(1), 5–32.

Goffman, E. (1959). *The presentation of the self in everyday life.* Garden City, NY: Doubleday Anchor Books.

Kloosterman, P., & Cougan, M. C. (1994). Students' beliefs about learning school mathematics. *Elementary School Journal, 94*(4), 375–388.

Mulford, W., & Silins, H. (2003). Leadership for organizational learning and student outcomes. *Cambridge Journal of Education, 33*(2), 175–195.

Noddings, N. (1992). *The challenge to care in schools.* New York: Teachers College Press.

Noddings, N. (2003). *Caring: A feminine approach to ethics and moral education.* Berkeley: University of California Press.

Pugh, M. D. (1976). Statistical assumptions and social reality: A critical analysis of achievement models. *Sociology of Education, 49*(1), 34–40.

Stronge, J. H. (2002). *Qualities of effective teachers.* Alexandria, VA: Association for Supervision and Curriculum Development.

AFTER THE BELL

Participation in Extracurricular Activities, Classroom Behavior, and Academic Achievement

Elizabeth Covay and William Carbonaro

Studies show that students from higher socioeconomic status (SES) backgrounds have higher achievement and attainment levels in school than students from lower SES levels. The result is that students from higher SES backgrounds have occupational and income advantages in the long run. In addition, there is mounting evidence that students' home environments have a major impact on the SES achievement differences. This reading considers whether students' participation in extracurricular activities influences the achievement advantage of higher SES students. Elizabeth Covay and William Carbonaro examine students' socioeconomic status and unequal access to learning opportunities outside of the school setting. They examine whether extracurricular activities provide an additional advantage, especially in noncognitive skills including "task persistence, independence, following instructions, working well within groups, dealing with authority figures, and fitting in with peers" (Covay & Carbonaro, 2010, p. 21).

Questions to consider for this reading:

1. What do social scientists know about the relationship between SES inequalities and the effects of extracurricular activities on student outcomes?

2. What did Covay and Carbonaro find about the link between extracurricular participation and noncognitive skills in school?

3. Should parents encourage their children to participate in extracurricular activities to improve long-term success? Why or why not?

Socioeconomic status (SES) differences in educational achievement and attainment are large and pervasive in modern industrialized societies. Students from higher-SES backgrounds have higher levels of academic achievement and are more likely to go further in school than lower-SES students. These SES inequalities in schooling outcomes are later translated into advantages in occupational attainment and income (Blau & Duncan, 1967; Jencks, 1972; Kerckhoff, Raudenbush, & Glennie, 2001; Sewell & Hauser, 1975). A growing body of evidence suggests that SES gaps in achievement are present before students enter formal schooling (Entwisle, Alexander, & Olson, 1997; Farkas, 2003; Hart & Risley, 1995). These important findings suggest that inequalities in students' home environments are critical factors that drive much of the SES gap in achievement in school. Our study contributes to the SES gap literature by examining inequalities in an additional context: extracurricular activities (EAs).

In this study, we focus on unequal access to learning opportunities that elementary school students receive outside both the conventional school curriculum and the immediate home environment. We examine whether EAs provide an additional source of advantage for high-SES students that helps them increase their chances of school success. In her recent ethnographic account of class differences in childhood experiences, Lareau (2003) focused on class differences in parenting styles that led some parents to provide enriched extracurricular experiences for their children. In our study, we examine SES differences in extracurricular participation in elementary school and consider their effect on students' noncognitive skills and achievement outcomes for students in the same age range as Lareau's study.

We argue that EAs improve students' noncognitive skills: a broad set of skills that include (but are not limited to) task persistence, independence, following instructions, working well within groups, dealing with authority figures, and fitting in with peers (i.e., skills that align with the hidden curriculum; Carneiro & Heckman, 2005; Dreeben, 1968; Farkas, 2003; Jackson, 1968; Rosenbaum, 2001). We focus on noncognitive skills as the mechanism that explains the link between extracurricular participation and increased academic achievement. Our results indicate that students from higher-SES families do participate in EAs more than students from lower-SES families. We also find that race and the percentage of minority students within a school are related to a student's likelihood of extracurricular participation. Overall, participation in EAs explains a modest portion of the SES advantage in both noncognitive and cognitive skills. Finally, the association between extracurricular participation on noncognitive and cognitive skills depends in part on students' SES.

UNEQUAL PARTICIPATION IN EAS

. . . In this study, we focus on structured EAs because (as we describe below) these activities are most likely to contribute to the development of noncognitive skills and greater student learning.

Prior research has suggested that participation in EAs varies by family background (Dumais, 2006; Lareau, 2003). In her in-depth ethnographic study, Lareau (2003) found important class differences in how students spent their leisure time: upper- and middle-class students had little unscheduled time and spent more time in structured EAs, whereas lower- and working-class students mostly participated in unstructured activities. Dumais (2006) analyzed nationally representative data and found that SES was positively related to extracurricular participation.

Interestingly, little research has examined why social class is related to extracurricular participation. Lareau (2003) identified two distinct parenting styles in her study, *concerted cultivation* and *accomplishment of natural growth,* which were related to EA participation. Lareau found that high-SES families pursued concerted cultivation, whereas lower-SES families embraced a natural growth approach. Thus, Lareau offered a cultural explanation for SES differences in extracurricular participation. Chin and Phillips (2004) challenged Lareau's conclusion with their study of how parents organized summer activities for their children. In their study, Chin and Phillips found that low-SES parents valued these EAs during the summer (just as high-SES parents did), but income and time constraints served as significant barriers that lowered participation rates for low-SES families. Because neither study used a nationally representative sample or statistical controls to estimate associations between SES and extracurricular participation, additional research is needed to disentangle the effects of parental education, occupation, and income on extracurricular participation.

Prior research has also indicated that race is a significant predictor of participation in EAs. Dumais (2006) found that black and Hispanic children participated in EAs in kindergarten or first grade at a lower rate compared to white children. In testing the larger construct of conceited cultivation, Cheadle (2008) found significant racial differences in concerted cultivation, although he did not focus specifically on extracurricular participation. Yet Lareau (2003) concluded that, after accounting for class differences, there were no racial differences in her study.

As with SES, little is known about why race is related to extracurricular participation. Although Lareau (2003) argued that racial differences are explained by differences in SES, we suspect that continued residential and school segregation (Clotfelter, 2006) creates different levels of access to extracurricular opportunities by SES and race. Research (see Eccles, [Barber, Stone, & Hunt,] 2003) suggests that at-risk adolescents tend to have less access to high-quality extracurricular programs. Moreover, Pattillo-McCoy (2005) found that middle-class black families live in more disadvantaged neighborhoods compared with middle-class and poor white families, which suggests that black families have less access to community resources. . . .

EAS AND NONCOGNITIVE SKILLS

Unequal participation in EAs takes on greater significance when we consider possible linkages between extracurricular participation and academic outcomes. If EAs improve student achievement, inequalities in participation may contribute to SES and racial-ethnic gaps in learning gains. . . . We hypothesize that EAs contribute to student achievement indirectly by enhancing students' noncognitive skills . . . which produces greater gains in students' learning. . . . In this section, we argue for the importance of . . . the link between EAs and students' noncognitive skills.

EAs resemble classroom settings in many important ways. Both settings promote and inculcate similar values among children. Dreeben (1968) identified four main values promoted in classrooms: independence, achievement, universalism, and specificity. Some EAs, such as sports and music, strongly promote and value achievement:

children must demonstrate mastery of a given set of skills by performing in public (or semipublic) settings in which they are evaluated by others (Lareau, 2003). Children must regularly deal with success and failure (e.g., winning and losing, missing notes and cues) in EAs, just as they do in the classroom (Lareau, 2003). Task persistence and a strong work ethic are also important in both classroom and extracurricular settings. Being on a team, in an orchestra, or in the cast of a play typically involves being a member of a general category (e.g., soccer player, percussionist), and participants are typically given specific roles to fulfill. These experiences promote the values of universalism and specificity (respectively).

EAs also resemble classroom environments in how social relationships are defined and structured. In both cases, children are subordinate to an adult authority figure who sets goals and expectations for children, organizes tasks designed to promote mastery of a given skill, and provides instruction, to promote skill development. Success in both the classroom and EAs requires an ability to successfully interact with, and learn from, authority figures. Interactions with peers are also important in each setting. Sometimes children are forced to compete with peers for learning resources (e.g., the teacher's or coach's attention), whereas other times, peers take the role of teammates in exercises that require cooperation and teamwork. EAs also provide children with an opportunity to interact with more privileged peers, who can model appropriate behavior in educational settings. We argue that the similar nonnative frameworks and social relations found in classrooms and EAs promote similar types of noncognitive skills in children. The tasks required in structured activities allow students to practice noncognitive skills that are also valued by schools (Gilman, [Meyers, & Perez,] 2004).

Both school- and community-based EAs help students develop their noncognitive skills through opportunities to learn and use social and intellectual skills, access to social networks of peers and adults, and opportunities to face new challenges (Eccles et al., 2003). EAs can help students to work as a team and to practice interpersonal skills as they work with others (Gilman et al., 2004). Children who participate in sports and clubs are seen by their teachers to exhibit better interpersonal skills than students who do not participate in EAs (Fletcher, [Nickerson, & Wright,] 2003). Participation in EAs exposes participants to peers and adults with important societal (including school) values and a variety of skills (Gilman et al., 2004). Students who participate in sports report higher levels of work orientation and self-reliance (Fletcher et al., 2003). If extracurricular participation has a positive effect on students' noncognitive skills, high-SES and nonminority students would disproportionately benefit because of their higher rates of participation in such programs.

EAs, Noncognitive Skills, and Achievement

In our conceptual model, EAs have an indirect relationship with achievement: EAs improve students' noncognitive skills, which are positively related to academic achievement. Numerous studies have found a positive relationship between extracurricular participation and academic achievement (see Broh, 2002; Fletcher et al., 2003; Guest & Schneider, 2003; Marsh & Kleitman, 2002). Among the different types of activities, sports activities consistently have significant (and positive) effects on achievement, while the evidence on other activities is more mixed (Broh, 2002; Marsh, 1992; Marsh & Kleitman, 2002; Steinberg, 1996).

It is important to note that nearly all of the research in this area focuses on middle and high school students; virtually no research with nationally representative data has examined the effects of EAs on student achievement in elementary school. This is an important omission, because Lareau's (2003) much cited study focused on elementary school students. Dumais (2006), using Lareau's theoretical framework, found that students participating in sports, clubs, and dance during either kindergarten or first grade had greater reading gains (and math gains for dance participants) between first and third grade compared with students who

did not participate in EAs. In addition, she found that sports participants were rated by teachers as having higher math skills compared with students who did not participate.

As Broh (2002) and Eccles et al. (2003) noted, there is very little empirical evidence regarding why EAs have positive effects on learning outcomes. Broh's analyses indicate that developmental variables (e.g., locus of control and effort/homework time), along with stronger social ties with adults, explained most of the positive effect of sports on achievement.

We have decided to focus most heavily on noncognitive skills as a possible mediating mechanism between EAs and achievement in our conceptual model because prior research suggests that peer relations and social ties outside the family are less important for students' outcomes among elementary school students (e.g., Steinberg, 1996). Thus, in our analyses, we examine whether the academic benefits of EAs are attributable to stronger work habits and engagement associated with noncognitive skills. Numerous studies have indicated that attitudes and behaviors associated with students' work habits and overall diligence are consistently related to higher achievement (e.g., Carbonaro, 2005; Farkas, [Grobe, Sheehan, & Shuan,] 1990; Olneck & Bills, 1980; Rosenbaum, 2001; Smerdon, 1999). However, very few studies of noncognitive skills have focused on elementary school achievement, and the results of such studies are somewhat mixed. A recent study by Duncan et al. (2007) found that attention skills predicted achievement, but socioemotional skills did not (net of other factors). In contrast, Bodovski and Farkas (2008) found that noncognitive skills are significantly and positively related to reading gains in first grade. Thus, noncognitive skills are a highly plausible candidate for explaining the EA-achievement relationship. . . .

Reexamining the Sources of SES Advantages: Research Questions

Much has been learned about SES inequalities and the effects of EAs on student outcomes. However, important questions about SES and extracurricular participation remain unanswered, especially for elementary school students. Our research questions address these important issues.

The first set of questions focuses on differential rates of participation in EAs:

> **Research Question 1a:** How much do students from different SES backgrounds differ in their participation in EAs?

> **Research Question 1b:** Which aspects of family background are most important in predicting EA participation?

> **Research Question 1c:** Does the school context affect students' chances of participating in EAs?

Our second and third questions focus on the relationship between extracurricular participation and noncognitive skills in school. Past research and theorizing suggest that SES predicts student mastery of the hidden curriculum in school (Farkas et al., 1990; Farkas, 2003; Lareau, 2003).

> **Research Question 2a:** Does extracurricular participation affect students' noncognitive skills in the classroom?

> **Research Question 2b:** Do these activities explain part of the relationship between SES and noncognitive skills?

> **Research Question 2c:** Do EAs matter more for the noncognitive skills of low-SES students than high-SES students?

Finally, we are interested in how SES, EAs, and noncognitive skills are linked to academic outcomes for students. We argue that part of the SES advantage in achievement works through EA participation and its relationship with mastery of the hidden curriculum in school.

> **Research Question 3a:** Do EAs explain part of the relationship between SES and academic skills, and do noncognitive skills serve as the mediating mechanism?

> **Research Question 3b:** Do EAs contribute more to the achievement gains of low-SES students than high-SES students?

Together, these research questions will help us better understand whether and how EAs serve as an important source of advantage for students from high-SES families.

DATA AND METHODS

The data set used for this study is the Early Childhood Longitudinal Study—Kindergarten Class of 1998–99 (ECLS-K) (National Center for Education Statistics, 2004). ECLS-K is a nationally representative sample of 21,260 children, and the data focus on students' early childhood experiences. The third-grade wave was collected in the spring of the students' third-grade year, and it is the main data source for our analysis. . . .

DISCUSSION: EAS AND SES ADVANTAGES

We examined whether participation in EAs serves as a source of advantage for students from high-SES families. Our study complements and extends Lareau's (2003) *Unequal Childhoods* by analyzing data from a nationally representative sample with multivariate methods that explore the relationship between EAs, social class, and academic outcomes. Moreover, we hypothesized that noncognitive skills would act as a key mediating mechanism that translated SES advantages in EAs into academic gains for high-SES students. Overall, we find partial support for our conceptual model.

The first set of research questions focused on differential rates of participation in EAs. Our findings indicate that education level, income, and occupational prestige are related to higher levels of participation in EAs, which is consistent with Lareau (2003) and our conceptual model. However, our results also expand on Lareau's findings. In Lareau's ethnographic study, she examined the levels of EA participation among a selected group of students, finding that children from higher-SES families participate more in structured activities compared with poor and working-class families. We find that participation levels are high among third graders from all SES levels. However, we do see that in general, as measures of SES increase, so do rates of participation in EAs, reaching near saturation points at the highest level. This finding is consistent with Chin and Phillips (2004), who found that parents from all social classes wanted their children to participate in summer camps, but lower-SES families experienced constraints that prevented their children from participating. Yet SES is not the only dimension on which participation in EA varies. In contrast with the results from Lareau's ethnographic study, white students are more likely to participate in EA compared with the other racial and ethnic groups. . . . However, white students are less likely to participate in dance lessons, music lessons, art lessons, and performing arts activities, net of SES, compared with other racial groups. Thus, participation in EAs is related to race as well as SES.

The different levels of extracurricular participation between black and white students are explained largely by the racial composition of the school, which we use as a proxy for the students' exposure to opportunities to participate in EAs. Continued school and neighborhood segregation in the United States creates different extracurricular opportunity structures for students, which drive unequal access and rates of participation. Moreover, black families tend to have tighter connections to extended families compared with white families (Gosa & Alexander, 2007). Combined with limited access to opportunities to participation in EAs, black children may be more likely to spend time with cousins and fictive kin. Although Lareau (2003) described lower- and working-class families spending more time with extended family compared with upper-class families, the same process may be working for black families, which is a characteristic of accomplishment of natural growth. Finally, our finding of increased participation in fine art programs in high-minority schools could be due to community projects targeted at maintaining music and art in areas that no longer have the programs within the schools. The higher participation of black children in fine art activities may also be related to

the emerging black middle class, which has emerged more recently than the white middle class (Gosa & Alexander, 2007). Black middle-class parents may encourage their children to participate in fine art activities as part of developing middle-class tastes and dispositions. However, it may take generations for the influence of the black middle-class parenting approaches to manifest in achievement gains (Phillips, [Brooks-Gunn, Duncan, Klebanov, & Crane,] 1998).

Our second set of research questions examined how EAs were related to the development of noncognitive skills. We found that some EAs are related to an increase in noncognitive skills, particularly participation in sports and dance. This suggests that there is a connection between how students spend their leisure time and their school performance. EAs provide students with an opportunity to interact with authority figures and privileged peers, providing them with access to important noncognitive skills that facilitate academic learning. The similar context between EAs and the classroom helps students practice skills that are valued within the classroom setting. However, we found that participation in EAs does not mediate much of the SES effect on noncognitive skills. SES continues to have a direct relationship on noncognitive skills net of other family resources and behaviors.

Our third set of research questions examined whether EAs affected achievement outcomes and whether this relationship was explained by differences in noncognitive skills. Much of the relationship between EAs and achievement is explained by differences in noncognitive skills. This is an important contribution of our study because little is known about why extracurricular activities matter for achievement, especially for children in elementary school. However, EAs explained only a small amount of the SES advantage in achievement. One reason EAs did not explain more of the SES effect on achievement may be that the differences in EA participation by SES may be too small to be an important mediator. As already noted, a majority of low-SES students are participating in EAs, and this likely constrains how much of the SES-achievement relationship can be explained by EA participation.

Finally, we examined whether EAs had different effects on outcomes for high- and low-SES students. We predicted that the relationship between EAs and student outcomes would vary by SES level, with low-SES students benefiting more than high-SES students. Our results are only partly consistent with this prediction. When examining the relationship of sports participation and noncognitive skills, students from higher SES families enjoy an additional benefit from participation. In terms of predicting academic skills, our interactions are in the direction we predicted. Our mixed findings are consistent with those of Dumais (2006), who found that higher SES students who participate in sports score higher on teachers' evaluations of math skills, yet participation in art and music lessons provided low-SES students an added advantage over high-SES students for teachers' evaluations of language art skills and actual reading gains.

In our theory, we suggest that EAs provide a location, in addition to home, where high-SES students learn noncognitive skills. When predicting noncognitive skills, higher-SES students benefit from sports because there is reinforcement of noncognitive skills among home, school, and EAs. Children are able to practice and receive reinforcement for their noncognitive skills in multiple contexts. Moreover, parents with high SES may have greater engagement with the EAs by observing their children participating in the EAs and may comment on their children's behavior during the EAs. The reinforcement of noncognitive skills in the home may explain why high-SES children benefit more from sports participation compared with low-SES children. . . .

CONCLUSION

It is important to consider a larger view of educational outcomes and refocus on the role of noncognitive skills in education. The classroom is one place that promotes the development of noncognitive skills. As with other skills, students benefit from being able to practice and develop their noncognitive skills, which are important for later learning and employment outcomes. Our study explicitly identifies EAs as a site for students to practice and develop their noncognitive skills. A large portion of elementary-age students spend time in EAs, and it is important to examine the connection between how students spend their leisure time and their classroom behaviors.

The findings of our study provide modest support for our expectation that participation in EAs and its relationship with noncognitive skills mediate the SES-achievement relationship. Although EAs and noncognitive skills help explain part of the association between SES and academic skills, SES still has a direct relationship with academic skills. Our results suggest that students who participate in sports benefit more than students who participate in other activities. . . .

Overall, the findings of this study provide limited support for our conceptual model. We did not find strong mediating mechanisms between SES and test scores, yet we did expand the focus of EAs to include EAs as an additional source of noncognitive skills. We expect that our findings may not apply to adolescents in high school, because they have greater agency, parental influence, and peer influence in decisions such as extracurricular participation. Despite high rates of participation among low-SES families, relative differences by SES levels further perpetuate educational inequality. Our findings indicate that EAs in childhood provide academic benefits for students by providing them with a site to practice and develop their noncognitive skills. Yet low-SES students are still less likely to participate in all types of EAs, providing students with disparate access and opportunities to develop their noncognitive skills. High-SES students have access to such sites in a variety of settings, continuing to provide these students with an advantage. Leveling the playing field requires many interventions in numerous different areas, but communities can begin by looking for opportunities after the school bell rings and offering affordable, high-quality extracurricular programs for students regardless of their socioeconomic backgrounds.

REFERENCES

Blau, P. M., & Duncan, O. D. (1967). *American occupational structure.* New York: John Wiley.

Bodovski, K., & Farkas, G. (2008). Concerted cultivation and unequal achievement in elementary school. *Social Science Research, 37*(3), 903–919.

Broh, B. A. (2002). Linking extracurricular programming to academic achievement: Who benefits and why? *Sociology of Education, 75*(1), 69–95.

Carbonaro, W. (2005). Tracking, student effort, and academic achievement. *Sociology of Education, 78*(1), 27–49.

Carneiro, P., & Heckman, J. J. (2005). Human capital policy. In J. J. Heckman & A. R. Krueger (Eds.), *Inequality in America: What role for human capital policies?* (pp. 77–239). Cambridge: MIT Press.

Cheadle, J. E. (2008). Educational investment, family context, and children's math and reading growth from kindergarten through the third grade. *Sociology of Education, 81*(1), 1–31.

Chin, T., & Phillips, M. (2004). Social reproduction and child-rearing practices: Social class, children's agency, and the summer activity gap. *Sociology of Education, 77*(3), 185–210.

Clotfelter, C. (2006). *After Brown: The rise and retreat of school desegregation.* Princeton, NJ: Princeton University Press.

Covay, E., & Carbonaro, W. (2010). After the bell: Participation in extracurricular activities, classroom behavior, and academic achievement. *Sociology of Education, 83*(1), 20–45.

Dreeben, R. (1968). *On what is learned in school.* Reading, MA: Addison-Wesley.

Dumais, S. (2006). Elementary school students' extracurricular activities: The effects of participation on achievement and teachers' evaluations. *Sociological Spectrum, 26*(2), 117–147.

Duncan, G. J., Dowsett, C. J., Claessens, A., Magnuson, K., Huston, A. C., Klebanov, P., . . . Japel, C. (2007). School readiness and later achievement. *Developmental Psychology, 43*(6), 1428–1446.

Eccles, J. S., Barber, B. L., Stone, M., & Hunt, J. (2003). Extracurricular activities and adolescent development. *Journal of Social Issues, 59*(4), 865–889.

Entwisle, D. R., Alexander, K. L., & Olson, L. S. (1997). *Children, schools, & inequality.* Boulder, CO: Westview.

Farkas, G. (2003). Cognitive skills and noncognitive traits and behaviors in stratification process. *Annual Review of Sociology, 29,* 541–562.

Farkas, G., Grobe, R., Sheehan, D., & Shuan, Y. (1990). Cultural resources and school success: Gender, ethnicity, and poverty groups within an urban school district. *American Sociological Review, 55,* 12–42.

Fletcher, A. C., Nickerson, P., & Wright, K. L. (2003). Structured leisure activities in middle childhood: Links to well-being. *Journal of Community Psychology, 31*(3), 641–659.

Gilman, R., Meyers, J., & Perez, L. (2004). Structured extracurricular activities among adolescents: Findings and implications for school psychologists. *Psychology in Schools, 4*(1), 31–39.

Gosa, T. L., & Alexander, K. L. (2007). Family (dis)advantage and the educational prospects of better off African American youth: How race still matters. *Teachers College Record, 109*(2), 285–321.

Guest, A., & Schneider, B. (2003). Adolescents' extracurricular participation in context: The mediating effects of schools, communities, and identity. *Sociology of Education, 76*(2), 89–109.

Hart, B., & Risley, T. R. (1995). *Meaningful differences in the everyday experience of young American children.* Baltimore: Paul H. Brookes.

Jackson, P. W. (1968). *Life in classrooms.* New York: Holt, Rinehart and Winston.

Jencks, C. (1972). *Inequality.* New York: Basic Books.

Kerckhoff, A. C., Raudenbush, S. W., & Glennie, E. (2001). Education, cognitive skills, and labor force outcomes. *Sociology of Education, 74*(1), 1–24.

Lareau, A. (2003). *Unequal childhoods: Class, race, and family life.* Los Angeles: University of California Press.

Marsh, H. (1992). Extracurricular activities: Beneficial extension of the traditional curriculum or subversion of the academic goals? *Journal of Educational Psychology, 84*(4), 553–562.

Marsh, H., & Kleitman, S. (2002). Extracurricular school activities: The good, the bad, and the nonlinear. *Harvard Educational Review, 72*(4), 464–514.

National Center for Education Statistics. (2004). *ECLS-K longitudinal kindergarten—third grade public-use data file: Data files and electronic code book* [CD-ROM]. Washington, DC: National Center for Education Statistics.

Olneck, M. R., & Bills, D. B. (1980). What makes Sammy run? An empirical assessment of the Bowles-Gintis correspondence theory. *American Journal of Education, 89*(1), 27–61.

Pattillo-McCoy, M. (2005). Black middle-class neighborhoods. *Annual Review of Sociology, 31*, 305–29.

Phillips, M., Brooks-Gunn, J., Duncan, G. J., Klebanov, P., & Crane, J. (1998). Family background, parenting practices, and the black-white test score gap. In C. Jencks & M. Phillips (Eds.), *The black-white test score gap* (pp. 103–148). Washington, DC: Brookings Institution.

Rosenbaum, J. (2001). *Beyond college for all.* New York: Russell Sage.

Sewell, W. R., & Hauser, R. H. (1975). *Education, occupation, & earnings: Achievement in the early career.* New York: Academic Press.

Smerdon, B. (1999). Engagement and achievement differences between African-American and white high school students. *Research in Sociology of Education and Socialization, 12,* 103–134.

Steinberg, L. (1996). *Beyond the classroom: Why school reform has failed and what parents need to do.* New York: Simon & Schuster.

Low-Level Violence

A Neglected Aspect of School Culture

David R. Dupper and Nancy Meyer-Adams

Recent stories of students committing suicide because they have been bullied and harassed in school have brought increased attention to low-level violence in schools. However, bullying does not make the headlines like school shootings and other violent crimes in schools. In reality, schools are among the safest places for young people to gather (Addington, Ruddy, Miller, DeVoe, & Chandler, 2002). What doesn't make the headlines are the millions of "little" acts of harassment and violence that leave some children afraid to go to school, tormented by peers and teachers, and lacking in self-esteem. These informal aspects of the school system affect students' ability to concentrate and achieve, and can result in anger, alienation, and hostile school environments. David Dupper and Nancy Meyer-Adams address several common forms of low-level violence. The authors suggest ways to create more positive school culture and climate.

Questions to consider for this reading:

1. Why is low-level violence often neglected by news media and the public?

2. How can the low-level violence discussed by the authors affect student performance in school?

3. What can be done to change the culture of schools, particularly as new technologies change the form and anonymity of harassment?

April, Age 13

Her mother said her daughter was being bullied and the ringleader was a popular girl who had targeted her for some unknown reason. Some kids called her fat, while others threw things at her and pushed her around, they even ridiculed her with rumors that she stuffed tissue in her bra. April took it all to heart. Faced with the prospect of juvenile detention as a truant or returning to a school to face taunting classmates, April decided against both. On Valentine's Day, she went into her bedroom, shut the door and hanged herself with a belt. ("Faced with 'go to jail' or 'go to school,'" 2000)

School shootings over the past several years, especially the carnage at Columbine High School in Littleton, Colorado, have propelled the issues of school violence prevention and school safety to the forefront in communities across the United States. Although high-level school violence (e.g., murder, rape, possession of weapons) is a serious problem that grabs the headlines and the public's attention, it is relatively rare (Astor, Vargas, Pitner, & Meyer, 1999; Centers for Disease Control and Prevention, 1998; Hyman & Snook, 1999; Kachur et al., 1996). In fact "there was a 40% decline in school-associated violent deaths between school years 1997–98 and 1998–99" (Brooks, Schiraldi, & Ziedenberg, 2000, p. 3). Unfortunately, relatively little attention has been paid to low-level or underlying forms of violence that occur in most secondary schools every day. The heartbreaking story of April illustrates the need to focus much more attention on low-level school violence such as bullying, peer sexual harassment, victimization based on known or presumed gay or lesbian sexual orientation, and the psychological maltreatment of students by teachers. Research over the past decade has shown that these forms of school violence, although not as overtly serious as weapons offenses, occur with greater frequency than most believe and have a profound impact on students' mental health and school performance (Elliott, Hamburg, & Williams, 1998).

BULLYING

Bullying refers to unprovoked physical or psychological abuse of an individual by one or a group of students over time to create an ongoing pattern of harassment and abuse (Batsche & Knoff, 1994; Hoover, Oliver, & Thomson, 1993; Olweus, 1991). It comprises direct behaviors (e.g., teasing, taunting, threatening, hitting, and stealing) and indirect behaviors (e.g., causing a student to be socially isolated by spreading rumors) (Smith & Sharp, 1994). Bullying victimization is estimated to affect 15% to 20% of the U.S. student population, with verbal teasing and intimidation being its most common form and boys reported to be victims at a higher rate than girls (Furlong, Chung, Bates, & Morrison, 1995). A study found that 88% of secondary school students reported having observed bullying and 76.8% stated that they had been a victim of

bullying at school (Hoover, Oliver, & Hazler, 1992). Bullying appears to peak in the middle school and junior high years (Batsche & Knoff, 1994). Students are bullied at school for a variety of reasons. These include girls being viewed by their peers as physically unattractive or not dressing stylishly, girls being physically well developed or not "fitting in" in some other way, boys not fitting a stereotypic macho male image, students having a different religion, students wearing unique or unusual clothes, students having physical weaknesses and/or being different in appearance (Furlong et al., 1995; Shakeshift et al., 1995).

The act of bullying has long-term implications for both victims and perpetrators. Negative impacts of chronic victimization include increased rates of truancy and dropping out as well as difficult psychosocial and psychosexual relationships (Hazler, Hoover, & Oliver, 1991). Hazler (1994) found that the impact of bullying on its victims includes a loss of self-esteem and feelings of isolation which, according to new research, can last into adulthood. He stated that

> their grades may suffer because their attention is being drawn away from learning. Being repeatedly victimized may push even "good kids" to extremes, such as starting fights or bringing weapons to school to exact vengeance on their tormentors, even students and adults who are witnesses are affected [in that] they must deal with the lowered self-esteem and loss of control that accompanies feeling unsafe and unable to take action. The result is children and adults who do all they can to avoid recognizing when someone else is being hurt. (p. 39)

It is harmful to those who witness peer harassment if this harassment is tacitly approved of and not acted upon by school personnel. For example, youth who are not direct victims of violence at school "may be victimized by the chronic presence of violence" (American Psychological Association, 1993, p. 42). "Students who must think about avoiding harm at school are diverting energy that should be expended on learning" (Chandler, Nolin, & Davies, 1995, p. 5). Bullies whose behavior is allowed to continue are 5 times more likely than their classmates to wind up in juvenile court, to be convicted of crimes, and, when they become adults, to have children with aggression problems (Hazler, 1994). A recent report that examined the profiles of school shooters concluded that in 66% of the cases, "the attackers felt persecuted, bullied, threatened, attacked or injured by others prior to the incident" and that a number of attackers had experienced longstanding and severe bullying and that "the experience of bullying appeared to play a major role in motivating the attack at school" (Vossekuil, Reddy, Fein, Borum, & Modzeleski, 2000, p. 7). Olweus (1993) found that 60% of students characterized as bullies in Grades 6 to 9 had at least one criminal conviction by age 24.

PEER SEXUAL HARASSMENT

The problem of peer sexual harassment appears to be pervasive in U.S. schools. A survey of 1,600 White, African American, and Hispanic students in Grades 8 through 11 sponsored by the American Association of University Women (AAUW) (1993) found that 85% of girls and 76% of boys reported experiencing some form of sexual harassment in school. Of that total, 25% reported being targeted "often." The types of peer sexual harassment in the AAUW study ranged from nonphysical forms (e.g., making sexual comments, spreading sexual rumors, flashing) to physical forms (e.g., touching, grabbing, pinching). The most common form of harassment, reported by 65% of girls and 42% of boys, was being the target of sexual comments, jokes, gestures, or looks. The second most common form of harassment was being touched, grabbed, or pinched in a sexual way. The AAUW study found that a child's first experience of sexual harassment is most likely to occur in middle or junior high school and that girls suffer more negative effects as a result of peer sexual harassment than boys. For example, girls reported "not wanting to go to school" (33%), "not wanting to talk as much in class" (32%), and "finding it hard to pay attention in school" (28%) as outcomes of being sexually harassed at school. Additionally, 64% of girls reported

experiencing "embarrassment," 52% reported feeling "self-conscious," and 43% of girls reported feeling less sure or less confident of themselves as a result of sexual harassment. Perhaps the most disturbing finding in the AAUW study was the response of students who engaged in sexually harassing behaviors at school. The majority of these perpetrators responded, "It's just part of school life," "A lot of people do it," "It's no big deal" (AAUW, 1993). Moreover, this indifference appears to extend to school personnel, because teachers and other school staff rarely, if ever, intervene to stop peer sexual harassment in schools (Batsche & Knoff, 1994; Hoover et al., 1992; Shakeshift et al., 1995; Stein, 1995). For example, in a study conducted by Shakeshift et al. (1995), a female respondent stated, "In science class, the boys snap our bras. The [male] teacher doesn't really care. He doesn't say anything the boys just laugh" (p. 42).

VICTIMIZATION BASED ON KNOWN OR PRESUMED GAY OR LESBIAN SEXUAL ORIENTATION

Victimization based on known or presumed gay or lesbian sexual orientation is the most common form of bias-related violence in the United States (Pilkington & D'Augelli, 1995). Being called gay or lesbian was the most disturbing form of unwanted behavior for boys (86%), and "being called gay would be more upsetting to boys than actual physical abuse" (AAUW, 1993, p. 23). In 1999, the Gay, Lesbian and Straight Education Network (GLSEN) conducted a survey of 496 lesbian, gay, bisexual, and transgender (LGBT) youth from 32 states. The authors of this survey found that over 91.4% of LGBT youth reported that they sometimes or frequently hear homophobic remarks (e.g., "faggot," "dyke," "queer") in their school. Homophobic remarks seem to be pervasive in schools. For example, the Massachusetts Governor's Commission on Gay and Lesbian Youth (1993) found that 97% of students in public high schools reported hearing homophobic remarks from their peers on a regular basis. This harassment often extends beyond verbal abuse. Pilkington and D'Augelli (1995) found that 22% of the males and 29% of the females reported having been physically hurt by another student because of their sexual orientation.

As is the case in peer sexual harassment, school personnel rarely intervene when students are victimized based on known or presumed gay or lesbian sexual orientation. For example, almost half the youth in the GLSEN (1999) study reported that someone intervened only some of the time, and one third reported that no one ever intervened in these circumstances. Compounding this problem is a finding by Sears (1992) that two thirds of guidance counselors harbored negative feelings toward gay and lesbian persons, less than 20% have received any training on serving gay and lesbian students, and only 25% consider themselves "highly competent" in serving gay and lesbian youth. Beyond their indifference and lack of training is the fact that school personnel are often perpetrators themselves. For example, almost 37% of respondents in the GLSEN (1999) study and over 53% of students in the Massachusetts Governor's Commission on Gay and Lesbian Youth study (1993) reported that they hear homophobic remarks from faculty or school staff. Given these findings, it is not surprising that gay and lesbian students keep their sexual orientation hidden from teachers and school counselors.

Victimization based on known or presumed gay or lesbian sexual orientation has a detrimental impact on the mental health and school performance of victims. Nearly half of the youth in the GLSEN (1999) study reported that they did not feel safe in their school because they are gay, lesbian, bisexual, or transgender. Furthermore, Krivascka, Savin-Williams, and Slater (as cited in Elia, 1993) reported that 80% of gays and lesbians had declining school performance, almost 40% had problems with truancy, and 30% had dropped out of school. Gays and lesbians also attempt suicide 2 to 7 times more frequently than heterosexual comparison groups (Saunders & Valente, 1987). In their survey of 194 lesbian, gay, and bisexual youth between the ages of 15 and 21, Pilkington and D'Augelli (1995) found that "approximately one-third of the males (30%) and females (35%) reported that being harassed or verbally abused in school currently limits their openness about their sexual orientation" (p. 44).

PSYCHOLOGICAL MALTREATMENT OF STUDENTS BY TEACHERS

Although emotional maltreatment of students by teachers "receives little pedagogical, psychological, or legal attention. data based on case studies, anecdotal reports, and some beginning research suggest that [the] psychological maltreatment [of students by teachers] may occur in schools more often than many think" (Hyman & Perone, 1998, p. 21). Psychological maltreatment of students by teachers and other adults in authority consists of discipline and control techniques that are based on fear and intimidation (Brassard, Hart, & Germaine, 1987). Too many teachers use screaming, sarcasm, threats, and ridicule to control students in their classroom (Hyman, 1997). Sakowski (1993) found that students who are psychologically maltreated exhibited behavior problems and poor interpersonal competencies. According to Hyman (1997), "Although psychological maltreatment is believed to occur more often than other forms of abuse [in schools], it is difficult to determine rate of occurrence in specific regions or schools, because schools are not anxious to investigate their own malfeasance" (p. 331).

BUILDING A MORE POSITIVE SCHOOL CULTURE AND CLIMATE

According to Davila and Willower (1996), in each individual school there is a culture that is owned by that school that embodies its values, norms, and beliefs. Additionally, each school has distinct yet overlapping climates that exist for the students, the faculty, and the staff. These climates play a critical role in the everyday performance and attitudes of these individuals and how these individuals can work together as a team to build a strong, positive culture in their school's environment. A school's culture and climate are important because we know that they significantly affect and influence students' behavior and learning (Wang, Haertel, & Walberg, 1997). Hamilton and Richardson (1995) defined a school's culture as "the beliefs and expectations apparent in a school's daily routine, including how colleagues interact with each other . . . culture is the socially shared and transmitted knowledge of what is and what ought to be symbolized in act and artifact" (p. 369). Freiberg and Stein (1999) stated that

> school climate is the heart and soul of a school. It is about that essence of a school that leads a child, a teacher, an administrator, a staff member to love the school and to look forward to being there each school day. The climate of a school can foster resilience or become a risk factor in the lives of people who work and learn in a place called school. (p. 11)

Culture affects students through the norms that drive behavior in a school environment, and climate reflects the perceptions that students have of the impact of that environment on their own well-being (Brown & Leigh, 1996; Glisson, 2000). Stolp (1995) contends that

> students work harder, attend school more often, and have stronger academic skills in schools with strong communities and student violence decreases in communal organizations . . . teachers work harder and enjoy their work more in an environment that puts social bonds above individual success . . . school community positively affects school culture. (p. 14)

Not only does a culture of low-level violence place students at risk, but it also deprives them of the opportunity to benefit from the educational opportunities a school provides.

PROGRAMS DESIGNED TO CHANGE THE CULTURE AND CLIMATE OF SCHOOLS

Based on our review, it is evident that bullying, peer sexual harassment, victimization based on known or presumed gay or lesbian sexual orientation, and the psychological maltreatment of students by teachers are problems that must be addressed in any comprehensive school violence prevention program. One way of reducing low-level, underlying violence in schools is to build a more positive school culture and climate. Interventions must be designed to change or modify the culture and climate of a school so that schools become safe havens and sanctuaries for all children and youth; places where teachers, students, administrators, parents, support staff, all feel invited to participate and welcome and share a psychological sense of community. The culture of a school must reflect a place where children and youth want to be, places they will respect. A recent publication by the National Association of Attorneys General (1999) concludes that research indicates that a supportive school climate is the most important step in ensuring that schools provide a safe and welcome environment for all students. Hansen and Childs (1998) stated that working toward a positive school climate involves "dedicated individuals [who] are making conscious efforts to enhance and enrich the culture and conditions in the school so that teachers can teach better and students can learn more" (p. 14).

Several programs have focused on building a more positive school culture and climate. These include the Bullying Prevention Program (Olweus, 1991, 1993), the School Development Program (Comer, 1988), and the Positive Action Through Holistic Education (PATHE) (Gottfredson, 1986). Of these, the Office of Juvenile Justice and Delinquency Prevention (OJJDP) has recognized the Bullying Prevention Program as one of its 10 Blueprint Programs that has been shown to be effective in preventing violence. Based on a large-scale study conducted in Norway in the early 1980s, the Bullying Prevention Program was shown to result in a substantial reduction in boys' and girls' reports of bullying and victimization; a significant reduction in students' reports of general antisocial behavior such as vandalism, fighting, theft, and truancy; and significant improvements in the "social climate" of the class, as reflected in students' reports of improved order and discipline, more positive social relationships, and a more positive attitude toward schoolwork and school (Olweus & Limber, 1999). More information about the School Development Program and PATHE Program may be found in the OJJDP publication "School and Community Interventions to Prevent Serious and Violent Offending."

Recently, two schools in California have been highlighted as a result of their efforts to reduce school violence by changing the culture and climate of the school. Epstein (1998) described Oakland's Emiliano Zapata Street Academy as "a public high school where there are no fights, no security guards, no metal detectors, no guns, and the police department visits to ticket meter violations rather than arrest students. It is like a 'private academy for poor kids'" (p. 1). Epstein goes on to describe four core components of this school: (a) This is a school of "tight relationships," where every staff member is a "consulting teacher" for 15 to 20 students. The teacher meets with his or her students twice a day to check on academic performance and behavior and responds immediately to problems by calling a parent or conferring with another student if there are conflicts—problems are not allowed to fester and grow! Even verbal altercations are taken seriously, and students are not sent back to class until they have worked out a solution. (b) This is a school that espouses multiculturalism—the staff's ethnic composition mirrors that of students and many staff live in the community. Racism is explicitly discussed and there is a stern response to cross-racial disrespect among students. (c) This is a small school with a closed campus. It treats its students as whole human beings; students tell teachers what is actually happening in their lives. (d) This is a school that is self-renewing, creating teachers who get better every year instead of burning out. According to Epstein, "teachers have enormous latitude in creating new teaching methods and procedures, but the school's leader is demanding of everyone, including herself, when it comes to meeting student needs" (p. 1).

Ruenzel (1997) described another school in California that is focusing on changing its culture and climate to reduce school violence. Ginger Hovenic, the principal of Clear View Elementary School, believes that a vital school culture is the "foundation for all learning that takes place in the classroom" (p. 1). In this school, 595 students speak 26 native languages, and 200 are from low-income families (Ruenzel, 1997). Hovenic and her teachers attempted to create a school environment where all children felt welcome and no child would fall between the cracks. In the end, she and her teachers came up with a variation of homerooms, something they call "families," and it has become the central feature of the school culture. According to Ruenzel, each family consists of two dozen students randomly drawn from every grade in her K–6 school. Students remain in the same family and with the same teacher until they go on to middle school. The families meet for an hour each week. They celebrate birthdays and holidays together, they go on outings, and keep hefty family scrapbooks. They take part in a number of social projects such as collecting food and clothing for families and helping out needier children in the school. The Peace Patrol involves student volunteers trained in the art of negotiation, wearing blue jackets and carrying clipboards, patrolling school grounds and mediating disputes before they spiral out of control. Part of the school culture is that kids get sent to the principal only for having done something positive. Parents are involved by attending a town meeting at the beginning of each year, where they are encouraged to pose questions and voice concerns; the principal also hosts regular coffees with parents throughout the school year to keep them up to date on the full range of school matters; routine parent conferences are not led by teachers but by students, who present their work to their parents. Teachers are encouraged to dream and scheme together about new things they can try—this type of collaboration takes time, so every Thursday afternoon, 2 hours are set aside for teachers to discuss everything from books they have read to workshops they are thinking of attending. They also discuss students who need academic help—with the aid of computer-generated spreadsheets that provide a statistical picture of each student's academic performance. Teacher evaluation is also a collaborative effort. Although neither of these programs has been formally evaluated, they each offer some promising ideas and directions for school personnel interested in reducing low-level violence in the schools they serve.

RECOMMENDATIONS

To prevent or reduce low-level, underlying violence in schools, we recommend that school personnel focus on changing a school's culture and climate by implementing interventions based on the following assumptions:

- Every individual should have the right to be spared oppression and repeated, intentional humiliation in school as well as in society at large. Schools must send a strong message to students and staff that all forms of low-level violence are inappropriate and that adults will actively intervene in all instances of low-level violence and that those who fail to recognize and stop low-level forms of violence as they occur actually promote violence.

- Because many school personnel do not acknowledge that low-level violence is a serious problem, it is essential that a needs assessment be conducted and all school personnel be informed about the extent of bullying, peer sexual harassment, victimization based on known or presumed gay or lesbian sexual orientation in their school, and the psychological maltreatment of students by teachers and other school staff. If ignored, low-level violence in schools can jeopardize students' academic achievement, undermine their physical and emotional well-being, and may provoke retaliatory violence.

- The best way to reduce low-level forms of school violence is to create a school culture and climate characterized by warmth, tolerance, positive responses to diversity, sensitivity to others' views, cooperative interactions among students, teachers, and school staff, and an environment that expects and reinforces appropriate behavior. In cases of violations of limits and rules, nonhostile, nonphysical sanctions should be consistently applied.

- Homophobia makes schools unsafe for all students, not only for those who are gay and lesbian. Antigay prejudice and homophobia can make any student who defies the narrowly defined gender roles a target for violence and harassment. A concerted effort is required to address homophobic attitudes among school personnel.

- Rather than focusing on the perpetrators or victims alone, effective interventions must happen at multiple levels, concurrently. These multiple levels include school-level interventions (e.g., conflict resolution and diversity training workshops for teachers and school staff), classroom-level interventions (e.g., regularly scheduled classroom meetings during which students and teachers engage in discussion, role-playing, and creative activities related to preventing all forms of low-level violence), and individual-level interventions (e.g., formation of discussion groups for victims of low-level violence).

The middle and junior high grades (6 through 8) are a critical time for intervention and should receive highest priority.

CONCLUSIONS

The pervasiveness of low-level school violence in the forms of bullying, peer sexual harassment, victimization based on sexual orientation, and the psychological maltreatment of students by teachers must be acknowledged and addressed in a more preventive and proactive manner. School personnel must assume a leadership role in conceiving and implementing interventions designed to change the culture and climate of schools to reduce low-level violence.

REFERENCES

Addington, L. A., Ruddy, S. A., Miller, A. K., DeVoe, J. F., & Chandler, K. A. (2002). *Are America's schools safe? Students speak out.* Washington, DC: National Center for Education Statistics, U.S. Department of Education.

American Association of University Women (AAUW). (1993). *Hostile hallways: The AAUW survey on sexual harassment in America's schools.* Washington, DC: Author.

American Psychological Association. (1993). Violence and youth: Psychology's response. Volume I. *Summary report of the American Psychological Association Commission on Violence and Youth.* Washington, DC: Author.

Astor, R. A., Vargas, L. A., Pitner, R., & Meyer, H. A. (1999). School violence: Research, theory, and practice. In J. M. Jenson & M. O. Howard (Eds.), *Youth violence: Current research and recent practice innovations* (pp. 139–171). Washington, DC: National Association of Social Workers Press.

Batsche, G. M., & Knoff, H. M. (1994). Bullies and their victims: Understanding a pervasive problem in the schools. *School Psychology Review, 23*(2), 165–174.

Brassard, M., Hart, S., & Germaine, B. (1987). *Psychological mistreatment of children and youth.* Elmsford, NY: Pergamon Press.

Brooks, K., Schiraldi, V., & Ziedenberg, J. (2000). *School house hype: Two years later.* Washington, DC: Justice Policy Institute and Children's Law Center.

Brown, S. P., & Leigh, T. W. (1996). A new look at psychological climate and its relationship to job involvement, effort, and performance. *Journal of Applied Psychology, 81*(4), 358–368.

Cantalano, R. F., Loeber, R., & McKinney, K. C. (1999). *School and Community interventions to prevent serious violent offending* (Juvenile Justice Bulletin). Washington, CC: U.S. Department of Justice, Office of Juvenile Justice and Delinquency Prevention.

Centers for Disease Control and Prevention. (1998). *Youth risk behavior surveillance—United States, 1997* (Morbidity and mortality weekly report, 47(SS-3), U.S. Department of Health and Human Services). Washington, DC: Author.

Chandler, K., Nolin, M. J., & Davies, E. (1995). *Student strategies to avoid harm at school* (National Center for Education Statistics 95–203). Rockville, MD: Westat.

Comer, J. P. (1988). Educating poor minority children. *Scientific American, 259*(5), 42–48.

Davila, A., & Willower, D. J. (1996). Organizational culture in a Mexican school: Lessons for reform. *International Journal of Educational Reform, 5*(4), 438–443.

Elia, J. P. (1993). Homophobia in the high school: A problem in need of a resolution. *The High School Journal, 77,* 177–185.

Elliott, D. S., Hamburg, B., & Williams, K. R. (1998). Violence in American schools: An overview. In D. S. Elliott, B. A. Hamburg, & K. R. Williams (Eds.), *Violence in American schools* (pp. 3–28). New York: Cambridge University Press.

Epstein, K. K. (1998, March 4). An urban high school with no violence. *Education Week on the Web.* Retrieved from http://www.edweek.org/ew/1998/25epstei.h17

Faced with "go to jail" or "go to school, get beat up," 13-year-old hangs herself. (2000, February 19). *Knoxville News-Sentinel,* p. A-6.

Freiberg, H. J., & Stein, T. A. (1999). Measuring, improving and sustaining healthy learning environments. In H. J. Freiberg (Ed.), *School climate: Measuring, improving and sustaining healthy learning environments* (pp. 11–29). London: Falmer Press.

Furlong, M. J., Chung, A., Bates, M., & Morrison, R. L. (1995). Who are the victims of school violence? A comparison of student non-victims and multi-victims. *Education and Treatment of Children, 18*(3), 282–298.

Gay, Lesbian and Straight Education Network (GLSEN). (1999). *GLESN's national school climate survey: Lesbian, gay, bisexual and transgender students and their experiences in school.* Retrieved from http://www.glsen.org/pages/sections/news/natlnews/1999/sep/survey

Glisson, C. (2000). Organizational climate and culture. In R. Patti (Ed.), *The handbook of social welfare* (pp. 195–218). Thousand Oaks, CA: Sage.

Gottfredson, D. C. (1986). An empirical test of school-based environmental and individual interventions to reduce the risk of delinquent behavior. *Criminology, 24*(4), 705–731.

Hamilton, M. L., & Richardson, V. (1995). Effects of the culture in two schools on the process and outcomes of staff development. *Elementary School Journal, 95*(4), 367–385.

Hansen, J. M., & Childs, J. (1998). Creating a school where people like to be. *Educational Leadership, 56*(1), 14–17.

Hazler, R. J. (1994). Bullying breeds violence: You can stop it. *Learning, 22*(6), 38–41.

Hazler, R. J., Hoover. J. H., & Oliver, R. (1991). Student perceptions of victimization by bullies in school. *Journal of Humanistic Education and Development, 29*(4), 143–150.

Hoover, J. H., Oliver, R., & Hazler, R. L. (1992). Bullying: Perceptions of adolescent victims in the midwestern USA. *Social Psychology International, 13,* 5–16.

Hoover, J. H., Oliver, R. L., & Thomson, K. A. (1993). Perceived victimization by school bullies: New research and future directions. *Journal of Humanistic Education and Development, 32*(2), 76–84.

Hyman, I. A. (1997). *School discipline and school violence.* Boston: Allyn & Bacon.

Hyman, I. A., & Perone, D. C. (1998). The other side of school violence: Educator policies and practices that may contribute to student misbehavior. *Journal of School Psychology, 36*(1), 7–27.

Hyman, I. A., & Snook, P. A. (1999). *Dangerous schools: What we can do about the physical and emotional abuse of our children.* San Francisco: Jossey-Bass.

Kachur, P., Stennies, G., Powell, K., Modzeleski, W., Stephens, R., Murphy, R., . . . Lowry, R. (1996). School-associated violent deaths in the United States, 1992 to 1994. *Journal of the American Medical Association, 275,* 1729–1733.

Massachusetts Governor's Commission on Gay and Lesbian Youth. (1993). *Making schools safe for gay and lesbian youth: Report of the Massachusetts Governor's Commission on Gay and Lesbian Youth.* Boston: Author.

National Association of Attorneys General. (1999). *Protecting students from harassment and hate crime.* Washington, DC: U.S. Department of Education, Office for Civil Rights.

Olweus, D. (1991). Bully/victim problems among schoolchildren: Basic facts and effects of a school based intervention program. In D. J. Pepler & K. H. Rubin (Eds.), *The development and treatment of childhood aggression* (pp. 411–448). Hillsdale, NJ: Lawrence Erlbaum.

Olweus, D. (1993). *Bullying at school.* Oxford, England: Basil Blackwell.

Olweus, D., & Limber, S. (1999). *Blueprints for violence prevention: Bullying prevention program.* Boulder, CO: Institute of Behavioral Science, University of Colorado.

Pilkington, N. W., & D'Augelli, A. R. (1995). Victimization of lesbian, gay, and bisexual youth in community settings. *Journal of Community Psychology, 23,* 34–56.

Ruenzel, D. (1997). One school that can. *Education Week on the Web.* Retrieved from http://www.edweek.org/ew/1998/25epstei.h17

Sakowski, L. (1993). *A study of pre- and post-trauma adjustment in corporally punished students* (Unpublished doctoral dissertation). Temple University, Philadelphia.

Saunders, J. M., & Valente, S. M. (1987). Suicide risk among gay men and lesbians: A review. *Death Studies, 11*(1), 1–23.

Sears, J. (1992). Educators, homosexuality, and homosexual students: Are personal feelings related to professional beliefs? *Journal of Homosexuality, 22*(3/4), 29–80.

Shakeshift, C., Barber, E., Hergenrother, M., Johnson, Y. M., Mandel, L. S., & Sawyer, J. (1995). Peer harassment in schools. *Journal for a Just and Caring Education, 1,* 30–44.

Smith, P. K., & Sharp, S. (1994). *School bullying: Insights and perspectives.* London: Routledge. Retrieved from ERIC Database. (ED 387 223)

Stein, N. (1995). Sexual harassment in school: The public performance of gendered violence. *Harvard Educational Review, 65*(2), 145–162.

Stolp, S. (1995). *Every school a community: The academic value of strong social bonds among staff and students.* Eugene: Oregon School Study Council.

Vossekuil, B., Reddy, M., Fein, R., Borum, R., & Modzeleski, W. (2000). *USSS safe school initiative: An interim report on the prevention of targeted violence in schools.* Washington, DC: U.S. Secret Service, National Threat Assessment Center.

Wang, M. C., Haertel, G. D., & Walberg, H. J. (1997). Learning influences. In H. J. Walberg & G. D. Haertel (Eds.), *Psychology and educational practice* (pp. 199–211). Berkeley, CA: McCuthan.

THE DROPOUT PROBLEM

Losing Ground

Paul E. Barton

The readings in this chapter provide a picture of how children, beginning at an early age, learn through the informal system how to fit into school and play their appropriate roles. They also learn what competing influences they face from peer groups, family problems, and other factors that can dominate the child's world. The ultimate failure for both schools and young people is when students drop out. Barton points out some aspects of student roles and the informal system that influence students to leave school. These include getting low grades, being absent frequently, and high turnover or changing schools—all of which disrupt the learning process. Many of his suggestions for improving retention and school climate focus on aspects of the informal system: small learning communities in schools, helping teachers recognize and deal with problems early and intervene with students having problems.

Questions to consider for this reading:

1. How extensive is the school dropout problem in the United States?

2. Which students are most likely to drop out of school, and why?

3. What can we learn from the previous reading by Dupper and Meyer-Adams on low-level violence and school climate that might be used to lower the dropout rate?

A recent upsurge of interest in the student dropout problem seems to have come as a surprise to U.S. school officials and policy-makers. During the last two decades, complacency had set in as reports from the U.S. Census Bureau's household survey suggested that high school completion among young adults was approaching 90 percent, the goal set by the first National Education Summit in Charlottesville, Virginia, in 1989. The long-dormant concern about dropouts revived several years ago, however, when half a dozen independent researchers in universities and think tanks began publishing estimates of high school completion rates that contradicted the official rates. As a result, the issue of high school dropouts has returned to the front burner.

MANY ESTIMATES, SIMILAR RESULTS

The recent independent estimates of high school completion rates are almost always lower than the official estimates—including those that states have reported to the U.S. Department of Education under the requirements of No Child Left Behind and the state estimates from the National Center for Education Statistics. These independent estimates—derived through different methods and not always pertaining to the same year—vary somewhat, but they are all in the same ballpark. Jay Greene at the Manhattan Institute estimated a high school completion rate of 71 percent for 1998; Christopher Swanson and Duncan Chaplin at the Urban Institute estimated 66.6 percent for 2000; Thomas Mortenson of *Post-secondary Education Opportunity* estimated 66.1 percent for 2000; Andrew Sum and colleagues at Northeastern University estimated 68.7 percent for 1998; and Walter Haney and colleagues at Boston College estimated 74.4 percent for 2001. (I describe these studies and their methodologies in detail in *Unfinished Business: More Measured Approaches in Standards-Based Reform*) (Barton, 2005a).

The well-publicized contradictions of official estimates led to a minor political explosion, particularly after the Education Trust (2003) attacked the accuracy of the states' reports to the Department of Education. Then-Secretary of Education Rod Paige appointed a task force to look into the matter. Later, the National Governors Association convened a Task Force on State High School Graduation Data to propose a plan for how states could develop a high-quality, comparable high school graduation measure. All of this is being weighed in Washington and in state capitals.

A CLOSER LOOK AT THE STATISTICS

My own analysis (Barton, 2005a) confirmed the estimates of other researchers. I relied on two numbers I knew to be actual counts. One was the census count of the population cohort that would be of graduation age (17 or 18) in spring 2000; the other was the number of regular public and private high school diplomas awarded that year as reported by the National Center for Education Statistics. My final analysis estimated that 69.6 percent of youth who were of graduating age had received diplomas in 2000.

To measure change over time, I made estimates for 1990 using the same approach and found a completion rate of 72 percent for that year. For both 1990 and 2000, I also estimated individual state completion rates, which varied broadly. For 1990, the spread was from 90.6 percent in Iowa down to 61.7 percent in Florida (and 59.9 percent in Washington, D.C.). In 2000, the percentage ranged from 88.2 percent in Vermont down to 55 percent in Arizona (and 48 percent in Washington, D.C.). Only seven states showed an increase in high school completion rates during the decade; rates in the remaining states declined (Barton, 2005b).

Other researchers have found that minorities have lower completion rates than white students. For example, Elaine Allensworth (2005) carried out an excellent study of Chicago schools, which had individual student records available to track students. Among boys, only 39 percent of black students graduated by age 19, compared with 51 percent of Latino students and 58 percent of white students. Girls fared better: Comparable rates were 57 percent for black students, 65 percent for Latino students, and 71 percent for white students.

Research on the path that students travel through the grades may also shed light on the dropout problem. For example, one study identified an important trend that has developed over the last decade: the "9th grade bulge." Compared with past years, an increasing number of 9th graders are failing to be promoted to the 10th grade. Haney and colleagues (2004) found that in 2001, 440,000 more students were enrolled in grade 9 than in grade 8 the previous year. By 2001 seven states had at least 20 percent more students enrolled in the 9th grade than had been enrolled in that grade in the prior year, and one-half had at least 10 percent more. We know that there is an association between failing a grade and dropping out. And we know that more students are dropping out at younger ages.

The research conducted in the last couple of years raises many questions. One issue is why the U.S. Census Bureau household survey estimates differ from the lower completion rates found by independent researchers. We can explain this difference in part by the fact that the census lumped regular diplomas and GEDs together. The GED is a well-respected substitute, but it is not a regular diploma earned after completing four years of high school. Numerous research studies show that GED recipients tend to fare better than dropouts, but not as well as graduates with diplomas (Boesel, Alsalam, & Smith, 1998). Although the number of GEDs has become a growing proportion of total graduates, inclusion of GED recipients does not entirely account for the gaps among the estimates. Further analysis is needed to reconcile the remaining discrepancies.

Another question raised by the research is why completion rates, in terms of regular diplomas, fell during the last decade in so many states. Some of the likely suspects include the decrease in two-parent families, the previously mentioned 9th grade bulge, and higher standards for graduation. However, my analysis did not produce evidence conclusively linking high school completion rates to any of these factors.

A Deteriorating Economic Position

At the same time that high school completion rates have fallen, labor market prospects for dropouts are becoming increasingly dire. In 2003, 1.1 million 16- to 19-year-olds did not have a high school diploma and were not enrolled in school. In the landscape of the economy, these dropouts are often lost travelers without a map. Only 4 in 10 of the 16- to 19-year-olds are employed, as are fewer than 6 in 10 of 20- to 24-year-old dropouts. Black and Latino youth are doing considerably less well than others (T. Morisi, U.S. Bureau of Labor Statistics, personal communication, July 14, 2004).

What about the earning power of those dropouts who do have jobs? Do they make enough money to support a household? For 25- to 34-year-old dropouts who manage to work full-time, the average annual salary of males dropped from $35,087 (in 2002 constant dollars) in 1971, to $22,903 in 2002, a decline of 35 percent. The

comparable annual earnings for females without a diploma were $19,888 in 1971, declining to $17,114 in 2002. Even when they work full-time, the average earnings of this age group of dropouts are not far above the poverty line for a family with children—and most dropouts do not even reach this level of earnings. The earnings of high school graduates also have declined since 1971, but not as steeply as those of dropouts (National Center for Education Statistics [NCES], 2004, Tables 14–1, 14–2, and 14–3).

Factors That Affect the Dropout Rate

Which student conditions and life experiences are correlated with failure to complete high school? A 2002 report from the U.S. General Accounting Office (GAO)[1] summarized the research. Factors that correlated with low completion rates included coming from low-income or single-parent families, getting low grades in school, being absent frequently, and changing schools. These factors vary considerably by state, as do high school completion rates.

These predictive factors do not determine completion rates, but they do show the conditions that schools need to overcome in their effort to maximize completions. Some schools rise above expectations, some schools meet them, and some schools do less well than expected.

To find out how the individual states performed in 2000 compared with what we might expect on the basis of conditions in each state, I computed the correlation of completion rates with expectations based on three factors: state average socioeconomic characteristics (family income, education, and occupation); the percentage of two-parent families; and the rate at which students change schools. I found that these factors accounted for almost 60 percent of the variation in state completion rates.

This comparison of the *expected* completion rates with the *actual* completion rates disclosed that the actual rate fell within 4 percentage points of the expected rate in 24 states. Except for

Rhode Island and Hawaii, actual rates in the remaining states were within 10 points of the expected rates. The states doing the best in exceeding their expected completion rates were Hawaii, Maryland, Vermont, Connecticut, and West Virginia. The states doing the worst were Rhode Island, Indiana, South Carolina, and Arizona (Barton, 2005a). To learn more about increasing school completion rates, we should study both those states that greatly exceed the expected high school completion rate and those that fall far below it for clues about what these states are doing differently.

INCREASING SCHOOL RETENTION

The factors identified in the GAO report—that low-income students and high-mobility students are high-risks, that low achievement and grade retention are precursors to leaving school—provide a guide for what we need to do to improve high school completion rates. In my research, the factor *most* predictive was coming from a single-parent family (even after controlling for socioeconomic status). The extra effort that schools make to support students in all these circumstances will likely determine whether schools achieve higher or lower high school completion rates then expected.

Evaluations have established the effectiveness of a number of programs and models designed to increase school retention. The following models, described in more detail in *One-Third of a Nation: Rising Dropout Rates and Declining Opportunities* (Barton, 2005b), merit a close look by any state, district, or school wishing to embark on efforts to retain students in school.

• **The Talent Development High School** was developed by the Center for Research on the Education of Students Placed At Risk (CRESPAR), a collaboration between Johns Hopkins University and Howard University. This model emphasizes small learning communities, curriculum reforms, professional development, interdisciplinary teams of teachers, longer class periods, and employer advisory boards. There are now 33 such high schools in 12 states.

• **Communities in Schools** is designed specifically to keep students in school. Schools and community agencies form partnerships to deliver services and provide resources to students, such as individual case management, counseling, volunteers and mentors, remedial education, tutoring, classes teaching life skills and employment-related topics, and a variety of after-school programs.

• **Maryland Tomorrow** is a large-scale statewide dropout prevention effort operating in 75 high schools and is directed at students considered at risk of dropping out. Among other components, the program includes counseling, intensive academic instruction during the summer and the school year, career guidance and exploration, a variety of summer activities, and adult mentors.

• **The Quantum Opportunities Program** was launched in 1989 with funding from the Ford Foundation and the U.S. Department of Labor. Although the funding ended in 1999, the program's features offer a roadmap for providing supplemental services to students in schools that have large proportions of low-income and minority families. The program targeted randomly selected at-risk 9th graders entering inner-city high schools with high dropout rates. Using a comprehensive case management approach, the program provided year-round services to the participants throughout their four years of high school. Components included tutoring and homework assistance, computer-assisted instruction, life and family skills training, supplemental after-school education, developmental activities, mentoring, community service activities, and financial planning.

The documented results of these programs, together with the growing research on public alternative schools (Kleiner, Porch, & Farris, 2002), provide a knowledge base about comprehensive approaches to increasing both academic achievement and high school completion rates—which generally go hand in hand.

When it comes to working with individual students to avert a decision to drop out, however, there is a serious impediment. Guidance counselors, working with teachers, are the logical people to identify, track, and help students who show the well-known predropout behaviors: frequent absenteeism, course failure, and negative attitudes. But these professionals can hardly perform such work given the current ratio of 1 counselor to almost 300 high school students—a ratio that is even worse in high minority schools (NCES, 2004, table 27–1). In addition, almost all of a counselor's time goes to scheduling courses, helping students with college choice and admissions, performing hall and lunchroom duty, and, increasingly, dealing with test administration (NCES, 2001).

Somehow, schools must recruit individuals who have the time to interact with students one-on-one: more counselors, more volunteers, and more paid and unpaid mentors and tutors. How schools achieve this aim will vary, but any viable approach will require additional effort and resources at the school, school district, or state level (or all three).

Schools attempting to tackle the dropout problem face strikingly different circumstances. At one end of the spectrum are the schools in suburban neighborhoods where most students graduate and go on to college. Here, the relatively few students who appear dropout-prone can be identified, and resources are likely to be available to help them. At the other end are the schools in poor inner-city neighborhoods where families may have less time to supervise after-school activities or interact with the schools to address student absenteeism, misbehavior, or concerns about homework. Here, efforts to increase high school completion will require considerable additional resources, including the help of the larger community. All sorts of school situations lie in between, and no handy formula will apply across the board. But policymakers, administrators, and legislators have a base of knowledge to draw on, as well as information about good practices that work at the school and classroom levels.

A Battle on Two Fronts

The growing demands for high school reform have emphasized the need for higher achievement levels for students who graduate from high school so that they are prepared to either succeed in college or go directly into academically demanding jobs. Although such efforts are important, any reform initiatives that do not also make inroads on the dropout situation can hardly be considered successful. We face a hard battle on two fronts—one to make high school more rigorous, and the other to keep more students in high school through graduation.

Note

1. Effective July 7, 2004, the GAO's legal name became the U.S. Government Accountability Office.

References

Allensworth, E. (2005). *Graduation and dropout trends in Chicago: A look at cohorts of students from 1991 through 2004.* Chicago: Consortium on Chicago School Research.

Barton, P. (2005a, January). *Unfinished business: More measured approaches in standards-based reform* (Policy Information Report). Princeton, NJ: Educational Testing Service, Policy Information Center. Retrieved from http://www.ets.org/Media/Education_Topics/pdf/unfinbusiness.pdf

Barton, P. (2005b). *One-third of a nation: Rising dropout rates and declining opportunities.* Princeton, NJ: Educational Testing Service, Policy Information Center. Retrieved from http://www.ets.org/Media/Education_Topics/pdf/onethird.pdf

Boesel, D., Alsalam, N., & Smith, T. M. (1998). *Educational and labor market performance of GED recipients.* Washington, DC: U.S. Department of Education, National Education Library.

Education Trust. (2003, December). *Telling the whole truth (or not) about high school graduation.* Washington, DC: Author.

Haney, W., Madaus, G., Abrams, L., Wheelock, A., Miao, J., & Gruia, I. (2004). *The education pipeline in the United States, 1970–2004.* Chestnut Hill, MA: National Board on Educational Testing and Public Policy.

Kleiner, B., Porch, R., & Farris, E. (2002, September). *Public alternative schools and programs for students at risk of education failure, 2000–01.* Washington, DC: National Center for Education Statistics.

National Center for Education Statistics (NCES). (2001). *Survey on high school guidance counseling.* Washington, DC: Author.

National Center for Education Statistics (NCES). (2004). *The condition of education 2004.* Washington, DC: Author.

U.S. General Accounting Office. (2002). *School dropouts: Education could play a stronger role in identifying and disseminating promising prevention strategies* (GAO-02–240). Washington, DC: Author.

Projects for Further Exploration

1. Using variables from the first reading on principals, plan and carry out an interview with a principal and write up your findings about the role of the principal. How closely do your interview findings coincide with Lortie's discussion of the principal's role?

2. Using an academic database, find the latest data on a topic related to teachers' roles that was described in the reading by Richard Ingersoll and Elizabeth Merrill on the status of teaching. Restrict your search to refereed journals.

3. Using an academic database, pick one variable, such as extracurricular activities, that might influence students' achievements and performance in school. Look up that variable in an advanced search with both school and achievement and find studies that explain the influence on student achievement. Some examples of variables you might consider are substance abuse, bullying, school violence, student employment, gang membership, absenteeism, participation in sports or extracurricular activities, and cliques.

6

WHAT WE TEACH IN SCHOOLS

Knowledge for What and for Whom?

Knowledge is the base of all education. Without knowledge to impart to students there would be no justification for schools, even though education fills many other functions in a society. In this chapter, we examine the social construction of knowledge and how it comes to be taught in schools. What knowledge is appropriate and what knowledge is included in the curriculum are determined by a number of both input and output factors as illustrated in the open systems model. The study of knowledge provides another way of thinking about how social forces shape what is taught in our schools.

Researchers often consider the social context of educational institutions and people's educational trajectories. Rarely, however, do they consider what is meant by knowledge or how it comes to be taught. When we consider knowledge, we assume that there are truths and that our educational systems are teaching those truths. The readings in this chapter suggest otherwise. Indeed, these readings suggest that the social construction of knowledge is very much a part of the process of education in society and that knowledge is what is created in society, particularly by those in power.

Swidler and Arditi (1994) explore different approaches, both past and present, that theorists use to study knowledge. They describe new ways of examining knowledge and review different theoretical perspectives that attempt to understand knowledge. One way to view knowledge is to investigate it as a characteristic of persons—such as viewing someone as knowledgeable or smart—or, once incorporated into individuals, as an output in the open systems perspective, which is used to teach others or to maintain or improve the structures of daily life.

As noted in the reading by Durkheim in Chapter 1, schools are expected to output individuals with the capabilities, attitudes, and orientations necessary to function in society. Both perspectives see knowledge as a component of our everyday world—something that frames people's expectations for themselves and others. All of these approaches to knowledge affect schools; each perspective views knowledge as something that individuals use to interpret their worlds, something that shapes their orientations to others and their place in institutions in society such as schools and work.

Swidler and Arditi (1994) also explore theories relating to larger societal inputs that produce knowledge. They argue that the role of authority and power in knowledge production is part of a stratification process that maintains and reproduces inequality. In many ways, knowledge is sold to schools, and textbooks are the final product in the production of knowledge. However, the process by which knowledge is sold to schools is very complex, as described in the reading by Joan DelFattore in this chapter. She examines one pattern that shapes the curriculum students receive in schools—the production of knowledge as a highly political process because views of what is appropriate knowledge vary considerably. Ideally, we should all be able to agree on one common core of knowledge; however, in reality, that rarely happens. It is important to think about the way societies construct knowledge and for what purposes. The reading by Stuart Foster and Jason Nicholls examines how textbooks in four industrialized countries describe the United States' role in World War II, illustrating how national interests and images vary depending on which country is presenting the "knowledge." Yet, the institutional perspective argues that there is a great deal of similarity in the curriculum provided for children around the world. McEneaney and Meyer (2000) contend that global pressures shape a common curriculum across cultures to form the basis for a larger global social order.

Another approach to studying knowledge focuses on the authority to define it and examines the organizational practices that shape knowledge as well as the structure and relations of power (Swidler & Arditi, 1994). The focus on authority within this framework can be at the level of the social organization of knowledge or the power of the individuals within that organization. At the more macrolevel of social organization, the production of knowledge within this framework is embedded in how society is organized to define legitimate authority. In our society, we define knowledge within the context of formal institutions, as opposed to apprenticeships or applied learning. Therefore, college professors in civil engineering have more authority in defining how bridges are to be built than the contractors who put up the bridges.

If we switch to an analysis of the gatekeepers who work within the organizational structure to generate knowledge, it is not surprising to find that many of the major scientific advances in history were discovered years before they were acknowledged as "discoveries." Thomas S. Kuhn, in a classic book on *The Structure of Scientific Revolutions* (1970), developed the idea of shared paradigms within the scientific community. That is, prestigious scholars and scholars at prestigious universities, often the same people, have the authority to define what is known within their disciplines. They share paradigms of what is known and are generally unwilling to have their paradigms challenged. Kuhn argued that "normal science" seeks confirmation, not disconfirmation of its theories. Because scientists are more concerned about maintaining their forms of knowledge than with discovering new forms of knowledge, a significant number of disconfirming findings must occur before gatekeepers allow new forms of knowledge to be recognized.

Pierre Bourdieu takes a different approach, examining how power creates knowledge or, as noted by Swidler and Arditi (1994), how those in power can manipulate knowledge. In this explanation, those who hold power in society also shape knowledge. Individuals with *cultural capital* fit the expectations of those in power in schools and, thus, have more power themselves. This is because they both understand and have access to the social and cultural artifacts and knowledge that are most valued in society. This is illustrated in the different treatment some parents received from schools, as reported in the reading by Lareau and Horvat in Chapter 2. They found that parents with more cultural capital were able to manipulate systems and increase the level of education and type of knowledge their children received in schools.

In fact, individuals get to define knowledge and can create ideologies or belief systems that support and maintain their positions of power. Interestingly, those groups that DelFattore discusses in her reading are not always persons with the most highly valued cultural capital. Rather they are individuals who have such a strong sense of what is appropriate knowledge that they mobilize using collective power to make sure their version of knowledge would be taught in schools. The persons DelFattore calls textbook censors have carefully used the system to impose their views on what is presented in textbooks. She shows how these individuals amassed power in an attempt to control the content of textbooks. Indeed, many individuals take very seriously what they consider to be their responsibility to safeguard students from receiving the wrong kind of knowledge. Yet, powerful people may be involved in financing the organizations that support these individuals in their causes, which would support Bourdieu's argument that the rich and powerful manipulate knowledge (Swidler & Arditi, 1994). To learn more about these ideas, you can look up some of the organizations that are mentioned in DelFattore's reading, many of which continue to operate today to monitor textbooks in schools.

DelFattore and others argue that such undue influence on textbook publishing leads to the "dumbing of America" because publishers are pressured to present "knowledge" that is acceptable to many diverse audiences. In her book, she describes the centralized nature of textbook decision making. In two states, California and Texas, textbooks are purchased at the state level for all students. The decision of what textbook to purchase is highly profitable for the publisher whose textbook is selected. Although we might argue that such a process helps to make knowledge more consistent for all students, DelFattore finds that this process results in washed-out, "dumbed-down" texts that would be acceptable to everyone involved in the selection process in those two states. Decision making is consolidated as administrators in these two states either set down standards for textbook publishers or refuse to adopt textbooks unless they have the option of rewriting sections of the books of which they do not approve (DelFattore, 1992). As a result, the selection process in California and Texas shapes textbooks for the other 48 states. Knowledge, therefore, is oftentimes embedded in politics rather than education.

A growing body of literature on pedagogy, or the process of teaching, addresses these concerns at all levels of education. Initially the focus of this literature was on introducing knowledge of women and other cultures into classrooms. Advocates of multiculturalism and feminism focus not simply on inclusion of women and nonmajority groups into the curriculum but also on the ways in which these groups are presented. In fact, it was these advocates for modernizing the curriculum who generated the backlash of textbook censors.

The latest concerns in the social construction of knowledge include the effect of new technologies or the mode of delivery of knowledge. Technology has been growing at a pace far faster than ever before in history (Tyack & Cuban, 1995). Swidler and Arditi (1994) discuss the impact of moveable type and the printed book on the social construction of knowledge. There is less theoretical speculation about the changes that current technologies may have on the way we formulate knowledge. Cyberspace is a large frontier that enters the classroom both formally and informally as more and more students from preschool through college own and use computers. Wenglinsky (2005/2006) argued that the computer-to-student ratio went from 1 to 20 in 1990 to 1 in 5 at the end of that decade, creating a revolution in how knowledge was delivered to students in the classroom. He used national data to assess the impact of the use of technology on student achievement and found that students did better when computers were used for higher-order thinking such as to write papers and generate ideas rather than for drill and practice exercises (Wenglinsky, 2005/2006). Therefore, the technology itself is not as important as how it is used in the classroom. Whether technology transforms the way we think and use knowledge is still open to question. Tyack and Cuban (1995) feel that technology and computers may be the innovations that could change education in the future. However, many questions remain. We will just have to wait to see if knowledge becomes more anonymous when it comes to us through a computer and whether teaching and learning will respond to technology's speeding up the process of generating knowledge.

Technology is not the only potential controversy in terms of how knowledge is constructed in classrooms. The reading by Harold Wenglinsky in this chapter discusses the impact of testing for accountability on the way knowledge is taught (do we teach basic facts or critical thinking?) and the effects of teaching methods on learning. While the subjects taught may be the same, standardized tests can shape the way materials are presented to students and ultimately affect the depth of understanding of what we learn in school.

At the conclusion of this chapter, we hope you are more aware of the complexity in the process of constructing and presenting knowledge and the impact of those processes on how we define the reality of children. An important part of the social organization of knowledge is that knowledge is perceived to be legitimate and provides a shared understanding of a common world. Although this seems to be a simple and straightforward matter, the readings in this chapter point to many problems and difficulties in defining what knowledge is legitimate.

REFERENCES

DelFattore, J. (1992). *What Johnny shouldn't read: Textbook censorship in America*. New Haven, CT: Yale University Press.

Kuhn, T. S. (1970). *The structure of scientific revolutions* (2nd ed., enl.). Chicago: University of Chicago Press.

McEneaney, E. H., & Meyer, J. W. (2000). The content of the curriculum: An institutional perspective. In M. T. Hallinan (Ed.), *Handbook of the sociology of education* (pp. 189–211). New York: Kluwer Academic/Plenum.

Swidler, A., & Arditi, J. (1994). The new sociology of knowledge. *Annual Review of Sociology, 20,* 305–329.

Tyack, D., & Cuban, L. (1995). *Tinkering toward utopia: A century of public school reform*. Cambridge, MA: Harvard University Press.

Wenglinsky, H. (2005/2006). Technology and achievement: The bottom line. *Educational Leadership, 63*(4), 29–32.

ROMEO AND JULIET WERE JUST GOOD FRIENDS

Joan DelFattore

Joan DelFattore discusses textbook censorship in the following excerpt from her book *What Johnny Shouldn't Read: Textbook Censorship in America* (1992). What is not always apparent to us as consumers of textbooks is the political struggles over what will be portrayed as knowledge in these books. As noted in the introduction to this chapter and referred to in this reading, the selection of elementary and secondary school textbooks is big business and highly centralized. DelFattore's discussion of textbook censorship investigates six federal court cases. Her discussion of this process illustrates the social construction of knowledge in textbooks, including issues of decision making and power that go well beyond the simple publication of a book.

Questions to consider for this reading:

1. How does the process of textbook censorship that DelFattore describes fit the theoretical approaches described in the first reading of this book by Ballantine and Spade?
2. What choices do parents have in selecting textbooks for their children?
3. What does the selection of textbooks have to do with the social construction of knowledge?

A few years ago, I taught a summer course in literary classics for high school English teachers. When the class began talking about *Romeo and Juliet,* two of the teachers had trouble following what the others were saying. Those two teachers were using high school literature anthologies; the rest of the class had read paperback versions of *Romeo and Juliet.* We compared the high school anthologies with the paperbacks and found more than three hundred lines missing from the play in each anthology. Neither textbook mentioned that its presentation of Romeo and Juliet was definitely not Shakespeare's.

In the anthologies, lines containing sexual material—even such mild words as *bosom* and *maidenhood*—were missing. Removing most of the love story shortened Romeo and Juliet considerably, but the publishers did not stop there; they also took out material that had nothing to do with sex. Both anthologies, for example, omitted Romeo's lines,

> When the devout religion of mine eye
> Maintains such falsehood, then turn tears to fires;
> And these who, often drown'd, could never die,
> Transparent heretics, be burnt for liars!
> (1, 2)

I later found that this speech is routinely removed from high school anthologies because it associates religion with falsehood and violence, thus offending people who demand that religion must always be presented favorably.

The realization that publishers can simply drop three hundred lines from a Shakespeare play was startling, and I set out to discover what other material is being deleted from textbooks, why, and by whom. I found excellent books and articles discussing various aspects of textbook censorship from the 1950s through the early 1980s. . . .

Along with books and articles, I was also reading newspapers. Throughout the 1980s, one censorship lawsuit after another made front-page headlines. [The lawsuit of] *Mozert v. Hawkins County Public Schools* was filed [by a group of] Tennessee parents who maintained that an entire elementary school reading series, including "Cinderella," "Goldilocks," and *The Wizard of Oz*, violated their fundamentalist religious beliefs. More than half a century after the Scopes "monkey trial," *McLean v. Arkansas Board of Education* and *Aguillard v. Edwards* evaluated attempts to promote the teaching of creationism in public schools. In *Smith v. Board of School Commissioners of Mobile County*, a federal district court ordered the removal of forty-four history, social studies, and home economics textbooks from public school classrooms on the grounds that the books violate the First Amendment by promoting the religion of secular humanism. *Farrell v. Hall* and *Virgil v. Columbia County School Board* pitted parents and teachers against school boards that had banned literary classics, such as *Lysistrata*, *Macbeth*, and *The Autobiography of Benjamin Franklin*.

Behind each court case was a red-hot local controversy fanned by national organizations that eventually funded the lawsuits they had helped to bring about. The dynamics leading up to legal action, the educational agendas of national lobbying groups, and the rulings in the lawsuits all have powerful implications for the future of education in this country. . . .

All six of the federal court cases discussed in [*What Johnny Shouldn't Read*] involve attempts by religious fundamentalists to influence the content of public education. *The American College Dictionary* defines fundamentalism as

"a movement in American Protestantism which stresses the inerrancy of the Bible not only in matters of faith and morals but also as literal historical record and prophecy." Trying to decide how to use the word fundamentalist in a discussion of textbook censorship is, however, more problematic than the dictionary definition suggests. Over the past five years, I have given more than a hundred talks on this subject at public gatherings as well as at professional conferences. That experience has made it clear that the term fundamentalist does not, in practice, describe a monolithic belief system. Time after time, audience members have stood up and said something to this effect: "I am a fundamentalist, but I do not agree with what the textbook protesters are doing. I am embarrassed when extremists use the name fundamentalist because it makes people think we are all like that." Conversely, others proclaim that they do not consider themselves fundamentalists but do oppose evolution or nontraditional female roles.

A similar dilemma arises with regard to the word conservative. Textbook protesters often describe themselves as conservatives, but when George Will and James Kilpatrick write scathing columns condemning a textbook challenge, it is difficult to believe that that challenge represents mainstream conservative thought. Problems also arise when it comes to identifying the locations in which textbook controversies take place. While visiting southern states where court cases and controversial textbook adoption activities had occurred, I often met people who opposed the textbook activists and were irritated that the names of their states were associated with them. The same thing happened in California with regard to textbook protesters who call themselves liberals but represent viewpoints that mainstream liberals consider extreme and that many Californians do not endorse. . . .

The reason for focusing on recent federal textbook lawsuits that involve fundamentalist ideology is simple: there is none that does not. In some cases, parents and teachers who describe themselves as fundamentalists initiate lawsuits against a school district for using books that violate their religious beliefs; in others, a school board bans books because of fundamentalist lobbying, whereupon other parents and teachers file suit.

Apart from lawsuits, there are hundreds of incidents every year in which parents or teachers try to convince school boards to include or exclude certain materials. Such controversies are reflected on a wider scale in the textbook adoption process in large states. Challenges initiated by people who identify themselves as fundamentalists not only outnumber the protests of all other groups combined but also involve far more topics. The National Organization for Women (NOW), for example, advocates the depiction of women in nontraditional roles, and the National Association for the Advancement of Colored People (NAACP) lobbies for more favorable presentations of African Americans. One may agree or disagree with the stands taken by NOW and the NAACP, but neither group is likely to comment on such issues as the age of the earth, the development of language, or the probable domestication of dinosaurs. Fundamentalist textbook activists, on the other hand, lobby for geology and history books that conform to their interpretation of Genesis by teaching that the earth is about five thousand years old and that dinosaurs once coexisted with humans Flintstones-style. Their interpretation of the Bible also rejects biological evolution and, by extension, gradual development of any kind, such as the evolution of language over time.

The fundamentalist textbook activists are determined to color the education of all students with their entire world view. Their protests therefore target a wide range of subjects, including personal decision making, imagination, conservation, world unity, tolerance for cultural diversity, religious tolerance, negative portrayals of religion, unflattering depictions of the military or the police, empathy toward animals, antipollution laws, pacifism, socialism, gun control, nontraditional roles for women, minority issues, and evolution.

Because the word *fundamentalist* means different things to different people, it is impossible to tell exactly how many fundamentalists there are in the United States. Estimates generally range from 3 percent to 20 percent of the total population, with a few enthusiasts claiming that more than half of all American citizens are fundamentalists. But even if no more than three Americans out of a hundred are fundamentalists, and some of them do not support all of the textbook protesters' views, they are effective out of all proportion to their numbers because of their intense dedication to what they see as the salvation of American children from political, social, economic, and spiritual ruin. In most local elections, a very small proportion of qualified voters shows up at the polls, and few of them have paid close attention to the candidates for school board seats. Under those conditions, how many determined voters does it take to elect a sympathetic candidate to the school board? It is also important to remember the cardinal rule of any political dynamic: the number of people needed to make a difference is inversely proportionate to their level of expertise at working the system. Saying that a relatively small number of intense activists cannot have much effect on textbooks is like looking at the shape of a bumblebee and saying, "That thing can't possibly get off the ground." Maybe it can't, but it does. Far Right national organizations have become very adept at supporting grassroots legal challenges and at influencing the state-level textbook adoption process, thus affecting the content of textbooks purchased by school districts and private schools throughout the country.

Textbook protests are nothing new to the United States. As Kenneth Donelson explains in "Obscenity and the Chill Factor" (1979), activists of one kind or another have influenced the selection of classroom materials since colonial times. Nevertheless, according to the American Library Association, challenges to reading materials, including textbooks, have increased dramatically since 1980 . . . [and] is probably related to the overall upswing in ultraconservative activism surrounding the Reagan victory. Moreover, the changing content of textbooks themselves has motivated protesters to proclaim loudly—and accurately—that education is not what it was in the old days. From presenting traditional family, religious, and patriotic themes, textbooks have moved to endorsing multiculturalism, environmentalism, and globalism while discouraging militarism, stereotyping, and unbridled capitalism. The gradual change in textbooks began in the 1960s, but it was not until the 1970s and early 1980s that nationally organized campaigns were mounted against the new books.

In the Dick and Jane readers some of us remember from our childhoods, a family consisted of a married couple, two or three well-behaved children, and a dog and a cat. Father wore suits and went out to work; mother wore aprons and baked cupcakes. Little girls sat demurely watching little boys climb trees. Home meant a single-family house in a middle-class suburban neighborhood. Color the lawn green. Color the people white. Family life in the textbook world was idyllic: parents did not quarrel, children did not disobey, and babies did not throw up on the dog.

With the advent of civil rights and feminism, and with the rise of pollution, overpopulation, drug use, and the threat of nuclear war, the key word in textbooks became *relevance*. People who were not white or middle-class and did not live in traditional nuclear families began to demand representation in textbooks. Textbooks also began to talk about the importance of international understanding and independent thinking in today's complex and troubled world.

The new books are deeply disturbing to people who do not want education to describe a changing social order or promote independent decision making. At its extreme, fundamentalist textbook activism is based on the premise that the act of creative thinking is evil in itself, regardless of content, because it might lead to thoughts that are displeasing to God. Pictures of little girls engaging in activities traditionally associated with boys, such as playing with toy cars or petting worms, threaten American family life because girls might grow up craving male roles. Pollution is a humanist myth promoting international cooperation, which could lead to world unity and thus to the reign of the Antichrist, which will signal the end of the world. Conservation is an act of human pride and an offense against God. Humans have no business worrying about the extinction of whales; if God wants whales to exist, they will exist. If not, then preserving them is an act of rebellion against God.

Textbook activism often begins at the grassroots level, but successful drives to ban or change books require the support of powerful national groups. The Far Right organizations that are most vocal about textbook content are the American Family Association, based in Mississippi and headed by Donald Wildmon; Citizens for Excellence in Education (California, Robert L. Simonds); Concerned Women for America (Washington, D.C., Beverly LaHaye); the Eagle Forum (Illinois, Phyllis Schlafly); Focus on the Family (California, James Dobson); and the National Legal Foundation (Virginia, Pat Robertson). These well-funded, politically sophisticated national organizations supply legal representation for local textbook protesters and support efforts to lobby school boards and state legislatures.

It would be misleading to suggest that all textbook activism—conservative or liberal—is censorship, since decisions about what to teach and what not to teach are a necessary part of every educational system. Some material may be too advanced, academically or socially, for students of a particular age. Besides, human knowledge is cumulative: as scientific discoveries are made, as poems and novels are written, as historic events occur, information previously taught is pushed aside to make room for newer material. The school day has just so many minutes, and the school year has just so many days. For every fact that is put into a textbook, something else is left out. Given that some degree of selectivity is essential to education, advocacy groups will, naturally, try to influence textbook content in directions they consider appropriate. A certain amount of activism is part of the normal functioning of an educational system in a nontotalitarian state; the challenge is to determine the point at which attempts to influence textbook content shade into attempts to censor education.

The verb *to censor* operates according to its own peculiar grammatical rules. It is used almost exclusively in the second or third person: "You are censoring" or "they are censoring." It is almost never used in the first person: "We are censoring." A much more common self-perception is "We are participating in the commonsense selection of material suitable for children and adolescents." In order to make the point that even by the most rigorous definition censorship is occurring in American schools, neither conservatives nor liberals are called censors in [*What Johnny Shouldn't Read*] unless their goal is to obliterate from the store of human knowledge all trace of ideas with which they disagree. By that stringent definition, relatively little of today's textbook activism is actually censorship, but the incidents that do fall under that heading are very serious indeed. Only two major groups thereby qualify as textbook censors: fundamentalists and politically correct extremists.

The changing image of textbooks has aroused liberal advocates who are as dedicated to intensifying the new trend as their opponents are to reversing it. Some liberal protesters call for an increase in the representation of women, minorities, and non-Western cultures in textbooks without specifically targeting anything for removal. It would be naive to suggest that such inclusion does not involve exclusion; given the constraints of textbook space and classroom time, something that used to be covered has to be eliminated to make room for the new material. "Inclusionary" liberal textbook activists also tend to encourage the selection of facts that place previously underrepresented groups in the best possible light. By the definition of censorship given above, however, such lobbyists are not censors. Their efforts certainly contribute to the fragmentation of textbooks, but they do not tend toward the systematic elimination of any particular idea or fact.

Somewhere along the continuum of liberal textbook activism, however, "inclusionary" advocates give way to liberal censors. *Battle of the Books*, Lee Burress's (1989) study of literary censorship in the schools, describes organizations whose attempts to eliminate racism and sexism from textbooks have become so extreme that they are themselves censoring part of the truth. Since Burress's book was written before the term politically correct came into vogue, it is clear that the movement preceded its current label. Regardless of what

liberal censors are called, the exact point at which they take over from "inclusionary" liberal activists is difficult to identify because the difference is in degree, not in kind. The noncensor leans toward additional, and favorable, representation of minorities and women. The politically correct censor is determined to eliminate all depictions of women in traditional roles, or every statement that could possibly be construed as disparaging a particular racial, ethnic, or religious group. The accuracy of a statement and the context in which it occurs are dismissed as irrelevant. Politically correct extremists, like their fundamentalist counterparts, operate on the assumption that education has two functions: to describe what should be rather than what is, and to reverse the injustices of yesterday's society by shaping the attitudes of tomorrow's. Balanced portrayals of reality—some women are full-time homemakers, while others do have careers—get lost in the shuffle.

Taken to its extreme, the term *political correctness* denotes a form of intellectual terrorism in which people who express ideas that are offensive to any group other than white males of western European heritage may be punished, *regardless of the accuracy or relevance of what they say.* Racism, sexism, and other forms of prejudice are abhorrent and cannot be tolerated by any culture that claims to be civilized. Nevertheless, if we were *trying* to perpetuate mutual hostility and suspicion, we could not find a better way to do it than by suppressing honest questions because somebody might not like the answers, or by selecting and altering facts solely to shape opinion. Politically correct censors, like fundamentalist censors, also ignore the broader implications of their activities. By what logic can people defend their own freedom of expression while denying the rights of others to state facts and express beliefs? Once a culture decides that the truth can be suppressed because it is offensive to some, all that remains is a trial of strength to determine whose sensibilities take precedence. In this regard, the only difference between fundamentalist and politically correct extremists lies in the specific truths they wish to promote or suppress; the principles on which they operate are the same.

What Johnny Shouldn't Read discusses only elementary and secondary school textbooks, not because college texts are immune from outside pressures, but because the same forces do not apply to them. College attendance is voluntary and most college students are legally adults, which makes college instruction less vulnerable to lawsuits than public education is. Moreover, the selection procedure for college textbooks is different from the method of adopting books for public school classes. Students in multisection college courses may use a common textbook selected by a faculty committee, but most college texts are chosen by the individual professor teaching a particular course. College professors in their right mind (admittedly not 100 percent of us) would simply refuse to use a version of *Romeo and Juliet* with three hundred lines missing. The book would not make a profit because it would not sell, and that would be that. At the pre-college level, however, textbook selection is handled in a more centralized way. A small proportion of elementary and secondary school teachers may serve on textbook selection committees, but on the whole, teachers at the pre-college level are assigned textbooks that have been developed and selected by a highly politicized process. Regardless of anyone's opinion about what the teaching profession should look like, the truth is that individual college professors generally have more autonomy and more power than individual elementary or secondary school teachers. As a result, college textbooks tend to be produced to the specifications of professors, whereas elementary and secondary school books are more likely to reflect the wishes of school boards, administrators, and other nonclassroom personnel.

College professors' relative freedom to select and shape course material does not mean that textbook censorship does not affect college education. When students have spent twelve years reading books based more on market forces than on scholarly excellence, they may not come to college prepared to do college-level work. The increasing use of short sentences and simple words—often called "dumbing down"—in

elementary and secondary school textbooks has generated a great deal of print since the mid-1970s, but the watering down of ideas is at least equally dangerous. In response to this problem, the American Association of University Professors (AAUP) (1986) recently published a report prepared by its Commission on Academic Freedom and Pre-College Education. The report, entitled "Liberty and Learning in the Schools: Higher Education's Concerns," points out that students whose pre-college education was based primarily on "official" textbooks are not likely to understand how to deal with shades of meaning or with controversial topics.

Religious private schools that want to promote a fundamentalist viewpoint can purchase textbooks from small presses specializing in religiously oriented instructional materials. . . .

Secular private schools, and religious private schools that do not use specifically religious textbooks, have no choice but to buy their books from the same publishers that supply public school districts. Private schools have far fewer students and operate in a less centralized way than public schools, which means that they do not have the economic clout to tell publishers what to include in textbooks or to induce publishers to produce special editions just for them. As a result, parents who think that they are sidestepping public school politics by sending their children to private schools are only partially correct. The same is true of parents who live in school districts that do not advocate censorship. . . .

Overall, the textbook development process in America has less to do with educating a nation than with selling a product. In the world of publishing, the consumers who matter most are not the students and teachers who use the textbooks but the school boards that buy them. Some school boards choose to accept the recommendations of teachers almost automatically, but recent federal court decisions have shown that school boards can, if they wish, simply order teachers to use certain textbooks. Since school boards are either elected themselves or appointed by elected officials, they are vulnerable to lobbying by pressure groups. What school children throughout America learn is heavily influenced by states like Texas and California in which large populations are combined with strong state-level textbook activism. . . .

Not surprisingly, national organizations representing educators and librarians play an important role in responding to censorship issues. . . .

Professional associations are not the only groups active against censorship. In each of the legal cases discussed in [*What Johnny Shouldn't Read*], the anticensorship side was underwritten by the American Civil Liberties Union (ACLU) or People for the American Way (PAW). The ACLU, PAW, and the National Coalition Against Censorship also mount mailing campaigns informing the public of challenges to reading materials and soliciting contributions for the fight against censorship. Dedicated as these national groups are, however, the real power lies with the people—conservatives, moderates, and liberals alike—who oppose the extremes to which the textbook censors go.

REFERENCES

American Association of University Professors (AAUP). (1986). Liberty and learning in the schools: Higher education's concerns. *Academe, 72*(5), 22a–33a.

Burress, L. (1989). *Battle of the books: Literary censorship in the public schools.* Metuchen, NJ: Scarecrow Press.

DelFattore, J. (1992). *What Johnny shouldn't read: Textbook censorship in America.* New Haven, CT: Yale University Press.

Donelson, K. L. (1979). Obscenity and the chill factor: Court decisions about obscenity and their relationships to school censorship. In J. E. Davis (Ed.), *Dealing with censorship* (pp. 63–75). Urbana, IL: National Council of Teachers of English.

AMERICA IN WORLD WAR II

An Analysis of History Textbooks from England, Japan, Sweden, and the United States

Stuart Foster and Jason Nicholls

Stuart Foster and Jason Nicholls reviewed two textbooks from four different countries to examine how America's role in World War II was described. Their findings are both surprising and not so surprising, given what you have already read relating to the social construction of knowledge and the role of knowledge in socializing members of society. This reading makes clear the influence of culture in producing knowledge. Their findings also suggest hesitation as we consider whether what we read is "true," even when what we read is from textbooks in school.

Questions to consider for this reading:

1. How do the findings in this reading relate to the arguments made in the introduction to this chapter?

2. What possible impacts would these differences in portrayal of national histories have on a global society?

3. What advantages result from textbooks in different countries putting their own "interpretations" on world events?

History is one of the few curriculum subjects typically mandated in schools throughout the world. Furthermore, the use of history textbooks to support student learning is also almost universally accepted practice. Of course, we should not assume that what is in the history textbook is what is taught; furthermore, we should not assume it has been learned. Nevertheless, as many researchers consistently have indicated, textbooks not only enjoy routine usage in history classrooms, but all nations, to some degree, appear to be guilty of using history textbooks as a means to promote a particular view of the past, to enhance the collective memories of a nation, and, more often than not, to appease social and political agendas in the present. Textbooks never appear as neutral sources. As a consequence, analysis of how textbooks in different nations portray common historical events such as World War II enables the development of broader cross-cultural and international understandings of approaches to teaching about

From "America in World War II: An Analysis of History Textbooks from England, Japan, Sweden, and the United States," by S. Foster and J. Nicholls, 2005, *Journal of Curriculum and Supervision, 20*(3), pp. 214–221, 226–233. Copyright 2005 by the Association for Supervision and Curriculum Development, a worldwide community of educators advocating sound policies and sharing best practices to achieve the success of each learner. To learn more visit http://www.ascd.org. Reprinted with permission.

the past and implications for the present day. In addition, textbook studies not only offer a window into the perspectives of others, but also provide invaluable opportunities to reflect critically on practices in one's own educational system.

Specific attention to the role of the United States during the Second World War is particularly intriguing. At the beginning of the 21st century, the United States has emerged as the world's sole superpower, and its global influence and economic dominance remain unquestioned. Arguably, the unique position of the United States in the contemporary world can be traced back to victories in North Africa, in Europe, and in the Pacific during World War II. By war's end the imperial powers of France and Britain were exhausted, Japan and Germany were defeated, and, with more than 20 million dead and its resources and infrastructure seriously depleted, the U.S.S.R. confronted overwhelming problems. In economic and military terms, the United States emerged from World War II without rival.

Accordingly, the inclusion of the significant role of the United States in World War II is guaranteed in school history textbooks used across the world. This study, therefore, offers a detailed analysis of the role of the United States during World War II as portrayed in the history textbooks of four selected nations: England, Japan, Sweden, and the United States. Its purpose is to appreciate, compare, and contrast the particular historical content included in each nation's history textbooks and to illuminate national and international differences in the portrayal of the actions of the United States during the war.

METHODOLOGY AND STUDY

Textbooks as Sources

Textbooks in these four countries were selected for analysis because potentially they offered different perspectives on events. Apart from appreciating how U.S. textbooks portrayed America's role, a central line of inquiry sought to understand how textbooks in Sweden (a neutral

nation), England (a close ally), and Japan (a wartime enemy) portrayed the United States' role in World War II more than 50 years after the war. Two textbooks were selected from each country, each with a publication date of within the past eight years (see Appendix A). All textbooks were designed for use in upper-secondary school. These textbooks were among the most popular used in each of the respective countries.

Although the study analyzed the textbook treatment of America's role during World War II in four different nations, it cannot claim to compare similar data sources because textbooks are fashioned and employed for different reasons and different purposes in each nation. Furthermore, coverage issues and the place and status of history in different countries ensure that like-for-like comparisons are not possible. The situation is further complicated by awareness of the complex relationship between the production, selection, and deployment of history textbooks and the relative influence of government agencies, national curricula, standardized testing, and the practices of individual schools and teachers in the different countries. Despite these different contexts, however, examination of textbook content offers intriguing and illuminating points of contrast that help critics better understand how history is used and portrayed in different national settings. . . .

THE BEGINNING OF WORLD WAR II

U.S. Textbooks

Although U.S. history textbooks mention the outbreak of war in Europe in 1939, their extended treatment of the war begins with the Japanese attack on Pearl Harbor on December 7, 1941. Strikingly apparent in both U.S. textbooks is the dramatic impact that the Japanese assault on Pearl Harbor had on the American nation. These textbooks unequivocally hold that Japan's attack both "shocked and united" an American nation previously divided on isolationist and interventionist issues. According to the textbooks, after Pearl Harbor the nation pulled together under President

Roosevelt's leadership and united for the war effort. Thus, although both U.S. textbooks detail the rise of Benito Mussolini and Adolf Hitler in Europe and note that "democracy everywhere was threatened by the dictators" (US1, p. 500), they tacitly imply that the Second World War did not become America's war until December 1941.

The U.S. textbooks ascribe responsibility for the outbreak of hostilities in Europe and the Pacific to the aggressive policies of Germany, Italy, and Japan (the Axis nations) and their partnership "as three of the world's major fascist powers" (US1, p. 503). Reasons for Japan's recourse to war in the Pacific receive limited attention. Where mentioned, however, Japan's actions typically are explained in terms of that nation's being "ever hungry for more resources, materials, and markets" (US1, p. 503). As one textbook notes, "Japan was determined to do whatever was necessary to attain its militaristic aims" (US1, p. 504).

A salient feature of the U.S. textbooks is their common assessment of the state of global affairs on the eve of U.S. entry into World War II. As one textbook asserts, "The Allies were in deep trouble by the time the U.S. entered the war. They found themselves on the defensive on every front" (US1, p. 506). The textbooks note that by December 1941, the Allies' situation was desperate. One text provocatively asks, "Only an exhausted Britain stood between the Nazis and their dream of dominating the European continent. The U.S. finally cast its lot with the British—but was it already too late?" (US1, p. 499).

This type of dramatic and emotive language is not uncommon in the U.S. textbooks. By portraying the United States as a nation battling against overwhelming odds, the textbooks emphasize the heroic struggles and sacrifices of the American people to dramatic effect. Accordingly, in describing the state of affairs following the declaration of war on the United States, *America: Pathways to the Present* (US1) proudly comments, "The American people were now committed to this war. Their contributions would make the difference between victory and defeat for the Allies" (US1, p. 505).

In a similar vein, U.S. textbooks are eager to relate to U.S. students that the war was fought to ensure a free and democratic postwar world as encapsulated in Roosevelt's "Four Freedoms" speech and in the Atlantic Charter. This quest for a more ideal world is neatly characterized by the following textbook extract:

> As soldiers huddled in filthy foxholes overseas, they dreamed of home and a cherished way of life. War correspondent John Hersey once asked a young marine on the Pacific front what he was fighting for. After reflecting for a moment, the soldier just sighed. "What I'd give for a piece of blueberry pie." (US1, p. 506)

The U.S. textbooks manifest the overriding impression that, despite the obstacles involved, the Axis powers represented an evil threat to the world that the United States had a duty and a responsibility to eradicate.

Japanese Textbooks

In contrast to U.S. textbooks, Japanese history textbooks portray Pearl Harbor as one event in a chain of historical occurrences that begins with the 1931 "Manchurian incident." Of note, one text, published by Jikkyo Shuppan, entitles the section dealing with events in the 1930s and 1940s "The Fifteen Years War and Japan," thereby embedding the Second World War into the flow of Japanese history and events in the Pacific region (J2, p. 315). As a result, by concentrating attention to affairs in the Pacific from 1930 to 1941, Japanese textbooks provide a rich context to the events that led to the bombing of Pearl Harbor in December 1941. Significantly, whereas the textbook published by Yamakawa Shuppan devotes 22 lines of text to the war itself, it provides 8 pages of coverage on the Japanese build-up to war (J1).

Central to the perspective offered by the Japanese textbooks is a sharp presentation of reasons for Japan's suspicion of British, Dutch, and, most important, U.S. intentions during the prewar years. Crucially, the textbooks inform students that

Japan's leaders were deeply troubled by the menacing shadow of the anti-Japanese "ABCD encirclement" (Americans—A, British—B, Chinese—C, and the Dutch—D). Contrary to the presentation of events in U.S. textbooks, Japanese textbooks note that the unreasonable U.S. demands on Japan, including "the withdrawal of Japanese forces from China . . . Manchuria, and French Indo-China, the rejection of the Tripartite Pact, and the dissolution of the Wang government," proved that "the U.S., too, had resolved on war against Japan," which, according to one textbook, the "U.S. had come to see as inevitable" (J1, p. 330).

The outbreak of hostilities in 1941, therefore, is portrayed in Japanese textbooks as the culmination of a chain of events for which several nations on both sides (Axis and Allies) shared responsibility. Unlike typical presentations in U.S. and English textbooks, Japanese textbooks portray the steady drift to war with the United States as understandable and, perhaps, inevitable. Of further significance, even Japan's failure to warn the United States of the attack on Pearl Harbor—often depicted as a "surprise attack" in Western texts—is portrayed in one Japanese textbook as an error perpetrated by senior Japanese naval officials who had been instructed to issue an ultimatum to the United States before the attack, but had failed to translate the coded message in a timely manner.

Overall, therefore, Japanese textbooks' portrayal of the war in the Pacific differs significantly from that of the U.S. textbooks. In American textbooks, the United States is portrayed as the victim of an aggressive and shocking surprise attack; the Japanese textbooks assert that U.S. attitudes and actions before Pearl Harbor in large part were responsible for the recourse to war.

English Textbooks

Although they recognize the global scale of World War II, English textbooks typically portray the war from a European perspective. In particular, in depicting the situation once war breaks out in Europe in September 1939, English textbooks devote significant attention to the period from June 1940 to December 1941, when Britain and its Commonwealth forces stood alone against the Nazi juggernaut. However, under the section heading "The USA's Concerns Grow," one book points out Americans' growing fear that their country would have to fight in another European war (E1, p. 276). Also portrayed is Roosevelt's recognition of this reality and the shift of opinion in the United States during 1941 toward the prospect of intervention.

English textbooks acknowledge the close relationship between Britain's Prime Minister Churchill and President Roosevelt. One quotes Churchill's telegram to FDR expressing his joy at his re-election in 1940: "I prayed for your success and I am truly thankful for it" (E1, p. 276). The book also remarks on the "vital supplies" that the United States and Canada gave to Britain before U.S. entry into the war, and one textbook claims that without the support of Canada and the United States and the Atlantic "lifeline, Britain could not have carried out the war" (E1, p. 284). Still, significantly, although U.S. entry is portrayed as a major event, it is never considered within the context of British gratitude or relief for the support of its most powerful ally. Indeed, rather than acknowledging the significance of U.S. support of the British war efforts, this involvement is simply portrayed as just another, but important, episode during the course of the war. Certainly the English textbooks do not specifically acknowledge the impact of U.S. entry into the war, as do U.S. textbooks.

In the British textbooks we analyzed, the outbreak of the war occupies an intriguing middle ground between the accounts in U.S. and Japanese textbooks. On the one hand, one of the English textbooks points out that Japanese military actions were part of that nation's aggressive desire "for dominance of the Pacific" (E1, p. 275). On the other hand, some events are interpreted from the Japanese perspective. Textbooks point out, for example, how the United States and the Western European powers had made life difficult for the Japanese by their repeated impositions of economic sanctions and tariffs during the prewar period. In this respect, although these books hold that the Japanese attack on Pearl Harbor was an act of aggression, they recognize Japanese actions as having been logical given the situation in which Japan found itself.

Swedish Textbooks

To an even greater extent than the English books, Swedish texts focus on the war from a European perspective. As such, the role of the Soviets and the British, on the whole, are accorded both more space and attention than is the role of the United States in the war. The Swedish textbooks follow the war chronologically. In this treatment, these books deal in some detail with German Chancellor Hitler's expansion through Europe, the situation in Scandinavia, and the German invasion of the Soviet Union. Only later do these texts offer increased attention to the U.S. role at the start of the war in Europe. Indeed, apart from reference to Roosevelt's lend-lease program and the plight of U.S. cargo vessels crossing the Atlantic, they provide very little mention of the United States.

The two Swedish books give substantial attention to Chancellor Hitler's 1941 invasion of the Soviet Union in Operation Barbarossa and to the rapid advance of German forces across Belarus and the Ukraine. Like the English texts, these books give little attention to the war in the Pacific. For example, one Swedish textbook includes a section on the entrance of the United States under the heading "The War Becomes a World War," although it fails to mention the important Battle of Midway anywhere in the textual narrative. Both Swedish textbooks place the war in the Pacific within the context of Japan's expansionist policies in East Asia that began in the 1930s. In this way, the attack on Pearl Harbor tends to be portrayed as another part of the unfolding story of Japanese imperialism in the region and as a result of the growing tensions between the United States and Japan (S1, p. 308). In the same textbook, the close and developing relationship between Roosevelt and Churchill is described along with the observation that, after Pearl Harbor, Britain now had "a powerful ally" (S1, p. 308). On the whole, although the importance of having the United States as a powerful ally is recognized, the Swedish textbooks accord greater coverage to the British and Soviet roles at the start of the war than to the actions of the United States. . . .

THE END OF THE WAR

U.S. Textbooks

Both U.S. textbooks include sections entitled "Victory in Europe." However, their principal focus is on the war in the Pacific and in Western Europe, and they refer to the role of the Soviets in the last stages of the war only briefly (US2, p. 760). Thus the end of the war in Europe is presented in terms of the changing fortunes of the Western Allies in the battle for the Atlantic, the air raids on German cities, the Normandy landings, and the push through the Benelux countries. No mention is made of Germany's two-year retreat from Stalingrad to Berlin due to the efforts of the Soviet Red Army. However, the collaborative nature of the final offensive by the Allies on Germany is recognized to a minor degree in *The American Nation,* including the Soviet occupation of Berlin (US2, p. 762). *Pathways to the Present* (US1), on the other hand, presents a quite different version. It acknowledges the Soviet advance into Germany but makes no subsequent mention of the Soviets' impact on the *Wehrmacht,* their occupation of Berlin, or that British and Canadian forces were significantly involved in the last push of the Allies into Germany from the west.

The final stages of the war in the Pacific receive strong coverage in both of the U.S. textbooks. However, even though the "Allies" are described as taking "the offensive" in the Pacific after the Battle of Midway, the actions of U.S. forces are most prominently described. For example, in *Pathways to the Present* (US1), although the battle for Guadalcanal is described as an Allied offensive, only the landing of U.S. troops is detailed. Furthermore, it is U.S. marines, and not combined Allied forces, who are depicted as winning the battle for that island (US1, pp. 509–510). A similar situation prevails in *The American Nation* (US2), in which the wrapping up of the Pacific war is described as an American affair.

The American use of the atomic bomb is described as a "tough decision" for President Truman against a Japan that "still had a well-trained army and strong inner defenses" (US2, pp. 764–765). Ultimately, *The American Nation* attributes Japan's surrender to the use of the atomic bombs and, to a lesser extent, the Soviet invasion of Manchuria, which is only briefly mentioned. However, the end of the chapter includes a commentary section on "Using the Atomic Bomb" in which different perspectives are offered. In particular, the use of the bomb "to strengthen the hand of the United States in its postwar dealings with the Soviet Union" is suggested (US2, p. 769). One book includes a six-page section about the decision to drop the atomic bomb and its effects. The alternatives available to Truman are described, as well as the ease with which he claimed to have arrived at the final decision to use this weapon. *Pathways to the Present* (US1) expresses some sympathy for the Japanese people; for example:

> The Japanese were dazed by the blasts. They were already considering surrender when the Soviet Union entered the war on the Chinese front two days after Hiroshima. Following the Nagasaki explosion, they sought to end the conflict any way they could. (US1, p. 521)

Both U.S. textbooks assert that the atomic bombs forced a quick Japanese surrender and the end of the war. Both draw close attention not only to the direct ethical and humanitarian controversy surrounding the use of the bombs, but also to the possibility that the United States dropped the bombs in order to strengthen its role in the postwar world.

Japanese Textbooks

The Japanese textbooks tend to focus almost completely on the Pacific theater of the war, giving only minor attention to wartime actions in Europe and North Africa. Thus key events toward the end of the war such as D-Day, the liberation of Paris, the Soviet advance into Berlin, and the liberation of Nazi concentration camps are markedly absent. In the Pacific, the tendency is to portray the United States defeating Japan single-handedly, with no reference to other Allied nations.

Further, the Japanese books note the decrease in the import of raw materials from Southeast Asia to Japan during the war and the ensuing fall in production levels, which are entirely attributed to the increased control of the sea and the air by U.S. naval and air forces. In one book, Japanese forces are described as literally overwhelmed by the United States' material superiority between the Battle of Midway and the end of the war (J2). With the fall of the islands of Saipan and later the Philippines, the launch of the U.S. bombing offensive on Japanese cities is described in both textbooks. The kamikaze suicide attacks are mentioned, however, in only one textbook (J2) as evidence of Japan's desperate military situation late in the war. With the fall of the island of Okinawa to U.S. forces in the spring of 1945, "Japan's defeat" is described as "imminent" (J1, p. 233).

By April 1945, Japan is thus portrayed as a nation on the verge of collapse and in search of some kind of peace. However, because of the Soviet decision not to mediate as well as the fact that Japan did not respond to the Potsdam Declaration, Japan's fate is sealed with the U.S. decision to drop atomic bombs on Hiroshima and Nagasaki. Of interest, Japan's response to the Potsdam Declaration is portrayed differently in the two Japanese textbooks. One suggests that Japan's failure to reply to the Potsdam Declaration prompted the United States to drop the atom bomb (J2, p. 409), whereas the other book (J1) portrays Japan as much more a victim of U.S. aggression. This latter book observes, "The Japanese government was still anguishing over its response [to the Potsdam

Declaration] when the U.S. dropped an atomic bomb on Hiroshima on August 6 and another on Nagasaki on August 9" (J1, p. 237). Accordingly, this book portrays the United States as the aggressor, with no suggestion that the bombs were necessary to end the war quickly and to avoid a bloody assault on the Japanese homeland.

Overall, Japanese textbooks provide only cursory detail of the end of the Second World War. They focus attention on the war in the Pacific, where the defeat of the Japanese army is attributed solely to the material superiority of the United States.

English Textbooks

On the whole, the English textbooks offer a diverse picture of the end of World War II. Ben Walsh's *Modern World History* (E1, p. 279) recognizes the war as "a truly world war with fighting on four continents." As such, although the importance of the U.S. role is acknowledged, similar roles of other Allies across all the military arenas are noted. Victory at the end of World War II is portrayed very much as a collaborative Allied effort against a broken and defeated Axis, with the European war receiving primary focus.

As background to the events leading to Truman's decision to drop the atomic bombs on Hiroshima and Nagasaki, both textbooks also note the significance of increasing U.S. military casualties. Lancaster and Peaple's *The Modern World,* for example, remarks that on Okinawa "over 7,000 American soldiers were killed," and this was "without doubt one reason why the atom bomb was dropped" (E2, p. 155). However, in contrast to the U.S. textbooks, which depict the invasion of Okinawa as only a U.S. affair, English students read that "in March 1945, British and U.S. forces took the island of Okinawa" (E1, p. 296). Walsh's *Modern World History* additionally points out that "some 120,000 Africans also fought for the Allies in the Burma campaign" and that "India provided over 2.5 million men and women for the armed forces and spent a staggering 80% of its wealth in 1943–44 on the war effort" (E1, p. 295).

The justification for the United States' dropping of the atomic bomb is portrayed as problematic in the English textbooks. Both textbooks offer a range of views and a variety of sources to portray conflicting viewpoints about Truman's decision. Students are then invited to use the information to reach a reasoned conclusion about this event. Despite this apparently evenhanded approach, however, both textbooks suggest that the dropping of the bombs, although bringing a speedy end to the war, may not have been necessary to win the war.

Swedish Textbooks

Having portrayed the events at Stalingrad and, to a lesser extent, North Africa as the important turning points of the war, Swedish textbooks describe the final offensive in Europe as a joint Allied affair. In *Living History,* under the heading "The Year 1944: The Invasion of Normandy," the U.S. role is portrayed as part of an essentially combined effort by the Western Allies in the final defeat of Germany (S1, pp. 312–313). The role of Stalin and the Soviet Red Army offensive in the east is given equal if not greater attention than are the actions of the Western Allies. Thus the Normandy landings are placed in the context of Stalin's insistence that the United States and Britain open a second front in the west. Moreover, although the magnitude of D-Day is fully recognized as "the largest invasion of its type in military history," students read that the "Red Army increased in strength and condition" and that "1944 saw 10 million men in an attack towards the west" (S1, pp. 312–313). Significantly, the only visual image to accompany the narrative account that depicts the fall of Berlin is the famous photograph of the Red Army soldier waving the Soviet flag from the roof of the German parliament buildings in May 1945 (S1, p. 314). Thus Swedish books portray the end of the war in Europe as an essentially collaborative effort between all the Allies, although they accord special attention to the importance of the Soviet role.

Both books describe the final stages of the war in the Pacific. Interestingly, *Living History* (S1) portrays the United States as the sole Allied power fighting against the Japanese in the Pacific and makes no mention of the actions of other nations. In contrast, *History: Life and Change* (S2) notes the importance of British contributions. Japan is presented as a "lesser threat" than Germany, soon on the defensive against a United States that quickly rearmed itself after Pearl Harbor. In addition, although the brutality of the island-hopping campaign and, in particular, the ferocity of Japanese resistance is described, many key battles and events are not acknowledged. The use of atomic weapons, for example, is described without mentioning the brutal battles for Iwo Jima and Okinawa or the kamikaze suicide attacks by Japanese pilots, all decisive events that may have influenced President Truman's decision. However, in the narrative, reasons given for using the "new weapon," the textbook alleges, were "to demonstrate the U.S.A.'s strength and to spare the lives of American soldiers" as well as to force an unconditional Japanese surrender and to bring the war to a speedy close (S1, p. 314).

Overall, the Swedish textbooks cover in some detail Allied military victories in the Western European, Eastern European, and Pacific theaters of war. The war effort also is seen as a collaborative affair in which the actions of the British, Soviet, and U.S. forces appear salient. Most apparent, however, is that Soviet successes on the eastern front are viewed as more significant than are the military successes of the British and Americans in the west. Furthermore, the Pacific War is portrayed as secondary to the more vital and momentous military campaigns fought in Europe.

DISCUSSION AND CONCLUSION

Around the globe, history textbooks are employed to serve different purposes. Typically they perform multiple functions simultaneously. For example, they are used to "cover" mandated historical topics, to conform to curriculum needs, and to address the demands of standardized tests. As often, they are used as a support mechanism and as the primary source of information for teachers, students, and parents. Occasionally they are used critically as an example of one representation among many of a particular historical perspective. However, no matter what they are used for, they inescapably represent a powerful means to render a particular version of a nation's past in the history classroom. Textbooks consciously attempt to shape and inform students' understanding of their national history and the relationship between their country and other nations.

Analysis of the central story lines and messages about World War II in textbooks regularly used by students in Japan, Sweden, England, and the United States reveals that in many respects, these textbooks examine the Second World War from each nation's own cultural, historic, and geopolitical perspective. Accordingly, U.S. textbooks emphasize the significant role that the United States played in crushing the Axis forces in Europe and the Pacific. Unequivocally the U.S. textbooks portray American entry into the war as decisive. They emphasize U.S. military commanders, battles in which the United States was a chief protagonist, and the ideals for which U.S. soldiers allegedly fought. They mention the involvement of other nations, but the contributions of those nations appear altogether secondary to those of the United States.

In contrast, although acknowledging the significant role of the United States during World War II, English textbooks do not portray the U.S. contributions as more significant than those of the British Empire or the U.S.S.R. Indeed, concentrated focus is given to the British war effort before U.S. entry and to the defeat of Hitler's German armies by the Soviet Red Army on the eastern front. Moreover, after the U.S. entry into the war, according to the implicit message presented by English textbooks, the Allied effort was a joint venture involving equal partners, and not one dominated by the United States.

Japanese textbooks offer a very different perspective on events. In the Japanese textbooks, the war in Europe is a secondary issue and receives substantially limited attention. Instead, these books' coverage of the war centers on events in the Pacific. Here, Japanese textbooks focus much detail on the context leading to the Japanese attack on Pearl Harbor. In contrast to the portrayal in U.S. textbooks, the United States does not appear to be an innocent victim of a "surprise attack." Rather, Japanese textbooks carefully explain how U.S.-Japanese antagonism before events in December 1941 all but rendered war inevitable. The defeat of the Japanese armies principally is attributed to actions of the United States, but details are limited and lack context. Significantly, according to Japanese textbooks, the eventual military success of U.S. military forces resulted from America's overwhelming material, not military, superiority.

Finally, the Swedish textbooks focus on the war in Europe and North Africa. As a result, the United States is portrayed as playing a supportive rather than a leading role in events. The Swedish textbooks place much emphasis on the war before U.S. entry, particularly on military action on the eastern front. Moreover, the German defeats at Stalingrad and, to a lesser extent, El-Alamein, are portrayed as not only the beginning of the end for Germany but also the cause of irreparable cracks in the Axis states. The United States is depicted as the unquestionable leader in the Pacific war against Japan. However, this arena of the war is portrayed as a secondary affair in the Swedish textbooks.

This study of history textbooks from four nations abundantly illustrates that historical information and interpretation conveyed to students in different parts of the world vary considerably. Moreover, it illuminates how textbook representations appear to be influenced by particular nationalistic bias, differing cultural and geopolitical perspectives, and the sociopolitical agendas of the nation in which the books are used in schools. Many individuals and organizations hold that the purpose of textbook studies is to construct more tolerant and more accurate versions of our shared past. For example, the Council of Europe, UNESCO, and the Georg Eckert Institute in Braunschweig, Germany,

value textbook research as a means to promote increased international understandings. Such objectives are important and worthwhile. However, the function of this study was not to call for more balanced and consensual history, but rather to explore how and why different nations treat historical events in different ways.

The nature of historical study is such that events inevitably will be interpreted differently in different cultures. The overall aim, therefore, is to recognize, understand, and appreciate national differences; to examine how and why they occur; and to offer the prospect that the information presented will lead educators and officials to critically examine existing practice and the nature and function of history in their society. In this respect, the study offers insights into issues associated with the teaching and learning of history in national settings.

Appendix A: Textbooks Used in the Study

US1—A. Cayton, E. I. Perry, and A. Winkler. (1998). *America: Pathways to the Present.* Upper Saddle River, NJ: Prentice Hall.

US2—P. Boyer. (1995). *The American Nation.* Austin, TX: Holt, Rinehart and Winston.

E1—B. Walsh. (2001). *GCSE Modern World History.* London: John Murray Publishers.

E2—T. Lancaster and D. Peaple. (1996). *GCSE History: The Modern World.* Ormskirk, Lancashire: Causeway Press.

S1—L. Hildingson and K. Hildingson. (1997). *Levande Historia 7–9 (Living History 7–9).* Orebro, Sweden: Natur och Kultur.

S2—K. Sjoebeck and B. Melen. (1995). *Historia: Liv i Foeraendring (History: Life in Transition).* Malmo, Sweden: Interskol.

J1—I. Susumu, K. Kazuo, K. Kota, S. Haruo, et al. (1994). *Shosetsu Nihon shi (Comprehensive Japanese History B).* Tokyo: Yama kawa Shuppan.

J2—N. Kojiro, et al. (1994). *Nihon shi (Japanese History B).* Tokyo: Jikkyo Shuppan.

FACTS OR CRITICAL THINKING SKILLS?

What the NAEP Results Say

Harold Wenglinsky

This reading by Harold Wenglinsky examines the role of teaching practices on what knowledge is presented. The debate between teaching basic skills and teaching critical thinking is not new, but it has become more heated with the No Child Left Behind (NCLB) and Race to the Top legislations' emphasis on accountability. Although the National Assessment of Educational Progress (NAEP) has been around since 1969, the new federal government emphasis on accountability uses other methods of evaluation that emphasize basic skills rather than critical thinking.

Questions to consider for this reading:

1. What national and local factors influence how knowledge is presented in schools?

2. What difference does it make if students learn basic skills rather than critical thinking?

3. Will NCLB's focus on changing testing to assess basic skills influence the type of knowledge presented in schools or only the presentation of the knowledge?

In the past 30 years, policymakers and educators have debated whether schooling should emphasize facts or critical thinking skills. Proponents of the first view argue that students need to know when the Civil War happened before they can accurately interpret its causes. Proponents of the second view counter that students will soon forget the exact dates of the Battle of Chancellorsville, but they will probably remember the insights that they gain from studying the battle's causes, leadership, military reasoning, and human costs.

State policymakers have responded to the shifting debate. Thus, the California legislature has gone back and forth between emphasizing phonics and whole language approaches in its reading curriculum. Maryland emphasizes critical thinking skills in its state standards and tests; just across the Potomac River, Virginia emphasizes basic facts.

For the most part, however, this debate has not been informed by actual empirical data. Fortunately, the National Assessment of Educational Progress (NAEP) offers relevant information. Administered every year or two since 1969 in various subjects—including mathematics, science, reading, and civics—the NAEP assessments are taken by representative samples of 4th, 8th, and

From "Facts or Critical Skills: What NAEP Results Say" by H. Wenglinsky, 2004, *Educational Leadership, 61*(1), pp. 32–35. Copyright 2004 by the Association for Supervision and Curriculum Development, a worldwide community of educators advocating sound policies and sharing best practices to achieve the success of each learner. To learn more visit http://www.ascd.org. Reprinted with permission.

12th graders throughout the United States (U.S. Department of Education, 2000). Because each student takes only a small subset of the examination, the full examination can cover a substantial breadth and depth of material. Test items include both multiple-choice responses and more complex written responses so that they assess both basic skills and critical thinking skills. In addition to the test, students and their teachers and school administrators also fill out questionnaires that furnish information about student and teacher backgrounds and the instructional practices used in the classroom.

By measuring the relationships between specific instructional practices and student performance, we can use NAEP data to compare the effectiveness of teaching for meaning with that of teaching basic skills. Using advanced statistical techniques, we can even take into account the potential influence of student achievement, thus isolating the effects of instruction oriented to teaching for meaning.

When we examine various analyses, some published and some unpublished (Wenglinsky, 2000, 2002, 2003), a clear pattern emerges from the data: Across subjects, teaching for meaning is associated with higher NAEP test scores. Although students must learn basic skills and facts at some point, these results suggest that instruction emphasizing advanced reasoning skills promotes high student performance.

MATH AND SCIENCE: EARLY TEACHING FOR MEANING

In mathematics, some educators advocate teaching students basic skills, such as the times tables, and reinforcing those skills through drill and practice. Others advocate teaching students mathematical reasoning, such as the principles behind algorithms for multiplication and division, and emphasizing such complex topics as data analysis and probability early in the curriculum. The NAEP data supports the latter approach. Among U.S. 4th and 8th graders, teaching that emphasizes higher-order

thinking skills, project-based learning, opportunities to solve problems that have multiple solutions, such hands-on techniques as using manipulatives were all associated with higher performance on the mathematics NAEP. Such methods reflect the idea that learning mathematics is an iterative process, rather than a linear process in which students progress from simple facts to more complicated ones (McLauglin & Talbert, 1993).

The Trends in International Mathematics and Science Study (TIMSS) provides further evidence. Stigler and Hiebert (1999), analyzing videotapes of classes in the United States, Germany, and Japan, found that the Japanese 8th grade teachers were more likely to emphasize critical thinking by having students fashion their own solutions to problems and by introducing advanced material (for example, algebra) at a relatively early stage. And overall, Japanese students outperformed their U.S. and German counterparts in mathematics.

In science, the curricular debate has been between those who advocate teaching students the facts of science and those who emphasize hands-on activities that allow students to explore theory. Basic skills advocates do not necessarily object to the use of hands-on activities, but they assign them a different role, in which the teacher defines laboratory procedures and students carry them out to demonstrate, for example, what happens when heat is placed under a balloon.

The NAEP data again suggest the benefits of teaching for meaning. Students tended to score higher on the 4th grade and 8th grade NAEP science tests when they had experienced science instruction centered on projects in which they took a high degree of initiative. Traditional activities, such as completing worksheets and reading primarily from textbooks, seemed to have no positive effect.

READING AND CIVICS: A MORE LINEAR PICTURE

In contrast to the NAEP results for math and science, the results in the humanities demonstrate the benefits of a more linear approach to teaching.

In reading, one debate has centered on how students should learn to identify words and develop fluency, and a second debate has centered on how students should develop reading comprehension. The first debate has played itself out in the reading wars between phonics and whole language advocates. The phonics approach emphasizes teaching students to sound out words, whereas whole language emphasizes identifying unfamiliar words from their context. Because the NAEP does not test students until grade 4, its results shed little light on this first debate. Reports by the National Reading Panel (2000) and the National Research Council (Snow, Burns, & Griffin, 1998) have supposedly resolved the issue in favor of a balanced approach that focuses on phonics but leaves some room for a contextual approaches (although some reading researchers question the reports' findings).

The second debate—regarding reading comprehension—has not been fully engaged. Some scholars have simply staked out positions on reading comprehension analogous to their position on word identification and fluency. Yet here, NAEP scores do offer some guidance—and they strongly suggest that when it comes to comprehension, basic skills approaches are inappropriate.

In both 4th and 8th grades, NAEP scores in comprehension favor teaching for meaning. Students tended to perform better on NAEP comprehension questions when they had experienced instruction in metacognitive skills (drawing meaning from text by asking questions, summarizing the work, identifying key themes, and thinking critically about the author's purpose and whether that purpose was achieved). In addition, students' comprehension was higher when they had been exposed to "real" texts—books and stories rather than short passages in basal readers. Finally, students improved their comprehension skills by reading literature and then writing about that literature, which gave them the opportunity to apply their metacognitive skills.

Thus, it appears that learning to read follows a linear trajectory. Previous studies suggest that students first need to learn the basic skills from phonics to sound out words and develop fluency.

Once they have done that, however, the NAEP scores indicate that students should move on to develop reasoning skills and critical thinking skills in order to comprehend texts.

In civics, the story is also linear. The debate in civics centers on whether students should learn facts about the government through textbooks and homework or through more hands-on civics activities, such as community service. The NAEP data indicate that the 4th graders, on the other hand, benefit both from reading textbooks and such hands-on activities as service learning. Thus, in the case of civics, students will likely do best with a developmental model in which they begin by learning the content and then go on to make sense of it through civic practice.

BASIC SKILLS AND TEACHING FOR MEANING IN PARTNERSHIP

These analyses of NAEP results suggest that although basic skills have their place in pedagogy, critical thinking skills are essential. In mathematics and science at both the 4th and 8th grade levels, practices that emphasize critical thinking skills are associated with higher student achievement, whereas practices that emphasize basic skills are not. Apparently, students more effectively learn simple content, such as the times tables, if they understand the conceptual framework that lies behind that content. Educators do not need to choose between basic and advanced skills in math and science, but we should introduce advanced skills early to motivate students to learn the basic algorithms—which, let's face it, are not very interesting in and of themselves.

In the humanities, on the other hand, the data suggest the value of a more linear process. Students should not begin their school lives as readers developing their own rules for spelling or creating their own vernacular language. But once they know how to take language from the page, students need opportunities to construct sense out of text by interpreting it, writing about it, and reflecting on what they have written. Similarly, civics students need to know what the branches of government do, what freedoms the Bill of Rights protects, and how to influence their elected officials. Once students have learned these facts, however, they need to put their knowledge into practice by performing community service activities, going on field trips, and communicating with elected officials on matters important to them. . . .

IMPLICATIONS FOR POLICYMAKERS AND EDUCATORS

These empirical findings about the importance of teaching for meaning suggest certain actions that public officials and education administrators need to take.

At the school level, principals need to encourage their teachers to spend more time teaching for meaning across subject areas—especially in math and science in the early grades. In the humanities, students may need to learn basic skills in reading and civics in elementary school. But by the time students reach middle school, teaching for meaning becomes crucial.

Unfortunately, school principals and superintendents may have difficulty moving in this direction because federal policy now intervenes in state and local curriculum choices in favor of basic skills and against teaching for meaning. The No Child Left Behind Act (NCLB) constitutes an unprecedented level of federal involvement in education.

NCLB's goals are highly laudable. Despite the complaints of many educators, creating a national infrastructure that holds schools accountable for the performance of their students and sanctions schools for a pattern of repeated failure is an appropriate role for the federal government. When the states demonstrated their inability during the Great Depression to provide social insurance and welfare benefits to their unemployed and elderly, and when states were unwilling during the civil rights era to educate black and white students together, federal intervention became necessary. These days, where

the states have demonstrated their inability to educate our children well—particularly minority children and those living in poverty—the federal government is again obligated to act. Only the federal government can create a common yardstick for measuring performance and take actions against states that do not make the fiscal effort to provide good schools for all students. My own state of New York provides a case in point: Education in New York City and other urban systems is woefully underfunded, and as a result, school and teacher quality is manifestly lacking. In the sense of holding states accountable, then, NCLB could do some good.

But NCLB has overextended itself. It has moved beyond accountability for student achievement results by providing professional development funds that exclusively support a basic skills approach. To qualify for the funds, such cities as New York—which desperately need money—must teach a basic skills curriculum across the board. In addition, the federal government is rewriting the NAEP so that the tests will reflect a greater emphasis on basic skills instead of their current balance between basic and higher-order skills. By squeezing out critical thinking skills, these actions put the cognitive development of our students at risk.

Many education leaders oppose NCLB on the wrong grounds. They should embrace the notion of being held accountable for the achievement of their students but demand autonomy in how to improve that achievement. And as the NAEP data suggest, the best way for school leaders to raise student achievement is by placing more emphasis on teaching for meaning.

REFERENCES

McLaughlin, M. W., & Talbert, J. E. (1993). Introduction: New visions of teaching. In M. W. McLaughlin & J. E. Talbert (Eds.), *Teaching for understanding* (pp. 1–10). San Francisco: Jossey-Bass.

National Reading Panel. (2000). *Teaching children to read: An evidence based assessment of the scientific research literature on reading and its implications for reading instruction.* Washington, DC:

National Institute of Child Health and Human Development.

Snow, C. E., Burns, M. S., & Griffin, P. (Eds.). (1998). *Preventing reading difficulties in young children.* Washington, DC: Committee on Prevention of Reading Difficulties in Young Children.

Stigler, J. W., & Hiebert, J. (1999). *The teaching gap: Best ideas from the world's teachers for improving education in the classroom.* New York: Free Press.

U.S. Department of Education. (2000). *Trends in academic progress: Three decades of student performance.* Washington, DC: Author.

Wenglinsky, H. (2000). *How teaching matters: Bringing the classroom back into discussions of teacher quality.* Princeton, NJ: Educational Testing Service.

Wenglinsky, H. (2002). How schools matter: The link between teacher classroom practices and student academic performance. *Education Policy Analysis Archives, 10*(12).

Wenglinsky, H. (2003). Using large-scale research to gauge the impact of instructional practices on student reading comprehension: An exploratory study. *Education Policy Analysis Archives, 11*(19).

Projects for Further Exploration

1. Using an academic database, look up the topic of *text* or *book* and *censorship, banned,* and *school* to see what additional research has been done in this area. Then look it up in a database that includes newspaper articles.

2. Try to find out how textbooks are selected in your school district using the Web, informal contacts with friends, or calls to your local schools or school district office.

3. Using the Web, see if you can find out more about the publication of textbooks. That is, check out a major publisher to see how many textbooks are sold (e.g., a fourth-grade reading series) and how that publisher markets the textbooks.

4. Examine textbooks from public schools in your area and ask whether the information presented is geared toward exploring ideas or reciting the cultural character of this country. Do these textbooks provide an opportunity for creative exploration or a focus on test-taking as described by Wenglinsky in the reading in this chapter?

7

WHO GETS AHEAD?

Race, Class, and Gender in Education

R anking people in categories is a process that pervades all institutions, including education systems. Social stratification has been a central concern for sociologists of education for some time. In this chapter we explore the role that education plays in stratifying individuals and groups in society and within schools. Although issues of stratification are discussed throughout this book, this chapter focuses on the ways schools stratify by race, class, and gender, while readings in Chapter 8 describe attempts to alleviate inequality in schools. Unfortunately, space does not permit us to explore all inequalities, such as the prejudice and discrimination in schools for students with alternative sexual identities (Pascoe, 2007) and those whose body types and learning styles do not fit the "norm" (physical and cognitive differences). As you study the readings in this chapter and in Chapter 8, we encourage you examine parallels between the ways different groups are treated in schools and to consider how and why inequality exists in education. In doing so, you will develop a deeper understanding of the role schools play in maintaining inequality at the microlevel and macrolevel.

Let's stop to take a look at America's schools by examining class, race, and gender compositions. First, while it would seem that the proportion of males and females in schools should be similar to the population as a whole—49.3% male to 50.7% female (U.S. Census Bureau, 2008)—this is not the case. The relatively even sex ratio changes as students move through the school system, with boys more likely to drop out of high school—8.5% vs. 7.5% for girls (National Center for Education Statistics, 2009a). Women obtain a higher percentage of college degrees at all levels (National Center for Education Statistics, 2010)—four-year degrees (57.3% vs. 56.1% for men), master's degrees (60.6% vs. 57.1%), first-professional degrees such as law or medicine (49.7% vs. 42.9%), and doctoral degrees (51% vs. 42%). This is a change in the gender distribution of higher education degrees and some people are concerned about boys not achieving as much as girls in schools. Roslyn Arlin Mickelson discusses this issue in her reading in this chapter and Leslie Miller-Bernal also considers gender issues in higher education as she reviews the history of women's colleges in Chapter 9.

There are concerns as well about educational outcomes related to racial/ethnic and social class differences. The Department of Education (National Center for Education Statistics, 2010) reports that in 2009, 48% of fourth graders attending public schools were eligible for free or reduced lunch, with the percentage varying widely by race—31% white, 80% black, 82% Hispanic, 45% Asian/Pacific Islander, and 67% American Indian/Alaska Native. These children living in poverty are more likely to be located in city schools (62%) and towns (52%) than suburbs (39%) or rural areas (42%) (National Center for Education Statistics, 2010).

The percentage graduating from high school also varies by race. The Department of Education (National Center for Education Statistics, 2009a) reports that in 2008, the percentages of individuals 16 through 24 years old dropping out of high school was 4.8% for whites (non-Hispanic), 9.9% for blacks, and 18.3% for Hispanics. The rates for college completion for individuals 25 to 29 years old in 2009 are also distressing: 37.2% for whites, 18.9% for blacks, 12.2% for Hispanics, and 56.4% for Asian/Pacific Islanders (National Center for Education Statistics, 2009a). In 2009, the percentage of 25- to 28-year-olds with bachelor's degrees was much higher for whites (34.8%) and Asian/Pacific Islanders (56.4%) than blacks (18.9%) and Hispanics (12.2%—Note: this last percentage is used cautiously and reported as "unstable") (National Center for Education Statistics, 2009b). Clearly these figures suggest considerable inequality in American education.

Sociologists focus on inequality within and between schools. This inequality in schools comes in a variety of forms, as you will soon see. However, the end result is always to give advantage to one group over another or put some children at a distinct disadvantage in what might otherwise be an equal playing field. Caroline Hodges Persell discusses various explanations for racial inequality in school. The readings by Heather Beth Johnson and by Joan Z. Spade, Lynn Columba, and Beth E. Vanfossen focus on social class as a barrier to equal educational opportunities. The reading by Michelson adds to this discussion by examining gender differences in educational experiences. The two readings by Edward Morris illustrate the interaction of race, class, and gender in determining school experiences by examining the microsocial interactions, with one reading focusing on an urban school and the other a rural school. Clearly, improving academic achievement for *all* individuals is very complex.

Stratification in schools has been studied either at the school level or by examining the effects on individuals. At the school level, researchers study stratification within schools or between schools. Stratification between schools refers to the different educational experiences offered in different schools. Stratification within schools includes the placement of students within certain courses or curriculum tracks, as well as structures that exclude or discourage some groups of students from programs or curricula. In this chapter, we look at both levels of stratification.

The reading by Spade, Columba, and Vanfossen helps us to understand how social class shapes schooling experiences from the perspective of social structure and the organization of schools. The authors examine between-school discrimination, showing how schools are segregated by social class. Their research looks at differences in resources between schools, more specifically the types of courses offered to students and the processes by which students are placed in courses. The authors find that the distribution of students to classes in school is linked to the social class of the community in which the school is located. Parents are aware of this process, as Johnson points out in her reading. She finds that parents think carefully about the type of schools their children will attend, selecting places to reside based on their desire to have their children attend "good schools," which is most likely if the school is in a middle to upper social class neighborhood. Although we would like to think all students have equal chances of succeeding in school, the readings by Johnson and Spade, Columba, and Vanfossen illustrate how the inputs in the form of the social class of students and the community can affect the organization of schools by shaping the resources that different schools offer to students. Between-school stratification occurs when, as Johnson points out, families think carefully about the type of school their children will attend when selecting housing, which reinforces social class differences between schools. In addition, some families in the United States chose to send their children to private schools. Educational opportunities are often better in private schools, but this privilege of better education typically comes with a price tag, which families living in poverty usually cannot afford.

One of the primary methods of within-school stratification affecting students across race and social class is the process of curriculum tracking described in the Spade, Columba, and Vanfossen reading. Curriculum tracking is a structural feature of schools in which students take classes at different levels of difficulty. Missing from this chapter are readings from the large number of quantitative studies that define or examine the effects of tracking on students. Vanfossen, Jones, and Spade (1987) categorize the early research on the effects of tracking on status maintenance into three categories. One category of research looked at the effects of tracking in maintaining social-class status from generation to generation. The second category assumed that tracking was based on ability; therefore, differential treatment in tracks is unrelated to social mobility. The third category of research concluded that the relationship between tracking and status maintenance is "irrelevant, because tracking in high school does not have a significant impact upon achievement, values, and educational outcomes" (p. 105). The first explanation is most likely. When children enter middle school, they are placed in ability groups based on achievement test scores; however, such placement is not based on academic factors alone (Dauber, Alexander, & Entwisle, 1996). This trajectory of ability grouping is reinforced as children enter high school. The correlation between social class and track placement is too strong to be explained away by chance. Although some lower-class students end up in more challenging tracks, many others do not. Assignment to a lower track typically exposes a student to less-rigorous instructional methods along with a less-challenging curricula (Gamoran, Nystrand, Berends, & LePore, 1995). Tracking students into lower-level curriculum is also related to attachment to school, self-esteem, and more limited views of future opportunities (Vanfossen et al., 1987).

Some of the more recent research on tracking focuses on defining tracking itself. Indeed, the procedure is more complicated than simply assigning students to academic or vocational programs of study, as envisioned at the beginning of the 20th century. The idea of differential courses of study was introduced at that time as one of many efforts to tailor schools to the needs of a society dealing with nascent industrialization and an influx of immigrants (Oakes, 1985; Tyack & Cuban, 1995). By 1970, the organization of tracking became less rigid as schools allowed students to select their own courses. Powell, Farrar, and Cohen (1985) called this array of choices the "shopping mall high school." Samuel Lucas (1999) describes the variations in patterns of course-taking across subjects that exist today, which continue to be organized in a hierarchical level of knowledge presentation tailored to different ability levels.

Most of the more recent literature in this area attempts to understand the effects of tracking on students' academic achievements and orientations toward school. Grouping students by ability or tracking begins in elementary school, disadvantaging children from lower-income families long before they enter the middle school. Children from lower-income families not only do not "catch up" to their wealthier peers in elementary school, but they fall further behind throughout the school years. Alexander, Entwisle, and Olson in their reading in Chapter 3 followed students over a period of time and found that lower-income children experience a "summer setback" in achievement, whereas their peers from higher-income families actually show gains on achievement tests over the summertime when they are away from school because they are exposed to more academic enhancing experiences during their time off. Therefore, placing students from lower-income households in classes with less rigorous academic expectations puts them farther behind their peers who come from more advantaged households.

The two readings by Morris in this chapter focus on aspects of within-school stratification, looking at the microlevel or interactional factors that shape children's schooling and life experiences. Persell also describes the interpersonal interactions that create inequalities within schools, reviewing various explanations for racial differences in achievement outcomes. As the readings by Morris and Persell illustrate, families can have a significant impact on the direction of their children's schooling; however, teachers' responses to parents of racial and social class backgrounds different from their own can frustrate parents and teachers alike, as Lareau and Horvat described in Chapter 2. From his observations within schools, Morris shows how race, class, and gender interact to influence how teachers and school officials discipline and relate to children.

The reading by Mickelson further examines gender differences within schools, as well as the unequal payoffs of education for females and males. These processes are subtle, yet they have a substantial impact on the ultimate success of women and minority students. These readings illustrate how the stratification process occurs in different school contexts and is reinforced by teachers, peers, and others in the process of educating our children.

The following readings are meant to provide you with a better understanding of the mechanisms that segregate students both between and within schools in terms of curriculum and learning experiences. This differential treatment results in unequal educational and occupational opportunities for students across social class, race and ethnicity, and gender.

REFERENCES

Dauber, S. L., Alexander, K. L., & Entwisle, D. R. (1996). Tracking and transitions through the middle grades: Channeling educational trajectories. *Sociology of Education, 69*(4), 290–307.

Gamoran, A., Nystrand, M., Berends, M., & LePore, P. C. (1995). An organizational analysis of the effects of ability grouping. *American Educational Research Journal, 32*(4), 687–715.

Lucas, S. R. (1999). *Tracking inequality: Stratification and mobility in American high schools.* New York: Teachers College Press.

National Center for Education Statistics. (2009a). *Digest of education statistics.* Washington, DC: U.S. Department of Education. Retrieved from http://nces.ed.gov/programs/digest/d09/

National Center for Education Statistics. (2009b). *Status and trends in the education of racial and ethnic minorities.* Washington, DC: U.S. Department of Education. Retrieved from http://nces.ed.gov/pubs2010/2010015/tables/table_7_5a.asp

National Center for Education Statistics. (2010). *Fast facts: What is the percentage of degrees conferred by sex and race?* Washington, DC: U.S. Department of Education. Retrieved from http://nces.ed.gov/fastfacts/display.asp?id=72

Oakes, J. (1985). *Keeping track: How schools structure inequality.* New Haven, CT: Yale University Press.

Pascoe, C. J. (2007). *Dude, you're a fag: Masculinity and sexuality in high school.* Berkeley: University of California Press.

Powell, A. G., Farrar, E., & Cohen, D. K. (1985). *The shopping mall high school: Winners and losers in the educational marketplace.* Boston: Houghton Mifflin.

Tyack, D., & Cuban, L. (1995). *Tinkering toward utopia: A century of public school reform.* Cambridge, MA: Harvard University Press.

U.S. Census Bureau. (2008). *2006–2008 American community survey 3-year estimates.* Washington, DC: Author. Retrieved from http://factfinder.census.gov/

Vanfossen, B. E., Jones, J. D., & Spade, J. Z. (1987). Curriculum tracking and status maintenance. *Sociology of Education, 60*(2), 104–122.

Schools

The Great Equalizer and the Key to the American Dream

Heather Beth Johnson

As is clear already, the educational system in the United States is based on local control of schools. This local control results in schools that vary considerably in terms of the educational opportunities they offer to the students who attend them. Heather Beth Johnson presents the results of interviews with 206 individuals in five major metropolitan areas across the United States. She explores the ways in which wealth and education are linked in maintaining inequality across race and social class. In these interviews with parents, she describes their view of education as the "great equalizer," their understanding of what a "good" school is, and their interpretations of meritocracy as it relates to educational and personal achievement. These images of equality and inequality combine in parents' minds to justify decisions about what schools their children will attend.

Questions to consider for this reading:

1. What interpretations do parents give to meritocracy and education as they relate to achieving the "American Dream"?

2. Are parents across social-class backgrounds similar or different in their interpretations of the power of education in achieving success in life?

3. What makes a "good" school in parents' minds? How are these views related to readings by Meyer and Rowan in Chapter 3 and Metz in Chapter 4?

I n the United States today, approximately 20 percent of children under the age of six are living below the official poverty line (Proctor & Dalaker, 2003). Many of these children's parents are desperately impoverished and unemployed, and the plight of these families—often single mothers and their children—is harrowing (Berrick, 1995; Edin & Lein, 1997; Ellwood, 1988; Kozol, 1988). Perhaps even more troubling, because of the irony, is how many poor children live in homes with at least one working parent; 40 percent of impoverished adults hold at least one job (Ehrenreich, 2001; Johnson, 2002; Levitan & Shapiro, 1987; Newman, 1999; Rank, 2004; Shipler, 2004). Many of these families have worked hard, they have played by the rules, and they are still coming up short. The working poor challenge our thinking about inequality in America: if people wind up where they do based on how hard they work, and if 40 percent of the poor are working hard, then why is it that those families are struggling so to even stay afloat? Such questions have been asked often and social scientists have revealed some of the structural arrangements contributing to the predicaments of the working poor (Marx, 1867/1967); only recently, however, have we begun to seriously consider ways that the structure of *wealth* ties into the dynamics of intergenerational inequality in the contemporary United States. . . .

This [study] examines the extent to which parents—black and white, wealthy, middle-class, and poor—believe in the ideology of meritocracy, while at the same time understanding and acknowledging the advantages that private wealth can confer to children and families. On one hand, the families interviewed recognize and acknowledge how significant structured wealth inequality is in shaping family trajectories and children's educational opportunities. On the other hand, they claim their social positions have been earned and deserved through hard work and individual achievement, or lack thereof. Wealthy families are particularly provocative to examine because their stories so clearly contradict the notion of meritocracy. The more privileged parents interviewed acknowledge the advantages they have received through family wealth, and acknowledge the advantageous educational opportunities they are now able to pass along to their children because of them. What is really intriguing, however, is that at the same time, these same families hold close to their hearts the idea that they have earned and deserved what they have, and they argue vehemently that their privileged positions have resulted from their individual hard work, efforts, and achievements.

Since family wealth is such a private matter, and normally so unspoken of, it is often largely invisible. Thus, families with wealth often take its privileges for granted as a "normal" part of life, and families without it are not always cognizant of what they are up against when they try to compare themselves to others. While families with wealth acknowledge their privilege and claim their positions are self-earned, the reverse is true as well: families who could not possibly compete with peers who are reaping the benefits of wealth legacies nonetheless blame themselves for coming up short. The families with which we spoke both believe in the ideology and acknowledge

structured inequality at the same time. They uphold the contradiction between the American Dream and the power of wealth. . . .

PARENTS' BELIEFS IN THE AMERICAN DREAM

Sitting on a plush leather couch in their living room, sipping ice water, Suzanne and Drew talked about the American Dream. A white, professional couple in their early thirties, the Wrights were each very accomplished and came from affluent family backgrounds. At the time of the interview, Suzanne was working for a small high-tech company of which she was part owner with her father. Drew was a very successful high-tech recruiter. Their condominium in an exclusive development in the metropolitan New York City area was beautifully appointed; they dressed meticulously, traveled frequently, and their lifestyle appeared to be more than comfortable. In their elevated status and social class positioning, the Wrights were somewhat exceptional in our sample, but in their perspectives on the American Dream, they were not.

The Wrights and other families repeatedly articulated a similar view: that the American Dream is a realistic explanation for how our social system operates and that it provides a sound justification for where an individual stands in the hierarchy of social class positioning. While they did not use the word *meritocracy* to describe it, meritocracy was, in effect, what was discussed most often. Families were consistent in their explanations that in the United States social class positions are earned, deserved, and merited based on individual achievement or lack thereof. Broaching the topics of wealth and inequality inevitably generated discussions of individualism and equal opportunity. In these discussions, people's perspectives were clear. Essentially, they believed that with hard work and aspirations, people's chances are equal regardless of their backgrounds. . . . [T]hese same families contradicted these sentiments by also claiming that some individuals are advantaged and disadvantaged by their access to family wealth. However, their first claim—and truly, a seemingly genuine one on their parts—was always that meritocracy is real. This was not just a rhetorical stance; families from across the race and class spectrum used notions of meritocracy to explain that their own social positions and the positions of others were legitimately the result of their own doing. Just as Suzanne and Drew articulated a strong meritocratic stance, Anjillette, a black single mother from the Los Angeles area who was working as a vocational nurse, was explicit about the same themes. . . .

Parents evoked, as Anjillette did, the American Dream's core credo of meritocracy to explain why people rise and fall. The underlying—or, in Anjillette's case, overt—presumption was that people independently *choose* their relative class circumstances. Regardless of their own social class positioning, and despite their vastly differing life experiences, the parents interviewed asserted that individual hard work is the main determinant of upward and downward social mobility. Lodged within this logic was a profound optimism about an individual's life chances. As one father from a wealthy white family in the New York City area insisted, "Hard work can go a long way toward overcoming most any obstacle!" But this adamant meritocratic belief had a flip side too: just as "success" was perceived as one's personal achievement, "failure," too, was seen as the direct result of one's own doing. In an interview with the Gordons, a well-off white couple from the Washington, D.C., area, James, a public relations director for a major D.C. media firm, was asked "What is 'the American Dream,' in your own opinion?" He responded, "The American Dream for me is equal opportunity. Second, no discrimination. Third, you have the right to be what you want to be. And the only other thing—which I feel—is you could do it if you want." . . .

THE GREAT EQUALIZER AND THE KEY TO THE DREAM

If the American Dream of meritocracy is our country's promise, public education is what ensures that promise to all children. Education—more than any other institution—is the system's way of making certain that achievement is independently earned, not tied to one's background. Parents emphasize that it was because of this that they saw their hopes for their children as not just a dream, but truly possible. Joyce and Elliston Meador, a black couple, both social workers, who lived in inner-city St. Louis, exemplified this emphasis in their interview. Elliston explained, "One of the things that helps a person move from poverty to financial independence, or at least having a decent income you can live off of, is education. I mean that's the level that everybody can ascend to regardless of race, creed, or color. If you're poor, I don't care if you're white, black, red, yellow—doesn't make any difference. If you don't have an education, you are not going to be upwardly mobile. So everybody has an opportunity to move up from poverty."

The American Dream does not guarantee that everyone will make it in America, but it presumes that despite inequalities in their circumstances each individual will have a fair chance, an equal opportunity, and no one will be unfairly advantaged or disadvantaged. Given that we are born into different families with very different backgrounds, the system must provide some way to balance our opportunities. A major role of the institution of education is to do just that; it is supposed to level out what is an initially uneven playing field. The parents interviewed clung to this idea. . . .

While . . . parents also did question its legitimacy, they repeatedly asserted the notion that education is the Great Equalizer. The idea of the Great Equalizer is that no matter who you are, no matter what financial or social background you come from, no matter what your family situation is, the school system diminishes inequalities of circumstance and provides opportunities to get ahead. In this way, the Great Equalizer is central to the proper functioning of the whole system: the institution of education is supposed to be where meritocracy is operationalized, actualized, and realized. It is supposed to ensure that regardless of background—regardless of whatever contexts of advantage or disadvantage we might be born into—our own positions in society are ultimately earned, deserved, and achieved by us and us alone. The families—including the Mitchels, an affluent white family with handsome homes in downtown Washington, D.C., and in rural Virginia—were consistent on this point. When asked how essential they thought education is to one's success in this country, Jacob responded right away: "I think that education is the Great Leveler. That's what sets me and my family apart is our education, advanced education. And everyone in my family has at least a master's or a double master's. And I think everyone has done well because of their education. We didn't start out with much. My father didn't have much. But I think the children, through education, ended up doing very well."

Education was viewed as the Great Equalizer making the American Dream real, and also as *the key* to the dream. Education provides, at least in theory, a clear route to follow: if you work hard enough in school, then you can be anything, do anything, rise up to any level you choose. In the minds of the parents, however, this was more than just theory—as Jacob's quote above illustrates, parents saw it as real. Whether it had been so in their own experience or not, parents seemed to genuinely believe in education as the key to their children's future success. As such, it held paramount importance in the raising of their children; they understood their role as parents to include—as an important part—navigating the education system for their kids. Kimberly Harmon, a black single mother who was working as a receptionist in a downtown Boston office, explained her perspective regarding her son:

Kimberly: Hopefully he can get a good education, 'cause that's the most important thing.

Interviewer: Why is it so important? Why do you think a good education is so important?

Kimberly: A good education is good because without education what are you going to be? You need your education. Everybody should know that!

For the parents with whom we spoke, education was of the utmost importance. When asked,

"Why do you think education is so important?" parents responded quickly and matter-of-factly. Their tones implied that—as Kimberly Harmon had said outright—"Everybody should know that!" Education was so important because, as Melissa Desmond, a white, unemployed mother from Boston, explained, it was perceived as determining life chances for a child. . . .

Previous studies of families from across race and class spectra confirm that since education is seen by people as the "principal means to economic advancement" in our current system, it thus becomes the focus of much parental energy (Kluegel & Smith, 1986, p. 42; see also Brantlinger, 2003; Lareau, 2000, 2003). . . .

"It's Not Necessarily Fair, and It's Not Necessarily Right"

. . . Since education is so crucial to the American Dream, this is—at least in part—why Americans care so deeply about their schools (Hochschild & Scovronick, 2003). The families interviewed were intent on making sure their own children got the best education possible but were concerned about the state of America's education system. Despite their faith in the American Dream and their claims that education was the Great Equalizer, they were also up-front about their perspectives that different schools provided vastly different opportunities for kids; for, as much as the families interviewed believed in the egalitarian principles of meritocracy, they were also faced with the reality of drastically disparate school systems. As Sarah Otis, a white freelance journalist from Boston, reflected on this reality, "I mean, it's just obvious to me that there's a severe problem in the United States with education right now. And it makes me so sad, though, that, you know, all kids—I mean, I just look at my daughter's class, you know? They're all bright, wonderful little kids, you know? They should all have an opportunity to receive a decent education. And, you know, it's just so profoundly unfair."

Of the 260 parents interviewed, not one of them claimed that schools in America are actually equal. One middle-class black father summed up their collective view when he said, "The more money you have, the better the neighborhood you live in. The better neighborhood, the more taxes, the better the school. Your kid goes where you live." Parents regularly brought up how they thought it unfair that some children had to attend poor-quality schools while others could attend excellent ones. They emphasized this inequality and criticized it. They were concerned about their own children and voiced concern for all children. . . .

Vivian articulated precisely the sentiments that parent after parent had stressed: that, given their emphasis on education, they "would do whatever they could to make sure their children get a good education." This meant they had to get their children into a good school. First and foremost, however, parents had to figure out which schools were the "good" schools.

A "GOOD" SCHOOL

What was considered to be a "good" school? Parents said that good schools had updated facilities and equipment, stimulating atmospheres, and high-quality educational programs. They said that they were safe, had teachers who were dedicated, small class sizes, computers, healthy environments, and successful graduates who went on to excel academically and occupationally. However, as much as parents described in detail the types of educational resources characteristic of "good" schools, rarely had they actually explored the availability of these traits when considering schools for their kids. Similarly, parents often emphasized the importance of a school's rankings or standardized test scores and were quick to point them out if they knew them—but they rarely did. A divergence between what these families said was important in considering schools and what actually had been determining factors in their decisions was transparent in the interviews.[1] What

they overwhelmingly *had* relied upon in determining whether or not a school was "good" was one thing: simply, if it was located in a "good" neighborhood. . . .

"Good" schools and "bad" schools were defined—first and foremost—by their location. Molisa Parks, a working-class, black single mother from St. Louis, put it bluntly: "I mean, we all know that kids in the country get a better education than kids in the city—as far as the atmosphere, the equipment they have to work with, the change of attitude of the kids. It's just class sizes, anything and everything, computer equipment!"

Even when parents mentioned specifics such as safety, class size, or equipment, they usually spoke of them in the context of location. Rarely did parents use any information other than its location to substantively inform their judgment of a school.

That parents judged schools by their location was not surprising since previous research has identified a strong link between school reputation and location (Holme, 2002). What was remarkable was that parents' perspectives on what makes a school's location a good one were so incredibly consistent. They all seemed to dictate the same basic formula: a good school is in a good neighborhood, and a good neighborhood is a wealthier and whiter neighborhood.

Race and class framed parents' thinking regarding the schools they wanted for their children to attend. This was true for white parents—who were often quite explicit about their desires to avoid schools with racially diverse populations. It was also true for black parents—who despite a desire for racial diversity in their children's schools, wanted the best quality schooling, which they generally presumed to be whiter and less diverse. And, for all of the parents, the more wealthy and affluent the area in which a school was located, the better the school was considered to be.

Elsewhere, Thomas Shapiro and I have argued that for the parents we interviewed, race was a defining factor, if not *the* factor, in determining a "good" school. In our interviews, parents tied a school's reputation directly to the race and class composition of its students. While claiming to be concerned about such things as safety and class size, the families we spoke with were ultimately seeking whiter—and, in their view, inextricably wealthier—school districts for their children, regardless of any other of the school's characteristics. Because we have focused on it previously, this social construction of school reputation and the race and class dynamics of school decisions are not major focal points here (Johnson & Shapiro, 2003; Shapiro & Johnson, 2005). I would be remiss, however, to not at least mention the enormous extent to which families' perspectives were explicitly framed by race and class, and by racism and classism.

Race played a significant role in parents' logic where schools for their children were concerned. Their views, decisions, actions, and experiences were informed and structured by race and racism, and, presumably, race and racism help to contribute to their maintenance (Johnson & Shapiro, 2003; Shapiro & Johnson, 2005). Indeed, the interviews provide evidence that, as sociologist Eduardo Bonilla-Silva argues, the contemporary United States is "a racialized social system" (1997, 2001, 2003). The families we studied were operating within a racial structure, where, as Bonilla-Silva (1997) discusses, racially motivated—or even racist—behavior such as choosing whiter schools is rational. Race and racism, however, were often conflated with class and classism in complex ways.

Class rigidly structured school reputation, as parents consistently asserted that the "good" schools were located in wealthier, more affluent areas. While I suspect that the frequently used phrase "more money" was often code for "whiter," parents clearly believed that better-funded schools were simply better schools. Class dynamics—as separate from, and as entwined with, race dynamics—helped to frame families' views, decisions, actions, and experiences.

Since schools are funded in large part by local property taxes, the schools that were located in more affluent areas were presumed by parents to have better funding and thus be better schools.

This was true regardless of whether or not a parent had gathered actual information about a school or visited it. . . .

SEPARATE AND UNEQUAL

Since American education has historically been structured around neighborhood schools, and since schools have traditionally been funded largely by local property taxes, schools and communities are inextricably linked. Just as parents considered schools to be "good" if they were in "good" neighborhoods, they considered neighborhoods to be "good" if they had "good" schools. . . .

With financial support from their families, Suzanne and Drew Wright were able to buy their first home soon after they got married. Although they could have bought a "huge house" for the same price in another area, they opted for a small townhouse because it was all they could afford in the specific town where they wanted to live in the New York City metropolitan area. Although other locations would have meant shorter commutes to work, a much lower cost of living, and, as they put it, "far more house for their money," the Wrights explained that they wanted to live where the best schools were located. For the families we interviewed, this was the norm. They most often cited schools as their primary consideration in deciding where to live. Figures from the U.S. Department of Education show this as the pattern nationally: at least one out of four families nationwide chose their neighborhood specifically for the schools there (U.S. Department of Education, 2004).

At least in terms of the public school system, where we live determines where we go to school. And, since perhaps more than any other variables race and class segregation characterize our residential living patterns, significant schooling differences go hand in hand. If all of us—from all walks of life, from all racial and ethnic backgrounds, and representing every point on the socioeconomic spectrum—were spread out evenly in the country's cities and neighborhoods, then perhaps school funding and student populations would be generally equivalent. If that were the case, then perhaps localized school systems might result in more or less equal education—which might correspondingly go a long way toward making neighborhoods more uniformly desirable (or undesirable, as some would argue). However, we are not spread out evenly throughout the neighborhoods of America. Residential segregation is a major linchpin in educational inequality.

Patterns of residential segregation in post–civil rights America have been well documented by scholars across disciplines (Meyer, 2000). Data from the past two decades, for example, show that while residential racial segregation declined slightly through the 1980s (Farley & Frey, 1994), that decline has since reversed and segregation is again on the rise (Orfield & Eaton, 1997; Yinger, 1995). In *American Apartheid,* sociologists Douglas Massey and Nancy Denton (1993) detailed the contours of race and class segregation and described the contemporary United States as categorized by "persistent" and "severe" segregation. Their work showed how racial groups—most acutely, African Americans—are intensely "hypersegregated": isolated from other groups, clustered in contiguous areas, concentrated in small areas, and centralized within urban areas (Massey & Denton, 1993). Other data—for example, a 2002 report from the U.S. Census Bureau—confirm that blacks are still the most residentially segregated of any racial or ethnic group (Iceland, Weinberg, & Steinmetz, 2002).

Due to the ways that race and class are linked (through, for example, the historic racial wealth gap [Oliver & Shapiro, 1995; Shapiro, 2004]), racial segregation is also, of course, inexorably class segregation. The resulting social inequalities are extreme, causing segregation scholars to conclude, as Massey and Denton did, that "racial residential segregation is the principal structural feature of American society responsible for the perpetuation of urban poverty and represents a primary cause of racial inequality in the United States" (Massey & Denton, 1993, p. iii). Others have noted the ways in which residential segregation has molded our society into "a country of strangers" (Hacker, 1992), and how we are, for

all intents and purposes, living in "two nations" with great divides between racial and class groups (Shipler, 1997). In Mary Jackman's words, residential segregation "achieves an unprecedented physical separation of the groups—it maximizes the spatial distance between the groups and it radiates over many domains of social life as separate schools, shopping, places of employment, and recreational facilities effortlessly form the existence of separate neighborhoods. Spatial segregation in neighborhoods thus spills over into all walks of life, creating de facto physical separation of the groups throughout social life" (1994, p. 136).

One of segregation's greatest fault lines lies in the fact that the nation's younger generations are perpetually educated in separate and unequal schools. A 2003 U.S. Department of Education report showed that 70 percent of white students attend schools that are at least 75 percent white. The same report revealed that 32 percent of black elementary and secondary school students are enrolled in schools located in large cities, compared to only 6 percent of white students (Hoffman & Llagas, 2003). Other studies' results are even more acute: Gary Orfield and John Yun's examination of school segregation shows that, in industrial states, over half of all black children attend schools that are of over 90 percent minority students; in large urban areas, over 90 percent of black children attend schools that are predominantly nonwhite (Orfield & Yun, 1999). In 2004, 70 percent of black students were eligible for free or reduced school lunches, compared to 23 percent of white students. Of those children who qualified, 76 percent of the black students lived in central cities, compared to 24 percent of the qualifying white students. In center-city schools, 61 percent of black students attended schools where over 75 percent of the students qualified for free or reduced-price lunches (U.S. Department of Education, 2004).

Rather than being a Great Equalizer, separate and unequal schooling presents a direct contradiction to the American Dream of meritocracy. If schools are segregated and unequal, then a major avenue of ensuring equal opportunity is blocked.

Efforts to reconcile this issue have been part of social justice agendas and education reform goals for decades. The U.S. Supreme Court's 1954 ruling in *Brown v. Board of Education* that "separate educational facilities are inherently unequal" is probably the most large-scale and well-known example. Fifty years have passed since the famous *Brown* opinion was declared, and while desegregation did achieve some very real gains in the school systems, substantive desegregation efforts have been more or less stalled for the past 25 years (Hochschild & Scovronick, 2003; Orfield & Eaton, 1997), levels of school segregation have been worsening since the early 1990's (Orfield & Eaton, 1997), and both integrated and equal education remain, for the most part, unrealized (Orfield & Eaton, 1997; Steinhorn & Diggs-Brown, 1999).

The result of what Jennifer Hochschild refers to as "deeply embedded patterns of inequality" is that, as she puts it, "the worst-off students and schools have a completely different educational experience from the best-off students, with predictably different outcomes" (Hochschild, 2003, pp. 825–826). Wealthier schools spend on average 56 percent more per student than do poorer schools (Children's Defense Fund, 1998). Seventy percent of teachers in schools located in low-income areas say they lack the books, supplies, and other materials necessary for them to successfully teach their students (Children's Defense Fund, 1998). Children from poor families disproportionately attend weaker schools and are at greater risk for serious academic failure (Pagani, Boulerice, & Tremblay, 1997). They are much more likely to drop out of their schools, attain fewer years of education, and earn less income later in life than children from more well-off families (Children's Defense Fund, 1998, p. xiv; Duncan & [Brooks-]Gunn, 1997; Fine, 1991; Haveman & Wolfe, 1994).

Essentially, the research literature supports what the parents we interviewed believed. The schools that were perceived as "good" and "bad" were indeed probably better or worse in terms of the resources they offered, the educational opportunities they provided, and the chances and outcomes of their students. While there are always exceptions, the funding, resources, opportunities, and student outcomes of poorer, more urban, disproportionately black public schools are generally weaker relative to the "whiter, wealthier," more suburban schools that the parents so often compared them to (Anyon, 1997; Fine, 1991; Hochschild, 2003; Orfield & Eaton, 1997; Wells, 1995).

"RUNNING WITH FAST HORSES"

. . . In regard to school inequality, it was not only differences in funding, resources, opportunities, and student outcomes that concerned parents. Parents were highly cognizant of what they perceived as enormous differences in schools in terms of the social status of the students who attended them. While they were clearly concerned with making sure their children received a high-quality education, they were exorbitantly *more* concerned with the caliber, social standing, and family backgrounds of their children's potential classmates. From their perspectives, enrolling their children in school meant providing them with reading, writing, and arithmetic skills, but it also meant choosing their social environment, determining who their classmates and friends may be, and selecting their peers.

Parents wanted their children to, as Carter Martin put it, "run with fast horses" so that they would "run fast, too." They emphasized the importance of a school's social environment in determining the prospects for student achievement—achievement educationally, and achievement in life. They talked about wanting their children to be "exposed to" and "surrounded by" kids who were "smart"; "striving to achieve"; "well-behaved"; and would "do well in life." As one father said, "The person's ability is one factor. But a good portion of the deal is that, as they say, 'It's not what you know, it's *who* you know.'"

Parents wanted their kids to attend schools with peers who would positively influence their work habits, social lives, and life chances. They were also quite clear regarding those with whom they did *not* want their children to attend school.

As Deborah Curley explained her logic, "I was just really concerned about the kinds of children that my child would be exposed to. I definitely didn't want her exposed to a lot of the kids that are in the population that I work with. So that's a consideration too, you know? So the more that you spend on a school, then you guarantee that that's not going to happen. You know that your children won't be exposed to, uh, kids that have been abused or neglected. You know, that kind of thing."

Impressions of student populations and perceptions of school reputations, whether grounded in direct experience (as was the case with Deborah), or based purely on ungrounded speculation (as was the case with the majority of parents we spoke with—especially white and middle-class parents) (Johnson & Shapiro, 2003; Shapiro & Johnson, 2005), often had deep race and class undertones. Often, of utmost importance in parents' minds (and often undoubtedly tied to race and class stereotypes) were questions about the "character" or "values" of the student population: Are the school's students "good kids," "from good families," with "the right values," and "bright futures?" Or are they not? The subtle—and not so subtle—subtext of such reasoning on the part of parents involved their questioning the race and class composition of schools. . . .

Often having never visited the schools they were judging, nor directly observed any of the students at them, parents' perceptions about their children's potential peers were based almost entirely on word-of-mouth or blatant presumptions. Thus, school reputations were constructed almost entirely around parents' subjective impressions of who attended the school. Results from other recent research show similar findings. For example, in a study by education researcher Jennifer Jellison Holme, parents of high socioeconomic status in California were found to know virtually nothing firsthand about the schools to which they chose to send their children. Parents' school decisions had been based solely on the subjective reputations of area schools. These reputations, as it turned out, were founded almost exclusively within parents' own social networks,

and were based almost entirely on the race and class characteristics of the families whose children were attending the schools (Ball, 2003; Brantlinger, 2003; Holme, 2002).

Research studies have documented that the social environment of a school does indeed significantly impact student achievement and student outcomes. The greater the proportion of wealthy students who attend a school, the higher the likelihood of that school's students completing high school, and the higher the chances for their successful educational outcomes (Mayer, 1997). Jennifer Hochschild and Nathan Scovronick's extensive review of the literature on this subject has concluded, "One of the few things we know for certain about schooling is that the class background of a student's classmates has a dramatic effect on that student's level of success. This finding has been documented over and over in various countries and schools and with different methodologies and sets of data" (Hochschild & Scovronick, 2003, p. 26).

Some may wonder if the schools themselves really make such a large difference at all, if we can even be certain that education is central to achievement or, ultimately, to an individual's social positioning later in life. Indeed, some experts have argued that schooling does not matter nearly as much as it is presumed to matter, that life chance outcomes would be similar regardless of educational experiences (Coleman, 1996; Jencks, 1979). For example, some claim that the supposedly poor parenting skills of black families and the supposed cultural deficits of poor families are actually the significant agents in negative outcomes of black students and the long-term intergenerational transmission of poverty (Thernstrom & Thernstrom, 2003). Surely family background and many factors besides schools and outside of the education system matter greatly to individuals' life chances, and variables well beyond school quality affect children's trajectories and chances for success (Conley & Albright, 2004). Schools cannot be isolated as the sole distributors of opportunity or even as the primary influence on a person's life course. However, ultimately it seems that not just the families we interviewed, but also most researchers and policy makers tend to agree that, as social welfare scholar Mark Rank puts it, "A quality education is one of the most vital assets that an individual can acquire" (2004, p. 207). It would be naïve to think that school experiences and school quality do not have at least a significant effect, if not profound effects, on a child's path in life.

As Rank argues, "It is blatantly wrong that some American children, simply by virtue of their parents' economic standing, must settle for a sub-standard educational experience, while others receive a well-rounded education" (2004, p. 210). As he discusses in his book *One Nation, Underprivileged,* due to the fact that public schools are funded primarily through their local tax bases (mostly property taxes), school districts in wealthier areas generally have more ample funding (for things such as teachers' salaries, smaller class sizes, purchasing books, supplies, equipment, and technological resources, etc.) and thus, can offer higher quality education to their populations. The sorts of things that wealthier school districts can afford for their students correspond directly to the key school quality benchmarks identified as positively influencing student learning and performance. A report by the U.S. Department of Education pointed to indicators such as a school's academic environment, teacher academic skills and pedagogy, technology, and class size as characterizing high quality educational environments (Mayer, Mullens, & Moore, 2001). Indeed, in their research, education scholars Jeannie Oakes and Marisa Saunders (2004) found that such things as textbooks, technology, and curriculum materials are "educationally important," and the consequences of not having such things (or having inadequate levels of them) on student learning and student outcomes are "particularly harsh." They also found that schools serving low-income students are the schools that are most affected by shortages of such resources (Oakes & Saunders, 2004). In the end, most of us would be hard-pressed to claim that differences in schools do not matter when, as Linda Darling-Hammond and Laura Post (2000) report, in the United States the wealthiest 10 percent of school districts spend ten times the amount on educating their students than the poorest 10 percent, where poor and minority students are concentrated, spend. Certainly none of the parents we interviewed made the claim that school inequalities did not matter. In fact, they claimed the opposite: they believed that the differences between "good" schools and "bad" schools mattered greatly to their children's experiences. And they attempted to act on that belief.

Regardless of the reasons why, and regardless of whether they thought it was "fair or right," the parents we interviewed believed that some children were advantaged and some were disadvantaged based on where they could go to school. Schools, in their view, were profoundly important; schools were seen as the ticket to the American Dream, the route to success in the meritocracy. So, for them, getting their children into "good" ones was critically important (Warren & Tyagi, 2003). While they believed in the American Dream and defended the education system as the Great Equalizer, parents at the same time emphasized the uneven landscape of school inequalities. With all of them intent upon sending their children to a "good" school, the question logically follows: Who gets to go where?

NOTE

1. The degree to which the parents were consciously aware of the discrepancies between what they said and what they did was not clear and would require further research to explore. For discussion and analysis regarding the relationship between what people say and what people do, see Deutscher, Pestello, and Pestello (1993).

REFERENCES

Anyon, J. (1997). *Ghetto schooling: A political economy of urban educational reform.* New York: Teachers College Press.

Ball, S. J. (2003). *Class strategies and the education market: The middle classes and social advantage.* London: Routledge Falmer.

Berrick, J. D. (1995). *Faces of poverty: Portraits of women and children on welfare.* New York: Oxford University Press.

Bonilla-Silva, E. (1997). Rethinking racism: Toward a structural interpretation. *American Sociological Review, 62*(3), 465–480.

Bonilla-Silva, E. (2001). *White supremacy and racism in the post-civil rights era.* Boulder, CO: Lynne Rienner.

Bonilla-Silva, E. (2003). *Racism without racists: Color-blind racism and the persistence of racial inequality in the United States.* Lanham, MD: Rowman & Littlefield.

Brantlinger, E. (2003). *Dividing classes: How the middle class negotiates and rationalizes school advantage.* New York: Routledge Falmer.

Children's Defense Fund. (1998). *The state of America's children: A report from the Children's Defense Fund.* Boston: Beacon Press.

Coleman, J. S. (1996). Summary report. In *Equality of educational opportunity* (pp. 3–28). Washington, DC: U.S. Government Printing Office.

Conley, D., & Albright, K. (Eds.). (2004). *After the bell: Family background, public policy, and educational success.* London: Routledge.

Darling-Hammond, L., & Post, L. (2000). Inequality in teaching and schooling: Supporting high-quality teaching and leadership in low-income schools. In R. D. Kalenberg (Ed.), *A nation at risk: Preserving public education as an engine for social mobility* (pp. 127–167). New York: Century Foundation Press.

Deutscher, I., Pestello, F. P., & Pestello, H. F. G. (1993). *Sentiments and acts.* New York: Walter de Gruyter.

Duncan, G. J., & Brooks-Gunn, J. (1997). *Consequences of growing up poor.* New York: Russell Sage Foundation.

Edin, K., & Lein, L. (1997). *Making ends meet: How single mothers survive welfare and low-wage work.* New York: Russell Sage Foundation.

Ehrenreich, B. (2001). *Nickel and dimed: On (not) getting by in America.* New York: Metropolitan.

Ellwood, D. T. (1988). *Poor support: Poverty in the American family.* New York: Basic Books.

Farley, R., & Frey, W. H. (1994). Changes in the segregation of whites from blacks during the 1980s: Small steps toward a more integrated society. *American Sociological Review, 59*(1), 23–45.

Fine, M. (1991). *Framing dropouts: Notes on the politics of an urban public high school.* Albany: State University of New York Press.

Hacker, A. (1992). *Two nations: Black and white, separate, hostile, unequal.* New York: Ballantine.

Haveman, R., & Wolfe, B. (1994). *Succeeding generations: On the effect of investments in children.* New York: Russell Sage Foundation.

Hochschild, J. (2003). Social class in public schools. *Journal of Social Issues, 59*(4), 821–840.

Hochschild, J., & Scovronick, N. (2003). *The American dream and the public schools.* New York: Oxford University Press.

Hoffman, K., & Llagas, C. (2003). *Status and trends in the education of blacks.* Washington, DC: U.S. Department of Education, National Center for Education Statistics.

Holme, J. J. (2002). Buying homes, buying schools: School choice and the social construction of school quality. *Harvard Educational Review, 72*(2), 177–205.

Iceland, J., Weinberg, D. H., & Steinmetz, E. (U.S. Census Bureau). (2002). *Racial and ethnic residential segregation in the United States.* Washington, DC: U.S. Government Printing Office.

Jackman, M. R. (1994). *The velvet glove: Paternalism and conflict in gender, class, and race relations.* Berkeley: University of California Press.

Jencks, C. (1979). *Who gets ahead? The determinants of economic success in America.* New York: Basic Books.

Johnson, H. B., & Shapiro, T. (2003). Good neighborhoods, good schools: Race and the "good choices" of white families. In E. Bonilla-Silva & W. Doane (Eds.), *White out: The continuing significance of racism* (pp. 173–187). New York: Routledge.

Johnson, J. (2002). *Getting by on the minimum: The lives of working class women.* New York: Routledge.

Kluegel, J. R., & Smith, E. R. (1986). *Beliefs about inequality: Americans' views of what is and what ought to be.* New York: Aldine de Gruyter.

Kozol, J. (1988). *Rachel and her children: Homeless families in America.* New York: Random House.

Lareau, A. (2000). *Home advantage: Social class and parental intervention in elementary education.* Lanham, MD: Rowman & Littlefield.

Lareau, A. (2003). *Unequal childhoods: Class, race, and family life.* Berkeley: University of California Press.

Levitan, S. A., & Shapiro, I. (1987). *Working but poor: America's contradiction.* Baltimore: Johns Hopkins University Press.

Marx, K. (1967). *Capital: A critique of political economy* (Vol. 1). New York: International. (Original work published 1867)

Massey, D. S., & Denton, N. A. (1993). *American apartheid: Segregation and the making of the underclass*. Cambridge, MA: Harvard University Press.

Mayer, D. P., Mullens, J. E., & Moore, M. T. (2001). *Monitoring school quality: An indicators report 2000* (NCES 2001–030). Washington, DC: U.S. Department of Education, National Center for Educational Statistics.

Mayer, S. E. (1997). *What money can't buy: Family income and children's life chances*. Cambridge, MA: Harvard University Press.

Meyer, S. G. (2000). *As long as they don't move next door: Segregation and racial conflict in America's neighborhoods*. Lanham, MD: Rowman & Littlefield.

Newman, K. S. (1999). *No shame in my game: The working poor in the inner city*. New York: Alfred A. Knopf/Russell Sage Foundation.

Oakes, J., & Saunders, M. (2004). Education's most basic tools: Access to textbooks and instructional materials in California's public schools. *Teachers College Record, 106*(10), 1967–1988.

Oliver, M. L., & Shapiro, T. M. (1995). *Black wealth/white wealth: A new perspective on racial inequality*. New York: Routledge.

Orfield, G., & Eaton, S. E. (1997). *Dismantling desegregation: The quiet reversal of Brown v. board of education*. New York: New Press.

Orfield, G., & Yun, J. T. (1999). *Resegregation in American schools*. Cambridge, MA: Civil Rights Project, Harvard University.

Pagani, L., Boulerice, B., & Tremblay, R. E. (1997). The influence of poverty on children's classroom placement and behavior problems. In G. J. Duncan & J. Brooks-Gunn (Eds.), *Consequences of growing up poor* (pp. 311–339). New York: Russell Sage Foundation.

Proctor, B. D., & Dalaker, J. (2003). *Poverty in the United States: 2002*. Washington, DC: U.S. Government Printing Office.

Rank, M. R. (2004). *One nation, underprivileged: Why American poverty affects us all*. New York: Oxford University Press.

Shapiro, T. M. (2004). *The hidden cost of being African American: How wealth perpetuates inequality*. New York: Oxford University Press.

Shapiro, T. M., & Johnson, H. B. (2005). Race, assets, and choosing schools: Current school choices and the future of vouchers. In A. S. Wells & J. Petrovich (Eds.), *Bringing equity back: Research for a new era in American educational policy* (pp. 244–262). New York: Teachers College Press.

Shipler, D. K. (1997). *A country of strangers: Blacks and whites in America*. New York: Alfred A. Knopf.

Shipler, D. K. (2004). *The working poor: Invisible in America*. New York: Alfred A. Knopf.

Steinhorn, L., & Diggs-Brown, B. (1999). *By the color of our skins: The illusion of integration and the reality of race*. New York: Penguin.

Thernstrom, A., & Thernstrom, S. (2003). *No excuses: Closing the racial gap in learning*. New York: Simon & Schuster.

U.S. Department of Education and National Center for Educational Statistics. (2004). *The condition of education 2004*. Washington, DC: U.S. Government Printing Office.

Warren, E., & Tyagi, A. W. (2003). *The two-income trap: Why middle-class parents are going broke*. New York: Perseus.

Wells, A. S. (1995). Reexamining social science research on school desegregation: Long- versus short-term effects. *Teachers College Record, 96*(4), 691–706.

Yinger, J. (1995). *Closed doors, opportunities lost: The continuing costs of housing discrimination*. New York: Russell Sage Foundation.

TRACKING IN MATHEMATICS AND SCIENCE

Courses and Course Selection Procedures

Joan Z. Spade, Lynn Columba, and Beth E. Vanfossen

This reading examines the courses offered and the procedures in place at six different high schools located in working-class, middle-class, and affluent communities in one state. The high schools described in this research were carefully selected to represent schools that had records of achievement in mathematics and science well above what could be expected for the social class of their community and backgrounds of the students, as well as schools that had average records. The reading compares these "excellent" schools to their average counterparts and examines differences across social-class communities. "Excellent" is used cautiously here; these schools were chosen because of their performance on statewide examinations in mathematics and science and are defined as excellent only within the context of this study. Not included in this excerpt is the detailed discussion of how tests are used to place students in high school classes. Such tests and extensive evaluation measures are used primarily in affluent communities as a way of justifying placement against potential parental objections, but not in working-class communities in which outstanding students could be targeted and encouraged. This reading illustrates the multitude of ways students are tracked and placed in curricula that ultimately determine their future work opportunities.

Questions to consider for this reading:

1. How does the pattern of course offerings affect student achievement?

2. What differences did these researchers find in course offerings and course placement procedures across the six schools they studied?

3. What reasons can you give for why they found these patterns across social-class communities?

For many years, researchers have argued that tracking in high schools contributes to stratification and status maintenance (Alexander, Cook, & McDill, 1978; Hauser, Sewell, & Alwin, 1976; Heyns, 1974; Oakes, 1986; Rosenbaum, 1976; Vanfossen, Jones, & Spade, 1987). They noted that small initial differences in students' achievement, derived mainly from differences in social-class background, become accentuated over time through a continuing process of organizational selection (McPartland & McDill, 1982). Whereas earlier research focused almost entirely on the effects of tracking on students, attention has shifted to an examination of

From "Tracking in Mathematics and Science: Courses and Course Selection Procedures," by J. Z. Spade, L. Columba, and B. E. Vanfossen, 1997, *Sociology of Education, 70*(2), pp. 108–127. Copyright 1997 by the American Sociological Association. Reprinted with permission.

how tracking is nested in the organizational structure of schools (Garet & DeLany, 1988; Hallinan, 1991; Kilgore, 1991; Oakes, 1990; Riehl, Natriello, & Pallas, 1992; Useem, 1992a). More recent studies focused on how organizational characteristics of schools define the social context for teaching and learning, funneling students of similar backgrounds into a hierarchy of tracks, programs, and schools that are associated with different learning environments.

Many researchers found that the availability of diverse course offerings and procedures used by counselors, teachers, and schools to place students in courses is important in linking students to different opportunity structures (cf. Garet & DeLany, 1988; Kilgore, 1991; Oakes, 1985, 1990; Riehl et al., 1992; Stevenson, Schiller, & Schneider, 1992; Useem, 1992a). Also important are differences rooted in the social-class backgrounds of the students who attend the schools. Unfortunately, much of the research looked at individual students, rather than school organization. Thus, researchers focused less on organizational differences among schools of various social-class compositions than on differences among students of different social-class backgrounds. Although enrollments in courses and course-placement procedures are related to the distribution of social classes in particular school districts (Garet & DeLany, 1988; Monk & Haller, 1993; Oakes, 1990), there is nevertheless a need for more systematic comparisons and analyses of the organization of curriculum in schools across different social-class communities.

In this article, we explore how social class interacts with the organization of curriculum by examining course offerings and placement procedures in six high schools, carefully selected from all high schools in one state to represent average and excellent achievement in mathematics and science in working-class, middle-class, and affluent communities. In doing so, we present a detailed analysis of how the organization of schooling across social-class communities exerts indirect control over the tracking of students, both via the course options available and the mechanisms that place students in classes.

LITERATURE REVIEW

Oakes (1986) argued that curriculum tracking reinforces social class by providing differential opportunities to students. Students from middle- and upper-class backgrounds are typically found in a track where they are exposed to "high-status" content (including science, mathematics, and foreign languages), while students from working-class backgrounds are often placed in the lower-track, where they are presented with a sharply limited range of topics and skills. Oakes (1985) carefully documented differences in the content presented, use of time, quality of instruction, classroom climate, and students' attitudes in different tracks. Because the curriculum for the lowest track is aimed at getting students to pass minimum-competency examinations, lower-track students have neither the opportunity nor the credentials to develop higher-order knowledge and skills (Darling-Hammond & Wise, 1985).

Tracking is often referred to as the placement of students in courses of similar levels across disciplines. In our research, however, we focus more on the practice of offering courses at different levels of difficulty within subject areas. Powell, Farrar, and Cohen (1985) defined this practice as the "vertical curriculum." In theory, the vertical curriculum allows students to take a mathematics course at one level and a science course at a different level or to switch back and forth between levels of difficulty from one year to the next (Garet & DeLany, 1988).

Garet and DeLany (1988) argued that the placement of students in courses is the result of a twofold process in which courses are created and then students are matched with courses. Others have suggested that a variety of school policy decisions influence which courses are offered and that there are considerable differences across schools (Riehl et al., 1992; Stevenson et al., 1992; Useem, 1992a). Differences in the patterning of vertical curriculum have been found both in the flexibility or rigidity of course sequencing and the range of course offerings available to students (Hallinan, 1991; Powell et al., 1985; Rosenbaum, 1976).

RANGE OF COURSE OFFERINGS

Unless a sufficient range of courses is offered, students cannot be encouraged to take courses at different levels or to move up to higher levels of study. Thus, decisions about the organization of curriculum can truncate or encourage further study (Useem, 1992a). Many factors intercede in the processes by which course offerings are determined. Organizational demands and intraschool politics are just as likely to shape course offerings as are the ability levels of students (Finley, 1984; Hallinan, 1992; Kilgore, 1991; Sanders, 1990). Students' social class and the social class of their communities also influence students' and administrators' expectations of what courses are preferred (Garet & DeLany, 1988; Oakes, 1990; Sanders, 1990; Useem, 1992a; Vanfossen et al., 1987). Yet, schools vary considerably in the way they pattern the curriculum, even within the same social-class communities. Useem (1992a) found differences in the policies adopted by schools in middle- and upper-class communities. The net effect of these differences was that some schools exclude students from higher-level courses and other schools promote such study.

COURSE PLACEMENT

Besides the opportunities offered or denied by the range of courses offered, schools also effect learning via the criteria and processes they use to place students in courses. Although tracking in high schools reflects students' orientation and ability to a certain extent (Alexander & Cook, 1982), we cannot ignore the correlation of track placement with the social class of students (Oakes, 1990; Vanfossen et al., 1987). Students are shuffled into different levels of the curriculum as early as kindergarten on the basis of extraneous, class-based characteristics, such as physical appearance (including cleanliness and the condition of their clothes), interpersonal behavior, use of language in the classroom, and parental influence (Bourdieu & Passeron, 1977; Lareau, 1989; Rist, 1970). By the time a student reaches high school, many social and interpersonal forces converge to make it appear that the process of course selection is based on personal choice. However, the procedures schools use to help students choose courses are a critical part of the puzzle in understanding students' achievement (Rosenbaum, 1976).

Most schools include parents and students in placement decisions. However, parents' and students' actual influence on the selection of courses varies, with some of this variation again linked to social class (Baker & Stevenson, 1986; Gamoran, 1990; Useem, 1992b). Gamoran (1990) found that schools in higher social-class districts emphasized testing and competition within schools in their course-placement decisions. Whereas Gamoran viewed testing as more equitable than parental influence in making placement decisions, others have argued that an emphasis on test scores excludes students from advanced classes by denying them the opportunity to enter the "fast track" (Oakes, 1985; Useem, 1992a).

Our study examined both the types of courses offered to assess the number of options available to students, as well as how students are placed in classes, by studying course-placement decisions and the criteria used to make those decisions in "excellent" and "average" schools across social-class communities. We addressed the following questions:

1. How do school policies and practices affect what courses students take?

2. Does the social-class composition of the district affect what courses students are offered, as well as the policies and procedures used to place students in courses?

3. Do excellent schools offer a different menu of courses and guide their students into courses differently from average schools?

. . .

RESULTS

The Structure of Curriculum

As earlier research indicated, college-preparatory and advanced honor courses differ in substantial ways from general or remedial courses.

In particular, college-preparatory courses cover more material, in more depth, and with more assigned homework and laboratory work, than do non-college-preparatory courses. Thus, the availability of courses is important in explaining differential access to learning opportunities and will affect the academic outcomes of the student body.

College-Preparatory Courses

An analysis of Tables 33.1 and 33.2 identifies a range of mathematics and science courses offered in the six schools and permits two important generalizations: (1) the number of advanced courses offered in both mathematics and science increases with the social class of the school and (2) excellent working- and middle-class schools offer one or two more advanced courses in their area of excellence than do the average schools of the same social class.

The effect of social class on course offerings is seen in the range of higher-level courses offered by affluent schools in this study. The higher the social class of the district, the greater the diversity in the college-preparatory or advanced courses offered in the schools. For example, both working-class schools had only one college-level advanced-placement (AP) course and four honors courses. In contrast, both schools in affluent districts offered six to seven accelerated, honors, or AP courses in both mathematics and science.

Patterns of course offerings also varied across excellent and average schools, particularly in the working-class schools. The working-average school offered no accelerated, honors, or AP courses in either mathematics or science, whereas the working-excellent school offered four honors courses in science (its area of excellence) and one AP course in mathematics. The orientation of these schools is reflected in the responses of the heads of the science departments of the working-excellent school and the working-average school, respectively, to the interviewers' question, "Next, would you describe the advanced science courses which are offered?"

Head of working-excellent science department: "We originally were concerned that those students who were above average in ability, interest, and motivation were not getting the science course they

deserved or needed from a regular Regents class. So, we created the E-program. These students are sometimes gifted and talented in the technical sense of that term. They are almost always above their peers in terms of IQ scores, DAT scores, CTBS scores. They are the kinds of students who can relate what's going on in science to something they heard in social studies, to a novel they've read, to something they've heard on the news. They see the connection to a lot of different areas. They've got inquiring, creative minds. They'll have questions that are just incredible."

Head of working-average science department: "We have no advanced placement. We have three courses that might be considered, well four, chemistry, physics, they are usually the top kids in our school. Then we have a problems and research class, which is for a few select kids, and then there is on the books, an advanced biology class that has not met in two years."

Differences in course offerings at the higher levels were less clear in the middle-class and affluent schools. Both the middle-excellent and middle-average schools offered one AP mathematics course, but the middle-excellent school had more college-preparatory courses in mathematics (its area of excellence). In science, the middle-excellent school offered one more course at both the college-preparatory and AP levels, the middle-average school offered one honors course, and the middle-excellent school offered none. In the affluent schools, the number of AP, honors, and accelerated courses was almost identical for both mathematics and science. Unlike the pattern in the middle-class schools, the affluent-average school offered more college preparatory courses in both mathematics and science than did the affluent-excellent school.

Non-College-Preparatory Courses

An examination of Tables 33.1 and 33.2 suggests that (1) variation in the social-class composition of the student body does not appear to have had a marked effect on the diversity of general and basic courses offered and (2) the excellent middle-class and affluent schools offered fewer non-college-preparatory courses in their areas of excellence.

Table 33.1 Range of Mathematics Courses Offered in the Six Schools

School	College Preparatory AP	General Honors	Basic or Accelerated	Regents	Non-Regents	Remedial
Working-Class Average						
9th grade	—	—	—	1	2	.5[b]
10th grade	—	—	—	1	1.5[b]	—
11th grade	—	—	—	1	1	—
12th grade	—	—	—	2[b]	1[c]	—
Working-Class Excellent						
9th grade	—	—	—	1	1	1
10th grade	—	—	—	2[d]	1	1
11th grade	—	—	—	1	1	—
12th grade	1	—	—	1[b]	—	—
Middle-Class Average						
9th grade	—	—	—	1	1	1
10th grade	—	—	—	1	2	—
11th grade	—	—	—	1	1	—
12th grade	1	—	—	—	—	—
Middle-Class Excellent						
9th grade	—	—	—	1.5[b]	1	—
10th grade	—	—	—	2	—	—
11th grade	—	—	—	1	—	—
12th grade	1	—	—	1[b]	—	—
Affluent Average						
9th grade	—	1	1	1	1	1
10th grade	—	1	—	1[e]	1	—
11th grade	—	1	—	2	1	—
12th grade	1	1	—	1	1	—
Affluent Excellent						
9th grade	—	1	1[b]	1	1	1
10th grade	—	1[b]	1[b]	1	1	—
11th grade	—	1	1	1	1	—
12th grade	2	—	—	1[b]	1[b]	—

Note.

a. The school's class schedules and descriptions of courses prepared for students, as well as interviews with department heads and teachers, were used to formulate this table. The table indicates the yearly equivalent of unique courses taught at this level.

b. The number includes at least one one-semester (half-year) course.

c. This course has not been taught for a number of years because of low enrollments.

d. One of these courses can be taken for Regents credit or not, depending on the student's preference.

e. In addition, a 10-week course in PSAT/SAT mathematics is offered.

Table 33.2   Range of Science Courses Offered in the Six Schools

School	College Preparatory AP	General Honors	Basic or Regents	Non-Regents	Remedial
Working-Class Average					
9th grade	—	—	2	1	—
10th grade	—	—	2[a]	1	—
11th grade	—	—	2.5[b]	1	—
12th grade	—	—	1	—	—
Working-Class Excellent					
9th grade	—	1	1	1	—
10th grade	—	1	1	1.5[b]	—
11th grade	—	1	1	1.5[b]	—
12th grade	—	1	2.5[b]	—	—
Middle-Class Average					
9th grade	—	—	1	1	—
10th grade	—	—	1	1	—
11th grade	—	—	1	1	1
12th grade	1	1	—	1	—
Middle-Class Excellent					
9th grade	—	—	1	1	—
10th grade	—	—	1	1	1
11th grade	—	—	1	1	—
12th grade	2	—	1	1	—
Affluent Average					
9th grade	—	1	2	3	—
10th grade	—	1	2	2[b]	—
11th grade	—	2[c]	1	1.5[b]	—
12th grade	2	.5[b]	2	1	—
Affluent Excellent					
9th grade	—	1	1	1	—
10th grade	—	1	1	1	—
11th grade	—	1	1	2	—
12th grade	3	—	1	1	—

Note.

a. In addition to a Regents biology class, two half-year courses in environment science are offered to students with either a Regents or non-Regents background.

b. This number includes at least one one-semester (half-year) course.

c. One of these courses is listed as advanced biology, with the prerequisite of Honors or Regents biology.

Course sequencing in science is not as apparent as in mathematics. Therefore, unless otherwise specified, we used a general guideline that includes earth science as 9th grade, biology as 10th grade, chemistry as 11th grade, and physics as 12th grade.

Most of the schools in the sample offered three to five general and basic courses in mathematics and science, regardless of the range of higher-level courses they offered. However, a comparison of the offerings of excellent and average schools in the same social-class category indicated that there were some differences. The middle-excellent school offered almost all its mathematics courses (its area of excellence) at the college-preparatory level, while two-thirds of the middle-average school's offerings were at the general or basic level. Several teachers in the middle-excellent school believed that all students should take mathematics at the Regents level. The pattern for science courses in the two schools in the affluent districts was similar; the average school offered more general science courses than did the excellent school.

The working-class schools did not follow this pattern. The working-excellent school offered one more general, non-Regents course in science (its area of excellence) than did the working-average school. Because it offered more courses across the spectrum of science, the working-excellent school might have been able to encourage students to study science and to keep students interested in the subject. In contrast, in mathematics, the working-average school offered one more general mathematics course than did the working-excellent school.

Course Enrollments

Course offerings alone do not indicate how learning opportunities are distributed. Whether students actually enroll in the courses offered is even more important. We used two different types of data to examine how students were distributed across the curriculum—estimates of enrollments given during interviews and data on enrollments furnished by the department heads. The combination of these two sources gave us a sense of the enrollment patterns in 11th-grade mathematics and science courses at the six schools when neither subject was required.

We found that the lowest social-class districts and the average schools were less successful in getting students to enroll in 11th-grade mathematics

and science courses. Less than half the 11th graders in the working-class schools enrolled in these courses, compared to from 60 percent to more than 100 percent of those in the middle-class and affluent schools. . . .

To summarize, we found that both social class and excellence of school interacted to affect the diversity of course selections in the schools in our study. In higher social-class districts, schools offered a broader selection of courses. The differences in course offerings were particularly apparent when we compared the schools in affluent communities to the others in our sample. However, at all social-class levels, the excellent schools offered a wider array of courses than did the average schools. The working- and middle-class excellent schools offered more courses for college-bound students, and the working-excellent school offered more courses at the general or basic level in its area of excellence. It is interesting to note that these differences in curricular patterns occurred in a state that prescribes the curriculum both formally, through carefully developed course outlines and materials, and informally, through statewide examinations.

However, offering courses in the course catalog did not always mean that the classes would actually be taught. For example, the working-average school had an impressive array of mathematics courses for non-college-bound students, but the 12th-grade course was not taught because of the students' lack of interest in it. The affluent-average school was considering dropping its 9th grade general science course, AP biology, and mathematics sequence for gifted students because of low enrollments. Also, the affluent-average school offered just as many courses as did the affluent-excellent school, but the number of enrollments in these courses in the 11th grade fell well below the enrollments at the affluent-excellent school and the middle-class schools in our study. Although both schools in the affluent districts have the resources to offer a variety of courses, the affluent-average school was not as successful in getting students to enroll in these courses. Therefore, it is important to understand not only what courses are offered, but the procedures used to assign students to classes.

Placement in Courses

Procedures for placing students in courses can range from a minimalist laissez-faire approach, in which students and parents are the main selectors, to an extensive selection program involving teachers and counselors, as well as students and parents, in an elaborate system of testing, recommendations, and counseling, designed to distribute students on the basis of multiple criteria.

We found that all schools formally included parents and students in the course-selection process. Common practices across the schools included orientation meetings held when students entered the school and forms sent home for parents to indicate approval of the courses selected for the coming year. The guidance counselors in all the schools also met with the students and directed their selection of courses. However, excellent schools and those higher in social class differed in the degree to which decisions were relegated to parents, the roles of the guidance counselors and teachers, and the reliance on tests and objective indicators to guide placements. . . .

In conclusion, the procedures used to place students in courses varied somewhat across the six schools we studied. School personnel in working-class communities were less active in the selection process, and more emphasis was placed on parents' and students' choices in course-placement decisions. In contrast, counselors and teachers in the middle- and upper-class communities are more central in the process, both in the use of objective measures and in how actively they were involved. Although the differences between average and excellent schools are more subtle, the excellent schools were more likely than the average schools to influence students' course decisions by relying on objective measures and having more formal advisory procedures.

Parents and students in the working-class and average schools appeared to be making course decisions with less guidance from teachers as well as counselors. We call this situation laissez-faire decision making, and it is characterized by statements such as "Parents and students decide courses and programs" (the working-average school) or "The family has the right to choose the courses they

wish [the student] to take" (middle-average school). The administrators and teachers in schools that seem to be doing the best job in educating students in mathematics and science took more active and systematic roles in placing students in courses. In these schools, the teachers did not "politick" or randomly recruit to get students in higher-level courses. Instead, the teachers and counselors talked with the students about the courses they should be taking and used students' own records in framing their recommendations. All staff in the excellent schools spent more time counseling students. Although the guidance departments had more influence in schools in higher social-class communities, all staff in the excellent schools tended to consider their role to be critical in course-placement decisions. This tendency is clear when the two schools in the affluent communities are compared. While both schools emphasized teachers' recommendations, the teachers appeared to take these recommendations more seriously in the affluent-excellent school. In fact, the middle-excellent and affluent-excellent schools were the only schools in which the staff indicated that they ignored or denied parents' requests for courses.

The criteria used in the procedures to place students in courses are an important component in determining students' academic trajectories (Oakes, 1985; Rosenbaum, 1976; Useem, 1992b). Our analyses of the procedures associated with course placement suggest that both scores on standardized tests and teachers' recommendations are used differently across schools in different social-class communities. A laissez-faire policy in higher social-class districts may increase students' opportunities to enroll in higher-level courses (Useem, 1992b), but not in working-class schools, where the backgrounds and experiences of parents often do not provide the information necessary to assess their children's potential in the school system. Consequently, parents in working-class schools are less likely to become involved in school decisions (for similar conclusions, see Baker & Stevenson, 1986; Lareau, 1989; Useem, 1992b). If guidance is not provided by counselors and teachers, working-class students and parents will be left on their own.

CONCLUSION

Evidence of structural differences in learning opportunities existed in all the schools in the form of hierarchical levels of courses offered in mathematics and science (the vertical curriculum), as well as in the patterns of placing students in those courses. Although curricular tracking was set into motion long before students entered high school via previous course placement and exposure to different learning opportunities, the organization of the schools we studied differed in the ways they structured opportunities to take higher-level courses. We found an interaction between course offerings and procedures for placing students in courses that was driven by both students' desires and administrative decisions (cf. Riehl et al., 1992).

Schools in higher social-class communities offer more advanced classes, reflecting both higher financial resources and expectations in the community. Furthermore, the social class of districts is related to the intensity of counseling activities around course selection, the use of standardized tests in making decisions on students' programs, and the greater number of advanced classes that are offered. Although there are clear differences in per-pupil expenditures among these schools, financial advantage does not automatically benefit a district. The best performer in this study was the affluent-excellent school, which operated with $600 less per pupil than did the affluent-average school. In our interviews at the affluent-excellent school, the science teachers complained of inadequate laboratory supplies and said that they repaired laboratory equipment themselves at the same time that they bragged about how many students worked into the evening on science projects and the number of Westinghouse Scholars (a prestigious science award for high school students) that they had at their school. This school's excellence clearly reflected more than additional financial support.

The financial and cultural resources in the community in which the working-excellent school was located were decidedly low; most of the children came from poor, rural families, and some were children of migrant farm-workers. Yet, this school used its resources within the school, with teachers and counselors encouraging students to take more difficult courses because knowledge of science is important in their lives.

Therefore, although we found that the organization of schooling reflects the social class of the communities in which schools exist, schools can improve learning by offering more demanding classes and channeling students into higher-level courses. For the schools in this country that continue to struggle with fewer monetary resources and less cultural capital, our findings show that there are still things they can do to change the organization of schooling and improve students' performance.

Although only six suburban-rural schools were examined, this research provided for a more systematic analysis of social-class differences than have other case studies. We found, as did Monk and Haller (1993), that the social-class composition of communities accounts for considerable differences in curricular offerings. The broadest array of course offerings and most elaborate course-placement procedures are in the mid-sized schools in the affluent communities—not, as may be expected, in the largest school (in the middle-class community). These findings suggest that one should use caution when drawing conclusions about school structure without considering the social-class composition of the community. Further research is needed to examine whether the relationships between the social-class composition of communities and structural characteristics of schools apply to urban schools as well as to suburban-rural schools and to analyze the interaction of race and social class.

Course taking is the most powerful factor affecting students' achievement that is under the school's control. In this study, excellent schools and schools in higher social-class districts offered the broadest assortment of courses in mathematics and science, including more college-preparatory classes. Our findings suggest that administrators, especially those in schools in working-class communities, should focus on expanding the number of courses, particularly honors courses, that are offered (cf. National Council of Teachers of

Mathematics, 1989). They also indicate that to encourage additional study, schools must offer an array of courses, rather than terminal courses in the first or second years of high school (Secada, 1990).

Although schools cannot do much about the social class of the students who attend them, they can do something about the patterning of courses and the procedures used to place students in classes. The very fact that we found subject specific differences in our analyses indicates that schools' course offerings and placement policies can make a difference in encouraging students to study particular subjects. Our findings suggest that schools can influence the achievement of students, even when the social-class origins of the students they serve may not be conducive to achievement, by restructuring the patterning of classes and facilitating the placement of students in more challenging courses.

REFERENCES

Alexander, K. L., & Cook, M. A. (1982). Curricula and coursework: A surprise ending to a familiar story. *American Sociological Review, 47*(5), 626–640.

Alexander, K. L., Cook, M., & McDill, E. L. (1978). Curriculum tracking and educational stratification: Some further evidence. *American Sociological Review, 43*(1), 47–66.

Baker, D. P., & Stevenson, D. L. (1986). Mothers' strategies for children's school achievement: Managing the transition to high school. *Sociology of Education, 59*(3), 156–166.

Bourdieu, P., & Passeron, J. C. (1977). *Reproduction in education, society, and culture.* Beverly Hills, CA: Sage.

Darling-Hammond, L., & Wise, A. E. (1985). Beyond standardization: State standards and school improvement. *Elementary School Journal, 85*(3), 315–336.

Finley, M. K. (1984). Teachers and tracking in a comprehensive high school. *Sociology of Education, 57*(4), 233–243.

Gamoran, A. (1990, August). *Access to excellence: Assignment to honors English classes in the transition from middle to high school.* Paper presented at the annual meeting of The American Sociological Association, Washington, DC.

Garet, M. S., & DeLany, B. (1988). Students, courses, and stratification. *Sociology of Education, 61*(2), 61–77.

Hallinan, M. T. (1991). School differences in tracking structures and track assignments. *Journal of Research on Adolescence, 1*(3), 251–275.

Hallinan, M. T. (1992). The organization of students for instruction in middle school. *Sociology of Education, 65*(2), 114–127.

Hauser, R. M., Sewell, W. H., & Alwin, D. F. (1976). High school effects on achievement. In W. H. Sewell, R. M. Hauser, & D. L. Featherman (Eds.), *Schooling and achievement in American society* (pp. 309–341). New York: Academic Press.

Heyns, B. (1974). Social selection and stratification within schools. *American Journal of Sociology, 79,* 1434–1451.

Kilgore, S. B. (1991). The organizational context of tracking in schools. *American Sociological Review, 56*(2), 189–203.

Lareau, A. (1989). *Home advantage.* Philadelphia: Falmer Press.

McPartland, J. M., & McDill, E. L. (1982). Control and differentiation in the structure of American education. *Sociology of Education, 55,* 77–88.

Monk, D. H., & Haller, E. J. (1993). Predictors of high school academic course offerings: The role of school size. *American Educational Research Journal, 30*(1), 3–21.

National Council of Teachers of Mathematics, Commission on Standards for School Mathematics. (1989). *Curriculum and evaluation standards for school mathematics.* Reston, VA: Author.

Oakes, J. (1985). *Keeping track: How schools structure inequality.* New Haven, CT: Yale University Press.

Oakes, J. (1986). Tracking, inequality, and the rhetoric of reform: Why schools don't change. *Journal of Education, 168*(1), 60–80.

Oakes, J. (1990). *Multiplying inequalities: The effects of race, social class, and tracking on opportunities to learn math and science.* Santa Monica, CA: RAND.

Powell, A. G., Farrar, E., & Cohen, D. K. (1985). *The shopping mall high school: Winners and losers in the academic market place.* Boston, MA: Houghton Mifflin.

Riehl, C., Natriello, G., & Pallas, A. M. (1992, August). *Losing track: The dynamics of student assignment processes in high school.* Paper presented at the annual meeting of The American Sociological Association, Pittsburgh.

Rist, R. C. (1970). Student social class and teacher expectations: The self-fulfilling prophecy in ghetto education. *Harvard Educational Review, 40,* 411–451.

Rosenbaum, J. E. (1976). *Making inequality: The hidden curriculum of high school tracking.* New York: John Wiley & Sons.

Sanders, N. M. (1990, April). *Tracking and organizational structure.* Paper presented at the annual meeting of the American Educational Research Association, Boston.

Secada, W. G. (1990). The challenges of a changing world for mathematics education. In T. J. Cooney & C. R. Hirsch (Eds.), *Teaching and learning mathematics in the 1990s: The 1990 yearbook,* *National Council of Teachers of Mathematics* (pp. 135–143). Reston, VA: National Council of Teachers of Mathematics.

Stevenson, D. L., Schiller, K., & Schneider, B. (1992, August). *Sequences of opportunities for learning mathematics and science.* Paper presented at the annual meeting of The American Sociological Association, Pittsburgh.

Useem, E. L. (1992a). Getting on the fast track in mathematics: School organizational influences on math track assignment. *American Journal of Education, 100*(3), 325–353.

Useem, E. L. (1992b). Middle schools and math groups: Parents' involvement in children's placement. *Sociology of Education, 65*(4), 263–292.

Vanfossen, B. E., Jones, J. D., & Spade, J. Z. (1987). Curriculum tracking and status maintenance. *Sociology of Education, 60*(2), 104–122.

"TUCK IN THAT SHIRT!"

Race, Class, Gender, and Discipline in an Urban School

Edward W. Morris

Using theoretical and methodological frameworks similar to Lareau and Horvat in Chapter 2, Edward W. Morris describes findings from an ethnographic study of a middle school located in a large Texas city. For more than two years, he studied this school, which included six months of regular visits. He describes the interaction between students and teachers over the school's dress code. Race, gender, and social class all intersect to create very different approaches by school personnel to student behaviors.

Questions to consider for this reading:

1. What motivates teachers to discipline children? Are the assumptions driving their motivations accurate?

2. How is the discipline received by girls different from that of boys? Why is race or ethnicity less salient for teachers when making decisions about girls' behavior?

3. Considering your own educational experiences, what do you find most surprising in this reading?

Virtually every day that I conducted research at Matthews Middle School,[1] a predominately minority, urban school, I heard an adult admonishing a student, "Tuck in that shirt!" The prevalence of this phrase represents the connections among dress, behavior, and discipline that composed a primary but unofficial emphasis at the school. In this article I incorporate the theoretical concepts of cultural capital and bodily discipline to analyze this concern with student dress and comportment. I show how educators identified students deemed deficient in cultural capital, especially regarding manners and dress, and attempted to reform these perceived deficiencies through regulating their bodies. This process differed by race, class, and gender as interconnected, rather than distinct, concepts. Perceptions of race, class, and gender guided educators' assumptions of which students lacked cultural capital and which students required disciplinary reform. Although many school officials viewed this discipline as a way of teaching valuable social skills, it appeared instead to reinforce race, class, and gender stereotypes and had the potential to alienate many students from schooling. . . .

FINDINGS

The Importance of Dress at Matthews

Matthews was a public school but required students to wear uniforms based on the school colors—navy blue, red, or white shirts, and navy blue or khaki shorts or pants. Girls could wear navy blue or khaki skirts or skorts (half skirt, half shorts) that fell below the knee. Most sneakers and dress shoes were allowed, except sandals and boots. The school expected students to have their shirts tucked in at all times. According to teachers, the movement for uniforms at Matthews began about eight years before I started my fieldwork. Teachers told me that this was a collaborative effort between parents and the school, and the few parents I spoke with supported the uniforms. Similar to many urban schools, the uniform dress code at Matthews was intended to decrease gang activity (to rid the school of the "flying colors," according to one teacher) and make student poverty less visible. The regulation of the dress code, however, was a constant source of conflict between teachers and students.

Teachers' profound interest in instilling discipline through dress was reflected in their nearly ubiquitous calls to "tuck in that shirt!" This phrase is peppered throughout my field notes, and although adherence to the dress code was not an initial concern of my study, I soon found it emblematic of the school's exhaustive focus on bodily discipline. According to the principal, a survey of teachers conducted by the school just before I arrived found that dress code violations and discipline problems were among the top issues teachers wanted improved. Indeed, like other urban schools that require uniforms, teachers and administrators at Matthews linked the dress code to student discipline and order in general (Stanley, 1996). The school sent an information sheet titled "Standard Mode of Dress" to each student's home. This document states that the purpose of the dress code is to "ensure a safe learning environment" and "promote a climate of effective discipline that does not distract from the educational process." It describes the dress code and emphasizes in bold print that "baggy and over-sized clothing *will not* be allowed" (original emphasis). Students who deviated from this code, typically those who did not tuck in their shirts, were often spotted by adults and disciplined into compliance.

For many of the educators at the school, policing the dress code extended to an emphasis on teaching students how to dress "well." Many even coupled this interest with genuine, caring concern for student upward mobility in this working-class context. For example, the school held what it called a "dress for success" day, when students were invited to dress as one might for the "business world." Also, many teachers encouraged their students to dress up when giving a presentation in class, and teachers at the school were expected to dress up (often suits and ties for men and dresses and nylons for women), lending a tone of formality to the school. Matthews devoted entire assemblies to instructing students on how to dress properly. . . .

Thus, beyond the uniforms, the school sought to discipline the kids[2] into wearing clothing considered appropriate on nonuniform school days and events. This discipline served as part of a hidden curriculum, emphasizing strict regulation of dress for working-class students whom adults thought did not possess knowledge of "appropriate" manners and clothing. . . . I also observed other school officials, all of them African American women, critiquing girls (who were almost always African American as well), for wearing "hoochie-mama" clothing. These adults appeared to identify the styles of black girls in particular as overly sexual and sought to reform them (see also Collins, 1990, 1998).

However, concerns over clothing and appearance were not just directed toward girls. Adults also feared that boys, especially black and Hispanic boys, might wear something considered inappropriate to formal events, such as over-sized pants that sagged below the waist. Several African American men and women at the school encouraged boys to dress like "gentlemen," even giving some practical advice such as not wearing white socks with a suit. In this sense, these boys appeared to educators to display "marginalized masculinities," interpreted as overly coarse and aggressive (Connell, 1995). Educators aimed to reform these styles and behaviors into what were perceived to be mainstream masculine forms. School officials viewed the gendered prescription of dress for both girls and boys as a central part of teaching the students appropriate manners. In this process, they distinguished "street" styles, which they deemed brash, from "appropriate," conservative styles of dress and behavior.

Many adults at Matthews saw making students adhere to the dress code and use proper manners as a way to provide them with social skills, including those needed for future employment. This concern is interesting, because research on cultural capital has rarely examined public institutions that attempt to transmit such cultural skills. . . .

Many adults thought that teaching students "the rules" of dress and manners, including adherence to the dress code, was an important way to prepare students for future success. School officials viewed their discipline of students' bodies, especially in appropriately masculine and feminine ways, as transmitting cultural capital—modeling the type of dress and conduct that could be linked to upward mobility.[3]

However, school officials did not appear concerned with the dress and manners of all students in the same way. Disciplinary action differed according to how perceptions of race and class interacted with perceptions of masculinity and femininity. In my observations, disciplinary focus at Matthews took three general forms, which I discuss in detail below. First, educators were concerned with "ladylike" behavior and dress, especially for African American girls. Second, educators were concerned with threatening and oppositional behavior and dress, especially for African American and Latino boys (because Ferguson [2000] has already provided an in-depth account of the disciplinary experiences of African American boys, I focus on the discipline directed at Latino boys below). Third,

many school officials assumed that some students, especially white and Asian American students, required little guidance or discipline in their behavior and dress. Fourth, I consider how these disciplinary patterns may have provoked alienation and resistance from many of the students targeted for reform.

Acting Like a Young Lady: Race and Perceptions of Femininity

Aside from "Tuck in that shirt!" the most often used phrase that I recorded in my field notes was some variation on "Act like a young lady!" Adults invariably directed this reprimand at African American girls; I never recorded it directed at Latina girls, Asian American girls, or white girls (although members of these groups did receive other reprimands). Adults occasionally instructed boys (primarily black boys) in how to act like "gentlemen," but this was far less common and was never used as a reprimand. Teachers and administrators used the phrase "Act like a young lady" to instruct black girls in how to sit and get up properly, dress appropriately, and speak quietly. . . .

According to my observations, the girls [that] adults thought needed to learn this ladylike behavior tended to be African American. One first-year teacher, a black man named Mr. Neal, told me in a conversation that black girls in particular required instruction in acceptable manners. . . .

Interestingly, however, this concern with the gendered comportment of black girls did not seem to affect teachers' perceptions of them academically. Although black girls were frequently disciplined, they were not viewed as particularly "bad." They were overrepresented in pre–Advanced Placement classes, and teachers frequently described them in "regular" classes as among their best students. In fact, stereotypically masculine behavior, such as the boldness many adults interpreted as "loud," often seemed to benefit black girls in the classroom. As Mr. Wilson, a veteran white teacher, said in describing some of the best students in his class, "The black girls up there I don't worry about, they can fend for themselves—they're loud, but they're a sharp bunch and do their work" (field notes, 10/3/01). Although many adults viewed training girls to "act like young ladies" as putting them on the path to upward mobility, their discipline of black girls seemed to curtail some of the very behaviors that led to success in the classroom. Despite adults' good intentions, this disciplinary pattern could actually serve to solidify racial and gender inequality by restricting the classroom input and involvement of black girls.

Symbolizing Opposition:
Race, Masculinity, and Style

In contrast to girls, adults saw many boys at Matthews as "bad" and occasionally threatening. This was particularly true for Latino and African American boys. In my observations, members of these groups were the most likely to "get in trouble." Unlike that for most girls, this discipline often entailed stern reprimands and referrals to the office for punishment. My findings of the negative disciplinary experiences of African American boys match those of Ferguson (2000). However, I found that school officials at Matthews also considered many *Latino* boys equally if not more dangerous and subjected them to constant surveillance and bodily discipline. The discipline directed at Latino boys was strongly mediated by their presentation of self, however, especially through their choice of clothing, hairstyle, and response to authority (Bettie, 2000; Goffman, 1973; West & Fenstermaker, 1995). Teachers interpreted Hispanic students who projected a "street" persona through their dress and behavior as indifferent to school. Markers of this persona included gang-related dress such as colored shoelaces, colored or marked belts, or a white T-shirt or towel slung over a particular shoulder. However, other markers of this street style were less directly related to gang involvement, such as baggy Dickies brand pants, shaved or slicked-back hair, or refusal to keep the shirt tucked in. Many of these markers appeared instead to reflect a working-class identity.

Latino boys provoked fear in many teachers, especially when the boys were suspected of gang involvement. One white teacher, for example, referred to a group of Hispanic boys she called "gangsters" as "the type that would get back at you" (field notes, 5/13/02). Although many adults and students told me that most kids affiliated with gangs at the school were wannabes rather than full-fledged members, and I never witnessed any gang violence on or near school grounds, teachers viewed any "gang-related" students as potentially dangerous and disciplined them accordingly. Students suspected of being in gangs were almost always Latinos and were monitored closely by adults, especially in terms of their dress. . . .

Although many of the students at Matthews resisted the dress code prescription to tuck in their shirts, it was the resistance of Latinos that was viewed as especially threatening and oppositional. As Mr. Wilson told me, "The gang influence is bad among these Hispanics" (field notes, 10/3/01). Many teachers expressed a similar othering of Latinos, constructing the group as exotic and untrustworthy and connecting them to negative gang activity. . . .

Some Hispanic boys at the school were indeed involved with gangs, including the Crips, and announced this verbally as well as through their bodily displays. But outright gang members constituted only a small percentage of Latino boys at the school. I also knew of Asian boys and Hispanic girls who were involved in gangs, for instance, but teachers did not generalize that these groups of students, defined by race and gender, were dangerous. In addition, many adults viewed Latino boys in general as having the potential for gang involvement or violence, even if they did not openly display gang markers. For example, in another class I observed with Mr. Pham, he reprimanded a Latino boy who was wrestling with another boy. The Latino boy protested, saying he did not think he was hurting the other boy. Mr. Pham told him to stop anyway and added, "One day you're gonna hurt someone and not know it and go to jail." This particular Latino boy did not wear any salient markers of gang affiliation typically used at the school. However,

Mr. Pham still interpreted his actions as overly aggressive and warned that they could one day land him in jail. . . .

However, bodily display, especially clothing choice, had a major influence on how educators viewed and treated Latino boys. The few Latino boys who wore Dockers brand pants and dark sneakers or dress shoes and kept their shirts tucked in signaled to teachers that they were good students. One Hispanic student of this type was named Thomas. Thomas projected a middle-class, "schoolboy" persona through his Dockers pants, tucked-in shirt, and parted hair (see also Ferguson, 2000). Although I heard him called a "little nerd" by some of his classmates, he received positive reactions from teachers in class. Thomas was rambunctious and did have a few referrals to the assistant principal's office. However, these referrals were not for severe and persistent behavior, and teachers did not interpret Thomas's actions as threatening.

Thomas serves as an example of how Latino boys, largely through their dress and manners, could signal to school officials that they were conscientious students and came from middle-class backgrounds. These students paralleled the African American boys that Ferguson (2000) terms "Schoolboys" because of their strict adherence to school rules (in contradistinction to boys considered "Troublemakers"). At Matthews I noticed a similar split between those considered "schoolboys" and "bad boys" among Latino students.[4] I suggest that this dichotomous view stemmed largely from educators' perceptions of social class. Teachers seemed to hold more polarized views of the potential class backgrounds of Latino students than they did for other students. Many told me that the Hispanic students' backgrounds could be relatively wealthy and upwardly mobile or very disadvantaged. A veteran white teacher named Ms. Phillips, for instance, explained in our interview that she thought many of the school's Hispanic students were middle class or at least stable working class and in a better economic situation than most of the white students: "I'm pretty sure most of the white kids who go here live in apartments, and are poor like a lot of the other kids. Now, if you drive through the neighborhood just down from here—the one with all the houses—it's all Hispanic. A lot of the Hispanic families here are home owners."

I found that many Latino students at Matthews actively "performed" (Bettie, 2000) class identity and membership, especially through their dress. A middle-class performance displayed the students' possession of cultural capital in the form of dress and grooming, indicating a middle-class or upwardly mobile background and mitigating the discipline they received. Although Latino boys in general were viewed as potentially problematic, social class-oriented signals, in the form of clothing and manners, could ameliorate the negative perceptions associated with being male and Hispanic. . . .

SELF-DISCIPLINE AND BENIGN RESISTANCE: RACE, CLASS, AND GENDER IN THE PERCEPTION OF ACCEPTABLE BEHAVIOR

Most research employing concepts of cultural capital and bodily discipline has given little attention to how these processes might work for white and Asian students, especially those in predominantly black and Latino urban areas. Matthews had a small minority of white students and a larger minority of Asian American students. I almost never saw these students disciplined in terms of dress or manners, even when I observed clear violations.[5] School officials appeared to view Asian students at the school through the lens of the "model-minority" stereotype of high academic achievement and discipline (see Lee, 1994, 1996). I never saw Asian American girls disciplined for behavior or dress; in many ways these girls exemplified the educators' ideal self-disciplined student. I rarely observed school officials discipline Asian American boys. Behaviors for which adults frequently rebuked African American and Latino boys (e.g., getting out of their seats without permission, being loud) often went unnoticed when engaged in by Asian American boys. Further, some Asian American boys exhibited behavior and dress almost identical to that considered dangerous and gang affiliated when engaged in by Latino boys, but the Asian Americans were still considered good students. . . .

Adults rarely disciplined white girls or boys, although, as was the case for Latinos, this was strongly mediated by race- and class-based performance. Some white students, through their interactive style, choice of clothing, and friendship groups, signaled a type of street persona similar to many other students. This persona incorporated styles of dressing and speaking commonly associated with urban black youth. Although I never saw these white students wear Dickies pants, some wore gold chains outside their shirts, like many of the black and Latino students, and used expressions and spoke in a cadence similar to many black students at the school, what many might call "Black English" or "ebonics" (Labov, 1972). Students affecting this persona tended to receive more disciplinary action than other whites. . . .

IMPACTS OF DISCIPLINARY CONTROL

Several scholars suggest that discipline, especially when harsh and controlling, often engenders resistance and alienation (Ferguson, 2000; Foucault, 1977/1995; McNeil, 1986). When directed at historically marginalized student groups, such discipline may only perpetuate their marginalization and inequality in the educational system. At Matthews, the different ways in which students and teachers interpreted discipline in dress and manners provide insight into how this discipline might actually reproduce educational inequalities.

Although most teachers at Matthews favored strict discipline in dress and manners, a few did not. A white teacher named Ms. Scott, for example, said this when I asked why she thought so many adults insisted on making the students tuck in their shirts: "Because it's an easy battle. You might not be able to get them to sit in their seat and do their work, but you can make them tuck their shirt in. It's an easy way for teachers to assert their authority over the kids and make it

look like they have control" (field notes, 2/1/02). Ms. Scott implied that teachers who did not have enough control over their students to make them do schoolwork could project a facade of control through the regulation of student clothing. Similarly, some teachers I observed also made their students tuck in their shirts before going to lunch while ignoring untucked shirts in their own classrooms. These findings emphasize how important teachers considered the visibility of student compliance with clothing rules and echo Foucault's (1977/1995, p. 187) assertions that "in discipline it is the subjects that have to be seen. Their visibility assures the hold of power that is exercised over them." Students displaying tucked in shirts symbolized and embodied the control and order sought by the school.

In contrast to adults, virtually all the students I talked to at Matthews expressed displeasure with the dress code, especially the policy of keeping shirts tucked in. Most complained that the dress code made them physically uncomfortable and stifled their ability to express creativity. The students most persistently targeted for dress code infractions—black and Latino boys—appeared most resistant to this policy. For example, I tutored Daniel, a Latino boy, on a persuasive paper he was writing against the school's tucked-in shirt policy. I asked him why he thought adults cared so much about this. He replied, "Because they think it makes us look like we're educated." When I asked him why he opposed that, he thought for a while and finally stated, "Because it doesn't matter what you look like to be educated, it's all up here [points to his head]." . . .

Student displeasure with the dress code often translated into resistance. This resistance, especially in the form of untucked shirts and baggy pants worn low on the hips, symbolized defiance of the school for many teachers. According to Mr. Simms, a veteran white teacher, "We've tried to get them to wear pants that fit around their waist, but that hasn't really worked. That baggy style with the pants hanging low came from the black community and the prisons—they use it as a way to defy authority" (interview, 5/8/02). . . . Although white and Asian American students also resisted the dress code, adults interpreted their resistance as benign and harmless. Mr. Simms, along with other school officials, interpreted the race- and class-based "street" styles of black and Latino children in particular as purposely oppositional. Many educators seemed to think that purging these styles from the school would also purge the opposition. However, as Valenzuela (1999) reported also, most youth I talked to at Matthews wanted to wear baggy pants and untucked shirts not specifically to oppose the school but because this was normative dress among youth in their neighborhood. The restriction of these styles perplexed many students and led them to see the school as an alien, unfairly punitive institution. Because of its restrictions, the school inadvertently transformed the expression of youth identity, encompassing relatively innocuous stylistic rebelliousness, into a mode of subversive opposition. This, it appeared, only promoted more resistance from many students and did little to bond them to the school.

Conclusion

Schools teach children many lessons. These lessons often transgress the formal elements of overt curricula and instruct children how to speak, what to wear, how to move their bodies, and, ultimately, how to inhabit different race, class, and gender positions. At Matthews, school officials helped implement and regulate dress and manners out of an expressed, genuine desire to help students.[6] Left hidden, however, were the assumptions of which students needed this discipline, and in what form.

I want to highlight two ways in which this study advances our understanding of inequality in education. First, it demonstrates how the production of difference and inequality in schooling takes place not just through gender, or just through race, or just through class, but through all of these at once. Similar to Collins's (1990) concept of a "matrix of domination," race, class,

and gender interrelate to profoundly alter one another in guiding expectations and sanctions of young people. We know that identity formation works through intersections of race, class, and gender (Bettie, 2000), but previous research has not fully developed how organizations respond to these overlapping concepts. We have also seen that schools shape how students will embody race, class, and gender positions (e.g., Lewis, 2003; Martin, 1998; Thorne, 1993; Willis, 1977), but previous research has not explored how this process works for various combinations of identities. I have examined how teachers and schools interpret and respond to students based on previously underexplored intersections of race, class, and gender. My study suggests that race, class, and gender profoundly alter each other in framing perceptions of different students, which translates into different methods of regulating and shaping their behaviors. Examining organizational discipline at these intersections is crucial to developing a more nuanced understanding of the role of schools in producing and reproducing social inequalities.

Further, I wish to emphasize how such race, class, and gender assumptions actually worked to subvert the goal of many educators at the school to provide students with the skills to gain upward mobility. Research using Bourdieu's reproduction theory has not often examined organizations that actually attempt to teach students the skills and styles of the dominant culture. Using evidence from a school that emphasized informal training in dress and manners, my research exposes the difficulty of transmitting cultural capital in a public organizational setting, even if this is ostensibly a "caring" pursuit (see Valenzuela, 1999). Educators' identification of which students lacked cultural capital was greatly influenced by their perceptions of students' race, class, and gender. Students identified as lacking or resistant would never measure up to those whose race and class position suggested the possession of social skills in and of itself. In addition, the methods for transmitting and instilling this form of cultural capital involved persistent bodily discipline, which many students experienced as confusing and alienating. My observations suggest that students targeted for disciplinary reform can internalize the discipline aimed at them, and while for some this may lead to self-regulation and complicity, for others it could produce resistance and disengagement from school.

Rather than create opportunities for advancement, the emphasis on regulating students into embodying dominant modes of dress and comportment only seems to bolster perceptions of poor and minority youth as flawed in some way. Schools employing disciplinary regimes steeped in race, class, and gender assumptions (however well intentioned) risk pushing many students away and, ironically, reproducing the very inequalities they are attempting to change. This study suggests that to truly advance toward equality of opportunity, schools and society should seek to value, rather than reform, marginalized forms of style and appearance.

Notes

1. A pseudonym, as are all names in this analysis.
2. I occasionally refer to adolescents as "kids" because that is how teachers often referred to them and how they often referred to themselves (see also Thorne, 1993).
3. This interest in gender-specific manners—particularly when invoked by black teachers—perhaps stemmed from the influence of African American fraternities, sororities, and other social clubs that have historically emphasized social etiquette.
4. To be sure, there were black boys who were considered "school-oriented" and "street-oriented" at Matthews as well. However, educators seemed to especially identify this distinction among Latinos, many of whom could be considered extremely polite and from upwardly mobile backgrounds and others of whom could be considered among the most dangerous students in the school. This polarity did not appear to exist for black students; compared to Latinos, few were described as middle class, and fewer were also described as threatening gang members.
5. One could argue that this stems from the fewer numbers of white and Asian American students

at the school and that I was simply less likely to encounter discipline aimed at these students. However, as this article is part of a broader research plan focusing on white students in this predominantly racial-ethnic minority school, I purposely observed more classes and interactions involving white students than other students. It is possible that I missed some instances of discipline aimed at Asian American students, but this is highly unlikely in the case of white students.
6. While certainly strict, Matthews's climate was not one of harsh and severe discipline, such as that described by Anyon (1997) in her study of an urban school. Indeed, many adults at Matthews, including the principal, expressed a desire to create a caring, family atmosphere at the school.

References

Anyon, J. (1997). *Ghetto schooling: A political economy of urban educational reform.* New York: Teachers College Press.

Bettie, J. (2000). Women without class: Chicas, cholas, trash, and the presence/absence of the class identity. *Signs, 26,* 1–35.

Collins, P. H. (1990). *Black feminist thought: Knowledge, consciousness, and the politics of empowerment.* New York: Routledge.

Collins, P. H. (1998). *Fighting words: Black women and the search for justice.* Minneapolis: University of Minnesota Press.

Connell, R. W. (1995). *Masculinities.* Berkeley: University of California Press.

Ferguson, A. A. (2000). *Bad boys: Public schools in the making of black masculinity.* Ann Arbor: University of Michigan Press.

Foucault, M. (1995). *Discipline and punish* (2nd ed.; A. Sheridan, Trans.). New York: Vintage. (Original work published 1977)

Goffman, E. (1973). *The presentation of self in everyday life.* New York: Overlook Press.

Labov, W. (1972). *Language in the inner city: Studies in the black English vernacular.* Philadelphia: University of Pennsylvania Press.

Lee, S. J. (1994). Behind the model-minority stereotype: Voices of high- and low-achieving Asian American students. *Anthropology and Education Quarterly, 25*(4), 413–429.

Lee, S. J. (1996). *Unraveling the model minority stereotype: Listening to Asian American youth*. New York: Teachers College Press.

Lewis, A. E. (2003). *Race in the schoolyard: Negotiating the color line in communities and classrooms*. New Brunswick, NJ: Rutgers University Press.

Martin, K. A. (1998). Becoming a gendered body: Practices of preschools. *American Sociological Review, 63*(4), 494–511.

McNeil, L. M. (1986). *Contradictions of control: School structure and school knowledge*. New York: Routledge.

Stanley, M. S. (1996). School uniforms and safety. *Education and Urban Society, 28*(4), 424–436.

Thorne, B. (1993). *Gender play: Girls and boys in school*. New Brunswick, NJ: Rutgers University Press.

Valenzuela, A. (1999). *Subtractive schooling: U.S.-Mexican youth and the politics of caring*. Albany: State University of New York Press.

West, C., & Fenstermaker, S. (1995). Doing difference. *Gender and Society, 9*(1), 8–37.

Willis, P. (1977). *Learning to labor*. New York: Columbia University Press.

"REDNECKS," "RUTTERS," AND 'RITHMETIC

Social Class, Masculinity, and Schooling in a Rural Context

Edward W. Morris

This second reading by Edward Morris examines interactions in another, very different, high school in Ohio—a white, poor, rural high school. In ethnographic research (see Chapter 2) questions often emerge after you enter the field. Morris found that girls did better in high school than boys and explains why this may be so based on one and a half years of observations in this school. He observed classrooms and afterschool activities, conducted interviews with students, and collected school records and other documents such as newspapers. He argues that the definition of masculinity is a very strong factor in explaining boys' performance in school and that their definition of masculinity is very closely linked to the characteristics of the community in which they reside. One conclusion from this research is that we cannot examine race, gender, or social class separately if we are to understand students' behaviors in school.

Questions to consider for this reading:

1. Look up the definition for hegemonic masculinity, or ask your professor. How does this concept fit the argument Morris is making in this reading?

2. What are the positive consequences of adhering to the above definition of masculinity for these young boys? What are the negative consequences?

3. Compare this article to the previous one by Morris. What similarities or differences do you see in the way boys and girls approach high school?

I first entered Clayton High School[1] with the intention of studying school disconnection in a rural area. The school was located in a rural community once dominated by a booming coal industry, but now largely impoverished. Although it was not the original focus of my research, I soon discovered that girls outperformed boys academically and showed more interest in school. . . . In this article I analyze this gender difference in academic perceptions and outcomes. My analysis illuminates contradictions of constructions of masculinity and demonstrates how social class and gender are intimately interwoven. My analysis also shines new light on the much-discussed academic "gender gap" favoring girls in disadvantaged contexts, suggesting that particular constructions of social class and gender are critical in producing these academic differences. . . .

My analysis builds on the established tenet that men tend to seek historically specific outlets for asserting dominance over women and other men. But my analysis will also clarify and expand new directions in the theory. First, by focusing on a rural area that has undergone economic restructuring, the study will emphasize the interrelationship of global, regional, and local levels in contextual conditions and practices of masculinity (Connell & Messerschmidt, 2005). I will show, for example, how particular local history and concepts, broader regional categories such as "redneck," and global forces such as deindustrialization all shaped the enactment of masculinity among boys in this school. However, my analysis will stay primarily local and will, through the use of observational and interview data, emphasize individual action in the face of larger structural forces (see also Messerschmidt, 2004). This framework accounts for differences in local definitions of hegemonic masculinity, as well as different patterns of action based on interpretations of these definitions. Second, I will highlight a more intricate relationship between class and masculinity than many previous studies. My analysis does not just explain how pre-established factors such as class or race shape masculinity into subordinated or marginalized forms. Instead, it will demonstrate how social class and masculinity are constructed simultaneously (along with sexuality and whiteness), and how strategies of masculine dominance may actually reproduce class disadvantage. Finally, I will add to literature on hegemonic masculinity and latent costs for men. While past research has examined this phenomenon in areas such as crime (Messerschmidt, 1997) and sport (Messner, 1992), I focus here on education, which I discuss more below.

MASCULINITY AND SCHOOLING

Hegemonic masculinity reveals the ironies of the quest of many men to position themselves as different from and superior to women. Some of the more interesting views of the complications of masculinity have been shown in classic ethnographic studies in education. Although neither invoked hegemonic masculinity, Willis (1977) and MacLeod (1995) both demonstrated how for working-class boys "being a man" meant resisting school, engaging in risky, physically challenging behaviors such as fighting or drug use, and embracing manual or illegal labor. Such constructions of masculinity promoted opposition to school and other institutions. This only calcified the boys' working-class position, hindering their chances for upward mobility and greater social and economic power.

I examine whether similar processes might apply to constructions of masculinity among white working-class rural students, and what this can tell us about gendered differences in educational outcomes among disadvantaged youth in general. In contrast to Willis (1977) and MacLeod (1995), my analysis reveals how masculinity is not just an ancillary factor in the deeper dynamic of class reproduction. Instead, I position particular constructions of masculinity through social class as critical to this reproduction. I show how factors contributing to academic disconnection were seen as important resources for the expression of local hegemonic masculinity. . . .

FINDINGS

Differences in Academic Achievement and Career Goals

Based on an analysis of school records, I found that girls overall outperformed boys academically and had greater ambitions for higher education. I obtained a listing from a guidance counselor of student grade point averages and class ranking at the beginning of the school year in 2006. Girls dominated the peaks of these rankings. For example, the top student in each grade level was a girl. In the senior class, eight of the top 10 were girls. Of the top 20 in the senior class, just five were boys. In the sophomore class, where I concentrated my observations, the top five students (with perfect 4.0 grade point averages) were girls. Nine of the top 10 and 17 of the top 20 in the sophomore rankings were girls. By contrast, many students with low grade point averages and those who were required to repeat a grade or repeat certain classes were boys. Of the 23 students who repeated ninth grade in 2006, 15 (65 percent) were boys. However, I should note that some girls were also low-performing. Of the eight students repeating tenth grade in 2006, for example, four were girls. And some girls appeared near the bottom of the class rankings in each grade. Overall, however, girls clearly performed better than boys.[2]

These differences in class rank corresponded to different ambitions for higher education. I obtained surveys regarding plans after graduation that a guidance counselor had distributed to the outgoing seniors in 2006. Of the students who reported that they had no plans for any sort of college, 84 percent were boys and 16 percent were girls. Of those reporting that they planned to attend four-year colleges, 33 percent were boys and 67 percent were girls. Many young men reported an interest in manual, blue-collar jobs typically done by men and requiring no college, such as auto mechanics, construction, and loading trucks. And some young men simply reported "no plans" or "nothing" after graduation. What caused such stark differences in career plans and academic achievement? Several themes appeared in my data.

Too Cool for School: Masculinity and Academic Nonchalance

Rather than gender having a specific effect on the educational behaviors of girls and boys, educational behavior itself became a vehicle for the construction of gender. The performance of gender in this setting employed educationally relevant behavior to accomplish masculine and feminine identities (Butler, 1999; Messerschmidt, 2000, 2004; West & Zimmerman, 1987), and this shaped academic performance. For example, in my observations girls tended to direct considerable effort and attention to school. Boys, by contrast, took pride in their *lack* of academic effort. No boy I interviewed reported that he studied outside of school. Indeed, if boys achieved well academically, they had to do so

without any overt sign of effort or planning. For instance, a boy named Preston was described by several teachers and students as the "smartest kid in the school." Yet Preston only had a 3.15 grade point average. . . .

Preston reveals the ultimate goal of schoolwork for many boys at Clayton—to just "get by." My observations in classrooms mirrored what Preston described: Boys were more likely to sleep, less likely to turn in homework, and less likely to take notes.

Despite this, teachers and students frequently described boys as "smart." A science teacher named Mr. Deering told me, "I think the girls are more conscientious. They will work more, do more of what you ask them," he then pointed to two boys in the class and said, "they're smart, but they don't do a whole lot." Similarly, girls at the school appeared to see boys as smart, while viewing their own abilities as more limited (see also AAUW, 1992; Luttrell, 1997). These gendered academic behaviors and perceptions emerged from a discourse that framed masculinity as something that should not include academic effort. Boys were understood by themselves and others as smart enough to "get by," but not expected to attend diligently to academic work. These actions were seen as representations of masculinity. . . .

MASCULINITY, SEXUALITY, AND SCHOOL ENGAGEMENT

Perceptions of masculinity and educational engagement tended to show an interconnection between gender and sexuality. Similar to Pascoe (2007), I found that students at Clayton used terms charged with connotations of sexuality to police the boundaries of masculinity. For example, boys (and to a lesser extent, girls) used the term "pussy," "gay," or "fag" to refer to boys whom they perceived as unmasculine (Eder, Evans, & Parker, 1995; Pascoe, 2007). While important in the everyday construction of gender, this discourse on feminized, lower-status masculinity also occurred through academics. Academically oriented behavior itself could be seen as not masculine. For example, boys perceived as "nerdy"—often those who put more effort into school and were involved in school activities such as band—were more likely to be called "gay" or "pussies." . . .

Masculinity and Perceptions of Academic Knowledge and Skills: "Booksmarts"

As the student career surveys demonstrated, many boys at Clayton valued manual labor. Gendered and classed views of work and education also emerged throughout my student interviews. One definitive gender difference concerned perceptions of "booksmarts." Virtually all the girls I interviewed responded that they thought "booksmarts"—the knowledge and competencies gained from books—were important to be successful. Few boys thought that booksmarts were as important. Instead, boys were more likely to value "common sense" and "working with your hands." . . .

To boys such as Robert, acquiring "book knowledge" required boring, inert activities such as reading or "listening to someone talk the whole time." In contrast, Robert and other boys perceived nonacademic, blue-collar work such as woodworking or construction as more active and enjoyable. In this way, these boys forged working-class identities. But such work was also perceived as more manly, as many boys referenced their fathers or other men in their family who did such work, and they praised the utility and vigor of manual labor. Thus, the boys simultaneously forged masculine identities.

In doing so, some boys disparaged academic work and "office jobs." . . . [A]cademic work was not seen as "hard work" and masculinity in this community had historically been defined through hard physical labor. Although the boys I interviewed tended to admit that "office jobs" could be lucrative, most did not see such careers as useful or gratifying. Much of this perception, however, stems from the local feminization of such work and the lower status placed on femininity in general. Academics and professions requiring "booksmarts" were feminized and

considered lower status, while physical labor aligned with masculinity. This relationship undergirded local hegemonic masculinity, even though economic restructuring reduced manual labor jobs. As I show below, local views of masculine dominance in heterosexual relationships and work roles influenced such perceptions.

Gender, Work, and Power in the Community

Teachers at Clayton noted the irony of girls' high academic performance because they perceived the community (and most teachers lived in the community) as traditional and patriarchal. . . .

These patriarchal views emerged in my student interviews. Boys and girls perceived family roles differently. Boys tended to see the man as the primary leader and provider within the family (all of the girls I interviewed thought it should be equal). A boy named Zack expressed this in an interview:

> *Do you think the man should be the main provider for the family?* Oh yeah! I think it's just kinda stupid how girls have to go to work. It happens a lot around here. You have it so the girls have to go to work. I don't like that. *Ok, so you think it's kind of a problem that that has to happen?* Yeah. *And that happens a lot around here?* Happens quite a bit. Most of the time it happens around here, it's not because it has to happen. It's because people—the guys are too lazy. We got a lotta lazy people in our community.

Zack states an interest in the traditional breadwinner role for men, similar to other boys I interviewed. But Zack adds a unique twist compared to other boys—he indicts men in the community as too lazy to fulfill this role properly. Zack was one of the highest-performing boys in his grade, and I suggest that this unique interpretation of local family life provoked him to work hard in school to obtain a good job (which he intended to do through going to college and the military). This example demonstrates the importance of viewing gender as a situated construction influenced by interpretation and agency. Zack's achievement is not an anomaly, rather it results from his interpretation of laziness and inability to support one's family as the true failure of masculinity, and his desire to construct his own (perceived stronger) masculinity through academic success. Many other boys, however, did not appear to see this same connection. They continued to eschew and feminize academics even as they revered a male-as-provider family role.[3] This stemmed from a strong local sense of masculine entitlement nested in industrial labor and familial economic power. Such traditionalism, however, was palpably fading economically. Thus, class-based concepts and practices in the peer culture offered regional and local springboards from which to assert and protect masculinity.

Constructing Masculinity, Class, and Whiteness: "Rednecks" and "Rutters"

Hegemonic practices of masculinity at Clayton focused on a carefree, almost rebellious attitude toward schoolwork, and physical toughness exemplified by manual labor. Both practices of masculinity were reflected, but also given new life, through a popular term and identity at the school: "redneck." The term "redneck" is a well-known popular culture identity that implies being blue-collar, rebellious, and southern (Hartigan, 2003; Shirley, 2003). On a more tacit level, "redneck" also strongly represents masculinity and whiteness. Shirley (2003) finds that "redneck" connotes more of a masculine than a feminine identity. Hartigan (2003) asserts that "redneck" reflects important internal dynamics of whiteness as a racial category. This identity is unabashedly white, but opposed to middle- and upper-class whiteness.

Such dynamics are important to recognize because economic decline in Clayton compromised whiteness as well as masculinity. White men, particularly in lower economic strata, may define themselves in opposition to nonwhites (particularly African Americans) through work and economic stability (Fine & Weis, 1998). When asked about race, the white boys I interviewed also defined whiteness through this sense of stability. When discussing differences between white and Black people, a boy named Harry said: "[When thinking about white people] I think of people that . . . have better lives—live in good neighborhoods—stuff like that." Where economic situations are tenuous or declining such as in Clayton, however, this understanding of whiteness can be threatened (Fine & Weis, 1998; Kimmel & Ferber, 2006). The concept of "redneck" can reflect and respond to these tensions by reasserting a white blue-collar identity imbued with rebellious toughness. Such an identity fit well with hegemonic masculinity in Clayton.

For instance, I only heard the term "redneck" used at Clayton in reference to white men or boys. The boys I heard called this were most often in lower-level classes or vocational classes, indicating that the concept was not connected to sophistication and academic interest. Indeed, in popular culture "redneck" represents opposition to these ideals (Jarosz & Lawson, 2002). Similarly, some teachers used the term in a whimsically derogatory way to describe certain boys as blue-collar, uncouth, and brazenly macho. Although the term "redneck" is largely derogatory, many people in this community, especially men, embraced it. For example, several trucks in the area proudly displayed bright red "Redneck" stickers. Preston described the attitude in the following way: "Around here, it's like 'yeah I'm a redneck, what are you gonna do about it?' (laughs)."

As Preston implied, "redneck" at Clayton represented the stereotypically masculine trait of physical toughness. Harry mentioned this when I asked him to describe the school: "It's a rough school. It's ah, (laughs), it's a redneck school!" Uses of the term "redneck" captured a sense of pride embedded in living in this "rough," white working-class, rural location. Through the implication of toughness and opposition to elitist sophistication, this regional category offered a classed and raced template consistent with local hegemonic masculinity. This was an identity that could protect white working-class masculinity, but one that was not academically inclined.

While "redneck" served largely as a positive identity at the school, another class-based identity was not embraced: "rutter." Unlike the broader, regional category of redneck, "rutter" was a distinctively local term. "Rutter" denoted people who were extremely poor, dirty, and lowly, similar to the concept "white trash" (Hartigan, 2003; Wray, 2006). Students used this word as a class-based insult, and while "redneck" affirmed whiteness, "rutter" could impair it. (I analyze this further in a separate work: Morris, 2008.) For boys, using "rutter" as an invective often instigated fights. . . .

Reclaiming Physically Tough Masculinity: Risk-Taking and Fighting

Several works discuss a "risk-taking" quality in masculinity (Connell, 1995; Connell & Messerschmidt, 2005; Messner, 1992). Ferguson (2000, p. 176) refers to a similar emphasis on "brinkmanship"—challenging rules, authority, and refusing to back down. Like the "redneck" identity, physical brinkmanship at Clayton provided avenues to reassert the power of masculinity.

Similar to Courtenay's (2006) research on injury and risk-taking for men in rural settings, I found that boys in Clayton often took bodily risks and incurred physical injuries. Boys were proud of their "battle scars" and excitedly regaled me with unadulterated stories of their accidents and pain. . . .

The basic sense of risk-taking and physical bravery underlying such behavior could translate into challenging school rules and authority and the physical expression of power, both of which could hinder academic progress. These qualities can be seen through the example of fighting. There were several "girl fights" at the school, but students and adults tended to associate "real" fighting with masculinity. According to students, the purpose of fighting for boys was less complicated than for girls, and the goals intrinsic to the fight itself. As a girl named Jamie said, "Most of the girls have a purpose to fight, like the other girl makes them mad for a pretty good reason or something. And guys they just— 'you wanna fight, yeah, okay' [mimics punching motions]." For many boys fighting itself became the goal; it became an important method of cultivating and displaying masculinity. Fighting provided these boys a crucible that could demonstrate the superiority of masculinity to femininity. As Kevin and Roger stated, even boys perceived to not fight well could be branded as "pussies." This allowed some boys to prove superiority over other boys and over girls—something that they perceived could not be guaranteed through academics.

Some boys, particularly those from poorer backgrounds and those more disconnected from school, emphasized the freedom and closure they found in fighting (see also Ferguson, 2000). Fighting defied middle- to upper-class norms of comportment,[4] and also openly opposed school rules. In the second year of my research, the school enacted a stricter approach to fights, diligently policing the cafeteria (where most school fights occurred) and giving mandatory suspensions to those caught fighting. Several boys derided this "zero tolerance" approach as inhibiting a primary method of conflict resolution and self-expression. . . .

Fighting conveyed a message of physical superiority consistent with hegemonic notions of masculinity. Perhaps because they felt marginalized in other ways, fighting gave these boys a sense of physical empowerment, freedom, and clarity lacking in other areas of their lives. But this entailed academic and bodily costs. Fighting not only led to suspensions, but negative judgments from teachers and school administrators that obstructed boys' attachment to school, and ultimately their achievement. Fighting was certainly detrimental to academic success, but resoundingly consistent with the physical toughness and power associated with local hegemonic masculinity.

CONCLUSION

This article develops a new view of the academic "gender gap," especially as it applies to disadvantaged students. I argue that gender should not be seen as a static cause of academic differences, but that academically relevant behavior is employed in the construction of gender. Despite the actual and potential inequalities faced by boys at Clayton and other disadvantaged contexts, I argue against a "boys as disadvantaged" perspective. I do this through applying and expanding the theory of hegemonic masculinity in relation to social class and education.

This research shows that definitions of hegemonic masculinity differ according to locale, and these differences might engender unique patterns of action and consequences. At Clayton, pursuing locally hegemonic practices of masculinity tended to hinder boys in school. Fighting as a display of physical masculine dominance, or viewing academic work and striving as feminized and lower status, are examples. Such perceptions and behaviors operated within local, as well as regional and global, patterns of masculinity and social class. Local history meant that hegemonic masculinity in this context stemmed (partly) from maintaining a "breadwinner" role within the family through physically demanding labor. But global dynamics of economic restructuring meant that such practices were difficult for men in Clayton to enact. Thus, I suggest that broader regional concepts such as the tough, rebellious "redneck," or displays of physical dominance such as fighting, were employed by these boys as alternative means to forge and prove hegemonic masculinity.

The findings further demonstrate how class is produced through masculinity and how masculinity is produced through social class (and in a less elaborated way, how whiteness and sexuality are enmeshed in this process). Class privilege and gender privilege can be considered two separate, but interconnected systems of hegemony, further complicated by different (local, regional, and global) levels of practice. Local hegemonic masculinity entailed a sense of superiority tied to physical labor and displays of physical activity, risk, and power—not academics. While perceived to be advantageous locally, this masculinity was a disadvantage within the larger class structure, primarily because globalization has reduced opportunities for industrial labor in many pockets of the United States. This constraining class structure further compromised white working-class masculinity in Clayton, fueling a need to prove masculinity, along with class and race identities, in other ways. Some boys such as Zack crafted practices to accomplish this academically, but most saw academic behavior as inconsistent with local definitions of masculinity. Thus, interwoven processes of class and masculinity led to unexpected outcomes—specifically girls' academic advantage. Far from showing that girls have gender privilege, this outcome actually stems from boys seeking masculine privilege, but under a definition of masculinity that tended to hinder them academically.[5]

NOTES

1. All personal and place names are pseudonyms.
2. The only other achievement data I had access to were the Ohio Graduation Test results. Students in the state of Ohio are required to pass this curriculum-based achievement test before graduating from high school. There was no large difference in results by gender on this test, but it is difficult to use this as a gauge of performance because the results are reported as passing rates, not actual scores.
3. There were alternative enactments of masculinity at Clayton that demonstrated less traditional notions of gender, along with higher academic performance. The few boys already mentioned as "band kids" engaged in such practices, which again underscores the variability of masculinity. This constitutes an important area of further analysis; however, in this article I focus on hegemonic practices of masculinity to explain the academic "gender gap."
4. Fighting in school is related to family income. As income rises, it is less likely that a student will be involved in a physical fight in school. Perceptions of fighting among men also vary by class. Pyke (1996, p. 532) argues that higher-class men use the violence they associate with lower-class men as an example of

brutality that "reemphasize[s] their superiority over lower-class men."

5. I am not arguing that these boys are responsible for their own disadvantage, but that local hegemonic masculinity promised a degree of relational power over women and other men. This local dynamic must be considered within larger relations of class and gender in which these boys face significant inequalities.

REFERENCES

American Association of University Women (AAUW). (1992). *The AAUW report: How schools shortchange girls.* Washington, DC: The AAUW Educational Foundation and National Educational Association.

Butler, J. (1999). *Gender trouble: Feminism and the subversion of identity.* New York: Routledge.

Connell, R. W. (1995). *Masculinities.* Berkeley: University of California Press.

Connell, R. W. (1996). Teaching the boys: New research on masculinity, and gender strategies for schools. *Teachers College Record, 98*(2), 206–235.

Connell, R. W., & Messerschmidt, J. W. (2005). Hegemonic masculinity: Rethinking the concept. *Gender & Society, 19*(6), 829–859.

Courtenay, W. H. (2006). Rural men's health: Situating risk in the negotiation of masculinity. In H. Campbell, M. Mayerfeld-Bell, & M. Finney (Eds.), *Country boys: Masculinity and rural life* (pp. 139–158). University Park: Pennsylvania State University Press.

Eder, D., Evans, C. C., & Parker, S. (1995). *School talk: Gender and adolescent culture.* New Brunswick, NJ: Rutgers University Press.

Ferguson, A. A. (2000). *Bad boys: Public schools in the making of black masculinity.* Ann Arbor: University of Michigan Press.

Fine, M., & Weis, L. (1998). *The unknown city: The lives of poor and working-class young adults.* Boston: Beacon Press.

Hartigan, J., Jr. (2003). Who are these white people? "Rednecks," "hillbillies," and "white trash" as marked racial subjects. In A. W. Doane & E. Bonilla-Silva (Eds.), *White out: The continuing significance of racism* (pp. 95–111). New York: Routledge.

Jarosz, L., & Lawson, V. (2002). Sophisticated people versus rednecks: Economic restructuring and class difference in America's West. *Antipode, 34*(1), 8–27.

Kimmel, M. S., & Ferber, A. L. (2006). White men are this nation: Right-wing militias and the restoration of rural masculinity. In H. Campbell, M. Mayerfeld-Bell, & M. Finney (Eds.), *Country boys: Masculinity and rural life* (pp. 121–138). University Park: The Pennsylvania State University Press.

Luttrell, W. (1997). *School-smart and mother-wise: Working-class women's identity and schooling.* New York: Routledge.

MacLeod, J. (1995). *Ain't no makin' it* (2nd ed.). Boulder, CO: Westview Press.

Messerschmidt, J. W. (1997). *Crime as structured action: Gender, race, class, and crime in the making.* Thousand Oaks, CA: Sage.

Messerschmidt, J. W. (2000). *Nine lives: Adolescent masculinities, the body, and violence.* Boulder, CO: Westview Press.

Messerschmidt, J. W. (2004). *Flesh and blood: Adolescent gender diversity and violence.* Lanham, MD: Rowman & Littlefield.

Messner, M. A. (1992). *Power at play: Sports and the problem of masculinity.* Boston: Beacon Press.

Morris, E. W. (2008). *"Rednecks" and "rutters": Constructions of social class and whiteness at a rural high school.* Paper presented at the North Central Sociological Association Meeting, Cincinnati.

Pascoe, C. J. (2007). *Dude, you're a fag: Masculinity and sexuality in high school.* Berkeley: University of California Press.

Pyke, K. D. (1996). Class-based masculinities: The interdependence of gender, class, and interpersonal power. *Gender & Society, 10*(5), 527–549.

Shirley, C. D. (2003). *"Rednecks" and "white trash": The gendering of whiteness.* Paper presented at the Southern Sociological Society Meetings, New Orleans.

West, C., & Zimmerman, D. (1987). Doing gender. *Gender & Society, 1*(2), 125–151.

Willis, P. (1977). *Learning to labor: How working class kids get working class jobs.* New York: Columbia University Press.

Wray, M. (2006). *Not quite white: White trash and the boundaries of whiteness.* Durham, NC: Duke University Press.

How Race and Education Are Related

Caroline Hodges Persell

In this reading, Caroline Hodges Persell, a highly regarded sociologist of education, explores various theories to explain unequal educational outcomes for children of different races. She examines genetic, structural, and cultural explanations and proposes a new approach that incorporates structural, cultural, and interactional factors. Persell's argument is important because the explanations we give for racial differences in education influence how we approach solutions to these problems.

Questions to consider for this reading:

1. Do Persell's arguments help you to understand Morris's results in "Tuck In That Shirt!"?

2. Which of the reasons that Persell discusses for racial inequality in education do you think are most plausible?

3. Given Persell's argument, what steps do you think should be taken to improve the educational experience of racial minority groups?

Racial differences exist in many aspects of education, including access, resources, experiences, and outcomes. This chapter begins by considering educational outcomes such as achievement and completion, why they are important, and how they vary by race/ethnicity. It then examines existing explanations, proposes a new synthesis, and considers relevant evidence.

Much of the research on racial differences has been based on black-white comparisons for several reasons. Historically and today, blacks[1] and Native Americans have been the most intensely "hyper-segregated" group, that is, isolated from other groups, clustered together in small concentrated areas. Moreover, slavery of blacks created a system of stratification based on race where whites enjoyed political, economic, legal, and social rights that were denied to blacks on the basis of race. Thus, in the U.S. blackness and whiteness "are the symbolic anchors of our racial hierarchy" (Morning, 2007). Where data exist on other racial/ethnic groups it is included here. It is important to stress

that race is a socially constructed, somewhat fluid, changeable, and complex concept, containing considerable variation within whatever categories are used (Omi, 2001). "Races are labels not people," and some individuals and groups can change races over time (Morning, 2007). Boundary crossing varies widely between racial/ethnic groups, as does the extent of domination experienced by groups.

VARIATIONS IN EDUCATIONAL OUTCOMES

Of the possible educational outcomes, considerable research has focused on differences in educational achievement. Despite individual exceptions, there are variations in the educational achievement of African American, Latino/a, and Native American students which, on average, is lower than that of whites and Asian Americans. Gaps occur in standardized test scores, grade point averages, rates of placement in gifted or special education programs, drop out rates, and college attendance and graduation rates (Hallinan, 2001; Kovach & Gordon, 1997; National Center for Education Statistics, 2001; Nettles & Perna, 1997). These differences in educational achievement outcomes are significant predictors of an individual's employment opportunities and wages, as is race.[2] Over the past 30 years, racial differences in reading achievement declined until 1988 when they increased some until 1992 before leveling off through 2004. Math achievement gaps declined until 1990 and remained pretty level through 2004 (Berends, Lucas, & Penaloza, 2008).

EXPLANATIONS FOR DIFFERENT OUTCOMES

For a long time, no research could fully explain the variation in academic achievement. Recently, researchers[3] using different datasets found that a small number of social factors could statistically eliminate racial differences in achievement. This means, for example, that black and white children of the same age and birth weight, whose mothers have the same test scores, education, occupation, income, and wealth, whose mothers were the same age when they had their first child, and who have the same number of children's books or similar cultural resources in their homes, scored the same on their reading and math tests. But, you may be thinking, black and white children are not equally likely to share these indicators of life chances, so we need to explain (or understand) why they do not. A second puzzle is why by the third grade the achievement gap between those same white and black children reappeared, and why the factors that explained it statistically among kindergarteners no longer fully explain the gap among older children. Scholars have considered genetic, cultural, and structural explanations for racial variations in achievement.

Genetic Explanations

There have been recurrent efforts to offer genetic explanations for racial differences in educational achievement (e.g., Herrnstein & Murray, 1994; Jensen, 1969). In their 1994 book, *The Bell Curve*, Herrnstein and Murray presented evidence showing that when socioeconomic status was controlled, racial differences in educational achievement remained. Their measures of social factors were very incomplete, however. They then went on to suggest that the remaining difference must be due to genetic differences in intelligence (IQ) between the races since it was not explained by social factors. However, intelligence is not a simple, one-dimensional concept (Fischer et al., 1996; Gardner, 1983, 1993). Nor is intelligence unchanging through time and experience, as evidenced by Flynn's research showing a rise in Western countries of roughly fifteen IQ points in a single generation (2007). Neither is intelligence rooted in a particular gene. In short, genetic explanations lack empirical support, and race is seen by social scientists as being a socially constructed concept, rather than a biological or genetic entity. Writing about the IQ test score gap, Nisbett (1998, p. 101) concluded, "The most relevant studies provide no evidence for the genetic superiority of either race, but strong evidence for a substantial environmental contribution to the IQ gap between blacks and whites. Almost equally important, rigorous interventions do affect IQ and cognitive skills at every stage of the life course." Studies of mixed-race children with one white and one black parent show that children with white mothers and black fathers have considerably higher IQs than those with black mothers and white fathers (Nisbett, 1998, p. 100). Although their genetic inheritance is similar, their social exposure to activities favored by a predominantly white society differs according to the race of their mothers. If environment not genes is central, what aspects of environment matter? Cultural explanations are frequently offered.

Cultural Explanations

Standing in apparent opposition to a genetic explanation for racial/ethnic differences in school achievement, sociocultural explanations tend to root the causes in the cultural values, parenting practices, and linguistic codes of families and children, and some research is consistent with such an explanation. A broader measure of family environment, including grandmother's education, explained two-thirds of the racial gap in achievement (Phillips, Crouse, & Ralph, 1998, p. 138), twice as much as earlier studies. Ogbu's (2003) observations of greater degrees of "disengagement" from school among black compared to white students are also a cultural explanation. While such cultural explanations—such as family environment, parenting practices, and student behavior—explain more of the achievement gap than do traditional measures of socioeconomic status (SES) alone, they fail to explain when and how such potentially important cultural differences arise.

Cross-cultural research suggests the importance of contextual factors for differences in the culture, IQ, and educational achievements of different racial/ethnic groups. For example in Japan, the ethnic-minority Buraku have lower IQs and educational achievement than the dominant, ethnic-Ippan group, even though the two groups are of the same race. However, when members of both groups migrate to the United States, they do equally well on standardized tests and in school (Ogbu, 2001, 2003; Ogbu & Stern, 2001). These cross-cultural findings are consistent with evidence that other social factors, which Herrnstein and Murray did not measure, affect different achievement levels (Fischer et al., 1996).

Both genetic and cultural explanations attribute the source of failure to children and their families and, unless the cultural explanation pushes beyond individuals to their social contexts, both may have self-fulfilling potency. That is, if people in the larger society come to believe these explanations, such beliefs may contribute to children being taught less. Both genetic and cultural explanations tend to legitimate inequalities and divert attention and reform efforts away from structural inequalities in society, which need to be considered as a source of racial differences in educational achievement.

Structural Explanations

The first structural condition to consider is race, which needs to be viewed not as an individual attribute, but as a system of social relationships that creates systematic advantages for members of one group while the members of another group are systematically disadvantaged (see the important work of critical race theorists such as Bonilla-Silva, 1996, 2001, 2003; Omi, 2001). They see race as a system of organized power in society.

A group's subordinate position in a racialized system of power relations affects its measured intelligence and school achievement through three processes according to Fischer et al. (1996, p. 174): (1) socioeconomic deprivation, (2) racial/ethnic segregation which concentrates disadvantages and accentuates them, and (3) stigmatization as inferior by the wider society's perception of them. Recent research has statistically eliminated the racial gap in achievement among 10 to 14 year-olds by considering grandparents' characteristics and parenting behaviors (Mandara, Varner, Greene, & Richman, 2009). Another study statistically eliminated the racial gap among 10 to 18 year-olds, suggesting that intergenerational inequalities in wealth and education as well as structural inequalities in neighborhoods, schools, and friends statistically explain the achievement gap (Yeung, Persell, & Reilly, 2010).

TOWARD A FULLER EXPLANATION

The explanation proposed here links structural, cultural, and interactional elements. Structurally, it is important to measure the degree of racial stratification (i.e., structured inequality). This includes the historical social, symbolic, economic, educational, and political domination of one race over another either in different nations or regions of the same country. Those historical legacies are related to economic, cultural, social, and symbolic capital (Lewis, 2003), wealth (Conley, 1999; Oliver & Shapiro, 1997), and an individual's sense of efficacy.

Historical and current racial stratification is related to *socialization contexts*, particularly neighborhoods, families, and schools. Racial stratification, ideologies, and socializing contexts shape and constrain *culture, interactions, and responses* that occur between parents and children, teachers and students, parents and teachers, and among peers. All three major components in the model are implicated in creating racial differences in *educational outcomes*. The importance of multiple, interrelated factors is consistent with the evidence that relatively small educational differences between children in kindergarten grow in magnitude the longer they are in school. Since both race and educational achievement are related to occupations, incomes, marital status, housing, social respect, and opportunities for the next generation, they have intergenerational consequences. One reason individuals may work hard in school is to help their children thrive. So the degree to which such "payoffs" of education vary for different races may undermine confidence in the system.

Historical and contemporary structural inequalities between races have been well documented in economics, politics, prison populations, and social status.[4] When the degree of racial inequality is measured, the achievement gap is greater in U.S. counties with more racial stratification. Roscigno developed a model including the local class context and the local racial context in which families, schools, and students were located (1999, p. 163). He stressed that family and school influences on educational achievement and attainment "are themselves embedded in, and partially a function of, broader structures and spatial variations in class- and race-based opportunity" (1999, p. 159). He found that class context (measured at the county level) is related to race, with blacks significantly more likely than whites to live in communities with larger numbers of families in poverty (1999). What is really important to notice is the way that black educational achievement is depressed in areas of high racial inequality, above and beyond the effects of higher rates of absolute poverty (Figure 36.1). Greater racial inequality at the county level strongly depresses black student achievement, but not white student achievement. In counties where racial inequality in the local labor market is low, in the left portion of Figure 36.1, there are only small achievement differences between blacks and whites, compared to highly unequal counties where racial achievement differences are three times as large, in the right side of Figure 36.1. Not only the absolute level of poverty, but also the degree of racial inequality in an area affects the racial gap by depressing the educational achievement of black students. Local racial inequality explains nearly half of the racial gap in achievement (Roscigno, 1999, p. 180). Children of color and white children are not equally likely to attend private schools, socio-economically advantaged schools, smaller schools, or have small classes.

Whites are more likely than blacks to attend private school, and attending private school is related to higher chances of taking an academic curriculum, being in smaller schools, having student bodies with higher socio-economic status, greater discipline, and higher rates of attending college (Coleman & Hoffer, 1987). Public school students are much more likely to drop out of high school than are Catholic or other private school students (24%, 12%, and 13%, respectively) (Coleman, Hoffer, & Kilgore, 1982). Moreover, the strong academic curriculum and homework required in many private schools is important for student achievement (Bryk, Lee, & Holland, 1993; Coleman & Hoffer, 1987).

In public schools, blacks are more likely than whites to attend schools with larger numbers of low income students and schools with higher proportions of racial minorities. Many studies find correlations between the percent minority, or low income, in school and student achievement (e.g., Roscigno, 2000). School segregation, measured by the racial and socioeconomic composition of students in the school attended, varies by race and is related to educational achievement (Berends et al., 2008).

Figure 36.1 As Racial Inequality in the County Increases, So Does the Achievement Gap Between White and Black Children

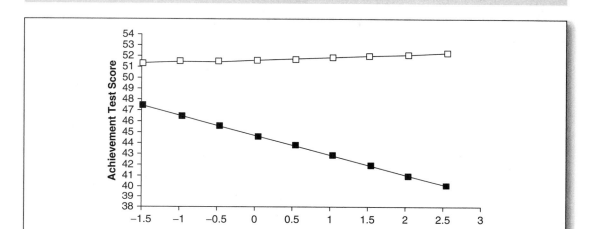

Note. From "The Black-White Achievement Gap, Family-School Links, and the Importance of Place," by V. J. Roscigno, 1999, *Sociological Inquiry, 69*(2), p. 179. Reprinted with permission.

Black students are more likely than whites to attend large urban schools. Both school size and percent minority students in a school are related to the amount of tracking in it (Lucas & Berends, 2002), and blacks and Chicano/as are more likely than whites to attend schools with curricular tracking. Track placement is often related to what is taught, what is learned, test results, and continuing one's schooling (Oakes, 1985; Persell, 1977; Persell, Catsambis, & Cookson, 1992), but not always (Dreeben & Gamoran, 1986; Hallinan, 1987). Other potential contributing factors include the time teachers expect students to spend on homework (Oakes, 1985) and teacher-student interactions (Good, 1987; Oakes, 1985; Persell, 1977).

By 2004, blacks and whites were almost equally likely to be in academic tracks, although not necessarily at the highest levels (Berends

et al., 2008). Between 1992 and 2004, blacks were increasingly more likely to attend schools with larger proportions of low income and minority students, and even less likely to attend private schools compared to whites (Berends et al., 2008).

Schools with more low income and racial minority students are more likely to have teachers who are not certified or are teaching out of their area of certification (Ingersoll, 2002), as well as teachers with lower achievement-test scores (Coleman, Campbell, Mood, Weinfeld, & York, 1966). Yet, teachers' test scores are related to students' test scores (Jencks & Phillips, 1998). Having a series of "high-achieving" teachers vastly increases the achievement of low-income and minority students.

Because schools are supported by local-property taxes and because there is so much housing segregation by social class and race in the United States, students who live in low-income areas are very likely to attend schools with lower per pupil expenditures on instructional program. Such disparities in educational opportunities affect how much children learn, how long they stay in school, their graduation rates, and the rates at which they successfully pursue further education after high school.

STUDENT ATTITUDES AND BEHAVIORS

Despite all these structured inequalities in the types of education received by students of color, numerous researchers have found that black students value education as much if not more than whites (Ainsworth-Darnell & Downey, 1998; Blau, 2003; Cook & Ludwig, 1998; Downey, Ainsworth, & Qian, 2009; Mickelson, 1990). Black students also value social goals and personal responsibility for achieving them more than white students do (Blau, 2003, p. 69). Among the differences in behavioral responses, black teens are less likely than whites but more likely than Asian or Latino students to report they have had discipline problems (Blau, 2003, p. 104). Blacks were more likely than whites, Asians, or Latinos, however, to report being unprepared for class and cutting classes (p. 104), reports that are consistent with higher rates of absenteeism among blacks in San Francisco high schools (Thernstrom & Thernstrom, 2003, p. 141). Overall, black students report doing fewer hours of homework per night and watching more TV or videos compared to other racial/ethnic groups. A panel analysis of a nationally representative sample of high school students found that extra time spent on math homework increased student test scores, while an extra hour of TV viewing negatively affected scores (Aksoy & Link, 2000).

Some of these behavioral responses have been taken as showing an "oppositional culture" among black or other minority race youths. A much contested cultural explanation, the concept of oppositional culture, emerged from a study of one all-black, inner-city, high school in Washington, D.C. (Fordham, 1988, 1993, 1996; Fordham & Ogbu, 1986). Subsequent researchers have found some (Downey & Ainsworth-Darnell, 2002; Farkas, Lleras, & Maczuga, 2002) or no empirical support (Cook & Ludwig, 1998; Ferguson, 2001; Kao, Tienda, & Schneider, 1996) for the concept. Overall, oppositional culture appears among some students of all races, is not uniform among all blacks, is class-linked, is most relevant for adolescents, and is more likely in schools where the race of students in all tracks does not reflect the racial composition of the school (Downey & Ainsworth-Darnell, 2002; Farkas et al., 2002; Horvat & O'Connor, 2006; Tyson, 2006).

We need to consider how racial inequalities in school practices may affect student responses including effort and achievement. Early academic performance and evaluations affect students' self-perceptions, and "these perceptions subsequently influence the decisions students make with respect to effort expended on schoolwork, course choices, and post high school plans, as well as how attached they feel to school" (Tyson, Darity, & Castellino, 2005, p. 16). The high value black students place on school and education may help to explain why doing poorly may be even more demoralizing for them than for whites and, thus be more consequential for their subsequent behavior (such as school disengagement). It may also be one reason for why school characteristics have more impact on black achievement compared to that of whites.

EDUCATIONAL PAYOFFS

Some students of color do complete higher education, despite the pitfalls of race inequalities in their neighborhoods, families, and schools. Do they receive the same "payoffs" from their educations as whites? Asian Americans have high levels of educational achievement. Do they earn the same as whites with similar education? The answer is yes, but only if they received that education in the U.S., not if their degree is from another country (Zeng & Xie, 2004). Among blacks who attended selective colleges, Bowen and Bok (1998) found that, even among the most highly educated males, racial differences in income remained—although no earnings differences existed among women.

Education does not afford members of all racial groups the same payoff in housing choices, treatment by the police, legal system, merchants, or restaurants, suggesting that educational achievement and attainment do not have the same "payoff" for blacks and whites, in material, symbolic, or social terms. Such unequal effects might corrode trust and educational effort among some members of the next generation.

Conclusions

Racial differences in educational achievement—that some have tried to explain by genes or culture—are better understood by rooting them in historical and current systems of race inequality which, in turn, affect the socializing contexts of neighborhoods, families, and schools, as well as individual responses, and rewards. When social class and/or racial differences are large, enduring, and institutionalized, they are consequential for the next generation and beyond and they affect educational experiences and outcomes in some of the ways we have delineated here. Without understanding the larger social constellations in which race and education are embedded we can never challenge and change them.

Notes

1. While mostly the word *black* is used in this chapter, it is used interchangeably with *African-American* (see Tatum, 1999).

2. According to Moss and Tilly (2003) and Pager and Quillian (2005), among others.

3. Fryer and Levitt (2004); Yeung and Conley (2006); Yeung and Pfeiffer (2006).

4. See Persell and Hendrie (2005) for more details.

References

Ainsworth-Darnell, J. W., & Downey, D. B. (1998). Assessing the oppositional culture explanation for racial/ethnic differences in school performance. *American Sociological Review, 63,* 536–553.

Aksoy, T., & Link, C. L. (2000). A panel analysis of student mathematics achievement in the U.S. in the 1990s: Does increasing the amount of time in learning activities affect math achievement? *Economics of Education Review, 19*(3), 261–277.

Berends, M., Lucas, S. R., & Penaloza, R. V. (2008). How changes in families and schools are related to trends in black-white test scores. *Sociology of Education, 81*(4), 313–344.

Blau, J. R. (2003). *Race in the schools: Perpetuating white dominance?* Boulder, CO: Lynne Rienner.

Bonilla-Silva, E. (1996). Rethinking racism: Toward a structural interpretation. *American Sociological Review, 62*(3), 465–480.

Bonilla-Silva, E. (2001). *White supremacy and racism in the post-civil rights era.* Boulder, CO: Lynne Rienner.

Bonilla-Silva, E. (2003). *Racism without racists.* Boulder, CO: Rowman & Littlefield.

Bowen, W. G., & Bok, D. C. (1998). *The shape of the river: Long-term consequences of considering race in college and university admissions.* Princeton, NJ: Princeton University Press.

Bryk, A. S., Lee, V. E., & Holland, P. B. (1993). *Catholic schools and the common good.* Cambridge, MA: Harvard University Press.

Coleman, J. S., Campbell, E. Q., Mood, A. M., Weinfeld, F. D., & York, R. L. (1966). *Equality of educational opportunity.* Washington, DC: U.S. Government Printing Office.

Coleman, J. S., & Hoffer, T. (1987). *Public and private high schools: The impact of communities.* New York: Basic Books.

Coleman, J. S., Hoffer, T., & Kilgore, S. (1982). *High school achievement.* New York: Basic Books.

Conley, D. (1999). *Being black, living in the red: Race, wealth, and social policy in America.* Berkeley: University of California Press.

Cook, P. J., & Ludwig, J. (1998). The burden of "acting white": Do black adolescents disparage academic achievement? In C. Jencks & M. Phillips (Eds.), *The black-white test score gap* (pp. 375–400). Washington, DC: Brookings Institution.

Downey, D. B., Ainsworth, J. W., & Qian, Z. (2009). Rethinking the attitude-achievement paradox among blacks. *Sociology of Education, 82*(1), 1–19.

Downey, D. B., & Ainsworth-Darnell, J. W. (2002). The search for oppositional culture among black students. *American Sociological Review, 67*(1), 156–164.

Dreeben, R., & Gamoran, A. (1986). Race, instruction, and learning. *American Sociological Review, 51*(5), 660–669.

Farkas, G., Lleras, C., & Maczuga, S. (2002). Does oppositional culture exist in minority and poverty peer groups? *American Sociological Review, 67*(1), 148–155.

Ferguson, R. F. (2001). Test-score trends along racial lines 1971 to 1996: Popular culture and community academic standards. In N. J. Smelser, W. J. Wilson, & F. Mitchell (Eds.), *America becoming: Racial trends and their consequences, vol. I* (pp. 348–390). Washington, DC: National Academy Press.

Fischer, C. S., Hout, M., Jankowski, M. S., Lucas, S. R., Swidler, A., & Voss, K. (1996). *Inequality by design: Cracking the bell curve.* Berkeley: University of California Press.

Flynn, J. R. (2007). *What is intelligence?* New York: Cambridge University Press.

Fordham, S. (1988). Racelessness as a factor in black students' school success: Pragmatic strategy or Pyrrhic victory? *Harvard Educational Review, 58*(1), 54–84.

Fordham, S. (1993). "Those loud black girls": (Black) women, silence, and gender "passing" in the academy. *Anthropology & Education Quarterly, 24*(3), 3–32.

Fordham, S. (1996). *Blacked out: Dilemmas of race, identity, and success at capital high.* Chicago: University of Chicago.

Fordham, S., & Ogbu, J. (1986). Black students' school success: Coping with the "burden of acting white." *The Urban Review, 18*(3), 176–206.

Fryer, R. G., Jr., & Levitt, S. D. (2004). Understanding the black-white test score gap in the first two years of school. *The Review of Economics and Statistics, 86*(2), 447–464.

Gardner, H. (1983). *Frames of mind: The theory of multiple intelligences.* New York: Basic Books.

Gardner, H. (1993). *Multiple intelligences: The theory in practice.* New York: Basic Books.

Good, T. L. (1987). Two decades of research on teacher expectations: Findings and future directions. *Journal of Teacher Education, 38*(4), 32–47.

Hallinan, M. T. (1987). Ability grouping and student learning. In M. T. Hallinan (Ed.), *The social organization of schools: New conceptualizations of the learning process* (pp. 41–69). New York: Plenum.

Hallinan, M. (2001). Sociological perspectives on black-white inequalities in American schooling. *Sociology of Education,* (extra issue), 50–70.

Herrnstein, R. J., & Murray, C. (1994). *The bell curve: Intelligence and class structure in American life.* New York: Free Press.

Horvat, E. M., & O'Connor, C. (Eds.). (2006). *Beyond acting white: Reframing the debate on black student achievement.* Boulder, CO: Rowman & Littlefield.

Ingersoll, R. M. (2002). *Out-of-field teaching, educational inequality, and the organization of schools* (Research Report No. R-02-1). Center for the Study of Teaching and Policy, University of Washington, Seattle.

Jencks, C., & Phillips, M. (1998). *The black-white test score gap.* Washington, DC: Brookings Institution Press.

Jensen, A. R. (1969). How much can we boost IQ and scholastic achievement? *Harvard Educational Review, 39*(1), 1–123.

Kao, G., Tienda, T., & Schneider, B. (1996). Racial and ethnic variation in academic performance. In A. M. Pallas (Ed.), *Research in sociology of education and socialization* (vol. 11, pp. 263–297). Greenwich, CT: JAI Press.

Kovach, J. A., & Gordon, D. E. (1997). Inclusive education: A modern day civil-rights struggle. *The Educational Forum, 61*(3), 247–257.

Lewis, A. E. (2003). *Race in the schoolyard: Negotiating the color line in classrooms and communities.* New Brunswick, NJ: Rutgers University Press.

Lucas, S. R., & Berends, M. (2002). Sociodemographic diversity, correlated achievement, and de facto tracking. *Sociology of Education, 75*(4), 328–348.

Mandara, J., Varner, F., Greene, N., & Richman, S. (2009). Intergenerational family predictors of the black-white achievement gap. *Journal of Educational Psychology, 101*(4), 867–878.

Mickelson, R. (1990). The attitude-achievement paradox among black adolescents. *Sociology of Education, 63*(1), 44–61.

Morning, A. (2007, August). *Teaching race.* Presentation at the American Sociological Association annual meeting, New York.

Moss, P., & Tilly, C. (2003). *Stories employers tell: Race, skill, and hiring in America.* New York: Russell Sage Foundation.

National Center for Education Statistics (NCES). (2001). *Bureau of the census, current population survey.* Washington, DC: Author.

Nettles, M. T., & Perna, L. W. (1997). *The African American education data book. Vol. I: Higher and adult education.* Fairfax, VA: Frederick D. Patterson Research Institute.

Nisbett, R. E. (1998). Race, genetics, and IQ. In C. Jencks & M. Phillips (Eds.), *The black-white test score gap* (pp. 86–102). Washington, DC: Brookings Institution.

Oakes, J. (1985). *Keeping track: How schools structure inequality.* New Haven, CT: Yale University Press.

Ogbu, J. (2001). Cultural amplifiers of intelligence: IQ and minority status in cross-cultural perspective. In J. M. Fish (Ed.), *Race and intelligence: Separating science from myth* (pp. 241–278). Mahwah, NJ: Lawrence Erlbaum.

Ogbu, J. (2003). *Black American students in an affluent suburb: A study of academic disengagement.* Mahwah, NJ: Lawrence Erlbaum.

Ogbu, J. U., & Stern, R. (2001). Caste and intellectual development. In R. J. Sternberg & E. L. Grigorenko (Eds.), *Environmental effects on cognitive abilities* (pp. 3–37). Mahwah, NJ: Lawrence Erlbaum.

Oliver, M. L., & Shapiro, T. M. (1997). *Black wealth/white wealth.* New York: Routledge.

Omi, M. A. (2001). The changing meaning of race. In N. J. Smelser, W. J. Wilson, & F. Mitchell (Eds.), *America becoming, vol. I* (pp. 243–263). Washington, DC: National Academy Press.

Pager, D., & Quillian, L. (2005). Walking the talk? What employers say versus what they do. *American Sociological Review, 70*(3), 355–380.

Persell, C. H. (1977). *Education and inequality: The roots and results of stratification in America's schools.* New York: Free Press.

Persell, C. H., Catsambis, S., & Cookson, P. W., Jr. (1992). Family background, high school type, and college attendance: A conjoint system of cultural capital transmission. *Journal of Research on Adolescence, 2*(1), 1–23.

Persell, C. H., & Hendrie, G. F. (2005). Race, education, and inequality. In M. Romero & E. Margolis (Eds.), *Blackwell companion to social inequalities* (pp. 533–612). London: Basil Blackwell.

Phillips, M., Crouse, J., & Ralph, J. (1998). Does the black-white test score gap widen after children enter school? In C. Jencks & M. Phillips (Eds.), *The black-white test score gap* (pp. 229–272). Washington, DC: Brookings Institution Press.

Roscigno, V. J. (1999). The black-white achievement gap, family-school links, and the importance of place. *Sociological Inquiry, 69*(2), 159–186.

Roscigno, V. J. (2000). Family/school inequality and African-American/Hispanic achievement. *Social Problems, 47*(2), 266–290.

Tatum, B. D. (1999). *"Why are all the black kids sitting together in the cafeteria?" and other conversations about race.* New York: Basic Books.

Thernstrom, A., & Thernstrom, S. (2003). *No excuses: Closing the racial gap in learning.* New York: Simon & Schuster.

Tyson, K. (2002). Weighing in: Elementary-age students and the debate on attitudes toward school among black students. *Social Forces, 80*(4), 1157–1189.

Tyson, K. (2003). Notes from the back of the room: Problems and paradoxes in the schooling of young black students. *Sociology of Education, 76*(4), 326–343.

Tyson, K. (2006). The making of a "burden": Tracing the development of a "burden of acting white" in schools. In C. O'Connor and E. M. Horvat (Eds.), *Beyond acting white: Reframing the debate on black student achievement* (pp. 57–87). New York: Rowman & Littlefield.

Tyson, K., Darity, W., Jr., & Castellino, D. R. (2005). It's not "a black thing." Understanding the burden of acting white and other dilemmas of high achievement. *American Sociological Review, 70*(4), 582–605.

Yeung, W.-J. J., & Conley, D. (2006). *Black-white achievement gap and family wealth* (Unpublished working paper). New York University.

Yeung, W.-J. J., Persell, C. H., & Reilly, M. C. (2010, August). *Intergenerational stratification, child development, and the black-white achievement gap.* Paper presented at the American Sociological Association annual meeting, Atlanta, GA.

Yeung, W.-J. J., & Pfeiffer, K. (2006). *The black-white test score gap: Age and gender differentials* (Unpublished working paper). New York University.

Zeng, Z., & Xie, Y. (2004). Asian-Americans' earnings disadvantage reexamined: The role of place of education. *American Journal of Sociology, 109*(5), 1075–1108.

READING 37

GENDER AND EDUCATION

Roslyn Arlin Mickelson

In 1989, Roslyn Mickelson published an article entitled "Why Does Jane Read and Write So Well?" She revisits those premises in this reading, asking why women's achievement is an anomaly—being particularly successful in school but not being able to parlay their successes into occupational and financial returns. She also examines the recent concern about underachievement of boys. She addresses these questions using several different explanations and applies test score data to test these theories.

Questions to consider for this reading:

1. Why does the article indicate that "Jane" reads and writes so well, and what are the concerns about her doing so?

2. How does the performance of girls in school compare to that of boys? What changes have occurred recently?

3. How are Mickelson's explanations for boys in schools similar to or different from those given by Morris in his two readings in this chapter?

Contemporary gender trends in educational outcomes reveal recognizable patterns. Familiar gender differences can be summarized as follows: net of race and social class, women do, on average, better in school and attain more education than do men; men's achievement and attainment patterns are somewhat bimodal in that men are more likely than women to be both academic stars and school failures; and women are less likely than men to excel in mathematics, science, and technical fields, while men are less likely to shine in reading, writing, social sciences, and humanities. Post–high school careers, college majors, and professional degrees reflect these same gender patterns in choices of college majors.

Since the middle of the 20th century, the historic male advantages in access to schooling and educational outcomes have largely disappeared. Women's educational achievements have closed many of gender gaps favoring men, and in some cases, new ones favoring women have emerged. To be sure, there are important social class and ethnic variations in gender differences. Nevertheless, overall, female students in the U.S. achieve at higher levels soon after they begin school and attain more education than their male counterparts at almost every degree level. However, at all degree levels, men receive larger occupational and income returns to their education.

This reading begins with a more detailed description of gender differences in educational processes, outcomes, and returns to schooling from the opportunity structure. Gender differences suggest two dilemmas: the first one concerns the underperformance of male students, especially males from disadvantaged ethnic minority backgrounds. The second dilemma involves why women do so well in school. In the face of continuing male income and occupational advantages in income returns for similar educational credentials, women's educational achievements and attainments appear anomalous. I conclude with observations on trends in gender and education.

K–12 EDUCATIONAL PROCESSES AND OUTCOMES

The years between children's birth and entry into kindergarten are critically important for readying them for school. There are very few gender differences in young children's access to preprimary school. Nonetheless, by kindergarten, females have a slight advantage in word recognition. By third grade males begin to perform slightly better in mathematics (U.S. Department of Education, 2005). These early, small gender differences in academic performance foreshadow the achievement patterns that continue through high school and postsecondary education.

TRACKING AND GROUPING

Ability grouping within elementary school classrooms and tracking of academic courses in secondary school are two of the most common organizational features of U.S. public education that shape educational outcomes. A student's gender alone rarely has a large effect on ability group or track placement, but elementary school placements in special education and gifted programs often reflect an intersection of students' gender, social class, and racial background. For example, although a majority of students are not identified for any special programs during elementary school, middle-class and white students are more likely to be identified as academically gifted, while ethnic minority and working-class students are more likely to be identified for special education. Disadvantaged minority males (especially African Americans, Latinos, and Native Americans) are disproportionately placed in special education while white, middle-class females are disproportionately identified for gifted education programs (Oakes, 2005). These

placements are consequential because elementary school ability groupings launch students onto educational trajectories that influence outcomes from elementary through postsecondary education (Lucas, 1999).

ACADEMIC PERFORMANCE K–12

A key reason that tracking and ability grouping are important is because they influence students' exposure to the formal curriculum. The National Assessment of Educational Progress (NAEP) is widely recognized as a measure of how well students learned the formal curriculum. NAEP assesses student academic performance in a given school at grades 4, 8, and 12 in a variety of subjects. NAEP results since 2000 show gender gaps exist in reading, writing, and mathematics. Overall, at each grade level, females outperform males in reading and writing. Males slightly outperform females in mathematics; however, when 12th grade NAEP performance is broken down into subject areas, male performance exceeds females' in only two of four mathematics content areas (U.S. Department of Education, 2005, p. 16). Males outperform females in science during the early grades but by 12th grade, their advantage disappears. Overall, the gender gaps in math and science have narrowed since the 1970s but the ones in reading and math persist.

SAT

College entrance exams such as the SAT are highly influential. The majority of SAT takers are females (54.6%) and overall scores reflect a large gender gap (1506 compared to 1532) in favor of males (College Board, 2006). It is worth noting that gender differences in SAT scores are dwarfed by ethnic differences in them. Males' SAT math scores exceed those of females. On average, males' scores in critical reading fall slightly above those of females, which is the opposite of the pattern found in NAEP scores, where females do much better than males in reading. Women's writing scores exceed those of men. The population of students who take the SAT includes those planning to attend college whereas NAEP tests reflect the overall population of students. This may be one reason that SAT scores do not reflect gender patterns found in NAEP results, where females excel in reading and writing relative to males.

HIGH SCHOOL CURRICULA

Students cannot learn what they have not been taught. Pallas and Alexander (1983) demonstrated that a major factor in SAT score gaps is students' differential enrollment rates in key high-level courses; students enrolling in higher-level courses in math and science generally score better on their college entrance exams. Analyses of high school transcripts reveal that large proportions of male and female students enroll in geometry, algebra II, chemistry, and biology (IES, 2007). In fact, compared to the gender gaps of 1970s, contemporary enrollment gaps in these courses are relatively small. With the exception of calculus and physics, females are slightly more likely than males to enroll in these math and science courses.

Today, there are few official systematic gender differences in curricular offerings for public school students. That was not always the case. Until the early 20th century, female students were unlikely to enroll in certain courses because of pervasive gender stereotypes about the proper kinds of knowledge for males and females. Curricula in coed schools varied but always reflected the local community's social construction of gender, especially the gendered nature of men's and women's public and private roles. Historically, some secondary science electives offered gendered curricula. For example, in a physics course for girls, students learned about the mechanics of vacuum cleaners and sewing machines (Tyack & Hansot, 1990). Observable gender differences in math and science enrollments that grew out of the ways that schools organized access to the curricula resulted in

females taking far fewer advanced math and science courses than males. Tyack and Hansot (1990) conclude that this historical gendering of the science curricula resulted in few if any females prepared for college science or engineering courses during the early decades of the 20th century.

At present there are no gender differences in the likelihood of students' placements in higher-level math and science secondary tracks once their prior achievement and previous track placements are taken into account. Research identifies persistent race and social class effects in track placements, though. Ethnic differences in higher-level course enrollments are related to many factors, including the fact that disadvantaged minority males were disproportionately placed in special education during elementary school. By high school, very few disadvantaged minority males are prepared to enroll in top-level academic courses.

ADVANCED PLACEMENT COURSES

Advanced Placement (AP) courses offer the most rigorous, college level coverage of subject matter. Compared to other high track courses, AP courses provide students with several advantages including exposure to college level course work. If they pass the AP exam, students receive college course credit. To pass the AP exam, students must score a 3 or 4 on the exam.

In 2002, 56% of AP exams takers were women. Females were the majority of exam takers in social studies, English, and foreign languages; males were the majority of exam takers in calculus, computer science, and sciences. Nevertheless, females fared relatively poorly compared to males in almost all categories of AP exams. Males' average AP scores in social studies, English, calculus, computer science, and sciences exceeded those of females. Females' average AP scores exceeded males' average scores only in foreign languages (U.S. Department of Education, 2005, p. 6). In fact, foreign languages is the only subject area in which females' average scores exceeded the threshold of 3.0 necessary for college credit;

whereas males' average scores exceeded the 3.0 threshold in all subject areas. The gendered patterns of achievement favoring male students in AP exam results are more similar to SAT scores than to NAEP gender patterns. It is important to remember that because the population of students taking AP exams is not the same as the population that takes NAEP tests, it is not appropriate to compare scores across tests.

EXTRACURRICULAR AND CO-CURRICULAR ACTIVITIES

For most students, high school is much more than academic courses. Extracurricular and co-curricular activities are important components of students' social lives as well as key contributors to their cognitive development, especially activities considered as co-curricular. Sociological research indicates that positive school outcomes are correlated with participation in extracurricular and co-curricular activities.

There are clear gender differences in the degree and type of participation in extracurricular activities. Females are more likely than males to participate in extracurricular and co-curricular activities, a fact that may be related to their overall higher academic performance. With the exception of student government, where participation rates are comparable among males and females, other activities are clearly gendered. Athletics are the only activity in which more males (45%) than females (32%) are involved. Females are much more likely than male students to participate in yearbook, newspaper, music and performing arts, and academic clubs.

RISKY BEHAVIOR IN HIGH SCHOOL

Students who dislike school or who engage in risky behavior are less likely to succeed academically and they are more likely to drop out of high school. NAEP data suggest that while most students are not involved in risky behavior, male students are more likely than female peers to have engaged in drug or alcohol use, to have carried a weapon to school, or to have been a participant in or victim of school violence. Childbearing has a negative effect on females' likelihood of completing high school, although young mothers from higher socioeconomic status are more likely to graduate than young mothers from low SES backgrounds (Freeman, 2004).

Nearly one-third of public high school students fail to graduate (Swanson, 2004). Nationally, an estimated 78% of whites, 72% of Asian Americans, 55% of African Americans, and 53% of Latinos graduated from high school in 2003 (Greene & Winters, 2006). Overall, male students are 8% less likely to graduate from high school than are females (Swanson, 2004). Gender differences in dropout rates exist in all ethnic groups: among whites, 5% fewer males than females graduate from high school; among Asian Americans the rate is 3% lower than for females; among African Americans 11% more women than males graduate; and among Latinos there is a 9% female graduation advantage (Greene & Winters, 2006). Dropout rates are declining for all male ethnic groups, except Latinos for whom rates are holding steady (Freeman, 2004).

POSTSECONDARY OUTCOMES

Postsecondary Enrollments

Forty years ago men were the majority of students at all levels of postsecondary education. Today, gender differences in postsecondary enrollments reflect patterns seen in earlier grades. Females are more likely to enroll in college and to graduate than their male peers. Fifty-six percent of undergraduates and 58% of graduate students are women. There are striking ethnic variations in undergraduate enrollments by gender: 49% of white, 37% of black, 34% of Latino, 30% of American Indian, and 54% of Asian undergraduate students are male.

Although men are still a majority of students in first-professional degree programs (medicine, dentistry, law, optometry, pharmacy, veterinary medicine, podiatry, and theology), women have made striking progress in first-professional degree enrollment since the 1970s when only 9% of students were women. In 1970, for instance, women received 5% of law degrees, 8% of medical degrees, and 1% of dentistry degrees (Freeman, 2004). By 2001, the percentages were 47, 43, and 39 respectively. In some fields, like veterinary medicine, a majority of recent recipients are women (Wright, 2006).

Postsecondary Attainment

Enrollment is the first step to obtaining a higher education. Persistence to graduation is the final and most important step. Males are less likely than females to persist in higher education. Fifty-nine percent of undergraduate degrees are awarded to female students. Important ethnic variations exist in undergraduate degree attainment: among white bachelor's degree recipients, 57% are female, among blacks 66% are female, and among Latinos, 60% are females.

Table 37.1 indicates students majoring in engineering, computer and information systems, and agriculture are disproportionately male; those majoring in biology and life sciences, accounting, education, psychology, and health fields are largely females. The only majors that approach gender balance are mathematics, business administration, and the social sciences and history.

These patterns both reflect and deviate from earlier trends in academic outcomes. Accounting, social science, mathematics, and history were fields historically dominated by males but are increasingly becoming female dominated. At the same time, the grossly disproportionate enrollment of males in engineering and computer and information systems majors is inconsistent with the minor gender disparities in high school course-taking and academic achievement. The virtual monopoly that men once enjoyed in engineering and computer and information sciences has been broken, but the fields of study are far from parity (Huang, Taddese, & Walter, 2000).

Table 37.1 Percentage of Bachelor's Degrees Granted by Field and Gender (2001)

	Female	Male
Engineering	20	80
Computer and Information Systems	28	72
Physical Sciences	41	59
Agriculture and Natural Resources	45	55
Mathematics	48	52
Business Administration	49	51
Social Sciences and History	52	48
Biology and Life Sciences	60	40
Accounting	61	39
Education	77	23
Psychology	78	22
Health and Related Services	84	16

Note. From *Trends in Educational Equity of Girls and Women: 2004* (p. 78), by C. E. Freeman, 2004, Washington, DC: U.S. Department of Education, National Center for Educational Statistics. Reprinted with permission.

Gender differences in fields of study have implications for labor force participation.

Labor Force Participation

Labor market outcomes for men and women have changed during the past 35 years in ways that reflect many of the trends in education. During the past half-century as the U.S. economy transformed from one based upon manufacturing to one dominated by services, gender roles became less rigid, more women obtained educational credentials, and greater proportions of them entered the labor force.

Women today are much more likely to work outside the home across all levels of educational attainment, and the occupational structure is much less sex segregated than it was a generation ago. Nonetheless, at every level of education, women's labor force participation rates are lower than men's. For example, in 2001 among 25- to 64-year-olds with less than a high school diploma, 75% of men compared to 52% of women were employed or looking for work. Labor participation rates for men and women increase as their educational credentials increase. Among those with some postsecondary education, 86% of men compared to 73% of women participated in the labor force; among those with a BA degree or higher, 92% of men and 81% of women were employed (Freeman, 2004, p. 96).

INCOME RETURNS TO EDUCATIONAL CREDENTIALS

Just as labor force participation rates increase with educational attainment levels, so do earnings. Both females and males enjoy a positive relationship between their educational credentials and income at every level of education; those with more education earn more. Still, females continue to earn less than males in comparable occupations. The 2000 U.S. Census shows that for all year-round full-time workers, overall females earned 69% of what males earned. The gap in female-male earnings ratio tends to narrow as occupations require greater education. Women in retail sales earn 65.5% of what males in retail sales earn, while women in computer programming earned 88.5% of what males in the same occupation earned. Still females in medicine earned 68.6% of the income of male physicians, most likely because they specialize in less lucrative fields such as family medicine as compared to orthopedic surgery, a specialty dominated by males (U.S. Census Bureau, 2004).

There is also a gender gap in income returns at every level of educational attainment. In 2000, women without a high school diploma earned 80% of men with similar education; women with a high school diploma earned 73% of what men earned; women with associate's degrees received 72% of men's income; women with master's degrees received 74% of men's income; and women with first-professional degrees earned 86% of their comparably educated male colleagues (Freeman, 2004, p. 105).

Economists and sociologists offer several possible reasons for the education-to-earnings gap and the within-occupation gender gaps in income. Structural explanations include the tendency for women to major in fields that are less lucrative (teaching versus engineering), sex-composition bias—whereby people who work in female dominated fields or subspecialties are paid less (Bellas & Reskin, 1994), the likelihood that women will drop in and out of the labor force to have children, and the relatively higher rate of part-time employment among women (Freeman, 2004, p. 98). Sociologists also recognize that sexist norms that devalue women's work may also contribute to the income gap.

THE FEMALE QUESTION: WHY DO FEMALES DO SO WELL IN SCHOOL?

Exploring structural reasons women earn less for their educational credentials is useful for understanding income differences by gender but it does not help to account for *why* women continue to achieve so well and attain so much education in the face of the education-to-earnings gender gap. Given that American society is purportedly a meritocracy that rewards those who accomplish more, the academic success of women relative to men in the face of such income disparities seems anomalous.

Mickelson (1989) proposed several hypotheses to account for the apparent anomaly of women's educational accomplishments. The various hypotheses draw from social scientific theories of human behavior that build upon the intersection between structural forces and individual components of achievement motivation.

The first one challenges the notion that discrimination in the labor force still exists. The Pollyanna hypothesis proposes that contemporary women believe men and women are rewarded equally by the opportunity structure based on their merit, not gender. For the young women who believe discrimination in labor force returns to women's education is a thing of the past, doing well in school is the rational course of action. Under this scenario, women's achievement is not anomalous because they expect to be equally rewarded for their efforts and accomplishments.

Even the young women who accept that gender discrimination still exists in the occupational structure nevertheless do well in school. The differential reference group hypothesis proposes that they gauge fairness of rewards to education by comparisons among women with different levels of education, not necessarily between men and women with the same education. Women with more education work in more lucrative, higher status occupations than women with less education; therefore, women's growing educational accomplishments make perfect sense.

Second, the social-powerlessness hypothesis proposes that well-educated young women expect to obtain returns on their own schooling through their husbands' occupational successes. They do well in school because better educated women make more desirable wives and mothers, and educational achievements will better position them in the marriage market. The social-powerlessness perspective rests on the premise that young women are keenly aware that the sex-segregated occupational structure and lower wages paid to women mean their educational efforts will not necessarily be rewarded based on merit. Given this reality, they expect academic achievement will reap the greatest rewards from the marriage market, not the labor market.

The next hypothesis rests on theories of gender-role socialization. According to this view women do well in school because they have been socialized to respond to external validation for their efforts, whereas males are more likely to have an internal orientation. "Good girls" comply with directives from authority figures like parents and teachers because they desire the praise of these significant others. Because their motivation to excel in school is not necessarily linked to external rewards such as occupational prestige or high incomes, the weaker returns they receive do not render their achievement anomalous.

The fifth hypothesis proposes that women are more likely than men to evaluate returns to education in terms not only of the income, status, and careers it brings, but of their education's potential to enhance the quality of their personal, familial, and community lives. Feminist theory challenges the traditional views that labor market rewards are the appropriate measure of returns to educational successes. Feminist theory suggests that there are fluid boundaries between women's public and private spheres. From a young age, women are socialized to approach their lives by weaving public and private roles into a single tapestry. For women, the public (the economy and the polity) and the private (family and community) exist as a continuum, rather than as a dichotomy.

Dumais (2002) observed that each of Mickelson's hypotheses for women's school success reflects a different habitus, one of three core components in Bourdieu's theory of practice, more commonly referred to as social action. According to Bourdieu, cultural capital, habitus, and field operate together to generate social action—in this case school success. The concept of cultural capital refers to objects that require special cultural abilities to appreciate, such as art; educational credentials and the credentialing system; and the capacity to appreciate and understand cultural goods (Dumais, 2002, p. 46). Schools reward students with greater cultural capital. Consequently, those who possess cultural capital excel in school. Middle-class girls are likely to possess more cultural capital than are boys. An important source of middle class females' cultural capital edge is their greater participation in private music, dance, or art lessons and co-curricular activities, all of which contribute to their stock of cultural capital (Dumais, 2002).

Bourdieu's concept of habitus refers to dispositions that influence a person's actions. The gendered nature of habitus is a consequence of the different possibilities that women and men perceive as available to them. Habitus is developed during childhood as a person grows to understand her or his place in the social structure. A student's habitus expresses perceived aspects of the gendered structure of opportunity that awaits her or him (race and social class are also relevant). Habitus plays a large role in school success because students' decisions to invest in their education, whether or not to study hard, and what college major and career to pursue depend on their expectations of whether people like themselves can and should be academically successful.

The research of sociologists like Dumais and Mickelson offers various theories to account for the female portion of the dilemma of gendered patterns in academic achievement, specifically the anomalous achievement of females in the face of relatively inequitable rewards for their accomplishments. While none of the theories provides a definitive explanation for women's academic successes, each one sheds some light on the ways that social structure and individual agency contribute to school outcomes. We now turn to the dilemma raised by male patterns of academic underperformance.

THE MALE QUESTION: IS THERE A MALE CRISIS IN EDUCATION?

The previous sections of this chapter described how, on average, beginning in elementary school males fall behind females on many measures of academic achievement. Even taking into account the striking ethnic and social class differences in these outcomes, overall, males demonstrate

lower verbal skills and are more likely to be identified for special education, to engage in more risky behaviors, to have lower high school graduation rates, and to attend and graduate from college at lower rates than females.

The gender gaps in primary, secondary, and postsecondary enrollments, performance, and outcomes have gained attention from policy makers, parents, and educators. Adherents to one school of thought consider the gender gaps as indicators that American society is leaving boys behind. Many of the observers who perceive "a boy crisis" believe that the societal focus on females' educational disadvantages (AAUW, 1992; c.f., Sadker & Sadker, 1995) during the past 30 years has resulted in neglect of the genuine problems of male students (Sommers, 2000). Some argue that the presence of so many female teachers in elementary school, behavioral norms that require students to sit still for extended periods of time in combination with a curriculum that emphasizes reading and verbal skills create learning environments that are less conducive to boys' early educational successes. Consequently, these critics argue, males fall behind their female counterparts beginning in the early grades and they are launched on less positive educational trajectories than females with similar backgrounds and cognitive strengths.

Many educators, parents, and scholars find the situation of black male students particularly troubling (Kunjufu, 1985; Jackson & Moore, 2006). Ferguson (2000) proposes that widely held negative societal images of black masculinity result in many educators, primarily whites, "seeing" black boys as adults. Educators' responses to black boys, especially the harsh discipline they dole out, contribute to the early educational failures that later become the high rates of special education placement, low test scores, high rates of dropping out, and consequent low rates of college attendance and graduation among black males. Lopez (2003) makes a similar argument about immigrant Caribbean males' negative educational experiences. She describes the toxic race-gender stigma that accompanies immigrant Caribbean male students to urban schools and educators' harsh responses to the stereotypes of them as "hoodlums."

A second school of thought, while acknowledging the existence of gender gaps, rejects the notion of a boy crisis. Those who hold this view note that when educational outcomes are broken out by social class and ethnicity, a much more nuanced view of the gender and education landscape appears. There is more within-gender variation in educational outcomes by ethnicity and social class than variation in outcomes between the genders. From this perspective, each gender faces unique problems, but the gender gap is dwarfed by race, ethnic, and social class gaps. Cynthia Fuchs Epstein (1988) calls this phenomenon a deceptive distinction, because gaps appear to be about gender when, in fact, they are about something else.

Those who reject the existence of a boy crisis in education point to evidence that contradicts the sweeping generalization that male students are being left behind. They note that wealthy males do not lag behind females in middle or high school. Poor and inner city males—primarily blacks, Latinos, and American Indian males—have significantly less educational success than females from their ethnic group (Kimmel, 2006). Throughout K–12 schooling, males tend to perform better than females in math and science, a longstanding pattern according to historians of education (Tyack & Hansot, 1990). On achievement tests, especially the important Advanced Placement exam, and SAT college entrance exams, males outperform females.

Postsecondary enrollment gaps are genuine, yet ethnicity and social class complicate the picture once again. For example, at most elite private institutions including Stanford, Harvard, Princeton, Duke, Yale, Chicago, there is no gender imbalance in enrollment. At UC Berkeley, the California Institute of Technology, and the Massachusetts Institute of Technology the gender balance in enrollment favors males (Kimmel, 2006). Male undergraduates are more likely than females to major in the STEM disciplines (science, technology, engineering, and math) that lead to lucrative careers. Importantly, labor force data indicate that compared to females, males earn more at all levels of the occupational structure and at all educational levels.

Whether or not one considers the relative underachievement of males to be evidence of a crisis or not, patterns of male underperformance require an explanation. Social conservatives, like Sommers (2000), argue that the educational system operates in ways that are destructive to boys. For example, the overwhelmingly female elementary teacher force means boys have little access to adult male role models during a critical period in their early development. She finds that schools are organized in ways that devalue or actually work against males' innate strengths. Moreover, she maintains, progressive educators and feminists have ignored boys' educational problems while focusing on girls' needs.

Kimmel (2006) and Lopez (2003) imply that the nature of some school subjects either work in support of or against certain norms of masculinity. From this perspective, succeeding in the humanities, reading, English, foreign language requires "feminine" ways of thinking; Kimmel (2006) argues that boys hate English for the same reasons that girls love it—there is no single correct answer. Science, mathematics, and technology, all of which have discrete correct answers, are more in tune with stereotypical masculine norms. Willis (1977) proposed a variation of this argument to explain why British working-class males rejected working hard in school. He found that working-class males defined schoolwork and other forms of intellectual labor as feminine in contrast to physical labor, which they considered to be masculine. These arguments are consistent with the data showing that working-class and low-income males, rather than elite males, are the most likely to underperform in school relative to females of the same social class background.

Sociologists also have proposed a more obvious reason that boys do less well in school. Essentially, why should men work so hard? Given the fact that males at every level of educational attainment will likely obtain greater occupational and income rewards than females even with less education—some studies show that male high school graduates earn as much or more than female college graduates—males have less incentive to achievement and attain to their full potentials.

CONCLUSION

Without doubt, gender differences in educational processes and outcomes exist. Because gender patterns in academic outcomes are consequential, they require continued attention by educators, parents, and policy makers. Nevertheless, it is important to consider the fact that there are greater within-gender variations by social class and ethnicity than there are differences between the genders. The ways that gender shapes a given student's educational experiences and eventual outcomes are intimately tied to her or his social class and ethnicity and to the larger social structural context in which the person lives.

The twin dilemmas of female achievement in the face of uncertain rewards and male underachievement are more than flip sides of the same coin. They raise important issues for sociologists trying to understand how the processes involved in educational stratification contribute to social stratification more generally.

REFERENCES

American Association of University Women (AAUW). (1992). *How schools shortchange girls.* Washington, DC: Author.

Bellas, M., & Reskin, B. (1994). On comparable worth. *Academe* (September/October), 83–85.

College Board. (2006). *College-bound seniors 2006: Total group profile.* Retrieved from http://www.collegeboard.com/about/news_info/cbsenior/yr2006/reports.html

Dumais, S. (2002). Cultural capital, gender, and school success: The role of habitus. *Sociology of Education, 75*(1), 44–68.

Epstein, C. F. (1988). *Deceptive distinctions: Sex, gender, and the social order.* New Haven, CT: Yale University Press.

Ferguson, A. A. (2000). *Bad boys: Public schools in the making of black masculinity.* Ann Arbor: University of Michigan Press.

Freeman, C. E. (2004). *Trends in educational equity of girls and women: 2004.* Washington, DC: U.S. Department of Education, National Center for Educational Statistics, U.S. Government Printing Office.

Greene, J. P., & Winters, M. A. (2006, April). *Leaving boys behind: Public high school graduation rates* (Civil Report 48). New York: Manhattan Institute.

Huang, G., Taddese, N., & Walter, E. (2000). Entry and persistence of women and minorities in college science and engineering education. *Education Statistics Quarterly, 2*(3), 59–60. Retrieved from http://nces.ed.gov/pubsearch/pubsinfo.asp?pubid=2000601

Institute of Educational Sciences (IES). (2007). *America's high school graduates: Results from the 2005 NAEP high school transcript study* (NCES2007-467). Washington, DC: U.S. Department of Education. Retrieved from http://nationsreportcard.gov

Jackson, J. F. L., & Moore, J. L. (2006). African American males in education: Endangered or ignored? *Teachers College Record, 108*(2), 201–205.

Kimmel, M. (2006). A war against boys? *Dissent,* (Fall). Retrieved from http://www.dissentmagazine.org/article/?article=700

Kunjufu, J. (1985). *Countering the conspiracy to destroy black boys.* Chicago: African American Images.

Lopez, N. (2003). *Hopeful girls, troubled boys: Race and gender disparity in urban education.* New York: Routledge.

Lucas, S. R. (1999). *Tracking inequality: Stratification and mobility in American high schools.* New York: Teachers College Press, Columbia University.

Mickelson, R. A. (1989). Why does Jane read and write so well? The anomaly of women's achievement. *Sociology of Education, 62*(1), 47–63.

Oakes, J. (2005). *Keeping track: How schools structure inequality.* New Haven, CT: Yale University Press.

Pallas, A. M., & Alexander, K. L. (1983). Sex differences in quantitative SAT performance: New evidence on the differential coursework hypothesis. *American Educational Research Journal, 20*(2), 165–182.

Sadker, M., & Sadker, D. (1995). *Failing at fairness: How our schools cheat girls.* New York: Simon & Schuster.

Sommers, C. H. (2000). *The war against boys: How misguided feminism is harming our young men.* New York: Simon & Schuster.

Swanson, C. B. (2004). *Graduation rates: Real kids, real numbers.* Washington, DC: Urban Institute.

Tyack, D., & Hansot, E. (1990). *Learning together: A history of coeducation in American public schools.* New Haven, CT: Yale University Press.

U.S. Census Bureau. (2004). *Population estimates.* Washington, DC: Author.

U.S. Department of Education. (2005). *National Center for Educational Statistics, 2005 mathematics assessment.* Washington, DC: Author, Institute of Educational Sciences.

Willis, P. (1977). *Learning to labor.* New York: Columbia University Press.

Wright, D. (2006, January). Animal attraction: Women in contemporary veterinary medicine. *S&T.* Retrieved from http://www.brynmawr.edu/sandt/2006_january

Projects for Further Exploration

1. Using an academic database, look up the topics of *"race"* and *"academic achievement"* to see what other research has been done in this area. How does this compare to the arguments made by Caroline Hodges Persell in this chapter?

2. Try to replicate the study by Joan Spade, Lynn Columba, and Beth Vanfossen by collecting information on what courses are offered at the schools on which you are collecting data. This information may be on the Web pages for those schools, or you could get a list of courses available from the school offices. How does what you find compare with the arguments in the reading by these authors?

3. Using the U.S. Census website, collect information about the poverty level of the school districts you are studying. Are there patterns between socioeconomic classes of districts and the measures of achievement on which you previously collected data?

8

EDUCATION AND OPPORTUNITY

Attempts at Equality and Equity in Education

Why is there inequality in the educational system and what can we do about it? As suggested by this book's introduction and the readings in Chapter 7, the U.S. education system is rife with problems of inequality. Many programs to bring about change have been designed to remedy these inequalities. This chapter contains descriptions of some of these efforts, most of which are current issues in education today. Although we cannot cover all attempts at equality and equity, we focus on those most salient, both from this historical record and at the present time. We do not cover general educational reforms in this part of the book, but leave the discussion of those efforts to Chapter 11 and other chapters.

In studying broad changes in education of any kind, we notice that the impetus for these changes comes from many different directions, with the most far-reaching changes generated at the federal level, either through judicial decisions or via massive funding efforts. This should not be surprising, given the preceding readings about the organization of schools in the United States (Chapter 4) and the way schools are financed (Reyes and Rodriguez, Chapter 3). In fact, loose coupling combined with local financing of schools makes broad-based reform efforts very difficult in the United States, as the readings in this chapter suggest.

School systems across the United States and other countries are very difficult organizations in which to introduce change, as illustrated by the many stakeholders in the open systems model. One of the most significant pieces of legislation to impact schools was targeted directly at increasing equality in education—*Brown v. Board of Education*. In 1954, the Supreme Court decision of *Brown v. the Board of Education of Topeka, Kansas* ruled that separate but equal education was unconstitutional. This decision set in motion many changes in public school education today and is thought to be responsible for changing the composition of cities and their schools as whites fled urban areas to avoid sending their children to desegregated schools. In 1964, James Coleman was commissioned by the U.S. Congress to assess changes in schools 10 years after this ruling. Coleman found that the 1954 decision had little impact on the segregation of America's schools. Pressure began to mount as school districts were "encouraged" to desegregate. These changes sometimes meant closing all-black schools and moving those students into formerly all-white schools (Cecelski, 1994). White residents also worked to alter the shape and structure of school districts during this period in an attempt to keep from desegregating their children (Rubin, 1972).

The early 1970s were active times, with courts mandating school desegregation across the country in a climate of outright racial conflict, particularly in the South. Both policies of desegregation and affirmative action are currently being challenged and overturned in the courts. Focus on minority status and social class is important because poverty is not distributed evenly across racial and ethnic households. In 2008, far more black (24.7%), and Hispanic (23.2%) households with children under the age of 18 live below the poverty level than white (8.6%) or Asian and Pacific Islander (11.8%) households (National Center for Education Statistics, 2009).

Issues of segregation, desegregation, and resegregation are addressed in the first two readings in this chapter. The first reading by Gary Orfield discusses the legal history of school desegregation and the current state of "resegregation" in American schools. The second reading by Jennifer Jellison Holme, Amy Stuart Wells, and Anita Tijerina Revilla use interviews with individuals who graduated in 1980 and were forced to attend desegregated schools in the early years of the implementation of the desegregation legislation to better understand the short-term and long-term impacts of these changes. Two more recent attempts by the federal government to achieve equality in education, No Child Left Behind (NCLB) and Race to the Top, were discussed in Chapter 3's reading by Kathryn Borman and Bridget Cotner. These two pieces of legislation designed to improve schools focused on increasing educational opportunities and experiences for all children. Borman and Cotner discussed a series of federal reform efforts that culminated in 2002 in the NCLB legislation and, in 2010, President Obama's Blueprint for Reform, both of which focus on accountability and innovation. One reform effort that is gaining momentum as a result of NCLB and the Blueprint for Reform is the charter school movement. Both pieces of legislation saw charter schools as an opportunity to provide alternative educational opportunities in public school systems and put more pressure on existing schools to improve the educational experiences they provide. Charter schools share many similarities with the earlier magnet schools; however, charter schools operate outside of most regulation by federal, state, and local authorities. The reading in this chapter by Linda Renzulli and Vincent Roscigno describes the rise of charter schools in the United States and considers the future of this recent school movement. The following reading by Linda Darling-Hammond uses her experience and background in researching school reform efforts to consider how charter schools, and all schools, can be more successful in educating children from disadvantaged backgrounds.

Although only briefly discussed in readings in this chapter, magnet schools, the precursors to charter schools, were one way that school districts attempted to desegregate without busing students involuntarily from one school to another. Magnet schools were organized in districts to attract students from different backgrounds around particular subject areas such as math and science or the arts. Successful magnet schools should have desegregated school districts; however, this was not always the case. In many cases, magnet schools enrolled only white students because those students had the cultural resources to both learn about and qualify for admittance to these specialized schools. Furthermore, teachers in magnet schools were trained in the particular area of the magnet, not necessarily in working with children from diverse racial backgrounds, as would be the case in desegregated schools (Metz, 1994).

A little background may be useful to understand the controversy surrounding the idea of parents choosing schools for their children. School choice became a political issue in the 1970s. At that time Americans were concerned about desegregation and the quality of education their children were receiving. Choice was seen as a way of improving education without increasing costs and getting parents more involved in the education of their children. Models of school choice, however, varied considerably; some were statewide, some only involved districts, while others included private schools. Whereas some people argue that school choice gives lower-class families an opportunity to get their children out of inferior educational settings and send them to better schools, others believe that lower-class parents will not have the "cultural capital" necessary to find their way through the system to the best schools (see the Johnson reading in Chapter 7; Saporito & Lareau, 1999) or to broker the best education for their children, as described by Lareau and Horvat in Chapter 2. Unfortunately, the first criterion in making a school choice for the white parents is the racial composition of the school their children will attend (Saporito & Lareau, 1999). The result of such choices reinforces the resegregation of schools, as illustrated in the reading by Holme, Wells, and Revilla in this chapter. It is unfortunate, but they found that both white and black students who benefited from desegregation still wanted their own children to attend "good schools" or predominantly white schools.

Attempts to achieve equality and equity in education face an uphill battle. The problems faced by schools are considerable and setting standards alone does not make up for inequality in society. As Richard Rothstein describes in his reading in this chapter, the achievement gap is rooted as much in the effects of poverty on children's lives as it is in the structure of our schools. He argues that children from poverty backgrounds have a considerable disadvantage in schools, regardless of what a school has to offer. As a result, he believes that reform efforts must go beyond the schools to address issues of poverty in general.

You will soon see that changing schools to make them more equal is clearly political. We include a selection by Michael W. Apple to explicitly discuss the politics of school reform. In the last reading in this chapter, Apple considers the conservative strategy toward education and suggests that liberals must think more politically if they are to effect change in schools.

All of these efforts to achieve equity and equality are very different; none are without controversy, but some are more controversial than others. It could be argued that none have been entirely successful because the condition of education for poor and minority children has not improved significantly. The readings in this chapter point to the problems of achieving equality, especially when doing so can affect the privilege of those who benefit from the unequal conditions.

REFERENCES

Cecelski, D. S. (1994). *Along freedom road: Hyde County, North Carolina, and the fate of black schools in the south.* Chapel Hill: University of North Carolina Press.

Metz, M. H. (1994). Desegregation as necessity and challenge. *Journal of Negro Education, 63*(1), 64–76.

National Center for Education Statistics. (2009). *Digest of education statistics.* Washington, DC: U.S. Department of Education. Retrieved from http://nces.ed.gov/programs/digest/d09/tables/dt09_021.asp

Rubin, L. B. (1972). *Busing and backlash: White against white in an urban school district.* Berkeley: University of California Press.

Saporito, S., & Lareau, A. (1999). School selection as a process: The multiple dimensions of race in framing educational choice. *Social Problems, 46*(3), 418–439.

LESSONS FORGOTTEN

Gary Orfield

Gary Orfield is a leading scholar on issues of civil rights and racial segregation in U.S. schools. He is currently codirector of the Civil Rights Project/El Proyecto de CRP, a center that was originally at Harvard University and renamed when it moved to UCLA in 2007. In this reading, Orfield describes the history of school desegregation in the United States. In addition to the legislation, critical to the desegregation and subsequent resegregation of American schools, he also describes the political climate and factors that influenced the attempts to provide more equal educational opportunities across race. Based on his research on school segregation and desegregation over time, this analysis and his other work suggest little hope that the current state of segregation in American schools will be reduced in the future.

Questions to consider for this reading:

1. According to Orfield, how did court cases fall short in ensuring desegregation of American schools?

2. What societal responses to the 1970s legislation made the resegregation of America's schools inevitable?

3. What difference does it make if schools are segregated?

In an era of great hope for this country's racial transformation from the mid-1960s to the early 1970s, we committed ourselves to creating integrated schools. There was a brief period in our history in which there was serious policy and research attention on how to devise racially diverse schools to achieve integration and equal opportunity. Civil rights leaders and participants in the hundreds of demonstrations demanding integrated education knew the sorry history of "separate but equal" and fought for access to the opportunities concentrated in White schools.

The desegregation experience has often been described by critics as little more than a mechanistic transfer of students, but it was often much more than that. From thousands of desegregation plans implemented around the nation we learned about the ways to operate successful integrated schools and classrooms. Now, as we deal both with resegregation, where court orders are dropped, and with the emergence of racial diversity in thousands of other schools, not as the result of court orders, but as the product of a great increase in the non-White population and of diversification of growing sectors of suburbia,

From *Lessons in Integration: Realizing the Promise of Racial Diversity in American Schools* (pp. 1–6), edited by E. Frankenberg and G. Orfield, 2007, Charlottesville: University of Virginia Press. Copyright 2007 by the Rector and Visitors of the University of Virginia. Reprinted with permission.

that experience and the unfinished agenda of the civil rights era are relevant again. Too many hard-earned lessons have been forgotten.

Most of the public struggle for desegregation involved opening the doors of White schools to students who had been historically excluded—Black and, in some cases, Latino students who attended segregated schools that were commonly inferior on many dimensions.[1] There was a fierce, two-decade struggle after *Brown v. Board of Education of Topeka* to desegregate the South, followed, in the 1970s, by a brief and usually losing struggle to desegregate northern cities. The Supreme Court's 1974 decision in the metropolitan Detroit case of *Milliken v. Bradley* rejected the only remedy that could have produced substantial and lasting school desegregation in much of the North, and instead built a massive legal barrier between city school districts and the surrounding suburban districts, where most White children resided and where typically the best schools were located. President Richard Nixon, who ran on the "southern strategy" promising to roll back desegregation, had dismantled much of the civil rights machinery of the federal government by this time (Panetta & Gall, 1971).

Critics often describe this period as one of mandatory race mixing with no educational components. Many educational experts, civil rights advocates, and officials, however, understood early that more must be done. Simply letting some minority' students into previously White schools operated by the same district officials was not likely to solve the problems of inequality. In fact, these officials often found new ways to discriminate within schools.

The deeper changes, in educational and social terms, involved going from the reality of desegregation—the fact that children of different racial and ethnic groups were now in the same school and faculties had been ordered to be desegregated—toward real integration, which required fair and equal treatment of each racial and ethnic group. Gordon Allport's classic book, *The Nature of Prejudice* (1954), published the year of the *Brown* decision, had concluded that creating desegregated settings could produce either positive or negative outcomes, which depended on how desegregation was done. The key, he said, was creating "equal status interaction" between the previously segregated groups. Allport wrote: "It required years of labor and billions of dollars to gain the secret of the atom. It will take a still greater investment to gain the secrets of man's irrational nature. It is easier, someone has said, to smash an atom than a prejudice" (as cited in Clark, 1979).

In the early days of desegregation there were too many reports of segregated classes, removal of minority teachers and principals, failure to integrate school activities, segregated classroom seating, discriminatory counseling, curricula that ignored minority history, and many other conditions that limited or prevented full access for minority students. Additionally, these conditions limited positive diversity experiences for White and minority students. Many educators, advocates, and researchers realized that factors influencing the nature of the transition from segregation to desegregation, and ultimately to integration, could shift the academic and social outcomes of students in these schools (Schofield, 1981). Most school staff members, who themselves attended segregated schools and were trained to work in one-race schools, did not have the knowledge and tools to address these issues.

Desegregation orders and plans by the late 1960s often went far beyond simply transferring students. The Supreme Court ended token desegregation that had been occurring through "freedom of choice" plans in 1968 and ordered "root and branch" desegregation to eliminate "dual school systems" organized on the basis of race (*Green v. County School Board of New Kent County,* 1968). To fulfill the constitutional requirement to create "unitary" school systems that were fully integrated, school desegregation plans had to include desegregation of teachers and students, and equalization of educational opportunities, facilities, and curriculum. The plans usually included strategies for informing the public of the plan, managing crises, retraining teachers and staff, developing new educational materials, and implementing policies for fair discipline and participation in student activities among the various groups of students.

Following the Supreme Court's decision in *Swann v. Charlotte-Mecklenburg Board of Education* (1971), there was massive controversy over court orders using tools such as busing to more thoroughly desegregate urban schools. Despite disagreements, both critics and supporters of desegregation recognized that help was needed in the suddenly integrated schools in hundreds of cities. Government responded, for a time. The Emergency School Aid Act was a bipartisan law initially intended to smooth the crises caused by sudden desegregation of urban school systems. In this act, negotiated between the Nixon White House and Senate liberals led by Senator Walter Mondale,[2] Congress enacted a policy of giving money to schools to support successful desegregation. Regardless of whether they supported desegregation plans, both sides could agree that if the plans must be implemented, schools required help to prevent dangerous cleavages in communities, such as those that did such severe damage to several cities, including Little Rock, Birmingham, and Boston, after racial violence flared. The programs funded under the desegregation assistance law did not provide money for busing itself, but they did provide hundreds of millions of dollars for helping the schools adapt.

The Emergency School Aid Act (Orfield, 1978, chap. 9) lasted from 1972 until 1981, when the Reagan administration ended it (Orfield & Eaton, 1996). While in operation, the law funded training, intervention programs, new curricula development, magnet schools for voluntary desegregation, and large-scale research or ways to improve race relations. Because courts were actively requiring desegregation, there was interest in obtaining help, and, as a result, school districts eagerly applied for these funds. The funding was so enthusiastically sought, in fact, that districts were often willing to do additional desegregation of students and teachers, not required by their own plan, to get it. Many magnet schools began and spread rapidly under this program, as school choice became a significant element in American education for the

first time. The law required that magnets be desegregated—choice was designed to combine equity with educational options.

During the Carter administration, the law was rewritten to incorporate the lessons of the major evaluation studies, which showed that aid made a substantial difference for both achievement and race relations, and was needed for at least several years to facilitate successful change. At the same time, the National Institute of Education supported research on desegregated schools and developed a research agenda for the field. Research on the effects of the programs and changes funded by the desegregation assistance law produced important findings about the conditions under which race relations and educational achievement gains were most likely to occur in interracial schools. During the desegregation era the Black-White gap declined sharply. Major studies documented the benefits of certain classroom techniques in mixed-race classrooms. Teachers and administrators facing racial change were given a great deal of inservice preparation.[3]

During this same period, education schools across the country and their national accreditation agencies made significant efforts to require training of teachers in multicultural education. Sensing a large new market, publishers supported substantial revisions of texts that had an exclusively White perspective. Many districts commissioned new curriculum about local minority contributions. At the same rime, the spread of bilingual education requirements and funding under the 1968 Bilingual Education Act, as well as the 1974 *Lau v. Nichols* Supreme Court decision about the rights of non-English-speaking students, brought into the schools an increasing number of Latino teachers and supported beginning education in a child's native language. Several desegregation orders, including those in school districts in Denver, Boston, and Texas, contained specific programs for language-minority students and their teachers.

The need for these efforts did not cease, but the support did. Training, school district programs, and research withered away. The Reagan administration in its first months opposed deseg-regation orders and eliminated the desegregation assistance program that had made desegregation plans work better; the research operation was shut down, and for the next quarter century there would be no significant federal funding for research or policy on effective race relations in diverse schools (Orfield & Eaton, 1996). The Reagan administration did, however, support research on "White flight," which it used to oppose desegregation in federal courts.

The country turned in a different direction when the standards movement emerged in the aftermath of the Reagan administration's *A Nation at Risk* report in 1983. The basic ideas of standards-based reform were that the social context of schools could be overlooked—both the problems of racial and economic inequality and the positive possibilities of racial diversity— and that standards, requirements, and sanctions would produce more equal outcomes in and of themselves or, if necessary, with the additional pressure of market competition from charter and private schools. Part of the basic analysis of the "excellence" movement was that schools had been diverted from traditional education responsibilities to counterproductive social reform efforts.

Virtually all states adopted this agenda, which was reinforced by the agreement between President George H. W. Bush and the nation's governors in 1989. At the Charlottesville Educational Summit, the National Governors Association's chair, Governor Bill Clinton of Arkansas, led the governors to agreement with the president on six national education goals to which the country should aspire by 2000, from school readiness to increasing high school graduation rates. Goal 3 (U.S. students should be first in the world in mathematics and science achievement) and goal 4 (all students should demonstrate achievement in core subjects) in particular spurred the bipartisan standards agenda (National Governors Association, 1989, 2000). The program to achieve the national goals became known as the America 2000 program, but it was not until the Goals 2000:

Educate America Act passed in 1993 during Clinton's first presidential term that the six goals were adopted as part of federal education law. In addition, the 1994 reauthorization of the Elementary and Secondary Education Act (known as the Improving America's Schools Act, or IASA) further drove the standards movement by requiring that all states adopt a system of standards, assessments, and account-ability to measure student performance in order to qualify for Title I funding. The IASA also required states to disaggregate student perfor-mance data for schools' annual yearly progress by race, gender, and socioeconomic status, but sanctions were not seriously enforced. Ultimately, none of the goals for closing the racial gap were realized and the gaps widened in some dimensions.

The No Child Left Behind Act of 2001 (NCLB), however, imposed more demanding goals and deadlines on all American schools. NCLB had strong goals and sweeping sanctions for equalizing achievement among minority and White children, but had no requirement to equal-ize the very unequal schooling opportunities or take any action to end segregation of minority students in inferior schools and improve race relations. By insisting on equal outcomes from patently unequal schools highly segregated by race and poverty, the 2001 law's sanctions tended to strongly penalize minority schools and teachers (Sunderman, Kim, & Orfield, 2005).

The effects of segregated education cannot be cured by merely enacting strong demands for achievement gains and changing nothing else in schools that are usually unequal in every major dimension relating to student achievement, including the quality of teachers, curriculum offered, and the level of competition (peer group). In fact, enforcing rigid standards without equalizing opportunity can exacerbate the inequalities by stigmatizing minority schools as failures, narrowing their curriculum to endless testing drills, and leading strong, experienced teachers to transfer to less pressured situations. The massive publicity given to test scores may also help destabilize residentially integrated communities, as realtors use test scores to steer White buyers to outlying White communities. Thus, the ironic impact of ignoring the inequality of the segregated schools in the name of standards is to worsen them.

In the past quarter century of incredible demographic transformation of the American school-age population there has been virtually no investment in either determining the best policies for extraordinarily complex school communities or even in applying well-documented programs and policies that are likely to make things better. Federal funding of desegregation research and experiments ended in the early 1980s, and private foundations do not generally support research about these topics, which has drastically limited the development of new knowledge that could assist schools with the racial transformation. This myopia makes school communities less effective internally and much weaker as anchors for multiracial communities dealing with pressures of racial stratification, fear, and racial transformation.

NOTES

1. The right for Latinos to desegregate was not acknowledged by the Supreme Court until 1973, after most active desegregation efforts had already ended. In striking contrast to the Johnson administration's role in the South, the Nixon administration did virtually nothing to enforce this policy.

2. Mondale, who became Jimmy Carter's vice president, chaired the Senate select Committee on Equal Educational Opportunity, which compiled 30 volumes of congressional hearings on all aspects of desegregation and issued a comprehensive report in 1972 that included a chapter on conditions for successful integration (U.S. Senate, 1972, chapter 17).

3. Much of that research is summarized in Hawley, Crain, Rossell, Schofield, & Fernandez (1983).

REFERENCES

Allport, G. W. (1954). *The nature of prejudice.* Reading, MA: Addison-Wesley.

Brown v. Board of Education of Topeka. 347 U.S. 483 (1954).

Clark, K. (1979). Introduction. In G. Allport, *The nature of prejudice* (pp. ix-xi). Cambridge, MA: Perseus.

Green v. County School Board of New Kent County. 391 U.S. 430 (1968).

Hawley, W. D., Crain, R. L., Rossell, C. H., Schofield, J. W., & Fernandez, R. (1983). *Strategies for effective desegregation: Lessons from research.* Lexington, MA: Lexington/D.C. Heath.

Lau v. Nichols. 414 U.S. 563 (1974).

Milliken v. Bradley. 418 U.S. 717 (1974).

National Governors Association. (1989). *Charlottesville summit.* Retrieved from http://www.nga.org/portal/sitc/nga/menuitem

National Governors Association. (2000). *America 2000 program.* Retrieved from http://govinfo.library.unt.ed/negp/reports/nego30.pdf

Orfield, G. (1978). *Must we bus? Segregated schools and national policy.* Washington, DC: Brookings Institution Press.

Orfield, G., & Eaton, S. E. (1996). *Dismantling desegregation: The quiet reversal of "Brown v. Board of Education."* New York: New Press.

Panetta, L., & Gall, P. (1971). *Bring us together: The Nixon team and the civil rights retreat.* Philadelphia: Lippincott.

Schofield, J. W. (1981). Complementary and conflicting identities: Images and interaction in an interracial school. In S. R. Asher & J. M. Gottman (Eds.), *The development of children's friendships* (pp. 53–90). Cambridge, England: Cambridge University Press.

Sunderman, G. L., Kim, J., & Orfield, G. (2005). *NCLB meets school realities: Lessons from the field.* Thousand Oaks, CA: Corwin Press.

Swann v. Charlotte-Mecklenburg Board of Education. 402 U.S. 1 (1971).

United States Senate, Select Committee on Equal Educational Opportunity. (1972). *Toward equal educational opportunity,* 92d Cong., 2nd Sess. Washington, DC: Government Printing Office.

LEARNING THROUGH EXPERIENCE

What Graduates Gained by Attending Desegregated High Schools

Jennifer Jellison Holme, Amy Stuart Wells, and Anita Tijerina Revilla

Jennifer Jellison Holme, Amy Stuart Wells, and Anita Tijerina Revilla present the results of their study of graduates of the class of 1980 from six high schools in six different states that desegregated as a result of *Brown v. Board of Education* and other court orders described in the previous reading by Gary Orfield. Using random sampling, they interviewed 40 to 45 graduates from each high school. Of the 245 individuals interviewed, 33% were African American, 56% white, 9% Latino, and 2% other race/ethnicity. The results of this study help us to understand both how desegregation worked in these high schools and what it meant for those individuals forced to attend the desegregated schools.

Questions to consider for this reading:

1. What was the effect of desegregation on the school lives of white, African American, and Latino students?

2. How did desegregation affect these students in their later lives?

3. How do their findings from interviews with students relate to the previous reading by Orfield that described the history of segregation and resegregation?

A t this 50th anniversary of the landmark *Brown* decision, one of the most important questions about desegregation policy has remained unanswered: What impact did school desegregation have on the "hearts and minds" of students who lived through it? Indeed, little is known about how graduates of racially diverse schools understand the ways in which their school experiences shaped their lives.

In an effort to answer this question, our team of researchers from Teachers College, Columbia University, and the University of California at Los Angeles (UCLA) set out to study what school desegregation meant to the people who attended racially diverse schools in the late 1970s.[1] We conducted in-depth case studies of six different school districts across the country, focusing on one racially mixed high school in each.[2] At these sites, we interviewed policymakers, activists, and educators, as well as students who graduated from these schools in 1980—during some of the peak years of school integration. In total, we interviewed 540 people, including 242 high school graduates from the Class of 1980.

In this article, we discuss one of the central findings from this study: what the graduates said about the impact of attending a desegregated high school on their understanding of race and on their lives in a racially diverse society. We found that all of the graduates—from each of the racial and ethnic groups—expressed gratitude for having had the opportunity to attend a racially diverse school. Reflecting back, these graduates said that their public high school years provided them rare opportunities to come together with and get to know people of other racial or ethnic backgrounds. This does not mean that attending a desegregated school was easy. In fact, in a number of cases racial tension and distance fostered mistrust, hurt feelings, and frustration. Furthermore, we know that in these schools, like most racially and ethnically diverse schools in this country, students were resegregated by classrooms where most of the students in high-track classes were white while most of the students in the lower-level classes were African American or Latino (see Wells, Holme, Revilla, & Atanda, 2008). Still, nearly all graduates we interviewed—even those who have few fond memories of high school—said that they learned invaluable lessons about race and living in a diverse society that they never could have learned elsewhere. In fact, these graduates emphasized that by living through the daily challenges of dealing with racial differences in high school, they gained insights and understandings that they could have never appreciated by simply reading about race or discussing it in the context of a one-race school.

The lessons these graduates said they took away from their high school years were all the more valuable because they realized just how unique these experiences were once they graduated. Most of them said that it was only when they got to college or to their workplaces that they realized what they had learned vis-à-vis their peers who had not attended diverse schools. Compared to these peers, the graduates said they were more open-minded, less prejudiced, and less fearful of other races. They attribute much of this to their experiences in racially diverse schools.

Despite these similarities, there were important differences across racial and ethnic groups in terms of what the students learned about race and how it has helped them as adults. In other words, while both white graduates and graduates of color said that their diverse schooling experiences prepared them to be more comfortable around people who are racially different from themselves, the specific skills they gained and the meaning they made of the lessons were quite different. For instance, many white graduates said they learned to be more comfortable in interracial settings in part because they had broken down stereotypes of what members of "other" races are like. While graduates of color also said they were more comfortable in interracial settings and had broken down some stereotypes of Whites, many of them added that one of the most valuable lessons they gained from high school was preparation for the discrimination they would face in a white-dominated society. Therefore, these graduates believe their schooling experiences helped them learn how to be less fearful of all-white or racially mixed environments, more confident in their ability to compete in such settings, and better able to cope with prejudice.

One of the most interesting aspects of the findings from our study is that graduates only came to understand what they learned from their high school experience *after* they left high school. While a small number of studies have been conducted on the effect of school desegregation on students' racial attitudes, the vast majority of that research has asked students to reflect on their views while they are still in school (Schofield, 1995). Our study, which interviewed graduates 20 years after they left high school, shows that much of what they understood about their school experiences was hindsight—lessons that they did not really appreciate until they had different experiences as adults and interacted with peers who had attended more racially segregated schools. We argue that our findings are highly significant in terms of efforts to fully appreciate the impact of high school desegregation on students' lives because the graduates we interviewed could not have fully articulated the "lessons they learned" from racially mixed schools when they were still in high school. Paradoxically, then, at the same time that these graduates were coming to understand what these experiences had meant to them, school desegregation has being curtailed and even eliminated in hundreds of school districts across the country (Orfield, Eaton, & The Harvard Project, 1996; Orfield & Lee, 2004). In this way, our study documents long-term consequences of a policy that the government had started to dismantle by the late 1980s, long before we even understood its impact on those who experienced it.

In this article, then, we explain the significance of our findings about what graduates learned from attending racially diverse schools in light of the current trend toward increasingly segregated schools in this country and policymakers' resistance to promoting diversity in public education. . . .

THE UNDERSTANDING RACE AND EDUCATION STUDY

As we noted above, our study consisted of historical case studies and interviews with graduates of the Class of 1980 from six racially diverse high schools in the U.S. We chose to study the history of these schools during this time because most desegregation in this country did not occur until the late 1960s and early 1970s when white resistance had finally been squelched by additional federal court orders. Thus, the Class of 1980, which entered kindergarten in 1967, was moving through the elementary grades just as the old system of segregation was finally breaking down. National data show that members of the Class of 1980, on average, were more likely to have classmates of other races than any class before them or more recent classes of the last 15 years. . . .

LIVING THROUGH SCHOOL DESEGREGATION: YOU HAD TO BE THERE

With very few exceptions, the graduates we interviewed said that, as a result of attending

their racially diverse high schools, they felt more prepared for a racially diverse society than they would otherwise be. All the graduates said that their high school experiences left them with a deeper understanding of people of other backgrounds and an increased sense of comfort in interracial settings. In fact, many of these graduates stressed the importance of their daily experiences of negotiating race in high school as one of the most challenging yet rewarding aspects of their education. The lessons they learned from these experiences, they said, could not have been taught through history books or documentary films; rather, many observed simply that they had to be there, living in these diverse schools on a daily basis. Furthermore, it is important to note that graduates of all races say that they often only appreciated how valuable their diverse schooling experiences were once they left high school and interacted with people who had not attended diverse schools. These findings highlight the need for policymakers and the public to pay attention to the voices of these graduates now—in their adult years—in evaluating whether desegregation was a success or failure and whether to reconsider our national retreat from policies designed to foster diversity in public schools.

Still, we do not mean to imply that these graduates learned exactly the same things in the same ways across racial groups and school context. In fact, we found that how these lessons were learned and what these lessons mean to our participants today, differ for the white graduates and graduates of color. The lessons graduates learned also varied across the six high schools, according to their context, in subtle but important ways.

EXPERIENCING INTEGRATION FIRST-HAND: AN ALTERED "WORLD VIEW"

Perhaps the most important testament to the power of policies designed to promote school integration is the strong belief by graduates that the type of lessons they learned in high school about diversity could only be gained through personal, day-to-day experience. In other words, these graduates reflected, such life-lessons could not be gained through books or courses on multicultural education or festivals celebrating diversity—they had to be lived first-hand in shared spaces and times. A number of graduates also recognized the role that the schools themselves played in teaching these lessons, as it was through their high schools that they had the opportunity to spend many years with the same cohort of students, and therefore had a chance to get to know members of other racial groups and learn how to negotiate racial differences.

Indeed, many graduates contrasted their own experience in high school with those of their friends and spouses who attended racially homogeneous schools—the type of schools that are becoming all the more common in the U.S. as schools resegregate across the country (Orfield & Lee, 2004)—and observed that those segregated settings provide no genuine opportunities for students to learn about race or to learn to negotiate racial difference. As a white female West Charlotte High School graduate said: "You cannot suddenly teach someone how to get along with someone [who's] different from them. You can't learn that from a book!"

Rather, many of these graduates note, having day-to-day high school experiences with members of other racial groups—the good and the bad—left them with a fundamentally altered way of seeing the world. As a white female Shaker Heights High School graduate explained in talking about what she learned by being there:

> I mean, that it's a world view thing . . . it's not just a sociological little experiment, it's your entire world view is altered by who you're growing up with, and it's not just who you're going to school with, but who you're growing up with, who you are sharing every minute of your day and every secret that you have. When that, when you have that experience, that alters your entire world view, which then is the lens that you're operating through every day.

Though some would argue that such lessons about race could be learned at any time in one's life, a number of graduates said that these lessons were all the more powerful to them because they were learned when they were in their youth. For instance, an African American graduate of Dwight Morrow High School reflected that having had interracial contact in schools from a young age was particularly helpful to her:

> That really put me ahead of the game being exposed to children, innocent children from other groups because there is no pretense about anything. You actually learn what people are about because you are kids, you don't have time to be pretentious.

Similarly, a graduate of John Muir High School who is of both white and subcontinent Indian descent said that while he faced some interracial conflict during his high school days, he also feels that learning about race at a young age was important to him:

> I found [John Muir HS] maybe a little bit harder than somewhere else, but I also knew that it was teaching me life lessons that no college can teach you. And those are invaluable. I know a lot of people who do a lot of college work and they test really well, but you put them out in the real world and . . . they can't make it.

While graduates of different racial backgrounds experienced their racially mixed high schools in very different ways, the one thing that all of them took away from that experience as they reflect back 20 years later was the impact that *living through* desegregation had on them. These lived experiences, as we shall show, taught graduates a number of important lessons about race that profoundly affected the way they interact with other racial groups, and the way they view the world. Below we discuss the racial and school-level variations on this theme of "having to be there" to show that Whites and students of color had slightly different ways of making meaning of the value of their experiences.

WHITE GRADUATES: INCREASED COMFORT, DECREASED FEAR

While all of the white graduates we interviewed said they believe attending a racially diverse school changed them in lasting, positive ways, we found that the more specific lessons that white graduates took away from their school experiences both differed from those of the graduates of color and varied to some degree by school.

Increased Comfort and Understanding

The one consistent finding from our interviews with white graduates across the six high schools was the increased sense of comfort that they say they gained in racially mixed and predominantly non-white settings as a result of their high school experiences. Many white graduates say that because they attended diverse high schools, as adults they were more at ease in interactions with people of different backgrounds and more willing to engage in conversations with people of color than many other Whites they know. As a white graduate from Austin High School said of his experience: "It gave me the ability to relate to just about any person and feel good about it, and to be sincere—not putting on an act." Similarly, a white female graduate from Topeka High noted, as a result of attending a racially diverse high school:

I can walk into any room or any situation and I don't care if they are black, yellow, white, orange or whatever. I feel that I can have a conversation with anybody or not be afraid to talk to somebody just because of their social status or because of the color of their skin.

Many white graduates say that they only realized how much more comfortable they were in diverse settings when they encountered racially mixed situations after high school with a friend or spouse who had attended predominately white schools. For example, a white graduate of Dwight Morrow High School recalled an evening when she attended a racially mixed retirement party for her mother, who taught in a predominantly black school district. Her husband, who attended predominately white rural schools, had a very different reaction to the experience from hers:

You know, the room is mostly Black, the families of the retired teachers, the other teachers that came, and a lot of them were teachers I had growing up, and you know, they'd see me, "Oh, how are you," and I introduced [my husband], and his comment, which was sort of a sad thing later on, he's like, "Wow." He had a great time, everybody was so nice. I don't remember his exact words but, "God, they were actually really nice." And I felt bad for him for a minute, I was like, "Yeah, they are." It was funny, but he doesn't know any different than that, and he still has that mindset although he's much more open-minded than his family . . . but he doesn't understand, he doesn't know a lot of things, so whenever he doesn't know he reverts back to what he knew growing up.

The point illustrated in this one story is reverberated throughout dozens of transcripts as these graduates came to realize how different they are from Whites who were educated in segregated schools.

Many white graduates traced their increased sense of comfort in racially mixed environments today to the way in which their experiences with members of other racial groups in high school challenged their own misconceptions about people of color. It was through daily, up-close interactions with members of other racial groups in high school, many white graduates observed, that allowed them to see through their previously held stereotypes. A white graduate from Topeka High noted:

[My high school experience] gave me an opportunity to know that some people that were Black or Hispanic that are not like stereotypes at all. . . . I think that my ideas about other races at that point in my life had been probably just formed by television stereotypes and there wasn't any real life experience before this for me.

A number of white graduates also recalled specific incidents with students of color during their high school years, which changed how they viewed those students. For example, a white West Charlotte High School graduate said that early on in her high school career she was afraid of the African American students at her school, but after having an experience where several African American students helped her stand up to a white high school bully, she said:

> It just changed that fear and it changed a lot of the prejudice that I had carried because of stories told to me by my neighbors. So at that point I just . . . I really lost a lot of my prejudice and that's why I'm so grateful, to this day, that . . . I did go to a desegregated school because I feel that just with family values, with my friend's ideas, I think I would have been extremely narrow minded, extremely prejudiced growing up.

Like this woman, many graduates told us that had they not attended their high schools and had an opportunity to have up-close interactions with students from different racial and ethnic backgrounds, they would be more prejudiced, closed-minded, and even fearful of people of color.

Decreased Fear

Part of feeling more at ease around people of color, the white graduates noted, is realizing that the fear that most white people have of African Americans and Latinos is unfounded. Many white graduates, in fact, said that their experiences with people of color in high school made them feel less fearful in interracial settings, particularly compared with Whites they know who had attended all-white schools. The decreased fear white graduates report as a result of going to a racially mixed school is particularly important in light of U.S. culture and media, which often suggests that people of color and predominately non-white settings are something to be feared and avoided (Williams, 2000).

Several graduates only recognized how much less fearful of non-white settings they were when they encountered a predominately non-white situation with a spouse or a friend who had attended majority-white schools. For instance, a white male graduate from Shaker Heights High School said that he realized how comfortable and unafraid he was around people of color on a recent family trip to Baltimore, when he and his wife got on a bus that was filled with Latinos and African Americans. He contrasted his sense of comfort in getting on the bus to his wife's unease:

> I think we were the only white people on the bus, there were some Hispanic people, African American. . . . My wife . . . went to pretty much an all white high school, and to listen to the way her father talks and, you know, he hadn't been around too many minorities . . . but I felt very comfortable, you know, getting on the bus and I really didn't feel out of place. . . . But I could definitely tell that my wife was not, you know, a hundred percent comfortable getting on that bus.

Another white male graduate from Austin High said that his white wife's lack of experience with students of color in high school left her extremely fearful in predominately non-white situations. He contrasts her fear with his own feelings of comfort, which he feels he gained through daily interactions in high school with members of different racial and ethnic groups:

> If you just hang out with a bunch of white people and . . . and you do everything that you can to say I'm going to act like a nice, open minded person when I get around these black folks and Mexican folks, you're not going to be as good at it. You're going to be more uptight. You're going to be stressed out. It's going to be a problem. There's . . . there are all kinds of things. Whereas because I was around black folks and Mexican folks and learned that they weren't going to kill me and you know, I can . . . I can go to the . . . to the Texas Relays where my girlfriend, now wife, is hyperventilating [and I said] "It is correct that we're in a group of 20,000 people and 75% of 'em are black people, but we're going to be all right. They're not going to hurt us. They're not going to knife us. They're not going to kill us. They're not going to

rob us. We're going to be okay. Just act nice and . . . treat people the way you like to be treated and . . . and you're going to be okay."

An interesting and unexpected finding of this study is that several of the white graduates who reported living through uncomfortable racial situations in high school, where they felt intimidated or physically threatened by members of another racial group, also said that, as a result of these experiences, they ultimately felt a decreased fear of people of color as adults.

For example, a white graduate of John Muir High School who reported feeling intimidated by the African American students said that ultimately her high school experience left her with not only a decreased fear of people of color, but a longing for more diverse environments than the all-white suburb she currently lives in. She notes:

I don't feel fear when I see a black person or a Hispanic person walking down the street. In fact, I feel kind of like . . . I feel kind of nostalgic 'cause it reminds me of growing up. . . . 'Cause around here, all I see are pretty much white people everywhere I look. So I'm grateful for that because I think some of the people that I knew and I met in San Diego grew up in an all-white neighborhood and I think they couldn't help but look at black people or Hispanic people as different or as, you know, a black person or a Hispanic person and not just a person. Yeah. So, like, in the workforce, I think, having . . . that background hopefully made me . . . look at people as equal. And I judge them based on their abilities, not based on the color of their skin. And when I encounter people that don't have that same belief, it makes me really uncomfortable.

Thus, even white graduates of the two high schools in our study in which Whites were in the minority—John Muir High School and Dwight Morrow High School—and where many Whites reported a higher level of racial uneasiness—and even fear while in school—say that those experiences ultimately left them more at ease in racially mixed settings, in part because they learned how to handle difficult interracial situations.

Increased Empathy and Insight

Another important outcome of attending racially mixed schools, at least for a small number of white graduates, was the better understanding they say they gained about what it was like to be a person of color in the U.S. In this way, these graduates' high school experiences played a very important role in opening their eyes to other ways of seeing and knowing the world. For instance, a white West Charlotte graduate said that he not only learned an appreciation for African American culture but he also learned what it was like to be a minority—an experience he realizes that most Whites have not had:

I mean, I think I'm more attuned a little bit more attuned towards black music, black history, black things that I might not have been exposed to. And at West Charlotte I . . . I mean, there were times when I felt like I was the minority and I think that was good for me, you know, in a way, to know a little bit what it feels like to walk down the hall full of these people and feeling like, ok, I'm the odd man out here, and to know what that feels like, you know, to not always be among the majority and on top of your game.

According to a white Topeka High School graduate, being exposed to different perspectives and points of view was one of the main ways he feels he was changed by attending his racially mixed high school. In such a setting, he said:

You get a lot of different input from different walks of life. . . . I have never been pulled over [by the police] simply because I met a profile. But I have friends who have been pulled over because they matched a specific profile. Those are issues that I wouldn't be aware of if I went to a totally Caucasian school. Or I wouldn't have experience with that.

A white male graduate from Shaker Heights High noted that his experience in his racially mixed community and in his schools gave him a critique of the larger society and caused him to question why most communities in the U.S. are so segregated. He notes,

> [Growing up] you develop a sense that this is the way the world is and then you go out in the world and you realize that that's not the way the world is, and then you can question the way the world is rather than the way Shaker Heights is . . . So, I think, in a subtle sense, it develops sort of a devil's advocate mentality.

While this finding was less universal across the white graduates, the ability of these graduates to see the world from the point of view of people of color and even to question the larger social structure was all the more profound because, more often than not, we found that in racially diverse high school classrooms there was very little discussion about race and racial inequity (see Revilla, Wells, & Holme, 2004). These lessons these graduates learned outside of the classroom about racial inequality—often in spite of their formal schooling experience—attest to the potential of policies promoting racially diverse schools to help promote a deeper understanding of racial difference and foster interracial understanding.

Graduates of Color: Survival Skills for a White World

Looking at racial understandings from the other side of the color line we also saw the powerful impact of desegregated schools on African Americans, Latinos, and other graduates of color more than 20 years later. Not only did these graduates' experiences differ to some degree from the white graduates but, like Whites, the lessons learned varied somewhat depending on the high school they attended. In particular, the racial make-up of these schools and the behaviors of the teachers and administrators in these schools seemed to matter a great deal.

Increased Comfort, Less Intimidation

Like Whites, graduates of color we interviewed said that going to a desegregated high school prepared them for a diverse society in that they had a greater sense of comfort in interracial settings. In saying that, many of these graduates of color meant that they were not simply prepared to get along with others but that they were prepared to function in predominately white work and social settings—often dominated by powerful Whites—that would otherwise be intimidating to many people of color.

An African American male graduate from Dwight Morrow High School said that his experience with Whites in high school gave him a confidence in racially diverse settings that he may not have otherwise gained. He reflects on what was gained from his high school experience this way:

> Today I would say that it makes me feel comfortable, that I can go anywhere and not feel intimidated, I just always feel like I belong and it didn't matter who was in the majority or minority, that I knew how to deal with all of them. . . . It definitely gave me the confidence to know that it didn't matter, people were people, and I could just interact.

Above all, graduates of color say that had it not been for desegregation, they would have gone through segregated schools with little or no exposure to Whites. The exposure that they did get in high school gave them a sense of comfort in interracial work and social settings that they find very useful today. As an African American female graduate from Dwight Morrow High School says:

> I feel that it really shaped me in terms of my ability to move into different circles of people. I'm not limited in terms of, you know, when I walk into a place, I can speak the same king's English, I can do that, and I can speak to my friends on a different level. So I think that it's made me a diverse person, and I was able to see other lifestyles and how people live. I mean, it's not, you know, you have some people in the inner city who never really experience, you know, rub shoulders with people that have six-figure incomes, and it's not, in other words, I don't get nervous when I'm dealing with someone who is a CEO of a company because his

experiences and my experiences are so different. You know, I've been around certain things that have afforded me a certain confidence.

As with Whites, the graduates of color reported they now feel a level of comfort in racially mixed or predominately white environments that could only be gained through the lived experience of attending a racially diverse school. In addition, what many graduates of color talked about in terms of the effect of their school experiences on their racial attitudes were understandings that they did not and could not appreciate until *after* they left those schools and were finding their way into college, jobs, families, and houses. Like Whites, these graduates said they only fully came to appreciate the skills they gained when, as adults, they met other people of color who had attended segregated, predominately minority schools. For example, an African American female graduate from West Charlotte High School said that she felt she had gained a useful set of skills vis-à-vis her African American friends who had attended all-black schools:

I know a lot of black people have only been around Blacks and they really can't see past being around anyone other than Blacks. So, you know, I feel like that has helped me in a way that . . . that I was already comfortable enough being around a different racial group to now, when there are so many different racial groups that I'm around on a daily basis, it doesn't bother me at all.

Similarly, an African American graduate of Topeka High School said his adult experiences in a large city in Texas, where he has lived for nearly 20 years, highlighted for him the comfort that he gained interacting with Whites by attending Topeka High. He says that as a result of attending such a diverse high school, he is far less intimidated by Whites than the African American people he has met in Texas who have not had the chance to interact with Whites in school.

For graduates of color, then, living through the experience of attending racially diverse schools gave them a greater sense of comfort in inter racial

settings compared with their peers who had attended segregated schools. Even those graduates who attended racially mixed schools where interracial relationships were not necessarily positive also say that they gained valuable skills from their high school experiences.

Learning to Face Prejudice

For the graduates of color, learning comfort in racially diverse settings has different implications given their different locations in the racial hierarchy of the U.S. society. This means that not only were they learning to feel more comfortable around people of different racial and ethnic backgrounds, but also that they were learning to deal with prejudice and cope with discrimination in ways they would not have learned had they attended all–African American or all-Latino schools.

The way they learned to cope with this discrimination differed, however, depending on the high school these graduates attended. For example, a number of graduates of color from Austin High School said that attending AHS helped them better deal with prejudice as adults because they encountered it so often at AHS. A Hispanic male graduate of AHS noted, had he not attended Austin High: "I wouldn't know what the word 'prejudice' was. I would have been in like a cocoon. . . . I was prepared. High school prepared me for prejudice. It did. That's what helped me."

Those graduates of color who had more positive experiences dealing with white students in their high schools said they were better able to cope with the prejudice they encountered because they knew first-hand that all Whites weren't as racist as the ones they met as adults. An African American female graduate of Shaker Heights High School reflected on her positive experiences with Whites at her high school:

It prepared me for the ignorance of college to understand everyone's not ignorant. I knew that, so it was able to probably help me have more confidence and be able to deal with the racial discrimination I *did* deal with in college [that] I [had] never dealt with in my life. So, I think having friends that were not African American probably prepared me for, you know, the ignorance that I had to deal with.

Even those graduates of color who say they had particularly painful racial experiences, such as being discriminated against by teachers or counselors, resegregated into lower level classes, or socially shunned or intimidated by white students, say that they are glad they had the opportunity to attend those schools, to learn the lessons that they did. As an African American female graduate from Austin High School reflects: "I'm glad I went to Austin High in spite of the pain and difficulty. I'm glad I went to school there. I think it prepared me in some ways for the real world. Not that I necessarily like the real world, the way it is, but you've got to start somewhere."

In this way, the graduates of color from our study show us that not all lessons learned in a racially diverse school are positive. In fact, some of the stories we heard from graduates of these schools—of all races and ethnicities—were quite upsetting and no doubt have had a lasting impact. Still, these experiences taught them lessons that they now find valuable as adults navigating a racially divided and unequal world.

NOTES

1. Our study, entitled "Understanding Race and Education," was funded by the Spencer Foundation, the Joyce Foundation, and the Ford Foundation. We are grateful to these foundations for their support, but the views expressed in this article are our own, based on our analysis and findings.

2. By "racially mixed," we mean between 40% and 75% of any one race, and no more than 25% of the racial balance of the city or town for any one race.

REFERENCES

Brown v. Board of Education of Topeka, Kansas. 347 U.S. 483, 74 S.Ct. 686, 98 L.Ed. 873. (1954).

Orfield, G., Eaton, S. E., & The Harvard Project on School Desegregation. (1996). *Dismantling desegregation: The quiet reversal of* Brown v. Board of Education. New York: New Press.

Orfield, G., & Lee, C. (2004). *Brown at 50: King's dream or Plessy's nightmare?* Cambridge, MA: Harvard University, The Civil Rights Project.

Revilla, A. R., Wells, A. S., & Holme, J. (2004). "We didn't see color": The salience of colorblindness in desegregated schools. In M. Fine, L. Weis, L. Powell Pruitt, & A. Burns (Eds.), *Off white: Readings on power, privilege, and resistance* (2nd ed., pp. 284–301). New York: Routledge Falmer.

Schofield, J. W. (1995). Review of research on school desegregation's impact on elementary and secondary school students. In J. A. Banks & C. A. McGee Banks (Eds.), *Handbook of research on multicultural education* (pp. 597–617). New York: Macmillan.

Wells, A. S., Holme, J. J., Revilla, A., & Atanda, A. K. (2008). *Both sides now: The story of school desegregation's graduates.* Berkeley: University of California Press.

Williams, L. (2000). *It's the little things: The everyday interactions that get under the skin of blacks and whites.* New York: Harcourt.

READING 40

CHARTER SCHOOLS AND THE PUBLIC GOOD

Linda A. Renzulli and Vincent J. Roscigno

In this reading, Linda Renzulli and Vincent Roscigno examine the growth and possible outcomes of the increase in the number of charter schools. These schools provide a radical approach to traditional schooling in the United States because they operate outside of many regulations that dictate the structure of schooling across the country. The idea of charter schools, embedded in a "market economy" framework, also involves parents in the selection of schools for their children. Yet, as the authors argue, by changing the focus of accountability in schools these new freedoms for school administrators, teachers, and parents come with problems as well as hopes for the future of education.

Questions to consider for this reading:

1. How and when did the charter school movement begin?

2. How do charter schools differ from public schools?

3. Do you think changes in accountability described in this reading will lead to improved education for the nation's poorest children? Why or why not?

According to the U.S. Department of Education, "No Child Left Behind is designed to change the culture of America's schools by closing the achievement gap, offering more flexibility, giving parents more options, and teaching students based on what works." Charter schools—a recent innovation in U.S. education—are one of the most visible developments aimed at meeting these goals. Although they preceded the 2002 No Child Left Behind (NCLB) Act, charter schools are now supported politically and financially through NCLB. Charter schools are public schools set up and administered outside the traditional bureaucratic constraints of local school boards, with the goal of creating choice, autonomy, and accountability.

Unlike regular public schools, charter schools are developed and managed by individuals, groups of parents, community members, teachers, or education-management organizations. In exchange for their independence from most state and local regulations (except those related to health, safety, and nondiscrimination), they must uphold their contracts with the local or state school board or risk being closed. Each provides its own guidelines for establishing rules and procedures, including curriculum, subject to evaluation by the state in which it resides.

Charter schools are among the most rapidly growing educational institutions in the United States today. No charter schools existed before 1990, but such schools are now operating in

40 states and the District of Columbia. According to the Center for Educational Reform, 3,977 charter schools are now educating more than a million students.

Charter schools have received bipartisan support and media accolades. This, however, is surprising. The true academic value of the educational choices that charter schools provide to students, as well as their broader implications for the traditional system of public education, are simply unknown—a fact that became obvious in November 2004, when voters in the state of Washington rejected—for the third time—legislation allowing the creation of charter schools. Driven by an alliance of parents, teachers, and teacher unions against sponsorship by powerful figures such as Bill Gates, this rejection went squarely against a decade-long trend. Reflecting on Washington's rejection, a state Democrat told the *New York Times,* "Charter schools will never have a future here now until there is conclusive evidence, nationwide, that these schools really work. Until the issue of student achievement gets resolved, I'd not even attempt to start over again in the Legislature."

all families, regardless of wealth, to take advantage of these new public educational options. Opponents contend that charter schools cannot fix broader educational problems; if anything, they become instruments of segregation, deplete public school systems of their resources, and undermine the public good.

Given the rationales for charter schools before and after the NCLB Act, it is surprising how few assessments have been made of charter school functioning, impacts on achievement, or the implications of choice for school systems. Only a handful of studies have attempted to evaluate systematically the claims of charter school effectiveness, and few of these have used national data. The various justifications for charter schools—including the desire to increase achievement in the public school system—warrant attention, as do concrete research and evidence on whether such schools work. The debate, however, involves more than simply how to enhance student achievement. It also involves educational competition and accountability, individual choice and, most fundamentally, education's role in fostering the "public good."

THE RATIONALE

Most justifications for charter schools argue that the traditional system of public schooling is ineffective and that the introduction of competition and choice can resolve any deficiencies. The leading rationale is that accountability standards (for educational outcomes and student progress), choice (in curriculum, structure, and discipline), and autonomy (for teachers and parents) will generate higher levels of student achievement. The result will be high-quality schools for all children, particularly those from poor and minority backgrounds, and higher levels of student achievement.

While wealthy families have always been able to send their children to private schools, other Americans have historically had fewer, if any, options. Proponents suggest that charter schools can address such inequality by allowing

IS THERE PROOF IN THE PUDDING?

Do students in charter schools do better than they would in traditional public schools? Unfortunately, the jury is still out, and the evidence is mixed. Profiles in the *New Yorker, Forbes, Time,* and *Newsweek,* for example, highlight the successes of individual charter schools in the inner cities of Washington, DC, and New York, not to mention anecdotal examples offered by high-profile advocates like John Walton and Bill Gates. While anecdotes and single examples suggest that charter schools may work, they hardly constitute proof or even systematic evidence that they always do. In fact, broader empirical studies using representative and national data suggest that many charter schools have failed.

One noteworthy study, released by the American Federation of Teachers (AFT) in 2004, reports that charter schools are not providing a better education than traditional public schools. Moreover, they are not boosting student achievement. Using fourth- and eighth-grade test scores from the National Assessment of Educational Progress across all states with charter schools, the report finds that charter-school students perform *less* well, on average, in math and reading than their traditional-school counterparts. There appear to be no significant differences among eighth-graders and no discernable difference in black-white achievement gaps across school type.

Because the results reported in the AFT study—which have received considerable media attention—do not incorporate basic demographic, regional, or school characteristics simultaneously, they can only relate average differences across charter schools and public schools. But this ignores the huge effects of family background, above and beyond school environment. Without accounting for the background attributes of students themselves, not to mention other factors such as the race and social-class composition of the student body, estimates of the differences between charter schools and traditional public schools are overstated.

In response to the 2004 AFT report, economists Carolyn Hoxby and Jonah Rockoff compared charter schools to surrounding public schools. Their results contradict many of the AFT's findings. They examined students who applied to but did not attend charter schools because they lost lotteries for spots. Hoxby and Rockoff found that, compared to their lotteried-out fellow applicants, students who attended charter schools in Chicago scored higher in both math and reading. This is true especially in the early elementary grades compared to nearby public schools with similar racial compositions. Their work and that of others also shows that older charter schools perform better than newly formed ones—perhaps suggesting that school stability and effectiveness require time to take hold. Important weaknesses nevertheless remain in the research design. For example, Hoxby and Rockoff conducted their study in a single city—Chicago—and thus it does not represent the effect of charter schools in general.

As with the research conducted by the AFT, we should interpret selective case studies and school-level comparisons with caution. Individual student background is an important force in shaping student achievement, yet it rarely receives attention in this research or in the charter school achievement debate more generally. The positive influence of charter schools, where it is found, could easily be a function of more advantaged student populations drawn from families with significant educational resources at home. We know from prior research that parents of such children are more likely to understand schooling options and are motivated to ensure their children's academic success. Since family background, parental investments, and parental educational involvement typically trump school effects in student achievement, it is likely that positive charter school effects are simply spurious.

More recently, a report by the National Center for Education Statistics (NCES), using sophisticated models, appropriate demographic controls, and a national sample, has concurred with the AFT report—charter schools are not producing children who score better on standardized achievement tests. The NCES report showed that average achievement in math and reading in public schools and in charter schools that were linked to a school district did not differ statistically. Charter schools not associated with a public school district, however, scored significantly *less* well than their public school counterparts.

Nevertheless, neither side of the debate has shown conclusively, through rigorous, replicated, and representative research, whether charter schools boost student achievement. The NCES report mentioned above has, in our opinion, done the best job of examining the achievement issue and has shown that charter schools are not doing better than traditional public schools when it comes to improving achievement.

Clearly, in the case of charter schools, the legislative cart has been put before the empirical horse. Perhaps this is because the debate is about more than achievement. Charter school debates and legislation are rooted in more fundamental disagreements over competition, individualism, and, most fundamentally, education's role in the public good. This reflects an important and significant shift in the cultural evaluation of public education in the United States, at the crux of which is the application of a market-based economic model, complete with accompanying ideas of "competition" and "individualism."

COMPETITION AND ACCOUNTABILITY

To whom are charter schools accountable? Some say their clients, namely, the public. Others say the system, namely, their authorizers. If charter schools are accountable to the public, then competition between schools should ensure academic achievement and bureaucratic prudence. If charter schools are accountable to the system, policies and procedures should ensure academic achievement and bureaucratic prudence. In either case, the assumption is that charter schools will close when they are not successful. The successful application of these criteria, however, requires clear-cut standards, oversight, and accountability—which are currently lacking, according to many scholars. Indeed, despite the rhetoric of their advocates and legislators, charter schools are seldom held accountable in the market or by the political structures that create them.

In a "market" view of accountability, competition will ultimately breed excellence by "weeding out" ineffectual organizations. Through "ripple effects," all schools will be forced to improve their standards. Much like business organizations, schools that face competition will survive only by becoming more efficient and producing a better overall product (higher levels of achievement) than their private and public school counterparts.

Social scientists, including the authors of this article, question this simplistic, if intuitively appealing, application of neoliberal business principles to the complex nature of the educational system, children's learning, and parental choice for schools. If competition were leading to accountability, we would see parents pulling their children out of unsuccessful charter schools.

But research shows that this seldom happens. Indeed, parents, particularly those with resources, typically choose schools for reasons of religion, culture, and social similarity rather than academic quality.

Nor are charter schools accountable to bureaucrats. Even though charter schools are not outperforming traditional public schools, relatively few (10 percent nationally) have actually been closed by their authorizers over the last decade. Although we might interpret a 10 percent closure rate as evidence of academic accountability at work, this would be misleading. Financial rather than academic issues are the principal reasons cited for these closures. By all indications, charter schools are not being held accountable to academic standards, either by their authorizers or by market forces.

In addition to measuring accountability through student performance, charter schools should also be held to standards of financial and educational quality. Here, some charter schools are faltering. From California to New York and Ohio, newspaper editorials question fiscal oversight. There are extreme cases such as the California Charter Academy, a publicly financed but privately run chain of 60 charter schools. Despite a budget of $100 million, this chain became insolvent in August 2004, leaving thousands of children without a school to attend.

More direct accountability issues include educational quality and annual reports to state legislatures; here, charter-school performance is poor or mixed. In Ohio, where nearly 60,000 students now attend charter schools, approximately one-quarter of these schools are not following the state's mandate to report school-level test score results, and only 45 percent of the teachers at the state's 250 charter schools hold full teaching certification. Oversight is further complicated by the creation of "online" charter schools, which serve 16,000 of Ohio's public school students.

It is ironic that many charter schools are not held to the very standards of competition, quality, and accountability that legislators and advocates used to justify them in the first place. Perhaps this is why Fredrick Hess, a charter school researcher, recently referred to accountability as applied to charter schools as little more than a "toothless threat."

INDIVIDUALISM OR INEQUALITY?

The most obvious goal of education is student achievement. Public education in the United States, however, has also set itself several other goals that are not reducible to achievement or opportunity at an individual level but are important culturally and socially. Public education has traditionally managed diversity and integration, created common standards for the socialization of the next generation, and ensured some equality of opportunity and potential for meritocracy in the society at large. The focus of the charter school debate on achievement—rooted in purely economic rationales of competition and individual opportunism—has ignored these broader concerns.

Individual choice in the market is a key component of neoliberal and "free-market" theory—a freedom many Americans cherish. Therefore, it makes sense that parents might support choice in public schooling. Theoretically, school choice provides them market power to seek the best product for their children, to weigh alternatives, and to make changes in their child's interest. But this power is only available to informed consumers, so that educational institutions and policies that provide choice may be reinforcing the historical disadvantages faced by racial and ethnic minorities and the poor.

We might expect that students from advantaged class backgrounds whose parents are knowledgeable about educational options would be more likely to enroll in charter schools. White parents might also see charter schools as an educational escape route from integrated public schools that avoids the financial burden of private schooling. On the other hand, the justification for charter schools is often framed in terms of an "educational fix" for poor, minority concentrated districts in urban areas. Here, charter schools may appear to be a better opportunity for

aggrieved parents whose children are attending poorly funded, dilapidated public schools.

National research, at first glance, offers encouraging evidence that charter schools are providing choices to those who previously had few options: 52 percent of those enrolled in charter schools are nonwhite compared to 41 percent of those in traditional public schools. These figures, however, tell us little about the local concentrations of whites and nonwhites in charter schools, or how the racial composition and distribution of charter schools compares to the racial composition and distribution of local, traditional public schools.

African-American students attend charter and noncharter schools in about the same proportion, yet a closer look at individual charter schools within districts reveals that they are often segregated. In Florida, for instance, charter schools are 82 percent white, whereas traditional public schools are only 51 percent white. Similar patterns are found across Arizona school districts, where charter school enrollment is 20 percent more white than traditional schools. Amy Stuart Wells's recent research finds similar tendencies toward segregation among Latinos, who are underrepresented in California's charter schools. Linda Renzulli and Lorraine Evans's national analysis of racial composition within districts containing charter schools shows that charter school formation often results in greater levels of segregation in schools between whites and nonwhites. This is not to suggest that minority populations do not make use of charter schools. But, when they do, they do so in segregated contexts.

Historically, racial integration has been a key cause of white flight and it remains a key factor in the racial composition of charter schools and other schools of choice. Decades of research on school segregation have taught us that when public school districts become integrated, through either court mandates or simple population change, white parents may seek alternative schools for their children. Current research suggests that a similar trend exists with charter schools, which provide a public-school option for white flight without the drawbacks of moving (such as job changes and longer commutes). While those from less-privileged and minority backgrounds have charter schools at their disposal, the realities of poor urban districts and contemporary patterns of racial residential segregation may mean that the "choice" is between a racially and economically segregated charter school or an equally segregated traditional school, as Renzulli's research has shown. Individualism in the form of educational choice, although perhaps intuitively appealing, in reality may be magnifying some of the very inequalities that public education has been attempting to overcome since the *Brown v. Board of Education* decision in 1954.

Regarding equality of opportunity and its implications for the American ideal of meritocracy, there is also reason for concern. Opponents have pointed to the dilution of district resources where charter schools have emerged, especially as funds are diverted to charter schools. Advocates, in contrast, argue that charter schools have insufficient resources. More research on the funding consequences of charter school creation is clearly warranted. Why, within a system of public education, should some students receive more than others? And what of those left behind, particularly students from disadvantaged backgrounds whose parents may not be aware of their options? Although evidence on the funding question is sparse, research on public schools generally and charter school attendance specifically suggests that U.S. public education may be gravitating again toward a system of separate, but not equal, education.

THE FUTURE OF PUBLIC EDUCATION

Variation across charter schools prevents easy evaluation of their academic success or social consequences for public education. Case studies can point to a good school or a bad one. National studies can provide statistical averages and comparisons, yet they may be unable to reveal the best and worst effects of charter schools. Neither type of research has yet fully accounted for the influence of family background and school demographic composition. Although conclusions about charter school effectiveness or failure remain questionable, the most rigorous national analyses to date suggest that charter schools are doing no better than traditional public schools.

Certainly some charter schools are improving the educational quality and experience of some children. KIPP (Knowledge Is Power Program) schools, for example, are doing remarkable things for the students lucky enough to attend them. But for every KIPP school (of which there are only 45, and not all are charter schools), there are many more charter schools that do not provide the same educational opportunity to students, have closed their doors in the middle of the school year, and, in effect, isolate students from their peers of other races and social classes. Does this mean that we should prevent KIPP, for example, from educating students through the charter school option? Maybe. Or perhaps we should develop better program evaluations—of what works and what does not—and implement them as guideposts. To the dismay of some policymakers and "competition" advocates, however, such standardized evaluation and accountability would undercut significant charter school variations if not the very nature of the charter school innovation itself.

Student achievement is only part of the puzzle when it comes to the charter school debate; we need to consider social integration and equality as well. These broader issues, although neglected, warrant as much attention as potential effects on achievement. We suspect that such concerns, although seldom explicit, probably underlie the often contentious charter school and school choice debate itself. We believe it is time to question the logic pertaining to competition, choice, and accountability. Moreover, we should all scrutinize the existing empirical evidence, not to mention educational policy not firmly rooted in empirical reality and research. As Karl Alexander eloquently noted in his presidential address to the Southern Sociological Society, "The charter school movement, with its 'let 1,000 flowers bloom' philosophy, is certain to yield an occasional prize-winning rose. But is either of these approaches [to school choice] likely to prove a reliable guide for broad-based, systemic reform—the kind of reform that will carry the great mass of our children closer to where we want them to be? I hardly think so." Neither do we.

FURTHER READINGS

[Editors' Note: No references were provided for this article; however, the authors recommend the following for further research into the subject.]

Fusarelli, L. D., & Crawford, J. R. (Eds.). (2001). Charter schools and the accountability puzzle (Special issue). *Education and Urban Society, 33*(2), 107–215.

Eight articles examine different models of charter school accountability.

Hening, J. R. (1994). *Rethinking school choice: Limits of the market metaphor.* Princeton, NJ: Princeton University Press.

In this early work on school choice, Hening discusses market-oriented choice programs, suggesting they may not work and are likely to make education worse in terms of segregation and outcomes.

Hoxby, C., & Rockoff, J. (2004). *Impact of charter schools on student achievement.* Unpublished manuscript. Retrieved from http://post.econom ics.har vard.edu/faculty/hoxby/papers/hoxbyrock off.pdf

Hoxby and Rockoff analyze the achievement of charter school students in Chicago, Illinois, compared to the achievement of students who do not attend charter schools.

Nelson, F. H., Rosenberg, B., & Van Meter, N. (2004). *Charter school achievement on the 2003 national assessment of educational progress.* Washington, DC: American Federation of Teachers.

The authors compare the math and reading scores of charter school and non–charter school students.

Renzulli, L. A., & Evans, L. (2005). School choice, charter schools, and white flight. *Social Problems, 52*(3), 398–418.

Renzulli and Evans show that integration in public school leads to increased proportions of white students in local charter schools.

Vergari, S. (2002). *The charter school landscape.* Pittsburgh, PA: Pittsburgh University Press.

Vergari examines charter school politics and policies in eleven states and the province of Alberta to show how charter schools are affecting public education.

ORGANIZING FOR SUCCESS

From Inequality to Quality

Linda Darling-Hammond

Linda Darling-Hammond elaborates on innovative schools, particularly charter schools discussed in the previous article. She brings to this discussion considerable experience working in schools to bring about change for low-income students. This excerpt from her book, *The Flat World and Education: How America's Commitment to Equity Will Determine Our Future,* illustrates what she has found does and does not work for low-income students in schools. This reading focuses more on the things that work, practices that she and her team of researchers have found to be effective in schools. While she echoes some of the concerns and problems with schools today that Linda Renzulli and Vincent Roscigno discussed in their reading, this one offers some structural and organizational changes that can make any schools more effective for those students who need it the most.

Questions to consider for this reading:

1. Does Darling-Hammond believe that charter schools are sufficient in and of themselves to provide the innovation we need in the organization of our schools?

2. What suggestion offered by Darling-Hammond do you think would be most effective in changing the type of education we offer to our children?

3. What factors do you think will inhibit change or make the changes she recommends in the structure of schools less likely to occur?

CREATING SYSTEMS OF SUCCESSFUL SCHOOLS

Designing schools that serve low-income students of color well is not impossible. Since the ground-breaking research of Ron Edmonds more than 3 decades ago,[1] many studies have documented the practices of unusually effective schools and have uncovered similar features of those that succeed with students who are historically underserved.[2]

However, to create such schools on a much wider scale, a new policy environment must be constructed that routinely encourages such schools to be developed and sustained.

Supporting Successful Innovation

Creating new schools and innovations is a great American pastime. Waves of reform producing productive new school designs occurred

From *The Flat World and Education: How America's Commitment to Equity Will Determine Our Future* (pp. 264–277), by Linda Darling-Hammond, 2010, New York: Teachers College Press. Copyright 2010 by Teachers College Press, Columbia University. Reprinted with permission.

at the turn of the 20th century when John Dewey, Ella Flagg Young, Lucy Sprague Mitchell, and others were working in Chicago, New York, and other Northern cities, and African American educators such as Anna Julia Cooper, Lucy Laney, and Mary McLeod Bethune were creating schools in the South. A wave of new school designs swept the country in the 1930s and 1940s when the Progressive Education Association helped redesign and study 30 "experimental" high schools that were found, in the famous Eight-Year Study, to perform substantially better than traditional schools in developing high-achieving, intellectually adventurous, socially responsible young people able to succeed in college and in life.[3] Urban school reform movements occurred in the 1960s and 1970s, producing schools such as the Parkway Program in Philadelphia and Central Park East Elementary in New York, for example; and in the 1990s when the impulse for innovation returned once again.

Despite more successful and more equitable outcomes than most traditional schools, few of these innovative schools were sustained over time. Any educator who has been in the field for any period of time has participated in what former Seattle teacher union leader, Roger Erskine, has dubbed "random acts of innovation"[4] that have come and gone, regardless of their success. Generally, this is because, like bank voles and wolf spiders, urban districts often eat their young. Changes in superintendents and school boards create swings in policies, including efforts to standardize instruction, go "back to the basics," and bring innovators to heel. Even when they achieve better outcomes, distinctive school models confront long-standing traditions, standard operating procedures, and expectations, including, sometimes, the expectation that the students who have traditionally failed should continue to do so, so that the traditionally advantaged can continue in their position of privilege. Indeed, Anna Julia Cooper's progressive M Street School in segregated Washington, D.C., which offered a "thinking curriculum" to Black students and outperformed two of the three White high schools in the city, was attacked for both of these reasons in the early 20th century.[5]

Sometimes, successful schools and programs fade because special foundation or government money has dried up, and the district does not have the foresight or wherewithal to preserve what is working. Other times, the challenges of replenishing the capable, dynamic teachers and leaders who have created a successful school prove too great to sustain the model. Historian Lawrence Cremin argued that the successes of progressive education reforms did not spread widely because such practice required "infinitely skilled teachers" who were never prepared in sufficient numbers to sustain these more complex forms of teaching and schooling.[6]

New York City's unusual renaissance was facilitated by the creation of an innovation silo in the form of the Alternative Schools Superintendency—which buffered schools from many regulations and forged new solutions to old bureaucratic problems, and by a rich array of professional resources in support of reforms, including expert practitioners who created networks of learning and support, a large set of public and private universities offering expertise and intellectual resources, and philanthropists and researchers who provided additional professional and political support to these efforts. The United Federation of Teachers (UFT) ran its own Teachers Center, and many of the teachers active in this professional development were involved in the new schools initiatives. Over time, the UFT incorporated many supports for reform-oriented schools into its contracts-first through waivers and later through changes in collective bargaining agreements—and, in some cases, became part of the protection for further reforms. Even when frequent changes in leadership might have led to abandonment of the new schools initiative, these forces kept the reform momentum going.

In most places, however, the lack of investment in professional education that would allow teachers and school leaders to acquire the knowledge they need to undertake sophisticated practices has proved to be an ongoing problem. Another recurring problem is the lack of policy development that could encourage the growth of such schools rather than keeping them as exceptions, on waiver, and at the margins. . . .

In the current environment, some, including Hill,[7] suggest that charters, contract schools, or performance schools that are essentially licensed by school boards to provide a particular model or approach may provide a way to spark innovation and protect it from the vicissitudes of district politics and changes of course. This strategy has the potential virtue of enabling continuity of educational direction and philosophy within schools—where, arguably, coherence is most important—and holding schools accountable for results, rather than for bureaucratic compliance.

Certainly, some important new school models have been launched through charters. In California, where the state has used chartering as a major lever for innovation, three of the five high schools we studied—Animo, Leadership, and New Tech—were charters. This allowed them to outline a specific approach to education and hold onto it, without being buffeted by changing district views or intruded upon by curriculum, testing, and management mandates. Although collective bargaining agreements from the industrial era often create cumbersome constraints in many districts, new approaches to bargaining have also begun to emerge, and two of these three charters employ unionized teachers.

Many other successful new small school models have been started and expanded through special arrangements for autonomy from district regulations or through charter organizations. Some, like Envision Schools, Asia Society, High Tech High, Uncommon Schools, and others, have introduced substantially new educational approaches, including performance assessments, exhibitions of learning, curriculum focused on global understandings, advisory systems, and more. Odds are that, within many districts, without formal protection, their adventurousness would have been quashed by some school board or superintendent's insistence on introducing a new standardized curriculum or testing system, or pressuring the schools to grow in size and revert to factory-model designs, or requiring the hiring of teachers or leaders who are not prepared for or

bought into the model. (Both district practices of centralized assignment and collective bargaining agreements that require seniority transfers can be culpable in this problem.) Even when there are good intentions to support innovation, local districts are subject to a geological dig of laws, regulations, precedents, and standard operating procedures that can be enormously difficult to untangle before they strangle change efforts.

For these reasons and others, Hill suggests an entirely new role for school districts as managers of a portfolio of relatively autonomous schools, rather than as school operators.

Today, boards oversee a central bureaucracy which owns and operates all the schools in a given district. It is time to retire this "command-and-control" system and replace it with a new model: portfolio management. In this new system, school boards would manage a diverse array of schools, some run by the school district and others by independent organizations, each designed to meet the different needs of students. Like investors with diversified portfolios of stocks and bonds, school boards would closely manage their community's portfolio of educational service offerings, divesting less productive schools and adding more promising ones. If existing schools do not serve students well, boards would experiment with promising new approaches to find ones that work.

This notion of a portfolio of schools—also advocated by the Gates Foundation—has many potential virtues to recommend it. Certainly, choice is better than coercion in the management of education. Students and families could find better fits with their interests and philosophies, and make a greater commitment to schools they have chosen. Choice could make schools more accountable and attentive to student needs. Schools that create successful designs should benefit from more autonomy to refine and maintain their good work. If a portfolio strategy works well it should "ensure a supply of quality school options that reflects a community's needs, interests, and assets . . . and [ensure] that every student has access to high-quality schools that prepare them for further learning, work, and citizenship."[8]

A portfolio structure is essentially what has emerged in New York City within the regular district structure (now divided into sets of school zones and networks) and, on a smaller scale, in Boston, which has launched a set of Pilot Schools—alternatives that provide a variety of educational options sharing the features described earlier in this chapter, which are succeeding at rates far above those of many other schools serving similar students.[9]

However, neither choice nor charters alone is a panacea. And not all innovations are useful ones. Although some public schools of choice have been successful, others have made little difference. For example, a recent evaluation of Chicago's Renaissance 2010 initiative, which replaced a group of low-performing schools with charters and other autonomous schools of choice run by entrepreneurs and the district, found that the achievement of students in the new schools was no different from that of a matched comparison group of students in the old schools they had left, and both groups continued to be very low-performing.[10]

Results for charters nationally have also been mixed. Reviews of the evidence have found positive impacts in some places and insignificant or negative impacts in others.[11]

A study of 16 states, covering 70% of all charter schools, found that only 17% of charters produced academic gains that were significantly better than traditional public schools serving demographically similar students, while 37[%] performed worse than their traditional public school counterparts, and 46% showed no difference from district-run public schools. The fact that outcomes differ across states suggests that different approaches to regulation and funding may be important. For example, in Ohio, where an unregulated market strategy created a huge range of for-profit and nonprofit providers with few public safeguards, charter school students were found to achieve at consistently lower levels than their demographically similar public school counterparts. Studies have also found lower average performance for charter students in the poorly regulated charter sectors in Washington, D.C.,

and Arizona, where charters can be granted for 15 years and fewer safeguards for students are required.[12] . . .

[T]he pressures under recent accountability regimes to get test scores up have led to growing concerns that some new schools—charters and otherwise—have sought to exclude those students who are the most challenging to teach, either by structuring admissions so that low-achieving students and those with special education or other needs are unlikely to be admitted, or by creating conditions under which such students are encouraged to leave. Studies of new schools created in New York City after 2000, for example, have found that these schools, unlike the earlier pioneers, enrolled more academically able students and fewer English language learners or students with disabilities than the large comprehensive schools they replaced. This enabled them to show better outcomes.[13]

Thus, it is not the governance mechanism or the degree of autonomy alone that determines whether schools will succeed. In places where new school models and redesigned schools have done well without ignoring or pushing out struggling students, attention has been paid both to sparking new educational possibilities and building schools' capacities for good instruction, and to removing unnecessary constraints and creating appropriate safeguards for students.

Sustaining Change

The goal, ultimately, is not just to support a vanguard group of unique schools, but to enable all schools to adopt practices that will be more successful for all of their students. For this to happen, districts must find ways to foster innovation and responsiveness without compromising equity, access, and the public purpose of schools to prepare citizens who can live, work, and contribute to a common democratic society. This will require redesigning districts as well as schools, rethinking regulations and collective bargaining, while building capacity and allocating resources in smarter and more equitable ways.

Redesigning Districts. For successful schools to become the norm, districts must move beyond the pursuit of an array of ad hoc initiatives managed by exception to fundamental changes in district operations and policy. Throughout the 20th century most urban districts adopted increasingly bureaucratic approaches to managing schools. They created extensive rules to manage every aspect of school life—from, curriculum, instruction, and testing to hiring, purchasing, and facilities—along with complex, departmentalized structures to manage these rules and procedures. Siloed bureaucrats have had the mission of administering procedures that often get in the way of practitioners' instructional efforts, rather than managing quality by being accountable for figuring out ways to support success. To create a new paradigm, the role of the district must shift

- From enforcing procedures to building school capacity
- From managing compliance to managing improvement
- From rewarding staff for following orders and "doing things right" to rewarding staff for getting results by "doing the right things"
- From rationing educational opportunities to expanding successful programs
- From ignoring (and compounding) failure in schools serving the least powerful to reallocating resources to ensure their success

To a large extent, these changes represent a switch from bureaucratic accountability—that is, hierarchical systems that pass down decisions and hold employees accountable for following the rules, whether or not they are effective—to professional accountability—that is, knowledge-based systems that help build capacity in schools for doing the work well, and hold people accountable for using professional practices that enable student success.

In a new paradigm, the design of the district office should also evolve from a set of silos that rarely interact with one another to a team structure that can integrate efforts across areas such as personnel, professional development, curriculum and instruction, and evaluation, with the goal of creating greater capacity in a more integrated fashion. These supports should include

- Recruiting a pool of well-prepared teachers and leaders from which schools can choose—and building pipelines to facilitate their training and availability
- Organizing access to high-quality, sustained professional development and resources, including skilled instructional mentors and coaches that schools can call upon and that can be deployed to diagnose problems and support improvements in schools that are struggling
- Ensuring that high-quality instructional resources—curriculum materials, books, computers, and texts—are available
- Providing services, such as purchasing and facilities maintenance, to school consumers in effective and efficient ways—if schools choose to acquire them from the district

If they incorporate choice, districts will need to ensure that all schools are worth choosing and that all students have access to good schools. This means they must continuously evaluate how schools are doing, seeking to learn from successful schools and to support improvements in struggling schools by ensuring that these schools secure strong leadership and excellent teachers, and are supported in adopting successful program strategies. Districts will need to become learning organizations themselves—developing their capacity to investigate and learn from innovations in order to leverage productive strategies, and developing their capacity to support successful change. Where good schools and programs are oversubscribed, districts will have to learn how to spread good models rather than rationing them, and where schools are failing, they will need to learn how to diagnose, address problems, and invest resources to improve them. These capacities are needed in all systems, whether or not they adopt choice strategies.

If education is to serve the public good, it is critical to guard against the emergence of a privatized system in which schools are separated by their ability to choose their students, rather than by the ability of students and families to choose their schools. For choice to work, districts must also not only provide information and transportation to parents; they must also manage parents' and schools' choices so that schools recruit and admit students without regard to race, class, or prior academic achievement, both to preserve the possibilities for integrated, common schools and to ensure that some schools do not become enclaves of privilege while others remain dumping grounds. Managed choice arrangements in cities such as Cambridge, Massachusetts, and (in some eras) New York City have created strategies for doing this, allowing parents to state several preferences and requiring schools to admit a diverse student body from all parts of the achievement range. However, these districts have also learned that such strategies require constant vigilance and are not by themselves enough to guarantee access to quality schools for all students. In particular, without the right support and incentives, many schools will seek to recruit the most advantaged students and deflect or push out the least advantaged ones. These incentives, as I discuss below, have to do with the level of capacity to serve students well, with resources, and with accountability measures.

Building Professional Capacity. [B]uilding professional capacity ultimately requires investments in effective preparation, hiring, mentoring, evaluation, and professional development for school leaders, as well as teachers and other staff. In addition, systems need to develop strategies for sharing good practice across schools, ranging from research that is widely disseminated to the establishment of networks of schools, teachers, and principals that develop and share practice with one another, to the creation of strategies such as school quality reviews that allow educators to examine one another's practice and get feedback that can help them grow.

Growing successful new schools or improving existing ones is not likely to be accomplished merely by a replication strategy in which external

agents seek to transplant programs or designs from one school into another. Replication efforts have an inglorious history, largely because they quickly run up against differences in staff knowledge and capacity resources, and contexts of receiving schools. Unless they are accompanied by intensive, long-term professional development support, schools can rarely attend to the nuances and implications of new strategies in ways that would permit strong implementation over the long run. When the purportedly effective techniques don't work immediately, especially for students who are challenging to teach, staff will tend to revert to old approaches and/or focus on reaching those who are easiest to teach given what teachers already know how to do and have the resources to support.

Another approach was used to achieve the surprisingly consistent and sophisticated practices we found across the Coalition Campus Schools we studied, which allowed them to be successful with normally low-achieving students. Following what might be called a birthing and parenting strategy, many of the new school "launchers" had been teachers in the older, successful schools. They were mentored by expert veteran principals and teachers while belonging to a set of networks that facilitated ongoing sharing of practice and supported problem solving.

Networking strategies have increasingly been found to be powerful for sharing practitioner knowledge. Teacher-to-teacher networks such as the National Writing Project help teachers develop effective pedagogical practices; principal networks have become critically important within many districts seeking to support stronger instructional leadership and create opportunities for shared problem solving; and, in both the United States and abroad . . . school networks are enabling educators to share departmental and schoolwide practices through collective professional development, observational visits, and pooling of intellectual resources.

Managing and Allocating Resources. For schools to succeed with all students, they also must be adequately resourced to do so. As we have seen, disparities in funding between states, districts, and schools often leave those working with the neediest students with the fewest resources. States can begin to change this by costing out what would be required to provide an adequate education to graduate all students, having met the state standards, and then allocating resources equitably to each student on a per pupil basis adjusted for regional cost-of-living differentials and pupil needs. The weighted student formula approach, advocated by many school finance reformers and adopted in some cities to equalize within-district funding, is intended to provide an added increment for students with disabilities, new English language learners, and low-income students, determined by estimating the costs of educating these students to the state's standards. Schools serving large concentrations of high-need students would receive additional funds to provide the services that so many of their students require.

Schools and districts also need the flexibility to spend their funds in optimal ways. Among the distinctive features of successful, redesigned schools is the fact that they use the resources of people and time very differently from traditional systems in order to provide more intense relationships between adults and students and to ensure collaborative planning and learning time for teachers, as schools in other nations do. [T]he United States spends much less of its educational budget on classroom instruction and on teachers—just over 50%, as compared to 70 to 80% in other countries.[14] This weakens instruction.

In part, this is because the United States spends more on several layers of bureaucracy between the state and the school, made necessary in part by the dizzying array of federal and state categorical programs schools are expected to manage because they are not trusted to make good decisions about resources. These categorical programs themselves create inefficiencies in spending, requiring administrative attention and audit trails, as well as fragmenting programs and efforts in schools in ways that undermine educational outcomes. Often, these programs and other regulations prescribe

staffing patterns and other uses of resources that reduce focus and effectiveness.

In addition, the United States spends more of its personnel budget on a variety of administrative staff and instructional aides rather than on teachers directly, implementing the outdated model that added a variety of pull-out programs and peripheral services to make up for the failures of a factory-model system, rather than investing in the instructional core of expert teachers given time to work productively with students whom they know well. Thus, whereas full-time teachers engaged in instruction comprise about 70 to 80% of education employees in most Asian and European nations, they are only about half of education employees in the United States.[15] In 2003, for example, whereas only 51% of school district employees in the United States were classroom teachers, the proportion of full-time classroom teachers in Japanese schools was 89% of all educational staff. The proportion is 72% of all employees, if one also includes the large number of doctors, dentists, and pharmacists who are based in Japanese schools.[16] Indeed, Japanese schools had, proportionately, as many doctors as there were instructional aides in U.S. schools, but only one-third the proportion of administrative staff.

Successful, redesigned schools often invest more of their resources in classroom teachers and organize teachers in teams that share students over longer periods of time, to create more sharing of knowledge, as well as to focus on accountability for student needs and success. They consolidate their resources to offer a strong, common core curriculum and key supports, resisting the temptation to diffuse their energies or spend on peripherals at the expense of the central goals of the school. The implications for staffing patterns, resource allocations, and the uses of teachers' and students' time are even more distinctive for schools that engage students in extended internships outside the school, as the Met and its network of schools do; for schools that are engaging students in a range of college courses while they are in high school; and for schools that are embracing technology-based approaches to project work as the New Tech network of schools does.

States and districts will need to encourage more thoughtful and inventive uses of resources by resisting the temptation to prescribe old factory-model requirements for staffing and uses of time and funds, and by providing supports for school leaders to learn how to design organizations that use resources in ways that are likely to produce the desired outcomes.

Deregulating Strategically. As I have suggested, a challenge in scaling up more effective school designs is that the century-old model of school organization that has shaped most schools is now reinforced by layers of regulations that often do not produce the most effective forms of education. Most state regulatory frameworks for schools have not yet shifted to accommodate or encourage the design choices made by new school models.

Where innovations are made possible by relief from regulations, they cannot spread unless the same regulatory relief is applied to other parts of the system. Few states have examined ways to deregulate public schools strategically in ways that would permit greater focus and success while preserving core public values. In recent years, as charters and other relatively autonomous schools have been created to permit flexibility in one part of the system, heavy-handed regulation has often increased in the remainder of the system.

The Boston Pilot Schools and the New York City alternative schools are proof that large public organizations can create organizational firewalls that allow space for successful innovation. But to do so, they must always be conscious of the impact of their policies on school-level practice, and they must, over time, allow innovators to help change the rules as well as avoid them. Regulations protecting access and providing equitable allocations of resources should provide the foundation of a redesigned system, while professional standards and investments in professional capacity that allow educators to be trusted should replace efforts to micromanage teaching and the design of schools.

Changing Contracts. Over time, many of the features of the factory model have been incorporated into collective bargaining agreements by both unions and school boards. Among the most problematic aspects for school reforms are constraints on how time and work are structured and procedures for faculty hiring and assignment that have assumed, in the assembly-line era, that teachers are interchangeable parts.

The success of schools committed to a set of educational principles depends on their ability to hire faculty who believe in those principles and have the capacity to enact them. Thus, centralized assignments of teachers can be a problem, whether in the initial hiring of teachers or due to seniority transfers that give teachers rights to transfer into schools where their skills and philosophy may not fit. Some districts have begun to change these traditions by taking on the responsibility to build a strong pool of well-prepared personnel from which schools can then recruit, and by placing teachers who want to transfer schools into this pool when openings are available, with rights to an early interview but not to placement in a specific school.

In New York, for example, the new school development process triggered important system reforms, including in the key area of selecting teachers. With the cooperation of the Board of Education, the United Federation of Teachers (UFT) and the CCS Project negotiated a process for selecting staff in which a committee of teachers reviews resumes, interviews prospective candidates—and often observes them teaching or planning collaboratively—and selects those most qualified for the available positions. Where teachers are equally qualified, seniority is the decisive variable. UFT representatives participated in these hiring committees, and were so pleased with the outcomes that the union introduced the process into contract negotiations and recommended its adoption more broadly. The contract now includes a peer selection process for teachers in all nontraditional schools, illustrating how innovation can be used as a lever to transform system policies.

In addition, in any New York school where 55% of teachers vote to do so, the school can trigger a School-Based Option that relieves it from many contract constraints and allows new arrangements to be substituted. Many innovative schools have created their own contracts for teachers which, for example, may recognize teachers' roles as advisors and acknowledge different uses of time during the day and week in return for smaller pupil loads and greater autonomy.

Rethinking Accountability. Finally, policymakers must learn new ways to manage the tension between fostering innovation and holding schools accountable to the other purposes of public education—equity, access, development of citizenship, and progress in learning. One critical aspect of the state's role is to ascertain that students are being adequately taught to become productive citizens of society. In recent years, accountability in the United States has largely come to mean tracking test scores on increasingly limited measures, rather than ensuring access to adequate and equitable learning opportunities and the achievement of a broader set of outcomes. As we have seen, the allocation of sanctions to schools based on these high-stakes measures also creates disincentives for schools to admit and keep the neediest students.

Some states, such as Nebraska and Rhode Island, have allowed schools to develop and implement broader, more ambitious assessments of student learning that are approved by the state and examined for accountability purposes along with other documented student outcomes. In New York, 31 schools in the Performance Standards Consortium, including many of those we studied, have developed their own graduation portfolio of challenging research papers and exhibitions. This collection of required products treats both academic outcomes and civic and social responsibility—the latter demonstrated through community service and contributions to the school—and is approved for use in lieu of some of the New York State Regents examinations, with the expectation that schools also track evidence of college admission and completion.

In the long run, accountability systems that provide the right incentives for school quality and equity will need to examine student growth and school progress on a range of high-quality measures, not just their status at a moment in time on one limited measure, include evidence of students' opportunities to learn as well as their outcomes, and enforce professional standards of practice that assure parents their children will be well taught, not just well tested.

CONCLUSION

A growing number of schools have disrupted the status quo by providing opportunities for low-income students of color to become critical thinkers and leaders for the future. Unless policy systems change, however, these schools will remain anomalies, rather than harbingers of the future. Creating a system that supports the learning of all students is not impossible. It will take clarity of vision and purposeful, consistent action to create a web of supportive, mutually reinforcing elements. In particular, dismantling the institutionalized inequities that feed the racial, socioeconomic, and linguistic achievement gap will require substantive policy changes in redesigning schools, developing teachers and principals, expanding our conceptions of curriculum and assessment, rethinking funding strategies, and reconceptualizing accountability.

NOTES

1. Edmonds (1979).
2. For a review; see Levine & Lezotte (1990).
3. Eight-year study.
4. Erskine (2002).
5. Robinson (1984).
6. Cremin (1961).
7. Hill (2006).
8. Gates Foundation (2005), p. 3.
9. French (2008).
10. Young et al. (2009).
11. Imberman (2007); Miron & Nelson (2001), p. 36.

12. Carnoy, Jacobsen, Mishel, & Rothstein (2005).
13. Advocates for Children ([2002]).
14. Darling-Hammond (1997); NCTAF (1996).
15. NCTAF (1996).
16. Japanese statistics are for elementary and lower secondary schools, as reported in Japanese Ministry of Education, Culture, Sports, Science, and Technology (2004); U.S. statistics are from National Center for Education Statistics (2005), Table 79.

REFERENCES

Advocates for Children. (2002). *Pushing out at-risk students: An analysis of high school discharge figures—a joint report by AFC and the public advocate.* Retrieved from http://www.advocates forchildren.org/pubs/pushout-11-20-02.html

Carnoy, M., Jacobsen, R., Mishel, L., & Rothstein, R. (2005). *The charter school dust-up: Examining the evidence on enrollment and achievement.* Washington, DC: Economic Policy Institute.

Cremin, L. (1961). *The transformation of the school: Progressivism in American education, 1876–1957.* New York: Vintage Books.

Darling-Hammond, L. (1997). *The right to learn: A blueprint for creating schools that work.* San Francisco: Jossey-Bass.

Edmonds, R. (1979). Effective schools for the urban poor. *Educational Leadership, 37*(1), 15–18, 20–24.

Erskine, R. (2002, February). *Statement on school reform and the Seattle contract.* Society for the Advancement of Excellence in Education. Retrieved from http://www.saee.ca/index.php?option=com_content&task=view&id=319&Itemid=90

French, D. (2008). Boston's pilot schools: An alternative to charter schools. In L. Dingerson, B. Miner, B. Peterson, & S. Walters (Eds.), *Keeping the promise? The debate over charter schools* (pp. 67–80). Milwaukee, WI: Rethinking Schools.

Gates Foundation. (2005). *High performing school districts: Challenge, support, alignment, and choice.* Seattle: Bill & Melinda Gates Foundation.

Hill, P. (2006). *Put learning first: A portfolio approach to public schools.* Washington, DC: Progressive Policy Institute.

Imberman, S. (2007). *Achievement and behavior in charter schools: Drawing a more complete picture* (Occasional paper 142). New York: National Center for the Study of Privatizations in Education.

Japanese Ministry of Education, Culture, Sports, Science, and Technology. (2004). *Japan's education at a glance, 2004: School education.* Tokyo: Author.

Levine, D., & Lezotte, L. (1990). *Unusually effective schools: A review and analysis of research and practice.* Madison, WI: The National Center for Effective Schools Research & Development.

Miron, G., & Nelson, C. (2001). *Student achievement in charter schools: What we know and why we know so little* (Occasional Paper No. 41). New York: Teachers College, Columbia University, National Center for the Study of Privatization in Education.

National Center for Education Statistics (NCES). (2005). *Digest of education statistics, 2005.* Washington, DC: U.S. Department of Education. Retrieved from http://nces.ed.gov/programs/digest/d05/tables/dt05_079.asp?referrer=list

National Commission on Teaching and America's Future (NCTAF). (1996). *What matters most: Teaching for America's future.* New York: Author.

Robinson, H. S. (1984). The M Street School. *Records of the Columbia Historical Society of Washington, D.C.: 1891–1916, 51,* p. 122.

Young, V. M., Humphrey, D. C., Wang, H., Bosetti, K. R., Cassidy, L., Wechsler, . . . Schanzenbach, D. W. (2009). *Renaissance schools fund-supported schools: Early outcomes, challenges, and opportunities.* Menlo Park, CA: Stanford Research International and Chicago: Consortium on Chicago School Research. Retrieved from http://ccsr.uchicago.edu/publications/RSF%20FINAL%20April%2015.pdf

THE ACHIEVEMENT GAP

A Broader Picture

Richard Rothstein

Richard Rothstein presents a very complicated picture of the factors that lead to student achievement in schools. The problems he describes in this reading are problems of poverty that children bring with them to school and that influence their abilities to learn. As such, the recommendations he makes in this reading go far beyond reforming schools and classrooms and link schools with the community to solve broader issues in society.

Questions to consider for this reading:

1. How does poverty shape children's ability to perform in classrooms?

2. Is it possible to solve issues related to children's health by only providing better health care?

3. What one thing would you change to enhance the learning environment for students living in poverty?

The large achievement gap between white and minority students is generally viewed as a failure of the U.S. education system. Policymakers almost universally conclude that this gap must result from ineffective school policy and practice: low expectations, unqualified teachers, badly designed curriculum, large classes, undisciplined school climates, unfocused leadership, or a combination of these.

Many well-intentioned people blame the achievement gap on "failing schools" because common sense tells them that it could not be otherwise. The amount of money a family has—or the color of a child's skin—should not determine how well that child learns to read. If teachers know how to teach and schools permit no distractions, all students should be able to learn.

This commonsense perspective, however, is misleading. For although income and skin pigment don't directly cause low achievement, the characteristics that in general define social-class differences inevitably influence learning. Here are some examples.

CHILD REARING PRACTICES

Parents from different social classes often have different child rearing habits, disciplinary philosophies, ways of communicating expectations, and even styles of reading to children. These differences do not hold true in every family, but they influence the average tendencies of families from different classes.

Social-class patterns in child rearing make sense when you think about them. If upper-middle-class parents have jobs in which they collaborate with fellow employees and resolve problems, they are more likely to show their young children how to figure out answers for themselves. Parents whose jobs require them to follow routines are less likely to encourage creative problem solving in their children. Therefore, youngsters raised by parents who are professionals will generally have a more inquisitive, active approach to learning than will youngsters raised by working-class parents.

Thirty-five years ago, Kohn (1969) found that parents whose occupations required creativity and decision making were less likely to punish their children for actions in which the children's intentions were desirable, even if matters did not work out as intended. Parents who were closely supervised at work were more likely to base punishment on their children's actions, regardless of the children's intentions.

More recently, two researchers visited homes of families from different social classes to record conversations between parents and toddlers (Hart & Risley, 1995). On average, professional parents spoke more than 2,000 words per hour to their children, working-class parents spoke about 1,300, and welfare mothers spoke about 600. At 4 years old, children of professionals had vocabularies that were nearly 50 percent larger than those of working-class children and twice as large as those of welfare children.

The researchers also tracked how often parents verbally encouraged or reprimanded their children. Toddlers of professionals received an average of six encouragements per reprimand. Working-class children got two. For welfare children, the ratio was reversed: They received an average of one encouragement for every two scoldings. It seems reasonable to expect that when these children eventually go to school, their teachers will not be able to fully offset such differences in early interactions. Students whose parents have encouraged initiative from an early age are more likely to take responsibility for their own learning.

HEALTH NEEDS

Many social and economic manifestations of social class also have implications for learning. Among these are differences in health.

For example, vision problems have an obvious effect on school success. Poor children have twice the average rate of severe vision impairment (Starfield, 1997). One reason for this higher rate of vision problems may be inadequate prenatal development resulting from mothers' poor medical care and nutrition. Visual deficits may also arise because low-income children are more likely to watch too much television, an activity that does not develop hand-eye coordination and depth perception. Forty-two percent of black 4th graders watch six hours or more of television a day, compared with 13 percent of white 4th graders (National Center for Education Statistics, 2003, table 117).

Typical vision screening in school only asks students to read charts for nearsightedness. Most students are never tested for farsightedness or for difficulty with tracking, problems that are most likely to affect academic performance. Even when testing leads to optometric referrals, low-income children are less likely to follow up. When they get prescriptions for lenses, they less frequently obtain them or wear them to school (Gould & Gould, 2003).

Vision problems make it difficult to read from a book or see the chalkboard. The disproportionate assignment of low-income black students to special education may partly reflect a failure to correct their vision. When students have puzzling difficulties learning to read, the explanation is often no more complex than their inability to see well.

Differences in dental care have a similar impact: Untreated cavities are nearly three times as prevalent among poor children as among middle-class children (U.S. General Accounting Office [U.S. GAO], 2000, Figure 1). Students with toothaches, even minor ones, will tend to pay less attention in class and to be more distracted during tests than will students with healthy teeth.

Low-income children have dangerously high blood lead levels—at five times the rate of middle-class children's—diminishing their cognitive ability (U.S. GAO, 1999). Although lead-based paint was banned from residential construction in 1978, low-income children more often live in buildings constructed prior to that date and in buildings that are not repainted often enough to prevent old layers of paint from flaking.

Low-income children, particularly those who live in densely populated city neighborhoods, are also more likely to contract asthma. The asthma rate is substantially higher for urban than for rural children, for those on welfare than for nonwelfare families, for children from single-parent families than for those from two-parent families, and for poor than for nonpoor families (Forrest, Starfield, Riley, & Kang, 1997). The disease is provoked in part by breathing fumes from the low-grade heating oil often used in low-income housing and from diesel trucks and buses. Excessive dust and allergic reactions to mold, cockroaches, and secondhand smoke also provoke it.

Asthma keeps children up at night; even if they make it to school the next day, they are likely to be tired and inattentive. Many children with asthma refrain from exercise and so are less physically fit. Drowsy and more irritable, they also have more behavioral problems. Middle-class children typically get treatment for asthma symptoms; low-income children often do not. Lower-class children with asthma are about 80 percent more likely than middle-class children with asthma to miss more than seven days of school a year because of the disease (Halfon & Newacheck, 1993).

Children without regular medical care are also more likely to contract other illnesses—some serious, others minor—that keep them out of school. Despite federal programs that make medical care available to low-income children, gaps between access and use remain. Many families do not enroll in such programs because they don't know of the programs' availability, are intimidated by the process, or are unaware of the importance of medical care. Even when enrolled, they are less likely to use the services to which they are entitled.

MOBILITY RATES

The growing shortage of affordable, adequate housing for low-income families also affects achievement. Urban rents have risen faster than working-class incomes have, forcing many families to move frequently because they fall behind in rent payments. Family breakups and bouts of unemployment also contribute to low-income children's high mobility rates. In some schools in minority neighborhoods, mobility rates are above 100 percent. For every seat in the school, two children were enrolled at some time during the year (Bruno & Isken, 1996; Kerbow, 1996).

A 1994 report found that 30 percent of the poorest students had attended at least three different schools by 3rd grade, whereas only 10 percent of middle-class students had done so. Black students were more than twice as likely as white students to change schools this often (U.S. GAO, [1994]). High mobility depresses achievement not only for the students who move—each move means readjusting to teachers, classmates, and curriculum—but also for other students in high-mobility schools. Teachers with ever-changing classrooms are more likely to review old material than introduce new material, and they are less able to adjust instruction to the individual needs of students they barely know.

FINANCIAL ASSETS

Differences in long-term economic security are also important predictors of student achievement. Most analysts overlook these differences and use only annual income to indicate economic status. But when we recognize that black families who earned a low income in one specific year are likely to have been poor for longer than white families who earned a similar income that year, it helps explain why black students, on average, score lower than white students with the same family incomes.

White families are also likely to own more assets that support children's achievement than are black families at the same current income level. Median black family income is now about 64 percent of median white family income, but black family net worth is only 12 percent of white family net worth (Mishel, Bernstein, & Boushey, 2003, tables 1.4, 4.6). So white middle-class families are more likely than black middle-class families to have adequate and spacious housing, even when their annual incomes are similar, not only because whites suffer no discrimination in real estate markets but also because white middle-class parents are more likely to have received capital contributions from their own parents—for a down payment on a first home, for example. Black middle-class parents are more likely to be the first generation in their families to have middle-class status, and their own parents are less likely to have been able to help financially. As with all these examples, not all middle-class whites get first-time down payments from their parents, and not all middle-class blacks fail to get them. But on average, more whites than blacks with similar incomes benefit from this practice, and this contributes to average differences in neighborhood resources and in housing quality that add to the test score gap.

Asset differences also influence how much families save for college educations. A student's awareness that his or her family has resources for college can influence whether or not that student believes that college attendance is within reach. Comparing black and white middle-class students whose families have similar current incomes, it would be reasonable to expect the white students to be more confident about affording college and thus more dedicated to working hard in school.

MAKING PROGRESS

To make significant progress in narrowing the achievement gap, we must pursue three tracks simultaneously.

Certainly, schools need to raise the quality of instruction. Better schools are important, and better school practices can probably narrow the gap. School reform, however, is not enough.

We must also invest resources to expand the definition of schooling to include crucial out-of-school hours in which families and communities are now the sole—and disparate—influences. Because the gap is already huge among 3-year-olds, this investment should probably concentrate initially on early childhood programs for infants and toddlers that provide the kind of intellectual environment that middle-class children typically experience. This goal probably requires professional caregivers and low child-adult ratios.

Another essential out-of-school focus is giving low-income students after-school and summer experiences similar to those that most middle-class students take for granted. These experiences should not consist only of remedial programs that provide added drill in math and reading. The advantage that middle-class children gain after school and in the summer comes mostly from the self-confidence they acquire and the awareness they develop of the world outside their homes and immediate communities as they participate in organized athletics, dance, drama, museum visits, recreational reading, and other activities that develop their inquisitiveness, creativity, self-discipline, and organizational skills. After-school and summer programs will narrow the achievement gap only if they duplicate such enriched experiences.

Finally, the federal and state governments need to develop social and economic policies that enable children to attend school more equally ready to learn. These policies include offering health services for low-income children and families, providing stable housing for working families with children, taking aggressive action against discrimination, and boosting the incomes of working parents employed in low-wage occupations.

Although many characteristics of social class are impervious to short-term change, many others would respond to achievable policy reforms. For example, establishing optometric clinics in schools to improve the vision of low-income students may raise their test scores more than spending the same money on instructional improvement. Likewise, schools could provide dental clinics at a cost that is comparable to what schools typically spend on less effective reforms. If the United States truly intends to raise the achievement of low-income students, however, we need to make a more expansive commitment and provide a full array of health services. We should also evaluate whether increasing low-income families' access to stable housing raises student achievement.

To date, there have been few experiments to test the relative benefits of these alternative strategies, partly because people are so wedded to the notion that school reform alone is sufficient. But we could easily design experiments of this sort, and we should make them a priority.

For nearly half a century, economists, sociologists, and educators have been aware of the association of social and economic disadvantage with student achievement gaps. Most, however, have avoided the obvious implication of this understanding: Raising the achievement of low-income children requires ameliorating the social and economic conditions of their lives, not just reforming schools.

References

Bruno, J., & Isken, J. (1996). Inter- and intraschool site student transiency. *Journal of Research and Development in Education, 29*(4), 239–252.

Forrest, C. B., Starfield, B., Riley, A. W., & Kang, M. (1997). The impact of asthma on the health status of adolescents. *Pediatrics, 99*(2), E1.

Gould, M. C., & Gould, H. (2003). A clear vision for equity and opportunity. *Phi Delta Kappan, 85*(4), 324–328.

Halfon, N., & Newacheck, P. W. (1993). Childhood asthma and poverty. *Pediatrics, 91*(1), 56–61.

Hart, B., & Risley, T. (1995). *Meaningful differences.* Baltimore: Paul H. Brookes.

Kerbow, D. (1996). Patterns of urban student mobility and local school reform. *Journal of Education for Students Placed at Risk, 12*(2), 147–169.

Kohn, M. L. (1969). *Class and conformity: A study in values.* Homewood, IL: Dorsey Press.

Mishel, L., Bernstein, J., & Boushey, H. (2003). *The state of working America 2002/2003.* Ithaca, NY: Cornell University Press.

National Center for Education Statistics. (2003). *Digest of education statistics—2002* (NCES 2003–060). Washington, DC: U.S. Department of Education.

Starfield, B. (1997). Health indicators for preadolescent school-age children. In R. M. Hauser, B. V. Brown, & W. R. Prosser (Eds.), *Indicators of children's well-being.* New York: Russell Sage Foundation.

U.S. General Accounting Office (U.S. GAO). (1994). *Elementary school children: Many change schools frequently, harming their education* (GAO/HEHS-94-45). Washington, DC: Author.

U.S. GAO. (1999). *Lead poisoning: Federal health care programs are not effectively reaching at-risk children* (GAO/HEHS-99–18). Washington, DC: Author.

U.S. GAO. (2000). *Oral health in low-income populations* (GAO/HEHS-00–72). Washington, DC: Author.

CAN SCHOOLING CONTRIBUTE TO A MORE JUST SOCIETY?

Michael W. Apple

In this excerpt from a larger piece, Michael W. Apple, a well-respected critical theorist, examines the attempts at equality from a political framework. This excerpt, which is solidly based in critical theory, examines both the politics of educational reform and the motivations driving conservative social movements in education. He looks at what makes these movements successful and suggests that liberals should consider such strategies in their attempts to change the educational process. This piece moves the issue of equality and equity in education to a new level, far outside the schools, to that of the politics of education.

Questions to consider for this reading:

1. Are politics important in deciding what happens in classrooms? If so, why?

2. According to Apple, why has the Right been successful in mobilizing people, even when participation is against their better interests?

3. What strategy for educational reforms is Apple suggesting as an alternative to the agenda for political reform put forth by conservative groups?

When a nation and its government and major institutions do not deliver on their promises and on the sets of values they officially profess in education and elsewhere, then substantive criticism is the ultimate act of patriotism. Such criticism says that "We are not just passing through. This is our country and our institutions as well, built by the labor of millions of people such as ourselves. We take the values in our founding documents seriously and demand that you do so too."

Of course, the arguments [I am] making in this article are quite political. But that is the point. Over the past three decades, many committed and critical educators have argued that education must be seen as a political act. They have suggested that in order to do this, we need to think *relationally*.

That is, understanding education requires that we situate it back into both the unequal relations of power in the larger society and into the relations of dominance and subordination—and the conflicts to change these things—that are generated by these relations. Thus, rather than simply asking whether students have mastered a particular subject matter and have done well on our all too common tests, we should ask a different set of questions: Whose knowledge is this? How did it become "official"? What is the relationship between this knowledge and who has cultural, social and economic capital in this society? Who benefits from these definitions of legitimate knowledge and who does not? What can we do as critical educators and activists to change existing educational and social inequalities and to create curricula and teaching that are more socially just (Apple, 1996, 2000; Apple & Beane, 2007)?

These are complicated questions and they often require complicated answers. However, there is now a long tradition of asking and answering these kinds of critical challenges to the ways education is currently being carried on, a tradition that has grown considerably since the time when I first raised these issues in *Ideology and Curriculum* (Apple, 1979; see also the more recent 3rd ed., Apple, 2004). Perhaps the best way of documenting why we need to keep these political issues at the forefront of our vision of what schools now do and what they should do is to focus on the life of a student, someone I knew very well. I hope that you will forgive me if at times throughout this article I use personal narratives to make larger points. But it seems to me that sometimes such a writing style can bring home points in ways that more abstract ways of presenting things cannot. Such a style also makes the politics of education not something "out there" in some abstract universe very far away, but puts it "right here" in terms of our personal choices inside and outside of education.

REMEMBERING REAL SCHOOLS AND REAL CHILDREN

Joseph sobbed at my desk. He was a tough kid, a hard case, someone who often made life difficult for his teachers. He was all of nine-years-old and here he was sobbing, holding on to me in public. He had been in my fourth-grade class all year, a classroom situated in a decaying building in an east coast city that was among the most impoverished in the nation. There were times when I wondered, seriously, whether I would make it through that year. There were many Josephs in that classroom and I was constantly drained by the demands, the bureaucratic rules, the daily lessons that bounced off of the kids' armor. Yet somehow it was satisfying, compelling and important, even though the prescribed curriculum and the textbooks that were meant to teach

it were often beside the point. They were boring to the kids and boring to me.

I should have realized the first day what it would be like when I opened that city's "Getting Started" suggested lessons for the first few days and it began with the suggestion that "as a new teacher" I should circle the students' desks and have them introduce each other and tell something about themselves. It's not that I was against this activity; it's just that I didn't have enough unbroken desks (or even chairs) for all of the students. A number of the kids had nowhere to sit. This was my first lesson—but certainly not my last—in understanding that the curriculum and those who planned it lived in an unreal world, a world *fundamentally* disconnected from my life with those children in that inner city classroom.

But here's Joseph. He's still crying. I've worked extremely hard with him all year long. We've eaten lunch together; we've read stories; we've gotten to know each other. There are times when he drives me to despair and other times when I find him to be among the most sensitive children in my class. I just can't give up on this kid. He's just received his report card and it says that he is to repeat fourth grade. The school system has a policy that states that failure in any two subjects (including the "behavior" side of the report card) requires that the student be left back. Joseph was failing "gym" and arithmetic. Even though he had shown improvement, he had trouble keeping awake during arithmetic, had done poorly on the mandatory city-wide tests, and hated gym. One of his parents worked a late shift and Joseph would often stay up, hoping to spend some time with her. And the things that students were asked to do in gym were, to him, "lame."

The thing is, he had made real progress during the year. But I was instructed to keep him back. I knew that things would be worse next year. There would still not be enough desks. The poverty in that community would still be horrible; and health care and sufficient funding for job training and other services would be diminished. I knew that the jobs that were available in this former mill town paid deplorable wages and that even with both of his parents working for pay, Joseph's family income was simply insufficient. I also knew that, given all that I already had to do each day in that classroom and each night at home in preparation for the next day, it would be nearly impossible for me to work any harder than I had already done with Joseph. And there were another five children in that class whom I was supposed to leave back.

So Joseph sobbed. Both he and I understood what this meant. There would be no additional help for me—or for children such as Joseph— next year. The promises would remain simply rhetorical. Words would be thrown at the problems. Teachers and parents and children would be blamed. But the school system would look like it believed in and enforced higher standards. The structuring of economic and political power in that community and that state would again go on as "business as usual."

The next year Joseph basically stopped trying. The last time I heard anything about him was that he was in prison.

This story is not apocryphal. While the incident took place a while ago, the conditions in that community and that school are much worse today. And the intense pressure that teachers, administrators, and local communities are under is also considerably worse (Kozol, 1991; Lipman, 2004). It reminds me of why large numbers of thoughtful educators and activists mistrust the incessant focus on standards, increased testing, marketization and vouchers, and other kinds of educational "reforms" which may sound good in the abstract, but which often work in exactly the opposite ways when they reach the level of the classroom (see Apple, 2006; Lipman, 2004; McNeil, 2000; Valenzuela, 2005). It is exactly this sensibility of the contradictions between proposals for reform and the realities and complexities of education on the ground that provides one of the major reasons so many of us are asking the questions surrounding how education can make a more serious contribution to social justice. I want to say more about this in the next section of this article.

THE POLITICS OF EDUCATIONAL REFORM

Critical educators have long demonstrated that policies often have strikingly unforeseen consequences. Reforms that are instituted with good intentions may have hidden effects that are more than a little problematic. We have shown for instance that the effects of some of the favorite reforms of neo-liberals and neo-conservatives, for instance—voucher plans, national or state-wide curricula, and national or state-wide testing can serve as examples— quite often reproduce or even worsen inequalities. Thus, we should be very cautious about accepting what may seem to be meritorious intentions at face value. Intentions are too often contradicted by how reforms may function in practice. This is true not only for large scale transformations of educational policies and governance, but also about moves to change the ways curriculum and teaching go on in schools.

The framework politically and educationally progressive educators have employed to understand this is grounded in what in cultural theory is called the act of repositioning. It in essence says that the best way to understand what any set of institutions, policies, and practices does is to see it from the standpoint of those who have the least power. Speaking personally, growing up poor myself made this almost a "natural" perspective for me to take. That is, every institution, policy, and practice—and especially those that now dominate education and the larger society— establish relations of power in which some voices are heard and some are not. While it is not preordained that those voices that will be heard most clearly are also those who have the most economic, cultural and social capital, it is most likely that this will be the case. After all, we do not exist on a level playing field. Many economic, social and educational policies when actually put in place tend to benefit those who already have advantages.

These points may seem overly rhetorical and too abstract, but unfortunately there is no small amount of truth in them. For example, in a time when all too much of the discourse around educational reform is focused on vouchers and choice plans on the one hand and on proposals for national or state curricula, standards, and testing on the other, as I have shown in a number of volumes (Apple, 1995, 1996, 2000, 2006, [2009a]; Apple et al., 2003), there is a good deal of international evidence now that such policies may actually reproduce or even worsen class, gender and race inequalities. Thus, existing structures of economic and cultural power often lead to a situation in which what may have started out in some educators' or legislators' minds as an attempt to make things better, in the end is all too usually transformed into another set of mechanisms for social stratification.

While much of this is due to the ways in which race, gender, class and "ability" act as structural realities in this society and to how we fund (and do not fund) schools, some of it is related to the hesitancy of policy makers to take seriously enough the complicated ways in which education is itself a political act. These very politics and the structurally generated inequalities that stand behind them provide much of the substance underpinning the organizational principles of my work.

A key word in my discussion above is *reform*. This concept is what might be called a "sliding signifier." That is, it has no essential meaning and, like a glass, can be filled with multiple things. As Wittgenstein (1953) reminded us, it is always wise not to accept the meaning of a concept at face value. Instead, one must contextualize it. The meaning is in its *use*. Let us look at this in a bit more detail.

The language of educational reform is always interesting. It consistently paints a picture that what is going [on] in schools now needs fixing, is outmoded, inefficient or simply "bad." Reforms will fix it. They will make things "better." Over the past decades certain language systems in particular have been mobilized. Not only will specific reforms make things better, they will make schools more democratic. Of course, the word democracy is one of the best examples of a sliding signifier. It carries with it an entire

history of conflicts over its very meaning (Foner, 1998). Like reform, democracy does not carry an essential meaning emblazoned on its head so to speak. Instead it is one of the most contested words in the English language. Indeed, one of the major tactics of dominant groups historically and currently is to cement particular meanings of democracy into public discourse. Thus, under current neo-liberal policies in education and elsewhere, there are consistent attempts to redefine democracy as simply consumer choice. Here democracy is not a collective project of building and rebuilding our public institutions. It becomes simply a matter of placing everything that was once public onto a market. Collective justice will somehow take care of itself as the market works its wonders.

As Mary Lee Smith and her colleagues have recently demonstrated in their powerful analysis of a number of educational reforms, the nice sounding and "democratic" language used to promote reforms is often totally at odds with the actual functioning of these reforms in real schools in real communities (Smith, 2004). A significant number of things that were advertised (and that is often the appropriate word) as making schools more responsive and "better" (increased testing and parental choice through marketization may serve as examples) may have exacerbated problems of inequality. (Think of Joseph and what happened to him in an earlier round of increased testing and "raising standards.")

One of the reasons this is the case is because the formation of a good deal of educational policy is actually a form of "symbolic politics," basically a kind of theater (Smith, 2004). This is not to claim that policy makers are acting in bad faith. Rather, because of the distribution (or not) of resources, tragic levels of impoverishment, the ways policies are implemented (or not), and the cleverness of economically and cultural dominant groups in using reforms for their own advantage, the patterns of benefits are not anywhere near the supposedly democratic ends envisioned by some of their well-meaning proponents. (Some reforms as well may simply be the result of cynical manipulation of the public for electoral advantage; but that's a topic for another essay.)

UNDERSTANDING CONSERVATIVE SOCIAL MOVEMENTS IN EDUCATION

The arguments I made above are related to a particular claim that is important to make. Many of us have spent a good deal of time showing that it is social movements, *not* educators, who are the real engines of educational transformations (Anyon, 2005; Apple, 2000, 2006, [2009]). And the social movements that are the most powerful now are more than a little conservative. I want to argue in fact that unless we think very tactically about what the Right has been able to accomplish and what the balance of forces now are, all too much of our attempts at putting in place more critically democratic reforms may be less powerful than we would like.

Over the past decade, a good deal of concerted effort has been devoted to analyzing the reasons behind the rightist resurgence—what I have called "conservative modernization"—in education and to try to find spaces for interrupting it (see Apple, 2006; Apple & Buras, 2006). My own aim has not simply been to castigate the Right, although there is a bit of fun in doing so. Rather, I have also sought to illuminate the dangers, and the elements of good sense, not only bad sense, that are found within what is an identifiable and powerful new "hegemonic bloc" (that is, a powerful set of groups that provides overall leadership to and pressure on what the basic goals and policies of a society are). This new rightist alliance is made up of various factions—neo-liberals, neo-conservatives, authoritarian populist religious conservatives and some members of the professional and managerial new middle class. These are complicated groups, but let me describe them briefly.

This power bloc combines multiple fractions of capital who are committed to neo-liberal marketized solutions to educational problems, neo-conservative intellectuals who want a "return" to higher standards and a "common culture,"

authoritarian populist religious fundamentalists who are deeply worried about secularity and the preservation of their own traditions, and particular fractions of the professionally oriented new middle class who are committed to the ideology and techniques of accountability, measurement and "management." While there are clear tensions and conflicts within this alliance, in general its overall aims are in providing the educational conditions believed necessary both for increasing international competitiveness, profit and discipline and for returning us to a romanticized past of the "ideal" home, family and school (Apple, 1996, 2006).

I have had a number of reasons for focusing on the alliance behind conservative modernization. First, these groups are indeed powerful, as any honest analysis of what is happening in education and the larger society clearly indicates. Second, they are quite talented in connecting to people who might ordinarily disagree with them. For this reason, I have shown in a number of places that people who find certain elements of conservative modernization relevant to their lives are not puppets. They are not dupes who have little understanding of the "real" relations of this society. This smacks of earlier reductive analyses within the critical tradition that were based on ideas of "false consciousness."

My position is very different. I maintain that the reason that some of the arguments coming from the various factions of this new hegemonic bloc are listened to is because they *are* connected to aspects of the realities that people experience (Apple, 1996; Apple & Pedroni, 2005). The tense alliance of neo-liberals, neo-conservatives, authoritarian populist religious activists and the professional and managerial new middle class only works because there has been a very creative articulation of themes that resonate deeply with the experiences, fears, hopes and dreams of people as they go about their daily lives. The Right has often been more than a little manipulative in its articulation of these themes. It has integrated them within racist nativist discourses, within economically dominant forms of understanding, and within a problematic sense of "tradition." But, this integration could only occur if they were organized around people's understanding of their real material and cultural lives.

The second reason I have stressed the tension between good and bad sense and the ability of dominant groups to connect to people's real understandings of their lives—aside from my profound respect for Antonio Gramsci's (1968, 1971) writings about this—has to do with my belief that we have witnessed a major educational accomplishment over the past three decades in many countries. All too often, we assume that educational and cultural struggles are epiphenomenal. The real battles occur in the paid workplace—the "economy." Not only is this a strikingly reductive sense of what the economy is (its focus on paid, not unpaid, work; its neglect of the fact that, say, cultural institutions such as schools are also places where paid work goes on, etc.) (Apple, 1986), it also ignores what the Right has actually done.

Conservative modernization has radically reshaped the commonsense of society. It has worked in every sphere—the economic, the political and the cultural—to alter the basic categories we use to evaluate our institutions and our public and private lives. It has established new identities. It has recognized that to win in the state, you must win in civil society. That is, you need to work at the level of people's daily experiences, not only in government policies. The accomplishment of such a vast educational project has many implications. It shows how important cultural struggles are. And, oddly enough, it gives reason for hope. It forces us to ask a number of significant questions. What can we learn from the Right about how to build movements for social transformation? If the Right can do this, why can't we?

I do not mean these as rhetorical questions. As I have argued repeatedly in my own work, the Right has shown how powerful the struggle over meaning and identity—and hence, schools, curricula, teaching and evaluation—can be. While we should not want to emulate their often cynical and manipulative processes, the fact that they have had such success in pulling people under their ideological umbrella has much to teach us. Granted there are real differences in

money and power between the forces of conservative modernization and those whose lives are being tragically altered by the policies and practices coming from the alliance. But, the Right was not as powerful 30 years ago as it is now. It collectively organized. It created a decentered unity, one where each element sacrificed some of its particular agenda to push forward on those areas that bound them together. Can we not do the same?

I believe that we can, but only if we face up to the realities and dynamics of power in unromantic ways—and think tactically about what can be done now even under conditions that we may not always control. And this means not only critically analyzing the rightist agendas and the effects of their increasingly mistaken and arrogant policies, but engaging in some serious criticism of some elements within the progressive and critical educational communities as well. Thus, as I argue in *Educating the "Right" Way* (Apple, 2006), the romantic, possibilitarian rhetoric of some of the writers on critical pedagogy is not sufficiently based on a tactical or strategic analysis of the current situation nor is it sufficiently grounded in its understanding of the reconstructions of discourse and movements that are occurring in all too many places. Here I follow Cameron McCarthy (2000), who wisely reminds us, "We must think possibility within constraint; that is the condition of our time."

We need to remember that cultural and educational struggles are not epiphenomenal. They *count*, and they count in institutions throughout society. In order for dominant groups to exercise leadership, large numbers of people must be convinced that the maps of reality circulated by those with the most economic, political, and cultural power are indeed wiser than other alternatives. Dominant groups do this by attaching these maps to the elements of good sense that people have and by changing the very meaning of the key concepts and their accompanying structures of feeling that provide the centers of gravity for our hopes, fears, and dreams about this society. The Right has been much more successful in doing this than progressive groups and movements, in part because it has been able to craft—through hard and lengthy economic, political, and cultural efforts—a tense but still successful alliance that has shifted the major debates over education and economic and social policy onto its own terrain. And the sometimes mostly rhetorical material of critical pedagogy simply is unable to cope with this. Only when it is linked much more to concrete issues of educational policy and practice—and to the daily lives of educators, students, and community members—can it succeed. This, of course, is why journals such as *Rethinking Schools* and books such as *Democratic Schools* (Apple & Beane, 2007) that connect critical educational theories and approaches to the actual ways in which they can be and are present in real classrooms become so important. Thus, while we should support the principles of critical theory and critical pedagogy in the USA and elsewhere, we also need to act as internal critics when it has forgotten what it is meant to do and has sometimes become simply an academic specialization at universities.

REFERENCES

Anyon, J. (2005). *Radical possibilities*. New York: Routledge.

Apple, M. W. (1979). *Ideology and curriculum*. Boston: Routledge Kegan Paul.

Apple, M. W. (1986). *Teachers and texts*. New York: Routledge.

Apple, M. W. (1995). *Education and power* (2nd ed.). New York: Routledge.

Apple, M. W. (1996). *Cultural politics and education*. New York: Teachers College Press.

Apple, M. W. (2000). *Official knowledge* (2nd ed.). New York: Routledge.

Apple, M. W. (2004). *Ideology and curriculum; 25th anniversary* (3rd ed.). New York: Routledge Falmer.

Apple, M. W. (2006). *Educating the "right" way: Markets, standards, God, and inequality* (2nd ed.). New York: Routledge.

Apple, M. W. (Ed.). (2009). *Global crises, education, and social justice*. New York: Routledge.

Apple, M. W., Aasen, P., Cho, M. K., Gandin, L. A., Oliver, A., Sung, Y.-K. . . . Wong, T.-H. (2003). *The state and the politics of knowledge*. New York: Routledge Falmer.

Apple, M. W., & Beane, J. A. (2007). *Democratic schools: Lessons in powerful education* (2nd ed.). Portsmouth, NH: Heinemann.

Apple, M. W., & Buras, K. L. (Eds.). (2006). *The subaltern speak: Curriculum, power, and educational struggles*. New York: Routledge.

Apple, M. W., & Pedroni, T. (2005). Conservative alliance building and African American support of voucher reform. *Teachers College Record, 107,* 2068–2105.

Foner, E. (1998). *The story of American freedom*. New York: Norton.

Gramsci, A. (1968). *The modern prince and other writings*. New York: International Publishers.

Gramsci, A. (1971). *Selections from the prison notebooks*. New York: International Publishers.

Kozol, J. (1991). *Savage inequalities*. New York: Crown.

Lipman, P. (2004). *High stakes education*. New York: Routledge Falmer.

McCarthy, C. (2000, January). Presentation at the International Sociology of Education Conference, University of Sheffield, England.

McNeil, L. (2000). *The contradictions of school reform*. New York: Routledge.

Smith, M. L. (with Miller-Kahn, L., Heinecke, W., & Jarvis, P. F.). (2004). *Political spectacle and the fate of American schools*. New York: Routledge Falmer.

Teitelbaum, K. (1993). *Schooling for good rebels*. New York: Teachers College Press.

Valenzuela, A. (Ed.). (2005). *Leaving children behind*. Albany: State University of New York Press.

Wittgenstein, L. (1953). *Philosophical investigations*. New York: Macmillan.

Projects for Further Exploration

1. Find the school report cards (part of the No Child Left Behind Act) for three school districts in your area (one from a rural area, one from a suburban area, and one from an urban area) and compare the data for each district on factors such as the graduation rates, percentage of students going on to college, and the racial composition of the districts.

2. Using an academic database, look for the most recent studies on charter schools and compare the findings from these studies to those presented in the readings by Linda Renzulli and Vincent Roscigno and by Linda Darling-Hammond.

3. Read your local newspaper for articles about education and schools, paying particular attention to political dimensions of the issues being discussed. Can you tell if those articles are coming from conservative or liberal political groups?

9

HIGHER EDUCATION

ducational systems provide knowledge and skills from basic literacy to professional training. Higher education is part of that system in most countries, providing specialized professional and vocational preparation. In this chapter, we include readings that examine the various issues faced by institutions of higher education. Some of these issues are similar to those at other levels of education—pressures from the environment for external funding, demands from businesses and communities, negotiating roles and relationships, interactions between students and teachers, and the role of higher education in maintaining inequality in society.

With more and more students seeking postsecondary educational experiences, higher education has become an important part of the structure of education, particularly in the United States. College enrollments in the United States are at an all-time high, with 18.25 million students enrolled in fall 2007, representing steady increases in full-time enrollment over the past several years (National Center for Education Statistics, 2009, table 3).

In the United States, higher education institutions vary considerably. A brief history of the development of higher education in the United States helps to explain where we are today. Harvard University, the first institution of higher learning in America, was founded in 1643, followed in 1693 by William and Mary College. By 1770, there were only nine colleges in colonial America. The growth of colleges during the next 90 years was spotty, with over 700 colleges failing to survive prior to 1860 (Rudolph, 1990, p. 219). Lawrence Veysey (1965) described college life prior to 1865 as "archaic" (p. 2), one in which the task of education was to instill discipline and piety. Despite the fact that postsecondary education was faltering and intended for white males only, three black colleges were established before the Civil War (Willie, 2003) and two women's colleges were opened in 1855 (see reading by Leslie Miller-Bernal in this chapter).

The end of the Civil War and nascent industrialization in this country, however, revitalized higher education. This growth included new colleges for blacks and women; these colleges were the only option for blacks and women as only a few blacks or women were allowed into colleges serving white, elite males (see Miller-Bernal in this chapter). Indeed, the greatest growth was in those colleges for white, elite men. According to Frederick Rudolph (1990, p. 244), "the movement for technological and scientific education, which had been underway before the war, spawned new and more popular colleges and institutes." Federal and state aid and bequests by wealthy industrialists led to the chartering of newer, more practical institutions such as the Massachusetts Institute of Technology (MIT) and Cornell, both in 1865. Changes in society also prompted changes in many of the older, established colleges. For instance, Princeton added its engineering school in 1871 (Rudolph, 1990).

In addition to the considerable growth in the number of colleges and universities, the post–Civil War era saw enrollments increase with the first waves of immigration in the 1890s. Higher education during this period continued to be limited to the wealthy, who at that time recognized the advantages of educating their children as a means of distinguishing themselves as a class above the newly arrived immigrants. Indeed, the enrollments in higher education grew at 4.7 times the rate of growth of the population during the years from 1890 to 1925 (Rudolph, 1990, p. 442). Higher education, however, was not necessarily focused around academics. According to Veysey (1965), the college experience at the end of the nineteenth century "meant good times, pleasant friendships, and, underneath it all, the expectation of life-long prestige resulting from the degree" (p. 269) at the most elite colleges.

The turn of the century saw a blending of worldly issues into the university, as business and academics mingled more so than in the past. Among the changes in higher education that occurred after the Civil War was the introduction of an elective curriculum in which students could choose from an array of courses; this curriculum replaced the rigid classical curriculum previously in use. However, at the same time that colleges worked to attract more students, they also raised standards (Veysey, 1965). In addition, the development of advanced programs in graduate studies transformed universities during this period (Rudolph, 1990).

Drawing on the ideas of progressivism at the early part of the 20th century, the ideal of service was introduced as a goal of higher education. During this period, universities developed extension courses and programs that attempted to serve community needs and provide expertise to the country (Rudolph, 1990). Scholarship, however, did not drop in significance as college and university professors formed learned societies, and the role of higher education was solidified in the early 20th century. Rudolph argues that the turn of the century was accompanied by a push toward more "organized" colleges and universities, with changes such as no longer installing only members of the clergy as college presidents.

World War I brought a counterrevolution, with pressures to return to a course of study that produced a well-rounded and academically grounded graduate. Thus, there was a push toward a general education or core curriculum. Service and practical learning, however, was still evident in land-grant universities and colleges of business administration (Rudolph, 1990).

The period from the depression of the 1920s through World War II was a time that tested higher education's resilience. Colleges and universities struggled to survive. With money scarce, college was a luxury neither society nor students could easily afford. Many students attending college during this period freely admitted to being "broke" (Rudolph, 1990, p. 466). The end of World War II brought enormous changes to college campuses previously enrolling only white, upper-class men. The GI Bill, which provided the means for many soldiers to attend college, was responsible for an enormous increase in the size of campuses, including what was once called "normal schools" that evolved into teachers' colleges. Across the country temporary classrooms and housing were hastily constructed to accommodate the returning soldiers. This growth in higher education continued through the end of the 20th century. In 1960, 3.5 million students attended higher education in the United States, a figure that doubled by 1970 (Rudolph, 1990, p. 486). As Kevin J. Dougherty notes in the third reading in this chapter, the demand for community colleges grew in response to the massive growth in higher education during the decade of the 1960s. Community colleges were not only cheaper than residential campuses, but they could accommodate weaker students, thus permitting existing colleges and universities to continue to be more selective. Dougherty also describes the role that community colleges play today, including close ties to business communities.

In contrast to the ideal of service to the community, higher education in the United States did not contribute to the development of new knowledge until they were called on during World War II (Graham & Diamond, 1997). Shortly after the war ended, the federal government created the National Science Foundation to fund scientific research. The funding was primarily in the physical sciences and engineering and used merit-based competition to distribute the research funds to universities and professors. The Department of Defense also provided support for research during the war and thereafter (Graham & Diamond, 1997).

The launching of Sputnik by the Soviet Union in 1957 unleashed even more federal funds for universities, as the United States raced to catch up in the new space-age technologies. The amount of federal funding to universities has waxed and waned over the years since World War II. The first reading in this chapter, by Zelda F. Gamson, describes how this influx of funding has fundamentally changed the mission of universities and indirectly changed the nature of faculties in colleges as well.

However, colleges and universities continued to receive pressure from the business community to make education useful. The push today is to focus more on preparing students to enter an increasingly global economy, evidenced by Europe's Bologna Agreement described by Fiona Hunter in the last reading in this chapter. Dougherty also states that American community colleges are responding to the business community's desire to educate workers for a global economy.

More than the direction in higher education is changing as we move into the 21st century. Indeed, the very structure of the institution is changing. The readings by Gamson, Dougherty, Miller-Bernal, and Hunter illustrate some of the most recent changes, but other changes are happening as well. We can now find universities online, where students complete a degree through distance learning. In these cases, campuses no longer are needed. The increase in the use of automation in higher education have led one scholar to call these universities "digital diploma mills" (Noble, 1998). Along with changes in the structure and purpose of college come changes in the composition of the student body. Among the most significant post–World War II changes in student composition are the increases in the numbers of women attending college in the United States, a change that began dramatically in the 1970s according to Miller-Bernal in this chapter. The numbers of women getting a bachelor's degree have grown considerably from 46.1% of all bachelor's degrees awarded in 1976–1977 to 57.3% in 2007–2008 (National Center for Education Statistics, 2009, table 268). A similar shift upward occurred in the percentage of degrees awarded for racial and ethnic minorities with blacks earning 6.4% of the bachelor's degrees in 1976–1977 to 9.8% of the degrees in 2007–-2008 and for Hispanics from 2.0% in 1976–1977 to 7.9% in 2007–2008 (National Center for Education Statistics, 2009, table 285). In contrast, white males earned 47.7% of bachelor's degrees awarded in 1976–1977 and 31.5% in 2007–2008 (National Center for Education Statistics, 2009, table 285). These numbers are not surprising since women and minority groups were kept out of most institutions of higher education, which were primarily all white and predominantly male, until the 1970s. Therefore, women's and historically black colleges and universities were basically the only avenue for higher education if you were not a white male prior to 1970. Although what was called "Negro colleges" were established in the South after the Civil War, and occasionally a black man graduated from college prior to the Civil War, the education of blacks and women in the United States continued to be an issue throughout the 20th century. Higher education was one of the issues that the civil rights movement of the 1960s addressed. By then, some strong black colleges had evolved and had graduated many people who went on to become early civil rights leaders. Those leaders, however, demanded access to primarily white colleges and universities. It wasn't until affirmative action legislation of the mid-1960s that there was legal support to enforce the admittance of women and minorities to attend previously all white, male colleges and universities.

Despite the gains in access in recent years, life on college campuses continues to be difficult for black students. Feagin, Vera, and Imani (1996, p. 17) refer to "educational apartheid" when describing the position of black students at white colleges and universities. Issues for other minority groups in higher education are also of concern, not only in terms of access but also in terms of quality of academic and social life once they are on campus.

384 • CHAPTER 9. HIGHER EDUCATION

The women's rights efforts of the 1970s opened up colleges and universities for women in many ways and women have been quite successful in gaining postsecondary degrees, except in some areas as discussed in the introduction to Chapter 7 and the reading by Mickelson in that chapter. However, the growth in women's enrollment in higher education has led to a decline in the number of women's colleges in the United States, as described by Miller-Bernal in this chapter.

Public colleges and universities have been important in providing pathways to higher education for people who might not otherwise have been able to afford college, with major expansion of public institutions of higher education occurring between 1960 and 1985 (Tobin, 2009). However, public institutions experienced problems with graduation rates, particularly among the less selective schools, as discussed by William G. Bowen, Matthew M. Chingos, and Michael S. McPherson in the reading in this chapter.

Many obstacles must be overcome for lower income students to achieve a college degree. Alejandro Portes and Patricia Fernández-Kelly describe factors in the lives of disadvantaged immigrant children that contributed to their success in college. Although the cases described are only a small portion of the children in their study, these stories help us to consider what things we might be able to change to help disadvantaged children achieve higher education degrees.

The system of higher education in America differs from the patterns and practices of advanced education in other countries. In Europe today, countries are working together to standardize higher education and ensure colleges and universities provide the same high standard of education across member countries. The Bologna Process, introduced in 1999 has generated considerable change across member countries and is continuing to affect higher education in Europe, as Fiona Hunter describes in her reading in this chapter.

As you can see, institutions of higher education have undergone and will continue to undergo many changes. The growth of private, for-profit institutions of higher education and the flexibility of technology in providing degrees are likely to lead to many more changes. This chapter is intended to familiarize you with some of the issues in higher education in the United States today and help you understand how the institution which you are currently attending fits into a history of higher education. All of the parts of the open systems model can be applied to understanding higher education in the readings that follow—organization, input and output, and feedback and influences from the surrounding environment.

REFERENCES

Feagin, J. R., Vera, H., & Imani, N. (1996). *The agony of education: Black students at white colleges and universities*. New York: Routledge.

Graham, H. D., & Diamond, N. (1997). *The rise of American research universities: Elites and challengers in the postwar era*. Baltimore: Johns Hopkins University Press.

National Center for Education Statistics. (2009). *Digest of education statistics*. Washington, DC: U.S. Department of Education. Retrieved from http://nces.ed.gov/

Noble, D. F. (1998). *Digital diploma mills: The automation of higher education*. Retrieved from http://www.firstmonday.dk/issues/issue3_1/noble/

Rudolph, F. (1990). *The American college and university: A history*. Athens: University of Georgia Press.

Tobin, E. M. (2009). The modern evolution of America's flagship universities. In W. G. Bowen, M. M. Chingos, & M. S. McPherson, *Crossing the finish line: Completing college at America's public universities* (Appendix A, pp. 239–264). Princeton, NJ: Princeton University Press.

Veysey, L. R. (1965). *The emergence of the American university*. Chicago: University of Chicago Press.

Willie, S. S. (2003). *Acting black: College identity and the performance of race*. New York: Routledge.

THE STRATIFICATION OF THE ACADEMY

Zelda F. Gamson

In this reading, Zelda Gamson looks at the effects of research activities by professors and students on colleges and universities. She describes the history of research expansion and contraction in major American universities, explores the effect of that trend on other colleges and universities, and considers the stratification of higher education within this context. Gamson also describes how external, societal forces changed expectations for colleges and universities and faculty to use their research for the greater social good. However, one of the consequences of this pressure was that teaching was no longer the main mission of colleges and universities and that faculty, across all institutions, including those primarily focused on teaching, expected faculty members to be productive researchers.

Questions to consider for this reading:

1. When did research activities expand and contract on university campuses, and what was behind these changes—government, business, or both?

2. How has research at major universities affected other colleges and universities?

3. What is the effect of research activities on the education of students?

Higher education is a mammoth industry. There are more than thirty-six hundred colleges and universities in this country with one million faculty members and fifteen million students. The property owned by colleges and universities has been estimated to be worth over $200 billion, total expenditures to be $175 billion, and annual university research and development expenditures to be about $20 billion.

This overall picture includes an enormous variety of institutions. Among four-year institutions, only 8 percent of private colleges and universities and 3 percent of public universities are very selective. All the rest, both public and private, are less selective or totally unselective, with the largest percentage concentrated at the bottom.

There are tremendous inequalities in the academy on almost any measure we might want to use. For example, the average family income of students in the very selective schools is three to four times that of students in the least selective schools. Faculty salaries do not show as extreme a ratio, but the differences are quite consistent: faculty in private research universities earn almost twice as much as faculty in liberal arts colleges. When we factor in total income—which includes consulting income, royalties, and other institutional income—faculty in private research universities are by far the highest paid, earning two and one-half times more than liberal arts college faculty. Average instructional and student services expenditures per student, a figure that is imperfect but the best measure of institutional resources available for educational (as opposed to research) purposes, decline markedly across the spectrum. Expenditures per student in private universities are more than twice those in liberal arts colleges and more than three times those in community colleges.

The Power of the Research Culture in the Expansionary Period

The academy is clearly at the end of the expansionary period that began after World War II and reached its pinnacle in the 1960s and 1970s. When Christopher Jencks and David Riesman published *The Academic Revolution* in 1968, the research university was at its height. The victory of the "academic revolution," as they called it, had been a genteel and well-funded affair underwritten by enormous amounts of federal support for higher education: government support in 1950 was 3 percent of what it was in 1980.[1]

Universities hired staffs of academics whose main work was doing research rather than teaching. If they did occasionally teach, these researchers were to be found in the graduate seminar, not the undergraduate lecture hall. The bargaining power of the faculty was heightened considerably during the early 1960s, especially in the research universities, when there were not enough college professors to teach the advance guard of the baby boom generation, which was beginning its march through higher education. College faculty began to be recruited nationally according to their scholarly research rather than their teaching ability. Faculty who never again did any scholarly work after their Ph.D. dissertations (and many did not) thought of themselves primarily as members of their [particular] disciplines—biologists, sociologists—not as educators.

In a general trend away from localism and single purposes, denominational colleges became more secular, single-sex colleges went coed, and teachers' colleges and other specialized institutions broadened their curricula. The exhilaration of expansion during this period propelled colleges across the country to broaden their missions and curricula. But in the process, older sources of legitimacy, such as commitment to a religious order or a particular population, became less serviceable, and the transformed institutions sought new markers of identity. The situation was ripe for what Paul DiMaggio and Walter Powell term "mimetic isomorphism," the imitation of apparently successful organizations by less successful ones.[2] Imitation is likely when organizations have ambiguous purposes or face uncertainty about their future. Many colleges and universities during the 1960s and 1970s allowed themselves to be pulled toward what appeared to be the only worthwhile model to emulate: the research culture.

The research culture draws its essential character from graduate faculty in research universities. It has three main elements: First, it is based on national rather than local allegiances. Second, it values research over teaching and service. Third, it prizes pure over applied research activities.[3] Through the socialization of new generations of faculty, through invisible colleges of scholars across the country working in similar subdisciplines, and through the peer review of grant applications and publications, these graduate faculty define the content, methods, and research problems addressed in funded projects, journals, and professional associations.[4]

The preeminence of the research culture is underscored by almost a century's worth of institutional ranking schemes. These ranking systems not only ensure visibility to those at the top but also legitimate an institutional hierarchy based on measures that are closely related to the research culture.[5] To some extent, this can be said of the category system invented by the Carnegie Foundation for the Advancement of Teaching and widely used by researchers and granting agencies. These categories have spurred many a doctorate-granting university to be reclassified as "research university," and "research university II" to be classified as "research university I." This giant classification sweepstakes can be seen as a kind of race whose winners are Harvard, the University of California at Berkeley, and Stanford.

By these means, a kind of invisible hand has guided the competition for faculty reputation, power, and prestige and, by extension, institutional prestige. In his study of the career mobility of faculty in a highly ranked department in a research university, Darwin Sawyer noted that "the professional status of an individual is as much an organizational resource in the institutional career of the department(s) which employ him/her as the institutional status of the department is a personal resource in the organizational careers of its members."[6] Prestige is a resource that enables universities to garner more tangible resources. An institution can offer its prestige by extension to its other constituents who, in return, place additional resources at its disposal. The greater the prestige generated by the institution, the more advantages it has in the competition for research funds, graduate students, and undergraduate enrollments.

It is no wonder that many formerly specialized colleges and universities aped the overwhelmingly successful culture of the research university. This mimicry became especially strong during the 1970s, when the scramble for resources became intense and administrators sought new ways to sustain the level of security and growth of the 1960s. The buyer's market of the 1970s allowed many institutions to hire faculty with more prestigious pedigrees than they had previously attracted.[7] This new breed of faculty brought a commitment to scholarly work that corresponded to administrators' desire for institutional prestige.

Faculty in liberal arts colleges, state colleges, and universities—places noted for their commitment to teaching and students—talked about needing more time for research. Faculty teaching loads declined everywhere but in community colleges, where the research culture never took hold. This correspondence of interests led relatively quickly to the inclusion of new criteria for hiring, promotion, and tenure that emphasized scholarly standards.[8] In other words, faculty who published a lot were favored with pay increases, leaves, sabbaticals, and release time. This shift toward a research culture is demonstrated by the change in faculty responses to a survey taken by the Carnegie Foundation. The survey, first taken in 1969, asked faculty to respond to the following statement: "It is difficult for a person to receive tenure if he/she does not publish." In 1969, 19 percent of the faculty in master's-level institutions agreed with this statement. Twenty years later, 65 percent agreed. In liberal arts colleges the change is not as dramatic but nevertheless striking for teaching institutions: 18 percent agreed in 1969, and 39 percent agreed in 1989.[9]

The march of the research culture throughout higher education was uneven, to be sure, but it took hold and delivered the goods—at least during the expansionary period—from donors and state budgets, if not from federal research programs, whose grants and contracts overwhelmingly went to research universities. As with the general economy in the post-war era, a rising tide raised all boats. All of higher education benefited from the expansion of the system, and the research culture legitimated that system. But while all the boats were rising, not all were rising at the same rate. The luxury liners—research universities, and the leading private ones in particular—led the way, followed by a variety of small yachts, sailboats, and tugboats.

THE TIDE TURNS

As the expansionary period peaked and then declined, the research culture began to lose its power. There are demographic, economic, and political reasons for this. Declines in the traditional college-going age group, whose impact has been greatest in the unselective colleges and universities, especially private ones, have led to great competition for a smaller pool of students in the last few years. The decrease in the eighteen-to-twenty-two-year-old, college-going population was balanced to some extent by increases in the attendance of older students overall, but not necessarily in the schools that have experienced the greatest enrollment stress—less selective private colleges with small endowments. Many of these colleges are barely surviving today, and some have gone under. It does not help them to know that the tide is shifting in the other direction, as the children of the baby boomers hit the campuses in full force.

College and university tuitions have been rising. In the thirteen years between 1976 and 1989, tuition and fees in public four-year colleges and universities almost tripled; in private institutions, they increased three and one-third times. Job insecurity, falling wages, and economic uncertainty have led students and their families to find paying for a college education, even in the public sector, a major hardship. Indeed, surveys show that one of the greatest concerns of the general public is the cost of higher education. This concern has found its way into public policy and the media. Higher education has increasingly been treated as just another entitlement burden on taxpayers; decreasing support for higher education can be used to offset state deficits and as a trade-off with claims from other constituencies.

A series of reports and books attacking higher education have appeared in rapid fire from the mid-1980s through the 1990s: in the mid-1980s, we had *Involvement in Learning*, a higher education sequel to the U.S. Department of Education's *A Nation at Risk*, which focused on schools; *To Reclaim a Legacy* under the leadership of William Bennett when he headed the National Endowment for the Humanities; and *Integrity in the College Curriculum*, issued by the Association of American Colleges. A critique by insiders and liberal reformers took shape in hundreds of reports from state and federal agencies and from higher education associations, which argued that undergraduate education was in serious trouble and that faculty seemed unable or unwilling to do anything about it. More recently, Bruce Wilshire in *The Moral Collapse of the University* and Page Smith in *Killing the Spirit* offered explanations about why this was

so, and those explanations rested squarely in a critique of the research culture.[10]

These critiques did not reach the general public. A campaign by conservatives, with a well-funded media program backed by right-wing foundations and think tanks, took higher education to the streets. First there was Allan Bloom's *Closing of the American Mind*, then in rapid fire Charles Sykes's *Profscam*, Dinesh D'Souza's *Illiberal Education*, Martin Anderson's *Imposters in the Temple*, and Roger Kimball's *Tenured Radicals*.[11]

These books attacked the faculty for "political correctness" and 1960s radicalism; the curriculum for faddishness and neglect of the canon; and administrators for lack of leadership. In less than ten years the sanctity of the academy was in serious jeopardy. State and federal governments have been taking more control over university budgets, admissions criteria, financial aid, outcomes, research conditions—and most recently faculty workloads. The story line from the states and Washington goes something like this: Colleges and universities are irresponsible and arrogant. They cannot explain what they do. They charge high tuition and misuse money. Faculty have lifetime employment and long vacations and do anything they want. What they want to do is research, not teach. Their research is silly and useless. (Remember Senator Proxmire's Golden Fleece Awards?) They need to be brought into line.

Tenure and promotion committees and college presidents playing the Carnegie sweepstakes may not know it yet, but the research culture is losing its currency. The gains brought by the research culture are beginning to erode: research grants are harder to get, overhead is down, and the cost to institutions of carrying out research is up. Declines in tuition dollars because of lower enrollment or large amounts of student aid lead to questions about faculty productivity and teaching loads. Assistant professors, those indentured for years before winning tenure, are gasping for air from the stratospheric publication requirements to which they are being held. They have been evincing surprising support for the abolition of tenure. Like other industries, universities are hiring casual labor. So-called part-time or non-tenure-track faculty have been a growing part of the faculty labor force outside of the top tier.

Attacks on the research culture have not seriously affected the schools in which that culture was created. In the leading research universities, faculty continue to reap the fruits of the research culture in low teaching loads, time and resources for research, and tenure. Despite efforts to spread their largess more widely than in the past, federal agencies, private foundations, and major donors still disproportionately fund a tiny group of leading research universities. Faculty salaries in most colleges and universities have been stagnant, whereas salaries in leading private research universities have been marching upward at a faster rate than those at equally eminent public research universities.

The stratification system in the academy is stronger than ever. The gulf is widening between a small number of affluent and highly selective institutions—where competition for admission is fierce and mostly privileges the wealthy—and hard-pressed public and private institutions. Low-income students are increasingly concentrated in community colleges. This divide mirrors the growing income inequality in the society as a whole.

What will replace the research culture in the majority of colleges and universities is still unclear, but we have glimmers of the future. Some colleges—women's colleges, sectarian colleges—are refocusing on the particular constituencies they had abandoned twenty or thirty years ago. Regional colleges and universities are rebuilding ties to regional and local organizations through service learning and mission-oriented research and professional expertise. There is much talk about recalibrating the faculty reward structure toward more recognition of teaching and service. Others are turning back to community as a way of enhancing their appeal to students and of recapturing faculty commitment to their institutions. It will be interesting for all of us to watch—better yet, to participate in—the process of finding new purpose in a world that has changed around us.

NOTES

1. See Table 95 in American Council on Higher Education, *1989–90 Fact Book on Higher Education* (New York: Macmillan, 1989).

2. Paul J. DiMaggio and Walter W. Powell, "The Iron Cage Revisited: Institutional Isomorphism and Collective Rationality in Organizational Fields," *American Sociological Review* 48 (April 1983): 147–60.

3. See Dorothy E. Finnegan and Zelda F. Gamson, "Disciplinary Adaptations to Research Culture in Comprehensive Institutions," *Review of Higher Education* 19 (Winter 1996): 141–77, for a fuller discussion of the research culture and its implications.

4. Tony Becher, *Academic Tribes and Territories: Intellectual Enquiry and the Culture of Disciplines* (Milton Keynes, England: Open University Press, 1989).

5. See David Webster, *Quality Rankings* (Springfield, IL: Thomas Crown, 1986), for a detailed analysis of the use of rankings in higher education.

6. Darwin O. Sawyer, "Institutional Stratification and Career Mobility in Academic Markets," *Sociology of Education* 54 (April 1981): 86.

7. A recent study of how this happened in "comprehensive" universities—institutions with both arts and sciences as well as professional degrees at the bachelor's and master's levels—is reported in Dorothy E. Finnegan, "Segmentation in the Academic Labor Market: Hiring Cohorts in Comprehensive Universities," *Journal of Higher Education* 64 (November/December 1993): 621–56.

8. Françoise A. Queval, "The Evolution Toward Research Orientation and Capability in Comprehensive Universities: The California State System" (PhD diss., University of California at Los Angeles, 1990).

9. Carnegie Foundation for the Advancement of Teaching, *National Survey of Faculty* (Princeton, NJ: Carnegie Foundation, 1989).

10. Study Group on the Conditions of Excellence in American Higher Education, *Involvement in Learning: Realizing the Potential of American Higher Education* (Washington, DC: U.S. Department of Education, 1984); National Commission on Excellence in Education, *A Nation at Risk: The Imperative for Educational Reform* (Washington, DC: U.S. Government Printing Office, 1983); National Endowment for the

Humanities, *To Reclaim a Legacy: A Report on the Humanities in Higher Education* (Washington, DC: U.S. Government Printing Office, 1984); Association of American Colleges, *Integrity in the College Curriculum: A Report to the Academic Community* (Washington, DC: Author, 1985); Bruce Wilshire, *The Moral Collapse of the University: Professionalism, Purity, and Alienation* (Albany: State University of New York Press, 1990); Page Smith, *Killing the Spirit: Higher Education in America* (New York: Penguin, 1991).

11. Allan Bloom, *The Closing of the American Mind: How Higher Education Has Failed Democracy and Impoverished the Souls of Today's Students* (New York: Simon & Schuster, 1987); Charles Sykes, *Profscam: Professors and the Demise of Higher Education* (Washington, DC: Regnery Gateway, 1988); Dinesh D'Souza, *Illiberal Education: The Politics of Race and Sex on Campus* (New York: Random House, 1992); Martin Anderson, *Imposters in the Temple: American Intellectuals Are Destroying Our Universities and Cheating Our Students of Their Future* (New York: Simon & Schuster, 1992); Roger Kimball, *Tenured Radicals: How Politics Has Corrupted Our Higher Education* (New York: Harper Perennial, 1991).

CHANGES IN THE STATUS AND FUNCTIONS OF WOMEN'S COLLEGES OVER TIME

Leslie Miller-Bernal

Sociologist Leslie Miller-Bernal examines the history of women's colleges in the United States as well as the changes in women's education over time. Her description of the changes in women's colleges tells us a great deal about the changing role of women in society and the use of education both to move women into appropriate roles in society and to contain them by keeping women from attaining too much or the wrong kind of education.

Questions to consider for this reading:

1. How has women's access to higher education changed in the United States?
2. What role did women's colleges play in maintaining gendered roles in society?
3. What is the future of women's colleges and why should they survive?

People tend to associate women's colleges with the past, when women's and men's spheres were more separate than they are today. For this reason it may be surprising to learn that the first college in the United States that accepted women was coeducational—Oberlin College in Ohio, which admitted women in 1837. And yet the generalization still holds: Most of the few women who attended college in the mid-nineteenth century did go to women's colleges. Most colleges and universities were for men only, so women's colleges were important to women who wished to receive higher education.

This chapter traces the rise and fall of women's colleges from their beginnings in the mid-nineteenth century to their precarious position in the early twenty-first century. Not only has the number of women's colleges declined dramatically, from 233 as recently as 1960 to about 58 today, but the types of students and their reasons for attending single-sex institutions have also changed markedly. Today many people question whether women's colleges will continue to survive, despite the ardent belief of many of their students and alumnae that they provide the best education for women.

ORIGINS OF WOMEN'S COLLEGES

Scholars debate which was the first women's college. Some institutions described themselves as "colleges" even though that designation seems unwarranted given the age of their students and the curriculum they offered. Candidates for the earliest women's college include Mary Sharp in Tennessee, which awarded its first degrees in 1855, and Elmira in upstate New York, which opened in 1855. Both these antebellum institutions required their students to study Greek, a hallmark of the curriculum of men's colleges of the time. Neither of these colleges fared well, however; Mary Sharp closed in 1896, and Elmira shut down for a while during the Civil War.[1]

Some women's colleges developed from seminaries, for example, Mills, Mount Holyoke, and Wheaton. Seminaries were not institutions for religious training but rather combined secondary education with some college work while they strictly regulated students' lives. Even if they were not first seminaries, early women's colleges often modeled themselves after seminaries. Vassar College, for example, opened in 1865 with one large seminary-like building in which all students and women faculty lived together. Such living arrangements enabled women teachers to monitor students closely to fulfill the colleges' claims that they provided a homelike atmosphere in which young women were trained to be "ladies." Students' posture and voice, for example, could be improved on a daily basis.

The heyday for women's colleges occurred at the end of the Civil War. Vassar, located in Poughkeepsie, New York, was the most famous women's college of that era because from its beginning, it had an endowment and a rigorous curriculum. Wells College in Aurora, New York, opened only three years later, in 1868. Only for its first two years was Wells called a seminary, but its lack of endowment, its weak academic standards, and its large preparatory department for students not ready to do collegiate work meant that it functioned as a seminary for many more years. By 1885 such famous women's colleges as Smith, Wellesley, and Bryn Mawr had opened.

OPPOSITION TO WOMEN'S HIGHER EDUCATION

While today it is common to ask why women were prohibited from studying at most colleges in the nineteenth century, at the time people often asked: Why should women go to college? After all, women's "natural" place was in the home, looking after their husbands and children. Even if a woman did not marry and needed to support herself, most occupations, including such prestigious ones as medicine and law, did not require a college degree; many practitioners in these fields learned through apprenticeships. Also retarding the development of collegiate education for women was the widespread belief that women harmed their reproductive organs by too much study. In a book that was very popular at the time, *Sex in Education; or a Fair Chance for the Girls,* retired Harvard professor and doctor Edward Clarke claimed that women would experience dire effects if they failed to obey the "law of periodicity." He based his research mainly on seven women, including a student at Vassar who fainted during gym because, Clarke argued, she should have been quiet at that time of the month. Moreover, when she was examined, she was found to have "an arrest of the development of the reproductive apparatus" and, in place of developed breasts, "the milliner had supplied the organs Nature should have grown."[2]

Women researchers and organizations that favored women's higher education, such as the influential Association of Collegiate Alumnae (ACA), refuted Clarke's research. Yet his book resonated with popular beliefs and managed to frighten young women, including the later president of Bryn Mawr College and famous feminist M. Carey Thomas.[3] Opposition to educating women may have been overcome more by practical concerns than by rational argument. As more and more communities established public schools, they favored hiring women as teachers since they received half or less of men's salaries. Teachers, of course, needed to be educated. A few other occupations opening up to women, such as clerical work, also required education.[4]

WOMEN'S EDUCATIONAL OPTIONS BY THE LATE NINETEENTH AND EARLY TWENTIETH CENTURIES

Women's colleges remained important for women's access to higher education throughout the nineteenth century. Many people saw them as more appropriate for women than were coeducational institutions, since their curricula could be modified in ways that were believed to fit women's talents and proclivities. The suspicion that women's colleges were thus not as intellectually challenging as men's colleges led most nineteenth-century women's rights advocates to favor coeducational institutions.[5] Yet women's colleges did improve academically in response to student and alumnae pressures, as well as to the exacting standards of the ACA, the forerunner of the American Association of University Women. They closed their preparatory departments and offered only collegiate-level education, all the time employing mainly women faculty, thus providing "critical entry points" for women wishing to enter academic life.[6] Nonetheless, even by 1880, a majority of women were being educated in coeducational institutions.[7]

Single-sex institutions for women and men were more prevalent in certain areas. Women's and men's colleges were mostly found in the Northeast, where many older colleges existed and which was a fairly wealthy region, and in the South, where people tended to adhere to traditional gender roles. In the Midwest and West, in contrast, frontier conditions often necessitated economizing through coeducation; gender roles were also more flexible and egalitarian, not as supportive of the separate-spheres ideology favored in more settled regions. Because of such practical and ideological factors, colleges like Oberlin (1833) and Antioch (1852) in Ohio, as well as some universities like Chicago (1892), opened as coeducational institutions.[8]

Significant differences in preferences for single-sex education also existed among segments of the population defined by religious and ethnic affiliation. Catholic institutions, almost all single sex, were founded later than were the first secular or Protestant-affiliated women's colleges. They developed as the daughters of Catholic immigrant groups increasingly sought higher education and would have attended secular institutions in their absence. They also provided education for nuns or, more generally, the women religious. The earliest Catholic women's college to grant a bachelor's degree was College of Notre Dame in Maryland, which awarded its first college degrees in 1899. The rate of founding of Catholic women's colleges increased over the first few decades of the twentieth century, with the greatest number, thirty-seven, opening between 1915 and 1925.[9]

Black colleges and universities, in contrast to Catholic institutions, were almost all coeducational, with a few notable exceptions. For about one hundred years, these separate institutions were virtually the only place African Americans could receive higher education. Two black women's colleges opened in the first two decades after the Civil War: Barber-Scotia in Concord, North Carolina (1867),[10] and Huston-Tillotson in Austin, Texas (1877),[11] but both later became coeducational. In contrast, Bennett College was founded in 1873 in Greensboro, North Carolina, as a coeducational institution, but it became a liberal arts college for women in 1926. The best-known historically black college for women is Spelman College in Atlanta, Georgia, which opened in 1881 and remains to this day a women's college.[12]

While most women's colleges were small and private, a few public institutions for women also existed. Some state women's colleges developed in the South and Southwest. The first state women's university was the Mississippi Industrial Institute and College (later called the Mississippi State University for Women), which opened in 1884. By 1908, state women's colleges had also been established in Georgia, North Carolina, Alabama, Texas, Florida, and Oklahoma.[13] New York City supported a women's college for the training of teachers—Hunter College, which opened in 1870 as the Normal College of the City of New York.[14] Many states developed colleges for teacher training; these were usually referred to as "normal schools" and enrolled all or mostly women.

Founding dates influenced the nature of women's colleges. Women's colleges that began in the nineteenth century tended to stress liberal education for women's refinement. Simmons, in contrast, which opened during the Progressive Era, focused on career preparation for working- and lower-middle-class women. Mills, in Oakland,

California, changed from a seminary to a college in the early twentieth century. Its curriculum changed over time, with more practical courses offered in the early part of the twentieth century and purely liberal arts later.

A HYBRID FORM: COORDINATE COLLEGES FOR WOMEN

In addition to women's colleges and coeducational institutions, a third form of higher education developed in the late nineteenth century: coordinate colleges. Essentially, coordinate colleges were "sister" colleges of men's institutions, established in response to pressure to educate women. Educators could point to Girton and Newnham, two women's colleges of Cambridge University, as models of how prestigious men's institutions could incorporate women without admitting them outright.[15] Some of the most famous examples in the United States were Radcliffe, the coordinate of Harvard; Sophie Newcomb, the coordinate of Tulane; Barnard, Columbia's coordinate; and Pembroke, Brown's coordinate. Many lesser-known men's colleges or universities had coordinate colleges for women, for example, William Smith, the coordinate of the men's college, Hobart; Westhampton, associated with University of Richmond; and Saint Mary's, affiliated with University of Notre Dame. Still other universities had what were essentially coordinate colleges, but because they did not have a different name, they tended not to be widely recognized as such. This was true, for example, of Cornell University and the University of Pennsylvania.

Coordinate colleges represented a desire to keep women separate from men students to retain the prestige of men's institutions. Nonetheless, such separation had unanticipated benefits for women in terms of the support they received, as well as leadership opportunities.[16] Coordination was also one of the ways coeducational institutions sometimes considered dealing with the "threat" of women, whose attendance rates were increasing faster than men's and who were receiving disproportionate shares of academic awards. Middlebury College and the University of Rochester, for instance, created coordinate colleges for their women students, although Middlebury lacked sufficient funds to implement coordination fully. Other coeducational institutions responded differently to the fears of "feminization" that were particularly acute at the beginning of the twentieth century. Stanford was one of the universities that established quotas on the number of women admitted. Wesleyan ceased to admit women altogether, thereby reverting to its previous all-male status.

WOMEN'S COLLEGES: PARADOXICAL ROLES AND IMAGES

Ambivalence about women's higher education did not cease as women's educational opportunities increased. In fact, the early twentieth century, when male dominance seemed less secure than it had earlier, was a period of backlash against women.[17] New arguments against educating women included the idea that educated women were less likely to get married or have children and hence caused "race suicide," a term popularized by Theodore Roosevelt in 1905.[18] Women's colleges were blamed in particular, although some commentators felt that coeducation caused greater damage, either by encouraging promiscuity or by contributing to the opposite problem—indifference to the opposite sex due to overfamiliarity.[19] In the early 1920s, Vice President Calvin Coolidge wrote that some of the eastern women's colleges fomented radicalism and Bolshevism.[20] The 1920s was also a decade when students experienced increased sexual freedom and when many Americans became familiar with Sigmund Freud's ideas. The "crushes" between women at women's colleges that had previously seemed innocent were now suspected of indicating lesbianism. Administrators at women's colleges felt compelled to take special measures to avoid such imputations.[21]

Another image of women's colleges was as "finishing schools" for privileged white Protestant women. Some researchers in the early twentieth century criticized them for not providing enough vocational guidance or training.[22] It was true that at many women's colleges, students received training in social graces, including how to be proper hostesses, how to talk in a refined manner, and how to develop good posture. While such training was not unknown in coeducational institutions, women's colleges generally gave more emphasis to the importance of women's refinement.[23]

Regardless of these conflicting images, women's colleges had a respectable place among institutions of higher education. By avoiding such applied subjects as home economics and keeping their student bodies homogeneous, many women's colleges retained or even enhanced their prestige. Women's colleges were known to be academically rigorous; some such as Wells College instituted demanding honor programs. By the late 1920s the most elite women's colleges—Barnard, Bryn Mawr, Mount Holyoke, Radcliffe, Smith, Vassar, and Wellesley—had come to be known as the Seven Sisters and were frequently seen as women's counterpart to what were later called the Ivy League colleges (Brown, Columbia, Cornell, Dartmouth, Harvard, Princeton, University of Pennsylvania, and Yale). In the 1920s some private women's colleges, including Wells, had many more applicants than they could admit. Wells considered expanding; since the president was concerned that this would mean the college would lose its "family" atmosphere, the college planned to open a "sister" college on the same grounds. This never happened, however, as the Great Depression intervened, affecting college enrollments and finances.[24]

Enrollment Trends Over the Twentieth Century

Increasing numbers of women attended institutions of higher education throughout the twentieth century, from about 141,000 in 1909–10 to more than one million in the mid-1950s. At the same time, the percentage that enrolled in women's colleges decreased. Even as early as 1920, more than four-fifths of women attended coeducational colleges and universities. This proportion gradually grew, so that by the mid-1950s, nine of ten women attending institutions of higher education were enrolled in coeducational institutions.[25] These increases in enrollments at coeducational institutions affected women's colleges not only directly but also indirectly, as more and more faculty were likely to have received their education at coeducational institutions. Thus most people connected to higher education began to take coeducation for granted.

The rise of state universities affected women's colleges, since most women's colleges were and are private.[26] Particularly at times of economic hardship—for instance, during the Great Depression—students found the lower tuition of state institutions attractive. Traditional private liberal arts women's colleges responded to enrollment threats by offering more scholarships and becoming slightly more diverse, enrolling some Catholics and a small percentage of Jews.[27] Nonetheless, some new private women's colleges opened—many Catholic women's colleges but also some secular ones, notably Sarah Lawrence (1928) and Bennington (1932) in the Northeast, and Scripps (1926) in California.[28]

After World War II, many veterans took advantage of support from the Servicemen's Readjustment Act, frequently referred to as the G.I. Bill, to enter colleges and universities. While the number of women students also grew, the rate of growth for men was much greater, so the proportion of women in higher education decreased to about 30 percent. As women had been about 55 percent of college students at the end of the war, this drop was dramatic.[29] At the same time, marriage rates were high, and college women, as well as administrators and faculty, began to raise the familiar question of what women should learn if they were almost all going to become mothers. Some women's colleges, such as Vassar and Barnard, instituted programs to respond to women's interrupted lives and their return to college after marriage and childbearing.[30]

The buoyant economy of the 1960s, with increasing foundation and federal support for higher education, had positive effects on many institutions, including women's colleges. In this halcyon period, colleges could both expand and be more selective. Wells College, for example, had its highest-ever enrollments—more than six hundred students—for seven consecutive years, from 1966 to 1972, while admitting only about half its applicants. New colleges were founded to meet the increased demand for higher education. Of approximately seven hundred new institutions established between 1960 and 1969, three-quarters were public institutions, including community colleges; some were experimental, for example, Old Westbury; and some were women's colleges.[31] These categories overlapped, of course. Traditional all-male Hamilton College in upstate New York established Kirkland College in 1968, for instance, as an experimental coordinate women's college. Similarly, Pitzer College opened as an innovative women's college in the Claremont cluster of colleges. Neither of these colleges lasted in this form, however. Hamilton College absorbed Kirkland a decade after it opened, and in less than ten years, Pitzer admitted men students.[32]

Enrollees also diversified during the 1960s. At many colleges, including women's colleges, students and faculty, influenced by the national civil rights movement, pressured their institutions to recruit minority students, staff, and faculty. The civil rights movement's push for integration and, slightly later, the women's movement's demands for women to be admitted to male bastions meant that separate institutions of all kinds, including women's and men's colleges, began to be seen as old-fashioned or even anachronistic.[33]

Men's colleges were some of the first to respond to this new cultural mood. Beginning in the mid-1960s, many men's colleges, particularly prestigious ones like Princeton and Yale, started to consider ways to incorporate women undergraduates. They were not motivated only by a desire to extend their educational privileges to women, however. Demographic trends favored women's admission: Women's enrollments were increasing at a faster rate than men's. Moreover, women

were known to be serious students. By the late 1960s, as inflation became a national economic issue, all colleges were anticipating financial problems. Some colleges that had borrowed money to expand during the 1960s began to be concerned about filling their campuses and paying back their loans during the high inflation period of the 1970s.[34] Men's colleges knew that by admitting women, they could increase enrollments, reduce debts, become more selective, and obtain hard-working students. And this, in short, is what happened. The admission of women to the remaining all-men Ivy League colleges, as well as to such prestigious men's colleges as Amherst and Williams, maintained or improved these institutions' finances and academic standings. By the 1990s, virtually no men's colleges remained, as almost all had become coeducational.[35]

Men's colleges' decision to become coeducational created problems for women's colleges. Given the sexism of society at large, anything male tends to be defined as superior to anything female.[36] Educators at women's colleges recognized that women students, particularly some of the academically strongest who previously would have attended their colleges, would now apply to formerly men's colleges. To avoid anticipated declines in enrollments and academic standards, some women's colleges decided to admit men. Vassar, which had been negotiating with Yale about developing a coordinate relationship, chose instead to become "coeducational."[37] Other women's colleges that made this transition in the late 1960s or early 1970s included Connecticut, Elmira, Sarah Lawrence, and Skidmore.

JUSTIFYING THE NEED FOR WOMEN'S COLLEGES

At the same time that the number of women's colleges declined—from 233 in 1960 to 90 in 1986—systematic research demonstrated their benefits to women.[38] For many years, journalists had noted the confidence of women who attended women's colleges and lauded the training for leadership these institutions provided.[39] The evidence was anecdotal, however. As the women's movement progressed, academics concerned with demonstrating how women fared under existing social arrangements began to conduct systematic studies of the relative advantages of single-sex education and coeducation.

Researchers coined the phrase the "chilly climate" to describe the many ways coeducational colleges discouraged women students' achievement and led to their loss of confidence. Studies found that professors called on men students more than on women students, were more likely to know men students' names, interrupted women more than men, asked women mundane questions but probed men students' answers for elaboration, and in general gave men students more of their time and attention.[40] Combined with information about women students' experiences of sexual harassment, date rape, lack of campus leadership positions, few female role models, and insufficient support for their sports, coeducational colleges and universities did indeed seem to be places where men consolidated their superior social position at the expense of women.

Women's colleges could correctly claim that they did not have "chilly climates." Moreover, a body of research, pioneered by M. Elizabeth Tidball in the early 1970s, began to accumulate that indicated that women who graduated from women's colleges were much more likely to succeed in later life than were women who graduated from coeducational institutions. Tidball's baccalaureate origin studies, which used listings in *Who's Who of American Women* and the *Doctorate Records File,* showed that graduates of women's colleges were two to three times more likely to become medical doctors, scientists, or recognized leaders in their fields.[41] These results fit with what some people already knew: Many women in Congress and successful women writers, for example, were graduates of women's colleges. And yet, other researchers criticized Tidball's methods—for her data sources (she used *Who's Who of American Women,* while some people argued *Who's Who in America* would be preferable), for not separating prestigious

women's colleges (the Seven Sisters) from more ordinary women's colleges, and for confusing the benefits of attending a women's college with the advantages of having a privileged family background.[42] The latter—the so-called selection effect—would mean that women's colleges are successful not because of what they do for women but because of qualities that students bring to these colleges.[43]

The debate over the value of women's colleges continues. Some researchers report no benefits of single-sex education for women once sufficient controls for preexisting or social background differences are taken into account.[44] Even after they control for students' family backgrounds, however, other researchers continue to find that women who attend women's colleges experience advantages in later life.[45] Several researchers have used Tidball's "baccalaureate origin" research method for studying more recent cohorts of women graduates. Such studies have found generally positive results for women's colleges, although the differences between graduates of women's colleges and of coeducational colleges have not been as large as Tidball reported for earlier cohorts of women graduates.[46] Research on recent graduates is particularly interesting since, over time, the social characteristics of women who attend women's colleges have changed dramatically. While students at private women's colleges used to come from elite families, since the late 1970s and the use of extensive financial aid to attract students, they are more likely to come from families whose income and education level are lower than those of the families of women at comparable coeducational private liberal arts colleges.

Another argument made against the idea that women still need and benefit from single-sex education is that coeducational institutions have improved. Some analysts, noting that the original "chilly climate" studies were conducted during the 1980s, contend that their findings are no longer relevant.[47] While women's experiences in many coeducational colleges and universities have undoubtedly improved, equality does not yet exist. Women do not comprise half the faculty, for example, and the more prestigious the institution, generally the fewer the women faculty there are. Similarly, while more women are found among top administrators, they are still only about one-fifth of college presidents.[48] Women students' college experiences are different from and more likely to be negative than those of men students. Sex offenses on campuses throughout the country, most of them committed against women and many perpetrated by members of fraternities or athletic teams, have been documented, even though institutions report only some of these offenses to the federal government.[49]

While gender equality remains more a goal than an actuality, what is different from the past is that many institutions are concerned about how their women students are faring and implement policies to promote equal opportunities for women and men. A panel at Duke University, for example, recently did a study of gender issues on campus. The panel found that women undergraduates feel pressure to exhibit "effortless perfection," that they worry about the possibility of acquaintance rape, and that their campus leadership tracks are "somewhat separate" from men's. With knowledge of such difficulties faced by women, administrators at Duke are developing appropriate programs to help overcome them. These include, for instance, a "sustained leadership program" that will give undergraduate women who participate "some of the benefits of a single-sex educational experience embedded within their otherwise coeducational college life."[50]

WOMEN'S COLLEGES TODAY

Despite the evidence that women's colleges not only have played a key role in women's access to higher education but also have enhanced their postgraduation success, most young women no longer consider attending them. The Women's College Coalition, formed more than thirty years ago to publicize the benefits of women's colleges, has not succeeded in changing high school girls' minds. Nor have the articles that appear in the popular press about women students'

attachment to and defense of their women's colleges. For more than two decades, a low percentage of girls, about 3 or 4 percent, says that they would "consider" a women's college, and a much lower percentage actually ends up attending one.[51] By 2006 only fifty-six women's colleges remained.

The persistent low interest in single-sex higher education continues to create enrollment and financial problems for women's colleges. Most women's colleges today no longer resemble people's images of a women's college—an isolated liberal arts college for women aged eighteen to twenty-two. Only a few very wealthy and prestigious women's colleges, such as Wellesley (whose endowment is over $1 billion), Smith, Mount Holyoke, and Agnes Scott, have been able to continue successfully in this mold.[52] . . .

CONCLUSIONS

Women's colleges appear to be a dying institutional form of higher education in the United States. Each year fewer remain, and most of those that do are struggling to survive. Forecasting the demise of women's colleges is not the same as arguing that they are not valuable, however. Indeed, the majority of studies of outcomes for women who were educated at women's colleges compared to those educated at coeducational colleges shows that women fare better in single-sex environments. And yet the overwhelming preference of young women today is for coeducational colleges. With fewer than 5 percent willing to consider women's colleges, these institutions' enrollment and associated financial problems remain severe. . . .

Even colleges that seem to be the same today as they were before the recent upsurge in coeducation about thirty-five years ago have tried various methods to stem enrollment declines or to prevent being taken over by another institution. In many other instances the changes in the women's colleges have been dramatic and hence easily visible. Whether college adaptations have been subtle or major, a basic question we have kept in mind. . . .

Women's colleges have played an important role in the lives of thousands of women. They are defended passionately by many students and alumnae who see them as having a unique environment in which women's interests and needs are given priority. It behooves all of us who are committed to gender equity to study women's colleges so that we can better understand the particular ways in which they have benefited women and so that we can use them as models for the increasingly prevalent coeducational institutions.

NOTES

1. Thomas Woody, *A History of Women's Education in the United States,* vol. 2 (New York: Science Press, 1929), 171–78.

2. Edward H. Clarke, *Sex in Education; or A Fair Chance for the Girls* (Boston: James R. Osgood, 1873/1972), 92–93.

3. See M. Carey Thomas's own assessment of her fears of Edward Clarke's conclusions: Refutations of Clarke can be found in Mary Putnam Jacobi, *The Question of Rest for Women during Menstruation* (London: Smith, Elder & Co., 1878); other refutations of Clarke's research are summarized in Sue Zschoche, "Dr. Clarke Revisited: Science, True Womanhood, and Female Collegiate Education," *History of Education Quarterly* 29 (1989): 545–69; and Rosalind Rosenberg, *Beyond Separate Spheres* (New Haven: Yale University Press, 1982), 20.

4. Barbara Sicherman, "Colleges and Careers: Historical Perspectives on the Lives and Work Patterns of Women College Graduates," in John Mack Faragher and Florence Howe, eds., *Women and Higher Education in American History* (New York: Norton, 1988): 130–64.

5. Leslie Miller-Bernal, *Separate by Degree* (New York: Peter Lang, 2000), 203–5.

6. The role that the ACA played in strengthening women's colleges is discussed in ibid., 33–34. On the role of women faculty at women's colleges, see Mary Ann Dzuback, "Gender and the Politics of Knowledge," historycooperative.press.uiuc.edu/journals/heq/43.2/dzuback.html, accessed June 28, 2005. Also available in *History of Education Quarterly* 43, 2 (2003).

7. Mabel Newcomer, *A Century of Higher Education for Women* (New York: Harper and Row, 1959), 40.

8. Rosalind Rosenberg, "The Limits of Access: The History of Coeducation in America," in Faragher and Howe, *Women and Higher Education in American History.*

9. By 1955, there were 116 Catholic colleges for women. See Mary J. Oates, ed., *Higher Education for Catholic Women: An Historical Anthology* (New York: Garland, 1987), 121. Other helpful discussions of Catholic women's colleges can be found in Susan L. Poulson and Leslie Miller-Bernal, "Two Unique Histories of Coeducation: Catholic and Historically Black Institutions," in Leslie Miller-Bernal and Susan L. Poulson, *Going Coed: Women's Experiences in Formerly Men's Colleges and Universities: 1950–2000* (Nashville: Vanderbilt University Press, 2004), as well as in Paula S. Fass, *Outside In: Minorities and the Transformation of American Education* (New York: Oxford University Press, 1989), chap. 6, "Imitation and Autonomy: Catholic Education in the Twentieth Century."

10. In 1867, this institution was called Scotia Seminary, dedicated to preparing black women for careers in teaching and social work. In 1916, it became Scotia Women's College; in 1930 it merged with Barber College and changed its name shortly thereafter. In 1954 it became coeducational. www.petersons.com/blackcolleges/profiles/barber-scotia.asp?sponsor=13, accessed July 4, 2005.

11. Tillotson opened in 1877 as a Collegiate and Normal Institute and went through various changes over time. In 1926 it was reorganized as a junior college and in 1926 as a women's college. In 1931 it became coeducational. In 1952 it merged with nearby Samuel Huston College. www.umcgiving.org/content/BCF/sc_huston.asp, accessed July 4, 2005.

12. A few black colleges for men were also established, probably the most famous being Morehouse, located adjacent to Spelman, and Lincoln University in Pennsylvania, which began admitting women in the 1950s. See Leslie Miller-Bernal and Susan Gunn Pevar, "A Historically Black Men's College Admits Women: The Case of Lincoln University," in Miller-Bernal and Poulson, *Going Coed.*

13. Archived Information Web site, Irene Harwarth, Mindi Maline, Elizabeth DeBra, "Women's Colleges in the United States: History, Issues, and Challenges," www.ed.gov/offices/OERI/PLLI/webreprt.html, accessed July 4, 2005.

14. See www.hunter.cuny.edu/news/inbrief.shtml, accessed July 4, 2005.

15. Thomas M. Landy, "The Colleges in Context," in Tracy Schier and Cynthia Russett, eds., *Catholic*

Women's Colleges in America (Baltimore: Johns Hopkins University Press, 2002), 61, cites an article written in 1898 that mentioned Girton as one of three prestigious institutions that women could attend.

16. Miller-Bernal, *Separate by Degree,* and Leslie Miller-Bernal, "Conservative Intent, Liberating Outcomes: The History of Coordinate Colleges for Women," in Amanda Datnow and Lea Hubbard, eds., *Doing Gender in Policy and Practice: Perspectives on Single-Sex and Coeducational Schooling* (New York: Routledge/Falmer, 2002).

17. Woody, *History of Women's Education,* 251; Rosenberg, "The Limits of Access"; Miller-Bernal, *Separate by Degree,* 65–66.

18. Patricia A. Palmieri, "From Republican Motherhood to Race Suicide: Arguments on the Higher Education of Women in the United States, 1820–1920," in Carol Lasser, ed., *Educating Men and Women Together* (Urbana: University of Illinois Press, 1987), 57.

19. The first president of the American Psychological Association, G. Stanley Hall, argued in his famous book on adolescence that the easy association between the sexes in coeducational institutions caused men and women to lose interest in each other: "Familiar camaraderie brings a little disenchantment [and] weakens the motivation to marriage." See Hall, *Adolescence,* vol. 2 (New York: D. Appleton, 1904), 620–21. At the same time, the then president of Stanford, David Starr Jordan, defended coeducational institutions because although they encouraged marriage, the unions were of the "best sort," based on "common interests and intellectual friendships." Jordan, "The Higher Education of Women," *Popular Science Monthly* 62 (1902): 107.

20. Calvin Coolidge, "Enemies of the Republic," *Delineator* 98 (1921): 4–5, 66–67.

21. Florence Howe, *Myths of Coeducation* (Bloomington: Indiana University Press, 1984), 277, 314; Dorothy Dunbar Bromley and Florence Haxton Britten, *Youth and Sex: A Study of 1300 College Students* (New York: Harper and Brothers, 1938), 118; Katherine Bennett Davis, *Factors in the Sex Life of Twenty-Two Hundred Women* (New York: Harper and Brothers, 1929), 245.

22. Marguerite Witmer Kehr, "A Comparative Study of the Curricula for Men and Women in the Colleges and Universities of the United States." *Journal of the Association of Collegiate Alumnae* 14 (1920): 3–26.

23. Miller-Bernal, *Separate by Degree,* 104–6.

24. Ibid., 99–101.

25. Newcomer, *A Century,* 49.

26. Enrollment in public institutions was about half of total enrollment by 1929–30, a proportion that remained fairly constant until the 1950s. Then the proportion increased, so that by 1977, it was a little over three-quarters, a proportion that has remained fairly constant since. For the earlier part of the twentieth century, see Thomas D. Snyder, ed., "Years of American Education: A Statistical Portrait," National Center for Education Statistics, nces.ed.gov/pubs93/93442.pdf. Figures from 1947 on can also be obtained at nces.ed.gov/programs/digest/d02/tables/dt172.asp.

27. Miller-Bernal, *Separate by Degree,* 101–3. See also Lynn D. Gordon, *Gender and Higher Education in the Progressive Era* (New Haven: Yale University Press, 1990): 47–48, on the treatment of Jewish women at Wellesley during the first two decades of the twentieth century. Gordon notes that there were fewer non-Protestant women in southern institutions than in colleges in the North (49).

28. These years refer to when these women's colleges opened, not their official founding dates.

29. Snyder, "Years of American Education."

30. See Fass, *Outside In,* 157–75.

31. Verne A. Stadtman, *Academic Adaptations: Higher Education Prepares for the 1980s and 1990s* (San Francisco: Jossey-Bass, 1980), 4.

32. For more information about Kirkland, see Miller-Bernal, *Separate by Degree.*

33. Miller-Bernal and Poulson, *Going Coed.*

34. Earl F. Cheit, *The New Depression in Higher Education* (New York: McGraw-Hill, 1971).

35. Three men's liberal arts colleges remain: Wabash in Indiana, Morehouse in Georgia, and Hampden-Sydney in Virginia. Deep Springs is an elite all-men two-year college in California.

36. For social-psychological evidence of this general principle, see the famous study by Goldberg on women's perception that essays are inferior if women are believed to have written them: Philip Goldberg, "Are Women Prejudiced against Women?" in C. Safilios-Rothschild, ed., *Toward a Sociology of Women* (Lexington, Mass.: Xerox College Publications, 1968), 10–13.

37. Most people refer to women's colleges that have admitted men students as having become "coeducational." This is ironic, since "coed" is a term that really pertains to women, and that originally had derogatory connotations. And yet, since this terminology is widespread, we sometimes also use it.

38. These figures come from Irene Hawarth, Mindi Maline, and Elizabeth DeBra, *Women's Colleges in the United States* (Washington, D.C.: National Institute on Postsecondary Education, Libraries, and Lifelong Learning, U.S. Department of Education, 1997), 28. Different researchers come up with somewhat different numbers, but they all show a dramatic decline in the number of women's colleges. For different estimates, see, for example, Erich Studer-Ellis, "Diverse Institutional Forces and Fundamental Organizational Change: Women's Colleges and the 'Coed or Dead' Question," paper presented at the annual meeting of The American Sociological Association, Washington, D.C., 1995.

39. Eunice Fuller Barnard, "Our Colleges for Women: Co-ed or Not?" *New York Times Magazine.* March 26, 1933: 4–5.

40. For overviews of this research, see Roberta M. Hall with Bernice R. Sandler, *The Classroom Climate: A Chilly One for Women?* (Washington, D.C.: Project on the Status and Education of Women, Association of American Colleges, 1982); Howe, *Myths of Coeducation;* Bernice Resnick Sandler, "The Classroom Climate: Still a Chilly One for Women," in Carol Lasser, ed., *Educating Men and Women Together* (Urbana: University of Illinois Press, 1987): 113–23; and Myra Sadker and David Sadker, *Failing at Fairness* (New York: Simon and Schuster, 1994). For examples of specific empirical studies of women and men's behavior in classrooms, see David A. Karp and William C. Yoels, "The College Classroom: Some Observations on the Meanings of Student Participation," *Sociology and Social Research* 60 (1975): 421–39; and Sarah Hall Sternglanz and Shirley Lyberger-Ficek, "Sex Differences in Student-Teacher Interactions in the College Classroom," *Sex Roles* 3 (1977): 345–52.

41. Some of Tidball's studies are the following: M. Elizabeth Tidball, "Perspective on Academic Women and Affirmative Action," *Journal of Higher Education* 54 (1973): 130–35; M. Elizabeth Tidball and Vera Kistiakowsky, "Baccalaureate Origins of American Scientists and Scholars," *Science* 193 (1976): 646–52; M. Elizabeth Tidball, "Women's Colleges and Women Achievers Revisited," *Signs* (1980): 504–17; M. Elizabeth Tidball, "Baccalaureate Origins of Entrants into American Medical Schools," *Journal of Higher Education* 56 (1985): 385–402; M. Elizabeth Tidball, "Baccalaureate Origins of Recent Natural Science Doctorates," *Journal of Higher Education* 57 (1986): 606–20; M. Elizabeth Tidball, "Comment on 'Women's Colleges and Women's Career Attainments Revisited,'" *Journal of Higher Education* 62 (1991): 406–9.

42. Mary J. Oates and Susan Williamson, "Women's Colleges and Women Achievers," *Signs* 3 (1978): 795–806; and Mary J. Oates and Susan Williamson, "Comment on Tidball's 'Women's Colleges and Women Achievers Revisited,'" *Signs* 6 (1980): 342–45.

43. For more detailed summaries of this research and its criticisms, see Miller-Bernal, *Separate by Degree,* 212–16, and M. Elizabeth Tidball, Daryl G. Smith, Charles S. Tidball, and Lisa E. Wolf-Wendel, *Taking Women Seriously* (Phoenix: Oryx Press, 1999).

44. Judith Stoecker and Ernest Pascarella, "Women's Colleges and Women's Career Attainments Revisited," *Journal of Higher Education* 62 (1991): 394–406.

45. Riordan found that attending a women's college for just a year had a positive effect on women's postgraduate education; attendance for more years was required for women's colleges to have a positive effect on women's obtaining higher-status occupations and higher incomes. See Cornelius Riordan, "The Value of Attending a Women's College," *Journal of Higher Education* 65 (1994): 486–510.

46. Joy K. Rice and Annette Hemmings, "Women's Colleges and Women Achievers: An Update," *Signs* 13 (1988): 546–59; Lisa E. Wolf-Wendel, "Models of Excellence: The Baccalaureate Origins of Successful European American Women, African American Women, and Latinas," *Journal of Higher Education* 69 (1998): 141–87. There have also been many studies that have examined differences between women at women's colleges and at coeducational colleges in terms of such factors as their satisfaction with college life, their self-confidence, and their choices of major fields. Almost all these studies have found that women's colleges have more positive environments for women students. See, for example, Sherrilyn M. Billger, "Admitting Men into a Women's College: A Natural Experiment," *Applied Economics Letters* 9 (2002): 479–83; Mikyong Kim and Rodolfo Alvarez, "Women-Only Colleges: Some Unanticipated Consequences," *Journal of Higher Education* 66 (1995): 641–68; and Daryl G. Smith, "Women's Colleges and Coed Colleges: Is There a Difference for Women?" *Journal of Higher Education* 61 (1990): 181–97.

47. An anonymous reviewer of Miller-Bernal and Poulson, *Going Coed*, made this comment, for instance, arguing that we were too negative about coeducational institutions.

48. Women's representation among the lowest faculty ranks is almost equal to men's, but women are much less likely to have tenure and to be full professors. Thus in 2001 45 percent of assistant professors were women, while only 20 percent of full professors were. At a prestigious institution like Princeton University, though, only 14 percent of full professors were women. See Karen W. Arenson, "More Women Taking Leadership Roles at Colleges," *New York Times,* July 4, 2002, www.nytimes.com/2002/07/04/education. Women are more likely to be presidents of two-year colleges than of doctoral universities, with their share being 22.4 percent of the former and 13.2 percent of the latter. See Kit Lively, "Diversity Increases among Presidents," *Chronicle of Higher Education,* September 15, 2000, chronicle.com/weekly/v47/i03/03a03101.htm.

49. For information about underreporting college and university sex offenses, see Sara Hebel, "U. of Calif. Failed to Report Crimes," *Chronicle of Higher Education,* April 18, 2003, chronicle.com/weekly/v49/i32/32a03203.htm, accessed July 19, 2004. A recent notorious example of sexual assaults involved seven rape charges brought against University of Colorado football players and recruits. The head football coach was placed on administrative leave after he made derogatory comments about one of the women who brought charges, and the governor of Colorado appointed a special prosecutor to investigate the situation. See Murray Sperber, "Sex and Booze: Two Steps to Winning Football," *Chronicle of Higher Education,* March 12, 2004, chronicle.com/weekly/v50,i27/27b02401.htm.

50. Women's Initiative Steering Committee, *Women's Initiative* (Durham, N.C.: Duke University, 2003), 15. A useful Web site that provides links to studies of women's status at more than thirty educational institutions is universitywomen.stanford.edu/reports.html#ureports. Most of the studies listed focus on issues concerning women faculty, however.

51. This figure is based on a 2000 College Board survey in which only 4 percent of college-bound high school girls said that they would "consider" a women's college. It is mentioned in an article about Hollins College: Andrew Brownstein, "Enrollment Falls, and a Small College Debates Its Future," *Chronicle of Higher Education,* May 4, 2001, p. A39. Other smaller studies report similar figures. A study conducted by Hood College of five Frederick-area schools, for example, found that only 3.6 percent of 1,200 high school girls surveyed said that they would prefer a single-sex college. See www.hood.edu/news/articles/index.cfm?pid=_executive_summary.htm, accessed April 4, 2004.

52. A few women's colleges that do not have very high endowments and are not as well known have attempted to stay essentially the same but have had a great deal of trouble attracting a sufficient number of students. Besides using extensive financial aid and intensive, expensive recruitment, some of these women's colleges have tried slashing tuition dramatically. Pine Manor College, outside Boston, reduced its tuition by 34 percent in 1998; Wells College reduced its tuition by 30 percent in 1999.

THE COMMUNITY COLLEGE

The Impact, Origin, and Future of a Contradictory Institution

Kevin J. Dougherty

Kevin Dougherty discusses the development of the community college and its role in American society. In doing so, he explores what he calls "the contradictory roles" of community colleges and considers the future of this important, but often neglected, part of higher education. As you read through this reading, consider how community colleges came to be and how educational trajectories and future work careers are shaped by the type of educational institution you attend.

Questions to consider for this reading:

1. What are the functions of community colleges? In what sense are they contradictory?

2. What is the role of community colleges in maintaining inequality in society?

3. How did business and government affect the growth of community colleges and how was their impact different from that on research universities?

ommunity colleges are one of the most important sectors of U.S. higher education. They are important because of their great number, their critical role in providing college opportunity (especially for nontraditional students), and the essential role that they play in providing postsecondary vocational training. These public two-year colleges—numbering 1,032 in 2007—comprise one-quarter of all higher educational institutions in the United States (U.S. National Center for Education Statistics, 2009, table 266). Community colleges enroll over one-third of all college students (some 6.3 million in fall 2007). This enrollment share is even greater for nontraditional students, whether older, part-time, minority, or disadvantaged (U.S. National Center for Education Statistics, 2009,

tables 192, 227). Finally, community colleges are important as key sources of postsecondary vocational education. Vocational enrollees at community colleges comprise over half of all students in all forms of postsecondary vocational training and provide a large share of our nation's graduates in such important occupations as nursing, computer operations, and auto repair (Cohen & Brawer, 2008; Dougherty & Bakia, 2000; Grubb, 1996, pp. 54–56).

Yet, because of this very importance, community colleges are contradictory institutions. Community colleges have taken on a host of different social functions, but some of these functions are partially incompatible. In this piece I explore these contradictory functions in closer detail and trace their historical origins.

Author's Note: I would like to thank Regina Deil-Amen, Floyd Hammack, James Jacobs, Vanessa Smith Morest, and Joan Spade for their comments on this chapter as it has evolved over the years.

CONTRADICTORY FUNCTIONS AND IMPACTS

Most community colleges are "comprehensive" institutions, offering a wide variety of programs to a diverse clientele. In most community colleges, a majority of students are enrolled in workforce preparation and economic development programs. However, three-quarters of all first-time community college students (including adults) aspire to get at least a baccalaureate degree and one-quarter transfer to a four-year college within five years of entering a community college (McCormick, 1997, pp. 32, 41).[1] In addition, community colleges operate sizable programs in remedial education, adult education, and community services (such as concerts and day camps) (Cohen & Brawer, 2008). Examining these functions in greater detail allows us to better understand the ways in which they are compatible or incompatible, synergistic, or contradictory.

COLLEGE ACCESS AND OPPORTUNITY

The community college is a central avenue into higher education and toward the baccalaureate degree, particularly for working class, nonwhite, and female students. Many baccalaureate recipients, particularly in states such as California and Florida, got their start at community colleges. In fact, several studies find that states and localities that are highly endowed with community colleges have significantly higher rates of college attendance and baccalaureate attainment than states and localities with a smaller community college presence (Dougherty, 1994, pp. 50–51; Rouse, 1998).

Several features of community colleges make them great avenues of college access. Community colleges are widely distributed across the country, located in urban, suburban, and rural areas. They are cheaper to attend than four-year colleges. Their tuitions are usually low and dormitory residence is not necessary because the colleges are nearby. And because of their open-door admissions ideal, they are more willing to take "nontraditional" students: high school dropouts, vocational aspirants, and adults interested in leisure education.

However, despite the community college's success in widening college access, there is concern about its role in providing college success. Many students entering the community college do not leave it either with a degree in hand or having transferred to another institution. Among students who entered a community college in fall 2003 and were followed up three years later, 45% had left higher education without a degree of any kind (Horn, 2009, pp. 22–23).

In explaining this high dropout rate, it is important to acknowledge that community college students tend to come from less advantaged backgrounds and be less prepared academically than four-year college entrants. However, it is also important to acknowledge the important role of *institutional* factors. Community colleges are less able to academically and socially integrate their students into the life of the college through such means as on-campus housing (Dougherty 1994, chap. 4; 2002, pp. 317–318). Moreover, community college faculty are less able to engage students because so many are part time. In fall 2007, 69% of all faculty in public two-year colleges were part-timers (National Center for Education Statistics, 2009, table 245). In studies that control for various student and institutional characteristics, there is evidence that higher proportions of part-time faculty in community colleges are associated with lower rates of student retention (Calcagno, Bailey, Jenkins, Kienzl, & Leinbach, 2008; Jaeger & Eagan, 2009). Finally, community colleges often do not adequately meet the needs of their students for extensive program and career advice (Rosenbaum, Deil-Amen, & Person, 2006).

PREPARATION FOR THE BACCALAUREATE (COLLEGE TRANSFER)

Historically, one of the leading roles of the community college has been to provide access to the baccalaureate. Originally, this took the role of fostering transfer to four-year colleges but in recent years, community colleges have begun increasingly to offer their own baccalaureate degrees (Floyd, Skolnik, & Walker, 2005). But despite the long-standing nature of this role of the community college, it has been fraught with controversy.

Many different studies find that entering a community college rather than a four-year college significantly lowers the probability that a student will attain a baccalaureate degree. Clearly, this gap in baccalaureate attainment could be simply due to the fact that community college students *on average* tend to be less well off, less prepared academically, and less ambitious educationally and occupationally than are four-year college entrants. But even when we compare community college entrants and four-year college entrants with the same family background, academic aptitude, high school grades, and educational and occupational aspirations, the community college entrants on average attain about 15% *fewer* baccalaureate degrees than their four-year college peers. This baccalaureate gap even holds in studies that systematically address issues of selection bias through the use of instrumental variables analysis or propensity score analysis (Alfonso, 2006; Dougherty, 1994, pp. 52–61; Doyle, 2008; Long & Kurlaender, 2009; Pascarella & Terenzini, 2005, p. 376). How do we explain this?

On closer inspection we find that—quite apart from the qualities students bring to college—entering the community college puts obstacles in the way of the pursuit of the baccalaureate degree. All other things being equal, baccalaureate aspirants who begin at a community college are more likely than comparable four-year college entrants to drop out during the first two years of college and not move on to become juniors at a four-year college.[2] As we have seen above, community college students more often drop out in the first two years of college because community colleges are less able to academically and socially integrate their students into the life of the college. In addition, fewer community college students go on to the junior year at four-year colleges because, in comparison to four-year college entrants, they receive weaker encouragement to pursue a bachelor's degree, less adequate financial aid, and less interest by four-year colleges in admitting them to popular campuses and programs (Dougherty, 2002, pp. 315–323). This lack of transfer to universities is more pronounced among students who are lower in socioeconomic status, nonwhite, and older (Cabrera, Burkum, & LaNasa, 2005; Dougherty & Kienzl, 2006).

WORKFORCE PREPARATION AND ECONOMIC DEVELOPMENT

The community college role in workforce preparation and economic development ranges from preparing students for their first job to retraining unemployed workers and welfare recipients, upgrading the skills of employed workers, assisting owners of small businesses, and helping communities with economic development planning (Dougherty & Bakia, 2000; Cohen & Brawer, 2008, chap. 8; Grubb, 1996; Jacobs & Dougherty, 2006).

In terms of initial job preparation, community colleges play a central role in supplying trained workers for "middle level" or "semiprofessional" occupations such as nurses, computer operators, and auto mechanics. In fact, about one-fifth of recent labor force entrants began at a community college (Grubb, 1996, pp. 54–56). These vocational graduates receive substantial economic payoffs. For example, students earning a vocational associate's degree from a community college earn 15% to 30% more in annual income than high school graduates of similar race and ethnicity, parental education, marital status, and job experience (Grubb, 2002; Marcotte, Bailey, Borkoski, & Kienzl, 2005).[3] In fact, there are community college vocational programs—particularly in nursing and certain technical fields—whose graduates earn more than many bachelor's degree holders. As a result, for many less privileged students who are only able to pursue short-term degrees, vocational education has emerged as a viable path to success (Deil-Amen & Deluca, 2010).

Still, the economic payoffs to community college degrees are, on average, not as good as those for baccalaureate degrees. Looking across all fields of study, the average baccalaureate degree pays about 40% to 50% more than the average high school degree, considerably more than the average vocational or academic associate's degree (Grubb, 2002; Marcotte et al., 2005). Moreover, community college students who pursue a vocational degree are significantly less likely to eventually transfer to pursue a baccalaureate degree, even when one controls for family background, educational aspirations, and high school preparation (Dougherty & Kienzl, 2006).

The community college's role in job retraining, small business assistance, and economic development planning—though less heralded than its role in job preparation—is important. Today, almost all community colleges retrain workers for new jobs or new tasks in existing jobs. In addition, many colleges assist small business owners by sponsoring small business development centers or simply offering courses that provide advice and training in management and personnel practices, marketing, finance, procuring contracts with government agencies, introducing new production technologies and work practices, and adapting to new government regulations. Finally, community colleges promote economic development by assisting local economic development planning efforts (Dougherty & Bakia, 2000).

While the community college's role in workforce preparation and economic development is very useful, it also can cause the community college considerable difficulties. Community colleges with very active workforce preparation programs can lose money on unpopular training programs, flood the market with too many graduates, provoke criticism by competing training providers, and give employers too much influence over the college curriculum (Dougherty, 1994; Dougherty & Bakia, 2000). Moreover, an active workforce preparation effort can interfere with other functions of the community college such as preparing students for transfer to four-year colleges and providing students with a general education.

REMEDIAL EDUCATION

From the beginning, community colleges have been gateways into higher education for students whom four-year colleges would turn away as unprepared for college. As a result, community colleges have long provided remedial education to many of their students (Cohen & Brawer, 2008). In 2000, 42% of freshmen in public two-year colleges were officially enrolled in remedial courses either in reading, writing, or arithmetic, as compared to 28% of college students generally (U.S. National Center for Education Statistics, 2003, p. 18). This remedial role grew during the 1990s as state legislators and four-year college boards pushed to have remedial education reduced or even eliminated at four-year colleges and relegated instead to community colleges (Shaw, 1997). This diversion of remediation into the community college poses a deep dilemma, one rooted in the contradictory effects of the community college. On the one hand, academically unprepared students pushed into community colleges may attain more education by perhaps receiving better remediation and occupational education than they would at four-year colleges. (However, there is no conclusive evidence that this is the case.[4]) But on the other hand, their long-run educational attainment may be harmed by receiving less assistance in pursuing a baccalaureate degree.

ADULT, CONTINUING EDUCATION, AND COMMUNITY EDUCATION

Adult, continuing, and community education (ACCE) is a catchall including vocational improvement and retraining for those already working, high school completion and adult literacy improvement, personal development and recreational courses, and community services such as arts events.

Adult-education students are a key community college constituency. Many adult students enter the community college to take high school equivalency (GED), adult basic education (ABE), and English as a second language (ESL) courses. It is estimated that 33% of adult-education enrollees are in community colleges and such students make up 7% of total credit and non-credit FTE enrollments in community colleges. About three-quarters of these community college adult-education students are in the bottom half in socioeconomic status and about half are non-white (Grubb, Badway, & Bell, 2003, p. 223; Prince & Jenkins, 2005). Despite the hopes for adult-education programs, there is little evidence that they bring significant income benefits if they do not lead to a degree (Grubb et al., 2003, pp. 229–233; Prince & Jenkins, 2005, pp. 5–6, 21). A study of first-time adult students entering Washington State community colleges in the late 1990s (the majority of whom did not have high school diplomas) found that the income payoff only becomes significant if students accrue at least a year's worth of credits and a credential. Unfortunately, the same study found that five years after entering the community college only 58% of adult education students had acquired *any* college credits (with only 13% of ESL entrants doing so) (Prince & Jenkins, 2005, pp. 13–16, 23).

The ACCE divisions of community colleges are often their most dynamic because community colleges can more easily develop new course offerings in this area because the courses usually do not carry credit and therefore are less subject to state regulation. Community colleges can use noncredit offerings to learn more about the demands of the labor market, particularly in fast changing technology fields, and then develop similar credit-bearing courses (Dougherty & Bakia, 2000; Downey, Pusser, & Turner, 2006; Van Noy, Jacobs, Korey, Bailey, & Hughes, 2008). However, ACCE divisions of community colleges usually are not well funded, with state funding often being absent or paying less per student than state funding for regular, credit-bearing academic and occupational programs (Cohen & Brawer, 2008, chap. 10; Grubb et al., 2003; Van Noy et al., 2008). In part because of this, ACCE courses, particularly in adult education, are often criticized for being of poor quality because they rely on too many part-time faculty and provide inadequate student support services (Grubb et al., 2003).

GENERAL EDUCATION

Community colleges have made a major commitment to general education, whether defined as transmitting a common culture or fostering skills of broad utility in a person's life, such as critical thinking and communication skills (Higginbotham & Romano, 2006). Unfortunately, this commitment is partially contradicted by the community college's other commitments, particularly to occupational education. An analysis of the catalogs of 32 community colleges found that all of them had some kind of general education requirement for their transfer programs and at least 90% had a general education requirement for their nontransfer programs. But though these figures are impressive, they also exaggerate the actual degree to which community college students receive a general education. For example, among the 90% of those 32 community colleges that had core curriculum requirements for their nontransfer programs, only half required taking even one course in U.S. government and only one-fifth required a course in ethnic studies or multiculturalism (Zeszotarski, 1999).

These apparent gaps in the provision of general education are not surprising because community colleges face great difficulties in providing general education for all their students. The rise of occupational education has meant that community colleges now enroll many students whose primary purpose is likely to be preparation for a job rather than preparation for a variety of life roles. This problem is exacerbated if employers are paying for the training. Contract training programs typically are narrowly focused on providing skills and usually devote little or no attention to broader social knowledge and life skills. Finally, it is easier for public authorities to hold community colleges accountable for inculcating work skills than general learning (Dougherty, 2002, pp. 333–338; Higginbotham & Romano, 2006).

THE ORIGINS AND LATER DEVELOPMENT OF COMMUNITY COLLEGES

Befitting their multiple and contradictory functions, community colleges have had equally mixed and contrasting origins. This is rarely acknowledged in the standard accounts of how community colleges were founded and later developed. Typically, these conventional accounts state that the community college was founded in response to calls by students, parents, and publicly interested educators and government officials for more college opportunities. And later, community colleges moved from an emphasis on academic education to a stress on occupational education primarily in response to the needs of students and employers for vocational training (Cohen & Brawer, 2008).

But other observers—particularly sociologists—have pointed out how these conventional chronicles miss much of the real history of the community college. For example, while these accounts mention the key role of state universities, they often misanalyze it. The state universities pushed the founding of community colleges not just to expand college opportunity, as is typically claimed, but also to keep the universities academically selective by channeling less able students toward the community colleges. Moreover, the universities unwittingly spurred the vocationalization of the community college by monopolizing greater status as "senior" colleges that trained for the most prestigious professional and managerial occupations. In order to escape the status of "junior" colleges, community colleges began in the 1920s to carve out an independent role as suppliers of a distinct training market of their own, the "middle level" or semiprofessional occupations such as technicians, nurses, etc. (Brint & Karabel, 1989; Dougherty, 1994).

Local and state government officials also played a key role in the establishment and later vocationalization of community colleges, motivated not just by a sincere belief in educational opportunity but also by self-interest. At the local level, school superintendents and high school principals were the prime instigators of local drives to found community colleges. While they were certainly moved by a commitment to expand college opportunity, they were also driven by the desires to earn prestige as college founders and to secure jobs as presidents of the new colleges (Dougherty, 1994).

At the state level, governors, state legislators, and state education departments strongly pushed the expansion and later vocationalization of community colleges. Again, their support was prompted by more than just a desire to widen college access. State officials were mindful that building more community colleges, rather than expanding existing four-year colleges, could meet the great demand for college access in the 1960s and 1970s at a much lower cost to state government. Unlike the four-year colleges, community colleges would not require expensive dormitories, libraries, and research facilities. These savings would translate either into lower taxes or more state funds for other politically popular programs, both of which would make elected government officials more popular. In addition, community colleges, because of their strong commitment to vocational and technical education, could help stimulate the growth of state economies by attracting business firms with the carrot of publicly subsidized training of employees. This economic growth in turn would enhance the reelection chances of officials when they ran again for political office (Dougherty, 1994).

Business firms usually did not play a powerful *direct* role in founding or vocationalizing community colleges. But business played a powerful *indirect* role, based on business's central position within the United States's economic and ideological systems. Economically, business controls jobs and investment capital. Hence, in order to get their graduates access to the jobs employers control, community college officials on their own initiative will develop occupational programs that employers find useful, even without business demand for such programs (Brint & Karabel, 1989; Dougherty, 1994). Business also owns investment capital and thus largely controls the pace and distribution of economic growth. Realizing that capital investment is key to economic growth and therefore their own political prospects, elected officials have taken the initiative to offer business publicly subsidized vocational education in order to secure business investment in their jurisdictions. Ideologically, business influences government officials because those officials subscribe to values and beliefs—such as that economic growth is vital and that this growth must come primarily through an expansion of jobs in the private rather than public sector—that have made them ready to serve business interests (Dougherty, 1994).[5]

different academic standards. But the reason community colleges are two-year schools is largely because university heads did not want the competition of many more four-year schools, state officials did not want the financial burden of a myriad four-year colleges, and local educators felt two-year colleges would be easier to establish and be staffed by local educators. The precipitate of these many different interests is an institutional structure that, unfortunately and largely unintentionally, often subverts the educational ambitions of baccalaureate aspirants entering community college, even as it opens up opportunities for students with nonbaccalaureate ambitions. In short, the complex origins of the community college have created a contradictory institution: one serving many, often conflicting, missions.

FROM COMPLEX ORIGINS TO CONTRADICTORY EFFECTS

An awareness of the community college's complex origins allows us to see how community colleges have come to powerfully hinder the baccalaureate opportunities of their students without this necessarily being an intended result. Because they lack dormitories, community colleges are less likely to keep their students in college by enmeshing them in a vibrant campus social life. But the reason community colleges lack dormitories is because this made the colleges cheaper to operate, a potent consideration in the minds of the local educators founding them and the state officials financing them. Because community colleges are heavily vocational, this may lead their transfer rate to be lower than it might otherwise be.[6] But a major reason community colleges are so strongly vocational is that this was a means of meeting elected officials' desire for economic investment and community college officials' desire for political support from business and jobs for their graduates. Finally, because community colleges are two-year schools, students are discouraged from pursuing a baccalaureate degree because they have to transfer to separate four-year institutions with

WHAT CAN COMMUNITY COLLEGES DO TO IMPROVE STUDENT SUCCESS?

Many of the difficulties the community college encounters are out of its control, lying in the nature of its students (who typically are less well off and less prepared than four-year college students) and the community college's very structure as a two-year nonresidential institution. Still, there is much community colleges can do to improve success rates for their students. They can reduce the number who leave without a degree by improving the academic and social integration of students and their academic achievement by creating learning communities and freshman seminars, employing more full-time faculty, improving advising and retention services particularly for minority students, working with high schools to improve the skills students enter college with, and developing more effective and transparent remedial education (Bailey, 2009; Bailey, Calcagno, Calcagno, Leinbach, & Kienzl, 2006; Dougherty, 2002, pp. 324–325; Jenkins, 2006; Kirst & Venezia, 2006; O'Gara, Karp, & Hughes, 2009; Rosenbaum et al., 2006; Scrivener et al., 2008; Zeidenberg, Jenkins, & Calcagno, 2007). Community colleges can increase transfer rates by encouraging transfer aspirations through better transfer advising, working to facilitate the transfer of course credits (especially for occupational students), and pushing state governments to provide financial aid specifically for transfer students (Bahr, 2008; Dougherty, 2002, pp. 325–328; Ignash & Kotun, 2005; Moore, Shulock, & Jensen, 2009).[7] In addition to these operational reforms, community colleges can also consider more far-reaching structural reforms, particularly themselves offering baccalaureate degrees rather than requiring students to engage in the often difficult process of transferring to a four-year college (Dougherty, 2002, pp. 328–330; Floyd et al., 2005).[8]

The Future of the Community College

The community college will not remain static. It will continue to change, perhaps sharply, due to its diffuse institutional mission and high responsiveness to its economic, social, and political environments (Townsend & Dougherty, 2006). As our economy globalizes, skilled and semiskilled jobs in offices and factories continue to be eliminated or moved abroad and class inequality increases. In response, community colleges are being asked to revamp their job preparation and economic development efforts to put more emphasis on high skilled jobs, including ones requiring baccalaureate degrees (Levin, 2001). Yet at the same time, community colleges still feel they should meet the needs of the many people who require remedial and adult basic education and preparation for semiskilled jobs (Jacobs & Dougherty, 2006). Meanwhile, as states conclude that their economies need more baccalaureate degree holders, community colleges are increasingly being asked by state officials to replace the more expensive public universities as the main site for the first two years of baccalaureate education (Wellman, 2002). But even as they respond to these demands, community colleges face increasing difficulties getting enough funds from state governments and rising competition from other colleges, whether four-year

colleges offering continuing education or for profit colleges offering occupational education with higher placement rates than community colleges typically produce (Bailey, 2006; Kenton, Huba, Schuh, & Shelley, 2005; Rosenbaum et al., 2006). As the focus for these many cross-pressures emanating from a socially stratified and conflictual society, the community college will continue to be an important, but also contradictory, institution.

Notes

1. These figures overstate the baccalaureate ambitions of community college students. Many of those holding baccalaureate ambitions are in no hurry to realize them. Moreover, for a good many, this ambition is not founded on a very solid basis. However, it is still important to realize that many students who enter community college, even if with the intention of securing vocational training, do hope to eventually get a baccalaureate degree.

2. Data from the 1980s indicated that baccalaureate attainment of community college transfer students was undercut as well by higher rates of attrition in the junior and senior year than was the case for students who had started at four-year colleges as freshmen. However, studies based on data from the 1990s apparently find that this is no longer the case (Melguizo & Dowd, 2009).

3. Lower degrees receive smaller payoffs. Students receiving one-year certificates outpace high school graduates by only about 10% in annual earnings, and students who attend community college but do not receive a certificate or degree lead high school graduates by only 5% to 10% in earnings for every year of community college. Moreover, the payoff to a given community college credential varies by the student's social background, major, and job placement. For example, women make more from associate's degrees and certificates than do men but make less when they have secured no credential. The payoff is considerably higher for associate's degrees in engineering and computers, business, and (for women) health than in education or humanities. Finally, community college students get much better returns if they find employment in fields related to their training, than if they do not (Grubb, 1996, pp. 90, 95, 99, 102; Grubb, 2002).

4. Despite the importance of remedial education, we have little hard data on how well community colleges actually remediate. A number of studies have found small positive impacts of community college developmental education but the areas of impact (whether grades on subsequent nonremedial courses, completing a degree, or transferring to a four-year colleges) are not consistent across studies. In addition, there is no consensus on what forms of developmental education are most effective (Bailey, 2009; Dougherty, 2002, pp. 311–312; Perin, 2006).

5. The argument laid out in the preceding paragraphs is indebted to the theory of the state in political sociology and institutional theory in the sociology of organizations. For more on these theoretical roots, see Dougherty (1994) and Brint and Karabel (1989).

6. There is some debate over how much transfer rates are negatively affected by whether a community college is high in the proportion of its students and degrees that are in vocational fields. Compare Dougherty (1994, pp. 93–97) and Dougherty and Kienzl (2006) to Roksa (2006). In any case, the growing push to facilitate the transfer of occupational credits and degrees will help reduce the negative impact of the vocational emphasis of community colleges on transfer rates.

7. It bears noting that studies of the impact of state policies to facilitate transfer and articulation do not find that seemingly stronger policies lead to higher rates of transfer or even lesser credit loss. However, the studies conducted so far have had to cope with less than ideal data so there is a need for further studies in this area (Roksa, 2009).

8. Community colleges in 14 states have begun to offer their own baccalaureate degrees (Dougherty, 2002, pp. 329–330; Floyd et al., 2005). In Florida, over a third of community colleges offer baccalaureate degrees, primarily in education, business management, nursing, and health care administration (Community College Baccalaureate Association, 2010).

REFERENCES

Alfonso, M. (2006). The impact of community college attendance on baccalaureate attainment. *Research in Higher Education, 47*(8), 873–903.

Bahr, P. R. (2008). Cooling out in the community college: What is the effect of academic advising on students' chances of success? *Research in Higher Education, 49*(8), 704–732.

Bailey, T. (2006). Increasing competition and the growth of the for profits. In T. Bailey & V. S. Morest (Eds.), *Defending the community college equity agenda* (pp. 87–109). Baltimore: Johns Hopkins University Press.

Bailey, T. (2009). Challenge and opportunity: Rethinking the role and function of developmental education in community college. In C. P. Harbour & P. L. Farrell (Eds.), *Contemporary issues in institutional ethics: New directions for community colleges #148* (pp. 11–30). San Francisco: Jossey-Bass.

Bailey, T., Calcagno, J. C., Jenkins, D., Leinbach, T., & Kienzl, G. (2006). Is student right-to-know all you should know? An analysis of community college graduation rates. *Research in Higher Education, 47*(3), 491–519.

Brint, S. G., & Karabel, J. B. (1989). *The diverted dream*. New York: Oxford University Books.

Cabrera, A. F., Burkum, K. R., & LaNasa, S. M. (2005). Pathways to a four-year degree. In A. Seidman (Ed.), *College student retention: Formula for student success* (pp. 155–214). Westport, CT: Praeger.

Calcagno, J. C., Bailey, T., Jenkins, D., Kienzl, G., & Leinbach, T. (2008). Community college student success: What institutional characteristics make a difference? *Economics of Education Review, 27*(6), 632–645.

Cohen, A. C., & Brawer, F. B. (2008). *The American community college* (5th ed.). San Francisco: Jossey-Bass.

Community College Baccalaureate Association. (2010). *Baccalaureate conferring locations*. Fort Myers, FL: Author. Retrieved from http://www.accbd.org/resources/baccalaureate-conferring-locations/

Deil-Amen, R., & Deluca, S. (2010). The underserved third: How our educational structures populate an educational underclass. *Journal of Education for Students Placed at Risk, 15*(1/2), 27–50.

Dougherty, K. J. (1994). *The contradictory college: The conflicting origins, impacts, and futures of the community college*. Albany: State University of New York Press.

Dougherty, K. J. (2002). The evolving role of the community college: Policy issues and research questions. In J. Smart & W. Tierney (Eds.), *Higher education: Handbook of theory and research*, Vol. 17. (pp. 295–348). Dordrecht, Netherlands: Kluwer.

Dougherty, K. J., & Bakia, M. F. (2000). Community colleges and contract training: Content, origins, and impacts. *Teachers College Record, 102*(1), 198–244.

Dougherty, K. J., & Kienzl, G. (2006). It's not enough to get through the open door: Inequalities by social background in transfer from community colleges to four-year colleges. *Teachers College Record, 108*(3), 452–487.

Downey, J., Pusser, B., & Turner, K. (2006). Competing missions: Balancing entrepreneurialism with community responsiveness in community college continuing education divisions. In B. T. Townsend & K. J. Dougherty (Eds.), *Community college missions in the 21st century: New directions for community colleges #136* (pp. 75–82). San Francisco: Jossey-Bass.

Doyle, W. R. (2008). The effect of community college enrollment on bachelor's degree completion. *Economics of Education Review, 28*(2), 199–206.

Floyd, D. F., Skolnik, M., & Walker, K. (Eds.). (2005). *The community college baccalaureate.* Sterling, VA: Stylus Press.

Grubb, W. N. (1996). *Working in the middle.* San Francisco: Jossey-Bass.

Grubb, W. N. (2002). Learning and earning in the middle, Part I: National studies of pre-baccalaureate education. *Economics of Education Review, 21*(4), 299–321.

Grubb, W. N., Badway, N., & Bell. D. (2003). Community colleges and the equity agenda: The potential of non-credit education. *Annals of the American Academy of Social and Political Science, 586*(1), 218–240.

Higginbotham, G. H., & Romano, R. M. (2006). Appraising the efficacy of civic education at the community college. In B. T. Townsend & K. J. Dougherty (Eds.), *Community college missions in the 21st century: New directions for community colleges #136* (pp. 23–32). San Francisco: Jossey-Bass.

Horn, L. (2009). *On track to complete? A taxonomy of beginning community college students and their outcomes 3 years after enrolling: 2003–04 through 2006. Statistical analysis report* (NCES 2009-152). Washington, DC: Government Printing Office.

Ignash, J. M., & Kotun, D. (2005). Results of a national study of transfer in occupational/technical degrees: Policies and practices. *Journal of Applied Research in the Community College, 12*(2), 109–120.

Jacobs, J., & Dougherty, K. J. (2006). The uncertain future of the workforce development mission of community colleges. In B. T. Townsend & K. J. Dougherty (Eds.), *Community college missions in the 21st century: New directions for community colleges #136* (pp. 53–62). San Francisco: Jossey-Bass.

Jaeger, A. J., & Eagan, M. K. (2009). Unintended consequences: Examining the effect of part-time faculty members on associate's degree completion. *Community College Review, 36*(3), 167–194.

Jenkins, D. (2006). *What community college management practices are effective in promoting student success?* New York: Columbia University, Teachers College, Community College Research Center. Retrieved from http://ccrc.tc.columbia.edu/Publication.asp?UID=419

Kenton, C. P., Huba, M. E., Schuh, J. H., & Shelley, M.C. (2005). Financing community colleges: A longitudinal study of 11 states. *Community College Journal of Research and Practice, 29*(2), 109–122.

Kirst, M., & Venezia, A. (Eds.). (2006). *From high school to college: Improving opportunities for success in post-secondary education.* San Francisco: Jossey-Bass.

Levin, J. (2001). *Globalizing the community college.* New York: Palgrave.

Long, B. T., & Kurlaender, M. (2009). Do community colleges provide a viable pathway to a baccalaureate degree? *Educational Evaluation and Policy Analysis, 31*(1), 30–53.

Marcotte, D. E., Bailey, T., Borkoski, C., & Kienzl, G. S. (2005). The returns of a community college education: Evidence from the national education longitudinal survey. *Educational Evaluation and Policy Analysis, 27*(2), 157–175.

McCormick, A. (1997). *Transfer behavior among beginning postsecondary students: 1989–94* (NCES 97-266). Washington, DC: U.S. National Center for Education Statistics.

Melguizo, T., & Dowd, A. C. (2009). Baccalaureate success of transfers and rising 4-year college juniors. *Teachers College Record, 111*(1), 55–89.

Moore, C., Shulock, N., & Jensen, C. (2009). *Creating a student-centered transfer process in California: Lessons from other states.* Sacramento: California State University, Institute for Higher Education Leadership & Policy.

O'Gara, L., Karp, M. M., & Hughes, K. L. (2009). Student success courses in the community college: An exploratory study of student perspectives. *Community College Review, 36*(3), 195–218.

Pascarella, E. T., & Terenzini, P. T. (2005). *How college affects students* (2nd ed.). San Francisco: Jossey-Bass.

Perin, D. (2006). Can community colleges protect both access and standards? The problem of remediation. *Teachers College Record, 108*(3), 339–373.

Prince, D., & Jenkins, D. (2005). *Building pathways to success for low-skill adult students: Lessons for community college policy and practice from a statewide longitudinal tracking study.* New York: Columbia University, Teachers College, Community College Research Center. Retrieved from http://ccrc.tc.columbia.edu/ContentByType .asp?t=1

Roksa, J. (2006). Does the vocational focus of community colleges hinder students' educational attainment? *Review of Higher Education, 29*(4), 499–526.

Roksa, J. (2009). Building bridges for student success: Are higher education articulation policies effective? *Teachers College Record, 111*(10), 2444–2478.

Rosenbaum, J. E., Deil-Amen, R., & Person, A. E. (2006). *After admission: From college access to college success.* New York: Russell Sage Foundation.

Rouse, C. E. (1998). Do two-year colleges increase overall educational attainment? Evidence from the states. *Journal of Policy Analysis and Management, 17*(4), 595–620.

Scrivener, S., Bloom, D., LeBlanc, A., Paxson, C., Rouse, C. E., & Sommo, C. (2008). *A good start: Two-year effects of a freshmen learning community program at Kingsborough Community College.* New York: MDRC. Retrieved from http:// www.mdrc.org/publications/473/full.pdf

Shaw, K. M. (1997). Remedial education as ideological battleground: Emerging remedial education policies in the community college. *Educational Evaluation and Policy Analysis, 19*(3), 284–296.

Townsend, B. T., & Dougherty, K. J. (Eds.). (2006). *Community college missions in the 21st century: New directions for community colleges #136.* San Francisco: Jossey-Bass.

Van Noy, M., Jacobs, J., Korey, S., Bailey, T., & Hughes, K. L. (2008). *The landscape of noncredit workforce education: State policies and community college practice* (Issue Brief 38). New York: Community College Research Center, Teachers College, Columbia University. Retrieved from http:// ccrc.tc.columbia.edu/Publication.asp?uid=634

U.S. National Center for Education Statistics. (2003). *Remedial education at degree granting postsecondary institutions in fall 2000* (NCES 2004-010). Washington, DC: Government Printing Office.

U.S. National Center for Education Statistics. (2009). *Digest of education statistics, 2009.* Washington, DC: Government Printing Office.

Wellman, J. V. (2002). *State policy and community college-baccalaureate transfer.* San Jose, CA: National Center for Public Policy and Higher Education.

Zeidenberg, M., Jenkins, D., & Calcagno. J. C. (2007). *Do student success courses actually help community college students succeed?* (CCRC Brief #36). New York: Community College Research Center, Teachers College, Columbia University. Retrieved from http://ccrc.tc.columbia.edu/Publication.asp? uid=667

Zeszotarski, P. (1999). Dimensions of general education requirements. In G. Schuyler (Ed.), *Trends in community college curriculum. New directions for community colleges #108* (pp. 39–48). San Francisco: Jossey-Bass.

Crossing the Finish Line

Completing College at America's Public Universities

William G. Bowen, Matthew M. Chingos, and Michael S. McPherson

In this selection from their book of the same title, William G. Bowen, Matthew M. Chingos, and Michael S. McPherson review their findings and make suggestions for improving educational experiences at public universities in the United States. Their findings are based on two data sets that they developed specifically for the purpose of examining retention rates at public colleges and universities, including a selection of public historically black colleges and universities. They included student information such as year entered, year graduated, financial aid, SAT and high school scores, and other indicators that might explain differences in the time it takes students to graduate. These data tell us a great deal about college completion at public universities in the United States.

Questions to consider for this reading:

1. Which of their five challenges do you think is most important in increasing college completion rates at public universities in the United States?

2. What do we know about college success from high school grades and academic placement tests?

3. What do the authors mean by undermatching and overmatching? Which is the best strategy for students of color?

Looking Ahead

Pervasive, persistent, but not intractable. That is how we view the disparities in educational attainment that we have documented in [*Crossing the Finish Line*]. Similarly, the failure of the overall level of educational attainment in this country to increase in recent years, as it did so steadily for most of our nation's history, does not have to be accepted as an immutable fact of life in 21st-century America. In this article we will look ahead to define the challenges before us and to identify ways of addressing them.

Challenges to Overcome

We have identified five principal challenges.

First, the overall level of educational attainment in the United States today is both too low and stagnant. The apparent inability of today's traditional college-age population to earn more bachelor's degrees is unacceptable. And it is finishing programs of study-earning degrees, not just starting out in college, that is the metric to be emphasized. The new Gates initiative in education clearly reflects a recognition of this central point, as do the statements and early initiatives of the Obama administration.

The current level of educational attainment in this country is particularly troubling when seen alongside the dramatic progress that is evident all around the world in overall levels of educational attainment and especially in degrees awarded in science and engineering.

Nor can the United States expect to continue to benefit to the extent it has in the past from its success in importing educated talent. Countries on many continents now work hard to keep their own educated citizens at home and, for that matter, to attract talented young people from abroad. China now imports more students than it exports. . . .

Over several decades, leading economists have done a great deal of work in documenting the large contribution to economic growth of investments in education, both in the United States and globally. Goldin and Katz (2008) have shown in persuasive fashion how America's success in expanding educational attainment in the 20th century proved decisive in driving this country's remarkable growth during that century and how the slowdown in growth of educational attainment evident in recent decades poses a serious risk to our nation's economic leadership.

Second, the U.S. educational system harbors huge disparities in outcomes, especially as measured by graduation rates that are systematically related to race/ethnicity and gender, as well as to socioeconomic status (SES). Moreover, these disparities appear to be growing rather than narrowing. This pattern is unacceptable because of its implications for social mobility and access to opportunity, as well as because of what it says about our collective failure to take full advantage of pools of latent talent.

Third, these two problems are linked: the only way to substantially improve overall levels of educational attainment is by improving graduation rates for the rapidly growing Hispanic population, for underrepresented minority students in general (with black men requiring special attention), and for students from low-SES backgrounds.

To be sure, we can and should graduate higher proportions of white students from middle- and upper-SES backgrounds. But this group already has above-average graduation rates, and it will decline in absolute numbers in the coming decades; it would be a mistake to count on progress with this group to solve the country's need for a higher overall level of educational attainment.

Fourth, time-to-degree matters as well as ultimate graduation rates. A long (and increasing) time-to-degree among underrepresented minorities and students from poor families harms access to later educational and career opportunities. Moreover, a long time-to-degree for students from all backgrounds carries high costs for the system as well as for individuals. Reductions in time-to-degree would allow universities to educate more students without adding proportionately to institutional outlays, a point of special consequence at a time when resources are so strained. Some legislators are again calling for colleges to offer three-year bachelor's degree programs, but we think it is more practical to focus on reducing the number of undergraduates who take more than four years to earn their degrees. Colleges could be more proactive in encouraging students to take less time to graduate. For example, West Virginia's PROMISE (Providing Real Opportunities for Maximizing In-State Student Excellence) Scholarship Program has introduced the idea of rewarding steady progress toward degree completion, not just maintaining a high GPA.[1]

Fifth and last, it is essential to recognize that public universities have to be the principal engines of progress in addressing these challenges. Important as it is, the private sector is not large enough, nor does its mission focus as strongly on social mobility as does that of the public sector. It is the public sector that has the historical commitment to educational attainment for all, as well as the scale, the cost-pricing structure, and the greatest extant opportunities to do better (given present graduation rates). As Eugene M. Tobin writes (2009), "America's flagship universities were created to meet the social and economic needs of the states that chartered them, to serve as a great equalizer and preserver of an open, upwardly mobile society, and to provide 'an uncommon education for the common man.' Any citizen, regardless of socioeconomic status, who fulfilled a standard set of academic requirements, would, in theory, be admitted to one of the state's public higher education institutions." Douglass and Thomson also see the unique purpose of public institutions: "It is not an exaggeration to say that the health of America's economy and the character of social stratification will remain dependent on the vibrancy of its public higher education institutions. For middle- and lower-income students, public institutions will remain the primary entry point."[2]

SORTING OF STUDENTS I: TEST SCORES AND HIGH SCHOOL GRADES

Outcomes, especially graduation rates, depend greatly on achieving an optimal match between students and institutions. We are dealing here with a double selection process—one in which colleges select students and students select colleges—that does not always work as well as it should. That is the theme of this section and the next.

In selecting students, colleges rely on a variety of criteria that often vary, as they should, from institution to institution. It is clear to us that different types of tests and other sources of evidence that can be used to predict academic potential and academic outcomes, such as high school grades, measure different things. The right question is not "Should we, or should we not, use tests?" Rather, the question is "In what settings can we expect various kinds of tests, and other measures, to be especially helpful?" A particular piece of evidence may be of great value for one purpose and of little or none for another. An instrument that is useful in predicting grades may have far less value as a predictor of graduation rates. Moreover, which measures are most useful depends on the relevant population of students; tests and other indicators that differentiate reasonably well among applicants to the

most selective universities may be of marginal value, at best, in the context of less selective colleges and universities. *A "one-size-fits-all" mentality is to be avoided.*

Still, several main story lines are straightforward. The mass of new evidence we have assembled on the predictive power of high school grades and standardized test scores is, we believe, nothing less than compelling. Here are the main take-aways:

- *High school grades are a far better incremental predictor of graduation rates than are standard SAT/ACT test scores—a central finding that holds within each of the six sets of public universities that we study.* The additional predictive power of high school GPA is especially strong—really overwhelming—in the setting of the less selective flagships, which we call selectivity cluster (SEL) IIIs, and the less selective state system public universities, which we call SEL Bs. Scores on general reasoning or aptitude tests add little if anything in these contexts once we have taken account of high school GPA. SAT/ACT scores have more value in predicting graduation rates at more selective institutions (and somewhat greater value yet in predicting college grades, again especially at the more selective institutions), but here too high school GPA is a stronger incremental predictor.

- *Overly heavy reliance on SAT/ACT scores in admitting students can have adverse effects on the diversity of the student bodies enrolled by universities.* The correlation between family background and aptitude tests is consistently stronger than the correlation between family background and high school GPA.

- *The strong predictive power of high school GPA holds even when we know little or nothing about the quality of the high school attended.* In general, students with high grades from a weak school are appreciably more likely to graduate than are students with weak grades from an academically demanding high school. We believe that the consistently strong performance of high school GPA as a predictor of graduation rates derives in large part from its value as a measure of motivation, perseverance, work habits, and coping skills, as well as cognitive achievements. This is not to say that the quality of the high school is of no consequence. The quality of the high school matters too, and high school GPA has even greater predictive power when combined with knowledge about the high school attended. But whatever the high school, the in-school performance of the student dominates the effect of the high school itself in predicting graduation rates.

• *Scores on achievement tests, especially Advanced Placement tests, are better predictors of graduation rates than are scores on the standard SAT/ACT tests. As a general rule, colleges and universities selecting students are well advised to use a judicious combination of information about high school GPA, achievement test results (including the results of tests of uniting skills), and the quality of the high school looked at in conjunction with standard SAT/ACT scores.* "Triangulating" the selection process in this way is a strong protection against tendencies to "game" the system, which could be encouraged by focusing on only one predictor.

• *Putting more emphasis on content-based achievement tests has the further advantage of sending clear signals to high schools that they should concentrate on teaching content, including basic skills such as writing and the ability to use mathematics.* High schools should not be encouraged to "teach to the test" when the test allegedly measures reasoning skills and general aptitude; instead, more weight should be given to content-based tests that measure how well students learn what high school classes aim to teach.

Finally, testing organizations and others interested in testing should be encouraged to continue developing new tests and techniques of assessment that will facilitate matching processes of all kinds. Recent efforts by scholars at the Berkeley Law School to develop instruments that will predict "successful lawyering" are one example of this approach, and there also appears to be renewed interest at the undergraduate level in developing broadly gauged tests of "college readiness."[3] A further example is the effort by the eminent psychologist and now dean of the faculty at Tufts University, Robert Sternberg, to base admission to that university partly on "assessing students' creative and practical abilities."[4]

SORTING OF STUDENTS II: "OVERMATCHING" AND "UNDERMATCHING"

Broadly speaking, educational attainment suffers, and students (and higher education in general) are harmed, whenever two types of sorting errors occur: (a) students are "overmatched" by enrolling in programs for which they are not qualified or (b) students are "undermatched" by failing to attend colleges and universities at which they will be appropriately challenged. The findings reported in this study fail to provide any evidence of overmatching but demonstrate that undermatching is a massive problem.

The Overmatch Hypothesis

. . . [O]pponents of affirmative action have often claimed that race-sensitive admissions policies harm the very minority students they purport to help by inducing them to attend colleges that are too demanding, thrusting them into harmful competition with white classmates of greater ability and demoralizing them as they fail to meet applicable standards. The data for the 1999 entering cohorts at the public universities we study offer no support whatsoever for this hypothesis.

In fact, our research indicates that black male students who went to more selective institutions graduated at *higher,* not lower, rates than did similarly prepared black students who went to less selective institutions. There is no evidence that black men were "harmed" by going to the more selective universities that chose to admit them.

- *Students from all backgrounds, including black students, are generally well advised to enroll at one of the most challenging universities that will accept them.*

Undermatching

An obverse proposition deserves much more attention than it has received.

- *The frequently disappointing graduation rate outcomes for students from underrepresented minority groups and for students from low-SES backgrounds are due in no small part to the fact that a number of them were "undermatched"— that is, appreciable numbers of these students enrolled in either two-year colleges or four-year colleges that were less demanding than the colleges for which they were presumptively qualified, and some enrolled in no college at all.*

Among all high school graduates in North Carolina (the state with the richest data connecting experiences in high school to later collegiate outcomes) whom we classified as presumptively eligible to attend one of the most selective public universities in that state, over 40 percent failed to do so—that is, they undermatched. Not surprisingly, disproportionate numbers of these students came from families with low incomes and low levels of parental education. Many highly qualified students from low-SES backgrounds went to a community college or to no college at all. Supporting evidence comes from impressive studies of Chicago high school students that found that 28 percent of black high school graduates in that city "enrolled in a college that was far below a match," that Hispanic students were even more likely than black students to undermatch, and that less than half of the students in the most academically demanding programs ended up enrolling at colleges that match their qualifications[5] (Roderick et al., 2008; Roderick, Nagaoka, Coca, & Moeller, 2009).

- *The scale of the undermatch phenomenon among students from modest backgrounds*

suggests that addressing this problem offers a real opportunity to increase social mobility and simultaneously to increase overall levels of educational attainment.

Undermatching occurs primarily at the application stage of the admission process; in the main, it is not a result of students applying and being turned down or of failing to accept an admission offer. The key is to find ever more effective ways of informing high-achieving high school students and their parents of the educational opportunities that are open to them and of the benefits they can derive from taking advantage of these opportunities. Then, better ways need to be found to help these students navigate the process of gaining access to strong academic programs. We were surprised to learn how powerfully eighth-grade test scores that are content-based predict later college outcomes, and there is much to be said for identifying high-performing students from disadvantaged backgrounds early and tracking them carefully to reduce risks of undermatching. At the same time, we also recognize that the undermatch problem is by no means confined to either low-SES students or students with off-the-scale high school records. Students in general would benefit greatly from improved advising and counseling—functions that are too often under-resourced and uninformed. Finding ways to improve the matching process should be a high priority. Consideration should be given to ways of improving the use of digital technologies and online resources, and to the possibility of assigning special "coaches" the task of helping high-achieving students from modest backgrounds complete their applications and financial aid forms.

TRANSFER PATTERNS

A major advantage of the new public university databases that we have built is that they include students who transferred into these public universities as well as first-time freshmen. We also studied "transfer-out patterns." Some students who withdrew from the university at which they first enrolled ultimately graduated from another four-year institution, but taking these students into account raises overall graduation rates by only about 5 percentage points on average at the flagship universities and 10 percentage points at the state system universities. Taking account of transfer-out patterns does not change any of the main findings based on analysis of graduation rates at the institution first attended.

It is the transfer-in population that is of greatest interest, and there are three main empirical findings from this part of our research that deserve to be highlighted.

- *High school seniors who wanted to earn a bachelor's degree eventually, but who began at two-year colleges, were much less likely to earn a bachelor's degree than were comparable students who went directly from high school to a four-year program.*

- *Overall, transfer-in students did well. Those attending the more selective universities in our study graduated at about the same rate as first-time freshmen in spite of entering with weaker pre-collegiate credentials; transfer students at the less-selective four-year universities in our study graduated at higher rates than did first-time freshmen even though they entered with weaker pre-collegiate credentials.*

- *Transfer students from two-year college were substantially more likely to be from low-income families than were first-time freshmen.*

It is not easy to draw policy conclusions from these findings at a system-wide level because there may be some conflict between incentives for students and incentives for institutions, and there are also complex issues of resource allocation to be considered. But it does seem clear that a number of the universities in our study might improve both their socioeconomic diversity and their graduation rates by accepting more transfer students—who have, after all, demonstrated both motivation and accomplishment by completing a two-year course of study and seeking admission to a bachelor's degree program.[6] It also seems clear

that states should not encourage students with bachelor's degree aspirations and the necessary qualifications to enroll in a two-year program when they could have enrolled in a four-year college directly out of high school (the undermatch problem yet again). Nor should the existence of transfer opportunities justify underinvestment in creating places at four-year institutions.

MONEY MATTERS

Our research confirms an obvious proposition: the net cost of going to college and a family's resources together significantly affect both the probability that a student will graduate and the probability that the student will graduate in four years.

- *At every point in our analysis we find that students from high-income families are significantly more likely to graduate from college, and to graduate "on time," than are students with comparable qualifications from low-income families.*

- *Need-based grant aid was available to students attending all groups of public universities in our study, and there is clear evidence that such aid boosts both the numbers who attend such institutions and their graduation rates. Nonetheless, despite the presence of need-based aid, the graduation rate for students from low-SES families at these public universities was lower than the graduation rate for other students. In contrast, at highly selective private colleges and universities, graduation rates were essentially the same among students who differed in SES.[7]*

- *Comparisons across states between "net price" (tuition less grant aid) and adjusted graduation rates demonstrate that low- and moderate-income students who reside in states where attendance at the flagship university involves a higher net price are less likely to graduate than are comparable students from states where they face a lower net price, and they are considerably less likely to graduate in four years. Thus, we conclude that making college less expensive for students from modest backgrounds has to be a key consideration in any concerted effort to raise graduation rates and shorten time-to-degree.*

• *The data also clearly show that there is no such relationship between net price and graduation rates among students from families in the top half of the income distribution—a less obvious and potentially more consequential conclusion.*

• *Finding more resources for need-based student aid, while obviously difficult at all times, especially when fiscal constraints are so tight, is demonstrably less expensive than keeping the net price low by reducing tuition across the board, a policy that provides further subsidies to well-off families without improving their graduation rates.*

During the period of our study, undergraduates fared severe limits on the amount of money they could borrow under the federal loan programs, limits that had not risen since 1992. Students who needed to borrow more than the limit had to find other lenders outside the federally supported system and generally faced higher interest rates, if indeed credit was available to them at all. In the face of these constraints, some students no doubt sought to fill financial gaps by working in off-campus jobs, which of course can slow progress toward a degree. A complicating factor, alluded to by many campus commentators, is that a significant number of students are unwilling to defer their desire for "stuff" like flat-screen televisions until they have reaped the rewards of graduation. As a result, they may perform less well in college and even drop out altogether as they seek to satisfy their consumption preferences through long hours of work. To go beyond these anecdotal speculations requires more information than is available even in our rich data set, including, crucially, information on off-campus work patterns.

A particularly sensitive aspect of financial aid discussions is the role played by merit aid. According to a College Board study, only 44 percent of grant aid dollars at public four-year institutions went to students who had financial need. Nearly 40 percent went to non-need students, and 18 percent went to recruited athletes (including, of course, a number with need). As already noted, there is no evidence in our data that grants to more affluent students actually influence the likelihood that these students will graduate.

• *Although it is easy to understand an institution's wish to attract better students, the "cost" of using scarce grant aid dollars to pursue such a policy (which may or may not be effective if peer institutions match offers) can be too high. Reallocating some amount of money from merit-based aid to need-based awards could make a real difference.*

There is broader agreement on another proposition: that the complexity and uncertainty surrounding the financial aid process is itself a serious problem. There is a growing consensus (reflected, for example, in the "Rethinking Student Aid" study sponsored by the College Board and in statements made by the Obama administration) in favor of restructuring the provision of student aid.

• *Reliable, simple, and predictable provision of financial aid is important not just to initial access to college but to success in graduating.*

In this day of increasing transparency and greater accountability, it is surely desirable that most financial aid be delivered according to well-understood general policies and rules. However, financial aid programs, like programs of all kinds, can become too rigid and too bureaucratic. There is considerable anecdotal evidence that students from low-income families, in particular, are forced to leave college, perhaps never to return, because of unanticipated emergencies or family crises of one kind or another. One major advantage of coming from a family with the financial capacity simply to "write a check" is that such crises can usually be buffered and prevented from changing one's life course.

• *We are increasingly persuaded that providing key campus actors (presumably deans in most instances) with a meaningful amount of truly discretionary money that can be quickly deployed to relieve distress could make a real difference to completion rates and time-to-degree.*

We regret our inability to say more about the effects of loan programs of various kinds on completion rates. The data are hard to assemble and, when assembled, hard to interpret. In any case, it is clear that there is a continuing role for borrowing, and perhaps an increasingly important role for well-conceived contingent repayment loan programs. Here again, more evidence is needed, especially from careful analysis of loan aversion tendencies on the part of low-income students and their families. We agree that students in general, and low-income students in particular, should not be asked to assume such large debt obligations that their future is compromised. But it is equally clear that students can be too reluctant to borrow. Unwillingness to take on reasonable amounts of debt can itself exact a high "price" if the consequence is a longer and more tortuous path to a degree or no degree at all.

Finally, money matters in terms of the effects of economy-wide woes on state funding of both two-year and four-year public institutions. Anticipated budget cuts (in 2009) are causing many state systems to consider capping or even cutting enrollment. In addition, reductions in faculty can cause key courses to be closed, with obvious implications for time-to-degree and, in some cases, for the ability of students to complete degree programs. The perverse effects of cyclical funding on higher education are all too apparent—and unresolved.[8] In the fiscal environment of the United States in late 2008 and 2009, there has been much talk of providing fiscal stimulus by investing in the nation's "infrastructure" of roads, bridges, and the like. There is much to be said for viewing expenditures on education as investments in "human infrastructure" that may well be equally productive in the near term and arguably more durable than investments in bridges and tunnels.

INSTITUTIONAL SELECTIVITY AND GRADUATION RATES

One of the most relentlessly consistent findings in this study is the powerful association between graduation rates and institutional selectivity as measured by a combination of the test scores and high school grades of entering undergraduates. To be sure, more selective universities, by *definition, enroll students with stronger entering credentials who are more likely to graduate regardless of where they go to college.*

- *We find, however, that controlling for students' high school GPAs, SAT/ACT scores, and demographic characteristics fails to remove anything like all of the pronounced differences in graduation rates related to institutional selectivity. Substantial differences remain.*

These persistent differences are, we believe, driven principally by five broad sets of factors:

1. *Peer effects.* Students learn from each other. Being surrounded by highly capable classmates improves the learning environment and promotes good educational outcomes of all kinds, including timely graduation.

2. *Expectations.* The high overall graduation rates at the most selective public universities unquestionably create a climate in which graduating, and graduating with one's class, are compelling norms. Students feel real pressure to keep pace with their classmates.

3. *Access to excellent educational resources.* In the main, highly selective universities also have superior faculty and distinctly above-average library and laboratory resources. It seems reasonable to suppose that these factors improve learning environments for at least some highly talented undergraduates, who may succeed in identifying stimulating faculty mentors, take some graduate courses, and benefit from having exceptionally able graduate students as teaching assistants.

4. *Financial aid and student work opportunities.* In general, students at highly selective universities—especially those who are members of ethnic and racial minorities—are, as our data indicate, likely

to have access to more generous financial aid than other students. Also, research grants and contracts obtained by faculty members can provide attractive on-campus work opportunities, especially in the sciences and engineering, that foster engagement with the academic process and facilitate degree completion.

5. ***Unobservable selection effects.*** Finally, we suspect that there is some modest association between enrollment at the most selective flagship universities and unobservable characteristics of entering students, such as ambition and drive.

Universities that lack the established pulling power of a Berkeley, a Michigan, or a Chapel Hill cannot instantly and easily acquire their advantages. But they can strive to create "sub-environments" such as honors colleges and structured learning communities that can be used to set high expectations and create peer effects that reinforce these expectations. There is evidence in our data that honors colleges improve graduation rates, even after controlling for differences in student characteristics, but it should also be noted that honors colleges generally enroll disproportionate numbers of high-SES students and so may accentuate rather than diminish disparities in outcomes related to SES.

There has been debate for years over whether a heavy emphasis on cutting-edge research by faculty and on building top-ranked graduate programs helps or hurts undergraduate instruction. . . . Some undergraduates thrive in such settings, while at the same time others suffer from what can be impersonal, uncaring, and even intimidating environments. It is hard to generalize. But it is possible that the strong positive association between institutional selectivity and graduation rates reflects to some degree the impact of stimulating research environments at truly excellent universities.

Pressures to focus on research and to build up graduate programs may be every bit as strong, perhaps even stronger, at mid-level universities. The quest for excellence—and for prestige—is entirely understandable, but we suspect that, unless managed with great skill, it can have unintended consequences for undergraduate education. An example is the amount of support universities below the top tier often provide for less-than-outstanding graduate programs. Seeking to improve such programs, while obviously desirable, can siphon off resources that might be better invested, at least in some settings, in strengthening undergraduate education.

One fact stands out: flagship public universities as a group have become much more selective since the 1960s, as measured by the percentages of incoming students with A or A+ high school grades rather than Bs or Cs. . . . These universities face a difficult challenge in remaining true to their historical "access" missions while at the same time competing for faculty and students with ambitious and well-resourced universities in the private as well as public sector. Because selectivity per se is associated with higher graduation rates, there is no inevitable conflict between attracting larger and larger numbers of outstanding students and the desirability of graduating ever-higher fractions of entering undergraduate classes. But because undergraduate qualifications are so strongly correlated with family background, there can be a quite direct conflict with the desire to serve egalitarian ends by reducing disparities in outcomes.

• *This tension between "egalitarian" and "elitist" goals is an important reason for thinking carefully about how admissions criteria, transfer policies, and decisions about pricing and financial aid can be used to find the most appropriate balance.*

These are difficult issues, and each university and university system has to decide for itself, in conjunction with the state government that oversees it and provides support, what priority to give to different aspects of its mission and how to allocate resources that are often much too limited. A temptation to avoid is for all public universities to seek to "be Berkeley"; after all, there are many ways to excel, and many worthwhile missions to serve. We would not want all universities to look alike.

PROMOTING PERSISTENCE IN INDIVIDUAL INSTITUTIONS

There is no substitute, at the end of the day, for addressing completion rate and time-to-degree issues at the level of the individual institution. This approach requires a type of micro-analysis that is beyond the scope of this study, which focuses mainly on macro relationships. Our derailed data on semester-by-semester patterns of persistence across large numbers of institutions are, however, directly relevant to the question of how institutions should think about this set of issues.

• *In contrast to transfers, which are heavily concentrated in the first two years of college attendance, we find that withdrawals continue to occur, quite regularly, all along the path to graduation. There are modest "spikes" in withdrawals at the end of the second and fourth semesters, but nearly half of all withdrawals occur after the second year (Chapter 3). This finding is an important reminder that, although some "front-loading" of efforts to increase persistence makes good sense, it would be a big mistake to believe that addressing the "early-days" problems of students is all that is needed to improve graduation rates.*

The detailed data on the power of institutional effects . . . referenced in the previous section of this chapter contain an important insight relevant to efforts that individual institutions can make to improve outcomes. In fact, at given levels of selectivity there is considerable variation in adjusted graduation rates (adjusted to take account of differences among institutions in entering student characteristics and demographic factors); thus, it is possible to measure the extent to which some universities have done better at graduating students than have others that operate at the same level of institutional selectivity.

Careful examination of the characteristics of universities that do better or worse in this regard than their students' characteristics predict fails to reveal broad patterns related either to scale or to educational expenditures per student. But the data do indicate that residential patterns matter.

• *Other things more or less equal, "campus-like" institutions have somewhat higher graduation rates and shorter time-to-degree. Students who lived in a university residence hall during their first semester were more likely to graduate than were off-campus students after controlling for differences in entering credentials and background characteristics, including family income. There is also evidence of institution-wide effects. All students appear to benefit from attending an institution where more students live on campus.*

The implication cannot be that all universities need to become more residential, a proposition that makes no sense in many contexts (urban universities confront very different choice sets than do those in more rural settings) and would often be too costly. It would be totally unrealistic to expect public universities in general to create residential arrangements like those at a William and Mary or a Penn State. What may be more realistic, and what in fact many universities are already doing, is to provide surrogates for on-campus living experiences in, for example, university-owned apartments reasonably close to campus. For those students who do commute, it may be valuable to provide a safe, easy, and attractive environment on or around campus for their use between or after classes. The general point is simply that on-campus or near-campus living and learning options can increase the engagement of students with their university, which in turn should encourage higher graduation rates and shorter time-to-degree.

One frequently cited impediment to raising graduation rates for minority students and students from low-SES families is the discomfort such students often feel on campuses very different from anything they have experienced before. Such problems are compounded when there are very few students "like them" on their campus and in their classes. We have become intrigued by an approach to this problem pioneered by Deborah Bial through her national "Posse" program, which recruits inner-city students and sends them to colleges in "posses" so that they can support one another. We do not know whether such a cohort-based recruitment effort would prove to be workable and cost-effective if applied in more large-scale public university settings, but we think there is merit in experimenting with pilot programs.

Of course, there are innumerable interventions that have proved successful in particular college and university settings, and we will not repeat here the references provided earlier to summaries of "high-impact" approaches provided by the Association of American Colleges and Universities, the Lumina Foundation, and a number of scholars, including Vincent Tinto. One broader thesis persuasively advanced by Kevin Carey of Education Sector is that "just paying attention" can make a tremendous difference. That is, universities are beset fore and aft by pressures of all kinds, and it is easy to allow a concern for student completion rates to fall "between the cracks." Carey's point is simply that a top-down commitment demonstrated by deeds and not just bywords can galvanize efforts of many different kinds to keep students on track.

Also, we suspect that too little attention is paid to timely completion of programs. One recent graduate of a highly selective flagship university said that at his university graduating in four years was like "leaving the party at 10:30 p.m." In light of the costs to the system and the need for more student places at many flagship universities (in part to deal with the undermatch problem), it should not be made too easy for students simply to "hang around." Shining a bright light on the dropout problem, on the need to monitor time-to-degree, and on specific steps designed to allow students to complete their programs of study—such as careful organization of learning communities and relentless tracking of students with at-risk characteristics—can have a surprisingly large impact. There is much to be said for self-conscious efforts to inculcate the right "norms," including timely completion of degree programs.[9]

The "accountability" movement, which is here to stay, can stimulate efforts to monitor progress in, for example, raising graduation rates for subsets of students. It is noteworthy that groups of colleges and universities, such as the Association of Public and Land-Grant Universities, the American Association of State Colleges and Universities, and the National Association of Independent Colleges and Universities, have taken the initiative to create Web sites that make available data on outcomes of many kinds. And we find it even more encouraging that there is a growing interest at all levels of education in evidence-based research on results that matter. There is certainly much to learn—and much to accomplish.

NOTES

1. See the comments by Lamar Alexander, reported by Sara Hebel in "Colleges Urged to Take Action as They Prepare to Reap Billions in Stimulus Bill," *Chronicle of Higher Education,* February 10, 2009, online edition. California's lieutenant governor has proposed a fast-track medical school that would cut three years from the time needed to become a physician (Katherine Mangan, "New Medical School Programs Put Students on a Fast Track to the White Coat," *Chronicle of Higher Education,* February 6, 2009, online edition). David Leonhardt (2009) quotes a student at Shepherd University in West Virginia as saying, in discussing time to degree, "People don't push you" (p. 50). Leonhardt's article also describes the PROMISE (Providing Real Opportunities for Maximizing In-State Student Excellence) Scholarship Program in West Virginia.

2. Douglass and Thomson (2008).

3. See Marjorie M. Shultz and Sheldon Zedeck, "Final Report: Identification, Development, and Validation of Predictors for Successful Lawyering," University of California, Berkeley, September 2008, available at http://www.law.berkeley.edu/files/LSACREPORTfinal-12.pdf. See also the report of the inaugural conference of the University of Southern California's Center for Enrollment Research, Policy, and Practice, including the comments by Wayne J. Camara, vice-president for research and analysis at the

College Board, on the desirability of developing reliable measures of non-cognitive traits (Eric Hoover, "Admissions Experts Call for Broader Definition of College Readiness." *Chronicle of Higher Education,* August 6, 2008, online edition). We think it is encouraging that the College Board, long strongly identified with the standard SAT test, is actively working to promote greater use of Advanced Placement tests, as well as to develop reliable tests of non-cognitive skills. ACT has for many years put considerable focus on tests of "college readiness" and also on tests designed to measure workplace-related skills (see the ACT Web page).

4. See Helene Ragovin, "Amplified Application Will Provide Additional Cues about Prospective Students," *Tufts Journal,* May 2006, online edition, available at http://tuftsjournal.tufts.edu/archive/2006/may/features/index.shtml, accessed November 22, 2008.

5. Roderick et al. (2008, p. 24) and Roderick et al. (2009, figure 16, p. 53).

6. The Jack Kent Cooke Foundation's Undergraduate Transfer Scholarship Program addresses this question directly. Available at. http://www.jkcf.org/scholarships/undergraduate-transfer-scholarships/.

7. See Bowen, Kurzweil, and Tobin (2005), especially chapter 4 and pp. 119–120.

8. For a good discussion of this entire set of issues, see Katherine Mangan, "Their Budgets Slashed, Public Colleges Share in Their Applicants' Economic Pain," *Chronicle of Higher Education,* November 19, 2008, online edition. Norma G. Kent, vice-president for communications at the American Association of Community Colleges, put it this way: "Turning away students is something of an anathema, but if your budgets are being cut and you don't have enough faculty or classes, it's a de facto closed door." According to this account: "For the first time in its history, California State University plans to cut systemwide enrollment by 10,000 students if the state doesn't provide more money" (see Katherine Mangan, "Rising Enrollments Buoy Some Colleges, Burden Others," *Chronicle of Higher Education,* November 28, 2008, online edition).

9. For a case study of the Amherst College experience with these issues, see Elizabeth Aries, *Race and Class Matters at an Elite College* (Philadelphia: Temple University Press, 2008). David Leonhardt (2009) cites Peter Orszag, now director of the Office of Management and Budget in Washington, as arguing that his fellow economists have made a mistake in paying so little attention to cultural norms (in the health care field, for example) and overemphasizing market signals divorced from norms (p. 50). Education is full of examples of this tendency. Assumptions and expectations matter greatly.

REFERENCES

Bowen, W. G., Kurzweil, M. A., & Tobin, E. M. (2005). *Equity and excellence in American higher education.* Charlottesville, VA: University of Virginia Press.

Douglass, J. A., & Thomson, G. (2008). *The poor and the rich: A look at economic stratification and academic performance among undergraduate students in the United States* (Research and Occasional Paper: Series CSHE.15.08). Center for Studies in Higher Education, University of California-Berkeley.

Goldin, C., & Katz, L. F. (2008). *The race between education and technology.* Cambridge, MA: Belknap Press of Harvard University Press.

Leonhardt, D. (2009, February 1). The big fix. *New York Times Magazine.* Retrieved from http://www.nytimes.com/2009/02/01/magazine/01Economy-t.html

Roderick, M., Nagaoka, J., Coca, V., & Moeller, E. (2009). *From high school to the future: Making hard work pay off.* Chicago: Consortium on Chicago School Research.

Roderick, M., Nagaoka, J., Coca, V., Moeller, E., Roddie, K., Gilliam, J., & Patton, D. (2008). *From high school to the future: Potholes on the road to college.* Chicago: Consortium on Chicago School Research.

Tobin, E. M. (2009). The modern evolution of America's flagship universities. In W. G. Bowen, M. M. Chingos, & M. S. McPherson, *Crossing the finish line: Completing college at America's public universities* (Appendix A, pp. 239–264). Princeton, NJ: Princeton University Press.

No Margin for Error

Educational and Occupational Achievement Among Disadvantaged Children of Immigrants

Alejandro Portes and Patricia Fernández-Kelly

This reading by Alejandro Portes and Patricia Fernández-Kelly provides a deep look into the background conditions of immigrant children that facilitate achievement in higher education. From their sample of 5,262 immigrant children who grew up in very disadvantaged conditions, they identified 50 individuals who went on to achieve a college degree or degrees. While this is a small percentage (less than 1%) of their original sample, they argue that understanding what factors influenced these individuals to achieve is important. In this reading, they use what they call the segmented assimilation theory to examine what features of four individuals' lives may have taken them on a different trajectory. They focus on three major factors: (1) human capital in the form of skills and education that their families brought with them from their home countries; (2) how they and their families are incorporated into their new culture by the government, society, and the community; and (3) the structure of their immigrant families.

Questions to consider for this reading:

1. How does having human capital help individuals to achieve higher levels of education? Do you think this could be true for nonimmigrants as well?

2. What do they mean by "modes of incorporation"? Give examples from the reading.

3. If you were a policy maker or person in a powerful role in your community, what changes would you make to ensure the successful college completion of disadvantaged youth?

Immigration since the 1960s has transformed the United States. Today, close to one-fourth of the American population is of immigrant stock—immigrants themselves or children of immigrants. The same rough proportion holds among young Americans, aged 18 or younger. Children of immigrants and immigrant children exceed 30 million and are, by far, the fastest growing component of this population. Hence, their destiny as they reach adulthood and seek to integrate socially and economically into the mainstream is of more than academic interest.

Past research into this bourgeoning population has shown that a conventional assimilation model based on a unilinear process of acculturation followed by social and economic ascent and integration does not work well in depicting what takes place on the ground. Instead, several distinct paths of adaptation have been identified, some of which lead upwards as portrayed by the conventional assimilation model; other paths, however, lead in the opposite direction, compounding the spectacle of poverty, drugs, and gangs in the nation's cities. *Segmented assimilation* is the concept coined to refer to these realities. This alternative model has both charted the main alternative path of contemporary second generation adaptation and identified the main forces at play in that process ([Portes & Rumbaut, 2006]; Portes & Zhou, 1992; Zhou & Bankston, 1998).

Specifically, three major factors have been identified: the human capital that immigrant parents bring with them, the social context in which they are received in America, and the composition of the immigrant family. Human capital, operationally identified with formal education and occupational skills, translates into competitiveness in the host labor market and the potential for achieving desirable positions in the American hierarchies of status and wealth. The transformation of this potential into reality depends, however, on the context into which immigrants are incorporated. A receptive or at least neutral reception by government authorities, a sympathetic or at least not hostile reception by the native population, and the existence of social networks with well-established coethnics pave the ground for putting to use whatever credentials and skills have been brought from abroad. Conversely, a hostile reception by authorities and the public and a weak or nonexistent coethnic community handicap immigrants and make it difficult for them to translate their human capital into commensurate occupations or to acquire new occupational skills. The mode of incorporation is the concept used in the literature to refer to these tripartite (government/society/community) differences in the contexts that receive newcomers ([Hirschman, 2001]; Portes & Rumbaut, 2001, chap. 3).

Lastly, the structure of the immigrant family has also proved to be highly significant in determining second generation outcomes. Parents who stay together and extended families where grandparents and older siblings play a role in motivating and controlling adolescents, keeping them away from the lure of gangs and drugs, play a significant role in promoting upward assimilation. Single-parent families experiencing conflicting demands and unable to provide children with proper supervision have exactly the opposite effect (Fernández-Kelly & Konczal, 2005; [Portes, Fernández-Kelly, & Haller, 2005]). . . .

RESEARCH QUESTIONS

Sociology deals with social facts, expressed in rates or averages, rather than with individuals. There are times, however, when the study of individual cases can say something important about how social outcomes come to be or how they can be modified. Segmented assimilation in the second generation offers a case in point. The structural forces leading to alternative paths of adaptation are clear and have been well documented. Yet, not all children advantaged by their parents' human capital, favorable contexts of reception, and stable families manage to succeed educationally, and not all growing up under conditions of severe disadvantage end up in permanent poverty or in jail. Some among the latter even make it to the top, achieving a college degree and moving into the professions. Those individual cases have sociological significance for the lessons they offer in how to overcome the power of structural forces. Put differently, exceptions and outliers are important insofar as they point to alternative social processes obscured in sample averages that, when present, can lead to unforeseen outcomes.[1] . . .

First Narrative:
Miguel Morales, Mexican,
Aged Twenty-Eight, San Diego

Miguel was born and grew up in Inglewood, a working-class neighborhood close to South Central Los Angeles.[2] His mother has a seventh-grade education and never worked after marriage. His father has a fourth-grade education and, for most of his adult life, has worked as a food preparer in the kitchen of the Los Angeles Airport Hyatt Hotel. Miguel has a B.S. with honors in physics from the University of California, San Diego (UCSD), and a master's in physics from San Diego State University. He will soon join a PhD program in computational science at Claremont. His strength is math. He works as a high school and junior college instructor in math and physics.

Miguel's parents were born in rural Mexico, met and married in Tijuana, and managed to obtain legal U.S. residence through family ties. In Inglewood, Miguel grew up in a sheltered, Spanish-only community. Although born in the United States, he did not speak English when entering elementary school and suffered accordingly. On the other hand, his father was so committed to his son's education that he spent a third of his meager salary on tuition so that Miguel could attend a Catholic grammar school. The child eventually overcame his language deficit and started to get good grades.

Not only was Inglewood a Mexican cultural enclave, but the parents did not tolerate anything that escaped their reach. No sleepovers, no strange friends. Miguel Sr. took his sons everywhere he went. When Miguel rebelled in early adolescence, wanting to wear baggy clothes, he had a serious encounter with his dad's belt. Later on, at age eighteen, he tried to sneak out of the house through a window to attend a party, only to be physically dragged back into the house by his father.

This kind of isolation and discipline focused Miguel's attention on his studies but also left him woefully unprepared to cope with the world outside. He successfully completed his studies at St. Joseph's School and transferred to Stanley Junior High. The confrontation with the multiethnic environment of a public school and the embarrassment of having to take showers naked in front of others in the gym proved too much for the Mexican Catholic boy. He begged his father to pull him out. Miguel Sr. agreed. He sold his van, his only possession of value outside of the house, so that his son could attend South Port Christian Academy in National City.

By then, the family had moved to San Diego to be closer to relatives on the other side of the border. After completing junior high, Miguel moved to Point Loma High School, close to La Jolla, a school frequented mostly by children of affluent white families. He was the only Mexican taking advanced courses at Point Loma, and he succeeded in graduating with As and Bs. Through AVID (Achievement via Individual Determination), a program designed to facilitate admittance to college for poor minority students, he gained access to several summer internships doing research in biochemistry at the University of California, San Diego (UCSD), under a faculty member. That was the single most important experience of his high school days and oriented him decisively toward medical school.

After high school, he was admitted to UCSD, sponsored, among others, by Percy Russell, dean of UCSD's Medical School. An African American, Russell was an active supporter of AVID and organized the summer internship program in which Miguel took part. At UCSD, Miguel accumulated a 3.7 GPA in the sciences and an overall 3.5 GPA, graduating with honors. In his junior year, he shifted his major to physics. Before leaving UCSD, Miguel became an AVID tutor teaching other minority students in nearby high schools.

After receiving his B.S., Miguel went straight for his master's at San Diego State. As a high school and junior college physics instructor, he earns $67,000 a year. Despite his high income, he is determined to join a doctoral program in computational sciences in the fall. He lives on his own, but several times a week he visits his parents' home, where the interview was conducted, with Miguel Sr. arriving just as the conversation was about to end. Having told his life history, our respondent turned toward his father and told him, "*Gracias, Papa, porque me disciplinaste; me enseñaste bien.*" ("Thanks, Dad, because you disciplined me; you educated me well.")

STERN FAMILIES; SELECTIVE ACCULTURATION

The childrearing and educational psychology literatures in the United States have converged in preaching to parents a tolerant, patient, nonauthoritative attitude toward their offspring and in promoting openness to new experiences and intensive socializing among the young.[3] In parallel fashion, schools and other mainstream institutions pressure immigrants and their children to acculturate as fast as possible, viewing their full Americanization as a step toward economic mobility and social acceptance.

A recurring theme in our interviews was the presence of stern parental figures who controlled, if not suppressed, extensive external contacts and who sought to preserve the cultural and linguistic traditions in which they themselves were reared. Talking back to such parents is not an option, and physical punishment is a distinct possibility when parental authority is challenged. These family environments have the effect of isolating children from much of what goes on in the outside world; they are expected to go to school and return home with few distractions in between. While such rearing practices will be surely frowned upon by many educational psychologists, they have the effect of protecting children from the perils of street life in their immediate surroundings and of keeping them in touch with their cultural roots.

In other words, while freedom to explore and tolerant parental attitudes may work well in protected suburban environments, they do not have the same effect in poor urban neighborhoods where what there is to "explore" is frequently linked to the presence of gangs and drugs. Furthermore, and contrary to conventional wisdom, full Americanization has the effect of disconnecting youth from their parents and depriving them of a cultural reference point on which to ground their sense of self and their personal dignity. As we shall see, this reference point is also an important component of success stories.

Maintenance of parental authority and strong family discipline has the effect of inducing *selective acculturation*, as opposed to the full-barreled variety advocated by public schools and other mainstream institutions. Selective acculturation combines learning of English and American ways with preservation of key elements of the parental culture, including language. Previous studies based on CILS show that fluent bilingualism is significantly associated with positive outcomes in late adolescence, including higher school grades, higher educational aspirations, higher self-esteem, and lesser intergenerational conflict (Portes & Rumbaut, 2001, chaps. 6, 9; Portes & Rumbaut, 2006, chap. 8). CILS-IV interviews confirm this result, indicating that instances of success-out-of-disadvantage are almost invariably undergirded by strong parental controls, which leads to selective acculturation. By early adulthood, young people like Miguel Morales can recognize the benefits of such practices and thank their parents, in their parents' own language, for having educated them well.

Second Narrative: Raquel Torres, Mexican, Aged Twenty-Nine, San Diego

Raquel is the oldest daughter of a Mexican couple that emigrated illegally to San Diego after living for years in Tijuana. Her mother has a ninth-grade education and did not work outside the home while her three children were growing up; her father has a sixth-grade education. While living in Tijuana, he commuted to San Diego to work as a waiter. At some point, his commuter permit was confiscated and the family decided to sneak across the border. They settled in National City, a poor and mostly Mexican neighborhood where Raquel grew up monolingual in Spanish. As a result of her limited English fluency, she had problems at El Toyon Elementary, but she was enrolled in a bilingual training program where children were pulled out of classes for intensive English training. "My teachers were wonderful," she says.

It was while attending elementary school that she realized how poor her family was. She wanted jeans, tennis shoes, and popular toys that she saw other children have, but her parents said no, stating that they did not have the money. On the other hand, discipline at home was stern: "My parents, they brought us up very strict, very traditional, there was no argument; you just got the look and knew better than to insist." In middle school, she made contact with the AVID program. While she was still struggling with English, AVID provided her with a college student tutor and took her on field trips to San Diego State University: "It was a fabulous field trip; we were paired up with other students and sat in class. Mine was on biology. Still, I hadn't thought of going to college."

The decisive moment came in her first year at Sweetwater Senior High in National City after she enrolled in Mr. Carranza's French class. Carranza, a Mexican American himself and a Vietnam veteran, took a keen interest in his students: "I mean, it wasn't so much the French that he taught, but he would also bring Chicano poetry, and within the first month, I remember he asked me, 'Where are you going to college?'" At Open House that year, Carranza took her mother aside, "Usted sabe que su hija es muy inteligente?" (Do you know that your daughter is very intelligent?) "De veras, mi hija?" (Really, my daughter?), asked the mother. "Yes," the teacher replied, "she can go to college." "All of a sudden, everything made sense to me; I was going to college."

Raquel graduated with a 3.5 GPA from Sweetwater and applied and was admitted at UCSD. At the time, her family had moved to Las Vegas in search of better work, but Raquel wanted to be on her own. She had clearly outgrown parents who, at this time, had started to become an obstacle. "When I was studying late at night in senior high, my mother would come and turn off the light. She would say, 'Go to sleep, you'll go blind reading so much.'" Raquel entered UCSD in the last year of the Affirmative Action Program in California. While she was criticized by several fellow students for getting an unfair advantage, she strongly defended the program: "Without Affirmative Action, I probably would not have made it into UCSD. Besides, the program made me work harder. Other students took their education for granted and didn't study as much, instead going to parties and fooling around."

Raquel graduated from UCSD with a 3.02 GPA and immediately went for a master's degree in education at San Diego State. After graduating, she took a job as a counselor in the Barrio Logan College Institute, a private organization helping minority students like herself attend college. She is planning to enroll in a doctoral program in education. Her advice to immigrant students: "Stop making excuses; there's always going to be family drama, there's always gonna be many issues. But it's what you want to do that matters."

REALLY SIGNIFICANT OTHERS; OUTSIDE HELP

Despite these "where there's a will, there's a way" parting words, it is clear that Raquel moved ahead by receiving assistance in multiple ways. First, the same strict upbringing that we saw in the case of Miguel Morales kept her out of trouble, although it set her back in English. Her own selective acculturation had to be nudged along by those "wonderful" language teachers at El Toyon Elementary. Then, like Morales, she encountered the AVID program, which provided her with personalized educational assistance and the first inklings of what college life would be like. Finally, she encountered Carranza and her future took a decisive turn. The French teacher went beyond motivating her to recruiting her mother to support Raquel's new aspirations. Stern immigrant parents may instill discipline and self-control in their children, but they are often helpless in the face of school bureaucracies and can even become an obstacle.

A constant in our interviews, in addition to authoritative, alert parents, is the appearance of a *really* significant other. That person can be a teacher, a counselor, a friend of the family, or even an older sibling. The important thing is that they take a keen interest in the child, motivate him or her to graduate from high school and to attend college, and possess the necessary knowledge and experience to guide the student in the right direction. Neither family discipline nor the appearance of a significant other is by itself sufficient to produce high educational attainment, but their *combination* is decisive.

The second element that Raquel's story illustrates is the important role of organized programs sponsored by nonprofits to assist disadvantaged students. Whether it is AVID; the PREUSS Program, also organized by UCSD; Latinas Unidas; the Barrio Logan College Institute; or other philanthropic groups, such organizations can play a key supplementary role by conveying information that parents do not possess: how to fill out a college application, how to prepare for SATs and when to take them, how to present oneself in interviews, how college campuses look and what college life is like, and so on. The creation and support of such programs is within the power of external actors and can be strengthened by policy. While the character of family life or the emergence of a significant other is largely in the private realm, the presence and effectiveness of special assistance programs for minority students is a public matter, amenable to policy intervention. The programs and organizations that proved effective were grounded, invariably, in knowledge of the culture and language that the children brought to school and in respect for them. They are commonly staffed by coethnics or bilingual staff.

Unlike the full assimilation approach emphasized by public school personnel, these programs convey the message that it is not necessary to reject one's own culture and history to do well in school. On the contrary, such roots can provide the necessary point of reference to strengthen the children's self-esteem and aspirations for the future. In this sense, programs like AVID both depend on and promote selective acculturation as the best path toward educational achievement.

Third Narrative:
Martin Lacayo, Nicaraguan,
Aged Twenty-Nine, Miami

Martin's mother, Violeta, was a businesswoman in her native Nicaragua until the Sandinista regime confiscated her properties. His father was a professional and, for a time, mayor of the city of Jinotega. The Sandinistas jailed him as a counterrevolutionary, and he left prison a broken man. When Violeta made the decision to leave the country to escape the conscription of her sons in the Sandinista army, Martin's father refused to leave. Violeta managed to send her two oldest sons to Miami to the care of relatives. She then used her savings to buy tickets to Mexico City for Martin, her younger daughter, and herself. They then traveled by land to the border and crossed illegally with the help of two *coyotes* (smugglers).

Arriving in Miami, they found themselves without money, without knowledge of the language, and without access to government help because of their illegal status. To survive, Violeta started cleaning houses for wealthy Cuban families. She rented an apartment in the modest suburb of Sweetwater, and Martin enrolled in the local junior high school. Having studied at the private Catholic La Salle School in Jinotega, he found the *One Potato, Two Potato* book he was assigned to read offensive. "It seemed that the teacher wanted us all to go work at the Burger King," Martin said.

At Sweetwater Junior High, he finally came under the protection of Mrs. Robinson, an African American teacher who took an interest in the boy. She managed to have him receive a "Student of the Week" award, and his picture was displayed prominently in the school's office. That meant the world to Martin, who had never received any distinction in the United States. Eventually, the family regularized its legal status under the NACARA law, engineered by Miami Cuban American congressmen for the benefit of Nicaraguan refugees. Violeta found a job as a janitor at Florida International University and combined it with her private maid service. The family's economic situation improved, although Violeta never rose above the status of a janitor and her husband never rejoined her.

Martin venerates his mother for the strength and decisiveness that she displayed in those difficult years and for her unwavering support of her children. After the family moved to a better part of town, he attended Ruben Darío Senior High School where he excelled, graduating with honors and immediately enrolling at the University of Miami. There, he completed a bachelor's degree in economics and accounting. He currently works as an accountant for Merrill Lynch and has just bought a luxury condominium in Miami Beach.

THE IMPORTANCE OF CULTURAL CAPITAL

Aside from the elements already noted, the most important feature illustrated by Martin Lacayo's story is the transferability of social class assets and their use in overcoming extremely trying conditions. The son of separated parents, with a cleaning woman as a mother, and living as an illegal migrant, Martin still managed to avoid the lures of gangs and street life, stayed in school, graduated from high school, and then swiftly completed his college education.

The La Salle School that he attended as a young child and the memory of the middle-class life that he and his brother enjoyed before escaping to Miami provided key points of reference as he confronted poverty and the prospect of going no further than a fast-food job. He knew the meaning of the dull books put in the hands of limited-English students in public school and set his sights on escaping that environment. His mother not only supported him in that goal but also never allowed him to forget his family's origins. She could be a cleaning woman in Miami, but she remained, despite appearances, an educated, middle-class person.

A recurrent theme in our interviews is the importance of a respectable past, real or imaginary, in the country of origin. Parents repeat stories of who they or their ancestors "really were" as a way to sustain their dignity despite present circumstances. Children exposed to such family stories often internalize them, using them as a spur to achievement. We heard references to uncles and grandparents who were "doctors" or "professors" in Mexico, to ancestors who were "landowners in California and put down an Indian rebellion," and to parents who were high government officials before having to leave to escape political persecution.

The "cultural capital" (Bourdieu, 1979, 1985) brought from the home country has actually two components. The first is the motivational force to restore family pride and status. Regardless of whether the achievements of the past are real or imaginary, they can still serve as a means to instill high aspirations among the young. The second is the "know-how" that immigrants who come from the upper or middle classes possess. This know-how consists of information, values, and demeanor that migrants from more modest origins do not have. Regardless of how difficult present circumstances are, formerly middle-class parents have a clear sense of who they are, knowledge of the possible means to overcome difficult situations, and the right attitude when opportunities arise. These two dimensions of cultural capital converge in cases like Martin Lacayo's where both family lore and the *habitus* of past middle-class life are decisive in helping second-generation youth overcome seemingly insurmountable obstacles. . . .

Fourth Narrative: Ovidio Cardenas, PhD; Cuban, Aged Twenty-Eight, Stanford, California

Ovidio Cardenas's family came from Cuba during the chaotic Mariel exodus of 1980 and settled in Union City, New Jersey. He was a young child then and barely remembers life in Cuba. His mother promptly separated from her wayward husband and eventually moved to Florida, settling with her son in the working-class city of Hialeah, next to Miami. With a grade-level education, she could not go far and eventually settled for a job as a seamstress in a local factory. She eventually remarried another Cuban man who worked as a janitor.

Ovidio attended public schools in Hialeah, some of the worst in Miami. Gang fights, the open sale of drugs, and a prison-like environment at school were everyday experiences. "Most students were lazy. I was different because my mom and stepdad drilled into me the idea that I should not end up like them." The parents worked long hours, often at two jobs. The stepfather was a strict, traditional Cuban man who spoke little but strongly supported Ovidio in his studies. At Hialeah High, an English teacher, a white American woman, also made a deep impression on the young man. She conveyed to him the fact that "Hialeah was not the world" and eventually took time to work with him on his college applications and personal statement.

Ovidio focused on the sciences, especially biology, and graduated with a near-perfect GPA. He was one of the few among his graduating class at Hialeah High to go on to college and the only one to gain admission to an Ivy League institution. He was seriously depressed during his first days at Cornell. Hialeah may not have been the world, but it was the only world that he knew. He felt himself torn from his roots and certain that he would fail. He even attempted suicide on one occasion. After that event, somehow Ovidio pulled himself together and focused on his work. "All I did was study, morning, afternoon, and night. No sports, little recreation." After four years, he graduated from Cornell with a major in biology with honors and was admitted to Johns Hopkins Medical School. Originally, motivated by the suffering of his grandmother who died of cancer, he wanted to be a doctor. Eventually, however, he shifted to the biological sciences and, after completing his dissertation research, received his PhD in cellular and molecular biology. He is currently a postdoctoral fellow at Stanford Medical School.

Ovidio's career aspiration is to pursue research on leukemia at a private lab and eventually make a contribution to eradicate that disease. He also wants to help "Hispanics" (meaning young Hialeah Cubans) improve their education and their careers, but he does not know quite how. A devout Catholic, he makes sizable donations to the church. He is single, but he lives with a partner, also a PhD student.

Ovidio's advice to young Hispanics: "Stay focused; education is everything." He does not agree, however, that in life you get what you deserve: "There is too much variation in the situations surrounding people; some good people face dire problems and many who don't deserve success prosper." Another of his projects is to complete his family tree through genealogical research on his ancestors in Cuba. His mother never tired of telling him that his family had deep roots and that her ancestors had been among the founders of the city of Cardenas, which was named after them.

THE MOTIVATING FEAR OF FAILURE

The story of Ovidio Cardenas is included here for several reasons. First, he is arguably the most successful member of our disadvantage-to-achievement sample, having reached the doctorate and attained a substantial income before age thirty. Second, his case summarizes all the themes explored previously: traditional authoritative parenting, a really significant other encountered in adolescence, and a cultural memory from the home country on which to base his self-esteem and reinforce ambition. While Ovidio has never been back to Cuba, his sense of self is inextricably linked to the hometown that he barely remembers from his early childhood. He plans to return to the ancestral land to complete the family tree to establish firmly who his ancestors were.

The new dimension illustrated by this story is a final theme common to many respondents: fear of remaining in the same class position as parents. Along with stern discipline, immigrant parents often dispense the advice that education is the only way to rise above the menial jobs, long hours, and modest housing that has been their own fate—a message that youth absorb. While it can lead to downward assimilation among those dropping out of school and seeking alternatives to poverty in deviant activities, a more common result is to spur youngsters to higher achievement. Theirs is a *defensive success* that owes as much to personal ability as to rejection of their present status.

Thus, if memories of a real or imagined exalted past in the home country lead *proactively* to higher ambition and effort, fear of stagnating into the lower classes strengthens resolve *reactively*. Both mechanisms are privy to the internal dynamics of immigrant families and, hence, less amenable to external intervention than others noted previously. . . .

CONCLUSION

While our interviews raised additional themes showing the complexity and diversity of individual adaptation paths, the cases highlighted above represent common threads running through the lives of successful young men and women who faced daunting obstacles as children. Given the smallness of the sample and the retroactive character of our interviews, the causal factors identified by the study can be read as hypotheses in need of further validation.

As noted earlier, several of the factors identified are internal to immigrant families and, hence, not readily amenable to external intervention. The presence of authoritative parents capable of controlling children and protecting them from outside perils; the existence of family retrospectives and middle-class cultural capital brought from the home country; the motivational messages that parents transmit to children; and the number, order, and gender of siblings are all dimensions about which little can be done from the outside.

On the other hand, organized voluntary programs to assist and inform minority students in inner-city schools, the presence of teachers and counselors who take a direct interest in these children and drive them to pursue their studies, and the availability of community colleges that provide skills for decent employment and serve as stepping stones to four-year institutions are all factors that can be strengthened by policy, including incentive schedules for school personnel and financial support for effective outside programs.

Finally, even with the best-intentioned policies and the most effective interventions in place, not all immigrant children who grew up in conditions of severe disadvantage will make it to college. Even fewer will repeat Ovidio Cardenas's feat of converting a Hialeah High education into an entrance ramp for an Ivy League degree. In addition to helping other exceptional students follow the path of these high achievers, it is necessary to understand and address the needs of others not so motivated and not so gifted. A good vocational education, such as that dispensed by many community colleges, is probably the most feasible path for immigrant youths who may manage to avoid downward assimilation but who lack the skills or drive for a university degree. We suspect that the average educational achievement registered by the CILS sample in our last survey—fourteen years—is indicative that this path has been the one followed by a large number of immigrant children.

NOTES

1. This is a clear case of "sampling on the dependent variable," a research strategy adopted deliberately in this case. Results of this exercise cannot be used to "test" particular propositions but can be valuable in suggesting patterns and relationships testable in future studies.

2. Most of the names of persons in this article are fictitious.

3. The educational and social psychological literatures on this point are too extensive to cite. They start with followers of various brands of psychoanalysis, such as Bettelheim, Fromm, Erikson, and Redl and Wineman, and culminate in a veritable library of practical, how-to books addressed to parents. See Bettelheim (1955), Erikson (1959), Fromm (1945), and Redl and Wineman (1951). For an example of a recent practical guide, see P. Portes (1995).

REFERENCES

Bettelheim, B. (1955). *Paul and Mary: Two case studies of truants from life*. Garden City, NY: Anchor Books.

Bourdieu, P. (1979). Les trois etats du capital culturel. *Actes de la Recherche en Sciences Sociales, 30* (novembre), 3–6.

Bourdieu, P. (1985). The forms of capital. In J. G. Richardson (Ed.), *Handbook of theory and research for the sociology of education* (pp. 241–258). New York: Greenwood.

Erikson, E. (1959). *Childhood and society*. New York: Free Press.

Fernández-Kelly, P., & Konczal, L. (2005). "Murdering the alphabet": Identity and entrepreneurship among second generation Cubans, West Indians, and Central Americans. *Ethnic and Racial Studies, 28*(6), 1153–1181.

Fromm, E. (1945). *Escape from freedom*. New York: Free Press.

Hirschman, C. (2001). The educational enrollment of immigrant youth: A test of the segmented assimilation hypothesis. *Demography, 38*(3), 317–336.

Portes, A., Fernández-Kelly, P., & Haller, P. (2005). Segmented assimilation on the ground: The new second generation in early adulthood. *Ethnic and Racial Studies, 28*(6), 1000–1040.

Portes, A., & Rumbaut, R. G. (2001). *Legacies: The story of the immigrant second generation*. Berkeley: University of California Press and Russell Sage Foundation.

Portes, A., & Rumbaut, R. G. (2006). *Immigrant America: A portrait* (3rd ed.). Berkeley: University of California Press.

Portes, A., & Zhou, M. (1992). Gaining the upper hand: Economic mobility among immigrant and domestic minorities. *Ethnic and Racial Studies, 15*(4), 491–522.

Portes, P. (1995). *Making kids smarter*. Louisville, KY: Butler Books.

Redl, F., & Wineman, D. (1951). *Children who hate*. New York: Free Press.

Zhou, M., & Bankston, C. (1998). *Growing up American: How Vietnamese immigrants adapt to life in the United States*. New York: Russell Sage Foundation.

Bologna Beyond 2010

Looking Backward, Looking Forward

Fiona Hunter

This reading by Fiona Hunter provides a brief look into the changes in higher education that are being made across European countries. The Bologna Process, begun in 1999, has barely gotten off the ground. However, member countries are cooperating in accepting degrees and higher education credits from other member countries and applying strict standards and assessment criteria to build a solid system of higher education across Europe. The Bologna Process likely will have an impact on higher education around the world. This reading reviews some of the changes that have already been implemented and some changes yet to come. In addition, we include a list of websites from this article for future exploration of the topic.

Questions to consider for this reading:

1. What is the Bologna Process and what are the advantages to European countries who participate in the process?

2. What are the advantages to individuals who attend college under this system?

3. How will the Bologna Process impact higher education in other countries?

A couple of years ago, I was discussing the Bologna Process and what it would be like in 2010, "when we would all wake up one cold January morning and discover life in the brand new European Higher Education Area (EHEA)." That morning has arrived (and it is cold) and since the word January comes from Janus, the two-headed Roman god of beginnings and endings, it seems an appropriate moment to look back to what has been achieved and look forward to what still lies ahead.

A Quick Reminder

Let's remind ourselves quickly about how the Bologna Process came about in 1999 when higher education systems all over Europe were struggling to modernize in response to a changing environment. Shared problems called for shared solutions, and the Bologna Process developed into an unprecedented landmark reform with 10 action lines and a 2010 deadline to restructure and harmonize historically diverse systems. The

29 signatory countries became 46, representing 5,600 institutions and 31 million students.

The main goal of the Bologna Process is to establish the European Higher Education Area (EHEA) and to promote the European system of higher education worldwide through tools that enhance the employability and mobility of people and boost global attractiveness. While it was undoubtedly inspired by the Erasmus experience[1] of interuniversity cooperation, it also introduced the idea of competition in the very early stages, a reality that still sits uncomfortably in many university environments.

GLOBAL BOLOGNA

While the principal focus in the beginning was on the internal dimension and putting the European house in order, the Bologna Process has very quickly acquired an important external dimension as other countries across the world have taken a strong interest in the European response. International competitiveness is now accompanied by international dialogue and connections to other world regions.

The Bologna Process has given an identity to European higher education, although that identity may not yet be completely formed or understood, and to that end, a new information and promotion strategy is currently being developed to communicate Bologna outside the EHEA both for the purposes of cooperation and competition.

The growing interest in Bologna worldwide has also led to the creation of a global policy dialogue that took place back to back with the 2009 ministerial meeting in Leuven/Louvain-La-Neuve in Belgium. It included 15 countries from all over the world that gathered to discuss the effects of Bologna in their countries as well as the broader role and identity of higher education in the new environment: Australia, Brazil, Canada, China, Egypt, Ethiopia, Israel, Japan, Kazakhstan, Kyrgyzstan, Mexico, Morocco, New Zealand, Tunisia, and the United States. The dialogue will continue. . . .

In many ways, the Bologna Process is offering new instruments and models for other world regions seeking collaborative agreements and solutions. If Erasmus has been hailed as the most successful European initiative ever, the Bologna Process has achieved in 10 years what many national governments failed to achieve in decades, a policy for reform and a framework of reference, that is now not only transforming European higher education but is having tangible impacts beyond its own borders.

The domino effect of reform in the different countries has been activated by the mechanisms of this voluntary intergovernmental agreement. The reform process is driven by the different stakeholder groups and structured via communiques announced at biannual ministerial meetings where results of the previous period are evaluated and priorities for the next two years set. The priorities are transformed into national reform and implemented by the institutions but it is essential to remember that this happens in different ways and at different speeds in each of the signatory countries and individual institutions will interpret and implement the reform according to their capacity and ambition. As has been said many times before, it is a process of harmonization not homogenization.

MASSIVE CHANGES

There can be no doubt that there have been massive changes and the most important to date has been structural reform. European higher education has converged into three cycles—bachelor's, master's, and doctoral degrees—but with diversification in length of study. Bachelor's degrees last between three and four years, master's between one and two years, and doctoral studies between three and four years.

The European Credit Transfer System (ECTS) has not only been adopted as the standard but has since been linked to learning outcomes, which have been collaboratively developed to create a common language and frame of reference at the level of both cycles and disciplines. Learning outcomes do not sound particularly exciting or powerful, but they have the potential to revolutionize the way in which universities organize educational delivery as well as bring greater transparency, recognition and flexibility across the Bologna agenda. They transform approaches to curricular design and assessment, provide building blocks for qualifications frameworks and transmit valuable information to employers or professional bodies. They act as a tool for greater integration across the sectors in lifelong learning and make an important contribution to mobility both for study and employment purposes. Credits and learning outcomes are key tools for the development of student-centered learning, which has the potential to revolutionize the way in which universities organize educational delivery.

The Diploma Supplement, a standard template to describe qualifications, is increasingly being issued along with the final qualification and progress is being made in all countries to develop a qualifications framework that describes national qualifications according to a commonly defined set of descriptors and these will be inserted into an overarching European framework, connecting the different national education systems.

The last 10 years have seen a convergence of degree structures, credit frameworks, learning outcomes, and descriptors, but there has never been the objective of standardised qualifications. As has been often repeated, there is no single Bologna degree, but a range of Bologna-compliant degrees that fit the overall structures but have emerged in line with national and institutional preferences and traditions.

The Bologna Process has often accelerated internationalization processes in the institutions resulting in stronger institutional cooperation in integrated curricula for double and joint degrees. There has also been a significant increase in teaching in English in European universities, particularly at master's level, to facilitate mobility for both student exchange and student recruitment, as the new European master's degrees begin to establish themselves on the global higher education market.

In a Europe, where many higher education systems had no quality assurance systems in place, there is now extensive European cooperation in quality assurance that has led to the development of European standards and guidelines providing a framework for the creation of the different national systems. And in a Europe where mobility was often hampered by lack of recognition principles, the Lisbon Recognition Convention gives the right to fair recognition and provides transparent and coherent criteria.

There can be no doubt that European higher education has undergone significant transformation in the space of one decade.

MESSY REALITIES

So, the new European university has readable and comparable degrees, operates a credit system linked to learning outcomes, places the student at the centre of the educational process, issues the Diploma Supplement to all its graduates, has its own internal quality assurance mechanisms, is externally accredited by a quality assurance agency, is part of a system that has developed a national qualifications framework, and has fully implemented the Lisbon Recognition convention.

However, 46 countries and 5,600 institutions with a wide range of higher education traditions across the EHEA are all at different phases of implementation and there is significant diversity in national and institutional contexts and response capacities. Reality at ground level is much messier than the official government reports and declarations.

While the structural reforms are in place across Europe, there are a number of issues that need to be addressed in the next decade. The first objective will be completion of the reforms not only at legislative level, but ensuring they are properly implemented and firmly embedded in the institutions.

It must be said that in many institutions there has often been only a cosmetic introduction of the reforms. They may have been forced to adopt the new structures, but have then failed to rework their programs, design new curricula in line with new professions and interact with employers. The bachelor's degrees are not universally accepted as an entry point to the labor market and while many consider the master's degree as the real exit point, there is much confusion in the proliferation and variety of master's degrees. Doctoral reform is at the very early stages. Cramming old courses into new structures has also had the effect of reducing mobility and the next decade will focus on guaranteeing mobility at all levels of study.

ECTS as a tool for measuring student work-load and linking to student outcomes is often misunderstood and seen as a bureaucratic requirement rather than an opportunity to inno-vate. Issuing the Diploma Supplement to all graduates has not yet become standard practice and national qualifications frameworks are still to be implemented in most countries. Quality assurance mechanisms may be in place but a quality assurance culture for institutional learn-ing and improvement is not yet embedded. The Lisbon recognition principles are not always in line with national legislation and recognition of degrees is often a long and cumbersome process.

Reaching the Bologna goals at institutional level requires culture change and that is the big-gest challenge of all. Culture change takes time, it requires energy and commitment from leader-ship, but it also calls for professional develop-ment and financial resources, which have often been lacking.

It cannot be ignored that the Bologna Pro-cess has also generated confusion and hostility. Overcoming these challenges and maintaining momentum will be essential to avoid the risk of "Bologna burnout" among stakeholders that have been instrumental in driving the process forward.

Beyond the internal and external dimension, the social dimension of the Bologna Process is mentioned less frequently in international dis-cussions, but it is gaining in importance and sense of urgency. The questions of access to higher education and lifelong learning are not yet high priorities in most European institutional agendas and will become a major policy chal-lenge in the next decade to ensure higher educa-tion is meeting societal needs.

Bologna 2020

It is clear that, despite the remarkable progress of the last decade, there is still a long way to go before the Bologna goals of employability, mobility, and global competitiveness are reached and the EHEA becomes a reality. The Bologna Process represents a major modernization agenda for Europe and it is destined to go deeper and broader in the next decade.

An important new tool decided at the 2009 ministerial meeting is data collection and evalu-ation which will increase understanding of the changes and inform future decisions. An inde-pendent assessment of the last decade will be presented at the next ministerial conference and policy forum March 11–12, 2010, in Budapest, Hungary, and Vienna, Austria. Indicators to mea-sure mobility and the social dimension will be in place by 2012.[2]

Future institutional reforms will need to move from structural change to enhancement and mod-ernization of the curricula and much emphasis will be put on ensuring optimisation in use of ECTS and learning outcomes, introduction of student-centered learning, employability espe-cially at bachelor's level, and access and quality of mobility.

One target for mobility has already been set and that is 20 percent of graduates should have had a study or placement abroad by 2020. Mobility stud-ies should provide data on mobility between cycles and countries, mobility and employability, mobil-ity in and beyond Europe, and instruments for quality of and access to mobility.

Data collection and evaluation should also provide input for the social dimension to ensure Europe's student bodies reflect the diversity of its populations. Universities will be called upon to develop action plans for more flexible educational delivery accessible to a wider range of students and to realise lifelong learning through better recognition of prior learning and development of adult learning. Each country will be required to set measurable targets for increasing the participation of underrepresented groups by 2020.

The external dimension will focus on enhancing relationships between the EHEA and the rest of the world and preparing its institutions to face global challenges. A strategy will be put in place to promote the EHEA around the world and create the EHEA brand but also to ensure international dialogue and cooperation. International reputation is closely tied to international rankings and European pilot projects are being developed to create new approaches and encourage institutional diversity. Quality assurance and recognition will take on stronger international dimensions and include transnational education.

Research and innovation have also been identified as a priority and there will be emphasis on creating strong links between the EHEA and the ERA (the European Research Area). Doctoral education will receive greater attention for reform to improve careers for young researchers and enhance opportunity for mobility. Diversity in institutional research profiles will be encouraged.

An open debate that will continue throughout the next decade will be the issue of funding higher education. Higher education has been declared a public good and public responsibility and governments have made commitments to maintaining investment levels in the current global crisis. Nevertheless, European higher education funding is low compared to the United States and has often decreased in the past decade. Discussions on the levels and balances of public and private funding, in particular student fee structures, will continue in the search for a sustainable funding model for Europe.

SEEING OPPORTUNITY

The Bologna Process has been considered the greatest higher education reform ever implemented in Europe, bringing about unprecedented change, and yet as it draws to its 10-year conclusion it already appears insufficient to provide the solutions that are required to make European higher education a truly global player.

Significant structural reform has been carried out and important tools for convergence have been introduced. But as the next decade begins, Europe will need to develop an even more ambitious reform agenda, driving forward and interlinking the internal, external, and social dimensions while creating the conditions for effective institutional implementation of the reforms.

Success will lie in the institutional capacity and ambition to change. Those institutions that see the Bologna Process as an opportunity rather than a threat will not only implement the changes but go beyond them to craft their own agenda to become active players in the new environment. For those who continue to resist and remain nostalgic about the past, the words of Eric Shinseki come to mind, "If you don't like change, you're going to like irrelevance even less." That is surely not an option for European universities.

BOLOGNA PROCESS WEB RESOURCES

Official Bologna Process Website

http://www.ond.vlaanderen.be/hogeronderwijs/Bologna/

European Qualifications Framework

http://www.ond.vlaanderen.be/hogeronderwijs/bologna/qf/qf.asp

European Credit Transfer and Accumulation System

http://ec.europa.eu/education/lifelong-learning-policy/doc48_en.htm

Diploma Supplement

http://ec.europa.eu/education/lifelong-learning-policy/doc1239_en.htm

The Bologna Handbook

http://www.bologna-handbook.com/

European Quality Assurance

http://www.eqar.eu/

Information on quality assured and accredited higher education institutions (in progress)

http://www.qrossroads.eu/about-qrossroads

Study in Europe

http://ec.europa.eu/education/study-in-europe/

Lisbon Recognition Convention

http://www.coe.int/t/dg4/highereducation/recognition/lrc_EN.asp

NOTES

1. The Erasmus program, begun in 1987, is a European Union cooperation and mobility initiative to promote European higher education in which students can take and transfer courses across countries in the European Union.

2. The March conference met in March 2010 and welcomed Kazakhstan to the countries already participating in the Bologna Process. Member countries committed themselves to future implementation, recognizing the variable implementation rates across countries and need for continued development in strengthening the educational experiences across members of this group. To review the entire Declaration developed at that forum, see http://www.ond.vlaanderen.be/hogeronderwijs/bologna/2010_conference/documents/Budapest-Vienna_Declaration.pdf. Further documentation is available at the official website (see websites at the end of this reading).

Projects for Further Exploration

1. Using the Web pages listed in the Appendix, compare the percentage of African American, Hispanic, Asian American, and Native American men and women graduates (BA/BS, MA/MS, and PhD) of college to those of Caucasians. How does this compare to the arguments in the readings in this chapter?

2. Using the Web, compare the number and size of institutions of higher education in your area. Go to the Web pages of two or three of these colleges and compare their missions and criteria for acceptance. How does this information compare with the arguments made by Gamson; Bowen, Chingos, and McPherson; and Dougherty?

3. Use a search engine to get the most recent news stories on higher education in Europe to find out how the Bologna Process has changed patterns of higher education there.

10

GLOBALIZATION AND EDUCATION

Comparing Global Systems

From Afghanistan to Zimbabwe, children around the world attend schools, but their access, goals, and experiences vary greatly. For some, the goal is a university education and professional degrees. For others, basic literacy is all children can hope to achieve, regardless of their ability. Not long ago in human history, education of children was carried out informally; during the socialization process, parents, relatives, and elders taught children the skills they would need to survive. Early scholars were primarily religious figures who studied to read and interpret religious texts. However, with advanced industrialization, globalization, and advances in technology, new forces are driving education and educational reform. The growth of industry, trade, international business, and demands for an educated workforce are now heard around the world (Stewart, 2005).

The term *globalization* means many things to many people. Attempts at a concise definition are difficult because some scholars define its historical beginnings; others look at the political, economic, or sociocultural aspects of the process; and still others use interdisciplinary analysis including business and economics. Some studying globalization focus on "globalization from above" and "globalization from below." Globalization from above looks at the big picture—major world patterns and trends related to globalization such as Westernization, internationalization, and marketization (Singh, Kenway, & Apple, 2005). The top-down globalization from above generally starts from two points. The first is scholars who consider historical shifts and cultural patterns resulting in globalization. The second considers the role of multinational corporations and global political and economic organizations in globalization. Globalization from below, on the other hand, focuses on fragmentation and inequalities caused by globalization, and what is happening in traditional and local communities, some of which are being hard hit by effects of globalization and the rich/poor divide.

Theories of educational change today assume that global political, economic, and social change affect educational systems in numerous ways. New theories are emerging to view this ongoing process of change (Carnoy & Rhoten, 2002). *Institutional theory*, for example, is concerned with influence from the environment, especially global environment, and broader cultural norms on educational systems. Several questions guide the studies of researchers who take this approach: Why do educational organizations located in different communities and even countries have similar practices and structures? How do these organizations adapt to changing conditions in their environments? How do broader forces in cultures result in change across organizations? (Ballantine & Hammack, 2012; Meyer, 2009).

Understanding the impact of globalization on educational systems is critical to understanding education in today's world. In the first reading in this chapter, Joel Spring begins with the meaning of globalization as it relates to education, and he follows this with a discussion of four major theoretical perspectives used to help us understand globalization and education: world culture, world systems, postcolonialism, and culturalism. For example, just as countries are divided by economic systems and wealth into center core areas and poorer peripheral areas (world systems theory), so too do educational systems reflect the economic and political institutions of a given society and its place in the world system. Within and between countries, educational levels reflect the economic status of families, communities, and societies. Distinctions between countries lie at the base of many comparative studies and sometimes reflect the former colonial status of countries (postcolonial theory).

Sociologists of education are particularly interested in the differences in world educational systems because those differences help to put their own systems into perspective. The following paragraphs summarize several areas of study in the field of comparative education.

Comparison of education systems: Most countries provide free education for basic literacy skills, and many require schooling to the age of 16. Some countries even provide free education through the university level for those who qualify. However, children do not have equal opportunity to attend schools. Although variations in educational systems around the world are great, there are also areas of similarity (Boli, Ramirez, & Meyer, 1985; Zhao, 2005). Comparisons of systems take the form of reviewing curricula, test results, structures of educational systems, and many other variables. There are attempts by various countries to copy successful strategies of other countries, or to impose educational systems on others. However, cultures and, therefore, educational systems cannot be transported easily from one culture to another. In the second reading, David Baker and Gerald LeTendre discuss the need of all societies to prepare children for future work, and the fact that each country must meet its own needs based on its unique situation. Still, similarities in content around the world have evolved, even when these systems provide education to meet national needs of citizens.

Transition from school to work: As mentioned above, every society expects schools to help prepare young people for the transition from school to work. This school-to-work transition has stimulated research in recent years, especially comparisons across societies. Much of this research is coming from Europe and South America. The third reading, by Alan Kerckhoff, explores the school-to-work transition and its effect on student placement, stratification systems, and societies. He compares school-to-work plans of several European countries with the United States and discusses differences in countries' preparation of students for the work world, pointing out that some societies have trajectories with apprenticeships while others do little to ease the transition. Although educational systems in these countries are changing, this reading provides an overview of different ways to structure and assess the school-to-work transition.

Race, class, gender, and different school experiences: Another subject of research is the experiences and preparation that schooling provides to children around the world. Children have very different experiences in schools. Race, class, and gender all affect what chances a child has to achieve in school. Edith W. King illustrates these differences in accounts of children around the world; most poignant are the cases of girls in some Middle Eastern and African countries who have limited opportunities in life, face female genital mutilation, and receive much less education than their brothers (King, 1999). Although many children from poor families in poor villages are at an educational disadvantage, girls are most severely affected (Sperling, 2005)—yet girls are the ones who raise and feed the children and often need to support the family. A measure of the development of a country is often seen in the statistics on education of girls. The fourth reading, by Maureen Lewis and Marlaine Lockheed, provides a picture of the situation for girls in poor countries today.

Influences on curricula: Sociologists of education have traced the origins of modern educational systems and curricula to former colonial systems. For instance, former British colonies often include classical British literature in their curriculum and require the British O-level and A-level (vocational and university entrance) examinations at the completion of high school and for entrance to university. However, critics argue that this type of system is not preparing all citizens for the realities of their world because O-level students do not always receive the same amount or quality of education (Ramirez & Boli-Bennett, 1987). Some former colonized countries have developed educational systems that meet the needs of the majority of their populations, often including information on agricultural practices, health care, and other essential subjects for their societies.

Although there are commonalities in educational systems around the world, many researchers question whether that convergence is good for all members of all societies, especially students from peripheral third world countries. These scholars suggest that learning to read materials relevant to the needs of rural farmers, for example, would be more appropriate for some members of society than learning Latin. This is a key point made by educational reformers Ivan Illich (see Chapter 11) and Paulo Freire (1973; also Freire & Macedo, 1995) with regard to Latin America and other developing regions.

International comparative testing: Another group of studies compares the curricula of nations and changes in those curricula with globalization to determine how similar and different they are. Findings generally support a convergence of curricular themes across nations, reflecting the interdependence of nations (Chabbott & Ramirez, 2000; McEneaney & Meyer, 2000). The National Assessment of Educational Progress (NAEP) and the International Association for the Evaluation of Educational Achievement (IEA) compare scores of children around the world in literacy, mathematics, science, civic education, and foreign language. These rankings provide information on the similarities, differences, and effects of development on educational systems. The low scores of U.S. students are of concern to U.S. educators and government officials. However, it is necessary to exercise caution when interpreting international data, because, despite United Nations guidelines, data gathered in countries is not always standardized. Therefore, when reporting results, comparative studies must take this into account (see the reading by Baker and LeTendre).

In the final reading in this chapter, Joel Cohen, David Bloom, Martin Malin, and Helen Anne Curry point out what has happened in educational changes—the good, the bad, and the ugly—and what needs to happen, including the challenges that lie ahead. As countries of the world become more interdependent and share institutional systems, including education, it will continue to be important to study the processes of globalization, urbanization, development, and change around the world as they impact on educational systems.

REFERENCES

Ballantine, J. H., & Hammack, F. M. (2012). *The sociology of education: A systematic approach* (7th ed.). Upper Saddle River, NJ: Prentice Hall.

Boli, J., Ramirez, F. O., & Meyer, J. W. (1985). Explaining the origins and expansion of mass education. *Comparative Education Review, 29*(2), 145–170.

Carnoy, M., & Rhoten, D. (2002). What does globalization mean for educational change? A comparative approach. *Comparative Education Review, 46*(1), 1–6.

Chabbott, C., & Ramirez, F. O. (2000). Development and education. In M. T. Hallinan (Ed.), *Handbook of sociology of education* (pp. 163–187). New York: Kluwer Academic/Plenum.

Freire, P. (1973). *Pedagogy of the oppressed.* New York: Herder and Herder.

Freire, P., & Macedo, D. P. (1995). A dialogue: Culture, language, and race. *Harvard Education Review, 65*(3), 377–402.

King, E. W. (1999). *Looking into the lives of children: A worldwide view.* Melbourne, Australia: James Nicholas.

McEneaney, E. H., & Meyer, J. W. (2000). The content of the curriculum: An institutionalist perspective. In M. T. Hallinan (Ed.), *Handbook of the sociology of education* (pp. 189–211). New York: Kluwer Academic/Plenum.

Meyer, J. W. (2009). Reflections: Institutional theory and world society. In G. Krücken & G. S. Drori (Eds.), *World society: The writings of John W. Meyer* (pp. 36–63). Oxford, England: Oxford University Press.

Ramirez, F. O., & Boli-Bennett, J. (1987, August). *The political construction of mass schooling: European origins and worldwide institutionalization.* Paper presented at the meeting of the American Sociological Association, Chicago.

Singh, M., Kenway, J., & Apple, M. W. (2005). Globalizing education: Perspectives from above and below. In M. W. Apple, J. Kenway, & M. Singh (Eds.), *Globalizing education: Policies, pedagogies, and politics* (pp. 1–29). New York: Peter Lang.

Sperling, G. B. (2005). The case for universal basic education for the world's poorest boys and girls. *Phi Delta Kappan, 87*(3), 213–216.

Stewart, V. (2005). A world transformed: How other countries are preparing students for the interconnected world of the 21st century. *Phi Delta Kappan, 87*(3), 229–232.

Zhao, Y. (2005). Increasing math and science achievement: The best and worst of the east and west. *Phi Delta Kappan, 87*(3), 219–222.

RESEARCH ON GLOBALIZATION AND EDUCATION

Joel Spring

The world is becoming increasingly interdependent. Part of the reason is globalization, a complex process that is changing the lives of individuals in the most remote areas of the world. Joel Spring tackles the process of globalization. After defining globalization, he proceeds to discuss four theoretical perspectives that help us to understand the relationship between globalization and education: world culture, world systems, postcolonial, and culturalist. Because this reading tackles both the meaning of globalization and theories that help us understand globalization's impact on educational systems, it is an excellent introduction to our discussion of education around the world.

Questions to consider for this reading:

1. From the discussion in the introduction of this chapter and Spring's discussion below, describe globalization and how it impacts educational systems around the world.

2. What different perspectives do each of the globalization theories discussed by Spring provide for our understanding of the relationship between globalization and education?

3. How is the study of comparative education different from the study of globalization and education?

4. Which theory discussed by Spring do you think is most useful for comparing educational systems?

Research on globalization and education involves the study of intertwined worldwide discourses, processes, and institutions affecting local educational practices and policies. Researchers come from a variety of disciplines and often take an interdisciplinary approach to their topics. The field is developing its own language and conceptual frameworks, in particular with regard to "flows" and "networks." Often, the terms *societies* and *civilizations* are used to identify groups of peoples sharing similar characteristics who see themselves as connected across the boundaries of nation-states. In addition, research on globalization and education is currently divided into four overlapping theoretical perspectives about the causes and processes of globalization.

In the first section of this article, I will define the field of globalization and education. The second section discusses the major theoretical frameworks for interpreting the field. . . .

DEFINING GLOBALIZATION AND EDUCATION

The economist Theodore Levitt is credited with coining the term *globalization* in 1985 to describe changes in global economics affecting production, consumption, and investment (Stromquist, 2002). The term was quickly applied to political and cultural changes that affect in common ways large segments of the world's peoples. One of these common global phenomena is schooling. . . . "Formal education is the most commonly found institution and most commonly shared experience of all in the contemporary world" (Dale & Robertson, 2003, p. 7). However, globalization of education does not mean that all schools are the same, as indicated by studies of differences between the local and the global (Anderson-Levitt, 2003).

The language of globalization has quickly entered discourses about schooling. Government and business groups talk about the necessity of schools meeting the needs of the global economy. For example, the U.S. organization Achieve, Inc. (2005a), formed in 1996 by the National Governors Association and CEOs of major corporations for the purpose of school reform, declared that "high school is now the front line in America's battle to remain competitive on the increasingly competitive international economic stage" (p. 1). The organization provided the following definition of the global economy with a publication title that suggested the linkages seen by politicians and business people between education and globalization: "America's High Schools: The Front Line in the Battle for Our Economic Future" [2005b]:

> The integration of the world economy through low-cost information and communications has an even more important implication than the dramatic expansion of both the volume of trade and what can be traded. Trade and technology are making all the nations of the world more alike. Together they can bring all of the world's companies the same resources—the same scientific research, the same capital, the same parts and components, the same business services, and the same skills. (p. 4)

In a similar fashion, the European Commission's (1998) document *Teaching and Learning: On Route to the Learning Society* describes three basic impulses for globalization:

> These three impulses are the advent of the information society, of scientific and technical civilisation and the globalisation of the economy. All three contribute to the development of a learning society. (p. 21)

. . .

Most of the world's governments discuss similar educational agendas that include investing in education to develop human capital or better workers and to promote economic growth. As a consequence, educational discourses around the world often refer to human capital, lifelong learning for improving job skills, and economic development. Also, the global economy is sparking a mass migration of workers, resulting in global discussions about multicultural education. Intergovernmental organizations (IGOs), such as the United Nations, the OECD, and the World Bank, are promoting global educational agendas that reflect educational discourses about human capital, economic development, and multiculturalism. Information and communication technology is speeding the global flow of information and creating a library of world knowledges. Global nongovernmental organizations (NGOs), in particular those concerned with human rights and environmentalism, are trying to influence school curricula throughout the world. Multinational corporations, in particular those involved in publishing, information, testing, for-profit schooling, and computers, are marketing their products to governments, schools, and parents around the world.

These intertwined global educational processes are analyzed in the framework of societies in contrast to nation-states. This framework makes it possible to talk about a global society or societies. The term *societies* is meant to encompass something broader than a nation-state by including economic and political organizations, civil society, and culture. In this definition, the nation-state does not disappear but becomes a subset of societies. In other words, particular societies might be identified as having similar political forms such as democratic and totalitarian, similar economic organizations such as market-driven and planned, or similar religions such as Islamic, Christian, and Hindu societies. . . .

The term *civilizations* can be used for the categories of east and west and north and south. However, these terms are so broad that they defy any clear definition. In comparing the thinking of Asian and Western students, Nesbitt (2003) defined his concept of Asian to be a civilization based on Confucian ethical values, such as China, Korea, and Japan, and Western civilization as based on the early works of Greek thinkers like Plato and Aristotle. Huntington (1996) popularized the idea of clashes of civilizations. His vision is of a world divided by religious, cultural, and economic differences that override the boundaries of the nation-state. His civilizational categories include Western, Latin American, African, Islamic, Sinic (China and Korea), Hindu, Eastern Orthodox Christianity, and Japanese. In the future, civilization clashes, he argues, will be between Western, Islamic, and Sinic civilizations.

How is the study of globalization and education different from the traditional field of comparative education? First, researchers on globalization and education are not drawn exclusively from comparative education, although many of those studying globalization are identified with the field of comparative education. As a new field of study, researchers into the processes and effect of globalization on educational practices and policies come from a variety of education disciplines, including anthropology, curriculum studies, economics, history, sociology, educational policy, comparative education, psychology, and instructional methodologies. For instance, the book *Globalizing Education: Policies, Pedagogies, & Politics* is edited by Michael Apple, a curriculum researcher; Jane Kenway, a sociology of education researcher; and Michael Singh, an educational policy researcher (Apple, Kenway, & Singh, 2005). As a consequence, at least in its initial stages, research in this new field tends to be interdisciplinary. This does not preclude the possibility that sometime in the future, researchers in the field of globalization and education will be specialists educated in doctoral programs devoted to the topic.

Second, comparative education has traditionally focused on comparing the educational systems of nation-states. Referring to the "new world for comparative education," Dale (2005) wrote that with globalization, the world "can no longer unproblematically be apprehended as made up of autonomous states, an assumption that had been fairly fundamental to much work in comparative education, indeed, the basis of the comparisons it undertook" (p. 123). Or, as Carnoy and Rhoten (2002) asserted, "Before the 1950s, comparative education focused mainly on the philosophical and cultural origins of national education systems" (p. 1). For Dale (2005), globalization studies have given comparative education "a new lease of life" (p. 118). In an editorial in *Comparative Education,* Broadfoot (2003) wrote that the topic of globalization had a positive effect on the historic swings in the perceived value of the field of comparative education: "At the present time we find ourselves at the latter extreme [key educational policy tool], with governments around the world anxious to learn about educational practices in other countries, as they scan the latest international league tables of school performance" (p. 411). Researchers in the field of comparative education have logically turned their attention to the issue of globalization as indicated by the articles appearing in the *Comparative Education* journal such as "Globalisation, Knowledge Economy, and Comparative Education" (Dale, 2005) and "Meeting the Global Challenge? Comparing Recent Initiatives in School Science and Technology" (Jordan & Yeomans, 2003). . . .

WORLD CULTURE, WORLD SYSTEMS, POSTCOLONIALIST, AND CULTURALIST

Currently, there are four major interpretations of the process of educational globalization. The first is an interpretation that posits the existence of a world culture that contains Western ideals of mass schooling, which serves as a model for national school systems. One premise of *world culture* scholars is that all cultures are slowly integrating into a single global culture. Often called "neo-institutionalist," this school of thought believes that nation-states draw on this world culture in planning their school systems (Baker & LeTendre, 2005; Boli & Thomas, 1999; Lechner & Boli, 2005; Meyer, Kamens, & Benavot, 1992; Ramirez, 2003; Ramirez & Boli, 1987).

The other three interpretive models are sometimes overlapping, in particular with regard to analysis of world knowledges and power. The *world systems* approach sees the globe as integrated but with two major unequal zones. The core zone is the United States, the European Union, and Japan, which dominates periphery nations. The goal of the core is to legitimize its power by inculcating its values into periphery nations (Arnove, 1980; Clayton, 1998; Wallerstein, 1984, 2004). What I will call *postcolonial* analysis sees globalization as an effort to impose particular economic and political agendas on the global society that benefit wealthy and rich nations at the expense of the world's poor (Apple, 2005; Brown & Lauder, 2006; Gabbard, 2000; Olson, 2006; Weiler, 2001). The third interpretation emphasizes cultural variations and the borrowing and lending of educational ideas within a global context (Anderson-Levitt, 2003; Benhabib, 2002; Hayhoe & Pan, 2001; Schriewer & Martinez, 2004; Steiner-Khamsi, 2004). This interpretive framework draws on anthropological research and a *culturalist* theorist perspective.

World cultural theorists argue that schooling based on a Western model is now a global cultural ideal that has resulted in the development of common educational structures and a common curriculum model (Meyer & Kamens, 1992; Ramirez, 2003; Ramirez & Boli, 1987). As an ideal, this model of schooling is based on a belief in educability of all people, the right to education, and the importance of education in maintaining economic and democratic rights. As a participant in the evolution of world culture theory by a group of sociologists at Stanford University in the 1970s and 1980s, Francisco Ramirez (2003) wrote, "The [world] culture at work, we later asserted, was articulated and transmitted through nation-states, organizations,

and experts who themselves embodied the triumph of a schooled world 'credential society'" (p. 242). In their pioneer survey of the world's curricula, world cultural theorists John Meyer and David Kamens (1992) concluded "that through this century [20th] one may speak of a relatively clear 'world primary curriculum' operating, at least an official standard, in almost all countries" (p. 166). Why is there a common global primary school curriculum? Meyer and Kamens claim that "as national elites define and develop auricular policy, they tend to draw from the best developed models they and their consultants can find" (p. 168). These ideal education models exist in a world educational culture.

In sharp contrast to world cultural theorists who believe that a Western school model globalized because it was the best, world systems analysts believe that the core countries are trying to legitimize their power by using aid agencies, in particular through support of education, to teach capitalist modes of thought and analysis (Arnove, 1980; Tabulawa, 2003; Wallerstein, 1984, 2004). In a similar manner, postcolonialist analysis argues that Western schooling dominates the world scene as the result of the imposition by European imperialism and their Christian missionary allies. Simply stated, Western-style schools spread around the globe as a result of European cultural imperialism (Carnoy, 1974; Spring, 1998, 2006; Willinsky, 1998). With the breakup of colonial empires after World War II, new forms of colonialism or postcolonialism appeared through the work of IGOs, multinational corporations, and trade agreements. In its current manifestation, postcolonialist power promotes market economies, human capital education, and neoliberal school reforms all designed to promote the interests of rich nations and powerful multinational corporations. In the framework of postcolonialism, these critics argue, education is viewed as an economic investment designed to produce better workers to serve multinational corporations (Becker, 2006; Crossley & Tikly, 2004; Rhoads & Torres, 2006; Spring, 1998; Stromquist, 2002; Stromquist & Monkman, 2000). In describing what they consider to be the negative effects of global IGOs and trade agreements on Latin American education, Schugurensky and Davidson-Harden (2003) wrote, "We take a postcolonial perspective in considering the historical inequalities . . . mark the region's relations with the world's richer countries. . . . [The WTO/GATS] has the potential to continue the cycles of imperialism which have subdued Latin American countries' development since the time of colonisation" (p. 333).

In general, postcolonial analysis (Crossley & Tikly, 2004)

> includes issues of slavery, migration and diaspora formation; the effects of race, culture, class and gender in postcolonial settings; histories of resistance and struggle against colonial and neo-colonial domination; the complexities of identity formation and hybridity; language and language rights; and the ongoing struggles of indigenous peoples for recognition of their rights. (p. 148)

Postcolonial analysis considers a prevailing form of knowledge to be the result of political and economic power. In contrast to world cultural theorists, those using postcolonialist analysis believe that the global influence of Western thought is not a result of it being right but of political and economic power. German political scientist Weiler (2001) identifies the relationship between global knowledge and power as involving a hierarchy of knowledge where one form of knowledge is privileged over another; where a particular knowledge is legitimated by power because it legitimizes that power; and where a transnational system of power working through global organizations, such as publishing corporations, research organizations, higher education institutions, professional organizations, and testing services, legitimates one form of knowledge.

A common thread between postcolonial analysis and "culturalists" is the belief in the existence of world knowledges and the subjugation of some knowledges by others. Culturalists reject what they consider to be a simplistic view of world cultural theorists that national elites select the best model of schooling from a world culture of education. They also question the idea that

models of schooling are simply imposed on local cultures. This group of theorists believes that local actors borrow from multiple models in the global flow of educational ideas. In contrast to the concept of the existence of a world culture reflecting a single form of knowledge, culturalists stress the existence of different knowledges and different ways of seeing and knowing the world (Hayhoe & Pan, 2001; Little, 2003; Rahnema, 2001; Zeera, 2001). In addition, culturalists argue that in the global flow, there are other educational ideas besides human capital, such as religious, Freirian, human rights, and environmental education, and multiple forms of progressive education (Anderson-Levitt, 2003; Benhabib, 2002; Schriewer & Martinez, 2004; Spring, 2004, 2006; Steiner-Khamsi, 2004). For instance, Beverly Lindsay (2005) argues that universities in Zimbabwe and elsewhere should adopt "dynamic paradigms to support peace and progressive development through university enterprises" (p. 194). Choosing from these multiple educational models, local actors adapt them to local circumstances sometimes against the desires of local elites. Summarizing the case studies in her edited book, Steiner-Khamsi (2004) wrote,

> Educational transfer from one context to another not only occurs for different reasons, but also plays out differently. For example, despite all the political and economic pressure on low-income countries to comply with "international standards" in education, imported policies do not have homogenizing effects, that is, they do not lead to a convergence of educational systems. (pp. 202–203)

In conclusion, I would like to reiterate that postcolonial analysis and culturalists often overlap in their research because they share similar perspectives concerning the existence of multiple knowledges and the subjugation of some knowledges by others. However, the four major interpretive divisions in the field of globalization and education do reflect differing approaches to the future of globalization. The first two interpretive frameworks advocate a particular political agenda. World culturalists support and want to improve the current dominant human capital model of schooling. World systems theorists see this as a process to legitimize the actions of rich nations. Believing in the value of a world culture, Baker and LeTendre (2005) stress the existence of "a world culture of education shaping similar values, norms, and even operating procedures in schools across all kinds of quite contrasting nations. Education change right now is a result of deepening of existing institutional qualities more than the effect of outside forces" (p. 169). In other words, the dominant model of schooling is okay and any educational change should be focused on its improvement. In contrast, postcolonial analysis posits that the dominant global school model is exploitive of the majority of humanity and destructive to the planet. They would like to replace the dominant model of human capital education with other more progressive forms designed to empower the masses. For example, Franzway (2005) asks:

> What can education policy actors and practitioners of new pedagogies do in a world where the pressures of political and economic forces have reached a global scale? What are the possibilities for progressive action when capital and the state grasp at the flows of globalization, while communities, individuals, and social institutions flounder in pessimism and passivity? (p. 265)

A general political agenda among culturalists is recognition of multiple knowledges, alternative cultural frameworks for schooling, and the importance of studying the interaction between the local and the global. . . .

CONCLUSION

Uniformity of global curriculum, instruction, and testing might be the result of worldwide trends discussed in this article. Global educational discourses on the knowledge economy, lifelong learning, and human capital education are influencing the decisions of national policy makers. Research shows that most IGOs and NGOs, in particular the World Bank and OECD, are also supporting educational plans tied to the knowledge economy and human capital development. Gender equality in education is a priority of most global organizations. Uniformity of global curricula is being supported by international comparisons of scores resulting from the TIMSS and PISA. Neoliberal discourses and the GATS have stimulated a push for global privatization of educational services, in particular in higher education and the sale of information services and books by multinational corporations. Brain circulation might also contribute to a growing uniformity of global educational practices because of local pressures to ensure an education that will help graduates participate in the global economy. The growth of English as the language of global commerce is making the teaching of English a fixture in most national curricula.

There is considerable criticism of the growing global uniformity in education. World systems theorists argue that it is part of a process for legitimizing the actions of rich over poor nations. Those using postcolonial analysis criticize the trend by arguing that it will ensure the hegemony of global elites. Along with many culturalists, postcolonial analysis supports alternative forms of education to those geared for the knowledge economy and human capital, such as progressive and Freirian educational methods. Research done by culturalists concludes that local populations adapt educational practices to local needs and culture, and therefore, rather than uniformity, there is developing hybrid educational practices combining the local and the global. NGOs, in particular human rights and environmental organizations, are supporting an agenda of progressive human rights and environmental education. And, in sharp contrast to dominant global trends, indigenous groups are demanding the right to use traditional educational practices. Also, some groups are concerned about the loss of local cultures and identity with the trend to making English the global language. These disputes are reinforcing the importance of global educational practices while, at the same time, ensuring possible changes in their current development.

REFERENCES

Achieve, Inc. (2005a). *An action agenda for improving America's high schools: 2005 national summit on high schools.* Washington, DC: Author and National Governors Association.

Anderson-Levitt, K. (2003). A world culture of schooling? In K. Anderson-Levitt (Ed.), *Local meanings, global schooling: Anthropology and world culture theory* (pp. 1–26). New York: Palgrave Macmillan.

Apple, M. (2005). Are new markets in education democratic? In M. Apple, J. Kenway, & M. Singh (Eds.), *Globalizing education: Policies, pedagogies, & politics* (pp. 209–230). New York: Peter Lang.

Apple, M., Kenway, J., & Singh, M. (Eds.). (2005). *Globalizing education: Policies, pedagogies, & politics.* New York: Peter Lang.

Arnove, R. (1980). Comparative education and world-systems analysis. *Comparative Education Review, 24*(1), 48–62.

Baker, D., & LeTendre, G. (2005). *National differences, global similarities: World culture and the future of schooling.* Palo Alto, CA: Stanford University Press.

Becker, G. (2006). The age of human capital. In H. Lauder, P. Brown, J. Dillabough, & H. Halsey (Eds.), *Education, globalization & social change* (pp. 292–295). Oxford, England: Oxford University Press.

Benhabib, S. (2002). *The claims of culture: Equality and diversity in the global era.* Princeton, NJ: Princeton University Press.

Boli, J., & Thomas, G. (Eds.). (1999). *Constructing world culture: International nongovernment organizations since 1875.* Palo Alto, CA: Stanford University Press.

Broadfoot, P. (2003). Editorial. Globalisation in comparative perspective: Macro and micro. *Comparative Education, 39*(4), 411–413.

Brown, P., & Lauder, H. (2006). Globalization, knowledge and the myth of the magnet economy. *Globalisation, Societies, and Education, 4*(1), 25–57.

Carnoy, M. (1974). *Education as a form of cultural imperialism.* New York: David McKay.

Carnoy, M., & Rhoten, D. (2002). What does globalization mean for education change? A comparative approach. *Comparative Education, 46*(1), 1–9.

Clayton, T. (1998). Beyond mystification: Reconnecting world-system theory for comparative education. *Comparative Education Review, 42*(4), 479–496.

Crossley, M., & Tikly, L. (2004). Postcolonial perspectives and comparative and international research in education: A critical introduction. *Comparative Education, 40*(2), 147–156.

Dale, R. (2005). Globalisation, knowledge economy, and comparative education. *Comparative Education, 41*(2), 117–149.

Dale, R., & Robertson, S. (2003). Editorial. Introduction. *Globalisation, societies and education, 1*(1), 3–11.

European Commission. (1998). *Teaching and learning: On route to the learning society.* Luxembourg: SEPO-CE.

Franzway, S. (2005). Making progressive educational politics in the current globalization crisis. In M. Apple, J. Kenway, & M. Singh (Eds.), *Globalizing education: Policies, pedagogies, & politics* (pp. 265–279). New York: Peter Lang.

Gabbard, D. (2000). Introduction. In D. Gabbard (Ed.), *Knowledge and power in the global economy: Politics and the rhetoric of school reform* (pp. xiii–xxiii). Mahwah, NJ: Lawrence Erlbaum.

Hayhoe, R., & Pan, J. (2001). A contribution of dialogue among civilizations. In R. Hayhoe & J. Pan (Eds.), *Knowledge across culture: A contribution to the dialogue among civilisations* (pp. 1–21). Hong Kong: Comparative Education Research Centre, University of Hong Kong.

Huntington, S. (1996). *The clash of civilizations and the remaking of the world order.* New York: Simon & Schuster.

Jordan, S., & Yeomans, D. (2003). Meeting the global challenge? Comparing recent initiatives in school science and technology. *Comparative Education, 39*(1), 65–81.

Lechner, F., & Boli, J. (2005). *World culture: Origins and consequences.* Malden, MA: Blackwell.

Lindsay, B. (2005). Initiating transformations of realities in African and African American universities. In J. King (Ed.), *Black education: A transformative research and action agenda for the new century* (pp. 183–194). Mahwah, NJ: Lawrence Erlbaum.

Little, A. (2003). Extended review. Clash of civilisations: Threat or opportunity? *Comparative Education, 39*(3), 391–394.

Meyer, J., & Kamens, D. (1992). Conclusion: Accounting for a world curriculum. In J. Meyer, D. Kamens,

& A. Benavot (Eds.), *School knowledge for the masses: World models and national primary curricular categories in the twentieth century* (pp. 165–179). Bristol, PA: Falmer Press.

Meyer, J., Kamens, D., & Benavot, A. (1992). *School knowledge for the masses: World models and national primary curricular categories in the twentieth century*. Bristol, PA: Falmer Press.

Nesbitt, R. (2003). *The geography of thought: How Asians and westerners think differently . . . and why*. New York: Free Press.

Olson, L. (2006). Ambiguity about preparation for workforce clouds efforts to equip students for future. *Education Week, 25*(38), 1, 18–20.

Rahnema, M. (2001). Science, universities and subjugated knowledges: A "third world perspective." In R. Hayhoe & J. Pan (Eds.), *Knowledge across culture: A contribution to the dialogue among civilisations* (pp. 45–54). Hong Kong: Comparative Education Research Centre, University of Hong Kong.

Ramirez, F. O. (2003). The global model and national legacies. In K. Anderson-Levitt (Ed.), *Local meanings, global schooling: Anthropology and world culture theory* (pp. 239–255). New York: Palgrave Macmillan.

Ramirez, F. O., & Boli, J. (1987). The political construction of mass schooling: European origins and worldwide institutionalization. *Sociology of Education, 60*(1), 2–17.

Rhoads, R., & Torres, C. (Eds.). (2006). *The university, state, and market: The political economy of globalization in the Americas*. Palo Alto, CA: Stanford University Press.

Schriewer, J., & Martinez, C. (2004). Constructions and internationality in education. In G. Steiner-Khamsi (Ed.), *The global politics of educational borrowing and lending* (pp. 29–54). New York: Teachers College Press.

Schugurensky, D., & Davidson-Harden, A. (2003). From Córdoba to Washington: WTO/GATS and Latin American education. *Globalisation, Societies, and Education, 1*(3), 321–357.

Spring, J. (1998). *Education and the rise of the global economy*. Mahwah, NJ: Lawrence Erlbaum.

Spring, J. (2004). *How educational ideologies are shaping global society*. Mahwah, NJ: Lawrence Erlbaum.

Spring, J. (2006). *Pedagogies of globalization: The rise of the educational security state*. Mahwah, NJ: Lawrence Erlbaum.

Steiner-Khamsi, G. (2004). Blazing a trail for policy theory and practice. In G. Steiner- Khamsi (Ed.), *The global politics of educational borrowing and lending* (pp. 201–220). New York: Teachers College Press.

Stromquist, N. (2002). *Education in a globalized world: The connectivity of economic power, technology, and knowledge*. Lanham, MD: Rowman & Littlefield.

Stromquist, N., & Monkman, K. (2000). Defining globalization and assessing its implications on knowledge and education. In N. Stromquist & K. Monkman (Eds.), *Globalization and education: Integration and contestation across cultures* (pp. 3–25). Lanham, MD: Rowman & Littlefield.

Tabulawa, R. (2003). International aid agencies, learner-centered pedagogy and political democratization: A critique. *Comparative Education, 39*(1), 7–26.

Wallerstein, I. (1984). *The politics of the world-economy: The states, the movements, and the civilizations*. Cambridge, England: Cambridge University Press.

Wallerstein, I. (2004). *World-systems analysis: An introduction*. Durham, NC: Duke University Press.

Weiler, V. (2001). Knowledge, politics, and the future of higher education: Critical observations on a world wide transformation. In R. Hayhoe & J. Pan (Eds.), *Knowledge across culture: A contribution to the dialogue among civilisations* (pp. 25–45). Hong Kong: Comparative Education Research Centre, University of Hong Kong.

Willinsky, J. (1998). *Learning to divide the world: Education at empire's end*. Minneapolis: University of Minnesota Press.

Zeera, Z. (2001). Paradigm shifts in the social sciences in the east and west. In R. Hayhoe & J. Pan (Eds.), *Knowledge across culture: A contribution to the dialogue among civilisations* (pp. 55–74). Hong Kong: Comparative Education Research Centre, University of Hong Kong.

THE GLOBAL ENVIRONMENT OF NATIONAL SCHOOL SYSTEMS

David P. Baker and Gerald K. LeTendre

All societies must prepare the next generation to carry out the roles necessary for their success and societal survival. In some societies education of the young is largely informal, received from parents, elders, and older siblings. More and more, formal schooling is necessary for making it in today's world, and the content seen as necessary for students to learn tends to be comparable across nations. This is because all nations have similar needs for an educated citizenry to carry out tasks for the nation's well-being as it competes in the global system. Yet each nation must also adapt education to meet its individual needs and cultural patterns. The authors, David Baker and Gerald LeTendre, discuss global trends in education as they impact national educational systems.

Questions to consider for this reading:

1. Why is spending money on schools a budget priority in most nations?

2. What aspects of education do nations adapt from global educational systems and trends?

3. Is it inevitable that global trends will influence local school systems around the world?

4. Compare this reading to those in previous chapters. How do you think school organization and roles, the informal system, school environments, and stratification systems are similar worldwide?

Whatever success human society has mustered over the past hundred years is in large measure a result of widespread educational investment by nations in the skills, attitudes, and behaviors of all children. Schools are part of the essential fabric of life in a modern society. Although schools are so commonplace we often overlook them, they play a crucial role in the making of our social world. In the global community, a high-quality public system of education is the sine qua non of a modern democratic society. Many economists and others who study how nations develop stress that high-quality schools are essential for the human capital development and economic growth of nations. Beyond economic development, a nation would be hard-pressed to consider itself a functioning country without a national system of education.

With all the importance attached to schools, it is no wonder that politicians and policy makers around the world place much emphasis on providing quality public education to their constituents. Operating and regulating a nation's schools—public or private—is of extreme importance to national leaders, and governments everywhere guide and direct the kind of education that children receive. In a very short time, public schooling has become the major means by which governments try to promote positive economic change, strengthen national identity, and inculcate citizenship values and behavior in entire populations of people. Consequently there is incessant public discussion about schooling, and political campaigns in all sorts of nations make educational policy and the performance of schools a central point.

By and large, most people most of the time think about education as solely a national undertaking. The trends we examine here, however, lead to quite a different vision, one where there is a considerable global process at work. To make sense of this contrasting globalized world of education, it is helpful first to describe the common image of schooling as a national enterprise. It is a vision with several components.

The everyday vision of schooling as a national enterprise sees it as chiefly a unique product of a nation's culture and governmental effort to foster prosperity for its citizens. This is thought to be true regardless of the particular level of governance of schools within the nation. It is common, then, to refer to French, Chilean, Japanese, American, and South African (or any nation's) schools as separate national entities. After all, what could be more deeply embedded in a nation's society than its schools preparing children for future adult lives in that country? The reigning image of education today is that schools are designed and managed within a national context for the specific needs and goals of a particular nation.

This vision also assumes that schooling is organized to educate and socialize children in a specific way that is directly linked to the future welfare of a particular nation. For example, German schools are thought to produce German adults with the technical skills, linguistic capabilities, and cultural awareness necessary to carry forth the entity of Germany into the future. A national product of educated citizens issuing forth from the school system is the main image of what schooling does in every nation. Educators may be aware of the larger global world, but their predominant image of a nation's schools is as a means to pass on a sense of national uniqueness

and heritage, as well as meet the technical needs of its particular labor market. This image implies that schooling is limited to the specific needs of a nation, therefore schooling would not expand except as is needed for national reasons. Nor would schools engage in education that is separable from traditional values of the nation. Additionally, this image of schooling holds that because labor markets are hierarchical, so should schooling be hierarchical. For efficiency, the argument continues, the best and the brightest of a nation deserve the best educational opportunities for the best national outcomes, and those with lesser endowments should receive less. All of this is wrapped up in the picture of a national system of education operating uniquely to produce efficiently adults with the kind of skill necessary for a range of tasks in the labor market and adult life within a national context.

This common image of schooling bound up in a national context is further reinforced by the rhetoric of official comparisons of education across nations (Schümer, 2004). Observing schooling across nations is thought to reveal significant differences in specific and unique national features causing relative differences in academic outcomes, such as national achievement among nations. A common extension of this idea is that the specific characteristics of a nation's schools are partly responsible for its relative position in the world's economy, and that nations are different enough from one another in their implementation of education to make it possible to learn unique lessons from one another on how to develop and manage schools better. Listen to how the founder of modern empirical comparison of academic outcomes of nations' schools in the late 1960s, Torsten Husén, describes the logic behind cross-national studies:

> The more we have recognized education as an investment in human resources and as an instrument for bringing about economic growth and social change, the stronger has been the *need to investigate the roots of the educational systems* of which the world around us shows such a striking diversity. In the *search for causative factors behind the development and "productivity" of educational systems* there is a need for empirical data and for

cross-nationally valid variables pertaining to these systems as they actually function. (Husén, 1967, p. 19, emphasis added)

Now listen to how he perceives schooling as inseparable from national context: "Any educational system can only be fully understood in the context of the culture, traditions, history and general social structure of the *nation it is designed to serve*" (p. 220, emphasis added).

This image of national schooling is how many think the educational world works, but ultimately it is mostly inaccurate, and becoming more so every moment. In spite of the fact that nations (and their subunits, provinces and states) have immediate political and fiduciary control over schooling, education as an institution has become a global enterprise. We show here that there are all kinds of trends suggesting that ideas and demands and expectations for what school can, and should, do for a society have developed well beyond any particular national context. The same global ideas, demands, and expectations filter into nations, greatly shaping their schools in union with schools all over the world. Over the last century, there have been both steady expansion of schooling into our daily lives and deepening of education's meaning for things people hold dear. The current situation in schooling across nations is wholly unpredictable from the image of unique national models of schooling.

All the while that schooling has been considered a national technical project, from nation to nation considerable global forces are at work shaping and changing schooling in fundamental ways that many people are unaware of as they view education mostly from a national perspective. But just like the shrinking of the world's marketplace, media, and politics, education too is undergoing intensive globalization. Whether you find them in Mexico City, a small town in Pennsylvania, or in rural Kenya, schools all over the world appear to run in much the same way everywhere. Whether we were educated in a public school in New York City or a Catholic school in Tokyo, we experienced the same basic patterns of education. Today we can walk into almost any

public school around the world and be able to understand what is going on, even though the specifics of the lesson might be totally incomprehensible. Even if we do not know the language, social mores, or dominant religious dogma of a country, we can still identify central features and make sense of the general patterns when we step into a school there. We all recognize schooling just about everywhere because it entails a similar set of ideas about education held consistently throughout the world. This commonality—and the amazing story of what produces it—often goes unobserved, and its substantial consequences on the everyday world of students, parents, teachers, and administrators remain mostly unappreciated.

. . . [W]orldwide forces interact with local ones to create educational change among students, their families, teachers, and administrators in your neighborhood school. Although we focus on mathematics and science in the fourth, eighth, and twelfth grades, we generalize to all academic subjects in elementary and secondary schooling. We tell this story of globalized education through nine separate tales of educational trends, using some of an ever-growing stream of complex information intended to compare schooling across many nations.

Over the past three decades, there has been an explosion of information comparing schools and their outcomes, particularly the academic achievement of their students across nations. In most nations, this kind of information has become part of the dialogue about education improvement. But this information is often misinterpreted or misused, deliberately picked through for certain results and highlighting a particular political position within a national debate. Two good examples are the massive debates resulting from the Reagan administration's *Nation at Risk* report, with its overly gratuitous negative misinterpretation of American student performance relative to other nations (Bradburn, Haertel, Schwille, & Torney-Purta, 1991), and last year's debate in Germany over the causes of achievement differences among its provinces on the international assessment called PISA, in which politicians attributed educational outcomes to all sorts of unrelated policies.

With this recent flood of international information about schooling in various nations, it is not clear that national policy makers, educators, and even some policy analysts really understand how to interpret such data in conjunction with the global forces driving their school systems. We recognize that educational policy for running and improving schools is mostly aimed at national or subnational issues, and always will be. As the saying goes, all politics is local. Policy makers all over the globe have been organizing and reorganizing national school systems nationally or seminationally since at least the end of World War II, and in some nations well before that. But there is another major part of the story (increasingly becoming the main part of the story), namely, the effects of the globalization of schooling. As national and local educators alike are bombarded with comparative information that shows the results of this international process, the need to understand education on a more global level is inescapable in today's world.

Further, how global trends affect the operation of local schools is little understood by legislators and administrators who regulate and oversee them. These effects, we strongly suspect, will only increase in the future, with yet more globalization accompanied and reinforced by a growing array of international tests, studies, and politically motivated comparisons as well as the workings of numerous multinational and regional agencies such as the World Bank, OECD, and development foundations (see, for example, Dale & Robertson, 2002). . . .

Using analyses of the data from the Third International Mathematics and Science Study (TIMSS), we give the reader a look at how schools work around the world, and how complex forces are affecting all nations, shaping both their understanding of educational problems and solutions to them. . . .

SUBPLOT ONE: THE WORLDWIDE SUCCESS OF MASS SCHOOLING

In developing tales about cross-national trends in education, we are struck by how successful schooling is in the world. But we don't mean just any kind of schooling; rather, we refer to a particularly successful type of schooling that has spread around the world and has become the *singular model* of educating children, regardless of a nation's political regime, level of economic wealth, cultural heritage, and social problems. This is often referred to as *state-sponsored mass schooling,* or "mass schooling" for short. It is mostly public schooling for large masses of children, hence the name.

The history of the spread of public mass schooling and its accompanying mass enrollments around the world is the biggest success story ever known about the implementation of education (Fuller & Rubinson, 1992). Funding for schooling now rivals military and other social welfare expenditures in most national budgets, and educational spending continues to grow worldwide.

Comparing mass schooling with that of the education in premodern societies that has gone on throughout most of the history of human civilization shows how revolutionary an idea mass schooling really is. For most of recorded history, education was practical, situational, and highly limited—as with an apprenticeship to gain a set of skills—and it often did not require literacy. Most of the time, children learned all they needed to know within their family, clan, or tribe. Much of the content of premodern formal schooling was "religious" in nature: learning the legends, beliefs, and sacred traditions of a people or culture, and some limited literacy for reading religious texts. It was in this situation that premodern schooling became most elaborated; a small, elite group of students were taught how to read, write, and memorize the texts important to that culture. Practical apprenticeships were education for some nonelites, but this was not available for all and was aimed at a specific craft.

This all started to change some 150 to 200 years ago with the rise of mass schooling in many Western nations. There were still elite forms of education, but over time schooling was developed in principle for all children to learn academic skills through a more or less common curricula. Since then mass schooling has become one of the most impressive cases of successful transmission of a cultural model in the history of human society, developing and spreading in a relatively short time without limitations. Using mass schooling, most nations have achieved mass literacy within just the last hundred years, and currently there are no real alternatives to mass schooling anywhere. Full enrollment in elementary education was achieved before the middle of the twentieth century in wealthier nations and over the next forty years in poorer nations. Mass secondary education expanded to the same full enrollment a decade or two after elementary reached full enrollment, and the growth of higher education continues unabated in many nations today. Mass schooling has developed and intensified over time as an institution, deepening its meaning for everyday life. A big part of our story is what effects this resilient institution has on students, families, teachers, and school administrators.

SUBPLOT TWO: SCHOOLING IS AN INSTITUTION

At the core of the spread of mass schooling is a set of fundamental ideas that were unique just a short time ago but now have become widely accepted and even cherished. For instance, the ideas that all children should be educated; that the nation has an interest in this and should furnish funds; that education is for the collective good; that children should start early and receive continuous instruction for a relatively large number of years; that tradition of statuses such as race, gender, religion, or language should not be barriers to mass schooling; and that academic cognitive skills are useful to all children, are institutional foundations that underpin and give modern schooling widespread meaning in society. Adding to these powerful ideas is the rise of the exclusive currency of the educational credential, required to hold almost any position in labor markets all over the world. Now in human society, formal schooling has an unprecedented monopoly on the issuing and control of these credentials that lead to so many aspects of adult life.

Our stories lead us to appreciate how these ideas about mass schooling have formed a broad globalizing process making schooling a pervasive and powerful institution. As we have just described, the schooling-as-a-national-enterprise perspective tends not to appreciate the complex institutional nature of education, or its ability to reach across national borders as easily as the ideas behind modern capitalism and democratic government have spread worldwide. A big part of this underlying subplot is what is happening to the institution of mass education, more than what is happening educationally in any one nation, or even type of nation.

Education is an institution, like modern health care or the family, that may take on differing forms from nation to nation and even from region to region within a nation, but that at a deeper level is strongly affixed to global norms and rules about what education is and how schools should operate. If one turns a blind eye toward the image of schooling as a world institution, one is easily led astray in interpreting trends in schools, particularly cross-national trends that appear to differ so much from our individual experience (chiefly with a particular nation's schooling).

The trends . . . are essentially meaningless without the aid of this institutional perspective. For example, why is it that in all the TIMSS nations the educational background of parents has a large impact on school achievement even though school quality has been on the increase over the past three decades? Why have gender differences in eighth grade mathematics almost vanished across so many national school systems? Why do teachers from diverse nations have similar core beliefs about the role of teaching and the role of the student? Why have so many national administrations of schooling produced a paradoxical mix of centralized and decentralized operating procedures for managing schools? The answers to these questions are found in understanding the consequences of the deepening of institutional ideas about mass schooling and how nations respond to this institutional force.

Certainly not all nations are alike; nor do they experience global institutional forces in exactly the same way. Patterns of cross-national differences within overall trends help us detect the larger institutional picture, but without the notion of a world institution these trends are little more than cross-national curiosities, like so many unexplained relics from a nineteenth-century travel adventure.

We admit that it is easier to say "institutional perspective" than it is to communicate exactly what that means. In part this is because institutions themselves are simultaneously so fundamental to our behavior and so powerful in constructing how we make sense of our daily world that they are hard to observe. All of us are part *of* institutions, within them more than we are outside observing them. Historians have long known that time offers a useful perspective on institutions, and to a degree we use that perspective here. Also, cross-national difference, or a perspective from multiple places, is a useful technique to observe institutions. If we hold the social world like a prism at just the right angle to the light, we can see something of its institutional structure underneath; cross-national analyses help make that happen.

Institutions are the building blocks of human society at any time or place. By *institution* we do not mean a specific place with bricks and mortar, as in the vernacular sense that a particular mental hospital is an institution. Instead we mean a set of rules for behavior and social roles to be played in a particular sector of life. Institution is more process than entity, more cognitive than physical, powerful in its control of human behavior through the production of shared meaning in all realms of human existence. The social world is a world of social institutions providing meanings and values about how to think and act in the everyday world. Individuals and collectives—formal organizations, informal groups, and the individual human—obtain realities through social institutions. From an institutional perspective, the very essence of social change is institutional change (see Berger, Berger, & Kellner, 1974). In terms of schooling as an institution, we borrow an analogy from educational historians Larry Cuban and

David Tyack: the institutionalness of education constitutes the "grammar" of how things work in schools.

Our point here is that to a large extent the grammar of schooling is global. This means that much of the grammar of schools and the ideas behind it are reproduced and reinforced at a global level. Every individual school is still influenced by local, regional, and national factors, but the basic image of a school—what it is and what it should do—is commonly defined in the same way globally. Consequently, the organization of national school systems (French, German, American, and so on) is now influenced by transnational forces that are beyond the control of national policy makers, politicians, and educators themselves yet appear to be part of their everyday world. We do not mean to say that the United Nations or other powerful multinational agencies overtly force nations to do and think in the same way about schooling. Rather, widespread understanding repeatedly communicated across nations, resulting in common acceptance of ideas, leads to standardization and similar meanings, all happening in a soft, almost imperceptible, taken-for-granted way.

As a global institution, schooling has developed powerful world values and beliefs about children, learning, teaching, and the administration of schools. Over a thirty-year research program with colleagues, institutional theorist and comparative sociologist John Meyer has convincingly established a strong case for thinking about schooling as a product of a world culture that renders education as a resilient and powerful institution in modern society (see, as examples, Baker, 1999; Fuller & Rubinson, 1992; Meyer, 1977; Meyer, Ramirez, & Soysal, 1992; Ramirez & Boli, 1987). They have shown that mass schooling takes similar forms throughout the world, and that there are common beliefs in what schooling can and should do for society. This process, they argue, has to a large degree been driven by a dynamic world culture.

By *world culture,* we do not mean a culture that is void, ersatz, or not historical. Institutionalists see a dynamic world culture that (for better or worse) evolved out of Western ideals of rationality and purposeful action (Berger, Berger, & Kellner, 1974). Rationality as a pervasive cultural product (some would say even a hegemonic product) of the historical rise of the West serves to bureaucratize, marketize, individuate, and homogenize the institutions of the world (Finnemore, 1996; Scott & Meyer, 1994; Thomas, Ramirez, Boli, & Meyer, 1987). Homogenization produces consistent norms of behavior across a set of modern institutions, thus tying institutions such as the modern nation state and formal education together in a tight political sphere. Rationality, along with its offshoots of marketization, individualization, bureaucratization, and homogenization, plays the tune that all modern global institutions march to, but it is itself a cultural product and acts as such throughout the social system.

All this is not to suggest that local and national cultures do not have influence in schooling; they do. Perhaps a better way to think of culture is in terms of a *dynamic mix of cultures,* as discussed in comparative, anthropological studies. Global institutions can traverse and shape local, regional, or national versions of particular areas of human life such as education. Thinking from the perspective of wide-open dynamics of culture, national cultures—if they exist at all—have only vague boundaries. Culture is far too dynamic to stay purely national, yet subglobal cultures do mix with global ones (see LeTendre, 2000; Spindler, 1974; Spindler & Spindler, 1990; Tobin, Wu, & Davidson, 1989).

Culture is a continuous transforming process, often shaped by economic, political, or social change (see Spindler & Spindler, 1990). From this perspective, schools do not simply transmit culture; they are themselves cultural products not contained within national borders. In Louise Spindler's important book on culture and society, *Culture, Change, and Modernization,* she writes:

> Culture . . . refers to shared designs for living. It is not the people or things or behaviors themselves. Culture can be equated with the *shared models* people carry in their minds for perceiving, relating to, and interpreting the world around them.

Sociocultural systems therefore include customary, agreed upon, *institutionalized solutions* which influence most individuals to behave in a predictable manner most of the time, but never all of the time. [1977, pp. 4–5; emphasis added]

One of the major consequences of a dynamic cultural model is that world cultures are easily imagined, as are global or transnational institutional solutions applied to common human problems across nations (Boli & Thomas, 1999).

An institution heavily shaped by a world culture of schooling more accurately depicts the cross-national trends we observe here than a vision of many national cultures of schooling operating independently. Further, such a perspective offers a rich description of how organizations such as schools and institutional ideas interact to produce consequences for the people participating in them. This also offers us a way to think about what will change in schooling in the future, and this leads us to the last of our subplots, educational change.

SUBPLOT THREE: EDUCATIONAL CHANGE IS INSTITUTIONAL CHANGE

Institutions by their very nature impart deep meaning to our everyday world; hence they are resistant to change. When we go to a hospital, we expect things to run in pretty much the same way [as] the last time we were there. If we were to experience a completely different organization each time we had to rely on a hospital for our health care, most of us would be extremely upset. The same is true for schools. Change does occur, but most of us expect that basic patterns of interaction have not changed all that much from when we were in school. But the schooling and the political discussions surrounding it, in most nations, are full of rhetoric about change.

In fact, institutions do change, and institutional theorists have recognized this for some time. They tend to see two main types of force that make for institutional change: those outside the institution itself and those working from within. Outside forces tend to be large and progress over a long historical period. They also interact between institutions over time. Forces from within an institution also make change, often in much shorter time. The stories here about cross-national trends lead us to think about change in both ways. In terms of the former, a number of our tales are about how school and family as institutions interact and create a situation for substantial change in both. Internal institutional change of mass schooling is also evident in other tales, and in fact we end up seeing far more of it than change from the outside.

There are primarily two types of internal force at work that have brought change and will likely continue to do so in the near future. First is the force of standardization and universalism, meaning that organizations and individuals within a particular institution tend to become more similar over time and place. The pioneering works of sociologists of neoinstitutionalism show that there are strong global tendencies toward homogeneity within the education sector. . . .

The second type of endogenous change in institutions occurs through the process of institutionalization itself. In other words, as a particular institutional pattern deepens and spreads, it creates wider consequences that in turn have an impact on the original pattern. We sense this kind of process is at play in a number of our stories. For example, the deepening link between school credentials from mass schooling and the labor market has created in recent times increased pressure on families to seek help outside school for children, which in turn has an impact on the way schools themselves are doing things. . . .

Mass schooling is the predominant model of education in the world today. It pervades every part of people's lives in modern society and creates a culture of education unparalleled in human existence. Although nations have made, and will continue to make, their own modifications to the model, mass education chiefly develops as a world institution. But it is far from static or monolithic; global forces dynamically

interact with national ones and schooling often changes unpredictably. This is the image of institutional change that we take to cross-national trends in schooling.

REFERENCES

Baker, D. (1999). Schooling all the masses: Reconsidering the origins of American schooling in the postbellum era. *Sociology of Education, 72*(4), 197–215.

Berger, P., Berger, B., & Kellner, J. (1974). *The homeless mind.* New York: Random House.

Boli, J., & Thomas, G. (1999). *Constructing world culture: International nongovernmental organizations since 1875.* Stanford, CA: Stanford University Press.

Bradburn, N., Haertel, E., Schwille, J., & Torney-Purta, J. A. (1991). Rejoinder to "I never promised you first place." *Phi Delta Kappan, 72*(10), 774–777.

Dale, R., & Robertson, S. (2002). The varying effects of regional organizations as subjects of globalization of education. *Comparative Education Review, 46*(1), 10–36.

Finnemore, M. (1996). Norms, culture, and world politics: Insights from sociology's institutionalism. *International Organization, 50*(2), 325–347.

Fuller, B., & Rubinson, R. (Eds.). (1992). *The political construction of education.* New York: Praeger.

Husén, T. (1967). *International study of achievement in mathematics: A comparison of twelve countries.* Stockholm: Almqvist & Wiksell.

LeTendre, G. (2000). *Learning to be adolescent: Growing up in U.S. and Japanese middle schools.* New Haven, CT: Yale University Press.

Meyer, J. (1977). The effects of education as an institution. *American Journal of Sociology, 83*(1), 55–77.

Meyer, J., Ramirez, F., & Soysal, Y. (1992). World expansion of mass education, 1870–1980. *Sociology of Education, 65*(2), 128–149.

Ramirez, F., & Boli, J. (1987). The political construction of mass schooling: European origins and worldwide institutionalization. *Sociology of Education, 60*(1), 2–17.

Schümer, G. (2004). Versuche zur aufklärung von leistungsunterschieden zwischen schülern aus verschiedenen ländern. In S. Gruehn, G. Kluchert, & T. Koinzer (Eds.), *Was schule macht: Schule, unterricht and werteerziehung: theoretisch, historisch, empirisch* (pp. 113–131). Weinheim, Germany: Beltz.

Scott, W., & Meyer, J. (1994). Institutions and organizations: Toward a theoretical synthesis. In W. Scott, J. Meyer, et al., *Institutional environments and organizations* (pp. 55–80). Thousand Oaks, CA: Sage.

Spindler, G. (1974). *Education and cultural process: Toward an anthropology of education.* Austin, TX: Holt, Rinehart and Winston.

Spindler, G., & Spindler, L. (1990). *The American cultural dialogue and its transmission.* New York: Falmer Press.

Spindler, L. (1977). *Cultural change and modernization: Mini models and case studies.* New York: Holt, Rinehart and Winston.

Thomas, G., Ramirez, F., Boli, J., & Meyer, J. (1987). *Institutional structure.* Thousand Oaks, CA: Sage.

Tobin, J., Wu, D., & Davidson, D. (1989). *Preschool in three cultures: Japan, China, and the United States.* New Haven, CT: Yale University Press.

EDUCATION AND SOCIAL STRATIFICATION PROCESSES IN COMPARATIVE PERSPECTIVE

School to Work

Alan C. Kerckhoff

All societies need schools to prepare students to participate in productive roles, yet what schools prepare students to do differs across societies. This transition from school to work affects students' future positions in the social stratification system of their society. Alan C. Kerckhoff explores differences in the entry into the labor force in several European countries and the United States; most successful are the systems that have trajectories for students to follow during the school-to-work transition. For instance, some countries make student entry into the wider social world a smooth transition with apprenticeships leading to jobs and clear trajectories for entry into the economic system. Other countries provide minimal transition.

Questions to consider for this reading:

1. What are some examples of international differences in school-to-work transitions discussed by Kerckhoff? Compare with your country.

2. What is it about the German system that Kerckhoff feels makes the transition to work smoother than in the United States system?

3. Is there a model that countries can follow to facilitate the transition?

This article reviews recent research and theorizing that have been concerned with the relationship between education and social stratification processes in advanced societies and suggests some directions in which future work could take social scientists to build on this foundation. Social stratification is a term that is used to describe both a condition and a process. Social stratification as a condition refers to the fact that members of a population have characteristics that differentiate them into levels or strata. Social stratification as a process refers to the ways in which members of a population become stratified. Most of the literature linking education and social stratification has viewed education as a major contributor to the process that differentiates the society's population into strata. Young people pass through a society's educational institutions and obtain varied educational credentials. These credentials have lasting effects on their adult lives. In particular, occupational attainment depends heavily on educational

From "Education and Social Stratification Processes in Comparative Perspective," by A. C. Kerckhoff, 2001, *Sociology of Education*, *74* (Extra Issue: Current of Thought: Sociology of Education at the Dawn of the 21st Century), pp. 3–18. Copyright 2001 by the American Sociological Association. Reprinted with permission.

attainment, and occupational attainment is the primary dimension of social stratification in advanced societies.

A society's educational institutions can be described as its "sorting machine" (Spring, 1976) because they are a major part of the society's institutional arrangements that serve to stratify its population. Educational institutions sort students into stratified levels of educational attainment, certified by socially recognized educational credentials. Each new generation passes through the society's educational institutions and emerges as a stratified student population whose adult prospects vary significantly according to the credentials they obtain in those institutions. It is difficult to compare societies' distributions of educational attainments, however, because the credentials awarded by the societies' institutions are so different. Americans refer to high school graduation as an important level of educational attainment, but the British do not graduate from high school. Instead, a variety of attainments are possible during secondary school that have different levels of recognition in British society.

Educational attainment is different from other types of attainments used in social stratification research. Advanced societies all have highly comparable distributions of occupations, and there are well-established standard measures of occupational prestige and status (Ganzeboom & Treiman, 1996). But advanced societies' educational credentials (what I refer to as their indigenous credentials) are defined in different ways.

Besides these differences in educational credentials, differences in the organization of the educational systems of advanced societies also lead to variations in the processes by which these adult outcomes are produced. Not all "sorting machines" work in the same way. Not only do they sort their students into different indigenous credential categories, but the ways in which these credentials are produced and affect adult outcomes also differ in important ways.

Just within the past decade, many informative comparative studies have shown the great significance of the variations in educational systems in societies that are, in most other respects, very much alike. I review some of the more salient results from this body of research in the next section with particular focus on the different ways that educational systems distribute each new generation into adult strata defined in terms of occupational positions. In later sections, I focus on some of the more pressing questions this recent research has brought to light and suggest directions in which future research and theorizing can profitably take us.

DIMENSIONS OF SYSTEM VARIATION

Our understanding of the differences among educational systems has been increased by efforts to define dimensions that differentiate them. Three dimensions are generally emphasized: stratification, standardization, and vocational specificity. Combinations of these dimensions are thought to determine the educational systems' "capacity to structure" the flow of young people out of educational institutions and into adult strata that are defined by occupational positions. To help emphasize the importance of the three dimensions of educational systems, I refer throughout to four major societies' educational systems: those of France, Germany, Great Britain, and the United States. These four systems are remarkably varied on the three dimensions, and they differ greatly in the ways they "structure" the flow of students into adulthood.

Stratification

Stratification refers to the degree to which systems have clearly differentiated kinds of schools whose curricula are defined as "higher" and "lower." The term most often refers to difference among secondary schools. The German system's sorting of secondary school students into the Hauptschule, Realschule, and Gymnasium is a clear example of a stratified system. The British differentiation among Secondary Modern, Comprehensive, and Grammar schools is similar, although the Comprehensive school is not so much a separate part of a stratified system as a merging of the traditional Secondary Modern and Grammar schools.

Neither the French nor the American system is as stratified as the German and British systems. The American system has nothing comparable to the others' stratified secondary schools. The French system had been nearly as highly stratified as the German system until the 1970s, but major changes have occurred since then (Lewis, 1985) that have sharply reduced its degree of stratification. There are types of French secondary schools that specialize in general or technical studies, but they all award the baccalauréat.

In a stratified system, the program offerings in the types of secondary schools are associated with different degrees of access to opportunities for additional, more advanced schooling. So, the term stratification refers to both the kinds of programs offered and their links to future opportunities (Allmendinger, 1989). That is clearly the case in the German system. The successful Gymnasium student obtains the Abitur, a certificate entitling him or her to attend a university. The successful Realschule student may qualify to attend an advanced vocational school (Fachoberschule), but Hauptschule students have few later options.

The British system gives students at Grammar schools and most Comprehensive schools the opportunity to study for A-level examinations that are a prerequisite to attending a university. Most Secondary Modern schools do not offer that program of study. Although the French school system is divided into two types of secondary schools, both award the baccalauréat, and a student with a baccalauréat from either of them has access to higher education. Those with a general (rather than a technical) secondary school background are more often successful in higher education, however (Goux & Maurin, 1998).

The American educational system has an even lower degree of stratification than has any of these European systems. This lower stratification is reflected in the fact that virtually all secondary schools offer essentially the same curricula and award the same general credential: the high school diploma. In contrast, most European secondary schools award an array of credentials that reflect their varied program offerings. American students who finish secondary school but do not receive any postsecondary schooling all have the same credential, but German and British students without postsecondary schooling have a variety of credentials. And those varied credentials have significant effects on the students' access to jobs.

In summary, then, the German system is the most stratified of the four. The British system is somewhat stratified, and the French and American systems have little stratification.

Standardization

Standardization refers to "the degree to which the quality of education meets the same standards nationwide. Variables such as teachers' training, school budgets, curricula, and the uniformity of school-leaving examinations are relevant" (Allmendinger, 1989, p. 233). Of the four systems discussed here, the French is by far the most standardized. The Ministry of National Education oversees teacher training, provides the means to evaluate both teachers and students, and sets out the specifics of the national curricula. Standardization is generally higher [when] the system is controlled by the central government.

There is less standardization in Germany than in France because the 16 states (Länder) are the main sources of financial support for education and have primary responsibility for organizing the educational programs. However, the Länder cooperate both with each other and with the federal government in ways that help to standardize programs. The local British districts have even more autonomy than those in Germany, although both funding and credential standards are more influenced by the national government and national certification agencies than is the case in the United States. The strong insistence on local control of education in the United States ensures that there is a low level of standardization.

In summary, then, standardization is the greatest in France, although it is a close second in Germany. Standardization is lower in Great

Britain than in either France or Germany, and it is by far the lowest in the United States.

Vocational Specificity

Educational systems vary in the extent to which they offer curricula that are designed to prepare students for particular vocations and award credentials that are vocationally specific. The German system is the most extreme case of vocational specificity. The great majority of German students enter what is known as "the dual system" during their midteens (Müller, Steinmann, & Ell, 1998). The dual system is an apprenticeship system that combines work experience in regular firms with schooling that is designed to improve students' occupation specific skills. Students who successfully complete a program are awarded credentials that certify their ability to perform the duties of that occupation. The training is highly specific to preparation for 498 occupations (Mortimer & Krüger, 2000). Successful completion may also open access to opportunities for postsecondary schooling.

The British system provides opportunities for secondary school students to take specialized examinations that certify skills that may be of interest to potential employers, but these credentials are generally less occupation specific than are the credentials the German students obtain in the dual system. Greater occupational specificity is associated with the postsecondary courses that British students take in colleges of further education or training centers. The credentials awarded for completing these courses are comparable to the certificates that some American students obtain from technical institutes or community colleges, but the British credentials are nationally standardized and are obtained by a much larger proportion of students than in the United States.

The French system is closest to the American in this respect. There is a division in secondary school between the general and technical tracks, and once students leave the general track, they do not return. However, the curricula in the technical track have few direct applications to positions in the labor force, and students in both tracks have access to postsecondary schooling (Goux & Maurin, 1998). Most specific job skills are learned by French workers on the job, and the training does not as often lead to nationally recognized credentials as does the training in programs in either Great Britain or Germany.

Highly stratified educational systems tend to award more vocationally specific credentials (Müller & Shavit, 1998). In fact, part of the reason for the stratification of the secondary schools in systems, such as Germany's, is to begin to identify groups of students who can be prepared to enter general divisions of the occupational hierarchy.

CAPACITY TO STRUCTURE

In a landmark volume, Maurice, Sellier, and Silvestre (1986) contrasted the ways in which the French and German educational systems affected the distribution of young people into the labor force. They referred to the German system's much greater "capacity to structure" that distribution. In the terms I used earlier, they pointed to the German system's greater efficiency as a "sorting machine." Once students had passed through the German educational system, especially the dual apprenticeship system, their future locations in the adult labor force were highly predictable, much more predictable than the locations of French students.

Of the dimensions of educational systems just reviewed, Maurice et al. (1986) emphasized stratification and vocational specificity as the reasons for the sharp German–French contrast they described. The German students were systematically sorted by the stratified secondary schools and the dual system into progressively more occupation-specific channels, whereas the French students generally obtained credentials that were primarily differentiated by attainment levels with little direct relevance to labor force locations. Thus, French students with any particular credential could end up in a variety of occupations.

Part of the value of Maurice et al.'s (1986) analysis is the emphasis on what happens to students after they leave the two educational systems, especially how they become established in the labor force. That is a core sociological question for those who are concerned with the role of education in the stratification process. Maurice et al. showed how German students more than fit smoothly into stable labor force locations and experience relatively orderly careers. In contrast, French students more often experience a period of "turbulence" during which they may move in and out of the labor force and change jobs with some frequency. Thus, the transition from school to work is different in the two societies, and the difference can be traced to the organization of the two educational systems and the credentials they award.

Using Maurice et al.'s (1986) analysis as a reference point and remembering the earlier discussion of the three dimensions of educational systems, one can estimate the British and American educational systems' capacity to structure the flow of students from school into the force. Clearly, the American system is similar to the French in this respect. The American credentials are also general, and students with the same credential can end up in wide variety of occupations. If anything, the American system has even less capacity to structure the flow of students into the labor force than the French system does because the credentials that French students obtain are highly standardized. Although the French credentials are not vocationally specific, employers at least know their general value on a national scale. Most American students obtain only general credentials (a high school diploma or a bachelor's degree) that seldom have vocational meaning, and they obtain them from educational institutions that are among the least standardized in the world.

The British system awards more differentiated credentials than either the French or American systems. Many British postsecondary vocational credentials are awarded by industry-based organizations (City and Guilds, Royal Society of Arts, Joint Industry Board), and they have direct vocational relevance. Credentials from both the British and the German systems direct their recipients toward positions in the labor force.

A special feature of the British system is relevant here, however. A large proportion of British students leave secondary school early (at age 16 or 17) before they obtain occupationally relevant credentials. Whatever vocationally relevant credentials they have as adults are obtained after they enter the labor force, usually from part-time courses in colleges of further education or training centers. A relatively strong association between British workers' credentials and the jobs the workers hold evolves during the early years in the labor force, but the association results from a different process than in Germany. Thus, the British system does have the capacity to structure the flow of students into the labor force because it awards credentials that have some occupational specificity, but the process through which that capacity becomes manifest is not the same as in the German system. I return to this difference in the next section.

Stratification, standardization, and vocational specificity are all valuable conceptual tools that help to differentiate educational systems in advanced societies, and they serve to show how the systems vary in their capacity to structure students' entry into the societies' stratification systems. However, I suggest another dimension that also differentiates these educational systems that has important effects on students' patterns of educational attainments and entry into the labor force but that has received almost no systematic attention in the literature. I refer to the degree to which the systems provide opportunities for students to choose among alternative paths to educational attainment.

STUDENTS' CHOICE

The contrast between the ways in which German and British students obtain their vocational credentials provides an example of the importance of choice in educational attainment. Both the German and British systems award a range of occupationally relevant credentials. However, the

German system more actively sorts students into increasingly differentiated groups and directs them along established routes leading to a set of occupationally relevant credentials, whereas the British system makes greater allowance for students' initiative in obtaining them. This contrast suggests that another dimension on which educational systems vary is the importance of students' choice in the process of educational stratification.

One of the earliest and most influential analyses of the role of educational systems in the stratification process implied the distinction between the structure of systems and students' choice, although it was not stated in those terms. Turner's (1960) analysis of the British and American secondary school systems referred to them as providing "sponsored and contest" channels of mobility. By "sponsored mobility," Turner meant the British system's formal separation of students into two stratified kinds of schools at age 11. A minority were enrolled in Grammar schools that provided an enriched curriculum that fostered their academic and overall social success. The majority attended Secondary Modern schools that offered a more basic curriculum. In contrast, Turner noted, the essentially unstratified American high schools provided a continuing open contest among students who have equal access to educational opportunities. In the terms used here, the British system more actively imposed a structure, while the American system provided more room for choice.

The British system has changed in two important ways since Turner's analysis. First, the Comprehensive school has become the most common type of secondary school (although some Grammar schools and Secondary Modern schools still exist). Comprehensive schools have diverse curricula that serve a full range of students, much like American high schools. Second, a much more elaborate postsecondary system has evolved that includes universities, polytechnics, colleges of further education, and training centers. University attendance is still highly restricted and requires students to complete demanding secondary school programs, but the colleges of further education and training centers offer courses that

lead to an array of technical credentials. Even students who leave secondary school early can obtain more advanced credentials on a part-time basis after they enter the labor force.

The current British system is thus much less a system of sponsored mobility than it used to be. It provides many more alternative channels to educational attainment at both the secondary and postsecondary levels. British students now obtain a much wider variety of educational credentials than were recognized in 1960, and they have greater freedom of choice in seeking to obtain them. Whereas in 1960 it was reasonable to make the sharp sponsored-contest distinction that Turner made, it is a less appropriate distinction today.

Yet, important differences still exist between the American and British systems. One of the most obvious is reflected in their secondary school credentials. The American high school diploma is an all-or-nothing credential. No other credential can be obtained during secondary school. In sharp contrast, British secondary schools provide levels of examinations (CSEs, O-levels, A-levels) in different substantive areas that have meaning to prospective employers.

There is a similarly sharp contrast at the postsecondary level. Only a small proportion of American students obtain technical postsecondary credentials, and those credentials are not nationally standardized. For American high school graduates, the postsecondary choice tends to be college or nothing. Many fewer British than American students attend universities, but many Britons attend colleges of further education and training centers. Young Americans' educational credentials are largely "high school diploma only" and "bachelor's degree only," whereas young Britons have a wide array of credentials. American students make choices within secondary or postsecondary schools, but these choices lead to a restricted set of credentials.

Despite the contrast between the British and American systems, however, they are both strikingly different from the German system. The clearly stratified German secondary schools and the tightly structured dual apprenticeship system appear to be the epitome of a well-designed and effective sorting machine that moves students through highly structured channels and provides few opportunities for changes of direction. The German and British systems are similar in that both offer a much wider array of educational credentials than does the American system. But the German system differs from both the British and American systems in providing fewer opportunities for students to make choices as they pass through school.

These comparisons among the American, British, and German systems suggest that in using the structure-choice comparison in analyzing educational systems, it is not a simple matter of a system providing structure or choice. The British and American systems both offer students greater freedom to make choices, but the British system offers more alternatives to choose from. The British and German systems have more complex structures and offer a wider array of credentials, but the German system offers students fewer opportunities to make choices as they move through secondary and postsecondary education.

The clearest index of an educational system's allowance for choice is the flexibility of the linkages between structural locations at successive stages of attainment. There are more such linkages in the complex British and German systems than in the simpler American and French systems. However, Germany's system has less flexibility than the other systems because the pathways leading to levels of educational attainment are more restricted. Where students are located in the structure at each stage limits their possible locations at the next stage. Attending the Gymnasium and obtaining the Abitur are prerequisites to attending a university. Realschule students can qualify for attendance at an advanced vocational school (Fachoberschule), but Hauptschule students cannot. And which apprenticeships are available to students depends on the type of secondary school they attended (Heinz, 1999).

The British system has some of these same features. For instance, one must pass A-level secondary school examinations to be admitted to a university, and passing O-level examinations is a prerequisite to taking A-level examinations. Few of these kinds of restricted linkages are found for other kinds of British postsecondary schooling, however. France and the United States are even more flexible. All American high school graduates and all French holders of the baccalauréat can attend universities, and there are few restrictions on the use of the available American pathways to postsecondary vocational certification.

This comparison indicates that the four societies' educational sorting machines differ in two important ways that affect the role of choice in the system. First, they differ in the variety of differentiated units in the systems and in the diversity of credentials they award that have direct relevance to adult levels in the society's stratification system. That is, they differ in the number of structural locations through which students pass. More important, they differ in the flexibility of the linkages between structural locations at different stages in students' passage through the system. The German and British systems both have complex structures and offer a large variety of credentials, but the British system is much more flexible than is the German. With this review of dimensions of educational systems as a background, I now shift the discussion to the ways in which these dimensions affect the education-occupation association in the four societies.

Assessing the Education-Occupation Association

Comparative analyses of the contributions of educational systems to the social stratification process have conventionally focused on some measure of educational attainment (defined in terms of the societies' indigenous credentials or a standard set of categories) and some measure of occupational position (defined in terms of class, status, or prestige). Shavit and Müller's (1998) edited volume is an excellent example of such comparative analyses, carried out in 13 societies. In each society, specialists in social stratification research conducted parallel analyses of the transition from school to work.

The strength of the education-occupation association varies in the 13 societies studied, and some of that variation is due to differences in stratification, standardization, and vocational specificity. However, differences in the forms of analysis used in the 13 societies show how difficult this kind of comparative research is. The difficulties can be made salient by considering two questions: What is a first job? and When does education end?

What Is a First Job?

This question is especially relevant whenever the German system is compared with others. The great majority of young Germans enter the so-called dual system, which involves a combination of on-the-job experience and schooling designed to prepare students to carry out the duties of a particular occupation. In most scholarly analyses, the dual system is considered to be part of the German educational system. Thus, apprenticed Germans' "first jobs" are defined as the first jobs students obtain after they complete their apprenticeships, even though they have a great deal of work experience before they obtain those jobs.

That definition of "first job" cannot be used in the other societies discussed here because large proportions of students in those societies enter their first jobs before they obtain specific job skills. This is the case either because the educational systems provide little occupation-specific training or certification (as in France and the United States) or because most students obtain their occupation-specific training certification after they enter the labor force (as in Great Britain). The unique German definition of a first job naturally produces a stronger education–first job association in Germany than elsewhere.

When Does Education End?

Much of the discussion of the education–first job association implicitly assumes that there is a onetime transition from school to work: Students leave full-time school and enter full-time work. That is a particularly flawed assumption

in societies in which individuals commonly obtain schooling and additional credentials after they enter the labor force.

Among the four societies discussed here, obtaining new credentials through part-time schooling after labor force entry is especially common in Great Britain. It is so partly because so many young Britons leave school and enter the labor force at early ages and partly because they can obtain a wide range of vocationally relevant credentials on a part-time basis while they are employed. Among the four societies, a return to full-time schooling after initial entry into the labor force is most common in the United States. Arum and Hout (1998) reported that about one-fifth of their American sample left school, entered the labor force, returned to school, and reentered the labor force at least once by age 26. These societal differences present problems when making intersocietal comparisons of the education–first job association.

The contributors to Shavit and Müller's volume dealt with these questions in different ways. In their British analysis, for instance, Heath and Cheung (1998) defined the first job as the job obtained after an individual first leaves full-time schooling. In contrast, in Arum and Hout's (1998) American analysis, the first job was defined as the job obtained after an individual leaves full-time schooling for the last time. And Müller et al. (1998) followed scholarly convention and defined their German sample's first jobs as those obtained after they completed their apprenticeships. All three of these different definitions of completing education and entering a first job are defensible, but they affect comparisons of the education–first job association in these societies.

Allmendinger (1989) recognized the difficulty presented by the apprenticeship period in Germany and referred to it as a "transition period" between full-time schooling and full-time work. I suggest that it would increase our understanding of the role of education in the social stratification process if we included the idea of a "transition period" in all comparative research. It is important to see that the transition from school to work is a process, not an event, and that the process varies across societies. Differences in systems become manifest during the transition period. In what follows, I consider how a careful examination of the transition period can help clarify the varied effects of educational systems on stratification processes.

The Transition from School to Work

Following Allmendinger's (1989) lead, one could define the beginning of the transition period as the time a student first leaves full-time school and enters the labor force (ignoring vacation or other short-term jobs). This definition could easily be applied in the four societies discussed here and in most other advanced societies. For German apprentices, that time is as early as age 15 or 16, but for those who attend a university, it is later. For most Britons, it is at an early age (16 or 17), but for those who complete the sixth form of secondary school and for those who enter higher education, it is later. The beginning of the transition period also varies for both American and French students, depending on their levels of educational attainment.

It is much more difficult to define the end of the transition period in such a way that it can be consistently applied both within and among societies. Allmendinger's definition implies that there is a onetime change from a mix of schooling and work to a full-time commitment to work. Evidence presented here shows that that is not the case for many people in Great Britain and the United States. It is also not the case for many people in other societies.

I suggest that, at least tentatively, the transition period in advanced societies should be defined more simply and uniformly in terms of an age span. All advanced societies specify a compulsory period of schooling, and the minimum leaving age in most of them is 16. Also, in almost all advanced societies in recent years, most people complete their schooling and enter the labor force by age 25. I suggest, then, that

we can learn a great deal about the effect of education on social stratification processes if we study what occurs in school and in the labor force between the ages of 16 and 25. This definition of the transition period has the advantage of examining the same life-course period for all cases in all societies, rather than adjusting the definition to fit different societies or educational levels.

What happens between those ages clearly varies a great deal both within and among societies. Within all societies, some leave school at the beginning of the transition period, and others remain in school during most or all of it. Most leave school during the early part of that period, however, and spend a significant part of the period in the labor force.

What happens after people leave full-time school also varies both within and among societies. In most societies, those who leave full-time school the earliest are the least likely to return for additional schooling (Arum & Hout, 1998; Bynner & Fogelman, 1993) and are the most likely to experience unstable employment. The analyses in Shavit and Müller's (1998) volume show a consistent tendency for the risk of unemployment during the early years in the labor force to decrease as the level of educational attainment increases. Unemployment between leaving school and entering a first job is also more common in France and Great Britain than in Germany (Brauns, Gangl, & Scherer, 1999). This is another result of the predictability of first-job placement in the German apprenticeship system.

Initial job placements also vary in other ways. A common feature of jobs obtained by young people in France is that they are specifically defined as temporary (referred to as involving "short-term contracts"). The lower the worker's educational attainment, the more likely he or she will enter an early job of this type or one that is part time (Goux & Maurin, 1998). Temporary and part-time jobs are becoming increasingly common in all advanced societies (Kalleberg, 1996), and the lower the workers' educational attainments, the more likely the workers are to have such jobs. These changes have led some analysts to see an increasing polarization of the labor force in advanced societies into a relatively small elite group of highly skilled workers and a larger group of disadvantaged workers (Coffield, 1999). Whatever the validity of this view it serves to remind us that the education-occupation association depends as much on the nature of the labor force as on the educational systems that prepare students to enter it.

What are the ramifications of systematically including a transition period in the analysis of the role education plays in the stratification process? When the differences in the educational systems' stratification, standardization, and vocational specificity; their capacity to structure; and their tolerance of choice are considered together, it suggests that students in the four societies follow different pathways as they pass through the transition period and into adult positions in the labor force. I refer to these pathways as "trajectories," and I define a trajectory as a set of linked locations in a society's differentiated educational and labor force structures. I use the term in much the same way that the term career line has been used previously in the analysis of labor force pathways (Spenner, Otto, & Call, 1982).

Some Evidence of Differences in Trajectories

Estimates of the trajectories in these four societies can be deduced from characteristics of the educational systems and patterns of early labor force experiences. However, there are few empirical analyses of the flows of young people through the educational systems and into the labor force. We do not have adequate information to chart these trajectories, but we should seek to obtain it. I present some fragments of the kinds of information that are needed. These fragments provide useful evidence, but they also show how much more needs to be done.

The primary bases on which educational trajectories in advanced societies can be differentiated are age and type of education. At what ages

do people first leave school? What kinds of educational programs have they engaged in by the time they leave? Do some combine school and work? If they return to school, what kinds of schooling do they return to, and at what age? When we attempt to link educational trajectories with the labor force, the picture becomes complex, and the available data are less adequate. In what follows, I review some limited evidence of the variety of trajectories that can be observed within and among societies. The available evidence is only suggestive of what more adequate evidence could tell us.

School-Leaving Age as a Division Point

Students are allowed to leave school at age 16 in France, Great Britain, and the United States (most states), but the proportion of students who leave at that time varies greatly. In a comparison of British and American cohorts, my colleagues and I (Kerckhoff, Haney, & Glennie, [2001]) found that between the ages of 16 and 18, 13.8 percent of the Americans left secondary school, compared to 69.6 percent of the British. About half the British "dropouts" were in postsecondary training programs at age 18, but they were no longer in secondary school. Few French students leave secondary school at the minimum leaving age of 16; only about one-fourth leave before they at least try to obtain the baccalauréat, normally completed by age 18 (Goux & Mourin, 1998).

The German pattern is different from the other three. Compulsory education lasts until age 18. However, there is a division at about age 15 into the various programs that lead to higher education (via the Gymnasium), the dual apprenticeship system, or basic vocational schools. At least two-thirds enter apprenticeships in the dual system (Heinz, 1999). If entering an apprenticeship in Germany is viewed as leaving full-time school, then two-thirds of the German students leave full-time school at about the same time that about two-thirds of the British students do. What happens after that, however, is markedly different in the two societies.

Most of those in the German dual system actually stay in that system continually past age 18, which is quite different from the pattern in Great Britain, where a combination of school and work is more likely to involve young workers taking part-time courses. Much depends on how one defines the combined activities. For instance in their comparison of school and work patterns in Germany and the United States, Büchtemann, Schupp, and Soloff (1994) treated apprentices as having left school but as having jobs. They thus concluded that many more American than German "school leavers" are employed a year after they leave school. Hence, it is apparent that, even by age 16 or 18, educational trajectories are highly varied both within and among societies. They are even more varied by older ages.

Continuing Into
Postsecondary Education

Americans are by far the most likely to complete secondary school and move directly into higher education. In my and my colleagues' comparison of Great Britain and the United States (Kerckhoff et al., [2001]), we found that 43.4 percent of the Americans had entered colleges or universities by age 22, but only 9.5 percent of the Britons had entered higher education by age 23. However, 51.9 percent of the British students had taken courses in colleges of further education or training centers, compared with 25.6 percent of the Americans who had attended vocational schools or community colleges.

Because so many German students take part in apprenticeship programs, only about one-fourth enter universities or polytechnical college (Heinz, 1999). However, even some of those who take apprenticeships later go on to universities (Büchtemann et al., 1994). Postsecondary education has been undergoing a great deal of reorganization in France recently, but it is estimated that about one-fourth of French students engage in some kind of postsecondary education (Brauns & Steinmann, 1997).

Education After
Entering the Labor Force

Among these four societies, part-time schooling after labor force entry is most common in Great Britain, and returning to school full time after labor force entry is most common in the United States. This variation in rates of return to school suggests that more Americans and Britons than French or Germans have some kinds of educational experiences at relatively late ages. That appears to be the case, but there is also a sharp British-American contrast. In my and my colleagues' comparison of British and American educational trajectories (Kerckhoff et al., [2001]), 33.3 percent of the Americans attended some kind of educational institution between ages 22 and 28, but only 17.6 percent of the Britons did so between ages 23 and 28. Even more striking, 21.6 percent of the Americans attended colleges or universities during that period, compared with only 3.3 percent of the Britons. Most Britons' courses were taken at training centers or colleges of further education.

Employment Patterns
in the Early Years

Early employment is much more stable in Germany than in the other three societies. Young Germans change jobs least often soon after they first enter the labor force, and even when they do change jobs, they are less likely to change occupations. In addition, job changing during the early years less often involves periods of unemployment in Germany (Brauns et al., 1999; Büchtemann et al., 1994).

In all the respects discussed here, the trajectories in the four societies are diverse. Many British students leave secondary school early, but few do so in the other societies. Some kind of postsecondary schooling is more common in Great

Britain and the United States, but British and American students engage in different kinds of postsecondary schooling. Americans are the most likely to reenter full-time school after they enter the labor force. Germans are the least likely to change jobs in the early years after they enter the labor force. If we had more adequate comparative longitudinal data for the transition period, one would find that the most prominent trajectories would certainly be quite different in these four societies.

STRUCTURES, CHOICES, AND TRAJECTORIES

The limited evidence about trajectories just reviewed leaves unspecified the processes through which the steps in the trajectories occur. The earlier discussion of the systems suggests that the British and American trajectories are more influenced by students' choices, whereas the German trajectories are more influenced by forces within the German educational system that sort students into increasingly diverse but restricted trajectories. Relatively speaking, that is probably true, but recent detailed descriptions of some aspects of the processes in Germany and the United States suggest that some of these deductions about trajectories may be oversimplified.

The overviews of the systems suggest that German students are selected to attend one of three kinds of secondary school and that most of them are then selected into occupation-specific apprenticeships that move them into particular kinds of jobs. Mortimer and Krüger (2000) described how young Germans enter apprenticeships, and their description involves a mixture of system restrictions and students' choice. German secondary school students twice enter a six-week training program for an occupation of their choice. Many change their minds about their initial choice and choose another occupation the second time. Many are also unhappy with their second choice. Students submit apprenticeship applications during their last six

months in secondary school. Some apply for dozens of different positions. A rigorous testing and interview period follows, and many students end up in different apprenticeships than they originally said they wished to enter. Many of the changes are due to rejection, but some are due to students changing their minds about what they want.

Heinz (1999) provided another image of a mix of system restrictions and students' choices in Germany. Studying samples of graduates of selected apprenticeship fields in two German cities, he found that five years after they completed their apprenticeships, the graduates were more scattered than would be expected, given the standard view of the German educational system. About one-fifth of the original sample had returned to school. It may be noteworthy, however, that the great majority of them had been in white-collar apprenticeships. Completing the apprenticeships may have given them sufficient future job security to permit them to invest in the more difficult university option. Of those who were employed, nearly one-third were in a different occupation than the one they had prepared for during their apprenticeship. There thus seems to be more flexibility in the German system than many discussions imply.

Recent research has also suggested a more mixed picture in the United States than the comparisons suggest. American high schools are not quite as "open" and unstructured as they are purported to be. It is true that, over the past 30 years, formal tracking has generally disappeared in American high schools, the variety of courses available has sharply increased, and students take many combinations of courses. However, there is more order in students' course sequences than these changes seem to suggest, and the pattern of courses taken affects students' later lives. Lucas's (1999) review of the historical decline of formal tracking and analysis of recent patterns of course taking showed that the kinds of courses taken have continuity across the high school years and in different subjects (such as mathematics, English, and science). Lucas argued that the combinations of courses can be viewed as "tracks" despite the system's tolerance for students' course selection. He noted that several methods of defining track location in the 11th and 12th grades are significantly linked to academic achievement and college entry.

Other American research has also found more order than may be expected. Kerckhoff and Glennie (1999) used the same data that Lucas used to demonstrate that curricular linkages in mathematics, science, and foreign languages in the 9th through the 12th grade serve to separate students into stratified course-defined educational career lines across the period from age 16 to 28. They showed that as students proceed along these career lines, the differences in their academic achievement increase. That is, there is a cumulative dispersing effect of the curriculum-based career lines. Arum and Hout (1998) also found that high school tracks are significantly associated with American students' later labor market placements.

These German and American findings add some fine-grained texture to the broad picture obtained from considering the structural features of the educational systems. They suggest that both systems provide structure and both allow for some choice by students, even though the balance between those two influences differs. They show that the structure of systems does not preclude choice, but they also show that patterned trajectories can emerge even within less structured systems. Regularity can be found even when no formal structure requires it. Locations in trajectories can be generated by informal social definition and processes as well as by institutional structural constraints.

These regularities that are not institutionally imposed remind us that important processes occur within educational institutions that are not wholly determined by the formal institutional structures. Students relate to each other and families influence students' school experiences, creating informal clusters of like-minded students. In James Coleman's terms (see Schneider, 2000), functional communities evolve within which educational norms emerge. Where educational systems permit students' choices, one can expect that there will be some consistent patterns of choices that have normative force and lead to differentiated educational attainment trajectories. The very existence of alternatives to choose from and the lack of structural constraints should increase the likelihood that functional communities will evolve and normative influences will emerge.

As additional analyses become available for these and other societies, it should be possible to chart with greater confidence the trajectories that young people follow through the transition period into positions in the labor force. The additional analyses should also make it possible to assess the degree to which the trajectories can be attributed to the systems' structural features, to patterns of individual choices, and to normative influences of functional communities. Undoubtedly, structure, choice, and normative influences affect the observed trajectories in all societies, but the nature, extent, and timing of their effects vary. Research that is designed to identify these contributions will increase our understanding of the role of education in the process of social stratification.

Overview

I have reviewed a recent body of literature that has presented a multidimensional picture of the role of educational institutions in the social stratification processes in advanced societies. Because these societies have such varied educational systems that award different kinds of credentials, the processes by which young people become sorted into categories of educational attainment differ. The three dimensions on which these educational systems are usually differentiated are stratification, standardization, and the degree of vocational specificity of the credentials they award. The combination of stratification and vocational specificity determines the degree to which the systems have "the capacity to structure" the flow of students into the labor force. I added another dimension of system differentiation to these three: the extent to which students have opportunities to make choices.

These differences in the educational systems shape the interface between the systems and the societies' labor forces. To understand the role of educational institutions in these societies' stratification processes, it is essential to examine carefully what Allmendinger (1989) referred to as the transition period. The construction of the education-occupation association largely occurs during that period. Only after examining the transition period in many societies can we derive an adequate comparative picture of the role of education in the process of stratification and clearly conceptualize the education-occupation association.

Charting the passage of young people through the transition period in differently structured systems involves identifying the trajectories that students follow as they move through school and become established in the labor force. Mapping these trajectories more clearly is the primary challenge in this area of inquiry in the foreseeable future. The literature on structural variations of educational systems has provided a framework within which to conduct that mapping, but it is a broad framework that requires further specification. The further specification will necessarily take into account informal social processes as well as system structures. The locations that constitute the stages in trajectories can be generated by consistent patterns of students' choices and be imposed by structural constraints.

In specifying the trajectories, it will be important to maintain a balance between recognizing their diversity in all societies and maintaining a focus on regularities. To some extent, each person's pathway through school and into the labor force is unique. We need to look for patterned pathways that differentiate societies' methods of sorting young people into the stratified labor force.

REFERENCES

Allmendinger, J. (1989). *Career mobility dynamics: A comparative analysis of the United States, Norway, and West Germany.* Berlin: Max-Planck-Institute für Bildungsforschung.

Arum, R., & Hout, M. (1998). The early returns: The transition from school to work in the United States. In Y. Shavit & W. Müller (Eds.), *From school to work: A comparative study of educational qualifications and occupational destinations* (pp. 471–510). Oxford, England: Clarendon Press.

Brauns, H., Gangl, M., & Scherer, S. (1999). *Education and unemployment: Patterns of labour market entry in France, the United Kingdom and West Germany* (Working Paper Number 6). Mannheim, Germany: Mannheimer Zentrum für Europäische Sozialforschung.

Brauns, H., & Steinmann, S. (1997). *Educational reform in France, West Germany, the United Kingdom and Hungary: Updating the CASMIN educational classification* (Working Paper Number 21). Mannheim, Germany: Mannheimer Zentrum für Europäische Sozialforschung.

Büchtemann, C. F., Schupp, J., & Soloff, D. (1994). From school to work: Patterns in Germany and the United States. In J. Schwarze, F. Buttler, & G. G. Wagner (Eds.), *Labour market dynamics in present day Germany* (pp. 112–141). Frankfurt, Germany: Campus Verlag.

Bynner, J., & Fogelman, K. (1993). Making the grade: Education and training experiences. In E. Feri (Ed.), *Life at 33: The fifth follow-up of the National Child Development Study* (pp. 36–59). London: National Children's Bureau.

Coffield, F. (1999). Education and employment in Great Britain: The polarizing impact of the market. In W. R. Heinz (Ed.), *From education to work: Cross-national perspectives* (pp. 284–297). Cambridge, England: Cambridge University Press.

Ganzeboom, H. B. G., & Treiman, D. J. (1996). Internationally comparable measures of occupational status for the 1988 International Standard Classification of Occupations. *Social Science Research, 25*(3), 201–239.

Goux, D., & Maurin, E. (1998). From education to first job: The French case. In Y. Shavit & W. Müller (Eds.), *From school to work: A comparative study of educational qualifications and occupational destinations* (pp. 103–141). Oxford, England: Clarendon Press.

Heath, A., & Cheung, S. Y. (1998). Education and occupation in Britain. In Y. Shavit & W. Müller (Eds.), *From school to work: A comparative study of educational qualifications and occupational destinations* (pp. 71–101). Oxford, England: Clarendon Press.

Heinz, W. R. (1999). Job-entry patterns in a life-course perspective. In W. R. Heinz (Ed.), *From education to work: Cross-national perspectives* (pp. 214–231). Cambridge, England: Cambridge University Press.

Kalleberg, A. L. (1996). Changing contexts of careers: Trends in labor market structures and some implications for labor force outcomes. In A. C. Kerckhoff (Ed.), *Generating social stratification: Toward a new research agenda* (pp. 343–358). Boulder, CO: Westview Press.

Kerckhoff, A. C., & Glennie, E. (1999). The Matthew effect in American education. *Research in Sociology of Education and Socialization, 12,* 35–66.

Kerckhoff, A. C., Haney, L. B., & Glennie, E. (2001). System effects on educational achievement: A British-American comparison. *Social Science Research, 30*(4), 497–528.

Lewis, H. D. (1985). *The French education system.* New York: St. Martin's Press.

Lucas, S. R. (1999). *Tracking inequality: Stratification and mobility in American high schools.* New York: Teachers College Press.

Maurice, M., Sellier, F., & Silvestre, J.-J. (1986). *The social foundations of industrial power: A comparison of France and Germany.* Cambridge: MIT Press.

Mortimer, J. T., & Krüger, H. (2000). Transition from school to work in the United States and Germany: Formal pathways matter. In M. Hallinan (Ed.), *Handbook of the sociology of education* (pp. 475–497). New York: Kluwer Academic/ Plenum.

Müller, W., & Shavit, Y. (1998). The institutional embeddedness of the stratification process: A comparative study of qualifications and occupations in thirteen countries. In Y. Shavit & W. Müller (Eds.), *From school to work: A comparative study of educational qualifications and occupational destinations* (pp. 1–48). Oxford, England: Clarendon Press.

Müller, W., Steinmann, S., & Ell, R. (1998). Education and labour-market entry in Germany. In Y. Shavit & W. Müller (Eds.), *From school to work: A comparative study of educational qualifications and occupational destinations* (pp. 143–188). Oxford, England: Clarendon Press.

Schneider, B. (2000). Social systems and norms: A Coleman approach. In M. Hallinan (Ed.), *Handbook of the sociology of education* (pp. 365–385). New York: Kluwer Academic/Plenum.

Shavit, Y., & Müller, W. (Eds.). (1998). *From school to work: A comparative study of educational qualifications and occupational destinations.* Oxford: Clarendon Press.

Spenner, K. I., Otto, L. B., & Call, V. R. A. (1982). *Career lines and careers.* Lexington, MA: Lexington Books.

Spring, J. (1976). *The sorting machine.* New York: David McKay.

Turner, R. H. (1960). Sponsored and contest mobility and the school system. *American Sociological Review, 25*(6), 855–867.

INEXCUSABLE ABSENCE

Who Are the Out-of-School Girls— and What Can Be Done to Get Them in School?

Maureen A. Lewis and Marlaine E. Lockheed

In rich global North (developed) countries, girls generally have the same chance to obtain an education as boys. Often they attend university at higher rates than males, although the fields women pursue may not pay as well as fields males pursue. The picture is different in poor global South countries, especially in rural areas. Many girls, especially those from rural areas and minority groups, have no opportunities to pursue even primary level education, leaving them illiterate. Maureen Lewis and Marlaine Lockheed discuss some of the reasons for this lack of opportunity for girls and what it means for the girls, their families, their communities, and their countries. Their discussion focuses on the sources of the problem for girls and the types of exclusions they experience. In addition, they look at the number of girls who do not receive education in different parts of the world and the cost to society and girls of their lack of educational opportunity. Finally, the authors indicate some strategies for advancing excluded girls' education.

Questions to consider for this reading:

1. Why are girls in some countries excluded from educational opportunity, what are patterns of girls' exclusion, and how many girls are excluded?

2. What are the consequences of excluding girls from educational opportunity?

3. What can be done to increase the educational opportunities for girls?

Impressive strides have been made in bringing girls into primary school over the past 25 years, with many countries achieving universal primary education and gender parity. But considerable disparity exists within and across countries, with intracountry differences stemming largely from the lagging involvement of excluded groups—rural tribes in Pakistan, lower castes in India, Roma in Europe, indigenous peoples in Latin America. Of the 60 million girls not in primary school, almost 70 percent are from excluded groups. If further progress is to be realized, educating these girls must be a priority.

Who are the 60 million girls who remain out of school nearly two decades after the worldwide declaration on Education for All? These are their faces:

Meera, 8, *lives with her family on a sidewalk in New Delhi, India. During the day she roams* major intersections, her infant sister hanging from her hip, begging drivers for coins in the few words of English she knows. She does not go to school. In a few years she will be married off to a stranger. She will have six children, one of whom will go to school. Or she will die young, possibly immolated in a kitchen fire for having brought with her an insufficient dowry.

Sonia, 10, lives on the outskirts of a capital city in Eastern Europe. Like her siblings, all of whom speak only Romani, she does not attend school. Instead, Sonia spends her days committing petty theft to support her family. Adults in the town spit at her and warn visitors to watch their purses when they see her.

Lia, 12, went to school for a few years in her remote hill village in Thailand. Then her family sent her to the capital to earn a respectable living in a factory, but she was sold into the sex trade instead. She lives in a brothel and services dozens of clients a day. She will die young, most likely from HIV/AIDs.

Wambui, 14, goes to boarding school because no secondary school is available in her Kenyan village. But she will soon be expelled from school because she is pregnant, having been raped at school by boy students from another tribe, who considered it a mere prank.

Many developing countries have achieved gender equity in education, with near-universal girls' participation converging with that of boys:

Indrani, 10, is the daughter of illiterate parents living in rural Bangladesh. She goes to school. Her older sister is finishing secondary school and plans to work in the garment factory in the market center. While her mother was betrothed at 12, her parents have decided that their daughters must finish school before marrying.

Monique, 12, is excelling in secondary school in Tunisia. She and her siblings have finished primary school with the exception of her eldest sister, whose arranged marriage interrupted her schooling. She expects to work before she marries and plans to have two children.

Are excluded girls simply the daughters of the poor, or are other, more subtle factors at work? Why do some countries make better progress? School participation figures from six low- and middle-income countries offer some clues:

- In Laos, a low-income country, Lao-Tai girls living in rural communities complete five years of school, whereas hill tribe girls living in comparable communities complete fewer than two years of school.
- In Bangladesh, a low-income country, 86 percent of primary school–age girls attend school and 69 percent complete primary school. There is no significant difference between girls living in urban and rural communities.
- In Guatemala, a lower middle-income country, 62 percent of Spanish-speaking girls but only 26 percent of indigenous, non-Spanish-speaking girls complete primary school.
- In Tunisia, a lower middle-income country, 95 percent of all girls complete primary school and 68 percent are enrolled in secondary school.
- In the Slovak Republic, an upper middle-income country, 54 percent of Slovak girls but only 9 percent of minority girls attend secondary school.
- In Botswana, an upper middle-income country, 95 percent of all girls complete primary school and 57 percent attend secondary school.

SOURCES, FORMS, AND LEVELS OF EXCLUSION

What accounts for these differences? Most obvious is the presence or absence of significant subgroups. Bangladesh, Botswana, and Tunisia are largely homogeneous, while Guatemala, Laos, and the Slovak Republic have excluded subgroups.[1] In homogeneous countries higher shares of girls complete primary school, enroll in secondary school, and see higher achievement than those in heterogeneous countries.

Excluded subgroups are based on tribal, ethnic, linguistic, or traditional occupational classifications, such as the "untouchable" occupations of the lowest caste groups in India. But ethnic or linguistic diversity within a country does not necessarily lead to a failure to educate girls. The Basques in Spain, for example, are linguistically diverse but have high levels of female education. It is diversity accompanied by derogation and discrimination that leads to exclusion. The main driver of the remaining gender inequalities in education is the existence of subgroups within countries, accompanied by social stratification and cultural norms that seclude women. This driver operates both culturally and structurally to exclude girls from school. It is thus a particularly pernicious barrier.

Exclusion can take many forms—the more severe, the greater its effect on school opportunities. . . . At one end are extreme forms of exclusion leading to genocide. Only somewhat less severe is the exclusion associated with ethnically based slavery (not slavery as an outcome of conflict), where education is denied to children of slaves, as was the case for African slaves in the southern United States or Brazil in the 1800s. The shunning of a group, such as the Dalits in India or the Roma in Europe, is less severe. It can result in lack of schools, inaccessible schools, segregated or "special" schools, corporal punishment of students, teacher absenteeism, and generally poor-quality schools. Moderate exclusion can result in schooling that is poorly matched with the needs of students. Consider the conditions faced by Berber children in Morocco before 2005; . . . teaching and school materials were not in their mother tongue, mild corporal punishment and ability tracking were used, and early qualifying exams excluded poorly performing children from further education.

A mild form of exclusion is that associated with individual social preferences, whereby teachers may overlook students from excluded groups or children from a minority group may not be included in social events. Exclusion can also result in decreased demand for education or for autonomy in the provision of education.

Severe exclusion has structural consequences: schools are not built, curricular materials are not supplied, roads to schools are not paved, and teachers are often absent. Milder exclusion is cultural. It can affect the behavior of teachers and schoolmates, making teachers insensitive to excluded students' needs.

Language and ethnicity are only two of the sources of exclusion. Children living in remote rural communities face structural barriers to education due to distance, and these barriers are most pronounced for girls. Poor children face barriers to education due to the direct and indirect costs of education. Because the poor in developing countries often show a strong preference for sons, education investments are biased toward boys. Residential segregation often results in access to poorer quality schools.

The cultures of subgroups can differ with respect to the status and roles accorded to women. Where women are secluded, or expected to work long hours performing domestic chores or agricultural labors, cultural beliefs and norms limit girls' educational opportunities. Girls face special cultural barriers associated with their roles in the home and as future wives. As a result, social exclusion from these multiple sources has severe consequences for girls' education and will require different, more tailored policies to remedy them. The degree and nature of exclusion dictates the approach and scope of interventions; often multiple efforts are needed.

How Many Girls Are Excluded?

How many girls are affected by exclusion due to multiple causes? No formal estimates of the numbers of excluded out-of-school girls are available, because most developing countries do not systematically collect or report data on school participation disaggregated by all of the subgroups subject to exclusion. Data from various sources can be used to estimate the figure, however. These data reveal a staggering finding: nearly three-quarters of girls who do not go to school come from excluded groups, while these groups represent only about 20 percent of the developing world's population.

Most out-of-school girls live in Africa and South Asia, which together account for 78 percent of all girls not in school (UIS, 2005). In some large countries a small share of girls are out of school, but the size of the country means that large numbers of girls are affected. In some small countries the share of out-of-school girls is high, which represents a huge national challenge but adds little quantitatively to the global problem. For example, in Guinea-Bissau 55 percent

Table 53.1 Most Primary School-Age Girls Out of Schools Are From Excluded Groups, 2000

Region	Girls out of school (thousands)	Excluded girls out of school[a] (thousands)	Excluded girls as percent of all girls out of school	Excluded subgroups
Sub-Saharan Africa	23,827	17,870[b]	75	Members of nondominant tribes
South Asia	23,552	15,780[c]	67	Rural people in Afghanistan, scheduled castes and tribes in India, lower castes in Nepal, rural tribes in Pakistan
Middle East and North Africa	5,092	1,680[d]	33	Berbers, rural populations
East Asia and the Pacific	4,870	4,383[e]	90	Hill tribes, Muslim minorities, other ethnic minorities
Eastern Europe and Central Asia, Commonwealth of Independent States	1,583	1,425[f]	90	Roma, rural populations in Turkey
Latin America and the Caribbean	1,497	1,482[g]	99	Indigenous and Afro-Latino populations
Total	60,421	42,620	71	

Source: UIS, 2005; India census, 2001; Pakistan household survey, 2001–02; Vietnam Living Standard Measurement Survey, 1998; Ringold, Orenstein, & Wilkens, 2003; Winkler & Cueto, 2004.

Note. Data are for girls 7–12 years old, unless otherwise noted.

a. Estimated. The percentages in column 3 provide the basis for estimating the total number of out-of-school girls by region reported in column 2.

b. Based on the density of heterogeneity and the assumption that most out-of-school children are from minority groups.

c. Based on 2001 census data from India for the number of girls 7–14 years old from scheduled castes and scheduled tribes, on tribal breakdowns in the Pakistan Integrated Household Survey, a household survey of Nepal, and linguistic and ethnic data from non-urban girls in Afghanistan.

d. Percent of Berbers used to determine the number of out-of-school children.

e. Assumes all children out of school come from excluded groups.

f. Includes Roma and Turkish girls out of school.

of school-age girls never attend school, but because the total population of the country is little more than 1.2 million, only about 60,000 school-age girls are not in school. By contrast, in India 20 percent of school-age girls are not in school, but with a national population exceeding 1 billion, 27.7 million girls (ages 7–14) are not in school (Census of India, 2001).

Data on excluded girls are limited. But recent Indian census data document how multiple exclusions can deter girls' participation in school. Of the nearly 50 million children 7–14 years old not enrolled in school in India, 55 percent are girls. This figure is disproportionately high, with girls representing just 48 percent of all children 7–14 years old. Of the 27.7 million girls 7–14 years old not enrolled in school, 33 percent come from scheduled castes or scheduled tribes.[2] This figure is also disproportionately high, because only 26 percent of girls this age come from scheduled tribes or scheduled castes.

The cost of excluding girls from school is high, and the benefits of inclusion significant. . . . The social benefits of educating girls have been widely documented, and studies have also found economic benefits from educating girls.

Mild forms of exclusion often affect girls once they enter school, but the evidence suggests that when girls from excluded groups are given the opportunity to go to school, they tend to go—and to succeed—at least through primary school. Their achievement is often comparable to that of girls from nonexcluded groups and equal to or better than that of excluded boys. Given that the quality of primary schools attended by excluded children is often poor, this is remarkable.

A concatenation of sources of exclusion—gender, ethnicity, area of residence—greatly reduces overall achievement by the time girls reach lower secondary school. Designing interventions and proposing solutions thus require assessing the demand for and supply of education and examining the school practices that affect girls and other excluded subgroups. . . .

Lessons from developed countries can guide donors and policymakers in developing countries. But even developed countries grapple with exclusion. In some, failure to establish a level playing field early on has resulted in a backlash that exacerbates rather than mitigates differences. In developing countries, the diversity of subgroups and the specificities of the cultural contexts make building a new body of knowledge essential. . . .

Ensuring that excluded girls go to school is a major challenge, requiring targeted interventions that address both the structural and cultural dimensions of discrimination in education. The costs of failing are tremendous in terms of lives lost and development opportunities missed.

ADVANCING EXCLUDED GIRLS' EDUCATION

Strategies for advancing excluded girls' education do not apply in all contexts—what works in one country may prove disastrous in another, and "one size does not fit all." Consider busing. In Bulgaria the largely urban and peri-urban Roma community benefited greatly from being bused to better schools. In rural Turkey, busing led parents to pull their daughters out of school over concern for their safety because the new school was in another village. Context is critical. . . .

Policies to spark progress with the remaining out-of-school populations will require actions on various fronts:

- Altering education policies and addressing discrimination by changing laws and administrative rules.
- Expanding options for educating out-of-school children, especially girls.
- Improving the quality and relevance of schools and classrooms by ensuring that excluded girls receive basic educational inputs and providing professional development to help teachers become agents of change.
- Supporting compensatory preschool and in-school programs that engage and retain excluded children, particularly girls.
- Providing incentives for households to help overcome both the reluctance to send girls to school and the costs of doing so. Donors could spearhead innovation by:

- Establishing a trust fund for multilateral programs targeted at excluded girls that supports experimentation, innovative programs, alternative schooling options, and the basic inputs for effective schools.
- Expanding the knowledge base about what works to improve the school participation and achievement of excluded girls through a girls' education evaluation fund. The fund could finance a range of evaluations to build the knowledge base for policy. It could also assist more heterogeneous countries in participating in international assessments of learning achievement to monitor changes over time.
- Creating demand by financing the compensatory costs associated with reaching excluded children; promoting outreach programs for parents; building partnerships for conditional, cash transfers; and providing school meals, scholarships for girls, and school stipend programs for books and supplies.

ALTERING EDUCATION POLICIES AND ADDRESSING DISCRIMINATION

Changes in policies and rules can help determine the environment in which excluded groups function and increase the credibility of government efforts to reach out-of-school children. Policies alone ensure little, however. Establishing clear mandates against discrimination, a legal system that enforces both entitlements and rights of all citizens, administrative rules that foster the completion of basic education for all children, and an articulated education policy for excluded groups are needed to strengthen the credibility of government, establish a foundation for action, and bring together target populations. These actions also provide a context for engaging donors in advocating for marginalized groups, particularly marginalized girls, and in reaching under-served regions with education programs.

Antidiscrimination laws undergird both legal and policy efforts in fighting exclusion. Clear legal protection offers a beginning in reversing implicit and explicit discrimination against minorities. It has proved critical in Canada,

New Zealand, and the United States, where official and public discrimination against minorities was once widespread. South African blacks suffered similarly during apartheid, as did Cuban blacks prior to the revolution of 1958. Unless discrimination is aggressively addressed in the labor market, returns to education will not materialize, reducing the demand for schooling, particularly by girls. Barring trained workers from jobs on the basis of ethnicity, language, or cultural differences has adverse consequences for education because it reduces demand for education by groups that believe the returns will not be positive.

Affirmative action—and the less controversial "preferential" action, which emphasizes bolstering the performance of disadvantaged students while maintaining common standards—has been effective in many countries. Summer math programs and after-school enrichment can strengthen the skills of disadvantaged children. Compensatory programs assume that the minority groups suffer from deficits that can be remedied through tutoring, behavioral guidance, or other compensatory interventions. Brazil, India, Malaysia, South Africa, and Sri Lanka use a combination of affirmative action and compensatory investments to mitigate the effects of discrimination.

Administrative rules often prevent girls from attending schools. In some communities, separate schools for boys and girls are required, which often results in too few schools for girls. Rules preventing children from studying in their mother tongue keep some children who do not speak the language of instruction out of school or make it harder for them to learn. Early ability-based tracking allows schools to provide unequal education programs and produces dropouts. Expulsion of pregnant girls from school and lack of flexibility in school hours for young mothers attempting to continue their schooling after giving birth severely limit their educational opportunities. Changes in all of these rules could increase the number of excluded girls attending school.

Donors could expedite integration by fostering alternative forms of positive discrimination and expanding opportunities for girls who would otherwise have no options. The Open Society Institute assisted local nongovernmental organizations and governments in their efforts to initiate laws and regulations to protect the Roma and make schools safe havens for Roma children. Donor initiatives could also help countries analyze the educational regulations in place that act as barriers to girls.

EXPANDING OPTIONS FOR SCHOOLING

One of the lessons from the high-income OECD countries is that targeted, tailored programs are essential to complement overall schooling investments in order to reach excluded populations and keep excluded children in school. A first step in improving access is making schools or school equivalents locally available. Increasing the number of local schools typically results in greater access for children who are historically excluded.

One way of increasing the number of locally available schools is to allow communities to establish their own schools. Community schools are formal schools that provide the basic elements of the school curriculum, adapted to local conditions, including variations in language of instruction and hours of operation. They are designed to shape schooling to meet the needs and ensure the involvement of community members. They are the ultimate means of giving parents voice in the running of schools. South Asia pioneered the approach in 1987 with its *Shiksha Karmi* Project in Rajasthan, India, which uses paraprofessional teachers, allows the community to select and supervise teachers, and hires part-time workers to escort girls to school.

Two alternatives to formal schooling are nonformal schools and distance education. Nonformal schools address gaps or compensate for limitations of existing schools, particularly for children who never started school or who dropped out early and are older than primary school students. In some cases nonformal schools provide basic literacy training. In others they serve as preparation for re-entry into mainstream schools. Nonformal schools can be highly important in preparing disadvantaged children academically and in developing appropriate social skills and self-discipline. Such schools have contributed to progress in primary education in Bangladesh, which has recently achieved gender parity in primary school.

When expansion of schooling requires the use of teachers with less education, radio or television can help provide better quality lessons. Primary education programs that combine radio delivery of a high-quality curriculum with local monitoring of children's progress have been rigorously evaluated and found to boost learning. The most widely used are interactive radio instruction programs, which use professionally developed curricula broadcast to children in remote regions. Thirteen countries have successfully applied such programs.

At the secondary level, distance education programs such as Mexico's *Telesecondaria* offer a full range of courses, which would be difficult to provide in schools serving small communities. For girls with limited access to information or learning outside the immediate community, such programs vastly increase educational opportunities.

What has not succeeded, though, is providing separate schools for children from ethnic, cultural, and linguistic minorities—often tried in earlier periods, as in the United States, Canada, and New Zealand. Separate schools, for example for the Roma throughout Eastern Europe or blacks in the United States pre-1954, are inherently unequal and suffer from poor quality. Similarly, creating separate schools for girls may fail to improve girls' educational outcomes. Separate schools for girls can also limit their access and, because of poor quality, their performance. Indeed, the lagging performance of Pakistan in girls' education can be attributed in part to the need for double investments in schooling, one for girls, the other for boys. Bangladesh, which has coeducational primary schools, has sped ahead while Pakistan continues to struggle with expanding separate access for both genders.

Lack of funding often prevents experimentation with innovative means of expanding schooling to difficult-to-reach groups or adapting effective programs to new contexts. A trust fund for multilateral programs targeting excluded girls could provide the financial basis for expanding successful efforts of donors and governments.

Donors could also play a catalytic role in devising and financing alternative schooling options, particularly for innovative programs for adolescent girls. Programs such as English language immersion classes or computer training provide an alternative to secondary school that equips girls with marketable skills. Creation of a girls' education evaluation fund to finance bilateral, multilateral, and nongovernmental organization evaluations of new or ongoing programs aimed at reaching girls would help fill a major gap and offer guidance to both policymakers and donors eager to use their resources to promote girls' education. . . .

CREATING INCENTIVES FOR HOUSEHOLDS TO SEND GIRLS TO SCHOOL

Cultural taboos, the opportunity cost of labor, low demand for education, and reluctance to allow children, especially girls, to enter mainstream schools contribute to low enrollment, low completion rates, and below-average achievement among excluded groups. Three types of programs—conditional cash transfers, girls' scholarships, and school feeding programs—have shown promise in meeting these challenges.

Conditional cash transfers provide resources to households to defray the costs of sending their children to school. They tie social assistance payments to desirable behaviors, in this case enrolling and keeping children in school. Although challenging to administer, conditional cash transfers provide financial incentives to

families and put the onus on them to ensure that children actually go to school, something that school officials often find impossible to do. Robust evaluations have shown that conditional cash transfers increase both school enrollment and retention rates. Excluded groups, who are often more difficult to attract to these programs, have not been identified in these evaluations, so the impact on those groups is not yet known.

Scholarships for girls offer financing for primary and secondary school. They also encourage girls to stay in school. Scholarships compensate families for the direct and indirect costs of education. They are effective when households view cost as the impediment to girls' schooling. Scholarships also provide an additional revenue stream for secondary schools. They have been effective for girls at the secondary level in several countries, notably Bangladesh.

Various types of school feeding programs have been associated with higher attendance, higher enrollment, and, in some cases, lower dropout and higher student achievement. School feeding programs are most effective in meeting school attendance objectives. They are particularly successful where attendance is relatively low at the outset and children come from poor households. A concern, however, is whether school feeding provides additional nutrition or simply substitutes for home meals, particularly for girls; this issue deserves attention.

Governments and multilateral donors have forged partnerships for conditional cash transfers in many countries in Latin America. Expanding those initiatives to other countries and to difficult-to-reach groups could increase the number of excluded girls who attend school. How successful such programs can be in attracting excluded girls, especially adolescent girls, to school remains an open question. Donors could finance and manage household stipend components of conditional cash transfers for low-income countries that lack the managerial capacity and resources to conduct a conditional cash transfer program.

Scholarships for girls have demonstrated enormous promise. Donor initiatives to expand such programs to lower secondary, higher secondary, and tertiary education would increase the number of educated women in low-income countries. Educated women from disadvantaged households could serve as both community leaders and role models for excluded girls.

Stipends could be used to finance uniforms, school supplies, and books for girls—items parents often cannot afford or refuse to pay for because they do not appreciate their value. Providing assistance through stipends avoids the bureaucratic management problems of subsidizing inputs.

Financing school meals can attract children to school. It can also provide employment for adults and help involve parents in school, reinforcing the school as a focus of community life. Such initiatives offer an entry point to help upgrade schools and provide the potential for additional help to children with faltering attendance or performance. School feeding programs have not been tested specifically among excluded groups. Donor funding could help determine whether these programs are effective among excluded children.

NOTES

1. The excluded subgroups are: indigenous peoples in Guatemala, hill tribes in Laos, and Roma in the Slovak Republic.

2. Scheduled castes are the lowest caste populations in India and include the "untouchables." Scheduled tribes include indigenous people. They are both on a government schedule of disadvantaged groups, hence the name.

REFERENCES

Ringold, D., M. Orenstein, & E. Wilkens, 2003. *Roma in an expanding Europe? Breaking the poverty cycle.* Washington, DC: World Bank.

UIS (UNESCO Institute of Statistics) 2005. Children out of school: Measuring exclusion from primary education. Montreal: UNESCO.

Winkler, D., & Cueto, S. (Eds.). (2004). *Etnicidad, raza, género y educación en América Latina.* Washington, DC: Inter-American Dialogue, Partnership for Educational Revitalization in the Americas (PREAL). www.preal.org/public-IpeLIBROSindex.php. January 2006.

EDUCATING ALL CHILDREN

A Global Agenda

Joel E. Cohen, David E. Bloom, Martin B. Malin, and Helen Anne Curry

The final reading in this chapter discusses the current state of universal education, including a discussion of the obstacles to global education and how we might move beyond them. The good news is that formal education has been spreading around the globe, encompassing more and more eligible and eager children. Literacy rose from 25% to more than 75% in the 20th century and access to education increased dramatically. However, there are still millions of uneducated children without the opportunity to move ahead. Those who can attend school may not receive quality education. The largest problem for would-be school attendees is that some regions of the world, income groups, and girls do not have equal opportunity, as noted in the previous reading. Spending on education varies widely as well. Why provide all children with quality educations? Here, the authors point to the advantages that accrue to those with education: economic benefits, strong societies, better health for themselves and their families, and fulfilment of what many believe is a basic human right. Yet to reach the goal of universal education, obstacles such as corruption must be dealt with. However, pressure on countries to increase educational opportunities in order to participate in the 21st century world is great, thus generating higher educational enrollments.

Questions to consider for this reading:

1. What is the current scene in world educational opportunities?

2. Describe some challenges that face poor countries in trying to improve their educational systems. What does the future for educating all children look like?

3. What are the benefits of universal education for recipients and for countries?

O ver the past century, three approaches have been advocated to escape the consequences of widespread poverty, rapid population growth, environmental problems, and social injustices. The *bigger pie* approach says: use technology to produce more and to alleviate shortages. The *fewer forks* approach says: make contraception and reproductive health care available to eliminate unwanted fertility and to slow population growth. The *better manners* approach

From "Introduction: Universal Basic and Secondary Education," by J. E. Cohen, D. E. Bloom, M. B. Malin, and H. A. Curry, in *Educating All Children: A Global Agenda* (pp. 1–8), edited by J. E. Cohen, D. E. Bloom, and M. B. Malin, 2006, Cambridge: MIT Press. Copyright 2006 by Massachusetts Institute of Technology. Reprinted with permission.

says: eliminate violence and corruption; improve the operation of markets and government provision of public goods; reduce the unwanted after-effects of consumption; and achieve greater social and political equity between young and old, male and female, rich and poor (Cohen, 1995). Providing all the world's children with the equivalent of a high-quality primary and secondary education, whether through formal schooling or by alternative means, could, in principle, support all three of these approaches.

Universal education is the stated goal of several international initiatives. In 1990, the global community pledged at the World Conference on Education for All in Jomtien, Thailand, to achieve universal primary education (UPE) and greatly reduce illiteracy by 2000. In 2000, when these goals were not met, it again pledged to achieve UPE, this time at the World Education Forum in Dakar, Senegal, with a target date of 2015. The UN Millennium Development Conference in 2000 also adopted UPE by 2015 as one of its goals, along with the elimination of gender disparities in primary and secondary education by 2015.

Educational access increased enormously in the past century. Illiteracy fell dramatically and a higher proportion of people are completing primary, secondary, or tertiary education than ever before. Despite this progress, huge problems remain for providing universal access and high-quality schooling through the secondary level of education. The UPE goal looks unlikely to be achieved by 2015 at the current rate of progress. An estimated 299 million school-age children will be missing primary or secondary school in 2015; of these, an estimated 114 million will be missing primary school. These statistics suggest that providing every child between the approximate ages of 6 and 17 with an education of high quality will require time, resources, and colossal effort. Should the international community commit the necessary economic, human, and political resources to the goal of universal education?

If so, how should it deploy these resources, and how much will it cost?

THE CURRENT SCENE

Current educational data indicate that the world has made significant progress in education, though shortfalls and disparities remain.

The Good

Over the past century, formal schooling spread remarkably, as measured by the primary gross enrollment ratio (GER)—the ratio of total primary enrollment, regardless of age, to the population of the age group that officially belongs in primary education. In 1900, estimated primary GERs were below 40 percent in all regions, except that in northwestern Europe, North America, and Anglophone regions of the Pacific, collectively, the ratio was 72 percent (Williams, 1997, p. 122). Within the past few years, the estimated global primary net enrollment ratio (NER)—the number of pupils in the official primary school-age group expressed as a percentage of the total population in that age group—reached 86 percent (Bloom, chapter one [of *Educating All Children*], Appendix A). The NER is a stricter standard (i.e., it gives lower numbers) than the GER, so the achievement is all the more remarkable. Secondary-school enrollment shows similar progress. The number of students enrolled in secondary school increased eight-fold in the past 50 years, roughly from 50 million to 414 million (calculations by Bloom, based on UNESCO online data).

Measures distinct from enrollment round out this picture. Over the twentieth century, literacy tripled in developing countries, from 25 percent to 75 percent. The average years of schooling in these countries more than doubled between 1960 and 1990, increasing from 2.1 to 4.4 years

(Bloom & Cohen, 2002). That figure has risen further since 1990. This growth in enrollment and literacy was supported by more global spending on primary and secondary education than at any previous time. According to Glewwe and Zhao [in chapter 7 of *Educating All Children*], developing countries spent approximately $82 billion on primary schooling in 2000; Binder, in chapter eight, estimates that spending for secondary education in developing countries in 2000 was $93 billion per year. Although the data and methods of estimation underlying these figures differ, they both indicate large expenditures.

As access to education and literacy increased, global monitoring of students, schools, and educational systems also increased. Developing countries are participating in international measurements of educational status in greater numbers. More statistical measures of schooling have been defined (for example, net and gross enrollment ratios, attendance rates, completion rates, average years of attainment, and school life expectancy). Though not all are well supported by reliable, internationally comparable, comprehensive data, several organizations are working toward this goal. The UNESCO Institute of Statistics, Montreal, maintains the highest-quality data (for example, UNESCO, 2000; [UNESCO-UIS,] 2004).

The Bad

This progress is considerable, but large deficits remain. Roughly 323 million children are not enrolled in school (23 percent of the age group 6–17); roughly 30 percent of these children are missing from primary school, the rest from secondary school (Bloom, chapter one). In developing countries, 15 percent of youth aged 15 to 24 are illiterate, as are about one in every four adults (UNESCO, 2005).

Moreover, enrollment does not necessarily mean attendance, attendance does not necessarily mean receiving an education, and receiving an education does not necessarily mean receiving a good education. High enrollment ratios may give the mistaken impression that a high proportion of school-age children are being well educated. Some 75–95 percent of the world's children live in countries where the quality of education lags behind—most often far behind—the average of OECD countries, as measured by standardized test scores. That standard may not be universally appropriate. However, it is uncontested that educational quality is too often poor.

In addition, indicators of educational quality are scarce. Though participation in international and regional assessments of educational quality has increased, countries most in need of improvements are least likely to participate. As a result, important comparative data on quality continue to be lacking for the developing world. The problem of inadequate or missing data is pervasive.

The Ugly

Gross disparities in education separate regions, income groups, and genders. The populations farthest from achieving UPE are typically the world's poorest. Net primary enrollment ratios have advanced in most of the developing world but remain low in Sub-Saharan Africa. . . .

Girls' education falls short of boys' education in much of the world. Although enrollment rates sometimes do not differ greatly, many more boys than girls complete schooling, especially at the primary level. Although we know that gender, proximity to a city, and income level interact in influencing educational deficits, a systematic global analysis remains to be done of how much each contributes to differences in children's educational opportunities and achievements. In India in 1992–93, the enrollment rate of boys aged 6–14 exceeded that of girls by 2.5 percentage points among children of the richest households; the difference in favor of boys was 24 percentage points among children from poor households (Filmer, 1999). The study also shows that wealth gaps in enrollment greatly exceeded sex gaps in enrollment. The boys from rich households had enrollment rates 34 percentage points higher than those of boys from poor households; the gap in favor of rich girls compared to poor girls was 55.4 percentage points.

Developing countries differ widely in spending on primary education, ranging from $46 per student per year in South Asia and $68 in Sub-Saharan Africa to $878 in Europe and Central Asia (see Table 54.1). Spending per student in secondary education shows a similar range, from $117 per student per year in South Asia and $257 in Sub-Saharan Africa to $577 in Latin America and the Caribbean.

CHALLENGES

Closing the gap between the current state of global education and the goal of providing all children with high-quality primary and secondary education schooling requires meeting several distinct challenges.

- Educate the roughly 97 million children of primary-school age who are not currently enrolled in school. As a majority of these students are female and most live in absolute poverty, the underlying conditions that create disparities in educational access will likely need to be addressed.
- Educate the 226 million children of secondary-school age not in school. Improved access to primary education fuels the demand for secondary education. As more and more children attend school, more and more teachers—who should have at least a secondary education—will also be needed (UNESCO[-UIS], 2006).
- Develop the capacity to educate the 90 million additional children 5–17 years old in developing countries in the next 20 years (United Nations, 2004).

Table 54.1   Recent Public Current Expenditures on Primary Schooling in Developing Countries

Region	Public Spending per Student (U.S. $)	Total Public Spending (millions U.S. $)	Fraction of Population with Public Spending Data*
South Asia	46	6,910	0.98
Sub-Saharan Africa	68	6,100	0.98
East Asia and Pacific	103	21,200	0.96
Latin America and the Caribbean	440	28,200	0.90
Middle East and North Africa	519	14,200	0.60
Europe and Central Asia	878	5,210	0.22
All developing regions	151	81,800	0.88

Source: Glewwe and Zhao, chapter seven [*Educating All Children*].

Note. *Public spending figures are more reliable in regions where public spending data are available for a higher fraction of the population.

- Improve the quality of primary and secondary education, assessed according to constructive goals and clear standards.
- Provide policymakers with clear, empirically supported rationales for why education matters.

Achieving these goals requires a realistic appraisal of the obstacles that have thus far prevented educational opportunity for all children. It requires fresh thinking about what the goals of education should be, and how best to pursue those goals. And it demands an assessment of the costs, which are likely to be significant, as well as an assessment of the consequences of educational expansion and the returns on this investment, which are essential to securing societal and political support. . . .

WHY UNIVERSAL PRIMARY AND SECONDARY EDUCATION?

Although education is not available to hundreds of millions of children, neither are health care, adequate nutrition, employment opportunities, and other basic services available to these children or their families. Why should universal primary and secondary education be a development goal of high priority?

Several rationales support the pursuit of universal primary and secondary education. Education provides economic benefits. Education builds strong societies and polities. Education reduces fertility and improves health. Education is a widely accepted humanitarian obligation and an internationally mandated human right. These rationales are commonly offered for universal primary education, but many benefits of education do not accrue until students have had 10 or more years of education. Completion of primary education is more attractive if high-quality secondary education beckons.

Economic Benefits

. . . Extensive sociological and economic studies have found that education generally enables individuals to improve their economic circumstances. Although the benefits of education for the individual are clear, the aggregate effects on economic growth are more difficult to measure and remain a matter of dispute (Krueger & Lindahl, 2001; Pritchett, 1997; Bloom & Canning, 2004).

It is clear, however, that more education contributes to a demographic transition from high fertility and high mortality to low fertility and low mortality, and Bloom and colleagues (2003) find this change is associated with accelerated growth. When fertility rates fall, the resulting demographic transition offers countries a large working-age population with fewer children to support, although only for a transient interval before population aging begins. In this interval, the large fraction of the population that is of working age offers an exceptional opportunity for high economic growth (Bloom et al., 2003).

Women who attend school, particularly at the secondary or tertiary level, generally have fewer children than those who do not. An increase by 10 percent in primary GERs is associated with an average reduction in the total fertility rate of 0.1 children. A 10 percent increase in secondary GERs is associated with an average reduction of 0.2 children. In Brazil, women with a secondary education have an average of 2.5 children, compared to 6.5 children for illiterate women. In some African societies, total fertility is reduced only among girls who have had 10 or more years of schooling (Jejeebhoy, 1996).

Education contributes to reduced fertility through numerous pathways. Maternal education can lead to increased use of contraceptives. Education can enable women more easily to work outside the home and earn money. This improvement in status leads to empowerment and increased decision-making authority in limiting fertility. Educated women tend to delay marriage and childbearing, perhaps because of the increased opportunity costs of not participating in the paid labor force. Education and income may also become intertwined in a virtuous spiral: as incomes grow, more money is available to finance the spread of education, which leads to further increases in income.

Strong Societies and Polities

Although the evidence is not definitive, education has been shown to strengthen social and cultural capital. Absolute increases in educational attainment can shift disadvantaged groups, such as ethnic minorities or females, from absolute deprivation to relative deprivation compared to more advantaged groups. Educated citizens may be more likely to vote and to voice opposition. Among states, higher enrollment ratios at all levels of education correspond to increases in indicators of democracy. If the content of the education encourages it, education can promote social justice, human rights, and tolerance. As the percentage of the male population enrolled in secondary school goes up, the probability of civil conflict goes down (Collier & Hoeffler, 2001). These desirable effects depend on the content of education and do not flow from the fact of education per se (Cohen, [in press]).

Health

Controlling for income, educated individuals have longer, healthier lives than those without education. Children who are in school are healthier than those who are not, though causation could flow in either direction or both.

Many effects of education on health are indirect effects through increased income. Education increases economic status, and higher-income individuals have better access to health care services, better nutrition, and increased mobility. Education also has direct impacts on health, unrelated to income. It can provide vital health knowledge and encourage healthy lifestyles. For example, the offspring of educated mothers have lower child and infant mortality rates and higher immunization rates, even when socioeconomic conditions are controlled statistically. . . .

Improved health may in turn enhance education. . . . Randomized evaluations of school-based health programs in Kenya and India suggest that simple, inexpensive treatments for basic health problems such as anemia and intestinal worms can dramatically increase the quantity of schooling students attain. . . .

A Basic Human Right

Universal education is justified on ethical and humanitarian grounds as right, good, and fair. Education enables people to develop their capacities to lead fulfilling, dignified lives. High-quality education helps people give meaning to their lives by placing them in the context of human and natural history and by creating in them an awareness of other cultures. Article 26 of the United Nations' Universal Declaration of Human Rights, adopted in 1948, asserts: "Everyone has the right to education." It maintains that primary education should be free and compulsory. The Convention on the Rights of the Child, which entered into force in 1990, obliges governments to make universal primary education compulsory and also to make different forms of secondary education accessible to every child.

OBSTACLES

The rationales for continued educational expansion are powerful, but the barriers too are numerous and formidable. The cost to governments of providing universal primary and secondary schooling, discussed later in this introduction and in chapters seven and eight [of *Educating All Children*], are significant. The cost of education to individuals and families is sometimes a strong disincentive. Because governments face competing demands for the allocation of state resources, education is often pushed down the list of priorities. And even if financial resources for education were plentiful, then politics, corruption, culture, poor information, and history among other factors would conspire to block or slow the achievement of access to high-quality education for all children.

Economic Disincentives

Millions of children have access to schooling but do not attend. Some families may place greater value on the time children spend in other activities, such as performing work for income or handling chores so other household members are free to work in market activities. In developing countries, a troubled household economic situation may more often be a deterrent to enrollment than lack of access to a school. For example, in Ghana, almost half of parents, when asked why their children were not in school, answered, "school is too expensive" or "child needed to work at home"; another 22 percent believed that education was of too little value (World Bank, 2004).

Economic barriers disproportionately harm girls. Some parents perceive the costs—direct, indirect, and opportunity costs—of educating daughters to be higher than that of educating sons (Herz & Sperling, 2004).

Political Obstacles

Education competes for scarce national resources with many worthy projects such as building roads, providing medical care, and strengthening a country's energy system. Limited resources can hamper educational expansion in many ways. Organized interest groups may divert funding from education to their own causes. When social crises, such as crime, unemployment, or civil war, demand the time and resources of the government, citizens are perhaps unlikely to focus on education. Popular demand for education is frequently weakest in poor regions or countries where it is most needed.

Directing adequate funds to education requires a national commitment to education

that many countries lack. Government decisions guided by the short-term interests of those in power are unlikely to reflect the importance of education, as educational returns accrue over much longer time horizons. When politicians devote funds to education, the funding sometimes flows to political supporters rather than to programs and regions where it is most needed. Moreover, a limited capacity to oversee the implementation of education programs and the limited political status of education ministries within many governments may blunt reforms as they are enacted.

Corruption

As with any large public sector, the education sector is rife with opportunities for corruption. When funds are diverted for private gain at any level, educational expansion and improvement may be harmed. At the highest levels of government, corruption can affect the allocation of funds to the education budget; at the ministry level, it can influence the distribution of funds to individual schools; and at the school level, it can involve the diversion of money from school supplies, and the payment of bribes by parents to ensure their children's access to or success in school and by teachers to secure promotions or other benefits (Meier, 2004).

International donors may be deterred by a recipient's history of poor spending accountability, and may curtail funding or impose accountability measures that are themselves costly. The loss of financial resources is always harmful. It is most detrimental at the local level, where the poorest children may be denied access to education because they are not able to afford bribes or where systems of merit—both for students and teachers—are distorted through the widespread use of bribes to secure advancement (Chapman, 2002). Heyneman (2003) argues that if pervasive corruption leads to the public perception of education as unfair or not meritocratic, then this distrust of the school system may lead to distrust of the leaders it produces. As a result, he says, a country's "sense of social cohesion, the principal ingredient of all successful modern societies," may be undermined.

Lack of Information

Reliable, internationally comparable, useful data on many aspects of primary and secondary education are lacking. For example, the mechanisms that keep children out of school are poorly understood in quantitative (as opposed to qualitative) detail. Most routine data focus on measures of "butts-in-seats" such as enrollment, attendance, and completion. Data on educational processes, such as pedagogical techniques and curricula, and on learning outcomes, are inadequate.

Political incentives sometimes work against accurate reporting on even basic quantitative measures. In Uganda, enrollment was historically under-reported because schools were required to remit private tuition receipts to the government in proportion to the number of students they reported. When schools became publicly funded on the basis of enrolled pupils, the incentive for schools to report higher numbers resulted in a leap in official enrollments. In addition, governments may be reluctant to publish potentially unflattering data on their school systems, for fear of political consequences.

Failing to provide data on education feeds a vicious circle. Lack of accurate data impairs the formulation of effective education policy; citizens lack the information they need to hold their school administrators and elected officials accountable; unaccountable officials have few incentives to collect information that would help them to improve the system. Improving educational data could help to transform this vicious circle into a virtuous one by providing necessary information to citizens, administrators, and officials to monitor and improve the quality of schooling.

Historical Legacies

The history of efforts to expand education provides a rich source of models and lessons. These historical legacies can also present impediments to those who underestimate their importance. Benavot and Resnik examine in chapter two [of *Educating All Children*] the emergence of compulsory education laws, the transformation of diverse educational frameworks into formal school systems, the problems of inequality that have arisen, and the role played by international organizations in creating an increasingly interconnected global education system.

Despite the apparent uniformity in contemporary schooling, past educational models took many forms and motivations for educational expansion varied widely. Because national contexts differ, international organizations seeking to facilitate educational expansion need to be attuned to this varied history if their interventions are to succeed. Solutions that ignore the history of education in a particular country are likely to be less effective than solutions tuned to context. For example, when leaders advocated the decentralization of public schools in Latin American countries in the 1980s, they ignored the specific social and political purposes for which those schools had been founded, which included ending severe socio-economic segregation. Decentralization led to a growth of private schools and renewed fragmentation along socio-economic lines, which exacerbated the social divide that school centralization was initially intended to correct.

Though the past must not be ignored, it is not always a useful guide to present educational reform. Past state motivations to provide education—to consolidate national identity, win citizen loyalty, or neutralize rival political groups—were most prominent when nationalist, revolutionary, and totalitarian ideologies drove political development. Today, these rationales are less relevant.

REFERENCES

Bloom, D. E., & Canning, D. (2004). *Reconciling micro and macro estimates of the returns to schooling* (Working Paper of the Project on Universal Basic and Secondary Education). Cambridge, MA: American Academy of Arts and Sciences.

Bloom, D. E., Canning, D., & Sevilla, J. (2003). *The demographic dividend: A new perspective on the economic consequent of population change.* Santa Monica, CA: RAND.

Bloom, D. E., & Cohen, J. E. (2002). Education for all: An unfinished revolution. *Daedalus, 131*(3), 84–95.

Chapman, D. (2002, November). *Corruption and the education sector.* Sectoral Perspectives on Corruption Series. Washington, DC: USAID/MIS.

Cohen, J. E. (1995). *How many people can the earth support?* New York: W.W. Norton.

Cohen, J. E. (Ed.). (in press). *Education for all, but for what? International perspectives on the goals of primary and secondary education.*

Collier, P., & Hoeffler, A. (2001, October). *Greed and grievance in civil war.* Washington, DC: World Bank. Retrieved from http://www.worldbank.org/research/conflict/papers/greedgrievance_23oct.pdf

Filmer, D. (1999). The structure of social disparities in education: Gender and wealth. In *Engendering development through gender equality in rights, resources, and voice* (World Bank Background Paper). Washington, DC: World Bank. Retrieved from http://www.onlinewomeninpolitics.org/beijing12/g%26w.pdf

Herz, B., & Sperling, G. B. (2004). *What works in girls' education: Evidence and policies from the developing world.* New York: Council on Foreign Relations.

Heyneman, S. P. (2003). *Education and corruption.* Retrieved from http://tistats.transparency.org/index.php/content/download/23772/355754/file/heynemann_education_2003.pdf

Jejeebhoy, S. J. (1996). *Women's education, autonomy, and reproductive behaviour: Experience from developing countries.* New York: Oxford University Press.

Krueger, A. B., & Lindahl, M. (2001). Education for growth: Why and for whom? *Journal of Economic Literature, 39*(4), 1101–1136.

Meier, B. (2004). *Corruption in the education sector: An introduction.* Working Paper, Transparency International, July.

Pritchett, L. (1997). *Where has all the education gone?* (World Bank Policy Research Working Paper 1581). Washington, DC: World Bank.

UNESCO. (2000, April). *Education for all 2000 assessment: Statistical document.* Prepared for the International Consultative Forum on Education for All, World Education Forum, Dakar, Senegal. Retrieved from http://unesdoc.unesco.org/images/0012/001204/120472e.pdf

UNESCO. (2005). *Education for all: Literacy for life.* Paris: Author.

UNESCO-UIS. (2004). *Global education digest 2004: Comparing education statistics across the world.* Montreal: Author.

UNESCO-UIS. (2006). *Teachers and educational quality: Monitoring global needs for 2015.* Montreal: Author.

United Nations. (2004). *World population prospects: The 2004 revision.* Retrieved from http://esa.un.org/unpp

Williams, J. H. (1997). The diffusion of the modern school. In W. K. Cummings & N. F. McGinn (Eds.), *International handbook of education and development: Preparing schools, students and nations for the twenty-first century* (pp. 119–136). New York: Pergamon, Elsevier Science.

World Bank. (2004). *Books, buildings and learning outcomes: An impact evaluation of World Bank support to basic education in Ghana.* Washington, DC: Author.

Projects for Further Exploration

1. Various tests are used to compare academic achievement across countries. Using an academic database, search *international, "test results,"* and *education* to find a listing of test results across countries. How do students from the United States compare with those of other countries?

2. Using the Web, look up at least two colleges or universities from three countries in different regions of the world. Compare the criteria for admission, different curriculum offerings, methods for funding education, and format for instruction in these three different countries.

3. Interview a student or person from another country. Ask the interviewee about the structure of educational systems in the country and how the educational system prepares students for entry into the workforce.

11

CAN SCHOOLS CHANGE?

Educational Reform and Change

We have examined various parts of the open systems model throughout this book. Many of these readings pointed to places in which change and reform are desirable. In this chapter we conclude by focusing on the "whole" education system and look at the possibility of change. These four readings include historical analyses of change, comparative studies of educational reforms, and recommendations for the future.

Why even discuss change in education when sociologists define institutions as stable clusters of roles, norms, and values? It would seem that the tendency is for education to remain "as is" rather than to change rapidly. The first reading, by Larry Cuban, examines attempts at changing the time we spend in schools in the United States. In studying the history of change in schools, Tyack and Cuban (1995) found that change in the structure of schooling is complicated and likely to be rejected because interest in change may conflict with other interests in keeping things as they are. Many changes from the past are all too familiar and form the basis of what we consider to be "real schools" today. One example is the graded school, which began in 1860, and the school calendar, which Cuban discusses in this chapter. It can be baffling at times to try to understand why change is so difficult. Cuban discusses how different constituencies and the historical and personal meanings and relationships that revolve around how we structure time in schools help to maintain current patterns and practices in schools in the United States. He also discusses reforms related to this one issue—the school calendar.

However, there is a history of broader-based reform efforts in the United States. A brief review of these reform efforts since the 1980s helps us to understand the patterns inherent in these attempts at change. Race to the Top and No Child Left Behind (NCLB) (discussed by Borman and Cotner in Chapter 3) are the most recent in a series of reform strategies. Looking back, the publication of *A Nation at Risk* by the National Commission on Excellence in Education began what some called the first wave of reform in 1983. This report called for tightening requirements for students and qualifications for teachers. This was followed by calls from the National Governors' Association for school restructuring, including school-based management and school choice. When these efforts did not produce results by the late 1980s, the National Governors' Association defined goals for American schools. These goals called for systemic reform at all levels of education using both top-down and bottom-up strategies for implementation, including outcome-based education (Dougherty & Hall, 1997). The next wave of reform was initiated in 1989 with the specification of eight goals that were set for the year 2000. Goals 2000 focused on outcomes such as higher graduation rates and improved performance, including higher achievement in mathematics and science. Not surprising, these goals were accompanied by a focus on evaluation and assessment. The year 2000 arrived, and clearly these goals had not been reached.

The current focus on educational standards and testing, discussed in the second reading by Thomas Rohlen, is a natural outgrowth of these reform efforts and is specified clearly in NCLB and Race to the Top. Rohlen compares current educational reforms in the United States to the structure of the Japanese educational system. Although some progress has been made with NCLB, it will be interesting to watch the responses of politicians and educators and to follow the next wave of educational reform as it emerges. One conclusion we can draw from this brief review of recent reforms is that the federal government is playing an increasingly greater role in shaping education even while local control continues to exist. One example of the greater federal role in education is described in a 2010 *New York Times* article indicating that within two months of the release of recommendations for national educational standards by the governors and state school chiefs, 27 states had adopted the recommendations and more were expected to follow (Lewin, 2010).

All too often we get caught up on issues within schools and forget why these became issues in the first place. The reading by Richard Rothstein in Chapter 8 considered the attempts to improve academic achievement for all children from the perspective of the factors schools can't control. Many of these factors are related to the burdens of living in poverty. In the third reading in this chapter, Jean Anyon describes the role of social movements in effecting educational change. She argues that change in schools comes from connections of overlapping networks, including parents, unions, minority groups, academics, and others—all working together to call for change in the way schools work. She approaches the problem of change in schools historically, but takes a slightly different approach from that of Cuban. Anyon believes that social movements, or the merging of interests of multiple groups, can create a context for change in schools and promote equity in education.

We close this book with a classic piece by Ivan Illich that proposes an entirely different system of schooling and challenges the need for what Mary Metz called "real school" in Chapter 4. In his classic piece, published in 1971, Illich does not propose educational reform; rather he calls for radical changes in the way we "do" education. Illich argues for abolishing traditional schooling and replacing it with an entirely elective system in which individuals can learn whenever they wish from whomever they wish. Although his proposals may not stand a chance of implementation in the near or even distant future, it is useful in raising questions about what we are really trying to accomplish in our schools.

We, of course, are only providing a brief glimpse into the area about which many studies and reports proposing educational reform have been written. As you read this chapter, recall the open systems model in the introduction to this book. Think about how all these elements of the open systems model facilitate as well as inhibit change. We hope these readings stoke your creative juices and provide a framework for you to look at the parts of the educational system and envision the future of education in new and productive ways.

References

Dougherty, K., & Hall, P. M. (1997). Implications of the Goals 2000 legislation. In K. M. Borman, P. W. Cookson, Jr., A. R. Sadovnik, & J. Z. Spade (Eds.), *Implementing educational reform: Sociological perspectives on educational policy* (pp. 459–467). Norwood, NJ: Ablex.

Lewin, T. (2010, July 21). Many states adopt national standards for their schools. *New York Times*. Retrieved from http://www.nytimes.com/2010/07/21/education/21standards.html

Tyack, D., & Cuban, L. (1995). *Tinkering toward utopia: A century of public school reform*. Cambridge, MA: Harvard University Press.

THE PERENNIAL REFORM

Fixing School Time

Larry Cuban

The present is not always separated from the past, as Cuban notes in this reading on reform efforts to change the amount of time students are in school. The very extensive analysis he gives of this one educational reform helps us to understand the complex terrain on which educational change is built. Issues such as length of the school year, the school day, or even class periods are an important part of how schools are structured, as Barr and Dreeben suggested in Chapter 4. This reading suggests that any changes to this structure involve many players with very different motives and provides a framework for us to understand both why schools may change and why they remain the same.

Questions to consider for this reading:

1. As you read this article, think about which parts of the open systems model are involved in educational reforms.
2. Try to identify those factors that you think are most significant in driving reforms involving school time and those that are most involved in stopping such reforms.
3. Do you think that Cuban believes that these reforms to change schools will happen in the near future?

In the past quarter century, reformers have repeatedly urged schools to fix their use of time, even though it is a solution that is least connected to what happens in classrooms or what Americans want from public schools. Since *A Nation at Risk* in 1983, *Prisoners of Time* in 1994, and the latest blue-ribbon recommendations in *Tough Choices, Tough Times* in 2007, both how much time and how well students spend it in school has been criticized no end.[2]

Business and civil leaders have been critical because they see U.S. students stuck in the middle ranks on international tests. These leaders believe that the longer school year in Asia and Europe is linked to those foreign students scoring far higher than U.S. students on those tests.

Employers criticize the amount of time students spend in school because they wonder whether the limited days and hours spent in classes are sufficient to produce the skills that employees need to work in a globally competitive economy. Employers also wonder whether our comparatively short school year will teach the essential workplace behaviors of punctuality, regular attendance, meeting deadlines, and following rules.

Parents criticize school schedules because they want schools to be open when they go to work in the morning and to remain open until they pick up their children before dinner.

Professors criticize policy makers for allotting so little time for teachers to gain new knowledge and skills during the school day. Other researchers want both policy makers and practitioners to distinguish between requiring more time in school and academic learning time, academic jargon for those hours and minutes where teachers engage students in learning content and skills or, in more jargon, time on task.[3]

Finally, cyberschool champions criticize school schedules because they think it's quaint to have students sitting at desks in a building with hundreds of other students for 180 days when a revolution in communication devices allows children to learn the formal curriculum in many places, not just in school buildings. Distance learning advocates, joined by those who see cyberschools as the future, want children and youths to spend hardly any time in K–12 schools.[4]

TIME OPTIONS

Presidential commissions, parents, academics, and employers have proposed the same solutions, again and again, for fixing the time students spend in school: Add more days to the annual school calendar. Change to year-round schools. Add instructional time to the daily schedule. Extend the school day.

What Has Happened to Each Proposal in the Past Quarter Century?

Longer School Year. Recommendations for a longer school year (from 180 to 220 days) came from *A Nation at Risk* (1983) and *Prisoners of Time* (1994) plus scores of other commissions and experts. In 2008, a foundation-funded report, *A Stagnant Nation: Why American Students Are Still at Risk,* found that the 180-day school year

was intact across the nation and only Massachusetts had started a pilot program to help districts lengthen the school year. The same report gave a grade of F to states for failing to significantly expand student learning time.[5]

Year-Round Schools. Ending the summer break is another way to maximize student time in school. There is a homespun myth, treated as fact, that the annual school calendar, with three months off for both teachers and students, is based on the rhythm of 19th-century farm life, which dictated when school was in session. Thus, planting and harvesting chores accounted for long summer breaks, an artifact of agrarian America. Not so.

Actually, summer vacations grew out of early 20th-century urban middle-class parents (and later lobbyists for camps and the tourist industry) pressing school boards to release children to be with their families for four to eight weeks or more. By the 1960s, however, policy maker and parent concerns about students losing ground academically during the vacation months—in academic language, "summer loss"—gained support for year-round schooling. Cost savings also attracted those who saw facilities being used 12 months a year rather than being shuttered during the summer.

Nonetheless, although year-round schools were established as early as 1906 in Gary, Indiana, calendar innovations have had a hard time entering most schools. Districts with year-round schools still work within the 180-day year but distribute the time more evenly (e.g., 45 days in session, 15 days off) rather than having a long break between June and September. As of 2006, nearly 3,000 of the nation's 90,000 public schools enrolled more than 2.1 million students on a year-round calendar. That's less than 5% of all students attending public schools, and almost half of the year-round schools are in California. In most cases, school boards adopted year-round schools because increased enrollments led to crowded facilities, most often in minority and poor communities—not concerns over "summer loss."[6]

Adding Instructional Time to the School Day. Many researchers and reformers have pointed out that the 6½-hour school day has so many interruptions, so many distractions, that teachers have less than five hours of genuine instruction time. Advocates for more instructional time have tried to stretch the actual amount of instructional time available to teachers to a seven-hour day (or 5½ hours of time for time-on-task learning) or have tried to redistribute the existing secondary school schedule into 90-minute blocks rather than the traditional 50-minute periods. Since *A Nation at Risk,* this recommendation for more instructional time has resulted only in an anemic 10 more minutes per day when elementary school students study core academic subjects.[7]

Block scheduling in public secondary schools (60- to 90-minute periods for a subject that meets different days of the week) was started in the 1960s to promote instructional innovations. Various modified schedules have spread slowly, except in a few states where block schedules multiplied rapidly. In the past decade, an explosion of interest in small high schools has led many traditional urban comprehensive high schools of 1,500 or more students to convert to smaller high schools of 300 to 400 students, sometimes with all of those smaller schools housed within the original large building, sometimes as separate schools located elsewhere in the district. In many of these small high schools, modified schedules with instructional periods of an hour or more have found a friendly home. Block schedules rearrange existing allotted time for instruction; they do not add instructional time to the school day.[8]

Extended School Day. In the past half century, as the economy has changed and families increasingly have both (or single) parents working, schools have been pressed to take on childcare responsibilities, such as tutoring and homework supervision before and after school. Many elementary schools open at 7 A.M. for parents to drop off children and have after-school programs that close at 6 P.M. PDK/Gallup polls since the early 1980s show increased support for these before- and after-school programs. Instead of the familiar

half-day program for 5-year-olds, all-day kindergartens (and prekindergartens for 4-year-olds) have spread swiftly in the past two decades, especially in low-income neighborhoods. Innovative urban schools, such as the for-profit Edison Inc. and KIPP (Knowledge Is Power Program), run longer school days. The latter routinely opens at 7:30 A.M. and closes at 5 P.M. and also schedules biweekly Saturday classes and three weeks of school during the summer.[9]

If reformers want a success story in fixing school time, they can look to extending the school day, although it's arguable how many of those changes occurred because of reformers' arguments and actions and how many from economic and social changes in family structure and the desire to chase a higher standard of living.

Cybereducation. And what about those public school haters and cheerleading technological enthusiasts who see fixing time in school as a wasted effort when online schooling and distance learning can replace formal schooling? In the 1960s and 1970s, Ivan Illich and other school critics called for dismantling public schools and ending formal schooling. They argued that schools squelched natural learning, confused school-based education with learning, and turned children into obedient students and adults rather than curious and independent lifelong learners. Communication and instructional technologies were in their infancy then, and thinkers such as Illich had few alternatives to offer families who opted out.[10]

Much of that ire directed at formal public schooling still exists, but now technology has made it possible for students to learn outside school buildings. Sharing common ground in this debate are deeply religious families who want to avoid secular influences in schools, highly educated parents who fear the stifling effects of school rules and text-bound instruction, and rural parents who simply want their children to have access to knowledge unavailable in their local schools. These advocates seek home schooling, distance learning, and cyberschools.[11]

Slight increases in home schooling may occur— say from 1.1 million in 2003 to 2 to 3 million by the end of the decade, with the slight uptick in numbers due to both the availability of technology and a broader menu of choices for parents. Still, this represents less than 3% of public school students. Even though cheerleaders for distance learning have predicted wholesale changes in conventional site-based schools for decades, such changes will occur at the periphery, not the center, because most parents will continue to send their children to public schools.[12]

Even the most enthusiastic advocates for cyberschools and distance education recognize that replacing public schools is, at best, unlikely. The foreseeable future will still have 50 million children and youths crossing the schoolhouse door each weekday morning.

THREE REASONS

Reformers have spent decades trotting out the same recipes for fixing the time problem in school. For all the hoopla and all of the endorsements from highly influential business and political elites, their mighty efforts have produced minuscule results. Why is that?

Cost is the usual suspect. Covering additional teacher salaries and other expenses runs high. Minnesota provides one example: shifting from 175 to 200 days of instruction cost districts an estimated $750 million a year, a large but not insurmountable price to pay.[13] But costs for extending the school day for instruction and childcare are far less onerous.

Even more attractive than adding days to the calendar, however, is the claim that switching to a year-round school will save dollars. So, while there are costs involved in lengthening the school calendar, cost is not the tipping point in explaining why so few proposals to fix school time are successful.

I offer two other reasons why fixing school time is so hard.

Research showing achievement gains due to more time in school are sparse; the few studies most often displayed are contested.

Late 20th-century policy makers seriously underestimated the powerful tug that conservative, noneconomic goals (e.g., citizenship, character formation) have on parents, taxpayers, and voters. When they argued that America needed to add time to the school calendar in order to better prepare workers for global competition, they were out of step with the American public's desires for schools.

SKIMPY RESEARCH

In the past quarter century of tinkering with the school calendar, cultural changes, political decisions, or strong parental concerns trumped research every time. Moreover, the longitudinal and rigorous research on time in school was—and is—skimpy. The studies that exist are challenged repeatedly for being weakly designed. For example, analysts examining research on year-round schools have reported that most of the studies have serious design flaws and, at best, show slight positive gains in student achievement—except for students from low-income families, for whom gains were sturdier. As one report concluded: "[N]o truly trustworthy studies have been done on modified school calendars that can serve as the basis for sound policy decisions." Policy talk about year-round schools has easily outstripped results.[14]

Proving that time in school is the crucial variable in raising academic achievement is difficult because so many other variables must be considered—the local context itself, available resources, teacher quality, administrative leadership, socioeconomic and cultural background of students and their families, and what is taught. But the lack of careful research has seldom stopped reform-driven decision makers from pursuing their agendas.

CONFLICTING SCHOOL GOALS

If the evidence suggests that, at best, a longer school year or day or restructured schedules do not seem to make the key difference in student achievement, then I need to ask: What problem are reformers trying to solve by adding more school time?

The short answer is that for the past quarter century—*A Nation at Risk* (1983) is a suitable marker—policy elites have redefined a national economic problem into an educational problem. Since the late 1970s, influential civic, business, and media leaders have sold Americans the story that lousy schools are the reason why inflation surged, unemployment remained high, incomes seldom rose, and cheaper and better foreign products flooded U.S. stores. Public schools have failed to produce a strong, post-industrial labor force, thus leading to a weaker, less competitive U.S. economy. U.S. policy elites have used lagging scores on international tests as telling evidence that schools graduate less knowledgeable, less skilled high school graduates—especially those from minority and poor schools who will be heavily represented in the mid-21st century workforce—than competitor nations with lower-paid workforces who produce high-quality products.

Microsoft founder Bill Gates made the same point about U.S. high schools:

> In district after district across the country, wealthy white kids are taught Algebra II, while low-income minority kids are taught how to balance a checkbook. This is an economic disaster. In the international competition to have the best supply of workers who can communicate clearly, analyze information, and solve complex problems, the United States is falling behind. We have one of the highest high school dropout rates in the industrialized world.[15]

And here, in a nutshell, is the second reason why those highly touted reforms aimed at lengthening the school year and instructional day have disappointed policy makers. By blaming schools, contemporary civic and business elites have reduced the multiple goals Americans expect of their public schools to a single one: prepare youths to work in a globally competitive economy. This has been a mistake because Americans historically have expected more

from their public schools. Let me explore the geography of this error.

For nearly three decades, influential groups have called for higher academic standards, accountability for student outcomes, more homework, more testing, and, of course, more time in school. Many of their recommendations have been adopted. By 2008, U.S. schools had a federally driven system of state-designed standards anchored in increased testing, results-driven accountability, and demands for students to spend more time in school. After all, reformers reasoned, the students of foreign competitors were attending school more days in the year and longer hours each day, even on weekends, and their test scores ranked them higher than the U.S.

Even though this simplistic causal reasoning has been questioned many times by researchers who examined education and work performance in Japan, Korea, Singapore, Germany, and other nations, "common sense" observations by powerful elites swept away such questions. So the U.S.'s declining global economic competitiveness had been spun into a time-in-school problem.[16]

But convincing evidence drawn from research that more time in school would lead to a stronger economy, less inequalities in family income, and that elusive edge in global competitiveness—much less a higher rank in international tests—remains missing in action.

THE PUBLIC'S GOALS FOR EDUCATION

Business and civic elites have succeeded at least twice in the past century in making the growth of a strong economy the primary aim of U.S. schools, but other goals have had an enormous and enduring impact on schooling, both in the past and now. These goals embrace core American values that have been like second-hand Roses, shabby and discarded clothes hidden in the back of the closet and occasionally trotted out for show during graduation. Yet since the origins of tax-supported public schools in the early 19th century, these goals have been built into the very structures of schools so much so that, looking back from 2008, we hardly notice them.[17]

Time-based reforms have had trouble entering schools because other goals have had—and continue to have—clout with parents and taxpayers. Opinion polls, for example, display again and again what parents, voters, and taxpayers want schools to achieve. One recent poll identified the public's goals for public schools. The top five were to:

- Prepare people to become responsible citizens;
- Help people become economically sufficient;
- Ensure a basic level of quality among schools;
- Promote cultural unity among all Americans;
- Improve social conditions for people.

Tied for sixth and seventh were goals to

- Enhance people's happiness and enrich their lives; and
- Dispel inequities in education among certain schools and certain groups.[18]

To reach those goals, a democratic society expects schools to produce adults who are engaged in their communities, enlightened employers, and hard-working employees who have acquired and practiced particular values that sustain its way of life. Dominant American social, political, and economic values pervade family, school, workplace, and community: Act independently, accept personal responsibility for actions, work hard and complete a job well, and be fair, that is, willing to be judged by standards applied to others as long as the standards are applied equitably.[19]

These norms show up in school rules and classroom practices in every school. School is the one institutional agent between the family, the workplace, and voting booth or jury room responsible for instilling those norms in children's behavior. School is the agent for turning 4-year-olds into respectful students engaged in their communities, a goal that the public perceives as more significant than preparing children and youths for college and the labor market. In elite decision makers' eagerness to link schools to a growing economy, they either overlooked the powerful daily practices of schooling or neglected to consider seriously these other goals. In doing so, they erred. The consequences of that error in judgment can be seen in the fleeting attention that policy recommendations for adding more time in school received before being shelved.

TEACHING IN A DEMOCRACY

Public schools were established before industrialization, and they expanded rapidly as factories and mills spread.

Those times appear foreign to readers today. For example, in the late 19th century, calling public schools "factory like" was not an epithet hurled at educators or supporters of public schools as it has been in the U.S. since the 1960s.[20] In fact, describing a public school as an assembly-line factory or a productive cotton mill was considered a compliment to forward-looking educators who sought to make schools modern through greater efficiency in teaching and learning by copying the successes of wealthy industrialists. Progressive reformers praised schools for being like industrial plants in creating large, efficient, age-graded schools that standardized curriculum while absorbing millions of urban migrants and foreign immigrants. As a leading progressive put it:

> Our schools are, in a sense, factories in which the raw products (children) are to be shaped and fashioned into products to meet the various demands of life. . . . It is the business of the school to build its pupils to the specifications [of manufacturers].[21]

Progressive reformers saw mills, factories, and corporations as models for transforming the inefficient one-room schoolhouse in which students of different ages received fitful, incomplete instruction from one teacher into the far more efficient graded school where each teacher taught students a standardized curriculum each year. First established in Boston in 1848 and spreading swiftly in urban districts, the graded school became the dominant way of organizing a school by 1900. By the 1920s, schools exemplified the height of industrial efficiency because each building had separate classrooms with their own teachers. The principal and teachers expected children of the same age to cover the same content and learn skills by the end of the school year and perform satisfactorily on tests in order to be promoted to the next grade.[22]

Superintendents saw the age-graded school as a modern version of schooling well adapted to an emerging corporate-dominated industrial society where punctuality, dependability, and obedience were prized behaviors. As a St. Louis superintendent said in 1871:

> The first requisite of the school is Order: Each pupil must be taught first and foremost to conform his behavior to a general standard. The pupil must have his lessons ready at the appointed time, must rise at the tap of the bell, move to the line, return; in short, go through all of the evolutions with equal precision.

Recognition and fame went to educators who achieved such order in their schools.[23]

But the farm-driven seasonal nature of rural one-room schoolhouses was incompatible with the explosive growth of cities and an emerging industrial society. In the early 20th century, progressive reformers championed compulsory attendance laws while extending the abbreviated rural-driven short hours and days into a longer school day and year. Reformers wanted to increase the school's influence over children's attitudes and behavior, especially in cities where wave after wave of European immigrants settled. Seeking higher productivity in organization, teaching, and learning at the least cost, reformers broadened the school's mission by providing medical, social, recreational, and psychological services at schools. These progressive reformers believed schools should teach society's norms to both children and their families and also educate the whole child so that the entire government, economy, and society would change for the better. So, when reformers spoke about "factory-like schools" a century ago, they wanted educators to copy models of success; they were not scolding them. That changed, however, by the late 20th century.

As the U.S. shifted from a manufacturing-based economy to a post-industrial information-based economy, few policy makers reckoned with this history of schooling. Few influential decision makers view schools as agents of both stability and change. Few educational opinion makers recognize that the conservative public still expects schools to instill in children dominant American norms of being independent and being held accountable for one's actions, doing work well and efficiently, and treating others equitably to ensure that when students graduate they will practice these values as adults. And, yes, the public still expects schools to strengthen the economy by ensuring that graduates have the necessary skills to be productive employees in an ever-changing, highly competitive, and increasingly global workplace. But that is just one of many competing expectations for schools.

Thus far, I have focused mostly on how policy makers and reform-minded civic and business elites have not only defined economic problems as educational ones that can be fixed by more time spent in schools but also neglected the powerful hold that socialization goals have on parents' and taxpayers' expectations. Now, I want to switch from the world of reform-driven policy makers and elites to teachers and students because each group views school time differently from their respective perch. Teacher and student perspectives on time in school have little influence in policy makers' decision making. Although the daily actions of teachers and students don't influence policy makers, they do matter in explaining why reformers have had such paltry results in trying to fix school time.

DIFFERING VIEWS OF TIME IN SCHOOL

For civic and business leaders, media executives, school boards, superintendents, mayors, state legislators, governors, U.S. representatives, and the President (what I call "policy elites"), electoral and budget cycles become the timeframe within which they think and act. Every year, budgets must be prepared and, every two or four years, officials run for office and voters decide who should represent them and whether they should support bond referenda and tax levies. Because appointed and elected policy makers are influential with the media, they need to assure the public during campaigns that slogans and stump speeches were more than talk. Sometimes, words do become action when elected decision makers, for example, convert a comprehensive high school into a cluster of small high schools, initiate 1:1 laptop programs, and extend the school day. This is the world of policy makers.

The primary tools policy makers use to adopt and implement decisions, however, are limited and blunt—closer to a hammer than a scalpel. They use exhortation, press conferences, political bargaining, incentives, and sanctions to formulate and adopt decisions. (Note, however, that policy makers rarely implement decisions; administrators and practitioners put policies into practice.) Policy makers want broad social, political, economic, and organizational goals adopted as policies, and then they want to move educators, through encouragement, incentives, and penalties, to implement those policies in schools and classrooms that they seldom, if ever, enter.

The world of teachers differs from that of policy makers. For teachers, the time-driven budget and electoral cycles that shape policy matter little for their classrooms, except when such policies carry consequences for how and what teachers should teach, such as accountability measures that assume teachers and students are slackers and need to work harder. In these instances, teachers become classroom gatekeepers in deciding how much of a policy they will put into practice and under what conditions.

What matters most to teachers are student responses to daily lessons, weekly tests, monthly units, and the connections they build over time in classrooms, corridors, during lunch, and before and after school. Those personal connections become the compost of learning. Those connections account for former students pointing to particular teachers who made a difference in their

lives. Teacher tools, unlike policy maker tools, are unconnected to organizational power or media influence. Teachers use their personalities, knowledge, experience, and skills in building relationships with groups of students and providing individual help. Teachers believe there is never enough time in the daily schedule to finish a lesson, explain a point, or listen to a student. Administrative intrusions gobble up valuable instructional time that could go to students. In class, then, both teachers and students are clock watchers, albeit for different reasons.[24]

Students view time differently as well. For a fraction of students from middle- and low-income families turned off by school requirements and expectations, spending time in classrooms listening to teachers, answering questions, and doing homework is torture; the hands of the clock seldom move fast enough for them. The notion of extending the school day and school year for them—or continuing on to college and four more years of reading texts and sitting in classrooms—is not a reform to be implemented but a punishment to be endured. Such students look for creative shortcuts to skip classes, exit the school as early as they can, and find jobs or enter the military once they graduate.

Most students, however, march from class to class until they hear "Pomp and Circumstance." But a high school diploma, graduates have come to realize, is not enough in the 21st-century labor market.

COLLEGE FOR EVERYONE

In the name of equity and being responsive to employers' needs, most urban districts have converted particular comprehensive high schools into clusters of small college-prep academies where low-income minority students take Advanced Placement courses, write research papers, and compete to get into colleges and universities. Here, then, is the quiet, unheralded, and unforeseen victory of reformers bent on fixing time in school. They have succeeded unintentionally in stretching K–12 into pre-K–16 public schooling, not just for middle- and upper-middle class students, but for everyone.

As it has been for decades for most suburban middle- and upper-middle class white and minority families, now it has become a fact, an indisputable truth converted into a sacred mission for upwardly mobile poor families: A high school diploma and a bachelor's degree are passports to high-paying jobs and the American Dream.

For families who already expect their sons and daughters to attend competitive colleges, stress begins early. Getting into the best pre-schools and elementary and secondary schools and investing in an array of activities to build attractive resumes for college admission officers to evaluate become primary tasks. For such families and children, there is never enough time for homework, Advanced Placement courses, music, soccer, drama, dance, and assorted after-school activities. For high-achieving, stressed-out students already expecting at least four more years of school after high school graduation, reform proposals urging a longer school year and an extended day often strike an unpleasant note. Angst and fretfulness become familiar clothes to don every morning as students grind out 4s and 5s on Advanced Placement exams, play sports, and compile just the right record that will get them into just the right school.[25]

For decades, pressure on students to use every minute of school to prepare for college has been strongest in middle- and upper-middle-class suburbs. What has changed in the past few decades is the spread of the belief that everyone, including low-income minority students, should go to college.

To summarize, for decades, policy elites have disregarded teacher and student perspectives on time in school. Especially now when all students are expected to enter college, children, youths, and teachers experience time in school differently than policy makers who seek a longer school day and school year. Such varied perceptions about time are heavily influenced by the socialization goals of schooling, age-graded structures, socioeconomic status of families, and historical experience. And policy makers often

ignore these perceptions and reveal their tone-deafness and myopia in persistently trying to fix time in schools.

Policy elites need to parse fully this variation in perceptions because extended time in school remains a high priority to reform-driven policy makers and civic and business leaders anxious about U.S. performance on international tests and fearful of falling behind in global economic competitiveness. The crude policy solutions of more days in the year and longer school days do not even begin to touch the deeper truth that what has to improve is the quality of "academic learning time." If policy makers could open their ears and eyes to student and teacher perceptions of time, they would learn that the secular Holy Grail is decreasing interruption of instruction, encouraging richer intellectual and personal connections between teachers and students, and increasing classroom time for ambitious teaching and active, engaged learning. So far, no such luck.

Conclusion

These three reasons—cost, lackluster research, and the importance of conservative social goals to U.S. taxpayers and voters—explain why proposals to fix time in U.S. schools have failed to take hold.

Policy elites know research studies proving the worth of year-round schools or lengthened school days are in short supply. Even if an occasional study supported the change, the school year is unlikely to go much beyond 180 days. Policy elites know school goals go far beyond simply preparing graduates for college and for employability in a knowledge-based economy. And policy elites know they must show courage in their pursuit of improving failing U.S. schools by forcing students to go to school just as long as their peers in India, China, Japan, and Korea. That courage shows up symbolically, playing well in the media and in proposals to fix time in schools, but it seldom alters calendars.

While cost is a factor, it is the stability of schooling structures and the importance of socializing the young into the values of the immediate community and larger society that have defeated policy-driven efforts to alter time in school over the past quarter century. Like the larger public, I am unconvinced that requiring students and teachers to spend more time in school each day and every year will be better for them. How that time is spent in learning before, during, and after school is far more important than decision makers counting the minutes, hours, and days students spend each year getting schooled. That being said, I have little doubt that state and federal blue-ribbon commissions will continue to make proposals about lengthening time in school. Those proposals will make headlines, but they will not result in serious, sustained attention to what really matters—improving the quality of the time that teachers and students spend with one another in and out of classrooms.

NOTES

1. I wish to thank Selma Wasserman for her most helpful comments and suggestions on the penultimate draft and Bruce Smith for inviting me to do this special report.

2. National Commission on Excellence in Education, *A Nation at Risk* (Washington, D.C.: U.S. Government Printing Office, 1983); National Education Commission on Time and Learning, *Prisoners of Time* (Washington, D.C.: U.S. Government Printing Office, 1994); New Commission on the Skills of the American Work Force, *Tough Times or Tough Choices* (San Francisco: Jossey-Bass, 2006).

3. David Berliner, "What's All the Fuss About Instructional Time?" in *The Nature of Time in Schools: Theoretical Concepts, Practitioner Perceptions,* ed. Miriam Ben-Peretz and Rainer Bromme. (New York: Teachers College Press, 1990).

4. See, for example, North Central Regional Educational Laboratory, "E-Learning Policy Implications for K–12 Educators and Decision Makers," (2001). Accessed from http://www.ncrel.org/policy/pubs/html/pivolll/apr2002d.htm.

5. Strong American Schools, *A Stagnant Nation: Why American Students Are Still at Risk* (Washington, D.C.: Author, 2008), 3–4.

6. Joel Weiss and Robert Brown, "Telling Tales Over Time: Constructing and Deconstructing the School Calendar," *Teachers College Record*, (2003): 1720–57; Shaun P. Johnson and Terry E. Spradlin, "Alternatives to the Traditional School-Year Calendar," *Education Policy Brief Center for Evaluation & Education Policy*, (Spring 2007): 3. For a description of the "Gary Plan" of year-round schooling, see Ronald Cohen, *Children of the Mill: Schooling and Society in Gary, Indiana, 1906–1960* (Bloomington: Indiana University Press, 1990).

7. Strong American Schools, 4.

8. Robert Canady and Michael Rettig, *Block Scheduling: A Catalyst for Change in High Schools* (Larchmont, N.Y.: Eye on Education, 1995); personal communication from Michael Rettig, 28 April 2008.

9. Lowell C. Rose and Alec M. Gallup, "38th Annual Phi Delta Kappa/Gallup Poll of the Public's Attitudes Toward the Public Schools," *Phi Delta Kappan,* (September 2006); Sarah Huyvaert, *Time Is of the Essence: Learning in School* (Boston: Allyn & Bacon, 1998): 59–67; for KIPP, see http://www.ldpp.org/01/whatisaldppschool.cfm.

10. Ivan Illich, *Deschooling Society* (New York: Harper & Row, 1971).

11. For a politically conservative view on home schooling and its history, see Isabel Lyman, "Home Schooling: Back to the Future?" Cato Institute Policy Analysis No. 294, (January 1998), Accessed from http://www.cato.org/pubs/pas/pa-294.html. Beginning nearly a decade ago, state- and district-funded cyber schools, such as Florida Virtual School, provide courses for homeschoolers, parents who want more learning options for their children, and students in isolated rural areas who lack access to advanced high school courses. Florida Virtual School served over 50,000 students in 2006–07 and expects to reach 100,000 in 2009. See http://www.flvs.net.

12. For predictions from the 1990s and current ones for distance learning and students' use of the Internet, see "Predictions Database" in Elon University's "Imagining the Internet," (http://www.elon.edu/predictions/ql3.aspx). For an astute analysis of distance learning, see Clayton M. Christensen and Michael B. Horn, "How Do We Transform Our Schools?" *Education Next,* (Summer 2008). Accessed from http://www.hoover.org/publications/ednext/18575969.html. For the 2003 figure on home-schooled children, see "Fast Facts" from National Center for Education Statistics (http://nces.ed.gov/fastfacts/display.asp?id=65-).

13. The Minnesota example comes from Elena Silva, "On the Clock: Rethinking the Way Schools

Use Time," *Education Sector Reports,* (January 2007): 8; for cost savings in year-round schools, see Nasser Daneshvary and Terrence M. Clauretie, "Efficiency and Costs in Education: Year-Round Versus Traditional Schedules," *Economics of Education Review,* (2001): 279–87.

14. Johnson and Spradlin, 5; Harris Cooper et al., "The Effects of Modified School Calendars on Student Achievement and on School and Community Attitudes," *Review of Educational Research,* (Spring 2003): 1–52.

15. Bill Gates, "What Is Wrong With America's High Schools?" *Los Angeles Times,* March 3, 2005, B11.

16. One of the better summaries of how schools had become the central problem to the future of the nation in the 1980s can be found in Chester E. Finn, Jr., *We Must Take Charge: Our Schools and Our Future* (New York: Free Press, 1991); also see Diane Ravitch, "The Test of Time," *Education Next,* (Spring 2003), accessed from http://www.educationnext.org/20032/32.html; and, in the same issue, see a reprint of Albert Shanker's retrospective (9 May 1993) on A Nation at Risk report. For analyses of other countries compared to the U.S., see Norton Grubb and Marvin Lazerson, *The Education Gospel: The Economic Power of Schooling* (Cambridge, Mass.: Harvard University Press, 2004): 170–72.

17. John Goodlad, *A Place Called School* (New York: McGraw-Hill, 1984); and David Labaree, "Public Goods, Private Goods: The American Struggle Over Educational Goals," *American Educational Research Journal,* (Spring 1997): 39–81.

18. Lowell C. Rose and Alec M. Gallup, "The 32nd Annual Phi Delta Kappa/Gallup Poll of the Public's Attitudes Toward the Public Schools." *Phi Delta Kappan,* (September 2000): 47.

19. There are other personal values, such as honesty, trustworthiness, etc., that are highly prized and reinforced by teachers and school policies, but I will focus on the obvious societal values embedded in the structures and processes of tax-supported schooling. See Robert Dreeben, *On What Is Learned in School*

(Reading, Mass.: Addison-Wesley, 1968); Steven Brint, Mary C. Contreras, and Michael T. Matthews, "Socialization Messages in Primary Schools: An Organizational Analysis," *Sociology of Education,* (July 2001): 157–80; and Philip Jackson, *Life in Classrooms* (New York: Holt, Rinehart, and Winston, 1968).

20. For examples of the pejorative use of "factory-like schools," see Samuel Bowles and Herbert Gintis, *Schooling in Capitalist America: Educational Reform and the Contradictions of Economic Life* (New York: Basic Books, 1976); and Joel Spring, "Education as a Form of Social Control," in *Roots of Crisis: American Education in the 20th Century,* ed. Clarence Karier, Paul Violas, and Joel Spring, (Chicago: Rand McNally, 1973): 30–9.

21. Quote cited in Raymond Callahan, *Education and the Cult of Efficiency* (Chicago: University of Chicago Press, 1962): 152. It comes from Stanford Professor Ellwood P. Cubberley in his textbook, *Public School Administration,* written in 1916.

22. David L. Angus, Jeffrey E. Mirel, and Maris A. Vinovskis, "Historical Development of Age-Stratification in Schooling," *Teachers College Record,* (Winter 1988): 211–36.

23. David B. Tyack, *The One Best System: A History of American Urban Education* (Cambridge: Harvard University Press, 1974): 43.

24. Marty Swaim and Stephen Swaim, *Teacher Time: Wiry Teacher Workload and School Management Matter to Each Student in Our Public schools* (Arlington, Va.: Redbud Books, 1999); Claudia Meek, "Classroom Crisis: It's About Time," *Phi Delta Kappan,* (April 2003): 592–95; and National Center for Education Statistics, *Time Spent Teaching Core Academic Subjects in Elementary Schools* (Washington, D.C.: National Center for Education Statistics, 1997).

25. Although aware of anxiety-stressed teenagers, I was surprised by an article that described students in an affluent high school being required to eat lunch because they skipped eating in order to take another Advanced Placement class. See Winnie Hu, "Too Busy to Eat, Students Get a New Required Course: Lunch," *New York Times,* May 24, 2008, A1, A11.

WIDER CONTEXTS AND FUTURE ISSUES

National Standards and School Reform in Japan and the United States

Thomas P. Rohlen

Thomas P. Rohlen brings together conclusions from some of the articles in a book edited by Gary DeCoker, *National Standards and School Reform in Japan and the United States*, to consider future issues for the educational system in the United States. In this reading, Rohlen compares current standards-based reforms in the American educational system (see the reading on No Child Left Behind and Race to the Top in Chapter 3) to the Japanese system. He looks historically at the Japanese educational system and also considers critiques of that system. This excerpt summarizes considerable research on the educational systems of both countries as it examines both standards-based education and the hierarchical structures of education in the two countries. It is particularly valuable because the American educational system and achievement therein has been compared to that of Japan for some time.

Questions to consider for this reading:

1. In what ways is the educational system in the United States less hierarchical than that of Japan?

2. What features of the Japanese educational system contribute to higher achievement in that country?

3. Explain why Rohlen believes that standards-based testing will be effective in the United States.

C urrently there is strong interest in establishing and raising educational standards in the United States. Presumably, what appears to work so well in Japan to maintain high average levels of achievement (with smaller standard deviations in test results) could provide instructive insight for Americans seeking the same ends. Perhaps. But first we need to take another look at the American system. If in the past we have erroneously stereotyped the Japanese approach as centralized and hierarchical, we also have some rethinking to do about the nature of reform in the American system.

What is clear to the point of almost being a truism is that in its origins, and still very largely today, the American system is one that rests squarely on the assumption of local school board autonomy. The centralized qualities that have developed in our system are relatively recent developments that have arisen separately in each state and in an ad hoc fashion at the national level, resulting eventually in the creation of the U.S. Department of Education, which is given the task of administering a hodgepodge of congressionally mandated and largely peripheral programs. The U.S. Department of Education is hardly even comparable to the MOE (Ministry of Education in Japan). Nothing is more indicative of this state of affairs, to my way of thinking, than the fact that private textbook publishers in the United States occupy a more central ground in the shaping of instruction nationally than does any single government organization.

The nature of our educational system has built into it another kind of autonomy as well. The American teacher in his or her classroom has a degree of autonomy that is inconceivable to a Japanese teacher used to fitting in and working in highly interactive peer situations. American teachers generally decide for themselves how they will use the textbooks, what supplemental materials they will introduce, at what pace they will proceed, what they will cover, and how they will conduct instruction. Lee and Zusho (2002) confirm this fundamental difference, reported by a generation of comparative studies of the two systems.

It should come as no surprise that in the American educational system the degree of disconnection on both the vertical and horizontal dimensions is much greater than in Japan, and, as a result, the organizational fabric of the American system seems weak and unwieldy by comparison. The fact that there are regular calls from the political right for the elimination of the Department of Education is but one illustration of this condition. The complex and confusing process of state and local textbook adoption is another. That we cannot find common ground on which to establish standards in even mathematics is also telling. In fact, we have entered the 21st century with what is essentially an early 19th-century system, one that grew unplanned and largely from the bottom up. Our system predates the rise in Japan and Europe and elsewhere of the state-centered constructions arising as part of the ideology of the strong nation state. Japan's basic system was developed in the 1880s as part of a powerful nation-building agenda.

The fit between our locally funded and locally controlled system and American social reality is curious and quite different from that in Japan. It is deeply allied with cultural and political forces here that have an enclave mentality, protecting various kinds of class, regional, and religious differences from outside forces representing something like the national common denominator. Wealthy and middle-class suburbs, religious sects, and agricultural communities, for example, believe they find protection in this highly diffuse system. One result is the perpetuation of a degree of socioeconomic and cultural diversity unimaginable in Japan. The current level of residential mobility in the United States, on the other hand, puts our system in a very different light. Most Americans are not being educated today in a single local system. Rather, the typical educational career is one that embraces at least several, if not many, school districts. Nor are local investments in education likely to pay off in reliable human capital pools, given the way we Americans move around. Whether we are considering textbooks or standards or teaching methods, local authority appears sadly anachronistic in this light. Geographically mobile parents, strongly interested in their children's schools, are a common aspect of the educational landscape in both Japan and the United States today, yet the choices offered by the two systems are not the same. In the United States, without a national system in terms of budgetary equity, standards, or regulatory authority, parents struggle to find viable levers to effect broad reforms. In other words, opinion polls and electoral rhetoric may imply that our public concern is with education as a "national" problem, but the essential nature of our institutional arrangements makes centralized solutions exceedingly difficult.

Our efforts to reform education appear to follow two quite different paths, neither of which is at all like what we find in Japan. On the one hand, we are experimenting with standards and testing as something new and forceful that works top-down and across the board, and on the other, we continue at that local level to experiment in a massive way with every kind of initiative that holds out some kind of promise of improvement. Because of the disconnected nature of our system, we have few convenient institutions in the middle that might connect the two kinds of efforts.

This explains, I think, why when we seek to raise average achievement or raise the level of poorly performing districts and schools, we end up relying heavily on what are basically very coercive methods. We do not typically define these as coercive, but when compared with the Japanese approach they certainly have such a character. Take the many cases of legal intrusion into school system management as one example. Whether mandated by the U.S. Supreme Court, some state court, or a lower federal court, these intrusions have little or no real teacher input; almost intentionally ignore the realities of school and classroom; and force change primarily with threats of dismissal and closure. Also typical of this approach is close, aggressive, and often naïve supervision by the courts. The will of the courts, and their impatience, becomes central to reform once it is determined that the law is being broken. That judges could decide educational policy is unthinkable in the Japanese context.

A second common form of top-down intervention in the American case is the effort to legislate systemwide improvements by establishing universal standards coupled to standardized tests and other mechanisms of measurement and enforcement. Again, this kind of leverage can be found at all levels from the local to the national, and again without any clearly coordinated teacher input or consensus. Standards without tests have no teeth, obviously, and even tests without penalties are a weak form of coercion. Naturally, then, the movement to leverage average achievement by these means seeks to tie such things as graduation requirements, teacher pay, tenure, and other incentives and punishments to test results. The problems with this approach are so well known as to require no more than a brief list of its major defects: teaching to the test, debasing content, perpetual political disagreement on standards, issues of equity, ideological squabbling, the absence of critical skill development, widespread teacher resistance, and so forth. As with the case of legal intrusion from above, the time frames mandated tend to be too short for concerted reform, the consultation with teachers tends to be minimal, and the unintended consequences turn out to be quite large. The

middle ground where goals and means are adjusted and where teachers collectively join in the process of improvement and change hardly exists. One reason is that the institutions of consultation between national policy discussions and school-level change, so central to the Japanese approach, are absent. Instead, we delegate such communications to scholars, academic and professional journals, schools of education, district training sessions, and the like, areas very weakly developed in the Japanese system.

What have been the results of the American movement to establish a standards-based approach? Compared with Japanese students, American students certainly take more standardized tests annually. This may be surprising, but between testing at various grade levels and practicing to take such tests (not to mention teaching-to-the-test activities), American students are increasingly focused on tests imposed from outside the district. Eventually this will result in improved test scores, but probably will not lessen inequality or significantly improve general levels of skills or knowledge. The critical tests in Japan, those governing entrance to high school and university, cluster at the secondary level. These put enormous muscle behind the textbooks and the curriculum, as DeCoker (2002) shows, and they also give a prominent role to private tutoring schools. Russell (2002) illustrates how these are organized to fill the gap between the national guidelines and the competitive realities of the much condemned university entrance exams. Japanese secondary students are also thrust into practice test taking in a major way by the prospect of entrance exams. And, no doubt about it, entrance exams have all of the flaws just mentioned in regard to American standardized tests. The differences are, first, when the exams occur in the developmental process, and, second, that in Japan students are individually differentiated and ranked by their efforts (LeTendre, 2002; DeCoker, 2002), whereas in the American case the teacher and the school are likely to be punished for low results. The one emphasizes positive motivations; the other, negative ones. The Japanese approach makes students accountable; the American one makes teachers accountable. It is not surprising that in the United States the standards movement is often pushed most strongly by persons who harbor suspicions about teachers' qualifications and commitment. Furthermore, in Japan, it is the more talented and socioeconomically better off two-thirds of the population that are most affected by the entrance exam system, whereas in the United States, the effort to raise standards targets the lowest-performing one-third of the population. Most of our coercive efforts are aimed at the districts, schools, and teachers working with low-income, ethnic, rural, and disadvantaged students.

Standards per se are not the essence of our problem. Of course, there will be controversies when standards are first imposed, especially for easily politicized matters of language and social studies. Far more critical is the problem that any system designed to enforce standards contradicts the historic nature of American education. The attempt to establish strict accountability, furthermore, confronts some of the most basic organizational realities of education anywhere. Schools are limited instruments of social change, and accountability is a highly flawed concept when judgments are made simply on the basis of testing. Teachers, furthermore, are not motivated primarily by monetary or other easily manipulated incentives. Nor can accurate calculations be made of the appropriate time frames and support requirements needed to effect the levels of change intended.

Having arrived at a point in the United States where we as a nation have identified our greatest educational failures and acknowledged that they are intolerable, we still rely heavily in the policy realm on very crude top-down methods of change, ones that generally alienate most teachers and local administrators—the very people central to actually effecting the improvements needed. It is telling that Japanese high standards and high average achievement levels are not accomplished in the manner we have been inclined toward in public debate. Despite a few superficial similarities stemming from the fact that Japan is a centralized system, the fact remains that in Japan teachers and political

policy meet in the middle. History has dealt us a notably poor hand when it comes to administrative approaches to reform. It is not that standards and tests are inherently bad, but that alone they are woefully inadequate.

The second path I identify as characteristic of American efforts to improve education is marked less by a desire to create systemwide change than simply to demonstrate that there are "better ways" to accomplish education. Thus we witness a constant flow of new experimental programs and initiatives, most at local levels, funded by an amazing variety of private and public sources of support. These are largely disconnected from one another and philosophically as heterogeneous as one can imagine. In the same district and even in the same school there can be conflicts among them, but typically a state of churn and flux prevails. At one extreme, we find home schooling becoming popular—the ultimate in American-style autonomy. Perhaps as many as a million children are currently schooled by their parents. Also reflective of parental choice and the autonomy of private initiatives are the many kinds of "alternative" schools arising and disappearing on the educational landscape. If we include the full range of religious schools, charter schools, Montessori schools, Waldorf schools, cultural and language preservationist schools, and so forth, they number perhaps in the tens of thousands. The largest category of experimental schools, however, is comprised of public schools enrolled in one or more experimental programs. Who knows how large this category really is? It is unusual to visit an urban public school at any level that is not involved in an innovative program of some kind, whether in math teaching, values education, bilingual instruction, citizenship, community involvement, teacher collaboration, back-to-basics, sex education, abstinence education, drug education, or one of literally hundreds of other types of initiatives. Most of these efforts, we know, prove to be short-lived, so highly dependent are they on teacher enthusiasm, short-term funding, and extra effort. When the leadership changes, or the money goes away, or burnout arrives, or teachers transfer, the momentum typically wanes. Yet nothing about American education is more impressive to Japanese visitors than the lively innovation and teacher optimism exemplified by this vast array of local-level change efforts. Such diversified, exuberant, and uncoordinated innovation is unimaginable in Japan.

Seen in this light, voucher schemes, while generally discussed as systemwide and policy-driven initiatives, actually turn out to be an ingenious, if deceptive, mix of the two typical American approaches to reform. They are proposed by legislators and officials at the top, yet speak to the spirit of local autonomy and the promise of independent innovation. A major shift in the direction toward vouchers would greatly amplify our already massive inclination to piecemeal innovative diversity. While national standards and formal testing offer a highly specified if awkward and limited approach to reforming education, the "let a thousand flowers bloom" experimentalism path of vouchers is formless, but actually closer in spirit to what teachers and many parents take education to be. Combining the two, as is now commonly proposed, speaks to both inclinations.

Whether, if such proposals were followed, we would get the best of both or the worst of both is the essential question. It is worth recalling that before the formation of the Meiji state in 1868, Japan, too, had an educational landscape of great diversity and little if any inclusive organization. It chose a centralized, nation-state-oriented path, which has been modified considerably, but not fundamentally changed (Hall, 1973; Lincicome, 1995). Interestingly, the voices in Japan calling for a reorientation of education cite the American example as the ideal. It seems, ironically, that the grass is readily seen as greener on the other side of the Pacific.

Returning to the perspective granted us by this comparison, we can see that America's several paths to educational reform ignore the administrative middle ground. We have precious few noncoercive means of effectively coordinating instruction in the schools and classrooms across the nation. There are few national curricular guidelines of real merit, but many

national laws regulating a host of peripheral trivial matters. Nor are our textbooks the product of consultative processes arising from interaction in the administrative middle. The erratic way they are received at the local level and used by teachers reflects this. We also lack plausible mechanisms for significant (as opposed to token) teacher participation in our larger reform processes. Our policymakers, like our textbook writers, rarely come from within the system. The trust in and respect for teachers is low. Public impatience and ideological polarities arising outside education tend to determine our policy agendas and, given the enormity of the task, almost guarantee that systemwide efforts will fail. We have been in a chronic state of "crisis" for decades with little to show for all the reform rhetoric and "new" and creative programs. Is this evidence that the absence of an institutional middle ground in American education is a fundamental flaw? The contrast with Japan suggests precisely this.

The weakness of an institutional middle ground where adjustment and improvement efforts are routine and nationally coordinated certainly helps explain why our two kinds of responses, coercive and centripetal, tend toward the extremes of the range of administrative options set forth at the beginning of this discussion. Ironically, if both options continue to be popular, they are likely to become, in theory at least, increasingly interdependent. On the one hand, the heterogeneity of experimentalism will require a central core of standards if there is to be any framework legitimizing public expenditures. On the other hand, a system of standards and testing will have to discover reliable models of instruction and improvement to be dynamic. Perhaps this potential for interdependence is a key ingredient of a new design for American education.

Clearly, America is not Japan. The authors of chapters [in *National Standards and School Reform in Japan and the United States*] are properly reluctant to make recommendations or to claim that Japan has something to teach America. It is not hard to see in their accounts, however, an admiration for Japan's approach and accomplishments.

Implicit is the message that when it comes to the challenge of organizing and moving a large national system of instruction toward improvements and high achievement, Japan is worth studying, since it appears to have learned a great deal from a century of experience. The only way this experience will be of value to American policymakers, however, is if they become concerned with our lack of a viable middle ground, whether at the national or the state level. That concern is not much in evidence at present.

Our two distinct American paths to change could take us to a place far more unlike Japan than where we currently are. Whether we are engaged in the accidental invention of a quite new system is anybody's guess at present. Trends point, however, toward a circumstance in which public standards, standardized tests, and continued public funding form a kind of general context for a growing diversity of schools (increasingly private) and an accountability system that rests primarily on parental choice. Elements of this have been in place for a long time, but what is far from clear is whether this approach will actually address the hard core problems of the underperforming bottom third of the population any more effectively than the system we currently operate.

REFERENCES

DeCoker, G. (2002). Deregulating Japan's high school curriculum: The unlimited consequences of educational reform. In G. DeCoker (Ed.), *National standards and school reform in Japan and the United States* (pp. 141–145). New York: Teachers College Press.

Hall, J. P. (1973). *Mori Arinori*. Cambridge, MA: Harvard University Press.

Lee, S.-Y., & Zusho, A. (2002). Comparing Japan and U.S. teachers' manuals: Implications for mathematics teaching and learning. In G. DeCoker (Ed.), *National standards and school reform in Japan and the United States* (pp. 67–92). New York: Teachers College Press.

LeTendre, G. K. (2002). Setting national standards: Educational reform, and political conflict. In G. DeCoker (Ed.), *National standards and school reform in Japan and the United States* (pp. 19–32). New York: Teachers College Press.

Lincicome, M. E. (1995). *Principle, praxis, and the politics of educational reform in Meiji Japan*. Honolulu: University of Hawaii Press.

Russell, N. U. (2002). The role of the private sector in determining national standards: How Juku undermine Japanese educational authority. In G. DeCoker (Ed.), *National standards and school reform in Japan and the United States* (pp. 158–176). New York: Teachers College Press.

Progressive Social Movements and Educational Equity

Jean Anyon

In this excerpt from a longer article, Jean Anyon discusses educational reforms resulting from pressure by social movements. In addition to defining what a social movement is, she uses previous educational reforms to illustrate the role of social movements in changing schools. Anyon's approach is that the problem of attaining educational equity extends far beyond school walls and requires a coalition of community groups who can identify the barriers to educational equity.

Questions to consider for this reading:

1. In your own words, describe how Anyon defines a social movement.

2. How does Anyon's approach to educational change in this article differ from the discussion of school time in Cuban's article in this chapter?

3. Consider how the three recent organizing efforts she describes in this article—Southern Echo, Logan Square Neighborhood Association, and Community Collaborative for District 9—fit her definition of social movements. What types of change are they likely to achieve?

A social movement connects what may feel like personal, individual exclusion or subordination to social structure and political causes. Social movements also provide a way of connecting with other individuals and groups across neighborhoods, cities, regions, and states to forge collective solutions to social problems. They offer a forum for working together to develop community power and to collaborate with others in making fundamental shifts in the political and social arrangements that have caused inequities, exclusions, and subordination. Thus, social movements are not symptoms of a "dysfunctional" political system, as some earlier scholars argued (e.g., Neil Smelser, 1962). Rather, in a healthy democracy, social movements are part and parcel of the process of change.

The concept of a social movement does not apply just to workers in struggle for unions and higher wages. The concept applies to all people and groups struggling for what political philosopher Nancy Fraser (2000) calls recognition or redistribution—for racial rights, economic justice, women's reproductive freedom, or educational opportunities. Social movements can also strive for negative goals like ending unpopular wars or seemingly unwarranted invasion of other countries.

There have of course been movements on the political Right (e.g., the "Right to Life" movement). But this chapter concerns progressive social movements and what those involved in school reform and public engagement can learn from them (to garner lessons from the Right, see Apple, 2006. An excerpt from another article by Apple is in Chapter 8.).[1]

From "Progressive Social Movements and Educational Equity," by J. Anyon, 2009, *Educational Policy: An Interdisciplinary Journal of Policy and Practice, 23*(1), pp. 194–215. Copyright 2009 by Sage Publications. Reprinted with permission.

A comprehensive definition of social movements, summarizing several decades of sociological research, is as follows: We have a social movement in process when individuals and organizations are involved in "collective conflictual relations with clearly identified opponents" (Della Porta & Diani, 2006, p. 20). The conflict involves "an oppositional relationship between actors who seek control of the same stake—be it political, economic or cultural power—and in the process make . . . claims on each other which, if realized, would damage the interests of the other actors" (Tilly, 1978, as cited in Della Porta & Diani, 2006, p. 21). Thus, the conflict can be cultural and/or political-economic. The conflict typically has as a goal to promote or oppose social change. In a social movement, the actors engaged in the collective action are linked by dense informal networks of organizations and individuals. They share a collective identity or sense of shared mission. The networks and interactions between groups and members yield social and cultural capital, which are important to bridging locales, groups, and opportunities, and provide the skills involved in planning, mobilizing, and executing actions and campaigns. People involved in a social movement typically feel a collective identity. They feel connected by a common purpose and share commitment to a cause; they feel linked or at least compatible with a broader collective mobilization (Della Porta & Diani, 2006; Touraine, 1981).

It is important to note that one organization, no matter how large, does not make a movement. The dense and sometimes overlapping networks that constitute a social movement are made up of multiple organizations, all of which are in pursuit of a common goal (Della Porta & Diani, 2006; see also Tilly, 2004; Touraine, 1981).

Nor are social movements isolated protest events or short-lived temporary coalitions that form around an issue. They involve episodes of action that are perceived as components of longer lasting action, over time—typically multiple years of effort. Social movements use various forms of protest against the specified targets and may also involve cultural expressions of belief as in group singing and the production of art and music that contain a social message.

In sum, when people feel excluded or subordinated, when people face governments or other groups whose actions they believe are unjust, and when they belong to networks or organizations that share goals and collaborate over long periods of time to attempt to increase equity through protest and sustained political and social contention against the targeted groups, they are engaged in a social movement, or social movement building. . . .

Past Impacts of Social Movements on Educational Equity

Although not the only source of equity—upper class reformers, business groups, and politicians have at times advocated successfully for new educational resources or opportunities—progressive social movements have made substantial gains in increasing educational equity in America. Although we do not usually think of social movements as characterizing U.S. educational history in the early/mid-19th century, one can document substantial pressure from below that contributed to important educational change during those years.

The 19th Century

Horace Mann and his colleagues were not the only force pressing for the establishment of common schools in America in the 19th century. Historian Joel Spring (2008) points out that

> [t]raditional labor history . . . stresses the key role of working men's parties in the late 1820s and 30s in fighting for common school reforms. This interpretation places the American worker at the forefront of the battle for common schools. Of particular importance . . . is the opposition of workers to the . . . charity schools, which they felt reinforced social-class distinctions. (p. 100)

Active in the northeastern states of the United States, the Workingmen's Parties believed that "kept in ignorance, workers could be deprived of their rights, cheated in their daily business, and 'gulled and deceived' by . . . 'parasitic politicians,' 'greedy bank directors,' and 'heartless manufacturers'" (Russell, 1981, as cited in Spring, 2008, p. 100). These early union members believed that knowledge was power. Knowledge, to be acquired in schools available to everyone, was essential to protect workers' rights in the economic system.

Irish Catholics also fought against the public schools they faced. Between 1850 and 1900, Irish church officials and Catholic parishioners fought tenaciously against the public schools created by upper class reformers. Catholics rebelled against the Protestantism and anti-Catholic sentiment expressed in reading materials and personnel of the public schools. By 1900, they had established a wide network of Catholic schools for their children (Ravitch, 2000; Spring, 2008). In addition to providing opportunities for Irish families around the turn of the 20th century, the establishment of a system of Catholic schools in America provided opportunities later for children of color in cities as an alternative to public schools deemed deficient by parents. The existence of a system of religious schools had ramifications as well on federal education policy that continues to this day.

Foreshadowing later Civil Rights struggles, in the 1820s Boston's African American community, led by Black Abolitionist David Walker, began a 30-year fight against segregated public schools in that city. Their contestation ultimately led to a formal decision by the Massachusetts governor to end legal segregation in the state. In September 1855, the Boston public schools were legally integrated "without any violent hostilities" (Spring, 2008, p. 121). As we are aware, there would be more struggle necessary in the next century.

The 20th Century

During the Progressive Era, labor organizations, settlement house reformers, and immigrant families all put pressure on public school administrators to respond to the needs of the immigrant working-class population. Although there was a substantial effort in these reforms to "Americanize" newcomers, the schools were also responding to the pressures of the working-class majority in cities like New York. Schools as social centers with services enjoyed by many thousands of students and immigrant adults were the result; the school as a social center soon developed throughout the country at the turn of the 20th century (Spring, 2008).

The movement to establish teachers' unions radically changed the politics of U.S. public education and increased equity for the teaching force. Unionization of teachers increased their salaries and removed the most egregious forms of administrative control over their employment.

Most teachers associations in the early part of the 20th century were politically conservative. But teacher organizations in those years in New York and Chicago had a radical ideology and developed out of the Labor Movement (in the case of Chicago, there were close ties to the early women's movement as well). The teacher federations in both cities fought openly with conservative business interests and school administrators (Spring, 2008). Out of these struggles—and in concert with less radical pressures exerted by the more cautious teachers organizations—policies regulating the teaching force were instituted that made teachers' salaries and working conditions considerably more equitable than they had been.

The 20th century Civil Rights Movement, of course, achieved many educational victories for minorities. Although the *Brown* decisions in the 1950s did not initially bring about education integration in the South, they did renew and strengthen activist organizing toward that end, and ultimately, the decision delegitimated separate but equal accommodations in the civil sphere. As a consequence of the national social movement for political rights of Black Americans, this decision and others following it produced vastly increased opportunities in education for people of color—in educational admissions, the availability of administrative positions, K–16 curriculum offerings, expanded programs for students of color in public school, and in federal, state, and local policies and programs that supported these and other advances.[2]

The Head Start program, for instance, was a product of pressure from the Civil Rights Movement. Black and White Civil Rights workers, most of whom were involved in the 1960s in building Freedom Schools and the 1964 "Freedom Summer" (when scores of Northern college students went South to assist in voter registration drives), developed a program in rural Mississippi that provided education and services for poor children. Funded with War on Poverty money, the centers were staffed by Civil Rights activists and local people. After 2 years, in 1966, southern White politicians in Congress succeeded in defunding these early Head Start centers in Mississippi. With money from wealthy Northern supporters, activists and families took two busloads of preschool children to Washington in protest.

There, with their teachers and teacher's aides, they would show what Head Start in Mississippi was all about. "A romper lobby from Mississippi petitioned Congress today for a redress of grievances," was *The New York Times'* lead in its February 12 story on what others were calling "the children's crusade." Forty-eight Black children and their teachers turned the hearing room of the House Education and Labor Committee into a kindergarten, complete with pictures and children dragging "quacking Donald Ducks across the floor" (Dittmer, 1994, pp. 374–375).

Two weeks later, the Office of Economic Opportunity awarded the group a grant to continue operations. Head Start moved to center stage in the Johnson administration's efforts to support the education of low-income minorities and has remained a major source of opportunity for the education of young low-income children.

The women's movement of the 1960s and 1970s also was responsible for increased opportunities in education, specifically for female students. A confluence of Civil Rights and feminist organizing during these decades yielded not only laws and programs to protect and support people of color but women as well. . . .

On June 23, 1972, 2 years after the hearings, Title IX of the Education Amendments of 1972 was passed by the Congress and on July 1 was signed into law by President Richard Nixon.

The historic passage of Title IX was hardly noticed (by the press). I remember only one or two sentences in the Washington papers.

But Title IX would have a huge impact on education. It protects students, faculty, and staff in federally funded education programs at all levels. Title IX also applies to programs and activities affiliated with schools that receive federal funds (such as internships or School-to-Work programs) and to federally funded education programs run by other entities, such as correctional facilities, health care entities, unions, and businesses. The act covers admissions, recruitment, educational programs and activities, course offerings and access, counseling, financial aid, employment assistance, facilities and housing, health and insurance benefits and services, scholarships, and athletics. It also protects from discrimination against marital and parental status. Both male and female students are protected from harassment regardless of who is committing the harassing behavior.

A further example of increases in opportunities and resources resulting from social movement pressure is the right to learn and be taught in one's native language. Federal legislation creating bilingual programs was implemented in most parts of the nation originally as a result of organizing by Puerto Ricans in New York City and Chinese residents of San Francisco (Miguel & Miguel, 2004). . . .

RECENT ORGANIZING FOR EDUCATIONAL EQUITY

The past 15 years have witnessed the appearance and rapid growth across the nation of community organizing specifically for school reform, or education organizing. This type of advocacy involves the actions of parents and other community residents to change neighborhood schools through an "intentional building of power" (Mediratta, Fruchter, & Lewis, 2002, p. 5). Education organizing aims to create social capital in communities and to encourage parents and other residents to use their collective strength to force system change. Education organizing attempts to build leadership in parents by providing skill training, mentoring, and opportunity for public actions. Parents conduct community and school surveys, speak at rallies, mobilize other parents and community residents, and plan and enact campaigns aimed at school and district personnel and practices.

Because education organizing gives parents a base outside of school—typically in alliance with other community groups—parents are not dependent on school personnel for approval or legitimacy. When successful, parent organizing in poor communities yields the clout that parents create among themselves in affluent suburbs—where, with their skills and economic and political influence, they closely monitor the actions of district educators and politicians.

Several studies of parent organizing groups in low-income neighborhoods around the country document their rapid increase in number and influence, especially since the early 1990s (Mediratta et al., 2002).[3] Moreover, 80% of 66 parent organizing groups studied by the Collaborative Communications Group are working not only in local neighborhoods but also in regional or state coalitions formed to improve district or state education policy. One such group is Mississippi-based Southern Echo, which has grassroots community organizations in Tennessee, Arkansas, Louisiana, South Carolina, Kentucky, Florida, North Carolina, and West Virginia.

Southern Echo is an exemplar in several ways: It is regional, multigenerational, and led by former Civil Rights and labor union activists. The group describes itself as a "leadership development, education and training organization working to develop new, grassroots leadership in African American communities in Mississippi and the surrounding region." Until 1992, their work focused on jobs, affordable housing, and rebuilding community organizations. When they shifted their attention to education in the early 1990s, they began to organize around minority rights in education.

Southern Echo worked to create a force that could put pressure on state education officials. They provided training and technical assistance to help community groups carry out local campaigns, created residential training schools that lasted 2 days or more, and published training manuals and delivered hundreds of workshops in communities. One result of the work of Southern Echo and an affiliate, Mississippi Education Working Group, is that on October 23, 2002, the Mississippi State Board of Education agreed to fully comply with federal requirements for providing services to special education students—for the first time in 35 years. Echo leaders report that this was "the first time the community came together to force legislators, the state board of education, superintendents, special education administrators and curriculum coordinators to sit down together."

A particularly impressive education organizing group in the North is the Logan Square Neighborhood Association (LSNA) in Chicago—founded in the 1960s to work with the variety of problems local residents faced in their community. In 1988, when the Chicago School Reform Law created local schools councils, LSNA began to assist parents and community members work to improve their schools (Mediratta et al., 2002, p. 27). Among the accomplishments of the LSNA and parents are construction of seven new school buildings, evening community learning centers in six schools, mortgage lender programs to offer incentives for educators to buy housing in the area, parent training as reading tutors and cultural mentors of classroom teachers, the establishment of bilingual lending libraries for parents, a new bilingual teacher-training program for neighborhood parents interested in becoming teachers, and collaboration with Chicago State University to offer courses at the neighborhood school at no cost to participants (Mediratta et al., 2002, p. 28).

The final example of education organizing comes from South Bronx, New York. This group, Community Collaborative for District 9 (CC9), is an important instance of coalition building—between parents, community-based organizations (CBOs), the teachers union, and a university partner (Mediratta et al., 2002, p. 29). Organizational members include ACORN (which has been organizing parents in Districts 7, 9, and 12 for a decade), the New York City American Federation of Teachers, Citizens Advice Bureau (a local CBO providing educational services to residents for 30 years), High Bridge Community Life Center (a CBO providing job training and educational services since 1979), Mid-Bronx Senior Citizens Council (one of the largest CBOs in the South Bronx), parents from New Settlement Apartments, Northwest Bronx Community and Clergy Coalition (which unites 10 neighborhood housing reform groups), and the Institute for Education and Social Policy (which conducts research and evaluation and provides other technical assistance to community organizing groups).

The CC9 coalition researched educational best practices to determine what reform it was going to pursue. It decided that stabilizing the teaching force was critical and that increased staff development and lead teachers at every grade level in the schools would give teachers skills to be more successful with their students and thus encourage them to remain in district classrooms. The coalition then organized residents, petitioned, demonstrated, and engaged in other direct action campaigns to obtain New York City Department of Education funding to pay for the reforms. At every step, neighborhood parents were in the forefront. In April 2004, New York City provided $1.6 million for lead teachers and staff development throughout the 10-school district. Since that time, CC9 has expanded to include collaborations across the city and has been engaged in efforts to improve middle school education system wide.

But these efforts have been confined to education. Although that is of course important for educational equity, it may be necessary to collaborate across social sectors, if we are to build the power to make changes that will be fundamental and sustainable. . . .

I have been arguing that progressive social movements are an important force for increasing equity in education, but it may be that to wring sustainable, systemic change from the education system, we will have to work with groups active on other fronts as well. Indeed, we would not have to build a collaborative

social movement for economic and educational rights from scratch. . . .

Late 20th- and 21st-century globalization has indeed made the problems that public engagement efforts seek to solve no longer purely local. The causes of neighborhood problems like poorly funded education or lack of jobs often lie outside of the neighborhood and city in regional, state, and often national and global developments and policies. But although the problems people face may not be local, Tilly (2004) points out that most organizing is still local. The vast majority of organizing, he notes, still takes place in communities rather than on the global stage.

It may be that the important challenge of globalization for social movement building efforts in education (and economic) justice is that our organizing campaigns need to transcend neighborhoods. By this, I mean to suggest that the issues public engagement groups develop campaigns around need to be those that affect people in most or all of the neighborhoods of a city and in most or all of the cities of the state and nation. And the analysis that informs public advocacy needs to make the link to global causes. In this regard, analyses ought to transcend local power sources as causes and be supplemented by the identification of national and global developments and policies that affect neighborhoods. For instance, a local campaign against an underfunded urban school or district might connect the lack of public monies available for education to 25 years of diminished state and federal tax rates on corporations or to the huge federal spending on foreign wars. And as I have suggested earlier, we could expect synergy if we connected this local effort for increased education funding to alliances across sectors and indeed across the nation, in this case by joining education funding struggles to national antiwar and other alliances.

NOTES

1. As Tom Pedroni (2007) importantly points out, however, there are some social movements (like the

Nation of Islam, for example) that are not clearly of the Left or the Right, in that they exhibit characteristics of both.

2. It is interesting to note here that, as Jack Dougherty (2003) demonstrates in *More Than One Struggle*, many African Americans in the South supported desegregation to obtain better educational quality but did not support integration as a social goal. Indeed, as Vanessa Siddle Walker (1996) has pointed out, the desegregation of Southern schools removed from Black communities the embeddedness of their educational institutions.

3. As Pedroni (2007) demonstrates, some of this organizing can have complex relationships with both the Left and the Right—as in the case of vouchers and some charter school movements.

REFERENCES

Apple, M. (2006). *Educating the "right" way: Markets, standards, God, and inequality* (2nd ed.). New York: Rutledge.

Della Porta, D., & Diani, M. (2006). *Social movements: An introduction*. Oxford, England: Blackwell.

Dittmer, J. (1994). *Local people: The struggle for civil rights in Mississippi*. Urbana: University of Illinois Press.

Dougherty, J. (2003). *More than one struggle: The evolution of black school reform in Milwaukee*. Chapel Hill: University of North Carolina Press.

Fraser, N. (2000). Rethinking recognition. *New Left Review, 3,* 107–120.

Mediratta, K., Fruchter, N., & Lewis, A. (2002). *Organizing for school reform: How communities are finding their voices and reclaiming their public schools*. Providence, RI: Annenberg Institute for School Reform.

Miguel, G., & Miguel, G., Jr. (2004). *Contested policy: The rise and fall of federal bilingual education in the United States, 1960–2001*. Denton: University of North Texas Press.

Pedroni, T. (2007). *Market movements: African American involvement for school voucher reform*. New York: Routledge.

Ravitch, D. (2000). *The great school wars: A history of the New York City public schools*. Baltimore: Johns Hopkins University Press.

Russell, W. (1981). *Education and the working class: The expansion of public education during the transition to capitalism* (Unpublished doctoral dissertation). University of Cincinnati.

Siddle Walker, V. (1996). *Their highest potential: An African American school community in the segregated South*. Chapel Hill: North Carolina University Press.

Smelser, N. (1962). *Theory of collective behavior*. New York: Free Press.

Spring, J. (2008). *The American school* (7th ed.). Boston: McGraw-Hill.

Tilly, C. (1978). *From mobilization to revolution*. Reading, MA: Addison-Wesley.

Tilly, C. (2004). *Social movements, 1768–2004*. Boulder, CO: Paradigm.

Touraine, A. (1981). *The voice and the eye: An analysis of social movements*. Cambridge, England: Cambridge University Press.

DESCHOOLING SOCIETY

Ivan Illich

It is appropriate to include in this final part a reading by one of the more creative educational reformers of the 20th century. In this excerpt from his book of the same title, Ivan Illich proposes a totally different educational system that does not rely on schooling as we know it. This book is a classic in educational literature, published in 1971, and provides an interesting way to rethink the function and structure of schools. Illich's idea of deschooling society provides a totally different approach to what we know as "real school." May this reading trigger your imagination and raise many questions as you consider changes in education.

Questions to consider for this reading:

1. What parts of education does Illich find to be most harmful?
2. Describe the type of education Illich would like to see in society.
3. What do you know about schools as educational organizations from other readings in this book that would make Illich's reforms difficult to implement?

Equal educational opportunity is, indeed, both a desirable and a feasible goal, but to equate this with obligatory schooling is to confuse salvation with the Church. School has become the world religion of a modernized proletariat, and makes futile promises of salvation to the poor of the technological age. The nation-state has adopted it, drafting all citizens into a graded curriculum leading to sequential diplomas not unlike the initiation rituals and hieratic promotions of former times. The modern state has assumed the duty of enforcing the judgment of its educators through well-meant truant officers and job requirements, much as did the Spanish kings who enforced the judgments of their theologians through the conquistadors and the Inquisition.

Two centuries ago the United States led the world in a movement to disestablish the monopoly of a single church. Now we need the constitutional disestablishment of the monopoly of the school, and thereby of a system which legally combines prejudice with discrimination. The first article of a bill of rights for a modern, humanist society would correspond to the First Amendment to the U.S. Constitution: "The State shall make no law with respect to the establishment of education." There shall be no ritual obligatory for all.

To make this disestablishment effective, we need a law forbidding discrimination in hiring, voting, or admission to centers of learning based on previous attendance at some curriculum. This guarantee would not exclude performance tests of competence for a function or role, but would remove the present absurd discrimination in favor of the person who learns a given skill with the largest expenditure of public funds or—what is equally likely—has been able to obtain a diploma which has no relation to any useful skill or job. Only by protecting the citizen from being disqualified by anything in his career in school can a constitutional disestablishment of school become psychologically effective.

Neither learning nor justice is promoted by schooling because educators insist on packaging instruction with certification. Learning and the assignment of social roles are melted into schooling. Yet to learn means to acquire a new skill or insight, while promotion depends on an opinion which others have formed. Learning frequently is the result of instruction, but selection for a role or category in the job market increasingly depends on mere length of attendance.

Instruction is the choice of circumstances which facilitate learning. Roles are assigned by setting a curriculum of conditions which the candidate must meet if he is to make the grade. School links instruction—but not learning—to these roles. This is neither reasonable nor liberating. It is not reasonable because it does not link relevant qualities or competences to roles, but rather the process by which such qualities are supposed to be acquired. It is not liberating or educational because school reserves instruction to those whose every step in learning fits previously approved measures of social control.

Curriculum has always been used to assign social rank. However, instead of equalizing chances, the school system has monopolized their distribution.

To detach competence from curriculum, inquiries into a man's learning history must be made taboo, like inquiries into his political affiliation, church attendance, lineage, sex habits, or racial background. Laws forbidding discrimination on the basis of prior schooling must be enacted. Laws, of course, cannot stop prejudice against the unschooled—nor are they meant to force anyone to intermarry with an autodidact [a self-taught individual]—but they can discourage unjustified discrimination.

A second major illusion on which the school system rests is that most learning is the result of teaching. Teaching, it is true, may contribute to certain kinds of learning under certain circumstances.

But most people acquire most of their knowledge outside school, and in school only insofar as school, in a few rich countries, has become their place of confinement during an increasing part of their lives.

Most learning happens casually, and even most intentional learning is not the result of programmed instruction. Normal children learn their first language casually, although faster if their parents pay attention to them. Most people who learn a second language well do so as a result of odd circumstances and not of sequential teaching. They go to live with their grandparents, they travel, or they fall in love with a foreigner. Fluency in reading is also more often than not a result of such extracurricular activities. Most people who read widely, and with pleasure, merely believe that they learned to do so in school; when challenged, they easily discard this illusion.

But the fact that a great deal of learning even now seems to happen casually and as a by-product of some other activity defined as work or leisure does not mean that planned learning does not benefit from planned instruction and that both do not stand in need of improvement. The strongly motivated student who is faced with the task of acquiring a new and complex skill may benefit greatly from the discipline now associated with the old-fashioned schoolmaster who taught reading, Hebrew, catechism, or multiplication by rote. School has now made this kind of drill teaching rare and disreputable, yet there are many skills which a motivated student with normal aptitude can master in a matter of a few months if taught in this traditional way. This is as true of codes as of their encipherment; of second and third languages as of reading and writing; and equally of special languages such as algebra, computer programming, chemical analysis, or of manual skills like typing, watchmaking, plumbing, writing, TV repair; or for that matter dancing, driving, and diving.

In certain cases acceptance into a learning program aimed at a specific skill might presuppose competence in some other skill, but it should certainly not be made to depend upon the process by which such prerequisite skills were acquired. TV repair presupposes literacy and some math; diving, good swimming; and driving, very little of either.

. . . At present schools pre-empt most educational funds. Drill instruction which costs less than comparable schooling is now a privilege of those rich enough to bypass the schools, and those whom either the army or big business sends through in-service training. In a program of progressive deschooling of U.S. education, at first the resources available for drill training would be limited. But ultimately there should be no obstacle for anyone at any time of his life to be able to choose instruction among hundreds of definable skills at public expense.

Right now educational credit good at any skill center could be provided in limited amounts for people of all ages, and not just to the poor. I envisage such credit in the form of an educational passport or an "edu-credit card" provided to each citizen at birth. In order to favor the poor, who probably would not use their yearly grants early in life, a provision could be made that interest accrued to later users of cumulated "entitlements." Such credits would permit most people to acquire the skills most in demand, at their convenience, better, faster, cheaper, and with fewer undesirable side effects than in school.

Potential skill teachers are never scarce for long because, on the one hand, demand for a skill grows only with its performance within a community and, on the other, a man exercising a skill could also teach it. But, at present, those using skills which are in demand and do require a human teacher are discouraged from sharing these skills with others. This is done either by teachers who monopolize the licenses or by unions which protect their trade interests. Skill centers which would be judged by customers on their results, and not on the personnel they employ or the process they use, would open unsuspected working opportunities, frequently even for those who are now considered unemployable. Indeed, there is no reason why such skill centers should not be at the work place itself, with the employer and his work force supplying instruction as well as jobs to those who choose to use their educational credits in this way.

In 1956 there arose a need to teach Spanish quickly to several hundred teachers, social workers, and ministers from the New York Archdiocese so that they could communicate with Puerto Ricans.

My friend Gerry Morris announced over a Spanish radio station that he needed native speakers from Harlem. Next day some two hundred teen-agers lined up in front of his office, and he selected four dozen of them—many of them school dropouts. He trained them in the use of the U.S. Foreign Service Institute (FSI) Spanish manual, designed for use by linguists with graduate training, and within a week his teachers were on their own—each in charge of four New Yorkers who wanted to speak the language. Within six months the mission was accomplished. Cardinal Spellman could claim that he had 127 parishes in which at least three staff members could communicate in Spanish. No school program could have matched these results.

Skill teachers are made scarce by the belief in the value of licenses. Certification constitutes a form of market manipulation and is plausible only to a schooled mind. Most teachers of arts and trades are less skillful, less inventive, and less communicative than the best craftsmen and tradesmen. Most high-school teachers of Spanish or French do not speak the language as correctly as their pupils might after half a year of competent drills. Experiments conducted by Angel Quintero in Puerto Rico suggest that many young teen-agers, if given the proper incentives, programs, and access to tools, are better than most schoolteachers at introducing their peers to the scientific exploration of plants, stars, and matter, and to the discovery of how and why a motor or a radio functions.

Opportunities for skill-learning can be vastly multiplied if we open the "market." This depends on matching the right teacher with the right student when he is highly motivated in an intelligent program, without the constraint of curriculum.

Free and competing drill instruction is a subversive blasphemy to the orthodox educator. It dissociates the acquisition of skills from "humane" education, which schools package together, and thus it promotes unlicensed learning no less than unlicensed teaching for unpredictable purposes.

There is currently a proposal on record which seems at first to make a great deal of sense. It has been prepared by Christopher Jencks of the Center for the Study of Public Policy and is sponsored by the Office of Economic Opportunity. It proposes to put educational "entitlements" or tuition grants into the hands of parents and students for expenditure in the schools of their choice. Such individual entitlements could indeed be an important step in the right direction. We need a guarantee of the right of each citizen to an equal share of tax-derived educational resources, the right to verify this share, and the right to sue for it if denied. It is one form of a guarantee against regressive taxation.

The Jencks proposal, however, begins with the ominous statement that "conservatives, liberals, and radicals have all complained at one time or another that the American educational system gives professional educators too little incentive to provide high quality education to most children." The proposal condemns itself by proposing tuition grants which would have to be spent on schooling.

This is like giving a lame man a pair of crutches and stipulating that he use them only if the ends are tied together. As the proposal for tuition grants now stands, it plays into the hands not only of the professional educators but of racists, promoters of religious schools, and others whose interests are socially divisive. Above all, educational entitlements restricted to use within schools play into the hands of all those who want to continue to live in a society in which social advancement is tied not to proven knowledge but to the learning pedigree by which it is supposedly acquired. This discrimination in favor of schools which dominates Jencks's discussion on refinancing education could discredit one of the most critically needed principles for educational reform: the return of initiative and accountability for learning to the learner or his most immediate tutor.

The deschooling of society implies a recognition of the two-faced nature of learning. An insistence on skill drill alone could be a disaster; equal emphasis must be placed on other kinds of learning. But if schools are the wrong places for learning a skill, they are even worse places for getting an education. School does both tasks badly, partly because it does not distinguish between them. School is inefficient in skill instruction especially because it is curricular. In most schools a program which is meant to improve one skill is chained always to another irrelevant task. History is tied to advancement in math, and class attendance to the right to use the playground.

Schools are even less efficient in the arrangement of the circumstances which encourage the open-ended, exploratory use of acquired skills, for which I will reserve the term "liberal education." The main reason for this is that school is obligatory and becomes schooling for schooling's sake: an enforced stay in the company of teachers, which pays off in the doubtful privilege of more such company. Just as skill instruction must be freed from curricular restraints, so must liberal education be dissociated from obligatory attendance. Both skill-learning and education for inventive and creative behavior can be aided by institutional arrangement, but they are of a different, frequently opposed nature.

Most skills can be acquired and improved by drills, because skill implies the mastery of definable and predictable behavior. Skill instruction can rely, therefore, on the simulation of circumstances in which the skill will be used. Education in the exploratory and creative use of skills, however, cannot rely on drills. Education can be the outcome of instruction, though instruction of a kind fundamentally opposed to drill. It relies on the relationship between partners who already have some of the keys which give access to memories stored in and by the community. It relies on the critical intent of all those who use memories creatively. It relies on the surprise of the unexpected question which opens new doors for the inquirer and his partner.

The skill instructor relies on the arrangement of set circumstances which permit the learner to develop standard responses. The educational guide or master is concerned with helping matching partners to meet so that learning can take place. He matches individuals starting from their own, unresolved questions. At the most he helps the pupil to formulate his puzzlement since only a clear statement will give him the power to find his match, moved like him, at the moment, to explore the same issue in the same context.

Matching partners for educational purposes initially seems more difficult to imagine than finding skill instructors and partners for a game. One reason is the deep fear which school has implanted in us, a fear which makes us censorious. The unlicensed exchange of skills—even undesirable skills—is more predictable and therefore seems less dangerous than the unlimited opportunity for meeting among people who share an issue which for them, at the moment, is socially, intellectually, and emotionally important.

The Brazilian teacher Paulo Freire knows this from experience. He discovered that any adult can begin to read in a matter of forty hours if the first words he deciphers are charged with political meaning. Freire trains his teachers to move into a village and to discover the words which designate current important issues, such as the access to a well or the compound interest on the debts owed to the patron. In the evening the villagers meet for the discussion of these key words. They begin to realize that each word stays on the blackboard even after its sound has faded. The letters continue to unlock reality and to make it manageable as a problem. I have frequently witnessed how discussants grow in social awareness and how they are impelled to take political action as fast as they learn to read. They seem to take reality into their hands as they write it down.

I remember the man who complained about the weight of pencils: they were difficult to handle because they did not weigh as much as a shovel; and I remember another who on his way to work stopped with his companions and wrote the word they were discussing with his hoe on the ground: "agua." Since 1962 my friend Freire has moved from exile to exile, mainly because he refuses to conduct his sessions around words which are preselected by approved educators, rather than those which his discussants bring to the class.

The educational matchmaking among people who have been successfully schooled is a different task. Those who do not need such assistance are a minority, even among the readers of serious journals. The majority cannot and should not be rallied for discussion around a slogan, a word, or a picture. But the idea remains the same: they should be able to meet around a problem chosen and defined by their own initiative. Creative, exploratory learning requires peers currently puzzled about the same terms or problems. Large universities make the futile attempt to match them by multiplying their courses, and they generally fail since they are bound to curriculum, course structure, and bureaucratic administration.

In schools, including universities, most resources are spent to purchase the time and motivation of a limited number of people to take up predetermined problems in a ritually defined setting. The most radical alternative to school would be a network or service which gave each man the same opportunity to share his current concern with others motivated by the same concern.

Let me give, as an example of what I mean, a description of how an intellectual match might work in New York City. Each man, at any given moment and at a minimum price, could identify himself to a computer with his address and telephone number, indicating the book, article, film, or recording on which he seeks a partner for discussion. Within days he could receive by mail the list of others who recently had taken the same initiative. This list would enable him by telephone to arrange for a meeting with persons who initially would be known exclusively by the fact that they requested a dialogue about the same subject.

Matching people according to their interest in a particular title is radically simple. It permits identification only on the basis of a mutual desire to discuss a statement recorded by a third person, and it leaves the initiative of arranging the meeting to the individual. Three objections are usually raised against this skeletal purity. I take them up not only to clarify the theory that I want to illustrate by my proposal—for they highlight the deep-seated resistance to deschooling education, to separating learning from social control—but also because they may help to suggest existing resources which are not now used for learning purposes.

The first objection is: Why cannot self-identification be based also on an idea or an issue? Certainly such subjective terms could also be used in a computer system. Political parties, churches, unions, clubs, neighborhood centers, and professional societies already organize their educational activities in this way and in effect they act as schools. They all match people in order to explore certain "themes"; and these are dealt with in courses, seminars, and curricula in which presumed "common interests" are prepackaged. Such theme-matching is by definition teacher-centered: it requires an authoritarian presence to define for the participants the starting point for their discussion.

By contrast, matching by the title of a book, film, etc., in its pure form leaves it to the author to define the special language, the terms, and the framework within which a given problem or fact is stated; and it enables those who accept this starting point to identify themselves to one another. For instance, matching people around the idea of "cultural revolution" usually leads either to confusion or to demagoguery. On the other hand, matching those interested in helping each other understand a specific article by Mao, Marcuse, Freud, or Goodman stands in the great tradition of liberal learning from Plato's Dialogues, which are built around presumed statements by Socrates, to Aquinas's commentaries on Peter the Lombard. The idea of matching by title is thus radically different from the theory on which the "Great Books" clubs, for example, were built: instead of relying on the selection by some Chicago professors, any two partners can choose any book for further analysis.

The second objection asks: Why not let the identification of match seekers include information on age, background, world view, competence, experience, or other defining characteristics? Again, there is no reason why such discriminatory restrictions could not and should not be built into some of the many universities—with or without walls—which could use title-matching as their basic organizational device. I could conceive of a system designed to encourage meetings of interested persons at which the author of the book chosen would be present or represented; or a system which guaranteed the presence of a competent adviser; or one to which only students registered in a department or school had access; or one which permitted meetings only between people who defined their special approach to the title under discussion. Advantages for achieving specific goals of learning could be found for each of these restrictions. But I fear that, more often than not, the real reason for proposing such restrictions is contempt arising from the presumption that people are ignorant: educators want to avoid the ignorant meeting the ignorant around a text which they may not understand and which they read only because they are interested in it.

The third objection: Why not provide match seekers with incidental assistance that will facilitate their meetings—with space, schedules, screening, and protection? This is now done by schools with all the inefficiency characterizing large bureaucracies. If we left the initiative for meetings to the match seekers themselves, organizations which nobody now classifies as educational would probably do the job much better. I think of restaurant owners, publishers, telephone-answering services, department store managers, and even commuter train executives who could promote their services by rendering them attractive for educational meetings.

At a first meeting in a coffee shop, say, the partners might establish their identities by placing the book under discussion next to their cups. People who took the initiative to arrange for such meetings would soon learn what items to quote to meet the people they sought. The risk that the self-chosen discussion with one or several strangers might lead to a loss of time, disappointment, or even unpleasantness is certainly smaller than the same risk taken by a college applicant. A computer-arranged meeting to discuss an article in a national magazine, held in a coffee shop off Fourth Avenue, would obligate none of the participants to stay in the company of his new acquaintances for longer than it took to drink a cup of coffee, nor would he have to meet any of them ever again. The chance that it would help to pierce the opaqueness of life in a modern city and further new friendship, self-chosen work, and critical reading is high. (The fact that a record of personal readings and meetings could be obtained thus by the FBI is undeniable; that this should still worry anybody in 1970 is only amusing to a free man, who willy-nilly contributes his share in order to drown snoopers in the irrelevancies they gather.)

Both the exchange of skills and matching of partners are based on the assumption that education for all means education by all. Not the draft into a specialized institution but only the mobilization of the whole population can lead to popular culture. The equal right of each man to exercise his competence to learn and to instruct is now pre-empted by certified teachers. The teachers' competence, in turn, is restricted to what may be done in school. And, further, work and leisure are alienated from each other as a result: the spectator and the worker alike are supposed to arrive at the work place all ready to fit into a routine prepared for them. Adaptation in the form of a product's design, instruction, and publicity shapes them for their role as much as formal education by schooling. A radical alternative to a schooled society requires not only new formal mechanisms for the formal acquisition of skills and their educational use. A deschooled society implies a new approach to incidental or informal education.

Incidental education cannot any longer return to the forms which learning took in the village or the medieval town. Traditional society was more like a set of concentric circles of meaningful structures, while modern man must learn how to find meaning in many structures to which he is only marginally related. In the village, language and architecture and work and religion and family customs were consistent with one another, mutually explanatory and reinforcing. To grow into one implied a growth into the others. Even specialized apprenticeship was a by-product of specialized activities, such as shoemaking or the singing of psalms. If an apprentice never became a master or a scholar, he still contributed to making shoes or to making church services solemn. Education did not compete for time with either work or leisure. Almost all education was complex, lifelong, and unplanned.

Contemporary society is the result of conscious designs, and educational opportunities must be designed into them. Our reliance on specialized, full-time instruction through school will now decrease, and we must find more ways to learn and teach: the educational quality of all institutions must increase again. But this is a very ambiguous forecast. It could mean that men in the modern city will be increasingly the victims of an effective process of total instruction and manipulation once they are deprived of even the tenuous pretense of critical independence which liberal schools now provide for at least some of their pupils.

It could also mean that men will shield themselves less behind certificates acquired in school and thus gain in courage to "talk back" and thereby control and instruct the institutions in which they participate. To ensure the latter we must learn to estimate the social value of work and leisure by the educational give-and-take for which they offer opportunity. Effective participation in the politics of a street, a work place, the

library, a news program, or a hospital is therefore the best measuring stick to evaluate their level as educational institutions.

I recently spoke to a group of junior-high school students in the process of organizing a resistance movement to their obligatory draft into the next class. Their slogan was "participation—not simulation." They were disappointed that this was understood as a demand for less rather than for more education, and reminded me of the resistance which Karl Marx put up against a passage in the Gotha program which—one hundred years ago—wanted to outlaw child labor. He opposed the proposal in the interest of the education of the young, which could happen only at work. If the greatest fruit of man's labor should be the education he receives from it and the opportunity which work gives him to initiate the education of others, then the alienation of modern society in a pedagogical sense is even worse than its economic alienation.

The major obstacle on the way to a society that truly educates was well defined by a black friend of mine in Chicago, who told me that our imagination was "all schooled up." We permit the state to ascertain the universal educational deficiencies of its citizens and establish one specialized agency to treat them. We thus share in the delusion that we can distinguish between what is necessary education for others and what is not, just as former generations established laws which defined what was sacred and what was profane.

Durkheim recognized that this ability to divide social reality into two realms was the very essence of formal religion. There are, he reasoned, religions without the supernatural and religions without gods, but none which does not subdivide the world into things and times and persons that are sacred and others that as a consequence are profane. Durkheim's insight can be applied to the sociology of education, for school is radically divisive in a similar way.

The very existence of obligatory schools divides any society into two realms: some time spans and processes and treatments and professions are "academic" or "pedagogic," and others are not. The power of school thus to divide social reality has no boundaries: education becomes unworldly and the world becomes non-educational.

Projects for Further Exploration

1. Use an academic database (with no restrictions to refereed journals) to look up *educational reform.* What are the reform efforts most cited in nonacademic journals? How do they differ from the reforms discussed in this book?

2. Using an academic database (with no restrictions to refereed journals), look up *"national standards"* and *education.* What is the current discussion around national standards and how does it relate to the arguments made in the reading by Thomas Rohlen in this chapter?

3. Using a Web search engine, look up community efforts to improve education and compare these efforts with those described in the Anyon reading.

CONCLUDING REMARKS

Many people hang their hopes on the institution of education and the schools and class-rooms within that institution. Ivan Illich, however, is not alone in his frustration with the educational systems in many countries. Other individuals also criticize components of the educational systems, and some offer solutions. Governments wrestle with these problems and look for research that proposes reforms. A number of readings in this book discuss possible reforms (see Chapters 8 and 11 in particular), and yet they only begin to describe the various reforms that have been attempted or speculate on those that will be tried in the future.

The purpose of this book has not been to propose solutions or reforms, although some of the readings do just that. Instead, we intended to provide readers with an overview of the theories, methods, and issues in sociology of education today. Sociologists provide a rather unique view of institutions, one that places institutions such as education, family, religion, and politics within a societal context. Although few sociologists set out with the goal of school reform, by raising questions about educational issues, they encourage critical analyses of schools. Sociological studies can inform debates and provide scientific findings to guide policy makers. Sociological researchers provide a unique perspective that can help those involved in decisions about our children's education to see schools in a new light.

Why haven't some of the major educational problems been solved? Many of the readings in this book point to reasons why things remain the same or, if changed, why schools still do not meet the needs of many students. We hope that by reading the articles in this book you have come to understand how complex educational systems are. We hope that you have come to understand that one person's sense of frustration can be another's sense of accomplishment. We hope that you now have a better sense of both the structure and the processes within schools and the many variations and permutations both structure and process have within educational systems. We hope that you now know that schools both mirror and reinforce existing social patterns in society. And we hope you understand that schools do not exist in a vacuum, that educational systems respond to many external conditions, in addition to internal factors, in shaping how we educate young people.

APPENDIX

Web Resources for Continued Exploration of the Topics in This Book

Research Literatures

ERIC can be searched online to find research and reflections on a wide variety of educational topics: http://www.eric.ed.gov/. When at this site, you can search the literature data base

Jstor: http://www.jstor.org (found at college and university libraries that subscribe.) Jstor contains electronic versions of journal articles more than 5 years old in such journals as Sociology of Education, American Journal of Sociology, American Sociological Review, and others.

National Library of Education: http://www2.ed.gov/NLE/

Online Journals and/or Abstracts

Anthropology and Education Quarterly: http://www.aaanet.org/cae/AEQ/

Black Issues in Higher Education: http://www.blackissues.com/

Chronicle of Higher Education: http://chronicle.com

Education Week: http://www.edweek.org/

Educational Leadership: http://www.ascd.org

Harvard Education Letter: http://www.edletter.org/

Harvard Education Review: http://www.hepg/her/

Phi Delta Kappan: http://www.pdkintl.org

Rethinking Schools: http://www.rethinkingschools.org/

Teachers College Record at: http://www.tcrecord.org

Free Online News Sources

Boston Globe: http://www.boston.com/bostonglobe/

LA Times: http://www.latimes.com

New York Times: http://www.nytimes.com

Libraries

Library of Congress: http://lcweb.loc.gov/homepage/lchp.html

New York Public Library: http://www.nypl.org/branch/iresources.html

Professional Associations

American Association of School Administrators: http://www.aasa.org/

American Educational Research Association: http://www.aera.net/

American Federation of Teachers: http://www.aft.org/

American Sociological Association (ASA): http://www.asanet.org/

Association for Supervision and Curriculum Development: http://www.ascd.org/

Council for Aid to Education: http://www.cae.org/

Council of Chief State School Officers: http://www.ccsso.org/intasc

Council of Great City Schools: http://www.cgcs.org/

Education Commission of the States: http://www.ecs.org

Institute for Educational Leadership: http://www.iel.org

National Board for Professional Teaching Standards: http://www.nbpts.org/

National Education Association: http://www.nea.org/

Sociology of Education Section, ASA: http://www.asanet.org (go to sections, then Education)

Research Organizations

AACTE Education Policy Clearinghouse: http://www.edpolicy.org/

Center for Social Organization of Schools: http://web.jhu.edu/csos

Consortium for Policy Research in Education: http://www.cpre.org/

Key National Indicators- Education: http://www.whitehouse.gov/fsbr/education.html

National Center for Research in Vocational Education: http://vocserve.berkeley.edu/

National Center for Research on Evaluation, Standards, and Student Testing (CRESST): http://www.cse.ucla.edu/index.htm

Office of Educational Research and Improvement: http://www2.ed.gov/offices/OERI/index.html

Office of Postsecondary Education: http://www2.ed.gov/about/offices/list/ope/index.html

RAND Organization: http://www.rand.org.

U.S. Department of Education: http://www.ed.gov.

U.S. Department of Education Nation's Report Card: http://nces.ed.gov/nationsreportcard

Educational Reform Organizations and Information

Accelerated Schools Project: http://www.acceleratedschools.net/

Achieve, Inc. (an organization of governors and business leaders): http://www.achieve.org/

Annenberg Institute on Educational Reform: http://www.annenberginstitute.org/

American Youth Policy Form: http://www.aypf.org

Center for Educational Reform: http://www.edreform.com/

Center on Reinventing Public Education: http://www.crpe.org/

Center on School, Family and Community Partnerships: http://www.csos.jhu.edu/p2000/center.htm

Coalition for Essential Schools: http://www.essentialschools.org/

Comer School Development Program: http://medicine.yale.edu/childstudy/Comer

Edison Schools: http://www.edisonproject.com

Modern Red Schoolhouse: http://www.mrsh.org

National Charter School Research Project: http://www.crpe.org/cs/crpe/view/projects/1

The National Center for Fair & Open Testing: http://www.fairtest.org

New American Schools Network (merged with American Institutes for Research): http://www.air.org

Public Education Network: http://www.publiceducation.org/

Success for All Foundation: http://www.successfulforall.net

Higher Education Resources

American Association of College and Universities: http://www.aacu.org./

American Association of Community Colleges: http://www.aacc.nche.edu/

Association for the Study of Higher Education http://www.ashe.ws

Association for Institutional Research: http://www.airweb.org

Center for International Higher Education: http://www.bc.edu/research/cihe

Community College Research Center: http://ccrc.tc.columbia.edu/

Fund for the Improvement of Postsecondary Education: http://www2.ed.gov/about/offices/list/ope/fipse/index.html

Historically Black Colleges and Universities: http://edonline.com/cq/hbcu/

League for Innovation in the Community College: http://www.league.org/

The Learning Alliance for Higher Education: http://www.irhe.upenn.edu/

National Center for Postsecondary Improvement: http://www.stanford.edu/group/ncpi/

National Center for Postsecondary Improvement, Links: http://www.standford.edu/group/ncpi/links.shtml

National Center for Public Policy and Higher Education: http://www.highereducatio.org/

Review of Higher Education: http://muse.jhu.edu/demo/review_of_higher_education/

Society for College and University Planning: http://www.scup.org/

Western Interstate Commission for Higher Education: http://www.wiche.edu/

International Materials

United Nations Educational, Scientific and Cultural Organization—UNESCO: http://www.unesco.org/new/un/education/

Education Around the World: http://www2.ed.gov/offices/OUS/PES/int_edworld.html

International Bureau of Education: http://www.ibe.unesco.org/

International Sociological Association: http://www.isa-sociology.org/

Sociology in Switzerland, including online journals: http://socio.ch/

Data

General Social Survey (GSS) is available online, and simple analyses may be conducted online at: http://www.icpsr.umich.edu

National Center for Educational Statistics (NCES): http://nces.ed.gov/

NCES Encyclopedia of Education Statistics and Annual Reports: http://nces.ed.gov/annuals

NCES Surveys: http://nces.ed.gov/surveys

Roper Center for Public Policy Research: http://www.ropercneter.unconn.edu/

School Report Cards: Go to your State Education website and search from there

U.S. Census Bureau, Home Page: http://www.census.gov/

U. S. Census State, County, and Community data: http://quickfacts.census.gov/qfd/states/00000.html/

U. S. Census Statistical Abstract of the U.S.: http://www.census.gov/compendia/statab

The preceding information is an updated list of Internet Resources originally compiled by Caroline Hodges Persell and Floyd M. Hammack and originally published in Teaching Sociology of Education by the American Sociological Association, 2001.